7 DAY LOAN

THE UNIVERSITY OF LIVERPOOL
SYDNEY JONES LIBRARY
RESTRICTED LOAN

Please return or renew, on or before the last date below. A fine is payable on late returned items. Items may be recalled after one week for the use of another reader. Items may be renewed by telephone:- 0151 794 - 2678.

For conditions of borrowing, see Library Regulations

A HANDBOOK OF COMPARATIVE SOCIAL POLICY

A Handbook of Comparative Social Policy

Edited by

Patricia Kennett

Senior Lecturer in Comparative Policy Studies, School for Policy Studies, University of Bristol, UK

Edward Elgar
Cheltenham, UK • Northampton, MA, USA

Published by
Edward Elgar Publishing Limited
Glensanda House
Montpellier Parade
Cheltenham
Glos GL50 1UA
UK

Edward Elgar Publishing, Inc.
136 West Street
Suite 202
Northampton
Massachusetts 01060
USA

A catalogue record for this book
is available from the British Library

Library of Congress Cataloguing in Publication Data

A handbook of comparative social policy/edited by Patricia Kennett.
    p. cm.
  Includes bibliographical references and index.
  1. Social policy. 2. Globalization. I. Kennett, Patricia, 1959– .
HN17.5.H3357   2004
361.6'1—dc22

2004044126

ISBN 1 84064 886 4 (cased)

Typeset by Manton Typesetters, Louth, Lincolnshire, UK.
Printed and bound in Great Britain by MPG Books Ltd, Bodmin, Cornwall.

Contents

PART III   COMPARING AND CATEGORIZING SOCIAL POLICY, PROVISION AND REDISTRIBUTION

PART IV   THE RESEARCH PROCESS

PART V   THEMES AND ISSUES

Figures

Tables

Contributors

Jochen Clasen is Professor of Comparative Social Research and Director of the Centre for Comparative Research in Social Welfare (CCRSW), University of Stirling. His research interests include comparative social policy, social security policy, unemployment and employment policy in cross-national context. Recent publications include *Comparative Social Policy. Concepts, theories and methods* (ed.) (Blackwell, 1999); 'Motives, means and opportunities. Reforming unemployment compensation in the 1990s', *West European Politics*, **23** (2), 2000; 'Social Insurance and the Contributory Principle. A paradox in contemporary British social policy', *Social Policy and Administration*, **35** (6), 2001 and (with W. van Oorschot) 'Changing Principles in European Social Security', *European Journal of Social Security*, **4** (2), 2002.

Graham Crow is Reader in Sociology at the University of Southampton where he has worked since 1983. His recent publications include *Comparative Sociology and Social Theory* (Macmillan, 1997) and *Social Solidarities* (Open Univerity Press, 2002). He is currently writing a book for Palgrave on modes of sociological argument.

Mattei Dogan is a sociologist and political scientist. He is Research Director at the National Centre of Scientific Research in Paris and professor at the University of California-Los Angeles. His recent publications are *Pathways to Power*; *Comparing Nations*; *Creative Marginality*; *How to Compare Nations*; *Comparing Pluralist Democracies*; *Elites Crises and the Origins of Regimes*; *Elite Configurations at the Apex of Power*; and *A World of Giants*. He is chairman of the Research Committee on Comparative Sociology of the International Sociological Association and Member of the Bureau of the International Institute of Sociology.

Ray Forrest is Professor of Urban Studies and Head of School for Policy Studies, University of Bristol, UK. He has published widely on housing policy and processes of urban change and is currently co-director (with Ade Kearns, University of Glasgow) of the ESRC Centre for Neighbourhood Research. He is a Visiting Professor in the Department of Urban Studies, University of Glasgow and Adjunct Professor, Department of Public and Social Administration at the City University of Hong Kong. He is on the editorial boards of *Housing Studies, Housing, Theory and Society* and *Policy* *and Politics*. He is a founding member of the Asia Pacific Network for Housing Research.

Norman Ginsburg has been Professor of Social Policy at London Metropolitan University (formerly the University of North London) since 1996. His research interests are the comparative impact of social policy on social injustice and inequality, and the social effects of urban regeneration and housing policy. He is the author of *Divisions of Welfare: An Introduction to Comparative Social Policy* (Sage, 1992). Recent publications include articles on globalization and the liberal welfare states, social policy in Sweden, and the social aspects of urban regeneration. Forthcoming work includes papers on social capital in the inner city, the demise of council housing, and globalization and racism.

Ian Gough is Professor of Social Policy at the University of Bath and is Honorary Editor of the *Journal of European Social Policy*. Since October 2002 he has been Deputy Director of the 5-year ESRC-funded Research Group Well-Being and Development (WeD) at the University of Bath. He is author of *The Political Economy of the Welfare State* (published in 1979 and translated into six languages, including Chinese, Japanese and Korean) and co-author of *A Theory of Human Need* (1991), winner of both the Deutscher and the Myrdal prizes. Other books include *Can the Welfare State Compete?* (1991), *Social Assistance in OECD Countries* (1996), *Capitalism and Social Cohesion* (1999) and *Global Capital, Human Needs and Social Policies: Selected Essays 1993–99* (2000). His latest co-authored book is *Insecurity and Welfare Regimes in Asia, Africa and Latin America* (2004). He is a fellow of the Academy of Social Sciences.

Linda Hantrais is Professor of European Social Policy and Director of the European Research Centre in the Department of Politics, International Relations and European Studies, Loughborough University. Her research interests span cross-national comparative research theory, methodology, management and practice, with particular reference to public policy and institutional structures in the European Union, and the relationship between socio-demographic trends and social policy. She has co-ordinated several European research projects and published widely on these topics, including: *Cross-National Research Methods in the Social Sciences* (edited with Steen Mangen, Pinter, 1996); *Social Policy in the European Union* (Palgrave, 2000, 2nd edn); *Gendered Policies in Europe: reconciling employment and family life* (ed., Palgrave, 2000); and *Family Policy Matters: responding to family change in Europe* (Policy Press, 2004).

Ian Holliday is Professor and Head of Department of Public and Social Administration, City University of Hong Kong. His research interests focus on social policy and e-government in East and Southeast Asia. His recent publications include *Welfare Capitalism in East Asia: Social Policy in the Tiger Economies* (Basingstoke: Palgrave, 2003) (edited with Paul Wilding), 'Building E-government in East and Southeast Asia: Regional Rhetoric and National (In)action', *Public Administration and Development*, **22** (2002), 323–35, and 'Productivist Welfare Capitalism: Social Policy in East Asia', *Political Studies*, **48** (2000), 706–23.

Bob Jessop is Professor of Sociology and Director of the Institute for Advanced Studies in Management and Social Sciences at Lancaster University. He is best known for his work on state theory, Thatcherism, the regulation approach, and welfare state restructuring; and is currently working on the discourses and contradictions of the knowledge-based economy. His best known work includes *The Capitalist State* (1982), *Nocos Poulantzas* (1985), *Thatcherism: A Tale of Two Nations* (with Kevin Bonnett, Simon Bromley and Tom Ling), *State Theory* (1990), and *The Future of the Capitalist State* (2002). He has also published more than 100 book chapters and 60 refereed journal articles on these and related topics. Information about his recent work and new papers can be downloaded from his homepage: http://www.comp.lancs.ac.uk/sociology/rjessop.html.

Patricia Kennett is Senior Lecturer in Comparative Policy Studies at the School for Policy Studies, University of Bristol. Her research interests focus on comparative welfare systems, particularly in the context of Europe and East Asia; citizenship and social exclusion; housing and homelessness. Her recent publications include *Comparative Social Policy: Theory and Research* (2001) published by Open University Press; 'Precariousness in Everyday Life: Homelessness in Japan' (2003) *International Journal of Urban and Regional Research*, **27** (1); *Homelessness: Exploring the New Terrain* (1999) (eds) Policy Press (with Alex Marsh).

Walter Korpi is Professor of Social Policy at the Swedish Institute for Social Research, Stockholm University, and works on comparative welfare state development, political sociology, political economy, class and gender. In English, he has published *The Working Class in Welfare Capitalism* (1978) and *The Democratic Class Struggle* (1983). Recent articles include 'Faces of Inequality: Gender, Class, and Patterns of Inequalities in different Types of Welfare States' (*Social Politics*, 2000) and 'Contentious Institutions: An Augmented Rational-Action Analysis of the Origins and Path Dependency of Welfare State Institutions in Western Countries' (*Rationality and Society*,

2001), and 'The Great Trough in Unemployment: A Long-Term View of Unemployment, Inflation, Strikes, and the Profit/Wage Ratio' (*Politics & Society*, 2002).

Steen Mangen convenes the MSc in European Social Policy at the University of London School of Economics. His main research interests lie in the contemporary Spanish and German welfare states, qualitative methods in cross-national settings, and urban regeneration policies in Western Europe. He is joint editor (with Linda Hantrais) of a special issue of the *International Journal of Social Research Methodology* on cross-national methods (**2** (2), 1999). He has contributed to Eva Kolinsky et al. (eds) *The New Germany in the East: Policy Agendas and Social Developments since Unification* (Cass, 2000). His book, *Spanish Society After Franco: Regime Transition and the Welfare State*, was published by Palgrave in 2001. His latest book, *Social Exclusion and Inner City Europe: Regulating Urban Regeneration*, is being published by Palgrave in 2004.

James Midgley is Harry and Riva Specht Professor of Public Social Services and Dean of the School of Social Welfare at the University of California, Berkeley. He has published widely on issues of social development, social policy, social work and international social welfare. His most recent books include: *Social Welfare in Global Context* (Sage Publications, 1997); *The Handbook of Social Policy* (with Martin Tracy and Michelle Livermore, Sage Publications, 2000); *Controversial Issues in Social Policy* (with Howard Karger and Brene Brown, Allyn & Bacon, 2003); and *Social Policy for Development* (with Anthony Hall, Sage Publications, 2004).

Ramesh Mishra is Emeritus Professor of Social Policy at York University, Toronto. His research interests are in the relationship of globalization and social protection and in comparative social policy. He is currently working on the globalization of social rights. Ramesh Mishra's recent publications include *Globalization and the Welfare State* (1999); 'The Political Bases of Canadian Social Welfare' in J.Turner and F. Turner (eds) *Canadian Social Welfare* (2000); 'Globalization and Poverty in the Americas', *Journal Of International and Comparative Social Welfare* (2002); and 'Social rights as human rights' *International Social Work* (forthcoming).

David Nelken is Distinguished Professor of Sociology at the University of Macerata in Italy, Distinguished Research Professor of Law at Cardiff Law School and Honorary Visiting Professor at the LSE. Recent publications include *Comparing Legal Cultures* (Dartmouth, 1997), *Contrasting Criminal Justice* (Dartmouth, 2000) and *Adapting Legal Cultures* (Hart, 2001).

Julia S. O'Connor is Professor of Social Policy at the University of Ulster. Her main area of research is welfare states in comparative perspective, focusing on OECD and EU countries including the accession countries. Current research projects include a study of convergence in social policy in the EU in the context of increased globalization and a study of knowledge of, and attitudes towards, the European Union in Northern Ireland in a comparative context. Publications include *States, Markets, Families: Gender, Liberalism and Social Policy in Australia, Canada, Great Britain and the United States*, Cambridge University Press (1999) (with Ann S. Orloff and Sheila Shaver); *Power Resources Theory and the Welfare State*, University of Toronto Press (1988) (edited with Gregg Olsen).

Else Øyen is Professor of Social Policy at the University of Bergen and Scientific Director of CROP (Comparative Research Programme on Poverty).[1] She is former President of the International Social Science Council and former Vice-President of the International Sociological Association. She also served as Chair of the ISA Research Council and former Chair of the ISA Research Committee on Poverty, Social Welfare and Social Policy. Her research interests include comparative studies of processes in the welfare state, comparative methodology, poverty in developed and developing countries and social policy theory. She has published over a dozen books on social policy issues, inequality, sociology of law and client research; edited volumes on comparative welfare state studies, comparative methodology, social policy and poverty; articles on poverty research, methodological and ethical issues, principles of confidentiality, social policy and social security.

Joakim Palme is Director of the Institute for Futures Studies in Stockholm and an associate of the Swedish Institute for Social Research at Stockholm University. His research focuses on the development of welfare state institutions, and the causes and consequences of this development. He has published on pension rights and pension reform, the public–private mix in social protection, as well as on health and social insurance. Recently, he chaired the Welfare Commission, a large survey of the state of welfare in Sweden. He is currently involved in research on recent welfare state transformations in a comparative perspective.

Andrés Pérez-Baltodano is an Associate Professor of Political Science at the University of Western Ontario, in Canada. He is a former director of the Nicaraguan Institute of Public Administration. Between 1983 and 1988 he worked with the International Development Research Centre in Canada, where he organized a multinational research programme in public policy and participation. He has published extensively in the areas of globalization, public policies and the state, with special emphasis on Latin America. He is the editor of the book *Globalización, Ciudadanía y Política Social en América Latina: Tensiones y Contradiciones*. His most recent book *Entre el Estado Conquistador y el Estado Nación* (2003) offers an interpretation of the role of culture in the process of state formation in Nicaragua.

Graham Room has been Professor of European Social Policy at the University of Bath since 1992. He has acted as consultant to the European Commission on the development of its programmes in the field of poverty and social exclusion and as Special Adviser to the UK House of Lords Select Committee on the European Communities, 1994. He was founding editor of the *Journal of European Social Policy*. His recent publications include 'Social Exclusion, Solidarity and the Challenge of Globalisation', *International Journal of Social Welfare*, **8** (3), pp. 166–74, 1999, 'Commodification and Decommodification: A Developmental Critique', *Policy and Politics*, **28** (3), pp. 331–51, 2000, 'Social Benchmarking, Policy-Making and Governance in the EU', *Journal of European Social Policy*, **11** (4), pp. 291–307 (with C. De la Porte and P. Pochet), 2001, and 'Education and Welfare: Recalibrating the European Debate', *Policy Studies*, **23** (1), pp. 37–50, 2002.

Jill Steans is Senior Lecturer in International Relations Theory at the University of Birmingham. Her main research interests are in the fields of gender and international relations theory and international political economy. She is the author of *Gender and International Relations*, Oxford, Polity Press, 1998; co-editor (with Neil Renwick) of *Identities in International Relations*, Basingstoke: Macmillian, 1996 and co-author (with Lloyd Pettiford) of *International Relations: Perspectives And Themes*, London: Longmans, 2001. She is currently working on a book on gendering globalization.

Julia Tao is Associate Professor in the Department of Public and Social Administration, City University of Hong Kong. She is also the Director of the Governance in Asia Research Centre. Her teaching and research interests are in the areas of social and political philosophy, applied ethics, and comparative values and social policy. Her recent writings include an edited book on *Cross-Cultural Perspectives on (Im)Possibility of Global Bioethics* (Kluwer Academic Publishers, 2002) and 'Confucian and Liberal Ethics for Public Policy: Holistic or Atomistic?', *Journal of Social Philosophy*, December 2003 (with A. Brennan)

Alan Walker is Professor of Social Policy at the University of Sheffield. He is also Director of the ESRC Growing Older Programme and of the UK National Collaboration on Ageing Research. He has a long-standing interest in social policy in China and East Asia. Recent publications include *The Social Quality of Europe* (with W. Beck and L. van der Maesen) (The Policy Press) and *Social Quality: A Vision for Europe* (with W. Beck, L. van der Maesen and F. Thomese) (Kluwer International).

Chack-kie Wong is a Professor in the Department of Social Work at the Chinese University of Hong Kong. His current research projects focus on comparative social policy and Chinese social welfare. He has published articles in *Social Policy and Society*, *Journal of Social Policy*, *Social Policy and Administration* and *International Social Work*.

Note

1. CROP is an interdisciplinary and international research programme on poverty in developed and developing countries. CROP now has a network of more than 1700 researchers and institutions working with poverty issues. For more information you may visit the web at www.crop.org.

Acknowledgements

The original idea for this collection came from the publishers Edward Elgar. Convinced that this was a timely and valuable contribution to the literature on comparative social policy analysis, I enthusiastically took over the task of selecting and bringing together the wide-ranging contributions. I would like to thank the authors for their willingness to contribute to the handbook, for the time and effort put into producing their individual chapters and for their patience during the editing process. I am also grateful to the publishers for their advice and support, and to Claudia Bittencourt for her technical and secretarial assistance.

Introduction: the changing context of comparative social policy

Patricia Kennett

The field of comparative social enquiry has grown dramatically since the 1960s, in terms of the amount of studies being undertaken, the range of approaches used and the countries analysed. The analytical emphasis on the notions of modernization and convergence, and social expenditure as a proportion of GNP as the measure of welfare effort, whilst still evident in contemporary cross-national research, ceased to dominate the comparative landscape during the 1980s. There is now much more interest in recognizing and explaining qualitative as well as quantitative differences in types of welfare systems, an acknowledgement that formal social policies are only one element in the arrangement of welfare and that social policy is not just about ameliorating the impact of social inequality or altruism but itself contributes to social divisions in society. There has been a greater recognition of diversity and the importance of analysing context, processes and the outcomes of social policies in different countries and their impact on different groups.

The changing discourse around social policy and the welfare state can also be associated with the economic and political conditions of the 1980s, which were in marked contrast to what had gone before. In many OECD countries post-1945 was an era in which the notion of Keynesian welfare capitalism, in its various institutional forms, incorporated a commitment to extended social citizenship and a certain minimum standard of life and security as a matter of right. National welfare regimes helped to underpin a global system of interacting national economies characterized by mass production and mass consumption. This model of institutionalized, bureaucratic provision and social rights was perceived as the inevitable outcome of a 'modern' or developed society. By the 1980s it was the political rhetoric of deregulation, privatization, the efficiency of the 'free market' and rolling back the frontiers of the state that had become the global economic discourse influencing both national and international policies. According to Taylor-Gooby (2001) in a European context '... Keynesianism (the view that state intervention is the best way to promote growth and employment) is quite simply dead, a result of the general acceptance that governmental capacity to manage investment within its borders is limited' (p. 19). At the same time many of the fundamental assumptions associated with the national welfare state and the social rights of citizenship have been discredited and renegotiated, and the discourse about the role of the state in welfare has moved in a new direction (Taylor-Gooby, 2001; Kennett, 2001). Harris (2002) contrasts the 'new' welfare of the last two decades which centres on personal and community relationships (Etzioni, 1995, 1997; Driver and Martell, 1997), community governance and the notion of active membership, with the 'old' welfare of the post-war period with emphasized society, universal citizenship rights and statutory state provision (King and Wickham Jones, 1999; Rose, 1999). Fundamental to the 'new' welfare is a re-balancing of the social contract between the state and the individual, between rights and responsibility and between different spatial scales.

The current context then is one in which many of the old certainties of the past have been eroded, and the predominantly inward-looking, domestic preoccupation of social policy has made way for a more integrated, international and outward approach to analysis. Central to this endeavour is a reassessment of the place of the state in contemporary social policy analysis. The pre-eminence of the national scale, the national state and the national citizen has been weakened by internationalization, the growth of multi-tiered networks and partnerships, and the re-emergence of the regional and the local within national states. There has been a proliferation of scales, channels, projects and social networks through which social interaction and active participation can be pursued. Thus, within the modern world system the notion of unfettered state sovereignty has become problematic and contradictory (Clapham, 2002; Weiss, 2003) and has presented new challenges for comparative analysis in the social sciences.

These challenges have been captured in recent academic debates relating to processes of globalization which have contributed to a de-centring of the state in social policy analysis. The burgeoning literature reflects the multifaceted nature of global processes, and indeed the vagueness and inconsistencies in the use of the concept (Geshiere and Meyer, 1998). General debates have been concerned with the economic, cultural, technological, social and political dimensions of the phenomenon. More recently, the relationship between globalization, social policy and the welfare state has generated interest amongst commentators (for example Deacon et al., 1997; Midgley, 1997; Mishra, 1999; Yeates, 2000; Scharf, 2000; Swank, 2002). This interest has emerged in the context of the retrenchment and reorientation of welfare mentioned earlier and the changing role of the state as its dominant position has increasingly been challenged by transnational institutions and the assertiveness of subnational governments. Global processes are said by some to have contributed to the erosion of the functions of nation-states and deprived national governments of their ability to establish and maintain an autonomous welfare model. Clearly there are differing opinions on the nature, extent and impact of global processes on social policy and welfare systems. What is more certain is that the current context of social policy is one which looks beyond the boundaries of the state in terms of incorporating transnational and subnational activities, and which is sensitive to the nature of the mixed economy of welfare and the range of conduits through which policies are made and delivered. For Gershiere and Meyer the concept of globalization is inspiring precisely because it requires social scientists to reconsider and reflect upon their objects of study as well as 'seek for more appropriate fields of investigation which take account of peoples actual entanglement in wider processes' (Geshiere and Meyer, 1998: 603).

So in de-centring the state the researcher is encouraged to reconsider established structures of 'boundedness' and to seek out alternative orientation points and identify reconstructed boundaries as individuals, communities and societies seek to make sense of a changing world.

It is in this context then that this handbook brings together the work of key commentators in the field of comparative analysis in order to provide comprehensive, but by no means exhaustive, coverage of contemporary debates and issues in cross-national research. Organized around five themes, the collection explores the contextual, conceptual, analytical and processual aspects of undertaking comparative social research. The first part – 'The state and social policy in a globalizing world' – is concerned with extending the epistemological framework through which cross-national analysis is explored. The four contributors to this part draw on the theme of globalization to explore the future of the nation-state and the nature of governance, and the implications for human security and social protection in different societies and for different groups of people.

Bob Jessop (Chapter 1) identifies the transfer of powers previously located at the national level to a more diverse, multi-level and multi-sector range of actors and institutions. In addition, he stresses the increasing importance of looking 'beyond the state' in order to understand the future of national and/or nation-states and recognize that it is 'embedded in a wider political system, other institutional orders, and the lifeworld' (p. 12 this volume). Whilst pointing out that the boundaries and institutional structures of states are socially constructed and vary over time and across space, Jessop identifies the demise of the Keynesian welfare national state and its replacement by a Schumpeterian workfare post-national regime. Within this regime the emphasis is on innovation, flexibility and open economies, the erosion of the social wage and a subordination of social policy to the needs of a flexible labour market and an economy able to compete in the global market place.

The implications of this and other aspects of recent structural change on women are the concern of Jill Steans (Chapter 2). Her emphasis is on the gendered nature of globalization and world order and the significance of the public and private realms in reshaping identities and roles in both developed and developing countries. The differential impact of globalization on the states and societies of the North and the South is also a concern of Andrés Pérez-Baltodano in Chapter 3. He investigates the range of social policy responses to the crisis of security created by processes of globalization. He outlines the formation and development of the democratic western European state and, drawing upon this 'universalist' model, considers the different levels of 'stateness' achieved by countries in the North and the South. He argues that an understanding of the varying capacities of states to respond to global pressures is vital in order to fully comprehend the varying conditions of human security across societies. To this end, his focus on the North and South provides a useful comparison in that they 'represent categories for differentiating levels of institutional and regulatory capacity to create conditions of order and security at the national level' (p. 57 this volume).

In the final chapter of Part I (Chapter 4), Ramesh Mishra focuses on Australia, Japan and the post-socialist countries of Eastern Europe and the former USSR as representative of societies with institutional patterns defined as 'social protection by other means'. He argues that these were developed during an era of relatively closed and insulated national economies and considers the extent to which they have been undermined by the opening up of national markets to international competition.

The reassessment of the role of the state in social policy analysis forms part of a fundamental reappraisal of the assumptions embedded in social science research which has been under way since the 1980s. The rationality, essentialism and universalism of policy discourse and practices through which the welfare state was established have been called into question. The emphasis on diversity, difference and contingency and the notion of spatial and temporal variation challenged many of the assumptions on which the theoretical and epistemological traditions of social policy have been built. With this in mind Parts II and III of this volume focus on the conceptual and theoretical frameworks for analysing social policy cross-nationally.

In Chapter 5 Jochen Clasen begins by exploring the distinctive features of and the meanings applied to comparative social policy over recent years. For comparativists the unit of analysis has traditionally been different national contexts. However, as the boundaries of state and society are becoming increasingly blurred the concerns for Graham Crow in Chapter 6 are 'What do social scientists compare? Are the concepts of state and society still relevant in cross-national analysis?'.

Chapters 7 and 8 question the dominance of the Western social research paradigm in comparative analysis. Alan Walker and Chack-kie Wong critically assess the way in which the concept of the 'welfare state' has been utilized in cross-national analysis. They conclude that the Western ethnocentric construction of the concept has resulted in the exclusion of large sections of the globe from comparative research. Julia Tao reconceptualizes the nature of human need and social obligation from the Chinese Confucian moral tradition.

Attempts to categorize and typologize different aspects of welfare systems across countries have been an extremely popular feature of comparative social research. This approach is exemplified in the work of Gøsta Esping-Andersen (1990) which represents a major contribution to the field of cross-national analysis. His identification of the 'Three Worlds of Welfare Capitalism' is referred to in many of the chapters in this collection. The five chapters in Part III are concerned with extending and broadening the analytical, conceptual and substantive aspects of categorizing and typologizing welfare states. Walter Korpi and Joakim Palme begin by building a typology of welfare states based on their institutional characteristics and the consequences for inequality and poverty of different types of welfare system (Chapter 9). In Chapter 10 Julia O'Connor links the contested concepts of gender, citizenship and welfare regimes to explain the variations in the range and quality of social rights. She urges that 'gender, race and class and their interaction must be integral parts of comparative analysis' (p. 197 this volume). This is echoed by Norman Ginsburg in Chapter 11 who adopts a 'critical structured diversity' approach to explore cross-national developments in social policy. For Ginsburg this approach enables the researcher to retain the specificity of each national context, whilst also incorporating elements 'beyond the state' within the analysis. It also incorporates consideration of the relationship between the welfare state and the social divisions of race, class and gender.

The final two chapters in this section are concerned with the relevance of classificatory and explanatory models for analysing social welfare in the countries of the South. In Chapter 12 James Midgley points to the need for 'appropriate, normative frameworks that can address the persistence of global poverty, mass deprivation, oppression and other pressing problems' (p. 218 this volume) both in the North and in the South. He outlines the social development perspective and argues that this approach can make a major contribution to this effort. In contrast, Ian Gough's response (in Chapter 13) has been to 'radically recast' the welfare regime paradigm. He provides a variegated, middle-range model that can facilitate fruitful and integrated analysis across the North and South of the globe.

In Part IV – The Research Process – the focus, as the title suggests, is the day-to-day reality of preparing for and carrying out cross-national social policy analysis. It is concerned with recognizing and exploring the issues that emerge when researching in more than one country. In Chapter 14 Linda Hantrais discusses the relevance and implications of recognizing and understanding different research cultures and disciplinary traditions. In the following chapter (Chapter 15) Else Øyen uses research on poverty to highlight the difficulties and advantages of adopting a comparative focus. Chapter 16 (Patricia Kennett) emphasizes and demonstrates the need to develop appropriate and robust concepts and an understanding of the ways in which social problems are constructed in order to effectively analyse issues in different national contexts. Homelessness is used as a concrete example to highlight the 'elasticity' of definitions not only within national contexts but also internationally, and the implications of this for data collection. Chapters 17 and 18 respectively (Steen Mangen and Mattei Dogan) are concerned with qualitative and quantitative approaches in cross-national analysis.

The final part of this collection is intended to highlight continuing and emerging themes and issues which could prove of particular relevance to understanding the contemporary social world. There is evidence of increasing inequality and polarization in the distribution of wealth as the opportunities of globalization are unevenly distributed between nations and people. Graham Room (Chapter 19) considers the various ways in which social exclusion has been analysed in the European Union during the last 30 years and considers the possibilities for future research, whilst Ray Forrest (Chapter 20) explores the nature of the housing question for the 21st Century. For David Nelken (Chapter 21) it is not just the emergence of new types of crime such as transnational organized crime or sexual tourism that can be associated with globalization. Global processes have also exacerbated differences between countries, regions, cities and even parts of cities which, according to Nelken, has provided 'both the conditions and alibi for much crime' (p. 377 this volume). In the final chapter in this volume Ian Holliday (Chapter 22) discusses the rapid developments in information technology and e-government and considers the ways in which the policy process and social policy are being re-shaped. He points to the strengthening of global networks, the potential for new forms of political participation, policy making and social policy, as well as the deepening of inequalities and the international digital divide. These are aspects of The Informational Age that should and could be integrated into and better understood through comparative policy analysis.

References

Clapham, Christopher (2002), 'The challenge to the state in a globalized world', *Development and Change*, **33** (5), 775–95.

Deacon, Bob, with Michelle Hulse and Paul Stubbs (1997), *Global Social Policy. International Organizations and the Future of Welfare*, London: Sage Publications.

Driver, Stephen and Luke Martell (1997), 'New Labour's communitarianisms', *Critical Social Policy*, **17** (3), 27–44.

Esping-Andersen, Gøsta (1990), *The Three Worlds of Welfare Capitalism*, Cambridge: Polity Press.

Etzioni, Amitai (1995), *The Spirit of Community*, London: Fontana.

Etzioni, Amitai (1997), *The New Golden Rule, Community and Morality in a Democratic Society*, New York: Basic Books.

Geshiere, Peter and Birgit Meyer (1998), 'Globalization and identity: dialectics of flow and closure. Introduction', *Development and Change*, **29**, 601–15.

Harris, Patricia (2002), 'Welfare rewritten: change and interlay in social and economic accounts', *Journal of Social Policy*, **31** (3), 377–98.

Kennett, Patricia (2001), *Comparative Social Policy: Theory and Research*, Buckingham: Open University Press.

King, Desmond and Mark Wickham-Jones (1999), 'Bridging the Atlantic: the Democratic (Party) origins of welfare to work', in M. Powell (ed.) *New Labour, New Welfare State? The Third Way in British Social Policy*, Bristol: The Policy Press.

Midgley, James (1997), *Social Welfare in Global Context*, Thousand Oaks, CA and London: Sage Publications.

Mishra, Ramesh (1999), *Globalization and the Welfare State*, Cheltenham, UK and Northampton, MA, USA: Edward Elgar.

Rose, Nicolas (1999), *Powers of Freedom: Reframing Political Thought*, Cambridge: Cambridge University Press.

Scharf, Fritz W. (2000), 'The viability of advanced welfare states in the international economy, vulnerabilities and options', *Journal of European Public Policy*, vol. 7, pp. 190–228.

Swank, Duane (2002), *Global Capital, Political Institutions and Policy Change in Developed Welfare States*, Cambridge: Cambridge University Press.

Taylor-Gooby, Peter (ed.) (2001),*Welfare States under Pressure*, London: Sage Publications.

Weiss, Linda (ed.) (2003), *States in the Global Economy. Bringing domestic institutions back in*, Cambridge: Cambridge University Press.

Yeates, Nicola (2000), *Globalisation and Social Policy*, London: Sage Publications.

PART I

THE STATE AND SOCIAL POLICY IN A GLOBALIZING WORLD

1 Hollowing out the 'nation-state' and multi-level governance

Bob Jessop

Lively debates over the future of the nation-state resurfaced in the 1980s as scholars and politicians began to suggest that it had become too small to solve the world's big problems and too big to solve its little ones. These problems include: (1) the rise of global capitalism, (2) the emergence of a global risk society, especially regarding the environment, (3) the growth of identity politics and new social movements based on local and/or transnational issues; and (4) the threat of new forms of terrorism and dispersed network warfare. But what exactly these problems imply for the future of the state remains unclear. Prognoses include the development of an entirely new kind of state; the re-scaling of the nation-state's powers upwards, downwards or sideways; a shift from state-based government to network-based governance; or incremental changes in secondary aspects of the nation-state that leave its core intact.

More radical predictions of the future of the state include: the hollowing out of the nation-state, the rise of the hollow state, the internationalization of the state, the fragmentation of the modern system of nation-states into a convoluted and tangled 'neo-medieval' system; the decline of large nation-states in favour of medium-sized 'region-states' that organize dynamic regional economies across national frontiers; and the rise of a global state or, at least, a western hemispheric state under American hegemony. More modest predictions include references to 'holed power containers', 'perforated sovereignties', the 'unbundling' of national state powers, an uneven process of 'denationalization–renationalization' of the state, and growing intergovernmental cooperation based on the continued primacy of nation-states. Compounding this confusion, others have suggested that the powers of the territorial state are being replaced on all scales by non-hierarchical forms of coordination with highly variable territorial geometries. This development is often termed 'governance without government'. Yet others have suggested that the nation-state remains very much alive. The two main explanations for this continuing vigour are that it was never as strong before and is not now so weak as talk of its 'hollowing out' suggests; and/or that it is 'self-substituting' as state managers continually redesign the state to ensure its survival in response to new challenges.

1.   Five conceptual clarifications

An adequate response to this confusion requires five clarifications. First, all forms of state are based on the territorialization of political power. A formally sovereign national state exercising unchallenged sovereign control over a large territorial area is a relatively recent institutional expression of state power. It is the historical product of a specific, socially constructed demarcation of the political system and divides the latter into many territorially exclusive, mutually recognizing, mutually validating, sovereign states. These in turn provide the main reference point for political struggles and, indeed, the distinction between domestic and international politics. Other modes of territorializing political power have existed, new expressions are emerging, yet others can be imagined. Earlier modes include city-states, empires, the medieval state system, absolutism, and modern imperial–colonial blocs. Emerging modes include cross-border regions, triad regions (for example, the European Union), a western conglomerate state, and even an embryonic world state. Thus, the modern territorial national state must be seen as a very late – and by no means final – development in state formation.

Second, we should distinguish between the national state and the nation-state. Territorial delimitation long preceded nation-formation and, whereas territorial statehood is now almost universal, nation-statehood is not. Even when national identity is the basis of state formation, it can have different, potentially overlapping, sometimes antagonistic bases. These include ethnic identity, based on a socially constructed ethnonational community (for example, Germany); a cultural nation based on a shared national culture that may well be defined and actively promoted by the state itself (for example, France); and a civic nation based on patriotic commitment to the constitution and belief in the legitimacy of representative government (for example, the USA). These three forms can reinforce each other (for example, Denmark), be combined in a hybrid multinational state (for example, mainland Britain), or provoke conflicts over the proper basis of the nation-state (for example, Canada, New Zealand). Pressures exist to grant significant autonomy to regionally based national minorities (for example, Spain) or institute 'consociational' forms of government to share power between nations in a given state (for example, Belgium, New Zealand).

Third, addressing the future of national and/or nation-states requires us to look beyond the state. This does not exist in majestic isolation overseeing the rest of society but is embedded in a wider political system, other institutional orders, and the lifeworld. The state's delimitation as an institutional ensemble relative to its encompassing political system is historically variable and socially constructed. So are its multiple demarcations from other institutional orders (for example, the economy, religion, science, education, art) and from civil society. Indeed, '[t]he essence of modern politics is not policies formed on one side of this division [between the state and society] being applied to or shaped by the other, but the producing and reproducing of this line of difference' (Mitchell, 1991: 95). Thus an important aspect of state transformation is the redrawing of this 'line of difference' (or demarcation) as the state redefines its priorities, expands or reduces its activities, and is dis-embedded or re-embedded.

Fourth, despite the formal equivalence among mutually recognizing sovereign states in the modern state system, not all states are equally capable of exercising power internally and/or internationally. They face different problems at home and abroad; they have different histories; they have different capacities to address these problems and reorganize themselves in response; and, in international encounters, some states are more powerful than others. More specifically, in regard to recent debates on globalization and the state, whereas some political elites try to resist globalization in order to preserve some measure of formal sovereignty, other elites elsewhere actively promote it in their perceived national interests and even hope thereby to enhance state capacities. The most important example of the latter case is, of course, the US federal state, which has been the most vocal and forceful advocate of globalization for many years.

Fifth, as the previous clarification indicates, it is highly misleading to conceive of the relationship between globalization and the power of national territorial states in zero-sum terms. For this would involve treating the current, partly globalization-induced crisis of the territorial national state – whether in its post-war Atlantic Fordist form, developmental statist, national security state, or other forms – as signifying the present and future impossibility of any other institutional form(s) for the territorialization of political power. Instead it is likely that attempts will be made to redesign the national territorial state in response to globalization and/or to establish new territorial scales as the primary nodal point around which state power is exercised. In both cases this could include the redrawing of the line of demarcation between state and society (see above) to enhance the overall effectiveness of state power in achieving particular political objectives through sharing its exercise.

2. The Keynesian welfare national state

This contribution cannot consider recent changes in all forms of national territorial state, whatever their location in the international state system. Instead it focuses on changes in Keynesian welfare national states (or KWNS). This is the form of state that became dominant in North Western Europe, North America, Australia and New Zealand during the 1950s to 1970s and that was closely linked with the post-war Fordist growth dynamic based on mass production and mass consumption. Each term in this fourfold ideal type refers to a major aspect of state involvement in securing the continued expansion of capital accumulation and, in this sense, it interprets the state from a broadly economic perspective. This is not the only way to examine changes in the state; adopting alternative entry points would highlight other aspects of state transformation or, indeed, reveal certain continuities in the state. But the approach adopted here illuminates many of the issues noted above. Accordingly I now define the main features of the KWNS as a benchmark against which to assess recent changes in the state.

First, in promoting the conditions for profitable economic growth, the KWNS was distinctively *Keynesian* insofar as it aimed to secure full employment in a relatively closed national economy and did so mainly through demand-side management and national infrastructural provision. Second, in contributing to the day-to-day, lifetime, and intergenerational reproduction of the labour force, KWNS social policy had a distinctive *welfare* orientation insofar as it (a) instituted economic and social rights for all citizens so that they could share in growing prosperity (and contribute to high levels of demand) even if they were not employed in the high-wage, high-growth Fordist economic sectors; and (b) promoted forms of collective consumption favourable to the Fordist growth dynamic. Third, the KWNS was *national* insofar as these economic and social policies were pursued within the historically specific (and socially constructed) matrix of a national economy, a national state and a society seen as comprising national citizens. Within this matrix it was the national territorial state that was mainly held responsible for developing and guiding Keynesian welfare policies. Local and regional states acted mainly as relays for policies framed at the national level; and the leading international regimes established after World War II were mainly intended to restore stability to national economies and national states. And, fourth, the KWNS was *statist* insofar as state institutions (on different levels) were the chief supplement and corrective to market forces in a 'mixed economy' concerned with economic growth and social integration.

There was never a pure KWNS. Instead it had different national instantiations within the broader international economic and political framework of Atlantic Fordism. Nor has there been a generic crisis that affects all such national states identically. Nonetheless, they have all faced similar pressures from recent changes. The first signs of crisis in Fordist growth emerged in the mid-1970s and the situation worsened in the 1980s. In addition, the structured coherence of national economy–national state–national society was weakened by changes associated with globalization, internationalization, the rise of multi-tiered global city networks, the formation of triad economies (such as European Economic Space), and the re-emergence of regional and local economies. The unity of the nation-state has also been weakened by the (admittedly uneven) growth of multi-ethnic and multi-cultural societies and of divided political loyalties (with the resurgence of regionalism and nationalism as well as the rise of European identities, diasporic networks, cosmopolitan patriotism, and so on).

3. Six trends in the restructuring of national states

The current reorganization of the national state and the modalities of state power in response to these and other pressures can be summarized in terms of six sets of analytically distinct but empirically interrelated and often overlapping trends. Each trend is also associated with a counter-trend that both qualifies and transforms its significance for the state's form and functions. These counter-trends can be viewed in the first instance as specific reactions to the new trends rather than as survivals of earlier patterns. This is why they are presented as counter-trends to the trends.

Denationalization of statehood

This involves the transfer of powers previously located at the national territorial level upwards to supra-regional or international bodies, downwards to regional or local states, or outwards to relatively autonomous cross-national alliances among local metropolitan or regional states with complementary interests. In addition, new state powers have been allocated to scales other than the national. This de- and re-territorialization of specific state powers is reshaping national states *qua* mutually exclusive, formally sovereign, spatially segmented instantiations of the modern interstate system. Given the primacy of the national scale in the KWNS, this trend is sometimes described as the 'hollowing out' of the national state. However labelled, it reflects attempts by state managers on different territorial scales to enhance their respective operational autonomies and strategic capacities.

De- and re-statization

This involves redrawing the internal demarcation between state and non-state apparatuses within the political system as activities are re-allocated across this division. While denationalization concerns the territorial dispersion of the national state's activities (hence de- and re-territorialization), de-statization involves redrawing the 'public–private' divide and modifying the relationship between organizations and tasks across this divide on whatever territorial scale(s) the state in question acts. In other words, some of the particular technical–economic, juridical, administrative, narrowly political, and ideological functions performed by states (on any scale) have been transferred entirely to, or shared with, other (that is, parastatal, non-governmental, private or commercial) actors, institutional arrangements or regimes. This is often described as a shift from govern*ment* to govern*ance* but this slogan misleads in depicting a one-way shift. For there is also traffic in the other direction as states on different scales gain new responsibilities that were previously ascribed, if anywhere, to the market or civil society. Overall, this trend involves the increased importance of quite varied forms (and levels) of partnership between official bodies, parastatal organizations and non-governmental organizations (NGOs) in managing economic and social relations in which the state is often only first among equals. This blurs the division between public and private, expands and reinforces the principle of subsidiarity, strengthens the informal sector as well as private enterprise (especially in delivering welfare and collective consumption), and reinforces mechanisms such as 'regulated self-regulation' and 'private interest government'. It is also linked to the state's growing involvement in decentred societal guidance strategies based on growing recognition of functional interdependencies, the division of knowledge, and the need for mutual learning, reflexivity and negotiated coordination between state and non-state actors. This need not entail a loss in the overall power of government, however, as if power were a zero-sum resource. Resort to governance could enhance the state's capacity to project its influence and secure its objectives by mobilizing knowledge and power resources from influential non-governmental partners or stakeholders.

The retreat of the state

At stake here is the growth of modes of exercising power that do not rest on imperative coordination by a territorialized state apparatus and that are formally independent of its borders, even if the latter have been re-scaled. This process weakens territorial 'power containers' on any scale relative to non-territorial forms of political power. As such it is often subsumed under the shift from govern*ment* to govern*ance* but it differs from this trend because it dissociates the exercise of political power from imagined political communities whose interests are tied to territorialized state power. One way to distinguish between these two trends is to see de-statization as involving public–private partnerships in which the state devolves responsibilities to the private sphere but attempts to remain *primus inter pares*; and to consider the growth – perhaps at the behest of state managers themselves – of functionalized forms of power as involving self-organization that bypasses or circumvents direct top-down state intervention. The increasing importance of international regimes for the relative stabilization of a globalizing economy and the rise of cybernetworks in an extra-territorial, telematic space allegedly beyond state control are two contrasting examples of the third process.

Re-articulating the economic and extra-economic

The boundaries and division of labour between the political and economic systems are being redefined to take account of changed understandings of the economy and the conditions making for sound economic performance. The economy is no longer interpreted in narrow terms but has been extended to include many additional factors, deemed 'non-economic' under the KWNS regime, that affect economic performance and competitiveness. This requires attention to a growing range of economically relevant social practices, institutions, functional systems, and domains of the lifeworld that affect competitiveness. This has two interesting and paradoxical effects on states and politics. First, whilst it expands the potential scope of state intervention for economic purposes, the resulting complexity renders the typical post-war forms of top-down intervention less effective – requiring that the state retreat from some areas of intervention and redesign its institutional forms and functions in order to intervene more effectively in other areas. And, second, whilst it increases the range of stakeholders whose cooperation is required for successful state intervention, it also increases pressures within the state to create new subjects to act as its partners. Thus states are now trying to transform the identities, interests, capacities, rights and responsibilities of economic and social forces so that they become more flexible, capable and reliable agents of the state's new economic strategies – whether in partnership with the state and/or each other or as autonomous entrepreneurial subjects in the new knowledge-driven economy.

Re-ordering political hierarchies

Political hierarchies are also being re-ordered. The nested hierarchy of state power within territorially exclusive sovereign states and formal equality among such states was never fully realized in the modern interstate system, but it did provide the institutional framework within which forces struggled to control state power and/or modify the balance of international forces. Many of the changes discussed above have tended to undermine the coherence of this nested hierarchy and to produce increasing unstructured complexity as different scales of economic and political organization proliferate and different scale strategies are pursued. This is reflected in, *inter alia*, the internationalization of policy regimes. This means that the international context of domestic state action (whether national, regional or local) has expanded to include a widening range of extraterritorial or transnational factors and processes; that the international context has become more significant strategically for domestic policy; and that key players in policy regimes have expanded to include foreign agents and institutions as sources of policy ideas, policy design and implementation. This trend affects local and regional states below the national level as well as supranational state formations and international regimes. It is also evident in the development of the interregional and cross-border linkages connecting local and regional authorities and governance regimes in different national formations.

Re-imagining political communities

The political communities (or publics) around which forces in the political system orient their actions are being re-imagined in various ways. Among them are new 'imagined nations' seeking autonomy within and/or control of a defined territory below, above, or transversal to existing national states; a global civil society based on cosmopolitan patriotism, the primacy of human rights over national citizenship, or some other global identity; new 'communities of fate' defined by shared risks regardless of specific territorial location and, perhaps, global in character (for example, global warming); and new communities of interest defined by shared identities, interests and values regardless of specific territorial location (for example, cybercommunities). Such new territorial or extraterritorial conceptions of political community are linked to struggles to redefine the nature and purposes of the state, find alternatives to territorialized forms of political power, and redefine the imagined general interest which political power, whether it remains territorial or not, should serve.

4.   And six countertrends

Countering the denationalization of statehood and the re-ordering of political hierarchies are the attempts of national states to control the articulation of different spatial scales and the transfer of powers between them. It might seem that there is a simple continuity of function here but the loss of primacy of the national scale introduces a major discontinuity in two respects. On the one hand, it enhances the need for supranational coordination and opens the space for subnational resurgence. On the other hand, it extends the scope for the national state itself to mediate between the increasing number of significant scales of action. Thus, while the national state may have lost some formal sovereignty through the upwards, downwards and sideways transfer of powers, it seeks to play a central role in interscalar articulation. This can be seen not only in the forms and scope of functional networks and cyberspace(s) and their associated activities but also in the re-articulation of terrestrial and territorial scales. Thus national states have an important role in producing and regulating extraterritorial spaces, such as offshore financial centres, export processing zones, flagging out, and tax havens. They are involved in developing and institutionalizing the new *lex mercatoria* governing international economic relations in the effort to benefit their own economic spaces. The same holds for the governance of cyberspace and its associated *lex cybertoria*. States on other levels of state may also try to engage in interscalar management, of course, but even the European Union, the most advanced supranational political apparatus, still lacks the powers and legitimacy to do this to the same extent as national states – especially its larger member states. This does not exclude strategic alliances among states on various scales to steer interscalar articulation or an eventual new scale of territorial state that has gained the necessary powers and legitimacy to coordinate the proliferating scales of action and to institutionalize new spatio-temporal fixes around this new primary scale.

Regarding the dual shift from government to governance included in the second and third trends noted above, we must resist the idealistic fallacy that expansion of non-governmental regimes renders the state redundant. It retains an important role precisely because of these trends. It is not only an important actor in many individual governance mechanisms, but also retains responsibility for their oversight in the light of the overall balance of class forces and the maintenance of social cohesion. This can be described in terms of a counter-trend in the form of a shift from government to meta-governance.

Even as states cede their claim to formal juridical sovereignty in the face of growing complex interdependence and seek to enhance their political capacities by participating in public–private partnerships or delegating public responsibilities to private institutions and actors, they are also becoming more involved in organizing and steering the self-organization of partnerships, networks and governance regimes. This shift from governance to meta-governance should not be confused with the survival of state sovereignty as the highest instance of government nor with the emergence of some form of 'megapartnership' to which all other partnerships are subordinated. Instead, it involves a shift from the top-down hierarchical political organization characteristic of sovereign states to an emphasis on steering multiple agencies, institutions and systems that are both operationally autonomous from one another and structurally coupled through various forms of reciprocal interdependence. It falls to the state to facilitate collective learning about functional linkages and material interdependencies among different sites and spheres of action. And it falls to politicians – local as well as national – to participate in developing the shared visions that can link complementary forms of governance and maximize their effectiveness. Such tasks are conducted by states not only in terms of their contribution to particular state functions but also in terms of their implications for political class domination and social cohesion.

The expanded definition of the economic at the expense of the extra-economic clearly involves a key role for states (on whatever scale) in mediating this re-articulation, steering the resulting commodification and re-commodification of social relations, and dealing with the effects of the increasing dominance of capitalist logic on social cohesion and social exclusion. Moreover, whereas the promotion of the micro-social conditions for capital accumulation in these changing circumstances may well be better handled at other levels than the national, problems of territorial integration, social cohesion and social exclusion are currently still best handled at the level of the large territorial national state. For the latter is still currently irreplaceable given its fisco-financial powers and its scope for redistributive politics in rearranging spatio-temporal fixes.

The emergence of new imagined political communities is too complex to discuss in detail here because it is shaped by a wide range of processes from technological change and economic globalization to crises of class and national identity and the rise of new social movements. Nonetheless it has led states to introduce policies to counteract the newly perceived problem of social exclusion and to seek new bases of legitimation to counteract threats posed by growing political disenchantment with the prevailing forms of state. These policies are being pursued across different scales and involve multiple agencies but the national state generally retains the leading meta-governance role in these areas.

5.   Multi-level government or multi-level governance?
A key concept introduced by scholars and politicians in recent years is 'multi-level governance'. It is used to capture the denationalization of statehood, the de-statization of politics, and the re-articulation of territorial and functional powers – especially as these trends are developing in the European Union. The fact that it is being used to describe the interaction of three analytically distinct trends (each with its counter-trend) or, at least, to characterize their combined impact, suggests that the concept may obscure as much as it discloses about recent changes. Some conceptual clarity can be introduced by distinguishing between state- and governance-centred approaches.

State-centred approaches tend to adopt the ideal-typical sovereign national state as their reference point and examine the European Union in one of two ways. Some commentators identify a tendential, emergent, upward *re-scaling* of the traditional form of the sovereign state from the national to the supranational level. They argue that this re-allocation of formal decision-making powers leads to multi-level govern*ment* based on joint decision-making among different tiers of government under the overall authority of a supranational superstate. Other observers note the emergence of a *new supranational arena* for the pursuit of national interests by sovereign national states. This new arena is a site of intergovernmental (here, international) relations rather than a site to which important sovereign powers have been transferred. In the former case, then, we have multi-level government that could lead to a federal United States of Europe; in the latter case, we have multi-arena government, leading at most to a confederal United Europe of States or *Europe des patries*.

Governance-centred approaches argue that the legitimate monopoly of violence and the top-down modes of intervention associated with the modern nation state are becoming impotent, irrelevant, or even harmful in an increasingly complex and increasingly global social order. They therefore focus on the de-statization of politics rather than the denationalization of statehood and emphasize the enhanced role of reflexive self-organization in solving complex coordination problems. This provides two ways to distinguish government from governance. On the one hand, the sovereign state is the quintessential expression of hierarchy (imperative coordination) because it is, by definition, the political unit that governs but is not itself governed. Hence, beyond the sovereign state, lies the anarchy of interstate relations and/or a self-organizing international society. In contrast, governance is based on self-organization (networks, negotiation, negative coordination) rather than imperative coordination. On the other hand, the sovereign state is primarily concerned with governing activities within its own territorial domain and defending its territorial integrity against other states. In contrast, governance manages functional interdependencies, whatever their scope (and perhaps with a variable geometry), rather than activities occurring in a defined and delimited territory. Thus this sort of approach would see the EU as an emerging centre of governance that involves a plurality of state *and non-state actors* on different levels that are concerned to coordinate activities around a series of functional problems rather than exclusively in terms of a distinct territorial basis. In this context state actors would cooperate as negotiating partners in a complex network, contributing their sovereign authority and other distinctive capacities to help realize collectively agreed aims and objectives on behalf of the network as a whole. Other stakeholders would contribute other symbolic media or material resources (for example, legitimacy, money, knowledge, organizational capacities) to the solution of coordination problems.

One sign of the development of multi-level governance is that it involves tangled hierarchies and complex interdependence. This contrasts with the case of multi-level government or multi-tiered intergovernmentalism – where states operate directly as immediate holders of sovereign authority within a hierarchical command structure and insist on their supremacy vis-à-vis non-state actors. The key question for the development of European governance thus becomes how state and non-state actors organize their common interests across a range of territorial levels and/or across a range of functional domains. In this respect it seems that the principal trend in the operation of EU institutions at present is the development of multi-level governance. The EU functions less as a re-scaled, supranational sovereign state apparatus than as a nodal point in an extensive and tangled web of governance operations concerned to orchestrate economic and social policy in and across many different scales of action with the participation of a wide range of official, quasi-official, private economic interests, and representatives of civil society.

A close examination of the EU nonetheless reveals that the same counter-trends operate here as we found on other levels. In short, there is a struggle between national (and regional and local) states to shape the emerging forms of multi-level governance, including what governance powers are re-scaled and to which levels of governance; there is a struggle over the governance of governance (meta-governance) to shape the rules of the game and likely outcomes for different participants in governance arrangements; and there is a struggle between the relative primacy of territorial and functional identities and interests in the development of multi-level governance arrangements. It seems, then, that much of what now goes under the heading of multi-level governance in the EU domain takes the form of multi-level governance *in the shadow of (multi-level) hierarchy (or government)*. In other words, it involves the strategic use of multi-level governance by states at one or more levels to realize their own aims and objectives. States increasingly resort to multi-level governance to solve problems that cannot be resolved primarily in and through imperative coordination. In pursuing such strategies in the face of a complex, changing political environment, states will also engage in more or less complex forms of meta-governance (that is, the governance of governance).

This conclusion is consistent with the general analysis of state transformation given above. For, if the national state is changing in the ways suggested in sections three and four, then changes in the EU must be considered as part of a re-territorialized, de-statized, and internationalized political system. What we are witnessing is the re-scaling of the complexities of government *and governance* rather than the re-scaling of the sovereign state or the emergence of just one more arena in which national states pursue national interests. The development of multi-level governance is only one aspect of the overall reorganization of statehood and politics in the conditions of contemporary capitalism. It is best understood, therefore, in relation to the growth of multi-tiered government; the proliferation of arenas for intergovernmental relations (involving various tiers of government, not just the national state); the redefinition of the boundaries between the political and non-political and the economic and extra-economic as state intervention changes in response to changed understandings of economic competitiveness and the demands of social cohesion; and the development of a growing number of interest groups, stakeholders, lobbying activities, and so on, on a growing range of scales and in an expanding range of policy fields. A key feature of this complex re-articulation of statehood is the redistribution of competencies at the expense of the sovereign national state – but not necessarily at the expense of its operational autonomy and capacities to pursue state projects. In this sense, the national state is being re-invented rather than superseded but needs to operate in new ways to fit the changing demands upon it.

6. Conclusions

Drawing on the concepts and arguments presented above, I now conclude that the Keynesian welfare national state (KWNS) is being tendentially replaced by a Schumpeterian workfare post-national regime (SWPR). This can be presented in ideal-typical terms along the same lines as its predecessor. Thus, first, the new state form is *Schumpeterian* insofar as it tries to promote permanent innovation and flexibility in relatively open economies by intervening on the supply-side and to strengthen as far as possible their structural and/or systemic competitiveness. This invokes Schumpeter, the theorist of innovation, entrepreneurship and competition, rather than Keynes, the theorist of money, employment and national demand, as its emblematic economist. Second, as a *workfare* regime, the SWPR subordinates social policy to the demands of labour market flexibility and employability and to the demands of economic competition. This includes putting downward pressure on the social wage *qua* cost of international production but, given the economic and political limits to welfare cuts, it is especially concerned with the re-functionalization of the inherited welfare state to serve economic interests. The state also attempts to create subjects to serve as partners in the innovative, knowledge-driven, entrepreneurial, flexible economy and its accompanying self-reliant, autonomous, empowered workfare regime.

Third, the SWPR is *'postnational'* insofar as the national territory has become less important as an economic, political and cultural 'power container'. This is associated with a transfer of economic and social policy-making functions upwards, downwards and sideways. On a global level, this can be seen in the growing concern of a growing number of international agencies (such as the IMF, World Bank, OECD and ILO) and intergovernmental forums (such as the G8) with the shaping of current social as well as economic policy agendas. In part, the European Union acts as a relay for these agenda-shaping efforts and, in part, it has itself played an active role in developing its own agenda for countries beyond its borders. The EU level is also imposing more numerous and tighter restrictions on national economic and social governance, especially through the norms of the Single Market and the economic policy and performance criteria of the Eurozone. This is reflected in the tendential Europeanization of labour market policies, the transformation of national corporatist and bargaining arrangements to allow for greater local and regional differentiation, and the development of 'social pacts' that bundle economic and social policies together to advance worker, business and national interests. What is emerging in this context is a series of multi-level government and/or multi-level governance regimes oriented to issues of the interscalar re-articulation of the economic and political – with the European Union just one among many such emerging regimes. At the same time there are tendencies to devolve some economic and social policy-making to the regional, urban and local levels on the grounds that policies intended to influence the micro-economic supply-side and social regeneration are best designed close to their sites of implementation. In some cases this also involves cross-border cooperation among regional, urban or local spaces. In all three regards, welfare regimes have become more post-national. Paradoxically, this often leads to an enhanced role for national states in controlling the interscalar transfer of these powers – suggesting a shift from sovereignty to a *primus inter pares* role in intergovernmental relations.

The *post-national* moment of economic and social policy restructuring is complex because of the proliferation of scales and the relativization of scale with which it is associated. There are clear differences among the triads here. All three regions/triads have experienced the internationalization of policy regimes not only in economic but also in the juridical, political and social fields. However, the European Union provides the only example among the three triad regions of a clear commitment to economic, political, and social integration and, more ambivalently, to the development of supranational state structures. This excludes any easy generalization from the EU case to the other two triads – or vice versa. This is itself a sign that one should not push globalization too far as a general explanatory framework of recent changes.

Fourth, and finally, the SWPR relies increasingly on forms of governance to compensate for market failures and inadequacies. There is an increased role for non-state mechanisms in shaping and delivering state-sponsored economic and social policies. One aspect of this is the increased importance of private–public networks to state activities on all levels – from local partnerships to supranational neo-corporatist arrangements. The shift from govern*ment* towards govern*ance* means that traditional forms of intervention are less important now in economic and social policy. This does not mean that law and money have disappeared, of course; instead, active economic and social steering now tends to run more through soft regulation and reflexive law, additionality and private–public partnerships, organizational intelligence and information-sharing. A key role is also played by 'meta-governance', that is, the organization of the institutional framework and rules for individual modes of governance and the 'collibration' (or re-balancing) of different modes of governance.

Throughout this chapter I have emphasized the complexities of the recent structural transformation and strategic reorientation of the modern national state. This implies that any hypothesis or prediction about its future that can be expressed in a simple formula is likely to be one-dimensional and one-sided and that any collection of such hypotheses or predictions will be inconsistent and contradictory. Accordingly I have introduced some conceptual distinctions to cut through the theoretical morass and provide the basis for a more sophisticated (but also, necessarily, more complicated and dialectical) analysis of the future of the modern state as it developed in the post-war period in advanced capitalist societies. Even this account is simplified and neglects different national traditions and trajectories as well as important differences between variant forms of KWNS and SWPR (on which see Jessop, 2002). Nonetheless enough has been said to indicate that the future of the national state involves more than hollowing out and multi-level governance.

Bibliography

Albert, Mathias, Lothar and Brock, Klaus Dieter Wolf (eds) (2001), *Civilizing World Politics: Society and Community beyond the State*, Lanham, MD: Rowman and Littlefield.

Blatter, Joachim (2001), 'Debordering the world of states. Towards a multi-level system in Europe and a multi-polity system in North America? Insights from border regions', *European Journal of International Relations*, **7**(2), 175–210.

Goldmann, Kjell (2001), *Transforming the European Nation-State*, London: Sage Publications.

Held, David, Anthony McGrew and Jonathan Perraton (1999), *Global Transformations: Politics, Economics, Culture*, Cambridge: Polity Press.

Jessop, Bob (2002), *The Future of the Capitalist State*, Cambridge: Polity Press.

Mann, Michael (1997), 'Has globalization ended the rise and rise of the nation state?', *Review of International Political Economy*, **4**(3), 472–96.

Mitchell, Timothy (1991), 'The limits of the state: beyond statist approaches and their critics', *American Political Science Review*, **85**(1), 77–96.

Scharpf, Fritz Wolfgang (1999), *Governing in Europe: Effective and Democratic?*, Oxford: Oxford University Press.

Shaw, Martin (2000), *Theory of the Global State. Globality as an Unfinished Revolution*, Cambridge: Cambridge University Press.

2 Globalization, the state and welfare: gendering the debate

Jill Steans

Introduction

This chapter reflects on issues of gender in the globalization and social policy debate, from the perspective of one whose interests lie primarily in feminist International Political Economy (IPE). Within IPE the issue of welfare has been largely subsumed within a debate about globalization and the changing roles and functions of the state, focusing, in the main, on the problems that deregulation (particularly in financial markets) pose for national economic policy-makers. Feminist scholars have paid much closer attention to the gendered nature of globalization/global restructuring,[1] highlighting the so-cially embedded nature of economic activity and the social impact of global restructuring and adjustment. (See, for example, Enloe, 1989; Peterson and Runyan, 1993; Pettman, 1997; Sassen, 1998; Steans, 1998, 1999; Youngs, 1999; Marchand and Runyan, 2000; Breman et al., 2000; Wichterich, 2000; Dickenson and Schaeffer, 2001.)

The first section of the chapter considers the way in which 'critical' IPE (meaning in the context of neoGramscian IPE) has understood the nature of the global 'world order'. It is suggested that to some degree the conception of historically constituted structures and practices within which political and economic activity takes place, which one finds in neoGramscian IPE, is helpful to feminists seeking to elucidate the gendered nature of world order. However, whatever the achievements of critical IPE, conceptions of 'world order' have been largely gender blind (Tickner, 1992; Krause, 1994; Sylvester, 1994). The empirical focus of much critical IPE is on class relations and class politics. Conceptions of world order have largely ig-nored the significance of the public and private spheres. The main implications of feminist critiques of existing scholarship in IPE are that the public/private divisions which underpin such conceptions of economic and political activity render invisible deep social relations of power. The debate about the role of the state and welfare provision/retrenchment has to be seen in a broader context of shifts in the global economy, transformations in gender relations and the reshaping of the public and private identities and roles (Marchand and Runyan, 2000).[2] An analysis of world order that is sensitive to gender must necessarily problematize the public/private conceptual boundary and draw attention to the connections between the two realms.

In the second section of the chapter, the focus turns to the link between specific periods of capitalism, notably the relative openness of national economies and the ability of states to deliver effective social/welfare provision. As Mishra argues, the structural dependence of the welfare state on a relatively closed economy has become a crucial issue in current debates about globalization and social policy (1996: 5). The competitive pressures of an increasingly global capitalist economy, generate trade and investment flows and impel changes in the organization of production as multinational corporations (MNCs) seek out a cheap, abundant, flexible and non-unionized workforce (Dicken, 1992). Multinational corporations and Western finance houses have had a large impact on government policies to ameliorate the social impact of unemployment.

The post-war 'social settlement' in many OECD countries was a class settlement, but it was also a gender settlement in that it rested on a male breadwinner/female homemaker division as the 'norm' of gender relations (Mishra, 1996: 25; Dickenson and Schaeffer, 2001). It is evident that the 'fit' between the welfare state, the capitalist economy and the patriarchal family has broken down under the strain of changing economic and social conditions. In the past two decades, women have entered the paid workforce in all OECD countries in increasing numbers, partly as a consequence of de-industrialization and shifts to a service economy. These changes have benefited some women, particularly those with high levels of education and marketable skills.

However, the picture is complicated somewhat by issues of ethnicity and class. It is also evident that many of the changes and transformations taking place have gender-specific impacts that belie the neoliberal view of globalization as expanding the realm of 'opportunity' and 'choice', breaking down traditional forms of authority and challenging conventional ideas about gender roles and expectations. Globalization, liberalization and the move to free market economies in many countries is rewarding people with the skills to take advantage, but it is increasing inequalities, insecurities and risks. 'Expanding opportunities' for women are often in the informal sector, or in low skilled and/or low waged sectors of the economy. While women's employment has indeed expanded significantly in the past two decades, women have often been employed in preference to men because they are seen to be cheaper, less likely to organize into labour unions and more likely to accept hazardous working conditions (Enloe, 1989; Marchand, 1994; Meyer, 1998).

Moreover, the operation of global markets and other mechanisms allocates political power or economic resources unevenly across countries/territories and among specific social groups (Lundberg and Milanovic, 2000). Poverty and income inequality, regardless of where one lives, determines access to food or other basic needs. There is much diversity among women, but it is important not to lose sight of how gender relations in many societies continue to 'operate to construct life chances differently for women and men' (Maynard quoted in Crompton, 1999; UN Human Development Report, 1997). Poverty and inequality continue to have a significant gender dimension.

While there are a 'variety of arrangements, both formal and informal, in place around the world, for securing human welfare' (Yeates, 2001: 18), to a large degree the welfare of families and communities has depended upon women's unpaid labour. In the twentieth century, the state has assumed a larger role in welfare provision. As will be elaborated below, just how far this expanded role for the state has served to reinforce conventional patterns of gender relations and roles is a matter of some debate. In OECD countries, to varying degrees, globalization has called into question the role of the state as a guarantor of social security through the provision of a range of welfare goods and service. This has encouraged a redefinition of citizenship and ideas about entitlement (Hay and Watson, 2003). The move to market economies in the former Eastern bloc states and in countries across the global South has been encouraged by neoliberal ideas about the benefits of unfettered capitalism. Former Eastern bloc countries have increasingly been faced with conditionality on loans and in this new competitive climate have tended to see social protection as a burden on taxpayers, business and industry. Since the late 1970s, in many countries in the global South, attempts to improve health and social welfare provision have been undermined by debt and structural adjustment policies dictated by the 'realities' of global economic competition. It is well documented that welfare reform, or cutbacks more generally, work to transfer the burden of care from the public to the private sphere and, thus, often have a disproportionate impact on women.

The third section of the chapter focuses on the increasingly multi-layered nature of governance. The extent to which significant factors that impinge upon welfare provision are now beyond the control of individual nation-states is also at the core of the current interest in globalization and social policy. A global economy means that it is difficult for national policies to address economic and social problems 'without reference to what is going on in the rest of the world' (Hill, 1996: 187). Moreover, as Yeates argues, globalization requires more sustained attention to the global context of social policy, because 'the causes of social problems and their solutions are not necessarily confined to national institutions and structures' (Yeates, 2001: 17). Global social problems include growing poverty and inequality; inequitable access to health-care and medicines; inadequate supplies of safe and nutritious food; social dumping; diminishing social and economic rights of workers; growing numbers of political and economic migrants; environmental degradation and associated risks.

Globalization raises issues of redistribution both in jobs and/or the benefits of production in ways that enable all people to share the fruits of global growth (Hill, 1996: 200). Not only states, but also regional and international bodies and non-governmental organizations might have some role to play in the making and implementation of policies that directly or indirectly impinge on social welfare. Governance embraces organizations like the IMF and World Bank, regional bodies like the European Union, trading organizations such as the WTO, NAFTA or APEC, international and national development agencies and a range of NGOs, who have developed both informal and formal links with inter-governmental bodies.

The work of UN agencies, along with a range of international non-governmental organizations, represents 'the other side of globalization' (Mishra, 1996: x). For example, in what was hailed at the time as a notable step forward towards finding global solutions to a range of human ills, world leaders at the World Summit for Social Development, held in Copenhagen in 1995, committed themselves to, among other things, the eradication of poverty, full employment as a policy goal, the enhancement and protection of human rights, equality between men and women, increased resources to social development programmes and the incorporation of social development goals into structural adjustment policies.

However, the UN is losing influence to major powers (particularly the G10 group), the Bretton Woods institutions and the WTO who collectively dominate international economic and social policy settings, and have a disproportionate impact upon the global environment. During the 1980s and for much of the 1990s, bodies like the OECD and international organizations like the IMF, World Bank and World Trade Organization encouraged policies under-pinned by neoliberal ideology, that promoted deregulation, commodification and the privatization of economic activities as well as the down-sizing of government and the scaling down of social programmes.

In the international context, women's NGOs have worked within the system to try to influence directly the political agendas of international organizations like the UN and they are increasingly finding spaces opening up for participation in the policy-making process in multilateral economic institutions like the World Bank. In the past three decades a transnational feminist movement has emerged pushing a global agenda, and a network of relationships have grown up between NGOs, states, and regional and international institutions. At the international level, women's NGOs and feminist groups have been among the most vocal critics of unregulated globalization. The women's movement has challenged the neoliberal economic development paradigm that the Bank promotes and which might be responsible for accelerating rates of female immiseration in developing countries (Meyer and Prugl, 1999). The UN Women's Conferences and accompanying NGO forums have provided an international forum in which to debate and to lobby governments on key gender issues (Bystydzienski, 1992; Meyer and Prugl, 1999). The chapter concludes with some reflections on the possibilities that now exist for women's NGOs specifically to influence policy debates in both national and international contexts and the dilemmas and possible dangers in engaging in such a project.

Gendering 'world order'

Critical IPE

In neoGramscian IPE, the concept of 'world order' embraces social modes of production and social structures of accumulation with their own characteristic politics. Cox argues that there are different kinds of political organization – the state being a distinctly modern invention – and different forms of world order whose conditions of existence, constitutive principles and norms vary over time. In the contemporary world order, the globalization of production and finance now constitute a distinct sphere of power relations and a new social structure of production relations superseding the nation-centred, labour–capital relations of the previous era of organized capitalism (discussed at greater length below). Since the 1970s, the shift from Fordism to post-Fordism, from economies of scale to economies of flexibility, has accelerated, giving rise to a new social model based on a core-periphery structure of production (Cox, 1986). A novel feature of contemporary world order is the 'internationalization of the state', with different states and organizations performing some of the state's traditional regulatory and 'policing' functions.

Globalization is not just driven by material forces, but also by powerful ideas and discourses that work to further the political projects of particular social groups. In the contemporary world order, the activities of transnational corporations, transnational investment, global restructuring and the creation of global markets are legitimized by dominant discourses of globalization, modernization, and social progress. A transhistoric bloc has emerged comprised of multilateral economic organizations, multinational corporations, major capitalist states and elite social classes (Cox, 1986; 1987). Dominant transnational elites have used liberal, and latterly neoliberal discourses of 'modernization' and globalization to legitimize policies that have often served to insulate economic policy from popular pressures, specifically the demands of poor groups. While the impact of globalization/global restructuring is uneven and the relationship between global trends and national specificities never simple, it is meaningful to speak of a 'world hegemony' of liberal capitalism supported by a range of institutions, practices and a dominant ideology, enveloping the globe.

Critical IPE rejects the reductionism and determinism of much orthodox Marxist political economy. To understand the dynamic of change in international political economy one must understand how 'world order' is embedded in socio-political structures at both the national and transnational levels and how social forces are engendered by different and changing production processes (Gill, 1993). One of the strengths of critical IPE is that it provides a theoretical and analytical framework that puts individual and intentional acts within the context of structural constraint, but that also opens up issues of agency. The trajectory of social change is seen to be, in part, determined by deeply embedded organizing principles of social relations. These configurations of social relations include the structure of production relations, the embedded nature of social relations, a dominant-rationalist-knowledge structure; and a governance structure that comprises states and international organizations (Scholte, 2000). The notion of 'structure' encompasses the configuration of forces, material capabilities, ideas and institutions that create pressures and impose constraints on action. Social interactions are seen to produce and reproduce social structures that then shape identities, perceptions of interests and actions and circumscribe the range of 'options' available to social actors in any given historical context. However, since structure is seen to be partly constituted by the consciousness and actions of individuals and groups, at moments of structural instability and flux, agents can be influential in shaping and reshaping social, political and economic orders.

According to Cox, capitalist classes, global finance and multinational corporations are dominant in the current globalized world order, but oppositional and (potentially) transformative social forces emerge from the contradictions and conflicts generated by the expansion of capitalism to a global scale. The globalization of economic activity encourages new forms of politics at spatial scales above the nation-state. Gill and Law suggest that the contemporary world order is characterized by the growing globalization of aspects of social life and the disintegration of previous forms of identity and interest between internationalist and nationalist groups of interest. Transformation and struggle involve, therefore, the dialectical interplay between forces that are relatively cosmopolitan and others that are territorially based movements founded on nationality and linguistic identity (Gill and Law, 1988). However, the transnational social and economic order is one in which elites merge into a common structural force and in which counter-hegemonic groups are relatively powerless, fragmented by nationality, ethnicity, religion and gender (Cox, 1986).

Feminist IPE

Potentially, neoGramscian IPE has much to offer feminists seeking to elucidate the gendered nature of world orders old and new. In the contemporary world order, economic restructuring, debt, even the negotiation of trade agreements, can and does have a gender-specific impact (Runyan, 1996). A central feature of the global economic, social and political order is the naturalization of women's social subordination and the marginalization of women's labour. There is growing empirical evidence of the negative impact of economic globalization on many women; increased levels of poverty and decreasing access to welfare and healthcare, for example (see summary in Krause, 1994). However, while the constraints of dominant forms of power relations must be recognized, women are not passive victims of globalizing forces beyond their control. Feminist work has been valuable in drawing attention to the importance of political economy in understanding the changing position and experience of women caught up in global economic and political processes. Feminist scholars have also pointed out that international political economy is both a site of gender inequalities and a site of resistance (Marchand and Runyan, 2000).

However, critical IPE remains wedded to certain conceptions of 'economics' and 'politics' that privilege social class. IPE scholars have concentrated on the changing nature of production and labour relations (on an increasingly global scale), but the main focus has been the changing face of labour in the public realm – men's labour. It is assumed that 'political' activity is carried out in the public realm, while 'economics' involves the production of goods and services for the market, thus ignoring women's unpaid work.

Gender is a key factor in the social division of labour that underpins the distinction between the public world of work and the so-called 'informal economy' of the home and so-called domestic labour. Social reproduction and servicing might not appear in any set of public statistics, but this is of great significance to human welfare and security. As Benhabib has argued, along with the development of commodity relations in capitalism and the decline of the subsistence household, there was a privatization of the intimate sphere – the production of daily necessities, reproduction, and care of the young, the old and the sick (1992). After a period in which states have largely accepted that they have a role to play in welfare provision, the 'rolling back of the state' has meant that responsibility for social reproduction has once again been shifted back into the private realm.

Marchand and Runyan argue that feminist analysis investigates the interconnected material, ideological and discursive dimensions of globalization and offers more complex sightings or conceptual readings of global restructuring (2000). A key concern of feminist IPE has been the need to develop a richer, more nuanced conception of world order that addresses social relations of inequality marked by gender, culture, race and class. Material conditions comprise more than the class position of the individual, while social identities and subjectivities are not constituted in relation to public roles and activities alone. Ling and Bell argue that IPE is curiously silent on issues of race, gender and culture, since it subsumes all identities under generalized labels such as producers and consumers, workers and investors. Such an approach offers little by way of insight into how different subjectivities are constructed, sustained and mobilized and is particularly damaging to those denied their own subjectivity and agency (Ling and Bell, 1998).

Gender relations are often held to be deeply embedded in social institutions and everyday practices and so are resistant to change, but gender relations are not locked into the realm of the cultural or private. Feminist analysis interrogates how gender relations are socially produced and reproduced in relation to the 'public' and 'private' divisions. Inequality and power have been core themes in feminist analysis. As Youngs contends, 'gendered dimensions of power are deeply embedded in political economy, as witnessed by the high degree of differentiation in the structure of and rewards – or lack of them – for contrasting productive and reproductive functions and their definition in societies.' (Youngs, 1999: 25). States are involved in institutionalizing arrangements that demarcate the public from the private, through, for example, support for the institution of marriage, or by devising and implementing policies in the realm of family planning and sexual health, welfare and unemployment entitlement, labour legislation, taxation and rights of citizenship more generally (Sassoon, 1987, MacKinnon, 1989). However, gender relations are open to bargaining like other forms of social relations. Feminists have critiqued gendered notions of citizenship but at the same time have engaged with the state at the political level to further citizenship rights for women (Vargas, 1999). In this way, gender issues – previously considered private or cultural – have been brought into the realm of politics.

Organized capitalism, globalization and welfare

Organized capitalism
In the wake of World War II, the Bretton Woods System provided a framework for regulating international financial transactions and flows and set up a trading regime (GATT) that was designed to progressively reduce barriers to trade, but which nevertheless, permitted a fairly wide scope for government intervention in national economies to mitigate the most damaging and divisive impacts of capitalism. States were thus able to devise and implement macro-economic policies that fostered full employment. This combined with Fordist methods of production and the increased power of organized labour meant that jobs, for men at least, were full-time and relatively secure.

In many Western countries, in the post-Second World War period, the notion of duties and obligations between citizens and the state and among the citizen body expanded to embrace the social and economic dimensions of security. The nature and extent of entitlements that citizens had on the state, whether these were universal or based on specific needs, and the way in which these provisions were met, varied across countries, during different periods and according to the ideological predisposition of governments and their political/social constituencies. Nevertheless, during the twentieth century, and particularly after the end of the Second World War, political elites in Western countries largely accepted that the state had some role to play in the provision of basic health, education and welfare services and that citizens were entitled to basic standards in order to live a dignified life.

There is persuasive evidence that mass warfare, conscription and rising demands and expectations among returning servicemen were significant factors in the growth and expansion of citizenship. In Britain, for example, the war 'transformed social attitudes and social expectation' and 'produced a growing concern for the health and welfare of an ever-growing circle of people' (Fraser, 1984: 210; 208). As notions of citizenship expanded, both in the sense of a broadening franchise and wider conception of rights or entitlement, states frequently treated men and women differently. Moreover, these differences were justified on the grounds of gender differences that were held to be either natural and immutable, or socially relevant (Linklater, 1998). At the end of the war, women, who had entered the workforce in unprecedented numbers were encouraged to return to the home (Braydon and Summerfield, 1987). Women's citizenship came to be mediated through the patriarchal family structure; their 'duty' primarily one of bearing and raising children (Crompton, 1997: 65).

While there were differences between countries, generally Western economies were characterized by social security provision based on the notion of a 'national minimum standard of life' and paid for by full employment and relatively high levels of taxation and social insurance. The male breadwinner was the major source of income guarantee and maintenance, while Fordism helped to reproduce the male wage earner/female homemaker mode of social organization (Mishra, 1996). Thus women's rights as 'social citizens' were mediated through the male-headed family. Marriage and the family unit was assumed to be based on affection and it was taken for granted that men were the actors in the public realm and that their experiences could represent the family.

The male breadwinner and dependants paradigm profoundly influenced the way in which the role of the state was conceived. The state role in welfare began, when and where the family was unable to adequately fulfil this role, through family breakdown for example, or where the male head of household could no longer provide financially, as in the case of unemployment or widowhood (Dominelli, 1991; Crompton, 1999). Thus, while ideas about greater equality and social justice led to the redistribution of some resources in order to lessen inequality among households and provide a safety net from poverty, the breadwinner model tended to reinforce the gendered division of responsibilities between men and women and thus 'contributed directly to women's oppression by reinforcing their subordinate position within the family and legitimizing their dependent status' (Dominelli, 1991: 3).

Unsurprisingly, feminists were somewhat ambivalent towards and sometimes overtly critical of the welfare state, because of its perceived patriarchal nature. Social policy was seen, in some respects, as working to subordinate women. In Western countries gender roles had been constructed in such a way that women have been primarily responsible for housework, childcare and servicing, while men took on the role of 'breadwinner' or provider for the family. Feminist criticism was tempered somewhat by the recognition that the welfare state did benefit women to some degree. Labour market participation and the social insurance link meant that women, especially full-time carers, were often disadvantaged. Women's unpaid domestic work was not regarded as making an independent or productive contribution to society and so worthy of social insurance (Crompton, 1999: 12). However, welfare feminists believed that the task was to highlight the family as a site of social care and ensure that women's contribution to the welfare of families and communities was recognized and supported. Women's needs could best be met by policies that supported and improved the situation of women within their gendered determined life-styles. Amongst feminists who rejected the women-carers/men-providers dichotomy, there was recognition that some benefits accrued to women through state provision of welfare, for example, income support for single (often female-headed) families, state-funded child-care programmes, universal healthcare provision and 'family allowance' schemes. Historically the expansion of public services also provided a major source of employment for women.

Moreover, the goal of advancing the status of women necessitated a degree of pragmatism in that strategies for change had to be devised that worked through existing social and political structures. From the late 1960s the politics of the New Left, the shift away from class politics and the new emphasis on diverse social identities, served to extend the idea of reducing inequality to other social groups (Mishra, 1996). As women were brought into the policy debate, feminists were able to challenge gender-biased policies.

Thus far the discussion has centred on developed or OECD countries. In developing countries the provision of social and economic security depended upon an array of informal arrangements, but the welfare and well-being of families and communities largely depended upon the unpaid labour of women.

The expansion of the role of the state into the realm of welfare was predicated upon successful development. At the same time, advancing the status of women around the world came to be seen, by elites at least, as at once essential to and dependent upon successful economic development. Thus, developing countries, states and international organizations sought to exploit the labour of women in the development process, ostensibly with the aim of allowing women access to some independent income and thus improving their economic and social status.

In the context of Cold War ideological and political divisions, the United States functioned as a global hegemony, promoting institutions and a global system of economic regulation that would 'embed' liberal principles in the international economic order. Modernization strategies that fostered growth and industrialization according to basically free-market principles were actively promoted. Aid policies were frequently tied to the broader strategic interests and political objectives of the US. As the International Bank for Reconstruction and Development gradually assumed a role in facilitating development, its policies largely reflected Western modes of thought and analysis and Western – particularly US – political objectives, which were coloured by the Cold War context.

In the early modernization literature very little regard was given to the status and role of women (Jacquette, 1982). In theories of modernity, notions of kinship and family were often used interchangeably to describe important facets of social organization, which were seen as essentially outside the modernization process. However, during the first 25 years of its life, the UN Commission on the Status of Women began a programme of work that in time stimulated action in favour of women by UN specialized agencies and other UN organs (Reanda, 1992).

By the 1960s there was accumulating evidence that women were disproportionately affected by poverty, while inequalities between men and women manifest in, for example, barriers to land ownership and access to credit, perpetuated the low status of women in many countries. The status of women was, in turn, seen to be intimately tied up with issues of access to resources, levels of education, good healthcare, the reduction of poverty and so on. In the 1970s, feminists were documenting the contribution made by women in developing countries to the overall welfare of families and communities, as the main producers of food and many other home produced goods and services (Boserup, 1989). By the 1970s a link was being made between women's status and the social and economic well-being of whole societies and, largely thanks to the efforts of NGOs, development agencies gradually incorporated some analysis of gender, or 'women's needs' at least, into development strategies and specific projects (Pietila and Vickers, 1994).[3] This was the genesis of programmes that focused on women's needs in development.

Issues previously thought private and/or cultural began to be openly debated in an international forum (Reanda, 1992).

It is beyond the scope of this chapter to engage in a detailed discussion of the impact of development on women in countries across the South. The 'South', while a useful means of categorization for some purposes, disguises the diversity that exists among these states in terms of ethnic, linguistic and cultural composition, levels of economic development and growth and so on. There is no monolithic group who can be identified as 'third world women' (Mohanty, 1988; Mohanty et al., 1991; see also Grewal and Kaplan, 1994). Suffice to say that the issue of the status and role of women in non-Western countries was always deeply politicized and increasingly came to be linked to the politics of North/South relations. Waves of decolonization across the world resulted in an expansion of the UN and a change in the composition of the organization. Many countries in the so-called developing world had a history of colonial or imperialist domination and, unsurprisingly, were sceptical of the idea that progress and freedom would come from following the Western model of social and economic development.[4] Under-development came to be seen as a consequence of deeply rooted and enduring structural inequalities between the North and South. Appeals for development aid, a New International Economic Order, and a Charter of Economic and Social Rights and Duties, were made by developing states sometimes on humanitarian grounds, but often articulated as entitlement and obligations that arose from the experience and historical legacy of colonialism or imperialist domination.

Globalization
Since the 1980s, waves of global restructuring have seen changes in production and investment strategies and an increasingly complex international division of labour. Global restructuring is a consequence of the competitive pressures generated by a capitalist world economy and has been largely a Western-driven phenomenon. The first phase of global restructuring can be traced to the 1973 oil crisis, the dismantling of state-run enterprises and the opening of markets in many parts of the global South which accelerated in the wake of the debt crisis in the 1980s. The end of the Cold War and the collapse of communism in the former Soviet Union and throughout Eastern Europe have resulted in a marked consolidation of capitalism throughout the world (Birdsall and Graham, 2000).

During the past two decades there has been a shift towards the adoption of neoliberal economic policies in many parts of the world, the essence of which has been the deregulation of markets and flexibility in labour markets – achieved by weakening trade unions – market economies and export-led growth strategies. In the wake of the collapse of the Bretton Woods regime, neoliberal politicians and think tanks resisted renewed efforts at state regulation of markets, so much so that by the early 1980s most Western countries with big financial markets had abolished exchange controls.

Just how far states have been compelled to respond to the 'realities' of globalization and to undertake necessary adjustment and policy revisions, or conversely how far Western states, particularly, have played a key role in facilitating globalization is a matter of some debate.[5] Contrary to the neoliberal contention that the autonomy of states and consequently national policy-makers has been significantly undermined by globalization (Ohmae, 1996), key states have played an important role in facilitating globalization. The rhetoric of globalization widely embraced by elites within business and commerce and among national and international policy-makers during the 1980s and for much of the 1990s, has functioned as a powerful, transnational ideology of neoliberalism that has sought to establish its ascendancy world-wide (Murphy, 2000). Neoliberalism involves dominant interpretations and claims about the nature and extent of the complex and interrelated political, economic, social and technological processes that are extending and deepening relations between countries and peoples across the world, normative judgements about the perceived benefits of these trends and, following from this, policy prescriptions that set the boundaries of what is deemed to be 'appropriate' and 'feasible'. As Hay and Watson argue, it might be that, 'the political discourse of globalisation, rather than globalisation per se summons the "inevitability" of welfare retrenchment' (Hay and Watson, 2003; see also Youngs, 1996).

The impact of various aspects of globalization on gender relations, and on the position and status of women particularly is now being documented and it is evident that this has been uneven and inequitable. Today, in many OECD countries, the decline of the male 'breadwinner' and female 'homemaker' roles and the gendered division of responsibilities embedded in such constructions have been undermined to some degree by the decline of traditional industries and increases in male unemployment. The demise of Fordism has coincided with a decline and weakening of organized labour. At the same time, there has been a growth of female employment in the expanding service sectors of the economy and growing financial independence among women (Crompton, 1999; Dickenson and Schaeffer, 2001).[6] To some degree, changes in social policy have reflected these new realities.[7]

Women who are highly trained and well educated have often benefited from expanding employment opportunities for women. This applies to OECD countries and seems to be reflected in the experience of women in the 'transitional economies' of the former Eastern bloc (Rueschemeyer, 1994; Harris and Seid, 2000; Terrell, 2000). However, while women now have greater access to earned income, on the whole women in OECD countries continue to receive lower rates of pay than their male counterparts (Birdsall and Graham, 2000). The fluid socio-economic environment generated by globalization might work to challenge to some degree the meaning and implications of the gender constructs in specific societies, but it might also work to constrain women into certain types of work, invariably that which is low-paid and with few rights, simply because it is in keeping with women's gender-determined lifestyles (Sabaté-Martinez,1996).

The EU claims that the global economic changes that have led to the creation of supranational organizations have brought great socio-economic benefits to women. The European economy has moved increasingly towards the service sector which, together with increasing technological advancements has enabled a greater flexibility in working times and locations, and has brought about changes in family roles. Consequently new gender relationships have emerged (Commission of the European Communities, 1995). However, the majority of jobs created have been low skilled and are often part-time. While women have entered professions once almost exclusively reserved for men in increasing numbers, female employment has been largely concentrated in specific sectors of the economy (Crompton, 1999; Birdsall and Graham, 2000; Barnard, 1999; Sabaté-Martinez, 1996). The feminization of the labour force in the 1980s occurred alongside the growth of temporary, part-time jobs. It is generally agreed that in many OECD countries the 'position of those on the margins of the labour markets has deteriorated considerably' in the past two decades and that 'to a significant extent this shift is driven by transformations in the global economy that have affected all industrial democracies' (Pierson, 1994: 182). The ability to exploit 'opportunities' associated with globalization has depended on personal circumstances, including class, age and gender (Sen, quoted in Birdsall and Graham, 2000).

In many former Eastern bloc countries some groups of women have suffered significant losses in the wake of economic transition and restructuring. For example, the Soviet Constitution accorded women equal rights with men in work, rest, leisure, social insurance and education. The state also provided assistance to mothers with large families and to unmarried mothers, including maternity leave with full pay and the provision of a wide network of maternity homes, nurseries and kindergartens. Similar provisions existed in many communist states (Duchacek, 1973). These safeguards are now disappearing under the combined pressure of liberalization, marketization and increasing levels of competition.

Notwithstanding the challenges to gendered public/private distinctions and social roles that have taken place, it seems that when the need to provide care within the family arises, women are still assumed to be mainly responsible. The nature of women's employment in part-time and flexible or casual jobs may have worked to reinforce this idea. The impact on women of shifts in policy and especially public provision undoubtedly varies according to class. Growing inequality and the polarization of incomes mean that the impact on upper and middle class women has been cushioned somewhat by their ability to obtain services from the market, while the position of lower class women has significantly worsened.

The curtailment of autonomy and choice for states in relation to welfare policies has seemingly been much more evident in the global South. As we enter the twenty-first century, the extent to which development has failed is evidenced in growing levels of poverty and inequality.[8] Inequalities between countries and specific groups have became more marked in the wake of globalization and the transition to market economies across the world (Dicken, 1992; Birdsall and Graham, 2000).[9] In the wake of the collapse of communism, developing countries of the global South are increasingly following a liberal model of growth. MNCs are seen as harbingers of investment and jobs and production, that might pull the developing world out of poverty, but MNCs have been accused of violating the human rights of their workers. The harmful effects of MNCs often fall disproportionately on women workers who largely comprise the labour force in export production and export processing zones in the global South (Meyer, 1998).

It has been well documented that in developing countries to varying degrees, 'structural adjustments' and reductions in state provision of health, welfare and education have increased the burden of work for women (see, for example, Elson, 1990). In some countries, the combined pressures of adjustment, debt and the urgent need to earn foreign currency has resulted in the export of female labour. The 'Filipino maid' working in more prosperous parts of the Asia-Pacific and in Western Europe is an example of the complex interconnections emerging between middle class, educated women in the West and the newly industrializing countries of East Asia and poorer women from the global South (Chang and Ling, 2000).

One should not entirely discount the realm of domestic politics and policy even among states in the South. Governments have sometimes embraced neoliberal policies without overt pressures from multilateral economic organizations. However, in the wake of the debt crisis, developing countries of the global South have often been required to implement neoliberal development strategies as a condition of structural adjustment loans. Typically this has involved an emphasis on export-led growth, growing marketization, cuts in public expenditure and sometimes the introduction of user charges (George, 1988). Western states, international development agencies and other multilateral economic institutions like the World Bank and International Monetary Fund have played a major role in devising development strategies, grounded in liberal economic principles, promoting marketization and moves to free trade and export-led growth strategies. Furthermore, in this context, there has been a new emphasis on self-help and the idea that poorer countries should take responsibility for their own choices and actions (Hurrell and Woods, 1999). To a much greater degree, in developing countries, global restructuring, combined with problems of debt and structural adjustment, has resulted in a weakening of what was already inadequate welfare provision. As noted above, the provision of services like health and welfare in developing countries has in part come through development aid and development funding of various kinds, which has also seen significant cutbacks since the end of the Cold War.

As with many OECD countries the impact of globalization on women in developing countries has varied to some degree according to class, ethnicity and levels of education. Increasingly, however, the negative impacts of economic globalization on women across the world are being highlighted (Hooper, 1994a, 1994b, 1994c; United Nations, 1996, Afshar and Barrientos, 1999). Assessing the overall impact of globalization on welfare in developing countries raises issues of debt and structural adjustment, but also the impact on land (re) distribution, micro-credits, agricultural and consumptions subsidies and food security programmes (Yeates, 2001: 20). As providers of basic health and social welfare needs, the effects of structural adjustment have fallen disproportionately on women whose labour is expected to 'stretch' in order to compensate for cuts in public services (Elson, 1990). Increasingly NGOs are taking on an expanded role in the delivery of services to people in developing countries, a role which might involve support for women at grass roots level. However, as will be elaborated below, taking on a greater role here raises dilemmas for NGOs.

Multi-layered governance, citizenship and welfare

The state, security and global governance
The role of the state as provider of security, broadly conceived, has been challenged by globalization in various ways. Global restructuring can generate unemployment, while poverty and debt contribute to migratory flows that in turn increase pressures on receiving states to provide some welfare services to non-nationals. Greater attention is now being paid to the role that various institutions and networks of governance have to play in discouraging practices that impinge directly or indirectly upon human security and developing appropriate and effective welfare provision in a variety of different countries and contexts. For example, while primary responsibility for implementation of the World Social Summit agenda, alluded to in the introduction, lies with national governments, the Declaration also assigns specific responsibilities to UN bodies, including ECOSOC, and the Bretton Woods institutions.

The degree to which states or regional and international bodies can develop effective policies to address this broad range of human welfare and security concerns depends upon a number of interrelated factors, but a key consideration is how far they remain wedded to economic liberalization, competition, privatization and a much circumscribed and limited role for the state in the regulation of markets and in the provision of social security, pensions, healthcare and education, for example. Falk argues that factors at work that obstruct the realization of a more humane global governance regime include the anti-utopian mood that currently prevails among elites and the dominance of a neoliberal world view that has acquired added force, because it has been embraced by influential global actors, including the IMF, World Bank and WTO (Falk, 1999). Ultimately, the realization of a global social agenda requires something of a 'paradigm shift' towards notions of economic regulation, corporate responsibility and accountability, human rights, and conceptions of citizenship that are at once more inclusive and expansive.

The problems of unregulated economic globalization have been extensively articulated in recent UN reports and studies (Mishra, 1996). At the regional level there have been some achievements. For example the European Union has developed a model of citizenship that embraces social rights. There have been notable developments at the World Bank in the latter part of the 1990s, where chief economist Stiglitz became something of a critic of unfettered economic globalization. (see, for example, Stiglitz, 2000). In the post-Cold War period the Bank sought to strengthen the linkages with NGO networks because this is seen as a way of promoting and consolidating democracy and encouraging greater participation in institutions and the mechanism of governance. This measure would ostensibly increase the accountability of multilateral institutions and national governments to civil society (Alvarez, 1999: 182). Under the leadership of Wolfensohn, the World Bank has begun to emphasize the need for a more 'effective state' which will distribute the benefits of growth through investments in basic health and education.

However, generally the achievements of these various regional and international institutions and organizations have been modest. The Social Charter of the EU, for example, is not legally binding, and the EU has little by way of a common social policy (Mishra, 1996: 13). Trading blocs such as NAFTA have been criticized for their lack of social provision and weak environmental safeguards, both of which encourage the relocating of corporations to areas where labour is cheap, health and safety standards are lacking and the polluter is not expected to pay too much. The UN Centre on Transnational Corporations has called for multinationals to respect human rights and abstain from involvement in and subversion of domestic politics, but any such regime relies heavily upon MNCs signing up to voluntary codes of conduct (Meyer, 1998). In practice regulation of MNC activity remains weak. The

United Nations' development agencies and bodies have increasingly lost influence over matters of economic and social policy, and while it appears that the Bretton Woods institutions are responding to growing criticisms and pressure from a wide variety of groups and organizations, there is some doubt about whether this indicates a substantive change in policy, or merely a change in rhetoric.

Governance and gender politics

Opposition to unfettered economic globalization is manifest in a number of sites and around a range of global issues. Alliances are forging among groups around issues of poverty, inequality, debt, ill-health, environmental degradation and human/social welfare. Despite the relative decline of organized labour in the past two decades, labour unions remain forces in resisting neoliberal globalization. Labour unions have pushed for a greater degree of social protection and also combined with public interest organization to pressurize MNCs to adopt codes of conduct on workers' rights and working conditions (O'Brien, 2000).[10]

The feminist movement, particularly in the Western world, has been portrayed as a somewhat unreliable ally in the defence of welfare provision, because of ambivilance towards the welfare state. (Mishra, 1999:61–5). However, this is something of an over-simplification. While the situation is complicated somewhat by differences in class, it is likely that measures – promoted at the national, regional or global level – that respond to their changing identities, roles and needs of women both in the workplace and in the home, will generate support among women. Indeed, labour unions are reaching out to women in the social protection agenda by taking up issues like maternity leave, protection against sexual harassment, equal pay for equal work and minimum rights for home-based workers (O'Brien, 2000). Political parties also use social welfare issues to appeal to women voters (Mishra, 1999: 62; Newman, 2001).

As was noted above, women's NGOs are now organizing globally to promote and protect the interests of women and to resist the further erosion of welfare, health, education and social support in countries across the world. In recent years, spaces have opened up for women's NGOs to become more involved in the work of the World Bank. However, the Bretton Woods institutions have embraced an ideology and set of values within which women's concerns with health issues, or the social impacts of restructuring and 'adjustment' can be seen as attempts to impose market distortions (Steintra, 1999; see also Steans, 2002).

Moreover, if this process of dialogue and consultation is to be meaningful, a wide range of groups representing diverse constituencies of women must be involved. In reality, gender 'mainstreaming' takes place only to the degree that it has proved useful in improving efficiency and contributing to economic growth. Increasingly, governments and international organizations rely on NGOs to provide specialized knowledge about women and gender relations in specific societies. NGOs are taking on a role in delivering development resources to poor, marginalized groups. In this context, gender equality has come to be seen as a technical issue or the technical dimension of welfare policy and poverty alleviation (Alvarez, 1999: 199; Vargas, 1999).

Globalization has also impacted on the ability of NGOs to engage in the policy-making process. On the one hand, technological advancements in communications have facilitated networking among women's groups across the world. On the other hand, there has been a reconfiguration of the feminist movement, pushing some sections to public prominence and marginalizing others (Alvarez, 1999; see also O'Brien et al., 2000). In addition, the worsening economic climate in many developing countries and cutbacks in state funding and aid have made it increasingly difficult for NGOs to engage in the policy-making process. The degree to which NGOs can follow up on commitments made at the international conferences depends upon the national political context, the policy environment and the commitment of governments, but it also depends upon the capacity and resources of NGOs. The decline in overseas aid and diversion of aid to emergency operations and to the transition countries in Europe has impacted adversely on NGOs in developing countries particularly (Meyer, 1998).

With regard to the hegemony of neoliberalism globally, clearly liberalizing forces are not the only ones at work (Yeates, 2001: 166). Yeates argues, 'there is no reason to think the political pendulum could not swing back in favour of forces emphasising redistribution and comprehensive public provision' (p. 168). Certainly, the politics of class is being replaced by a much more complex mix of social forces. However, as yet, there are few signs that groups promoting such agendas are winning the battle with neoliberal forces that continue to promote market mechanisms as the only long-term remedy for a range of social ills, despite growing evidence of the market's failure to deliver.

Notes

1.   Marchand prefers the term 'global restructuring' over globalization because the 'former explicitly refers to a process of partially breaking down an old order and attempting to construct a new one'. Quoted in Marchand and Runyan (2000: 7).
2.   Rates of women's employment are rising in all OECD countries. In 1992, 68 per cent of men and 44 per cent of women were 'economically active'. The EU estimates that women will make up 48 per cent of the workforce by 2020 (Crompton, 1999: 9). In the US the percentage of women in paid work increased from 38 per cent in 1970 to 43 per cent in 1980. The rate slowed after 1980, rising to 48 per cent by 1990 (Dickenson and Schaeffer, 2001: 58).

3. For example, the International Research and Training Institute for Advancement of Women (INSTRAW) was set up in 1976 to provide technical assistance and training programmes to support women in developing countries. The Voluntary Fund for the UN Decade for Women (UNIFEM) was set up in the same year.
4. The Western cultural bias of the WID movement and the inequalities and divisions between women in developed and developing countries became contention issues at the Third United Nations Conference on Women in Development, convened in Copenhagen in 1980.
5. In the first wave of the literature, there was a tendency to present globalization as a set of interrelated processes that had similar effects on countries throughout the world: greater attention is now being paid to the uneven and differential impacts of globalization. For example, the empirical evidence of welfare state 'retrenchment' in relation to OECD countries is rather mixed (Mishra, 1996: ix). Globalization is undoubtedly mediated through the political economy of nation-states and the influence of domestic politics on policy cannot be wholly discounted. See Crompton (1999); Newman (2001).
6. At the same time, the popularity of marriage has declined, while single parenthood, and especially female-headed households has grown. See Dickenson and Schaeffer (2001: 38–9); Chant (1999).
7. For example, New Labour's reforms have been aimed at shedding the class politics image of Old Labour and appealing to other constituencies, notably women (Newman, 2001).
8. While globally consumption levels have increased massively during the past two decades, the poorest 20 per cent of the world's peoples have been left out of the consumption explosion, with billions deprived of even the most basic amenities. A fifth of the world's population do not have enough dietary energy and protein, some two billion people around the world are anaemic, 800 million people are malnourished and 40 000 people die every day from hunger and related diseases (UNDP, 2000).
9. In 1999 the wealthiest 20 per cent of the world's population accounted for 86 per cent of world GDP, 82 per cent of world export markets and 68 per cent FDI. The rest of the world's population accounted for just 1 per cent in each category (UNDP, 1992: 3, reproduced in Thomas and Reader, 2001). In 1960, the income ratio between the top 20 per cent of the world population and the rest was 30:1, by 1997 it was 74:1 (UNDP: p. 3 reproduced in Thomas and Reader, 2001). In the USA, differences in household income between the top fifth and the bottom fifth of the populace narrowed between 1947 and 1973, but then increased by more than 50 per cent between 1973 and 1996 (Burtless, 1998: 3). During the 1980s, there was an increase from 12 per cent to 18 per cent in the number of workers whose earnings fell below the poverty line. In the 1980s and 1990s all OECD countries except Germany and Italy saw increases in wage inequalities. In the post-Cold War period, Russia moved from a position of greatest level of income equality in Europe in 1987 to greatest level of inequality in 1995. More recently, in Russia, the richest fifth of the population's share of national income rose from 32.7 per cent in 1990 to 46.7 per cent in 1997, while the poorest fifth had its share decline over the same period from 9.8 per cent to 6.2 per cent (UNDP, 1999: 8).
10. The ICFTUs has been exerting pressure on states and international organizations like the WTO to enshrine labour standards, but has met resistance from some development organizations and unions in developing countries on the grounds that it might work against developing countries who are structurally disadvantaged in the global economy. See O'Brien (2000).

Bibliography

Afshar, Haleh and Stephanie Barrientos (eds) (1999), *Women, Globalization and Fragmentation in the Developing World*, Basingstoke: Palgrave.
Allen, John (ed.) (1995), *A Shrinking World? Global Unevenness and Inequality*, Oxford: Oxford University Press.
Alston, Phillip (ed.) (1992), *The United Nations and Human Rights: A Critical Appaisal*, Oxford: Clarendon.

Alvarez, Sonia (1999) 'Advocating feminism', *International Feminist Journal of Politics*, **2**(1), 181–209.

Barnard, Catherine (1999), 'Gender equality in the European Union: a balance sheet', in Phillip Alston, Mara Bustelo and James Heenan (eds), *The European Union and Human Rights*, Oxford: Oxford University Press, pp. 21–35.

Benhabib, Seyla (1992), *Situating the Self: Gender, Community and Postmodernism in Contemporary Ethics*, Cambridge: Polity Press.

Birdsall, Nancy and Carol Graham (2000), 'Mobility and markets: conceptual issues and policy questions', in Nancy Birdsall and Carol Graham (eds), *New Markets, New Opportunities? Economic and Social Mobility in a Changing World*, New York: Brookings Institute, pp. 3–21.

Boserup, Ester (1989), *Women's Role in Economic Development*, London: Earthscan.

Braydon, Gail and Penny Summerfield (1987), *Out of the Cage: Women's Experiences in Two World Wars*, London: Pandora.

Breman, Jan, Arvind Das and Ravi Agarwal (2000), *Labouring Under Global Capitalism*, Oxford: Oxford University Press.

Burtless, Gary (1998), *Globaphobia: Confronting Fears about Open Trade*, Washington, DC: Brookings Institute.

Bystydzienski, Jill M. (1992), *Women Transforming Politics: Worldwide Strategies for Empowerment*, Bloomington, IN: Indiana University Press.

Chang, Kimberly A. and Lily H. Ling (2000), 'Globalisation and its intimate other: Filipino domestic workers in Hong Kong', in M. Marchand and A.S. Runyan (eds), *Gender and Global Restructuring: Sitings, Sites and Resistances*, London: Routledge, pp. 33–52.

Chant, Sylvia (1999), 'Women-headed households: global orthodoxies and grassroots realities', in H. Afshar and S. Barrientos (eds), *Women, Globalization and Fragmentation in the Developing World*, Basingstoke: Palgrave, pp. 17–25.

Chinkin, Christine (1999), 'Gender, inequality and international human rights law', in Andrew Hurrell and Ngaire Woods (eds), *Inequality, Globalization and World Politics*, Oxford, Oxford University Press.

Commission of the European Communities (1995), *A New Partnership Between Women and Men*, COM (95) 221, Luxembourg: Official Publications of the European Communities.

Cox, Robert (1986), 'States, social forces and world order', in R. Keohane (ed.), *Neorealism and its Critics*, Princeton, NJ: Princeton University Press, pp. 204–54.

Cox, Robert (1987), *Production, Power and World Order: Social Forces in the Making of History*, New York: Columbia University Press.

Crompton, Rosemary (1997), *Women and Work in Modern Britain*, Oxford: Oxford University Press.

Crompton, Rosemary (ed.) (1999), *Restructuring Gender Relations: The Decline of the Male Breadwinner*, Oxford: Oxford University Press.

Dicken, Peter (1992), *Global Shift: The Internationalization of Economic Activity*, London: Paul Chapman Publishing.

Dickenson, Torry and Robert Schaeffer (2001), *Fast Forward: Work, Gender and Protest in a Changing World*, Boston: Rowman and Littlefield.

Dominelli, Lena (1991), *Women Across Continents: Feminist Comparative Social Policy*, Hemel Hampstead: Harvester Wheatsheaf.

Duchacek, Ivo (1973), *Rights and Liberties in the World Today*, Oxford: Clio Press.

Elson, Diane (1990), *Male Bias in the Development Process*, Manchester: Manchester University Press.

Enloe, Cynthia (1989), *Bananas, Beaches and Bases: Making Feminist Sense of International Politics*, London: Pandora.

Falk, Richard (1999), 'Humane governance for the world: reviving the quest', *Review of International Political Economy*, **7**(2), 317–34.

Fraser, Derek (1984), *The Evolution of the British Welfare State*, Basingstoke: Macmillan.

García-Ramon, Maria Dolors and Janice Monk (eds) (1996), *Women of the European Union: The Politics of Work and Daily Life*, London: Routledge.

George, Susan (1988), *A Fate Worse than Debt*, London: Penguin.

Gill, Stephen (ed.) (1993), *Gramsci, Historical Materialism and International Relations*, Cambridge: Cambridge University Press.

Gill, Stephen and David Law (1988), *The Global Political Economy: Perspectives, Problems and Policies*, Brighton: Harvester Wheatsheaf.

Grewal, Inderpal and Caren Kaplan (eds)(1994), *Scattered Hegemonies: Postmodernity and Transnational Feminist Politics*, Minneapolis, MN: University of Minneapolis Press.

Harris, Richard and Melinda Seid (eds) (2000), *Critical Perspectives on Globalisation and Neoliberalism in Developing Countries*, Boston: Brill.

Hay, Colin and Matthew Watson (2003), 'The discourse of globalisaticn and the logic of no alternative: rendering the contigent necessary in the political economy of new labour, *Policy and Politics*, **30**(4).

Hill, Michael (1996), *Social Policy: A Comparative Analysis*, London: Harvester Wheatsheaf.

Hooper, Elizabeth (1994a), *Report on the UN ECE Regional Preparatory Meeting for the Fourth World Conference on Women*, Geneva: United Nations Publications.

Hooper, Elizabeth (1994b), *Report on the UN LAC Regional Preparatory Meeting for the Fourth World Conference on Women*, Mexico: UN Publications.

Hooper, Elizabeth (1994c), *Report on the UN ESCAP Regional Preparatory Meeting for the Fourth World Conference on Women*, Jakarta: United Nations Publications.

Hurrell, Andrew and Ngaire Woods (eds) (1999), *Inequality, Globalisation and World Politics*, Oxford: Oxford University Press.

Jaquette, Jane (1982), 'Women and modernization theory: a decade of feminist criticism', *World Politics*, **34**(2), 267–84.

Kofman, Eleonore and Gillian Youngs (1996), 'Introduction: globalisation – the second wave', in Eleonore Kofman and Gillian Youngs (eds), *Globalisation: Theory and Practice*, London: Pinter, pp. 128–43.

Krause, Jill (1994), 'The international dimensions of gender inequalities and feminist politics; a "new direction" for international political economy?', in John MacMillan and Andrew Linklater (eds), *Boundaries in Question: New Directions for International Relations*, London: Pinter, pp. 128–43.

Ling, L. and N. Bell (1998), 'Theorizing hegemony: a critical examination of gender, race and class in Gramscian globalism', conference paper, IR Standing Group of the ECPR, Vienna, September.

Linklater, Andrew (1998), *The Transformation of Political Community*, Oxford: Polity.

Lundberg, Magnus and Branko Milanovic (2000), '*Globalisation and Inequality: Are they Linked and How?*', Washington, DC: World Bank.

MacKinnon, Catherine (1987), *Towards a Feminist Theory of the State*, Cambridge: Cambridge University Press.

MacKinnon, Catherine (1989), *Towards a Feminist Theory of the State*, Cambridge, MA: Harvard University Press.

McIntosh, Mary (1978), 'The state as oppressor of women', in Annette Kuhn and Anne Marie Wolpe (eds), *Feminism and Materialism: Women's Modes of Production*, London: Routledge, pp. 237–49.

Marchand, Marianne (1994), 'Latin American voices of resistance: womens' movements and development debates', in Stephen Rosow, Naeem Inayatlluah and Mark Rupert (eds), *The Global Economy as Political Space: Essays in Critical Theory and International Political Economy*, Cambridge, Cambridge University Press, pp. 89–109.

Marchand, Marianne and Ann Sisson Runyan (2000), *Gender and Global Restructuring: Sitings, Sites and Resistances*, London: Routledge.

Maynard, Mary (1994), 'Race, gender and the concept of "difference" in feminist thought', in Haleh Afshar and Mary Maynard (eds), *The Dynamics of 'Race' and Gender*, London: Taylor & Francis.

Meyer, Mary and Elizabeth Prugl (1999), *Gender Politics in Global Governance*, London: Rowman and Littlefield.

Meyer, William H. (1998), *Human Rights and International Political Economy in the Third World*, Westport: Praeger Press.

Mishra, Ramesh (1996), *Globalisation and the Welfare State*, Cheltenham, UK and Northampton, MA, USA: Edward Elgar.

Mishra, Ramesh (1999), *Globalisation and the Welfare State*, 2nd edn, Cheltenham, UK and Northampton, MA, USA: Edward Elgar.

Mohanty, Chandra (1988), 'Under Western eyes: feminist scholarship and colonial discourse', *Feminist Review*, **30**, 61–88.

Mohanty, Chandra, Anne Russo and Lourdes Torress (1991), *Third World Women and the Politics of Feminism*, Bloomington: Indiana University Press.

Murphy, Craig N. (2000), 'Global governance: poorly done and poorly understood', *International Affairs*, **76**(4), 789–803.

Newman, Janet (2001), *Modernising Governance: New Labour, Policy and Society*, London: Sage.

O'Brien, Robert (2000), 'Workers and world order: the tentative transformation of the international union movement', *Review of International Studies*, **26**(4), October, 125–37.

O'Brien, Robert, Anne Marie Goetz, Jan Aart Scholte and Mark Williams (2000), *Contesting Global Governance: Multilateral Economic Institutions and Global Social Movements*, Cambridge: Cambridge University Press.

Ohmae, Kenichi (1996), *The End of the Nation State*, New York: Free Press.

Peterson, V.S. and Runyan, A.S. (1993), *Global Gender Issues*, Oxford: Westview.

Pettman, Jan Jindy (1997), *Worlding Women*, London: Routledge.

Pierson, Paul (1994), *Dismantling the Welfare State? Reagan, Thatcher and the Politics of Retrenchment*, Cambridge: Cambridge University Press.

Pietila, Hilkka and Jeanne Vickers (1994), *Making Women Matter: The Role of the United Nations*, London: Zed Books.

Reanda, Linda (1992), 'The commission on the status of women', in Phillip Alston (ed.), *The United Nations and Human Rights: A Critical Appraisal*, Oxford: Clarendon.

Rueschemeyer, Marylin (1994), *Women in the Politics of Post Communist Eastern Europe*, London: Sharp.

Runyan, Anne Sisson (1996), 'The place of women in trading places: gendered global/regional regimes and inter-nationalized feminist resistance', in Eleonore Kofman and Gillian Youngs (eds), *Globalization: Theory and Practice*, London: Pinter, pp. 139–56.

Sabaté-Martinez, Ana (1996), 'Women's integration into the labour market and rural industrialization in Spain: gender relations and the global economy', in Maria Dolors García-Ramon and Janice Monk (eds), *Women of The European Union: The Politics of Work and Daily Life*, London: Routledge.

Sassen, S. (1998), *Globalization and its Discontents*, New York: New Press.

Sassoon, Ann Showstack (ed.) (1987), *Women and the State*, London: Hutchinson.

Scholte, Jan Aart (2000), *Globalisation: A Critical Introduction*, Basingstoke: Palgrave.

Sen, Amartya (1995), 'The political economy of targeting', in Dominique Van de Walle and Kimberly Neads (eds), *Public Spending and the Poor: Theory and Evidence*, Baltimore: Johns Hopkins University Press, pp. 158–65.

Steans, Jill (1998), *Gender and International Relations*, Oxford: Polity.

Steans, Jill (1999), 'The private is global: global political economy and feminist politics', *New Political Economy*, **4**(1), 113–28.

Steans, Jill (2002), 'Global governance: a feminist perspective', in Anthony McGrew and David Held (eds), *Governing Globalisation*, Oxford: Polity.

Steintra, Deborah (1999), 'Of roots, leaves and trees: gender, social movements and global governance', in Mary Meyer and Elizabeth Prugl (eds), *Gender Politics in Global Governance*, London: Rowman and Littlefield.

Stiglitz, Joseph (2000), 'Reflections on mobility and social justice, economic efficiency and individual responsibility', in N. Birdsall and C. Graham (eds), *New Markets, New Opportunities? Economic and Social Mobility in a Changing World*, Washington: Brookings Institute, pp. 36–68.

Sylvester, Christine (1994), 'The emperors theories and transformations: looking at the field through feminist lenses', in Christine Sylvester and Dennis Pirages (eds), *Transformations in Global Political Economy*, London: Macmillan, pp. 109–26.

Terrell, Katherine (2000), 'Worker mobility and the transition to a market economy', in N. Birdsall and C. Graham (eds), *New Markets, New Opportunities? Economic and Social Mobility in a Changing World*, New York: Brookings Institute.

Thomas, Caroline and Peter Wilkin (1996), *Globalisation and the South*, Basingstoke: Macmillan.

Thomas, Caroline and Melvyn Reader (2001), 'Development and inequality', in B. White, R. Little and M. Smith (eds), *Issues in World Politics*, Basingstoke: Palgrave, pp. 74–92.

Tickner, J. Ann (1992), 'On the fringes of the global economy', in R. Tooze and C. Murphy (eds), *The New International Political Economy*, Boulder, CO: Lynne Rienner, pp. 34–46.

United Nations (1996), *NGO Forum on Women: Final Report*, United Nations Publications.

(UNDP) United Nations Development Programme (1997), *UNDP Development Report 1997*, Oxford: Oxford University Press.

(UNDP) United Nations Development Programme (1999), *United Nations Human Development Report 1999*, Oxford: Oxford University Press.

(UNDP) United Nations Development Programme (2000), *United Nations Human Development Report 2000*, Oxford: Oxford University Press.

Van Boven, Theo (1989), 'Human rights and development: the UN experience', in D. Forsythe (ed.), *Human Rights and Development*, Basingstoke: Macmillan.

Vargas, Gina (1999), 'Latin America Feminism in the 90s- Reflections by Gina Vargas', A Conversation with Gina Vargas, Interviewed by Nira Yuval Davis, *International Feminist Journal of Politics*, **1**(2).

Wichterich, Christa (2000), *The Globalised Woman*, London: Zed.

Yeates, Nicola (2001), *Globalisation and Social Policy*, London: Sage.

Youngs, Gillian (1996), 'Dangers of discourse: the case of globalization', in Eleonore Kofman and Gillian Youngs (eds), *Globalization: Theory and Practice*, London: Pinter, pp. 3–16.

Youngs, Gillian (1999), *International Relations in a Global Age: A Conceptual Challenge*, Oxford: Policy Press.

3 Globalization, human security and social policy: North and South

Andrés Pérez-Baltodano

Introduction

On the 100th anniversary of the Nobel Prize, 100 Nobel laureates signed a public statement in which they pointed out that the security of the planet depends on environmental and social reform at the global level: 'It is time to turn our backs on the unilateral search for security, in which we seek to shelter behind walls' (*The Globe and Mail*, 2001, A21).

In their statement, the Nobel laureates echoed an argument that has become almost universally accepted by scholars and people in general: increasing global interconnectedness has created a crisis of human security that demands the formulation of strategies that transcend national boundaries. This argument was the central message of the United Nations Development Report of 1994 entitled *New Dimensions of Human Security* (see UNDP, 1994). In this report, the UN defined *human security* as 'safety from the constant threats of hunger, disease, crime and repression'; and 'protection from sudden and hurtful disruptions in the pattern of our daily lives – whether in our homes, in our jobs, in our communities or in our environment' (UNDP, 1994: 3).

The UN has pointed out more recently that globalization exacerbates human insecurity in both rich and poor countries: 'In the globalizing world of shrinking time, shrinking space and disappearing borders, people are confronting new threats to human security – sudden and hurtful disruptions in the pattern of daily life' (UNDP, 1999: 3).

This chapter explores the phenomenon of globalization as a historical process that challenges the capacity of the state to generate conditions of ontological security. The concept of ontological security makes reference to people's confidence 'in the continuity of their self-identity and in the constancy of their surrounding social and material environments of action' (Giddens, 1990: 92). Moreover, this chapter examines the theoretical rationale behind some of the most common *global* social policy strategies designed to contribute to the generation of ontological security in the world today.

The first section reviews the formation of the democratic Western European state as an institutional arrangement designed to spatialize history and 'to overcome contingency' (see Luhmann, 1982, 1993). The 'universalization' of this model will also be reviewed to provide a general characterization of the different levels of 'stateness' achieved by countries in the North and in the South.

The second section will analyse the differential impact of globalization on the states and societies of the North and the South. This analysis will then be used in the third section to assess the framework of historical possibilities and limitations within which alternative uses of social policy are being currently proposed to respond to the crisis of security created by globalization.

I. Processes of state formation and social policy: North and South

The North

The Great Crisis of the mid-1500s in Europe expanded the territorial scope of social life beyond the precarious boundaries of the 'natural societies' of the Middle Ages (Ortega y Gasset, 1946: 75; see also Anderson 1974: 115–42). In these circumstances, the construction of social order required the institutionalization of expectations (see Luhmann, 1990: 21–79) in abstract space (rather than in place), and the fostering of 'relations between "absent" others, locationally distant from any given situation of face-to-face interaction' (Giddens, 1990: 18–19). In turn, this required the centralization of power and the creation of a new foundation for authority. The historical answer to these requirements was the emergence and consolidation of monarchical absolutism.

Monarchical absolutism re-created the territorial scope of social life by forming a centralized structure of political power that overran the political societies of the Middle Ages. The foundation of authority for this new structure of power was provided by the idea of sovereignty, which was best expressed by Hobbes in 1651.

The early modern idea of sovereignty involved a radical reconceptualization of medieval conceptions of territory, history and security, in that it created the foundation for the development of society's capacity to generate 'a strictly political history of chains of events', with the capacity to replace 'the archaic fusion of mythical and genealogical time' that prevailed in the Middle Ages (Luhmann, 1982: 333). In the creation of this new history, philosophy would gradually replace theology, and the 'omnipotent God' would become 'the omnipotent lawgiver' (Schmitt, 1985: 36). Moreover, with the emergence of the Great Leviathan, security would be not only politically created, but also planned and delivered by the state in a process guided by the doctrine of *raison d'état*, that is, by the subordination of public morality to state power (Koselleck, 1988: 25).

The institutionalization of the modern state, then, was accompanied by the development of its capacity to regulate social relations within its territorial boundaries. In turn, this capacity made it possible for the state to regulate social relations across time. This is because continuous regulation of social relations across territorial space results, over time, in the institutionalization of 'behavioral expectations' (see Luhmann, 1990: 21–79). As such, the institutionalization of the modern state came to represent what Gross calls the 'spatialization of time and experience', which implies 'the tendency to condense time relations – which are an essential ingredient for personal and social meaning – into space relations' (Gross, 1981–82: 59).

The role of the state as a synchronizer of social expectations and social experiences underwent significant change in the eighteenth century, when the Enlightenment introduced the idea of progress. An open future dissociated from the past represented a formidable challenge to society's ability to achieve security and overcome contingency. This challenge was met by the ideas of popular sovereignty and representative democracy that expressed a new faith in human beings' ability to control their destiny. Democracy placed sovereignty not in the king or in the state, but in 'the people'.

The democratic state responded to people's needs and demands, not simply as the result of a passive reading of the people's will, but as an active organizer of people's aspirations and memories. Through its bureaucratic apparatus, the democratic state actively participated in the creation of 'imagined communities' (see Anderson, 1991) tied together by administrative and legal structures. These structures made the development of nationalistic values and identities possible (see Nisbet, 1981).

The development of the administrative and regulatory capacity of the state required that the principle of sovereignty, as articulated by Hobbes in the seventeenth century, be redefined during the eighteenth century (see Hume, 1981: 20). These efforts were best illustrated by Jeremy Benthan's concern for 'the idea of rational rules as paramount standards of administrative behavior' (Bahmueller, 1981: 186). The ultimate objective of these rules was to contribute to 'the maximization of the Benthamite values of security, predictability, stability, and physical comfort' (Long, 1977: 118).

The opportunities offered by the administrative and regulatory power of the sovereign state were fully realized with the emergence of civil society, that is, with the constitution of free associations that were not under the influence or control of the state. The emergence of these associations provided the state with an opportunity to use the organizational capacity achieved by society as an extension of its own regulatory power (see Rose, 1996). At the same time, the creation of 'reproduction circuits' that connected society with the state, provided people with an institutional mechanism to 'determine or inflect the course of state action' (Taylor, 1990: 4; see also Giddens, 1984).[1] This new relationship between the state and society created the conditions for the emergence and consolidation of citizenship rights.

Citizenship rights not only represented a challenge to the state, but also to national class structures. In this sense, the concept of class has a relative meaning vis-à-vis citizenship and, conversely, citizenship is a category which has an explanatory value that is intimately linked with that of class. Citizenship, T.H. Marshall points out, should be seen as, 'the architect of legitimate social inequality' in class divided societies (Marshall, 1983: 48–9). From this perspective, both class and citizenship constitute evolving historical realities associated with the struggle over the distribution of power within sovereign political spaces. In England, according to Marshall's gender-blind characterization of this struggle, citizenship rights evolved from civil rights in the eighteenth century, to political rights in the nineteenth century, to social rights in the twentieth century (see Marshall, 1983).

From this perspective, the Welfare State, and more precisely, the 'three worlds of welfare capitalism' in the North (see Esping-Andersen, 1990) can be seen as the product of the consolidation of social rights, and more generally, as the institutional consequence of roughly 250 years of evolution of citizenship rights. Further expansion of these rights, according to Marshall, would continue to challenge and reduce social inequality.

Marshall's optimistic analysis has been shattered by the globalization of capital, the transnationalization of the power of the state, and the difficulties that societies in the North confront today to condition public policy priorities. The conquering of risk and contingency, which constituted one of the central objectives of the struggle that generated social rights and the Welfare State in the North, is currently being challenged by an attempt to legitimize the forms of insecurity created by the market, and by the presentation of 'risk aversion' as a dangerous 'ideology' (see Neal, 2000).

The South

In Europe, the modern democratic State represented an institutional product generated by history. This institutional product was transplanted as a normative model to the rest of the world through a combination of exporting and importing mechanisms that included imperialism, colonialism, the institutionalization of relations of political and economic dependency, and development strategies and programmes (see Badie, 2000).

It is well known that many of the dysfunctional aspects of social life in Africa, Asia and Latin America are the result of the imposition of the Modern State model over societies that are the product of a historical dynamic that is fundamentally different from that of Europe. The legal principle of sovereignty that was formally attached to the states in the South by international law lacked the social and political significance it had for European societies.

Most states in the South never achieved the social regulatory capacity they required to spatialize history and to control social relations within their territorial boundaries. After almost two centuries of independent republican life in Latin America the power of the state 'fades off' outside 'the national urban centers' (O'Donnell, 1993: 1358). In countries like Colombia, the state does not even have the capacity to monopolize coercive power.

In Africa, the regulatory weakness of the state is even more dramatic than in Latin America. The 'juridical' African state, created by European colonial powers, never developed the capacity to regulate social relations within its territorial boundaries. Today, in many African countries, the regulatory power of the state is declining. For some observers, this situation 'foreshadows descent into a Hobbesian state in which (as Hobbes himself hypothesized) pervasive individual rational self-interest might not allow for a possible escape into a secure political order' (Rothchild and Harbeson, 2000: 6).

In South Asia, the weakness of the state manifest itself more vividly in the persistence of ethnic, religious, and regional disintegration. For example, in India, there has been 'a gradual erosion of the authority of the central government and a failure to create a system of governance that takes account of the great regional diversity of the country' (Rahman Khan, 1998: 113–44).

Nevertheless, the imposition/adoption of the Modern State as a normative model for the organization of the history of the South facilitated the conformation of an international system of states. Through this system, states in the South became recipients of 'a set of cognitive models defining the nature, purpose, resources, technologies, controls, and sovereignty of the proper nation state' (Meyer, 1999: 123). These 'cognitive models' include parliamentarism, bureaucracy, democracy, social policies and the welfare state.

The transfer of social policy and welfare models from the North to the South was made possible by the 'choices' created by the international system, as well as by the legitimized discourses articulated by the international organizations that operate within this system (see Strang and Mei Yin Chang, 1993). These organizations include the International Labour Organization (ILO), the International Social Security Organization, and the Ibero-American Social Security Conference. The work of these organizations facilitated the 'standarization' of social security legislation around the world (see Collier and Messick, 1975).

The replication of the idea of social policy in the South, however, was only partial and relative. The low regulatory capacity of the state, the absence of effective state sovereignty, and the fragility – and in some cases virtual absence – of structures of citizenship rights with the capacity to domesticate the functions of the State, resulted in the restructuration and acculturation of the normative models of social policy and welfare institutions diffused by organizations like the ILO. Social policy and welfare models, in other words, became historically assimilated and reconstituted by the societies of the South. This process of assimilation and reconstitution generated two main types of social policy and welfare systems:

clientelistic and residual. Generally speaking, these two systems corre-
spond to the levels of state regulatory capacity and societal organization
achieved by the countries of the South.

Clientelistic welfare systems in the South developed within corporatist
structures of state–society relations. Social policies in corporatist regimes are
mainly formulated and implemented in response to the power of elites and
special interest groups rather than to broad social or class demands. Therefore, the coverage of social policies in these systems expresses the levels of
power that different sectors of society have to 'colonize' the state apparatus.
Malloy illustrates this situation when he explains the structuration of social
policy coverage in the corporatist societies of Latin America:

> The first and best coverage went to groups like civil servants and the military who
> controlled parts of the state apparatus itself; coverage of high quality next went to
> groups in strategic economic activities in export products such as railroads, docks,
> maritime, etc; these were followed by groups in critical urban services such as
> banks, electricity, transport, etc; the last to receive coverage, and of a lower order,
> were manufacturing workers… the rural sector as well as the urban informal
> sector were excluded (Malloy, 1993: 235).

Residual social policy and welfare systems emerged typically in the countries of the South where state power has been organized and exercised in a
neo-patrimonial manner. Jonathan Hartlyn explains that 'at the level of ideal
types, neo-patrimonial regimes can be distinguished most clearly from regimes that are based on rational–legal authority and impersonal law, as well
as from regimes that legitimize themselves through ideological means'
(Hartlyn, 1998: 14–15).[2] In neo-patrimonial countries, the power of the state
is predominantly coercive and civil societies are rather weak or non-existent.
Therefore, residual social policy and welfare systems are not generated by
the constitutive force of citizenship rights. In fact, residual social policy and
welfare systems can be seen as an alternative to citizenship. As in the case of
the Elizabethan Poor Law in England, residual welfare and social policy
systems are not designed to transform the structural conditions that generate
poverty and insecurity; rather, they are designed 'to preserve the existing one
with the minimum of essential change' (Marshall, 1965: 87). The Poor Law
in England, Marshall points out, 'treated the claims of the poor, not as an
integral part of the rights of citizen, but as an alternative to them' (Marshall,
1965: 88).

In the neo-patrimonial regimes of Central America and the Dominican
Republic, for example, social policies are designed to benefit segments of the
population that suffer systematic forms of social, political and economic
exclusion. The people in this category are citizens only in a formal manner.
They are recognized as recipients of social policy by the same states that

deny their rights and maintain their exclusion from effective political participation.

In Africa, the history of residual social policies goes back to colonial times. Akin Aina points out that social services were provided to African societies during the colonial period 'to maintain law and order and a local low-level administrative cadre to exploit effectively the natural and other resources of the colonies and to create colonial markets for metropolitan export' (Akin Aina, 1999: 76). For a relatively short period of time after independence, African states expanded their capacity to provide social services in an effort to legitimize their power. However, by the end of the 1960s the African state was in crisis: 'social services and social infrastructures either decayed from sheer neglect or, where they existed in rudimentary forms, were appropriated by local barons and misused for political patronage' (Akin Aina, 1999: 78).

Globalization, structural adjustment programmes and neoliberal economic policies since the 1980s have severely reduced the social policy capacity of the state in both the clientelistic and the residual welfare and social policy systems of the South. Fiscal pressures in the South, for example, negatively affected the delivery of state-provided care services. Tax revenues in these countries declined from 18 per cent of GDP in the early 1980s to 16 per cent in the 1990s (UNDP, 1999: 7; 92–4). At the same time, the instrumentalist and ahistorical approach used by the World Bank to promote state reform in the South contributed to the erosion of society's capacity to condition the policy priorities of the state (see Campbell, 2001; Akin Aina, 1999, Hoogvelt, 2000; Osei-Hwedie and Bar-On 1999; Osteria, 1999; Wangwe and Musonda, 1998; Pérez Baltodano, 1997).

II.   Globalization and the state: human insecurity North and South
Globalization, and the state reforms that have accompanied this process, constitutes a direct challenge to the preservation and expansion of human security in the North and in the South. In the North, the territorial and political spaces created by the modern state are undergoing radical transformations. Economic and political pressures against the welfare state, the increasing fluidity of labour markets, and the erosion of social rights, to name just a few of these pressures, have significantly reduced people's capacity to control risk (see Mishra, 1999).

In the South, the pressures towards regional economic integration, the increasing power of transnational financial organizations, and neoliberal state reforms have reduced the chances for many developing countries to achieve the levels of state sovereignty and national identity that allowed societies in the North to function as 'communities of aspirations and memories' (de Visscher, 1957: 206). Furthermore, many of the fragile national territories of the South, especially in Africa, have been transformed in recent years into deinstitutionalized spaces in which life is 'nasty, brutish and short'.

The intensity and the nature of the challenge that globalization represents for human security at the national level vary according to the different capacity that national states have to filter or adapt to external pressures without losing their domestic regulatory power and their capacity to respond to domestic needs and demands (see Weiss, 1998; Yeates, 2001). In this sense, the notions of North and South are useful in that they represent categories for differentiating levels of institutional and regulatory capacity to create conditions of order and security at the national level.

Understanding the differential effect of globalization on the countries of the North and the South is essential to understand the different frameworks of historical limitations and possibilities within which social policy responses to the crisis of security created by globalization can be formulated. As Patricia Kennett points out:

> Global processes are complex and contradictory. While opening up opportunities for some countries and people, others have been marginalized and excluded from the benefits of the information age. Each nation interacts in its own way with global, regional, national and local arenas. In the same way the nature of the welfare system and the form and content of social rights will vary (Kennett, 2001: 145).

Unfortunately, the national differences that Kennett points out in her analysis are not systematically considered by the bulk of the mounting literature dealing with globalization. Many academics in the North have assumed the representation of the entire globe, yet they avoid engaging in detailed analyses of the socio-political realities in the South. The results of this omission are discourses that present either a rather optimistic image of a 'Global Age'; or that refuse to accept the conceptual value of 'globalization' (see Held and McGrew, 2000; Lechner and Boli, 2000).

The perspective on globalization proposed herein emphasizes the differential effects of globalization as they are expressed in the diverse manifestations of the problem of security in different countries and regions around the world. From this perspective, the crisis of security in the North appears as the result of the breakdown of the 'symmetrical' and 'congruent' relationship between state and society that resulted from the expansion of state power and the evolution of citizenship rights over the last 300 years (Held, 1991: 198).

The transnationalization of state power in advanced liberal democratic capitalist societies opened a gap between those who make policies and those who live with the effects of those policies (see Held, 1991). This gap has diminished the value of democracy in the North and its capacity to generate and reproduce security because people see themselves affected by decisions that they don't make or control (see Luhmann, 1993).

The transnationalization of state power in the North creates tensions and contradictions between the liberal concept of the modern state – with its emphasis on domestic 'responsiveness' and 'accountability' – and the economic imperatives of the global market. The result is a crisis of authority arising from the state's increasing inability to respond to society's needs and demands (see Rosenau, 1992).

Therefore, the crisis of human security in the North is the result of a deficit of the democratic power of society to condition the functions and priorities of the state (see Kymlicka, 1997). From this perspective, the solution to the crisis of security in the North requires the democratization of the transnational power of the state. This, in turn, involves the creation of circuits of communication and control that can facilitate the subordination of the functions and priorities of the transnational arms of the state, to the needs and aspirations of 'we the people'. These transnational circuits of communication and democratic control have to be built as extensions of the domestic processes and structures that allowed societies in the North to democratize the power of the state. From this perspective, transnational political action in the North should be seen as a crucial complement of domestic politics rather than a substitute for it.[3]

The crisis of human security created by globalization in the South, on the other hand, is the result of double bind: a deficit of state power, which manifests itself in the inability for the states in the South to influence the organization of the transnational space of power created by globalization; and, a democratic deficit, which manifests itself in the inability for civil societies in the South to condition the power of the state and their national policy-making process.

States in the South lack the capacity to influence the structures and processes that govern competition and cooperation within the transnational space of power created by global forces. As the United Nations Human Development Report on globalization points out,

> the structures and processes for global policy-making are not representative. The key economic structures – the IMF, World Bank, G-7, G-10, G-22, OECD, WTO – are dominated by the large and rich countries, leaving poor countries and poor people with little influence and little voice, either for lack of membership or for lack of capacity for effective representation and participation (UNDP, 1999: 8).

Furthermore, globalization encourages the isolation of important components of the policy-making process from the pressures of domestic politics, and frequently reduces the capacity of states in the South to respond to society's needs and demands, especially when they contradict the rationale of the global market. This became painfully evident during the 1980s and 1990s. During these decades governments in the South were forced to negotiate with international financial institutions to obtain new credits to restore external balance. To secure these credits, these governments agreed to introduce economic and institutional reforms along neoliberal lines. The implementation of these reforms involved opening national economies to international competition, reducing the size of the state, reducing government services including health and education, and privatization.

The inability of the state in the South to provide people with the necessary social services, compounded with the inability of the market to provide people with employment and job security, creates the proper conditions for the intensification of ontological insecurity, a situation in which 'the ordinary circumstances of everyday life constitute a continuous threat' (Laing, 1971: 171).

Ironically, the introduction of neoliberal economic policies and state reform programmes in the South coincided with the 'Third Wave of Democracy' (see Huntington, 1991). The double process of economic and political reform created profound tensions and contradictions between the principles of democracy and the principles that determine the formulation of neoliberal policies in the South.

Electoral democracy has survived and continues to dominate the political landscape of the South. Electoral democratic systems allow people the capacity to choose the governments in charge of administering states that are increasingly subordinated to the organizations that regulate the transnational space of power and conflict created by globalization.

III. Global social policy solutions for the reconstitution of human security in the South

The deficit of state power and the democratic deficit confronted by the countries of the South need to be taken into consideration to assess the different global social policy strategies that have been formulated to confront the crisis of security faced by these countries. These strategies include: the participation of the South in the organization of a global governance system and a global civil society that can recreate at the transitional level, the congruent relationship between state power and 'we the people' that generated the conditions of democracy and security enjoyed by the societies of the North (the cosmopolitan position); the integration of social and economic policy within a global ethical framework to respond to the needs and demands of the people of the South (the liberal internationalist position); and, finally, the formulation and implementation of transitional social policies designed to palliate the most urgent human needs experienced by the poor countries of the planet (the pragmatic position).

Global democracy and global civil society: the cosmopolitan argument
Cosmopolitanism is 'a moral frame of reference for specifying principles that can be universally shared; and, concomitantly, it rejects as unjust all those practices, rules and institutions anchored in principles not all could adopt' (Held and McGrew, 2000: 401). Globalists argue that the transnational space of power and conflict created by globalization offers opportunities for the realization of cosmopolitan ideals. This transnational space is perceived as a 'new frontier' that is virtually unconstrained by the historical structural conditions within which power has been unequally distributed among countries and regions of the world. 'The challenge now', Martin Albrow says, 'is to escape the pessimism of the intellectual and to depict an age for all the people' (Albrow, 1997: 105). 'World society', he adds, 'the sum total of human interactions is now of a shape where its history leaves it with uncertain and unclear organization and its theory has yet to escape the confines of the Modern Age' (Albrow, 1997: 113).

Unfortunately, the idea of global citizenship and of a 'world society' that can function within the transnational space of power and conflict created by globalization is idyllic. It ignores the fact that globalization tends to reproduce the unequal power relations and the unequal distribution of 'life chances' that are responsible for the marginalization and the exclusion of the South.

There is no doubt that the transnational space created by globalization has increased interaction and communication among transnational actors and movements from the North and the South. However, these interactions and exchanges of information 'do not promote the expansion of a world that is intersubjectively shared' (Habermas, 1996: 292).

For a space to function as a political space, it has to be able to work as a 'reference framework'; that is, as a mental framework that is created as a result of the collective experience of sharing a similar set of life chances (Werlen, 1993: 3–8). In the absence of this framework, the intensification of 'transnational politics', or 'political activism at a distance', or 'ciberactivism', or 'ciberpolitics', (see Lins Ribeiro, 1998), do not necessarily translate in the construction of a democratic transnational political space and a 'global city' (see Magnusson, 2000).

The social actors from the North and the South that participate in the transnational space of power and conflict created by globalization, and the people that they represent, do not share the same type of life chances. The statistical record could not be more revealing: by the late 1990s, people from the North – the fifth of the world population that lives in the highest-income countries had: '86 per cent of world GDP, the bottom fifth just 1 per cent; 82 per cent of world export markets, the bottom fifth just 1 per cent; 68 per cent of foreign direct investment, the bottom fifth just 1 per cent; 74 per cent of world telephone lines... the bottom fifth just 1.5 per cent' (UNDP, 1999: 3).

Moreover, the possibility for social actors from poor countries to exercise power at the transnational level is limited by the gap that separates the states from the South from the space of power and politics created by globalization, and by the gap that separates societies from the states in these countries. People from the North do have the capacity to realize a vision of a supranational democracy for the new millennium. However, this vision cannot be presented as a vision for humanity.

A global ethic to frame the integration of economic and social policies: the liberal internationalist argument
In contrast to the cosmopolitan radical proposal to restructure global power relations, the liberal internationalist position advocates the incremental democratization of the structures and processes that operate within the transnational space of power and politics created by globalization (see McGrew, 2000). The UN position regarding global social policy responses to the crisis of security generated by globalization is rooted in this position.

The 'globalization of ethics', and more concretely, the identification of 'global public goods' as ethical imperatives that can guide the formulation of economic and social policy has been proposed by the United Nations as a key strategic component of its global social policy recommendations (see Artigas, 2001; see also UN, 2001). The 'global public goods' identified by the UN include equity and access to key basic social services that should be adopted as 'universal rights' (UN, 2001: 8).

The construction of a global consensus for the integration of social and economic policy, according to the United Nations, requires, 'inclusive consultations that involve government ministries and other social and economic partners, such as trade unions, employers and other civil society organizations ....Open, transparent consultations and dialogues are important for consensus building and bridging communications gaps' (UN, 2001: 13).

The ethical approach proposed by the United Nations to institutionalize universal rights, including the right to key social services, is highly desirable from a normative and humanitarian point of view. Unfortunately, this approach is based on a voluntaristic view of history and social change that obscures the structural conditions that reproduce social inequality across the world.

Voluntarism denotes any argument or explanation 'that stresses the place of choice, decision, purpose, and norms in human action' (Cashmore and Mullan, 1983: xii). Voluntaristic arguments for the formulation of global social policies ignore the fact that the democratization and moralization of state power and of public policy making has always been the result of a political struggle for power. Social policies and welfare state institutions in the North – as previously indicated – were the result of the struggle between the elites who determined the nature and organization of society and the groups excluded from the decision-making process that affected their lives. The struggle was about the definition of citizenship rights, the constitution of the 'social contract', and the political mechanisms to change it. As a result of this struggle, social policies and the welfare state emerged in the North as an institutionalized 'trade-off' between social equality and economic efficiency (see Esping-Andersen, 1994).

The integration of social and economic policy within a global ethical framework, as a strategy designed to reduce the levels of human insecurity created by globalization, can only be the result of political action against the national and the transnational power structures within which neoliberal economic policies are designed and enforced at the national and global levels.

The people from the North can organize this form of action using their state structures and processes. For the societies of the South, on the other hand, efforts to organize effective political action to 'moralize' economic policy need to confront the democratic deficit created by the historic gap that has separated states and societies in the South, the tendency for globalization to intensify this gap; and, the state power deficit that is reflected in the inability for the national states of the South to condition the transnational space of power and conflict created by globalization.

Palliative transitional social policy: the pragmatic argument
The transformation of the spatial foundations of international systems of modern states brought about by globalization has forced national and international organizations to move in the direction of transnational social policies. Several motivating factors for the emergence of this kind of social policy can be identified. Abram de Swaan points to the existence of two: ecological factors that create global interdependency and that give poor countries some bargaining power to improve the distribution of wealth around the world; and, global South–North migration that can have the capacity to motivate developed countries to promote better social conditions in the poor countries of the world (see de Swaan, 1992). To these two factors can be added the social requirements of the global market; that is, the requirements for global social order and stability required by the increasing interdependence of national markets, and the intensification of trade and capital mobility.

Within the context of reunification in Germany, Georg Vobruba has advocated the formulation of social policies that allow people in Eastern Germany 'to wait'. Vobruba explains:

> social policy lowers the danger of vicious circles – first in an economic sense, insofar as social policy stabilises the purchasing power; second in a political sense, insofar as social policy reduces the conflict level in the society. This

happens not by providing justice in the sense of income equality, but by facilitating the acceptance of growing income inequalities, which can be seen as both problematic and necessary (Vobruba, 1994: 88)

The same logic used by Vobruba to propose social policies that function as 'a buffer' is used by de Swaan to propose the transfer of resources from the North to the South. The idea of transnational social policy, according to de Swaan, 'may be located on a continuum somewhere between international charity and disaster relief on the one hand and infrastructural development aid on the other: charity and emergency relief tend to be consumption-oriented, as is social policy, in contrast to development aid which tends to be production-oriented' (de Swaan, 1994: 109).

Transnational social policies designed to placate the desperation of the poor in the South or in the transitional societies of Eastern Europe are based on a pragmatic view of politics and history: that is, on a rationalistic calculation of the self-interest of the North. The political dangers and the moral limits of pragmatism are many.

Pragmatism 'substitutes *expediency* for *accuracy* or *concreteness* as a term of epistemic approbation' (Rorty, 1995: 4, original emphasis). The logic of the pragmatic transnational social policies proposed by de Swaan and Vobruba excludes the values of equity and solidarity that have played a fundamental role in the struggle for justice and rights. These 'intangibles' are pushed aside in an effort to articulate social policies that are legitimized on purely instrumental grounds. Regardless of their short-term potential benefits, pragmatic transnational social policies cannot generate the long-term conditions of human security that are needed to promote human development in the South. These policies can only generate false forms of security that will be dependent, not in the basic moral premise that people in the South have to have rights, but on the will and convenience of the states and governments of the North.

IV. Conclusions

Globalization has created a 'gap' between the transnational power of the advanced liberal democratic state, and the power of civil society to condition this power (see Held, 1991). The resolution of the crisis of human security created by this gap requires the resynchronization of democratic state–society relations.

The crisis of human security created by globalization in the South, on the other hand, is the result of double bind: a deficit of state power, which manifests itself in the inability for the states in the South to influence the organization of the transnational space of power created by globalization; and, a democratic deficit, which manifests itself in the historic inability for civil societies in the South to condition the power of the state and its policy priorities.

Unfortunately, the historical specificity of the South is not considered by the dominant interpretations of globalization. The omission of the South in the current debate about globalization keeps the South 'invisible' and militates against the potential to design and implement global social strategies that can reduce global insecurity.

The task of making current global reality explicit is incredibly challenging. It requires intellectuals to transcend the linear perspective – typically extrapolated from the North – within which the future of the planet is currently analysed. It forces us to embrace theoretically the disjointed, contradictory, and yet unified-in-destiny world that Picasso sensed before anyone else. Carl Einstein pointed out that the 'wondrous harmonies' in Picasso's work were the result of 'contrasting elements' and that 'truth' in his paintings lay 'in the identity which underlies the tension between opposites' (Einstein, 1988: 190–91) The 'truth' of globalization – its risks and opportunities – can only be established by creating a vision of humanity that is based on a theoretical recognition of the structural heterogeneity of the human condition, as well as of the tensions and contradictions generated by the increasing interpenetration between North and South generated by globalization.

Notes

1. 'Reproduction circuits' are 'cycles of routinized activities and consequences which are reproduced across time and space and between institutionalized locales' (Cohen, 1989: 124).
2. 'Corporatism' and 'Neopatrimonialism' are used as 'ideal types'. Several variations of these two types of regimes can be found in the South. Robert Bianchi, for example, has studied 'unruly' forms of corporatism in the Middle East and Asia (see Bianchi, 1988). Michael Bratton and Nicholas van de Walle have studied 'neopatrimonialism' in Africa. In fact, they make too strong a demarcation between 'corporatist Latin America' and 'neo-patrimonialist Africa' (Bratton and de Walle, 1994: 458). Actually, most Latin American political regimes – for example, most Central American countries and the Dominican Republic – are 'neo-patrimonialists' (see Hartlyn, 1998).
3. The crucial relationship between domestic and transnational politics in the North was clearly demonstrated in 1997 when the power of civil society in the OECD countries played a fundamental role in the defeat of the Multilateral Agreement on Investment (MAI) see (McQuaig, 1999).

References

Akin Aina, Tade (1999), 'West and Central Africa: social policy for reconstruction and development', in Daniel Morales-Gomez (ed.), *Transnational Social Policies: The New Development Challenges of Globalization*, London: Earthscan, pp. 69–88.

Albrow, Martin (1997), *The Global Age: State and Society Beyond Modernity*, Stanford, California: Stanford University Press.

Anderson, Benedict (1991), *Imagined Communities: Reflections on the Origin and Spread of Nationalism*, London: Verso.

Anderson, Perry (1974), *Lineages of the Absolutist State*, London: NLB.

Artigas, Carmen (2001), *El Aporte de las Naciones Unidas a la Globalizacion de la Etica: Revision de Algunas Oportunidades*, Santiago de Chile: CEPAL.

Badie, Bertrand (2000), *The Imported State: The Westernization of the Political Order*, Stanford, California: Stanford University Press.

Bahmueller, Charles F. (1981), *The National Charity Company: Jeremy Bentham's Silent Revolution*, Berkeley: University of California Press.

Bianchi, Robert (1988), 'Interest group politics in the third world', in Louis J. Cantori and Andrew H. Ziegler, Jr (eds), *Comparative Politics in the Post-Behavioral Era*, Boulder: Lynne Rienner Publishers, pp. 203–30.

Bratton, Michael and Nicholas van de Walle (1994), 'Neopatrimonial regimes and political transitions in Africa', *World Politics*, **46** (4), 11–32.

Campbell, Bonnie (2001), 'Governance, institutional reform and the state: international financial institutions and political transition in Africa', *Review of African Political Economy*, vol. 88, 155–76.

Cashmore, E. Ellis and Bob Mullan (1983), *Approaching Social Theory*, London: Heinemann Educational Books.

Cohen, Ira J. (1989), *Structuration Theory: Anthony Giddens and the Constitution of Social Life*, London: Macmillan.

Collier, David and Richard E. Messick (1975), 'Prerequisites versus diffusion: testing alternative explanations of social security adoption', *American Political Science Review*, **48** (2), 147–60.

de Swaan, Abram (1992), 'Perspectives for transnational social policy', *Government and Opposition*, **27** (1), 33–51.

de Swaan, Abram (1994), 'Introduction', in Abram de Swaan (ed.), *Social Policy Beyond Borders*, Amsterdan: Amsterdam University Press, pp. 1–6.

de Visscher, Charles (1957), *Theory and Reality in Public International Law*, Princeton: Princeton University Press.

Einstein, Carl (1988), cited in Arianna Stassinopoulos Huffington, *Picasso: Creator and Destroyer*, New York: Avon Books.

Esping-Andersen, Gøsta (1990), *The Three Worlds of Welfare Capitalism*, Cambridge: Polity Press.

Esping-Andersen, Gøsta (1994), 'After the golden age: the future of the welfare state in the new global order', Occasional Paper No. 7, World Summit for Social Development.

Giddens, Anthony (1984), *The Constitution of Society: Outline of the Theory of Structuration*, Berkeley: Berkeley University Press.

Giddens, Anthony (1990), *The Consequences of Modernity*, Stanford: Stanford University Press.

Globe and Mail, The (2001), 'Our best point of view', 7 December, A21.

Gross, David (1981–82), 'Space, time and modern culture', *Telos*, vol. 50, 131–42.

Habermas, Jurgen (1996), 'The European nation-state. Its achievements and its limits: on the past and future of sovereignty and citizenship' in Gopal Balakrishnan (ed.), *Mapping the Nation*, London: Verso, pp. 281–94.

Hartlyn, Jonathan (1998), *The Struggle for Democratic Politics in the Dominican Republic*, Chapes Hill: University of North Carolina Press.

Held, David (1991), 'Democracy, the nation-state and the global system', in David Held (ed.), *Political Theory Today*, Stanford: Stanford University Press.

Held, David and Anthony McGrew (eds) (2000), *The Global Transformations Reader: An Introduction to the Globalization Debate*, Malden, MA, USA: Polity and Blackwell Publishers.

Held, David and Anthony McGrew (2000), 'World order, normative futures: introduction', in David Held and Anthony McGrew (eds), *The Global Transformations Reader: An Introduction to the Globalization Debate*, pp. 401–404.

Hoogvelt, Ankie (2000), 'Globalization and the postcolonial world', in David Held and Anthony McGrew (eds), *The Global Transformations Reader: An Introduction to the Globalization Debate*, Malden, MA, USA: Polity and Blackwell Publishers, pp. 355–60.

Hume, L.J. (1981), *Bentham and Bureaucracy*, Cambridge: Cambridge University Press.

Huntington, Samuel (1991), *The Third Wave*, Norman and London: University of Oklahoma Press.

Kennett, Patricia (2001), *Comparative Social Policy*, Buckingham and Philadelphia: Open University Press.

Kjeld Erik Brodsgaard and Susan Young (2000), *State Capacity in East Asia: Japan, Taiwan, China, and Vietnam*, Oxford and New York: Oxford University Press.

Koselleck, Reinhart (1988), *Critique and Crisis: Enlightement and Pathogenesis of Modern Society*, Oxford: Berg.

Kymlicka, Will (1997), 'The prospects for citizenship: domestic and global', in Thomas J. Courchene (ed.), *The Nation State in a Global/Information Era: Policy Challenges*, Kingston, Ont.: John Deutsch Institute for the Study of Economic Policy, pp. 315–25.

Laing, R.D. (1971), *The Divided Self: An Existential Study in Sanity and Madness*, Middlesex, UK: Penguin.

Lechner, Frank J. and John Boli (2000), *The Globalization Reader*, Malden, MA and Oxford, UK: Blackwell.

Lins Ribeiro, Gustavo (1998), 'Cybercultural politics: political activism at a distance in a transnational world', in Sonia Alvarez, Evelina Dagnino and Arturo Escobar (eds), *Cultures of Politics, Politics of Cultures: Revisioning Latin American Social Movements*, Boulder: Westview Press, pp. 325–52.

Long, Douglas C. (1977), *Bentham on Liberty: Jeremy Bentham's Idea of Liberty in Relation to his Utilitarianism*, Toronto: University of Toronto Press.

Luhmann, Niklas (1982), *The Differentiation of Society*, New York: Columbia University Press.

Luhmann, Niklas (1990), *Essays on Self-Reference*, New York: Columbia University Press.

Luhmann, Niklas (1993), *Risk a Sociological Theory*, New York: A de Gruyter.

Magnusson, Warren (2000), 'Hyperspace: a political ontology of the global city', in Richard V. Ericson and Nico Stehr (eds), *Governing Modern Societies*, Toronto: Toronto University Press, pp. 80–104.

Malloy, James M. (1993), 'Statecraft, social policy, and governance in Latin America', *Governance: An International Journal of Policy and Administration*, **6** (2), 220–74.

Marshall, T.H. (1965), *Class, Citizenship and Social Development: Essays by T.H. Marshall*, with an introduction by Seymour Martin Lipset, New York: Anchor Books.

Marshall, T.H. (1983), 'Citizenship and social class', in David Held et al. (eds), *States and Societies*, Oxford: Basil Blackwell, pp. 248–60.

McGrew, Anthony (2000), 'Democracy beyond borders', in David Held and Anthony McGrew (eds), *The Global Transformations Reader: An Introduction to the Globalization Debate*, Malden, MA, USA: Polity and Blackwell Publishers, pp. 405–19.

McQuaig, Linda (1999), *The Cult of Impotence: Selling the Myth of Powerlessness in the Global Economy*, Toronto: Penguin Books.

Meyer, John W. (1999), 'The changing cultural context of the nation-state: a world society perspective', in George Stenmetz (ed.), *State/culture: state formation after the cultural turn*, Ithaca and London: Cornell University Press, pp. 123–43.

Mishra, R. (1999), *Globalization and the Welfare State*, Cheltenham, UK and Northampton, MA, USA: Edward Elgar.

Neal, Mark (2000), 'Risk aversion: the rise of an ideology', in Laura Jones (ed.), *Safe Enough: Managing Risk and Regulation*, Vancouver: The Fraser Institute, pp. 13–30.

Nisbet, Robert A. (1981), *The Quest for Community*, Oxford: Oxford University Press.

O'Donnell, Guillermo (1993), 'On the state, democratization and some conceptual problems: a Latin American view with glances at some postcomunist countries', *World Development*, **21** (8), 1355–69.

Ortega y Gasset, José (1946) 'The state as pure dynamism', in Randolph Bourne (ed.) *Leviathan in Crisis*, New York: Viking Press. .

Osei-Hwedie, Kwaku and Arnon Bar-On (1999), 'Sub-saharan Africa: community-driven social policies', in Daniel Morales-Gomez (ed.) *Transnational Social Policies: The New Development Challenges of Globalization*, London: Earthscan, pp. 89–116.

Osteria, Trinidad S. (1999), 'Southeast Asia: the decentralization of social policy', in Daniel

Morales-Gomez (ed.) *Transnational Social Policies: The New Development Challenges of Globalization*, London: Earthscan, pp. 117–48.

Pérez Baltodano, Andrés (ed.) (1997), *Globalización, Ciudadanía y Política Social en América Latina: Tensiones y Contradicciones*, Caracas: Nueva Sociedad.

Rahman Khan, Azizur (1998), 'The impact of globalization on South Asia', in A.S. Bhalla (ed.), *Globalization, Growth and Marginalization*, London and New York: St. Martin's Press, pp. 103–24.

Rorty, Richard (1995), 'Between Hegel and Darwin', in Herman J. Saatkamp, Jr. (ed.), *Rorty and Pragmatism*, Nashville and London: Vanderbilt University Press.

Rose, Nickolas (1996), 'Governing advanced liberal democracies', in Barry Andrew, Osborne Thomas and Rose Nickolas (eds), *Foucault and Political Reason: Liberalism, Neo-liberalism and Rationalities of Government*, Chicago: The University of Chicago Press, pp. 37–64.

Rosenau, James N. (1992), 'The relocation of authority in a shrinking world', *Comparative Politics*, vol. 24, pp. 253–63.

Rothchild, Donald and John W. Harbeson (2000), 'The African state and state system in flux', in John W. Harbeson and Donald Rothchild (eds), *Africa in World Politics: The African State System in Flux*, Boulder: Westview, pp. 3–20.

Schmitt, Carl (1985), *Political Theology: Four Chapters on the Concept of Sovereignty*, trans. George Schwab, Cambridge: MIT Press.

Strang, David, and Patricia Mei Yin Chang (1993), 'The international labor organization and the welfare state: institutional effects on national welfare spending, 1960–80', *International Organization*, **47** (2), 235–62.

Taylor, Charles (1990),'Invoking civil society', Working Papers and Proceedings of the Center for Psychosociological Studies, Chicago.

(UN) United Nations (2001), 'Integration of social and economic policy: report of the Secretary General', Economic and Social Council (Advanced Unedited Version), December.

(UNDP) United Nations Development Programme (1994), *Human Development Report, 1994: New Dimensions of Human Security*, New York and Oxford: Oxford University Press.

(UNDP) United Nations Development Programme (1999), *Human Development Reiport, 1999: Globalization with a Human Face*, New York and Oxford: Oxford University Press.

Vobruba, Geog (1994), 'Transnational social policy in processes of transformation' in Abram de Swaan (ed.), *Social Policy Beyond Borders*, Amsterdam: Amsterdan University Press, pp. 83–100.

Wangwe, S.M. and Flora Musonda (1998), 'The impact of globalization on Africa', in A.S. Bhalla (ed.), *Globalization, Growth and Marginalization*, New York: St. Martin's Press, pp. 149–67.

Weiss, Linda (1998), *The Myth of the Powerless State: Governing the Economy in a Global Era*, Cambridge: Polity Press.

Werlen, Benno (1993), *Society, Action and Space: An Alternative Human Geography*, London: Routledge.

Yeates, Nicola (2001), *Globalization and Social Policy*, London; Thousand Oaks; New Delhi: Sage Publications.

4 Social protection by other means: can it survive globalization?

Ramesh Mishra

The implications of globalization for social welfare remain a matter of a great deal of contention and debate. Not unexpectedly much of this debate has focused on the 'welfare state', that is on the implications for state programmes of welfare and social expenditure (see for example Rhodes, 1996; Pierson, 1998; Mishra, 1999; Sykes et al., 2001). Far less attention has been paid to what globalization might mean for those institutional patterns identified in the literature as 'social protection by other means' (SPM) (Castles, 1989). SPM refers to the fact that besides those institutions typical of the Western welfare state – notably social insurance programmes for income security and medical care and demand management policies to maintain employment – there are other institutional arrangements which though not generally considered as being a part of the formal system of social protection, nonetheless perform broadly similar functions, that is providing economic security and maintaining basic living standards. What the idea of SPM recognizes is that the range of policies and institutions which, directly or indirectly, might contribute to social protection extend beyond those associated with the 'welfare state'.[1] Castles (1989: 7–8), for example, has employed the concept in relation to certain institutional arrangements in the Antipodes but has pointed out, quite rightly, that it has wider applicability. In this chapter the implications of globalization for SPM are examined in three different settings: Australia, Japan and the post-socialist countries of Eastern Europe and the former USSR. No doubt the countries in this last group vary enormously in terms of economic, political and social conditions as well as the current state of transition from state socialism. However, they have shared certain institutional patterns characteristic of state socialism. It is this systemic feature that justifies their being treated as a single category.

What form did SPM take in these three different sites? In Australia it involved economic protectionism – including tariffs and strict control over immigration – meant to nurture domestic industries and ensure plentiful employment, and a system of compulsory wage arbitration meant to provide the working man with a living wage (Castles, 1989). In Japan SPM, which has not eroded much thus far, comprises full employment and job security maintained through a system of lifetime employment, and enterprise welfare

(Pempel, 1989). In the case of state socialist countries distinctive forms of social protection involved guaranteed full employment for men and women and extensive consumer price subsidies to help maintain living standards (Standing, 1996). While the policies and institutions identified above do not necessarily exhaust all forms of SPM in these countries, the chapter proceeds on the basis that these constitute the most important forms of SPM and have been recognized as such in the literature (Castles, 1989; Pempel, 1989; Standing, 1996).

The basic argument of this chapter is that these forms of SPM developed in conditions in which nation-states could remain relatively insulated from the global economy. The opening up of national economies to market forces and international competition over the last couple of decades or so has tended to weaken, if not undermine, the foundations of these types of SPM. They have been dismantled to a large extent in Australia, virtually eliminated in former state socialist countries and have suffered significant erosion in Japan. The result of these changes can be seen as a form of *structural* convergence in systems of social protection towards what might be described as the mainstream Western welfare patterns. For example in former state socialist societies systemic full employment has been replaced by levels of employment determined largely by the market, together with unemployment benefits. Targeted forms of income support, social assistance and other familiar Western-style welfare patterns, which were virtually non-existent in the past, have been emerging. From this viewpoint, economic liberalization and the greater integration of national economies into the global market place can be seen as a source of increasing uniformity and 'Westernization' of welfare patterns. It is important to keep in mind that what is being claimed here is a convergence in the *form* or structure of social welfare. Whether the *content* of social provision is also converging is a different issue with which we are not here concerned. Much of the debate over the implications of globalization for social welfare has of course been concerned with the *content* or substance of social policy, for example retrenchment of programmes and benefits, rather than the *form* or structure which is the focus of this chapter.

Thus far we have used the term 'globalization' without defining it. It is time to clarify the meaning of the term as employed in this chapter. Essentially the reference here is to *economic* globalization, that is the closer integration of national economies into the global market economy through the liberalization of trade and financial flows. However the promotion of economic liberalization by supranational agencies, notably the International Monetary Fund (IMF) and World Bank (WB), through their influence on economic and social policies of nations will also be considered as an aspect of globalization (Deacon et al., 1997; Mishra, 1999). One problem of employing a broad-gauge concept such as globalization as, so to speak, an 'independent variable' is the difficulty of demonstrating that the change in question was in fact due to the influence of this particular variable. Clearly what is offered here is an interpretation of the relationship, an argument backed by evidence, and not for example a statistical demonstration of the nexus between increasing economic openness and the decline of SPM. Moreover the transformation of SPM involves influences other than that of globalization. For example national responses to global challenges differ and make a difference to the outcome. Thus Australia and New Zealand have responded quite differently to the problem of dealing with SPM in the context of globalization (Castles, 1996). In New Zealand the institutions of economic protection and wage arbitration, in short SPM, were virtually eliminated outright. In Australia, by contrast, the process of change was more gradual and elements of compulsory wage arbitration have been retained. In general both endogenous and exogenous influences have been involved in the process of change. Essentially the argument here is that globalization has been an important influence in the erosion of SPM in the countries under examination.

The rest of the chapter is organized as follows. We consider the nature of SPM and its transformation since the 1980s in Australia, Japan and the post-socialist societies of Eastern Europe and the former USSR. In each case the relationship between globalization and the decline or demise of SPM is a key issue to be explored. A concluding section summarizes the main arguments and evidence and discusses their broader implications for the relationship between globalization and social welfare.

Australia

In Australia SPM comprised a strategy of economic protectionism plus a system of wage arbitration both of which developed in the early years of the twentieth century. Protectionism consisted of two basic elements: i) a high level of tariff in order to restrict foreign competition and to promote the development of a domestic manufacturing industry and ii) a strict control on immigration designed to exclude low-wage labour, especially from Asia, and to maintain a tight labour market. The system of compulsory wage arbitration was meant to secure for the worker – typically a male wage earner with a dependent wife and children – a minimum wage which met his 'normal needs', in short something like a 'living wage'. These conditions sought to ensure a high level of employment as well as a reasonable family wage for the worker which made the need for a comprehensive system of social protection along West European lines less pressing. Castles (1989) argues that this is what accounts for the apparently 'residual' form of income protection in the Antipodes. Thus Australia never developed a system of social insurance, for income protection during one's working life and in old age, the essential core of income security provision in the welfare states of virtually every industrialized nation. The Australian welfare state which has been labelled the '"wage-earner's" welfare state' remained a laggard in this respect with largely means-tested social benefits and low social expenditure (Castles 1988: 31). Yet as Castles (1988: 18) points out, in terms of welfare outcomes Australia was by no means a laggard nation. In short, SPM acted as a functional alternative to regular forms of social welfare provision.

Despite some changes in immigration policy and a period of disruption of the system of wage arbitration in the 1960s, overall the basic structure of SPM remained in place until the 1980s. It seems to have provided an effective means of economic security and welfare down to the early 1970s (Castles, 1996). During 1960–73 unemployment remained below 2 per cent and, in common with most other OECD countries, Australia achieved high rates of economic growth. Australia was among the most prosperous of OECD nations in the 1960s with a relatively low rate of poverty and egalitarian income distribution (Castles, 1988: 14–18). However, in the 1970s the international economic situation began to change, making the policy of economic protectionism increasingly counterproductive. By 1975 Australia had become the third most closed economy, after the United States and Japan, in terms of trade (Castles, 1988: 43). High tariffs and protectionism had made Australian manufacturing, producing largely for the home market, relatively inefficient and uncompetitive. The bulk of Australia's export trade was in commodities and staples which was being lost gradually as a result of European Common Market policies. Moreover the long-term trend in worsening terms of trade for commodities was working against Australia (Castles et al., 1996). The result was a relative decline in GDP per capita. From ranking sixth among 18 OECD nations in the 1960s Australia had slipped below the OECD average by the early 1980s (Castles, 1988). Moreover since the OPEC price shock of 1973 and the resulting 'stagflation', unemployment had been rising. It averaged 5 per cent during 1974–9 and above 6 per cent between 1980–82. Overall Australia's macro-economic performance in the 1970s was one of the worst among OECD countries. Despite some effort to reduce tariffs and make Australian industry more competitive, protectionist policies, which included subsidies to primary and secondary industries, continued into the 1980s (Castles et al., 1996).

By the early 1980s economic protectionism was ceasing to be a viable option. Major developments were taking place internationally, with the US and the UK in the lead, to open up Western economies in terms of financial flows and trade and extend the scope of market forces, nationally and globally. Instead of growth based primarily on the domestic market the new circumstances demanded trade-led growth in a globally competitive market. In short, the globalization bandwagon was on the roll and a relatively small nation such as Australia had little choice besides trying to get on it. Isolationism could only mean further economic decline. Henceforth becoming 'internationally competitive' became the new mantra in Australia as elsewhere (Wiseman, 1998; Castles et al., 1996). What all this amounted to was the need for a substantial deregulation of the economy, including the financial system and the labour market. The latter had to be made more 'flexible' with wages more responsive to market forces. Financial liberalization implied removing capital controls and allowing national currencies to float, which in turn meant far greater influence – direct or indirect – of global markets and global investors on national policies. The implications for the system of SPM were clear. As a part of the old protectionist and regulated economy it had to be scaled down substantially, if not dismantled (Wiseman, 1998).

The change came in the early 1980s when the Labour government decided to float the Australian dollar and deregulate the financial system. Reduction in tariffs followed in the late 1980s. Further falls in tariffs and industry assistance were projected in order to bring Australia in line with most other OECD nations by the year 2000 (OECD, 1997a: 81). As Castles (1988, 28) remarks, the new economic strategy was based on the 'need to strip away all those policies and practices' which had insulated Australia from global trends and international competition. Growth was to come by way of reversing the decline of Australian manufacturing and creating a specialized export-oriented manufacturing sector.

The deregulation of the wage arbitration system followed a more circuitous path. The Labour government's agreement with the trade unions (the Accord) ensured that change was gradual and consensual. In the mid-1980s the system was used to hold down wages in order to reduce inflation and follow a reflationary policy of creating jobs and reducing unemployment. From the late 1980s the scope of wage arbitration has been steadily curtailed while that of free collective bargaining has been extended. By the end of the 1990s collective bargaining had also been very substantially decentralized allowing more free play of market forces and a smaller role of the government in the determination of wages (Wiseman, 1998; OECD, 2001).

The result of economic liberalization and the dismantling of large components of SPM can be seen in changes in the labour market, income equality and poverty. Full employment is a thing of the past.[2] Wage dispersion has increased. 'Non-regular' forms of employment, for example temporary and part-time work at low wage, have increased substantially. For example during 1983–92, part-time share of total employment grew by 40 per cent (Wiseman, 1998: 63) while casual employment grew from 17 per cent of the workforce in 1985 to 24 per cent in 1995, one of the highest in the industrialized world (Beresford, 2000: 196).

As far as social welfare is concerned Australia has chosen to retain and strengthen its selectivist system of income maintenance. However, a public system of medical care was introduced in 1983 and a mandated system of occupationally based superannuation has been substantially expanded in scope and coverage since the mid-1980s. The latter may be seen as a modernized form of SPM whose origins lie in the system of wage arbitration (Castles, 1996).

In sum, of the three components of Australia's SPM identified earlier, that is economic protectionism, immigration control and wage arbitration, the first has been virtually eliminated, and the third has been very substantially reduced in scope. As regards immigration, economic liberalization in Australia, as in other countries, stops short of the free mobility of labour across national borders. The 'white Australia' immigration policy is a thing of the past but controls remain in place. However in this respect Australia is no different from other industrialized countries. Overall, Australia's SPM has eroded substantially, as a result of changes in the international political economy over the last quarter century and, in particular, the closer integration of Australian economy with the global market economy.

Japan

In Japan SPM, which took shape after World War II, comprises two main elements. First of all there is a policy of full employment and job security institutionalized through a commitment to 'lifetime employment' by employers and employees. What is distinctive about this pattern of full employment is that it seeks to provide a job for everyone – or at least for all working-age males – based on the *preservation* of private sector jobs, within a long-term relationship between the employee and the employer. Secondly, and related to the above, is a system of wide-ranging workplace benefits, for example pensions and retirement allowances, housing, medical care, family allowance and family leave, provided by the employer. In fact lifetime or long-term employment and occupational benefits form a part of the broader system of industrial relations in which wages are based on seniority rather than 'merit' and unions are organized around the enterprise (Peng, 2000; Pempel, 1989). True, the system of lifetime employment, seniority pay and enterprise welfare is far more typical of the large firms. These conditions therefore apply to only about a third or so of the labour force. However, in a weaker form the norm of job security and workplace benefits is also prevalent in medium and small firms. Significantly the obligation on the part of the employer not to dismiss regular employees save in exceptional circumstances is not merely customary but also upheld by the law (Schregle, 1993). It is estimated that some 70 per cent of the Japanese labour force enjoys de facto job security leaving about 30 per cent of the workforce, including temporary, contractual and part-time workers, as 'non-regular' employees. The latter consist largely of women, older workers (who may have retired from their regular employment) and immigrants. Although the non-regular workforce is not a part of the lifetime system of job security, the national policy of maintaining full employment seeks to ensure that there is little or no unemployment (Schregle, 1993; Peng, 2000; Therborn, 1986).

In sum the majority of Japanese employees (especially males) do have job security and access to a range of occupational benefits and the labour force as a whole enjoys the conditions of full employment. To full employment and enterprise welfare we need to add another element, that is strongly institutionalized extended family obligations to support and care for family members which is enshrined in family law (Peng, 2000). This last element can be seen as a cultural norm reinforced by law. Together these three elements make up what is distinctive about Japanese patterns of welfare, in short SPM. All three are currently under pressure and changes are under way. However, globalization is mainly relevant to full employment and enterprise welfare and the chapter will focus on these. As we shall see below economic protectionism has been important for maintaining these patterns and is now facing the challenge of globalization.

Although Japan has developed a basic social safety net consisting of pensions and health insurance, workers' compensation, unemployment insurance and family allowance the role of state welfare remains limited. Japan's social expenditure is one of the lowest among OECD countries. In 1960 it was 8 per cent of GDP compared with the OECD average of 13.1 per cent. Thirty years later it was only 11.57 per cent of GDP compared with an average of 21.6 per cent for OECD countries (OECD, 1985; OECD, 1994). Yet Japanese people enjoy economic security, a high standard of living and an egalitarian distribution of income that bears comparison with Scandinavian countries. Indices such as life expectancy, infant mortality and enrolment in tertiary education put Japan among the top nations of the world (Rose and Shiratori, 1986; Pempel, 1989). Clearly Japan has developed its own indigenous version of economic and social security which, arguably, offers social protection comparable to the advanced welfare states of Europe.

In the 1970s the OPEC price shock and its economic aftermath disrupted the Japanese trajectory of high economic growth and tested the policy of full employment severely. However, Japan went through extensive industrial restructuring scaling down old industries and developing new ones. The Japanese economy managed to weather the impact of the recession and restructuring with patterns of full employment and welfare largely intact. However, government spending to counter the recession and help maintain employment resulted in budget deficits and a mounting national debt (Therborn, 1986; Peng, 2000). These developments and the slowdown in economic growth as well as the economic difficulties facing Western welfare states in the 1970s were important in turning Japan away from its earlier intention of developing a comprehensive welfare state along Western lines. The 1980s saw significant cutbacks in state welfare programmes, which had been expanded in the 1970s, along with the decision to maintain a 'Japanese-style' welfare society (Goodman and Peng, 1996). In short SPM was to be maintained and strengthened. This worked well through the 1980s with the country enjoying full employment, relatively strong economic growth, low inflation and surplus budgets. At a time when most of the OECD countries were suffering from high unemployment, inflation and chronic budget deficits Japan seemed to be amply vindicated in its distinctive way of welfare (Mishra, 1999: 86).

However, the situation has changed dramatically since then. Japan went through a period of a speculative investment boom in the late 1980s (the so-called 'bubble economy') followed by a collapse of the 'bubble' in 1990. Since then the economy has been mired in stagnation and recession. Repeated economic stimuli by the government in the form of huge spending on infrastructure have failed to set the economy on the growth path. Meanwhile the national debt has soared to unprecedented heights. Despite the government pumping billions of yen to prop up the economy and maintain employment, unemployment has kept on rising reaching above 5 per cent by the year 2000. While this may not seem high by OECD standards it must be remembered that Japan's rate of unemployment has been exceptionally low, averaging 1.8 per cent during 1960–89 and reaching 3 per cent only in 1995. Moreover unemployment has been held down by keeping redundant workers on the payroll of companies and the government having to run up massive deficits. The economy has been stagnating for over a decade now and the prospects of recovery in the near future look bleak. True, the proximate cause of Japan's economic difficulties is the collapse of the bubble economy and the inability of the nation to deal with the ensuing problems effectively. However, the crisis has underlined a) the systemic nature of Japanese capitalism which makes piecemeal reform difficult and b) the economic costs of maintaining a relatively closed and regulated domestic economy in the context of increasing trade openness and competitiveness worldwide. The big question is whether the economy can recover without major restructuring and reform and whether the country can ever return to its traditional pattern of full employment and reliance on occupational benefits as a major component of welfare.[3]

To understand the Japanese situation better it is useful to look at the distinctive character of the Japanese economy. It is a dual economy which combines a highly efficient and competitive export-oriented sector, represented by corporate giants such as Toyota, Sony, Hitachi and others, with a large and substantially less efficient domestic sector of services and small producers. The domestic economy is highly regulated – both formally and informally – justifying the label of a 'closed' economy. Not only is domestic competition restricted but non-tariff barriers of various kinds also limit foreign competition very substantially. Japanese consumers have to pay for this protectionist policy, literally, in considerably higher prices which dampen domestic consumption. In short, despite its successful export trade, substantial overseas investment and large multinational corporations Japan Inc. remains very much a protected economy (Thurow, 1996: 200–204; Katz, 1998). It is largely this relative insulation from the sway of market forces, domestic and international, that has enabled Japan to maintain its pattern of enterprise-based full employment and welfare benefits. The less efficient but labour-intensive domestic sector of the economy helps maintain jobs, as does the 'lifetime employment' system of large- and medium-sized firms. The broader social norm that employees will not be dismissed by the company as long and as far as possible means that 'millions of redundant' workers remain on the company payroll even when profits are falling (Greider, 1998: 375). This in turn is made possible by the distinctive nature of Japanese capital market and financial institutions. Unlike Western companies Japanese corporations have extensive cross-shareholding, are not profit-driven and work within a long-term perspective (Dore, 2000). In part, this is what has made it possible for Japan to live through its longest period of post-war recession without making a radical break with traditional practices. Moreover if the labour market is inflexible in terms of employment this is counterbalanced by a variety of 'flexibilities' (OECD, 1997b: 112–17). For example, a part of Japanese wages consists of biannual bonuses. These can be adjusted according to the financial health of the company thus reducing wage costs. Employees can be redeployed, within the firm or within the conglomerate. In addition, such measures as early retirement, restrictions on overtime, freeze on new hiring and dismissal of temporary staff provide employers with a great deal of flexibility in terms of overall wage costs making it possible to avoid dismissals. These have been used extensively in recent years (Michito, 1998; OECD, 1999: 33–4, 47–50).

Furthermore the Japanese system of 'companyism' or the concept of the company as a community and a focus of loyalty of employees within a long-term relationship is an institution valued highly by employers as well as employees (Dore, 2000; Sako and Sato, 1997). It has been a distinctive feature of Japanese social and industrial organization for nearly half a century. It must also be remembered that the Japanese economy is still the second largest economy in the world. Indeed it was not so long ago that Japan was the envy of the industrialized world and Japanese management and labour practices were not only an object of admiration but also emulation. No wonder that Japan is reluctant to turn its back on an economic and industrial system that has served the country, on the whole, very well in the past. SPM is an integral part of this system. And to a large extent its future is tied to the viability of the Japanese form of capitalism itself.

However, the protracted economic crisis has taken its toll on SPM. With open unemployment reaching or surpassing that of many OECD countries including the US, Japan can scarcely claim to remain a full employment economy.[4] Whether and when it will be able to return to conditions of full employment is an open question. On the issue of lifetime employment employer *attitudes* show more inclination to move away from the system than current *practice* (Imai, 1999; Japan, 1999, p. 147). Nonetheless employers are hiring more temporary and part-time employees whose share in total employment has been rising steadily. These employees do not have job security or company welfare benefits (Peng, 2000: 104, 109). As a result of the long recession many Japanese pension funds are facing bankruptcy (OECD, 2000: 129; Takayama, 2001). They cannot survive without government assistance. Meanwhile with the rising burden of insurance contributions for pensions and medical care, companies are cutting back on employee welfare in order to reduce non-wage labour costs and to prepare for a more competitive environment (Peng, 2000: 105). The practice of basing pay on seniority rather than merit is one aspect of the old pattern that is being phased out. In short SPM has suffered some erosion especially in respect of full employment. It is likely that the scope of state programmes will increase in Japanese welfare bringing it closer to Western welfare patterns. For example, if Japan has to live with open unemployment the system of unemployment benefits will have to be improved. Social assistance may need to be made more accessible and benefit levels raised. Active labour market policies may have to be instituted. In some areas of need, for example long-term care insurance for the aged and disabled, and to some extent child care the state has already made significant commitments although these developments have more to do with endogenous factors such as the ageing of the population, increasing participation of married women in the labour force and a sharp fall in fertility rates (Peng, 2000).

While Japan seems to be holding on to past patterns for the moment, the long-term survival of Japanese SPM is very much in doubt. Japanese-style welfare developed as an integral part of the distinctive nature of the country's post-WWII economy, a developing economy dedicated to rapid industrialization via export-oriented growth. With its 'strategic' integration into the global market, Japan has been extremely successful in the venture of 'catching up', enjoying sustained high rates of growth for a long time. In part it was the protected domestic economy but in part it was also the high rate of economic growth and the expectation that it will continue that made the system of full employment and enterprise welfare affordable. Many of these assumptions underlying Japanese economy are losing their validity. High growth rates are unlikely to return.[5] The country now has a mature economy and it can no longer go on selling on the world market without opening up its own economy to foreign imports which could help bring down prices and expand domestic consumption. The continuing stagnation and recession since the early 1990s has exposed the weaknesses of Japan's financial system and capital market which relies much more on the norms of trust and 'accommodation' rather than on the impersonal market criteria of performance, transparency and other 'objective' standards. With increasing ascendancy of market forces and competition worldwide Japan is under pressure to open up the economy to international competition (Katz, 1998; Greider, 1998: 374–9). Yet a radical deregulation and transformation of Japan's domestic economy could result in large-scale bankruptcies and mass unemployment as companies restructure to meet domestic and foreign competition and let go of redundant labour numbering in the millions. It could spell the end of an enterprise-based system of welfare. If full employment and company welfare were to go under, Japan's system of SPM could come to an end. This is one extreme scenario. The other extreme would be the present tendency of inaction and immobility to continue resulting in economic stagnation and decline. The systemic features of the Japanese economic and industrial organization, intertwined with politics, make reform difficult but by no means impossible. In any case it appears that Japan has yet to tackle the problem of restructuring its economic system in order to make a successful transition to a mature post-industrial economy and to come to terms with globalization. It is highly unlikely that Japanese SPM could survive such a restructuring in anything like its present form.

Post-socialist societies
The post-socialist countries of Eastern Europe and the former USSR provide the most dramatic example of the collapse of SPM in the late twentieth century. These countries, of course, vary enormously in many significant ways including how far they have moved away from their former social system. The shift from socialist forms of SPM is most evident in Central-Eastern European countries, for example Hungary, Poland and the Czech Republic. However, similar trends can be seen in many other post-socialist countries although it would be unwise to assume that they will necessarily follow in the footsteps of Central-Eastern Europe. The decline of socialist forms of SPM has mainly to do with the collapse of state socialism but globalization has played a significant role in hastening the process.

In state socialist countries SPM comprised two basic elements. First, there was a policy of guaranteed full employment for both men and women of working age. Secondly, there was a system of consumer price subsidies for a wide variety of basic goods and services which held down the cost of living for the general population very substantially. In addition these countries also provided a range of universalistic services, for example education and medical care, as well as income security programmes, for example pensions, sickness benefits and child allowances, broadly similar to those of Western countries. Given full employment and also the importance accorded to labour and production by the system there was also an array of services and benefits based on the enterprises, complementing and augmenting state welfare services. SPM together with the state welfare programmes formed the core of economic security and welfare under state socialism (Standing, 1996; Kapstein and Mandelbaum, 1997).

Guaranteed, indeed obligatory, full-time work and consumer subsidies formed a part of the political economy of state socialism which entailed state ownership of the means of production, the virtual elimination of the market and control over the entire economy by a one-party state. The 'right to work', emphasis on collective consumption, low wage differentials and egalitarian living standards were a part of the ideology of state socialism. Under state socialism, wages, prices and employment were not determined by market criteria. Thus employment was more a 'social' than an 'economic' concept and many more workers were on the payroll of enterprises than was justified by market criteria.[6] In the absence of the market forces of competition and profitability, productivity was low and quality of goods produced poor. Enterprises worked in order to fulfil production quota for a captive domestic market in which consumers had little choice. Foreign trade was conducted largely with other socialist bloc countries and was guided by political rather than economic criteria (Kramer, 1997: 81). No doubt Central-Eastern European countries, notably Hungary and Poland, did introduce elements of market in their economies and developed significant trading and economic relations with capitalist countries. But on the whole, it is true to say that the economies of state socialist countries were subject to very little competition, domestic or international. It was the subordination of the market and the insulation from the international economy – in terms of trade and finance – that enabled these countries to maintain full employment and to provide many basic necessities at a price far below not only what might represent a reasonable market price but below even the cost of production.

We need not rehearse the inherent weaknesses of state socialism as an economic, political and social organization which eventually led to its unravelling. By the end of the 1980s the communist regimes had virtually collapsed in Eastern Europe and by 1991 in the former USSR. Since then many of these countries have been in a process of transition towards some form of market-based economy and representative government. In the event transition has meant the integration of these countries into the global market economy. The exact timing, extent and process of integration has varied. Central-Eastern European countries, such as Poland and Hungary, and some Baltic countries have led the process, followed, to a varying degree, by Russia and other former state socialist countries. Integration has meant opening up the economies fully to market forces – domestic and global – with free trade and financial flows and convertible currencies (Gowan, 1995). The dramatic change from conditions of relative closure and insulation from the international economy to full exposure has meant the virtual elimination of SPM within a short space of time which has contributed to the rise of mass unemployment, economic insecurity, inequality and poverty (Standing, 1996; Ferge, 2001). Full employment is a thing of the past and consumer subsidies have been drastically reduced, if not eliminated (Kolodko, 1999; Ferge, 2001). It is now market forces – global and local – that largely determine employment levels.[7] With the acceptance of unemployment as a part of the new economy forms of unemployment benefits have been instituted. These did not exist under state socialism which claimed to have abolished unemployment. Social assistance was weakly developed and means-tested benefits were practically non-existent. They now form an important part of the system of social protection. Partial privatization of programmes such as pensions has been taking place in a number of countries (Standing, 1996; Ferge, 2001). The post-socialist countries differ a great deal in respect of economic, political and social conditions and it is the Central-Eastern European countries that have been more successful in transforming themselves into something like stable capitalist democracies. Their system of social protection now broadly resembles that of Western countries, at least in *form* or structural characteristics even if not in substantive content (Ferge, 2001: 135). In short, socialist forms of SPM are disappearing and a gradual 'westernization' of systems of social protection appears to be taking place.[8]

How much of the socialist forms of SPM might have survived the end of state socialism in the case of a gradual transition towards some form of social democracy – as hoped for by many – is largely a hypothetical question. Arguably a policy of maintaining high levels of employment and retaining consumer subsidies in a modified form might have worked in more favourable international circumstances. However, the collapse of state socialism coincided with economic globalization and the ascendancy of the Washington Consensus in the West (Ferge, 2001). Thus liberalization of trade and finance, deregulation of labour markets and the unleashing of market forces more generally were seen as providing the best conditions for growth for former socialist countries, as indeed for others. This translated into a policy of 'shock therapy', that is a rapid marketization and globalization of the economy. This policy has been followed, to a varying degree, by many post-socialist countries through a mixture of choice and necessity (Gowan, 1995; Standing, 1996). It has meant a radical dismantling of SPM. Here the influence of international financial institutions (IFIs) such as the International Monetary Fund (IMF) and World Bank (WB) has been important. Apart from providing general policy advice, agencies such as the IMF and WB have been directly involved in extending loans to many of these countries to help with the problems of transition (IMF, 2000). These loans have included conditionalities, for example that consumer subsidies be cut back drastically and market forces be allowed maximum possible scope in determining prices and levels of employment if not also wages. The marketization of the economy was to be complemented by a social safety net to include unemployment benefits and means-tested social assistance. Partial privatization of pensions was also strongly urged upon these countries by the IMF and WB (Standing, 1996; Ferge, 2001).

Thus the general context of economic globalization and the direct influence of IFIs have both worked in the same direction – towards a rapid dismantling of SPM. In Hungary, for example, the first Structural Adjustment Loan of 1990 required consumer and housing subsidies to be reduced substantially. In the event they fell from 7.0 per cent of GDP in 1989 to 1.5 per cent in 1993. In Poland subsidies fell from 8.2 per cent of GDP to 0.7 per cent over the same period (Ferge, 2001: 133). Apparently the removal of subsidies was considered 'absolutely necessary' by the IMF which was willing to back only those adjustment policies that would lead to the eventual liquidation of all subsidies (Kolodko, 1999: 162). The IFIs in fact favoured the rapid withdrawal of price subsidies without compensation (Ferge, 2001: 133). However, governments often found it difficult to implement such drastic measures which were highly unpopular and imposed a great deal of hardship on people. The extent to which countries compensated for the reduction of subsidies by way of wage increases, social assistance or other forms of protective measures varied a great deal (World Bank, 2000). Whereas old practices continue to a varying extent in Russia and other countries of the former USSR it is Central-Eastern Europe that has 'Westernized' the most, largely phasing out old SPM and instituting the *structures* and *forms* of Western welfare (Ferge, 2001: 132, 135).

Discussion

This chapter has looked at SPM in three different settings and considered its transformation over the last two decades. One element common to all three forms of SPM has been a policy of full employment albeit in each case the approach has been different. In state socialist societies it took a systemic form, entailing the virtual abolition of the market economy and the establishment of the 'right to work' for men *and women* as an integral part of socialism. Employment became more a social than an economic concept. In Australia it involved conventional methods of economic protectionism within a capitalist economy and control over immigration to ensure plentiful employment but essentially for the male breadwinner. The Japanese approach to full employment stands somewhere in between. It has shared with Australia the practice of economic protectionism in a capitalist economy and the idea of full employment essentially for male breadwinners. But the means of economic protection have been very different, involving non-tariff barriers and a dual economy. Japan also differs from Australia in that it has a far bigger and stronger economy with formidable export competitiveness and a strong currency. It has therefore been in a much stronger position to maintain its strategy of 'domestic defence' and its relative insulation from the global market economy. Moreover Japan's commitment to full employment has been far stronger than that of Australia. Its SPM has not therefore suffered a great deal of erosion thus far. What Japan has shared with state socialist societies is a *systemic* or *quasi-systemic* feature which involves economic, financial and industrial organization and makes Japanese capitalism quite distinct from its Western (both Anglo-Saxon and European) counterpart. These systemic features have made it possible for Japan to take an approach to employment which is, in part, 'social' rather than economic – in the sense of being market-rational – echoing state socialism. These systemic features have also allowed Japan to maintain full employment through periods of economic recessions and restructuring. Unlike state socialism, however, Japanese capitalism has been a story of economic triumph rather than failure. The Japanese form of welfare capitalism, which includes SPM, has on the whole served the nation well. It also appears to enjoy a great deal of support in the country. Not surprisingly, therefore, Japan is to a large extent holding on to its distinct form of capitalism and SPM in spite of serious economic difficulties and a long period of stagnation. However, in parallel with state socialism the *systemic* features of Japanese capitalism, including vested interests, are making reform and piecemeal adaptive changes difficult, thus perpetuating stagnation and immobility.

In any case Japan can no longer be called a full employment country. Whether this proves to be a temporary phase and the country returns to its pattern of full employment is an open question. But at the moment this looks very unlikely. Thus we have to say that full employment as a part of SPM has ended in all three systems and the countries concerned. In Japan, as elsewhere, the future seems to lie more in the direction of Western patterns, that is largely market-determined unemployment, developed systems of unemployment compensation as well as active labour market policies, and social assistance.

Extensive consumer subsidies were a feature of state socialist societies alone. It was the socialist economy that allowed prices to be determined by social and political rather than economic criteria. Neither Australian nor Japanese SPM involved consumer subsidies. It should be noted, however, that subsidies for food and other necessities of life are a form of social protection that has been a feature of many developing countries. Indeed in a limited form they also exist in many advanced capitalist countries, for example for housing and transport, and are by no means incompatible with a well-functioning market economy. No doubt the retrenchment, if not elimination, of subsidies in many former state socialist countries is in part due to the economic difficulties resulting from the sudden collapse of the system and the problems of transition to a market economy. However, transition to a market economy in the context of globalization as well as direct pressure from Western donors and IFIs such as the IMF and WB has been important in eroding subsidies. The IFIs have had considerable leverage in influencing the social policy of these countries by way of conditionalities for loans and other assistance. Indeed as Standing (1996: 230) observes, 'the revolution that has been taking place in Central and Eastern Europe is the first in history in which social policy has been shaped and influenced by international financial agencies'. It is worth noting, however, that for many years Structural Adjustment Loans made by these IFIs to Third World countries have included similar stipulations about the reduction, if not the elimination, of price subsidies. Restoration of market pricing, coupled with targeted assistance to the needy, has been the preferred policy. Consumer price subsidies as a method of social protection is very much out of favour with the Washington Consensus and the globalized market economy with their penchant for allowing market forces full play and limiting the nature and scope of state intervention in the economy.

Labour market 'flexibility', including wage flexibility, has emerged as a key requirement for competitiveness and growth in the global market economy. Australia's system of compulsory wage arbitration made for considerable rigidity in the wage structure by making annual wage awards which formed the basis of wage determination throughout industry and beyond. Wage flexibility, on the other hand, requires that wages be responsive to the market situation of firms and to labour productivity. This is not to say that centralized forms of wage agreements – tripartite or bipartite – are necessarily dysfunctional for a national economy in the context of globalization. Flexibilities can be built around a basic agreement on wages as a number of European countries, in varying degrees and forms, show (Hirst and Thompson, 1999, Ch. 6). Indeed the Labour government in Australia practised a form of centralized wage determination during its period of accord with the trade unions in the 1980s and early 1990s, which held down national wage costs while seeking to ensure fairness and protection for low wage earners. Australia posted good economic as well as job growth during this period. However, business and global investors were pressing for the decentralization of collective bargaining and the deregulation of wage structure. The Liberal government, which succeeded Labour in 1996, was more sympathetic to these objectives and took steps to decentralize bargaining and limit the scope of wage arbitration. Thus changes in the Australian wage arbitration system cannot be understood in terms of globalization alone. National, including, political responses to the phenomenon must also be taken into account. Indeed as the somewhat different outcomes in Australia and New Zealand in this regard show, policy responses of governments and other major actors are important in deciding the specific outcomes. What we have argued, however, is that the changed context of globalization, which called for labour market flexibility, provided the rationale for scaling down the wage-arbitration system.

Extensive welfare benefits provided by the enterprise have been a distinctive feature of Japanese SPM. However, occupational benefits are by no means unique to Japan. They exist in many other countries and function, in part, as an alternative to more comprehensive public provision. For example in the United States, health insurance benefits at the workplace act as a partial substitute for public provision of medical care for the working population. And globalization seems to be weakening the nature and scope of such benefits in the United States too. Over the last couple of decades employers have been cutting back on benefits in order to reduce labour costs. The 'non-regular' labour force has been growing which means that fewer workers are now covered by occupational benefits. Moreover intensified corporate re-structuring and downsizing has resulted in thousands of dismissed employees losing health insurance (Mishra, 1999: 26–8).

There is, however, an important distinction between the United States – and for that matter other Western countries – and Japan in respect of enterprise welfare. In Japan welfare benefits are generally associated with long-term secure employment with a company. They are an aspect of the system of 'lifetime employment'. Moreover work-related benefits are considered as an integral part of 'Japanese-style welfare' and an important element in the economic and social security of the population. The stability and continuity of employment, and benefits related to employment, are crucial for the Japanese welfare system as a whole. The situation in the United States is very different. Occupational welfare does not form a part of the state's overall design of social policy for the working population which is residual in nature. The uncertainties and instabilities associated with deregulation and competition pose a greater threat for the Japanese system of welfare since the 'developmental state' in Japan assumes far greater responsibility for the social security of the working-age population. However, given its association with lifetime employment the future of enterprise welfare in Japan as a part of SPM depends, to a large extent, on the future of lifetime employment itself.

Concluding remarks

The main concern of this chapter has been to draw attention to the transformation of certain major forms of SPM (social protection by other means) at the end of the twentieth century and to highlight the relevance of globalization to the process. It has argued that it was above all the relative insulation of national economies from the global market economy that enabled countries to fashion policies and institutions of social protection other than those typical of the post-World War II welfare state. At the close of the twentieth century it has proven increasingly difficult, if not economically untenable, for these countries to maintain their isolation from the global market economy. They have been under pressure, directly or indirectly, to open up their economies in terms of trade and financial flows. This openness and the integration into the global economy has meant scaling down or dismantling SPM. The process has been uneven across the countries examined in this chapter and Japan, in particular, still remains a relatively closed economy with rather limited erosion of SPM.

We have also pointed out that influences other than those associated with globalization are involved in the process of change. Moreover it is incorrect to see globalization as a force impinging on nations from 'outside'. It is a process which involves actors within the nation-state as well as without, including IFIs such as the IMF and WB. In any case it is clear that the imperatives of openness and closer integration with the global market economy have deprived nations of certain policy options available to them earlier. In this respect globalization does curtail the policy autonomy of nations.

This is not to say, however, that countries have no choice regarding the social provision that might replace SPM. How far globalization influences such a choice is a question that is outside the remit of this chapter. It appears, however, that a 'mainstreaming' of methods of social protection is taking place leading to the 'Westernization' of the form or structure of welfare systems. This is certainly evident in Central-Eastern Europe and, one might venture to predict, is also likely to occur in Japan where it will mean more *direct* state provision of such things as unemployment compensation, social assistance, medical care and pensions.

Australia has wound down a good part of its SPM but has chosen to strengthen and adapt existing forms of provision for income security, that is means-tested benefits, rather than develop social insurance programmes. Besides, Australia's mandated superannuation allowances provided by employers is a hybrid form of social protection which shows not only continuity with the past but also the possibility of innovative forms of social protection involving, for example, cooperation between the state and the enterprise. In short if globalization is leading to a measure of convergence it does not, by any means, imply the end of diversity and choice in national patterns of welfare.

Notes

1. This raises the question of the criteria for demarcating those arrangements which constitute 'social protection by other means' from those which do not. In our view there is no clear-cut divide between the two. Rather there is a continuum of relevance of policies and institutions to social protection. It is a question of focusing on those which appear to be more directly relevant.
2. Australia's unemployment rate averaged 7.5 per cent during 1980–89 (calculated from OECD, 1991, Table R 19, p. 193) and 8.3 per cent during 1990–2000 (calculated from OECD, 2002, Annex Table 14, p. 22). At 6.8 per cent in 2001 it was just above the OECD average of 6.4 per cent (ibid.).
3. On Japan's economic situation since the collapse of the bubble economy see, for example, Katz (1998), Japan (1996), Japan (1999), OECD (1997b), OECD(2000).
4. During 1995–2001 the unemployment rate was 4 per cent (calculated from OECD, 2002, Annex Table 14, p. 220). In 2001 it stood at 5 per cent compared with 4.8 per cent in the US. In that year 12 OECD countries had a lower rate of unemployment than Japan (ibid.). It should be noted, however, that employment protection legislation has not been weakened, and restrictions on temporary hiring also remain. In light of the protracted stagnation and recessions as well as the decline of profitability of firms, Japan's open unemployment rate is quite low.
5. Japan's annual rate of economic growth fell from 10.2 per cent during 1961–70 to 4.5 per cent in 1971–80 and to 4 per cent in 1981–90 (OECD, 1998, Table 1, p. 22). During 1991–2001 it was only 1.4 per cent, well below the OECD average of 2.35 per cent. The prospect of attaining the growth rates of the 1980s any time soon does not look too bright.
6. According to one estimate (Kramer, 1997: 87), a quarter of the employed workforce in Poland, Hungary and Czechoslovakia under the communist rule was redundant.
7. During 1993–2001 unemployment averaged 6 per cent in the Czech Republic, 8.9 per cent in Hungary and 13.8 per cent in Poland (calculated from OECD, 2002, Annex Table 14, p. 220). In 2001 the respective rates were 8.2 per cent, 5.7 per cent and 18.2 per cent (ibid.).
8. The situation in many other countries of Eastern Europe and the former USSR, including Russia, remains chaotic and in a state of flux. It may be a long time before stable patterns of employment and welfare emerge. In Russia, for example, many old practices, for example 'social' employment (at low wages or without wages) and consumer subsidies, continue in varying degrees in different regions. However, steps have also been taken to reduce housing and other subsidies and to privatize the economy. Private pension plans have been emerging. Despite the rise of open unemployment and increase in poverty, systems of unemployment compensation and social assistance remain weakly developed thus far (see for example Standing, 1996; Aslund, 1997; World Bank, 2000, Ch. 9).

References

Aslund, Anders (1997), 'Social problems and policy in postcommunist Russia' in Ethan B. Kapstein and Michael Mandelbaum (eds), *Sustaining the Transition*, New York: Council of Foreign Relations.

Beresford, Quentin (2000), *Governments, Markets and Globalization*, St. Leonards, New South Wales: Allen & Unwin.

Bray, Mark and David Neilson (1996), 'Industrial relations reform and the relative autonomy of the state' in Francis G. Castles et al. (eds), *The Great Experiment*, Auckland: Auckland University Press.

Castles, Francis G. (1988), *Australian Public Policy and Economic Vulnerability*, North Sydney, New South Wales: Allen & Unwin.

Castles, Francis G. (1989), 'Social protection by other means' in Francis G. Castles (ed.) *The Comparative History of Public Policy*, New York: Oxford University Press.

Castles, Francis G. (1996), 'Needs-based strategies of social protection in Australia and New Zealand', in Gøsta Esping-Andersen (ed.), *Welfare States in Transition*, London: Sage.

Castles, Francis G. et al. (1996), 'Introduction' in Francis G. Castles et al. (eds), *The Great Experiment*, Auckland: Auckland University Press.

Deacon, Bob et al. (1992), *The New Eastern Europe*, London: Sage.

Deacon, Bob et al. (1997), *Global Social Policy*, London: Sage.

Dore, Ronald (2000), 'Will global capitalism be Anglo-Saxon capitalism?,' *New Left Review*, 2nd Series (6).

Ferge, Zsuzsa (2001), 'Welfare and "ill-fare" systems in Central-Eastern Europe' in Robert Sykes et al. (eds), *Globalization and European Welfare States*, Houndmills, Basingstoke: Palgrave.

Goodman, Roger and Peng, Ito (1996), 'The East Asian welfare states' in Gøsta Esping-Andersen (ed.), *Welfare States in Transition*, London: Sage.

Gowan, Peter (1995), 'Neo-liberal theory and practice for Eastern Europe', *New Left Review* (213).

Greider, William (1998), *One World, Ready or Not*, New York: Touchstone.

Hirst, Paul and Thompson, Grahame (1999), *Globalization in Question*, 2nd edition, Cambridge: Polity Press.

Imai, Yutaka (1999), 'Reinvigorating business dynamism in Japan', *The OECD Observer* (215).

IMF (International Monetary Fund) (2000), *World Economic Outlook: Focus on Transition Economics*, Washington, DC: IMF.

Japan, Government of (1996), *Economic Survey of Japan 1996–1997*, Tokyo: Economic Planning Agency.

Japan, Government of (1999), *Economic Survey of Japan 1998–1999*, Tokyo: Economic Planning Agency.

Kapstein, Ethan B. and Mandelbaum, Michael (eds) (1997), *Sustaining the Transition*, New York: Council on Foreign Relations.

Katz, Richard (1998), *Japan: The System That Soured*, Armonk, New York: M.E. Sharpe.

Kolodko, Grzgorz W. (1999), 'Equity issues in policymaking in transition economies' in Vito Tanzi et al. (eds), *Economic Policy and Equity*, Washington DC: International Monetary Fund.

Kramer, Mark (1997), 'Social protection policies and safety nets in East-Central Europe' in Ethan B. Kapstein and Michael Mandelbaum (eds), *Sustaining the Transition*, New York: Council on Foreign Relations.

Michito, Nitta (1998), 'Employment relations after the collapse of the bubble economy' in Banno Junji (ed.), *The Political Economy of Japanese Society, Vol. 2*, Oxford: Oxford University Press.

Mishra, Ramesh (1999), *Globalization and the Welfare State*, Cheltenham, UK and Northampton, MA, USA: Edward Elgar.

OECD (Organisation for Economic Cooperation and Development) (1985), *Social Expenditure 1960–1990*, Paris.

OECD (1991), *Economic Outlook*, 49, Paris.

OECD (1994), *New Orientations for Social Policy*, Paris.

OECD (1997a), *Economic Surveys 1997–1998: Australia*, Paris.

OECD (1997b), *Economic Surveys 1996–1997: Japan*, Paris.

OECD (1998), *Economic Surveys 1997–1998: Japan*, Paris.

OECD (1999), *Economic Surveys 1998–1999: Japan*, Paris.

OECD (2000), *Economic Surveys 1999–2000: Japan*, Paris.

OECD (2001), *Economic Surveys 2000–2001: Australia*, Paris.

OECD (2002), *Economic Outlook*, 71, Paris.

Pempel, T.J. (1989), 'Japan's creative conservatism' in Francis G. Castles (ed.), *The Comparative History of Public Policy*, New York: Oxford University Press.

Peng, Ito (2000), 'A fresh look at the Japanese welfare state', *Social Policy and Administration*, **34**(1), 87–114.

Pierson, Paul (1998), 'Irresistible forces, immovable objects: post-industrial welfare states confront permanent austerity', *Journal of European Public Policy*, **5**(4), 539–60.

Rhodes, Martin (1996), 'Globalisation and West European welfare states: a critical review of recent debates', *Journal of European Social Policy*, **6**(4), 305–27.

Rose, Richard and Rei Shiratori (eds) (1986), *The Welfare State East and West*, Oxford: Oxford University Press.

Sako, Mari and Hiroki Sato (eds) (1997), *Japanese Labour and Management in Transition*, London: Routledge.

Schregle, Johannes (1993), 'Dismissal protection in Japan', *International Labour Review*, **132**(4), 507–20.

Standing, Guy (1996), 'Social protection in Central and Eastern Europe' in G. Esping-Andersen (ed.), *Welfare States in Transition*, London: Sage.

Sykes, Robert et al. (eds) (2001), *Globalization and European Welfare States*, Basingstoke: Palgrave.

Takayama, Noriyuki (2001), 'The Korean social security pension system: an evaluation with a special reference to Japanese experience', paper presented at the *International Symposium on Sharing Productive Welfare Experience*, Seoul.

Therborn, Goran (1986), *Why Some Peoples Are More Unemployed Than Others*, London: Verso.

Thurow, Lester (1996), *The Future of Capitalism*, New York: William Morrow & Co.

Wiseman, John (1998), *Global Nation? Australia and the Politics of Globalisation*, Cambridge: Cambridge University Press.

World Bank (2000), *Making Transition Work for Everyone: Poverty and Inequality in Europe and Central Asia*, Washington, DC.

PART II

CONCEPTS AND DEFINITIONS

5 Defining comparative social policy

Jochen Clasen

The above title implies that comparative social policy is something which can be defined. Why not provide a neat definition in the glossary, rather than devoting an entire chapter to it? The reason is that any attempt at defining the term within the space of a paragraph or two is bound to run into trouble. This is not only because of the difficulty in characterizing a composite term, but also due to the contested nature of both of its elements, that is the substantive focus of social policy and the comparative approach. Is social policy an academic discipline or a field of study? Which particular programmes should be regarded as social policy and which should not? What is comparative analysis and is it different from other qualitative or quantitative research strategies in social science? Is there any scientific research which is not, explicitly or implicitly, comparative in nature?

The first part of this chapter addresses some of these definitional problems. It does not make any claims to be exhaustive but aims to highlight instead the limitations of delving into an extensive definitional mapping exercise of what are ultimately ambiguous and amorphous substantive and methodological boundaries. A more useful approach to appreciating what comparative social policy is about is simply to review some of the major contributions to the field. As will be seen below, comparative social policy has not only grown enormously over the past three decades or so, but has also progressed to a considerable degree.

Boundaries

Unlike economic policy or environmental policy, social policy can be regarded as a 'diffuse, residual category' (Wilensky et al., 1987: 381). In academic discourse, the term tends to be confined to the publicly provided, or regulated, core programmes such as income maintenance (or social security), housing, health and social services. Yet beyond these generally accepted central areas, there is a range of other public policies which might legitimately be included in the definition given that they are aimed at securing or enhancing the well-being and the life chances of individuals. Tax allowances, tax credits or exemptions, for example, are in many ways simply alternatives to providing social security transfers in the sense that they raise the disposable income of certain social groups. Education, active labour market policies, occupational health and health and safety issues impinge on an individual's state of welfare by providing opportunities for, or by directly improving the level of social and material protection. Yet these areas have tended to be excluded from standard textbooks on social policy, while non-public forms of welfare production on the part of voluntary organizations, families or individuals are still given scant attention.

There is no consensus as to the academic nature of social policy analysis either. Is it a discipline in its own right, or is it a field of research which attracts scientists from different disciplines, such as sociology, political science, economics, history and legal studies, and is thus approached from within a number of theoretical perspectives, guided by different research questions, and subjected to a variety of methodological tools? The answer depends on the definition of 'academic discipline'. With reference to the situation in the UK, Alcock (1996) regards social policy as an academic discipline because of its institutional recognition, indicated by the existence of university departments and undergraduate and postgraduate degrees in social policy, academic journals devoted to publishing studies of social policy and the existence of a professional association. By contrast, Spicker (1995) points to scientific criteria and argues that social policy 'is not claiming to be a discipline' because it has no 'distinctive view of the world, or special methods or approaches. It is defined by what it studies, not by how it goes about it' (1995: 8). Similarly, Erskine (1998: 15) considers it to be a 'multidisciplinary field of study rather than a discipline' because it lacks a 'unique set of methods, concepts, theories or insights'.

Clearly, social policy is not a sub-discipline of another more recognized discipline within social sciences, such as sociology or economics. Instead, the study of social policy shares certain interests and core concepts with these and other established disciplines. Indeed, in most countries in which the analysis of social policy has achieved a certain level of recognition and academic output, there are no separate university departments which offer undergraduate degrees in social policy. More typical are academics who have been trained in one of a range of disciplines, are employed in departments of sociology, political science or economics, and have developed an interest and become specialists in the analysis of social policy. They might offer specialist university units or modules on questions on social policy, are engaged in a research framework which might revolve around a particular aspect of social policy, or work in social policy research centres. Their number seems to have grown in the past decades, and so has (for a variety of reasons, see Clasen, 1999) the number of them who have become involved in analysing problems of social policy not only in their own countries but in a comparative cross-national perspective.

Given its complexity, the multi-disciplinary analysis of social policy can pose methodological problems. Yet different perspectives of the same issue, say sociological and economic assessments of welfare-to-work policies, can be mutually challenging and, potentially at least, cross-fertilizing. The same applies to comparative social policy research. For example, between the 1960s and 1980s, the debate on determinants of welfare state change was dominated by scholars working within a macro-sociological frame of reference. Explanatory variables such as modernization, class and class alliances, risk groups and demographic change figured prominently. By contrast, large parts of the contemporary debate on change and stability in mature welfare states (for an overview see Sainsbury, 2001) concentrate on options and limitations for policy makers to engage in processes of welfare retrenchment. This shift in focus might be attributable to the direction of welfare state change which occurred in the 1970s and 1980s, that is from expansion to consolidation. In any case, it has drawn more political scientists into the debate and introduced other core independent (and partly also dependent) variables, such as institutions, veto points and party constellations (Green-Pedersen and Haverland, 2002). The dispute between adherents of the 'new' and 'old' politics of the welfare state (Pierson, 2001) is partly also a debate between political science and sociology which, potentially, benefits the analytical reflexivity and thus quality of contemporary scholarship of welfare state restructuring.

Central to social policy is the specific focus upon the trajectory and implementation of policies which influence the social circumstances, or well-being, of individuals. It is this focus on the content or substance of policy which makes social policy distinct from sociology and, in approach, similar to public policy. Indeed, comparative social policy might be regarded as a subset of comparative public policy which developed in the 1970s as a field of study within political science and comparative politics (Leichter, 1977, Landman, 2000). While many studies within comparative public policy cover policy fields which are only loosely connected to social policy, such as urban planning or environmental policy, the bulk of major texts and reviews in the area (Dierkes et al., 1987; Heidenheimer et al., 1990; Castles, 1998) include core social policy programmes such as social security, housing, health or education or cover 'the welfare state' as a whole. Depending on the particular aims and interests, that is discussing what and how policies are delivered in different countries, why policies have developed similarly or seem to diverge, or what outcomes they produce, analyses will draw on different disciplines. These include comparative politics and public administration, which can inform studies interested in modes of policy delivery. Researchers investigating the causes for policy emergence and for variation in policy development tend to draw on macro-sociology, political economy and history as frameworks which provide theoretical propositions or hypotheses. Others who are primarily interested in assessing the effects of social policies across countries might turn to evaluation and implementation studies, to economics and also to social philosophy. After all, social policy is based on redistribution and thus a contested terrain in which preferences, debates and strategies are, at least partly, informed by normative perceptions and values about 'the type of society in which we like to live' (Heidenheimer et al., 1990).

Comparative social policy as a methodology

As Higgins (1986: 24) pointed out, 'comparative analysis is a methodology, rather than a substantive area of study, and should be employed where it can illuminate specific questions and hypotheses'. In other words, rather than attempting to come to grips with the essence of comparative social policy via defining its ultimately ambiguous, contested and amorphous subject matter, its actual distinctive feature can be found in the adopted research strategy. However, while this claim might be relevant, it invites other types of boundary problems. All social science might be regarded as ultimately comparative in the sense that observed phenomena are compared against a certain point of reference, which is either explicitly stated or implicitly assumed, and which allows differences and similarities to be analysed, interpreted or evaluated. If that is the case, is there anything distinctive about cross-national research as opposed to other forms of research strategies? This question has been extensively deliberated in texts on methods within comparative and cross-national social research (Kohn, 1989; Øyen, 1990; Ragin, 1987, 1991; Hantrais and Mangen, 1996). Without rehearsing the arguments made there, a conservative response might point to particular and compounding methodological problems when it comes to generating comparable data, identifying appropriate functional equivalents and achieving an adequate sensitivity towards the different historical and cultural contexts in which national social policies are embedded. In other words, as with other forms of comparative research, the distinctive feature of comparative social policy is to be found within its methodological aspects rather than its substantive nature.

Comparative social policy analysts should be explicit about the ways in which they conceptualize and operationalize countries as units of analysis. Comparisons might be made between two or more cases or cover a large number of countries, for example all member states of the UN. Analyses of the latter type are generally based on statistical methods, and thus tend to conceptualize countries as representing a particular set of quantifiable variables, such as levels of GDP, social spending, income inequality or mortality rates. Hence, as Ragin (1991) points out, the analysis within these 'large-n' studies are constructed as co-variations between these generally few variables, while countries as entities beyond these variables tend to disappear. In contrast, 'small-n' studies tend to treat countries as multi-dimensional backgrounds for comparing the content of, or change within, particular social policy programmes or welfare states as a whole. In other words, the latter type of research conceptualizes national social policies as embedded within different, and not always quantifiable, social, political, economic, cultural and ideological contexts which impinge on the shape and impact of particular social policies.

Esping-Andersen (2000) has argued for 'intentional and purposeful empiricism' which combines 'cross-sectional' with what he calls 'diachronic' comparisons (that is comparing the present with particularly distinctive time periods in the past) as the most useful research strategy in macro-societal investigations which are grappling with the emergence of new societal equilibria. The approach of 'confronting extremes in the past with vanguards of the future' (ibid.: 75), he argues, is particularly appropriate at times like this which, as is widely agreed, is a time of rapid social change which makes it hard to analyse the shape of society to come.

Indeed, it has to be noted that comparative social policy research, or other types of comparative social research, are not necessarily cross-national in nature. The provision of social services in a particular region, for example, might be compared over time rather than across countries. Also, the nation-state might be an inappropriate unit for a cross-sectional analysis. For some purposes countries might be too small (for example analysing the role of Catholicism on social policy formation), for others too large (for example studying the impact of cultural factors on the provision of social care within India). Depending on the particular aim of a comparative study, subnational entities (local authorities, regions, federal states) or supranational organizations (such as the EU) might be the more appropriate unit of analysis. Indeed, much research which has been labelled cross-national or cross-country is in fact a comparison of particular (and not necessarily representative) regions or towns within different countries (for example Bradshaw et al., 1993). There are often good methodological reasons for such a strategy, and as long as these are made explicit there is no problem with such an approach.

In their review of the literature, Wilensky et al. (1987: 382) defined only those studies as comparative social policy which had systematically covered 'the same phenomena in two or more countries'. Such an approach excludes comparatively oriented case studies and systematic investigations of social policies in single countries. Yet, as Ragin (1987: 4) puts it with reference to major classical sociological texts by Alexis de Toqueville or Emile Durkheim, 'many area specialists are thoroughly comparative because they implicitly compare their chosen case to their own country or to an imaginary but theoretically decisive ideal-type case'. Indeed, particularly early texts on social policy arrangements in a country different from the author's own have helped to broaden the horizon and inspired new reflections on domestic forms of social policy delivery, principles and impacts. However, over the past two decades or so the ease of accessing information – that is in English – about national social policy arrangements of particular countries has considerably improved, due both to specialized texts (for example Jones, 1990; Olsson, 1990; Clasen and Freeman, 1994) and efforts made by supranational agencies such as the EU or the OECD. Thus, while some single-country based analyses of social policy will continue to be of scholarly value, their inclusion as a form of comparative social policy seems to stretch the notion too far.

At the same time, simply because a study might cover data and information from more than one country this does not make it comparative in any explicit sense. There are many books which describe, discuss or even analyse social policy instruments, outcomes and policy developments in a number of countries, with individual chapters devoted to particular countries. Yet, although providing a flavour of recent national policy developments, often these texts lack criteria which would make them comparative in any analytical sense. For example, series of disparate country chapters often come without a common analytical framework, systematic structure or even set of common topics covered. There is little attempt to introduce central concepts or a discussion of how these have been operationalized throughout the book and, subsequently, little synthesis of the material or effort to draw comparative conclusions. On a positive note, the number of books and articles which are published each year and which meet these criteria has grown considerably. In part this has been assisted by the growth of outlets for comparative social policy writing. Within a European context, for example, a number of new academic journals have been established within the past ten years, such as the Journal of European Social Policy, the European Journal of Social Security, European Societies, or the Journal of European Social Work. They have both helped to raise the profile of comparative social policy and are indications of the growing internationalization of the field.

The growth of comparative social policy

In the 1960s, and even the 1970s, the idea of producing a handbook on comparative social policy might have seemed strange. This was the time of early explicit comparative writing on, first, social administration (Rodgers et al., 1968) and later social policy (for example Kaim-Caudle, 1973; Rodgers et al., 1979), which devoted relatively little space to contemplating whether studying social policy across countries involved any specific conceptual, methodological or theoretical considerations. Instead, driven by the idea that there is considerable knowledge and insight to be gained from looking across countries, these pioneers of comparative social policy briefly designed an analytical framework and then proceeded with 'constructive descriptions' (Stebbing in Rodgers et al., 1979: xii) and intensive country-by-country discussions of social policy programmes, aims and delivery. This systematic empirical engagement with social policy principles and their manifestations in a range of countries was valuable at the time but, due to the dynamic nature of social policy, many aspects were quickly outdated. Also, there were very few comparative studies of a few countries which made any claims to theoretical advancement. Heclo's seminal book (1974) on differences and similarities in the development of unemployment insurance and pension programmes in the UK and Sweden was one of the rare exceptions in the 1970s. Similarly intensive comparative accounts of social policy developments within developed welfare states followed only in the 1980s, now originating within collaborative research frameworks, such as the one developed by Peter Flora and colleagues, which produced landmark publications (Flora and Heidenheimer, 1981; Flora 1986).

The core explanatory variables in these studies were changes in national 'welfare efforts', that is the relative share of the national product which is devoted to social policy programmes, as well as broad patterns of welfare state development indicated by the timing of social policy legislation and the growth in programme coverage. The interest in these dependent variables links them to earlier studies conducted in the 1960s and 1970s which, based on statistical observations, argued that the emergence and development of welfare states has to be regarded as a response to socio-economic pressures developed within industrialized societies and growing capacities to meet demands (Cutright, 1965; Wilensky, 1975). In the 1970s and 1980s, this line of argument was superseded by those which pointed to political factors, and in particular the strength of organized labour, as a crucial variable of welfare state expansion (see Shalev, 1983).

None of the authors within this strand of social policy analysis felt the need to stress the comparative nature of their work. Instead, extending the analysis of the causes for the emergence and growth of welfare states from single nation to a cross-national arena was treated as a method of testing and advancing the robustness of theoretical propositions. Indeed, for this distinctive tradition of macro-comparative welfare state research (for reviews see van Kersbergen, 1995; Pierson, 1998), comparative social policy is neither a discipline nor a substantive focus or field of study as such, but a methodological device or necessity. As Esping-Andersen (1993:124) put it, 'the macro-comparison of welfare states immediately implies cross-national research designs'.

The current version of this ongoing debate about explanations of welfare state development points to diversity and the co-existence of several paths towards post-industrialism in accordance with the notion of welfare state regimes (Esping-Andersen, 1990), and to the affinity and interdependence between national social policy arrangements and other policy sectors, such as industrial relations, labour market policy or financial markets, as well as other societal arrangements regarding the role of families and households (Ebbinghaus and Manow, 2001; Esping-Andersen, 1999). Pursuing similar questions but concentrating on few countries, other studies have restricted themselves to comparative investigations of whole welfare states belonging to a particular type (for example van Kersbergen, 1995; Kautto et al., 2001) or to the development of particular social policy programmes over time, such as unemployment protection (Clasen, 1994), pensions (Bonoli, 2000) or health policy (Freeman, 2000).

In parallel to this strand of literature with a focus on policy development, another strand of more evaluative cross-national social policy analysis developed in the early 1980s. These were studies which investigated the impact of social policy on particular groups (for example Bradshaw and Piachaud, 1980) or focused on particular problems, such as poverty (Walker, Lawson and Townsend, 1983). Later, the developments of new and improved datasets, such as the Luxembourg Income Study or the European Community Household Panel, provided more robust empirical bases for comparative research in this sub-set of comparative social policy, spurning new studies on, for example, the impact of national income transfer programmes (Mitchell, 1991) or the effect of unemployment on individuals and families (Gallie and Paugam, 2000).

As Higgins (1986) pointed out at the time, in the 1980s these two types of comparative social policy traditions were still quite distinct from each other. However, what they had in common was their focus on industrialized countries with sizeable welfare state programmes, largely ignoring the, by the 1980s, growing amount of social policy research in developing countries. While much of contemporary comparative social policy might still not have fully rectified this, the adoption of a 'narrow rather than inclusive approach' (Jones Finer, 1999) has become much more questionable due to the growth of research on social policy in countries outside the OECD, some of which has been explicitly comparative in nature (for example MacPherson and Midgley, 1987). This emergence of several branches of comparative social policy analysis and the proliferation of cross-national analyses within social policy writing in the 1980s seems to have reached a level sufficient to warrant early textbooks in the field (for example Jones, 1985), literature reviews (for example Wilensky et al. 1985), as well as sparking off the adoption of explicitly cross-national perspectives within particular theoretical approaches on social policy, such as feminist writing (Dominelli, 1990).

In 1990 Esping-Andersen's seminal book on welfare capitalism was published and impinged on much comparative social policy for the decade to come. Building on earlier categorizations of welfare states (Titmuss, 1974), Esping-Andersen's typology was original in the sense that it was derived from a systematic empirical investigation of similarities and differences across developed industrialized countries at the time. Praised as well as criticized on methodological, theoretical and conceptual grounds, it is still a major reference point within comparative social policy. Debates continue about the sense or nonsense of constructing clusters of welfare states, about the appropriateness of indicators for such typologies, about the number of categories, about the epistemological character of welfare regimes (ideal types or actual systems), about the assignment of particular countries to a particular welfare state type and about the dynamic or static nature of welfare regimes (see Abrahamson, 1999 and, unfortunately only for readers of German, the excellent collection by Lessenich and Ostner, 1998).

These debates have impacted on both the evaluative and the more theoretically inclined camps of comparative social policy. Within the debate on welfare state change, the notion of welfare regimes makes it much more difficult to maintain social spending as the 'proxy' variable for social policy (Esping-Andersen, 1993). Equally, treating differences in internal structures of national policy programmes merely as dependent variables has become increasingly questionable in the 1990s. At the same time, the periodical publications of more in-depth but largely descriptive or evaluative accounts of national social policy programmes and their effects has become rather limited without making at least some attempt to justify theoretically the selection of countries, and to connect individual country analyses to a wider conceptual framework which would allow inferences about, for example, causes for social policy convergence or divergence. This is not to say that the boundaries between the two strands have ceased to exist or that a sufficient degree of cross-fertilization has already been achieved. However, compared with the situation of 20 and even 10 years ago, some convergence has occurred and methodological and conceptual progress has been made along the lines which Alber et al. (1987:468) suggested in the 1980s. Databases for comparative social policy have been improved and much comparative work has accumulated which allows for a better mapping of similarities and differences in national paths of welfare state development. Equally, the focus on (path-dependent or otherwise) welfare reform of social policy arrangements has provided a new theoretical impetus. Finally, the call for enhancing aggregate data analyses with more historically and contextually sensitive analyses and case studies seems to have been received by an increasing number of writers in the field.

Conclusion

Attempting to define comparative social policy seems somewhat fruitless. Sharp distinctions are difficult to make. Academics will continue to discuss what exactly might constitute social policy vis-à-vis other policy fields and whether it is an academic discipline or a field of study. The overlap with other areas of comparative analysis (particularly comparative public policy) is substantial, while the methodological problems of analysing policies across countries or over time are not particular to social policy but inherent in any form of comparative social research. Yet the difficulty of exactly mapping the boundaries of comparative social policy does not mean that it has little chance of developing. On the contrary, the chapter has tried to indicate that there are several parallel discourses and analytical frames of reference, aims and approaches which can broadly be subsumed under the rubric of comparative social policy and which have emerged and evolved over time.

Since the early 1980s, these strands have developed and thrived, as indicated by the emergence of literature reviews, textbooks and the diversification into even more branches in the field. Initially without much contact between them, to some extent comparative social policy analysis continues to co-evolve along different paths. But there is now more mutual recognition, more cross-references are being made and some attempts towards the bridging of gaps (for example by combining theoretical macro-analyses of welfare state reform with case studies, or by enhancing research on the development of particular programmes with evaluative comparative analysis). The distance between the different strands seems to have diminished, which can only be a good sign for the future of comparative social policy.

References

Abrahamson, Peter (1999), 'The welfare modelling business', *Social Policy and Administration*, **33**(4), 394–415.
Alber, Jens, Gøsta Esping-Andersen and Lee Rainwater (1987), 'Studying the welfare state: issues and queries', in Meinolf Dierkes, H.A. Weiler and A. Berthoin Antal (eds), *Comparative Policy Research*, Aldershot: Gower.
Alcock, Pete (1996), *Social Policy in Britain. Themes and Issues*, London: Macmillan.
Bonoli, Giuliano (2000), *The Politics of Pension Reform. Institutions and Policy Change in Western Europe*, Oxford: Oxford University Press.
Bradshaw, Jonathan and David Piachaud (1980), *Child Support in the European Community*, London: Bedford Square Press.
Bradshaw, Jonathan et al. (1993), 'A comparative study of child support in fifteen countries', *Journal of European Social Policy*, **3**(4), 255–72.
Castles, Frank (1998), *Comparative Public Policy. Patterns of Post-war Transformation*, Cheltenham, UK and Lyme, USA: Edward Elgar.
Clasen, Jochen (1994), *Paying the Jobless. A Comparison of Unemployment Benefit Policies in Great Britain and Germany*, Aldershot: Avebury.
Clasen, Jochen (1999), 'Introduction', in Jochen Clasen (ed.), *Comparative Social Policy: Concepts, Theories and Methods*, Oxford: Blackwell.
Clasen, Jochen and Richard Freeman, (ed.) (1994), *Social Policy in Germany*, London: Harvester Wheatsheaf.
Cutright, P. (1965), 'Political structure, economic development, and national social security programs', *American Journal of Sociology*, vol. 70, 537–50.
Dominelli, L. (1990), *Women across Countries. Feminist Comparative Social Policy*, London: Harvester Wheatsheaf.
Ebbinghaus, Bernhard and Philip Manow (2001), *Comparing Welfare Capitalism*, London: Rôutledge.

Erskine, Angus (1998), 'The approaches and methods of social policy', in Pete Alcock, Angus Erskine and Margaret May (eds), *The Student's Companion to Social Policy*, Oxford: Blackwell.

Esping-Andersen, Gøsta (1990), *The Three Worlds of Welfare Capitalism*, Cambridge: Polity Press.

Esping-Andersen, Gøsta (1993), 'The comparative macro-sociology of welfare states', in L. Moreno (ed.), *Social Exchange and Welfare Development*, Madrid: Consejo superior de investigaciones cientificas.

Esping-Andersen, Gøsta (1999), *Social Foundations of Postindustrial Economies*, Oxford: Oxford University Press.

Esping-Andersen, Gøsta (2000), 'Two societies, one sociology, and no theory', *British Journal of Sociology*, **51**(1), 59–77.

Flora, Peter (ed.) (1986), *Growth to Limits*, Berlin: De Gruyter.

Flora, Peter and Arnold Heidenheimer (eds) (1981), *The Development of Welfare States in Europe and America*, New Brunswick: Transaction Books.

Freeman, Richard (2000) *The Politics of Health in Europe*, Manchester: Manchester University Press.

Gallie, Duncan and Serge Paugam (2000), *Welfare Regimes and the Experience of Unemployment in Europe*, Oxford: Oxford University Press.

Green-Pedersen, Christoffer and Markus Haverland (2002), 'The new scholarship of the welfare state', *Journal of European Social Policy*, **12**(1), 43–51.

Hantrais, Linda and Steen Mangen (eds) (1996), *Cross-national Research Methods in the Social Sciences*, London: Pinter.

Heclo, Hugh (1974), *Modern Social Politics in Britain and Sweden: From Relief to Income Maintenance*, New Haven: Yale University Press.

Heidenheimer, Arnold J., Hugh Heclo and Carolyn Teich Adams (1990), *Comparative Public Policy. The Politics of Social Choice in America, Europe, and Japan*, 3rd edn, New York: St. Martin's Press.

Higgins, Joan (1986), 'Comparative social policy', *The Quarterly Journal of Social Affairs*, **2**(3), 221–42.

Inkeles, Alex and Masamichi Sasaki (eds) (1996), *Comparing Nations and Cultures. Readings in a Cross-disciplinary Perspective*, London: Prentice Hall.

Jones Finer, Catherine (1999), 'Trends and developments in welfare states', in Jochen Clasen (ed.), *Comparative Social Policy: Concepts, Theories and Methods*, Oxford: Blackwell.

Jones, Catherine (1985), *Patterns of Social Policy. An Introduction to Comparative Analysis*, London: Tavistock Publications.

Jones, M.A. (1990), *The Australian Welfare State*, London: Allen & Unwin.

Kaim-Caudle, Peter R. (1973), *Comparative Social Policy and Social Security: A Ten-country Study*, London: Martin Robertson.

Kautto, Mikko, Johan Fritzell, Bjørn Hvinden, Jon Kvist and Hannu Uusitalo (eds) (2001), *Nordic Welfare States in the European Context*, London: Routledge.

Kohn, Melvin L. (ed.) (1989), *Cross-national Research in Sociology*, Newbury Park: Sage.

Landman, T. (2000), *Issues and Methods on Comparative Politics*, London: Routledge.

Leichter, H. (1977), 'Comparative Public Policy: Problems and Prospects', *The Policy Studies Journal*, vol. 5, 583–96.

Lessenich, Stephan and Illona Ostner (eds) (1998), *Welten des Wohlfahrtskapitalismus. Der Sozialstaat in Vergleichender Perspektive*, Frankfurt: Campus.

MacPherson, Stewart and James Midgley (1987), *Comparative Social Policy and the Third World*, Sussex: Wheatsheaf.

Mitchell, Deborah (1991), *Income Transfers in Ten Welfare States*, Aldershot: Avebury.

Olsson, Sven E. (1990), *Social Policy and the Welfare State in Sweden*, Stockholm: Arkiv.

Øyen, Else (ed.) (1990), *Comparative Methodology: Theory and Practice in International Social Research*, London: Sage.

Pierson, Chris (1998), *Beyond the Welfare State? The New Political Economy of Welfare*, 2nd edn, Oxford: Polity Press.

Pierson, Paul (ed.) (2001), *The New Politics of the Welfare State*, Oxford: Oxford University Press.

Ragin, Charles (1987), *The Comparative Method*, Berkeley: University of California Press.

Ragin, Charles (1991), *Issues and Alternatives in Comparative Social Research*, Leiden: Brill.

Rodgers, Barbara with Abraham Doron and M. Jones (1979), *The Study of Social Policy: A Comparative Approach*, London: George Allen & Unwin.

Rodgers, Barbara, J. Greve and J.S. Morgan (1968), *Comparative Social Administration*, London: George Allen & Unwin.

Rose, Richard (1995), 'Making progress and catching up: comparative analysis for social policy-making', *International Social Science Journal*, vol. 143, March, 113–25.

Sainsbury, Diane (2001), 'Welfare state challenges and responses: institutional and ideological resilience or restructuring?', *Acta Sociologica*, vol. 44, 257–69.

Shalev, Michael (1983), 'The Social Democratic model and beyond', *Comparative Social Research*, vol. 6, 315–51.

Spicker, Paul (1995), *Social Policy. Themes and Approaches*, London: Harvester Wheatsheaf.

Titmuss, Richard M. (1974), *Social Policy*, London: Allen & Unwin.

van Kersbergen, Kees (1995), *Social Capitalism: A Study of Christian Democracy and the Welfare State*, London: Routledge.

Walker, Robert, Roger Lawson and Peter Townsend (1983), *Responses to Poverty in Europe*, London: Heinemann.

Wilensky, Harald L. (1975), *The Welfare State and Equality: Structural and Ideological Roots of Public Expenditure*, Berkeley: University of California Press.

Wilensky, Harald L., Gregory M. Luebbert, Susan Reed Hahn and Adrienne M. Jamieson (1985), *Comparative Social Policy. Theories, Methods, Findings*, Berkeley: University of California.

Wilensky, Harald L., Gregory M. Luebbert, Susan Reed Hahn and Adrienne M. Jamieson (1987), 'Comparative social policy. Theories, methods, findings, (abridged version of Wilensky et al., 1985) in Meinolf Dierkes et al. (eds), *Comparative Policy Research*, London: Gower.

6 Conceptualizing state and society

Graham Crow

Introduction

The practice of comparison in social science requires us to make decisions about the unit of analysis to be adopted and the operational definition of that unit. The question, 'What do comparative social scientists compare?', may be met with the time-honoured answer, 'societies', but to do so is problematic for a number of reasons. Societies are notoriously difficult to define because their boundaries are not readily identifiable and are arguably becoming increasingly blurred. Furthermore, the economic, political, cultural and other dimensions of a society do not necessarily coincide, and as a result comparative social scientists have to 'cope with the patterned mess that is human society' (Mann, 1993: 4). This problem is arguably becoming increasingly acute in an age of heightened international mobility and global interconnectedness, but it is not a new one, as careful reading of the classical sociologists reveals (Crow, 1997: ch. 1). The distinction between 'societies' and 'states' can be traced back over several centuries. This is precisely because it has long been recognized that states emerged as institutions designed to administer, regulate and control populations whose members do not necessarily identify with the ideologies and agendas of those individuals and groups that occupy formal positions of power. States thus offer an alternative conceptualization of the social collectivities that social scientists seek to investigate comparatively, and their seemingly more concrete expression appears to give an analytical edge to approaches that focus on 'states' (or variants such as 'nation-states' or 'welfare states') rather than on the more amorphous and elusive 'societies'.

In turn, it can be noted that the comparison of 'states' is by no means problem-free. The difficulties associated with the comparison of states relate particularly to the arguments advanced by writers as diverse as Giddens (2001), Urry (2000) and Wallerstein (1999) that state power is being modified and possibly even superseded by increasingly successful challenges from other entities. It is readily apparent that individuals do not automatically give priority to the identity and loyalties derived from their membership of states. People's status as citizens (or in some constitutions as subjects) exists alongside a range of other statuses that reflect their membership of and participation in the host of non-state organizations and associations to which the label 'civil society' has been applied (Deakin, 2001; Keane, 1998; Kumar, 2001).

The institutions of the state and of civil society both have a bearing on the twin problems of scarcity and social solidarity that Turner (1999: ch. 15) has argued are central to the understanding of citizenship. Market forces offer one mechanism by which the allocation of scarce resources among members of a society may be determined, and they do go a long way towards providing an explanation of 'Who gets what?', in Westergaard's (1995) pithy phrase. There is only limited scope for market-based distributions to achieve legitimacy, however, and it is principally for this reason that one has to look elsewhere for the bases of social solidarity (Crow, 2002). Welfare states offer one such basis, and it is possible to regard them as a mechanism that has been 'used to integrate the masses into industrial societies' (Mény, 2001: 267). Experience indicates that they do not have the capacity to provide a comprehensive solution to the problem of generating a sense of common purpose among citizens, and it is against this background that the growing interest in social organizations that operate beyond the state needs to be placed. In many parts of the world this sphere of activity is understood, and actively promoted, as the realm of 'community' (Craig and Mayo, 1995; Roberts, 1995; Scott, 1994), but this is just as problematic a term on which to found comparative analysis as are 'society', 'state' and 'civil society'.

The existence of competing definitions of key concepts such as 'society' and 'community' reflects the essentially contested character of these terms. Rival understandings of the key concepts used in comparative social science are rooted in the different values held by researchers, as a result of which there is unlikely ever to be a consensus about what these terms really mean. This problem is compounded by the more prosaic but no less important issue of how these concepts are operationalized in empirical research. If it is to be at all systematic, comparison must involve the generation and analysis of evidence relating to similarities and differences in patterns of social relationships, but the methodologies by which this task is undertaken are fraught with difficulties (Ragin, 1987). The comparison of data collected about states and societies is hampered by the fact that there is relatively little uniformity in the way in which such data are generated. This is true of quantitative as well as qualitative data, as is noted by researchers in areas as diverse as cross-national class analysis (Marshall, 1997), poverty (Townsend, 1993), time use (Gershuny, 2000) and the study of social policy (Kennett, 2001). In none of these cases has the need for caution in the use of data derived from different sources and using different methodologies been an insuperable obstacle to valuable research being undertaken, but it has meant that certain questions can be answered with more confidence than others. It has also meant that efforts have been made to generate the data that will allow new questions to be answered. This point is nicely illustrated by the debate about welfare state regimes pioneered by Esping-Andersen (1990), among whose participants are feminists who argue that the contrasting positions of women in different regimes merit considerably greater attention (Sainsbury, 1999). The agenda of comparative research is continually enhanced by such debates over what the proper object of study ought to be, debates that are in turn influenced by changing perceptions of the world in which we live and of the long-term social trends that are unfolding.

The comparison of states and of societies

The history of the term 'society' is a long and complicated one, and so it should be no surprise that it does not provide a ready-made concept for social scientific analysis. As Williams has noted, the term 'society' is frequently used to denote 'the body of institutions and relationships within which a relatively large group of people live'. Alongside this definition there exists the rival meaning of 'society' as 'our most abstract term for the condition in which such institutions and relationships are formed'. Whether it is used as a generalization or as an abstraction, the term 'society' retains something of the sense of 'companionship or fellowship' that Williams identifies as its 'primary meaning'. A society is thus 'that to which we all belong' and 'a system of common life' (1983: 291–4), although Williams goes on to point out that there has been a long-term decline in the extent to which this is attributed to the intentions of the individuals who make up 'society'. By the nineteenth century a number of sociological theorists were able to counterpose 'the individual' and 'society', with the latter having analytical priority over the former. This was done most famously in Durkheim's analysis of how individuals are involuntarily constrained by society, which he insisted it was important to treat as more than 'the mere sum of individuals' (1982: 129). The idea of society as something existing over and above its individual members is by no means restricted to the Durkheimian tradition, however, and it became a key foundation of a variety of structuralist perspectives that have had an enduring legacy.

The notion that comparative social science involves the comparison of social structures led directly to evolutionary schema in which simpler forms of social organization give way progressively to more complex ones. In the modernization theory that was developed in the mid-twentieth century the idea of social evolution was captured in the notion that it was possible to identify a shift taking place from traditional societies to modern societies. The former were characterized by subsistence, while in the latter the stage of high mass consumption had been reached and even surpassed. This basic focus on *societies* undergoing such a transition remains influential even though modernization theory has justifiably been extensively critiqued (Crow, 1997). Inglehart's (1997) account of 'postmodernization' may have jettisoned certain elements of modernization theory (notably its determinism and ethnocentrism), but it is still a comparison of societies. Moreover, although he acknowledges the shortcomings of conceptions of society as economically, politically or culturally determined entities, Inglehart holds on to the claim that societies can be compared, and that the essence of this comparison can be captured in distinct sets of values. He does this by arguing that the various constituent parts of societies together form a coherent whole; his thesis is that 'the relationships between economics and culture and politics are mutually supportive' (1997: 10). Others who have examined the proposition that the boundaries of the various elements of a social system coincide have questioned this claim. Mann, for example, prefers to conceptualize societies as 'multiple, overlapping and intersecting networks of interaction' (2000: 146), and the implication of this is that an individual may have considerable difficulty in identifying the 'society' to which they belong.

One category of people for whom it is particularly difficult to identify the society to which they belong is that of migrant workers whose employment involves them in living and working in another country. Globalization has prompted the enormous expansion and diversification of migrant labour (Papastergiadis, 2000). Significant numbers of these modern migrants are care workers and domestic labourers whose work commitments and loyalties to families in their home countries mean that they feel themselves to be both 'here and there' (Hochschild, 2001). Hochschild's examples of Filipino and Latin American women living and working in the United States have parallels in many other parts of the world, and the question of belonging to a particular society is further complicated by the frequent denial of citizenship rights to migrant workers (Anderson, 2000). Against the background of the global movement of people on a grand scale it can be argued that the concept of 'society' has become redundant because this mobility has revealed the inappropriateness of the assumption that populations have discrete boundaries. The regularity with which people, resources and ideas now criss-cross the globe has led to the 'fragmentation' of societies, or at least to the recognition that societies and nation-states cannot sensibly be treated as conterminous (Albrow, 1996). Albrow goes onto argue that 'Societies extend over time and space and it's often difficult to say where they begin and end' (1999: 3–4). The implication of this is that the concept of 'society' is of limited value for comparative research, at least as it is conventionally understood.

The imprecision surrounding the concept of society helps to explain why many researchers have preferred to focus their attention on the state, and in particular the nation-state. The idea of the state is less general than that of society because, as Williams notes, 'the *state* is the apparatus of power' (1983: 293, emphasis in original). In other words, the state has a definite institutional expression, and it is because of this that states can be studied more readily. States not only have definite geographical boundaries marking out the extent of their jurisdiction, they also have constitutions which grant different rights and statuses to people according to precisely how their citizenship is enshrined. There has been a long-term tendency for the citizenship rights bestowed by states on their citizens to be extended, as Marshall (1963: ch. IV) famously showed. Citizenship's extension from civil rights, through political rights, to social rights may be understood as an evolutionary process, in the British case dating back to the eighteenth century in Marshall's view. On the basis of such evolutionary thinking some commentators considered it possible to trace the emergence of the welfare state as a distinct form of the state. Marshall expressed doubt about this idea on the grounds that to speak of a standard welfare state involved a dangerous generalization, one which overlooked the fact that 'social systems are deeply impregnated with the unique influences of the time and place in which they came into existence'. His preference was 'to study the "British Welfare State" in the post-war period, and to compare it with the welfare systems of other countries' (1963: 91–2), and this agenda has been explored further by other writers seeking to avoid imputing more uniformity to welfare states than is warranted.

By far the most influential recent contribution to this debate has been that of Esping-Andersen. Acknowledging that welfare states have emerged in many countries to replace previous state forms in which governmental concerns with social welfare were much more limited, his central theme is that 'welfare states are not all of one type' (1990: 3). This is more than a matter of some welfare states being engaged in higher levels of spending than others, although it is undoubtedly the case that this happens. It is because Esping-Andersen wants to compare welfare states in terms of their structural characteristics that he puts forward the idea that three distinctive welfare state *regimes* can be identified in contemporary capitalism. It is in his view crucial to recognize that 'state activities are interlocked with the market's and the family's role in social provision' (1990: 21), and that all of these factors play a part in determining the extent to which citizens' welfare is an expression of their social rights rather than a reflection of their economic power. Welfare state regimes can thus be compared according to the degree to which citizens' welfare has been un-coupled from their market position, a process that Esping-Andersen refers to as 'de-commodification'. Central to a welfare state regime in which de-commodification has been established is freedom from labour market dependence, expressed in terms of the ability of citizens to 'freely, and without potential loss of job, income, or general welfare, opt out of work when they themselves consider it necessary' (1990: 23). On the basis of extensive analysis of statistical data relating to the configurations of state, market and family relationships in 18 advanced capitalist countries, Esping-Andersen goes on to argue that three distinct clusters can be discerned: liberal, conservative and social-democratic welfare state regimes. The United

States, Germany and Sweden are then taken to be more or less 'representa-tive' (1990: 143), respectively, of the three types identified, and as such are subjected to detailed cross-national comparison. Esping-Andersen's (1996, 2001) subsequent work has continued to direct attention towards the diversity of *national* welfare state regimes, as has much of the debate generated by his ideas (Mabbett and Bolderson 1999). The difficulties and controversies that have emerged in doing so make it clear that the conceptualization of what is being compared needs to be kept under regular review.

Beyond the comparison of states and societies

Contemporary criticisms of using the state or society as the unit of compari-son have two broad strands to them. One strand emphasizes the increasingly globalized character of present-day life and argues on this basis that analysis at the national level is becoming redundant because so much traffic now crosses the frontiers of nation-states, which have only limited power to con-trol it. Against the backdrop of this globalization, Urry gives serious consideration to the idea that 'there is no such thing as society', since global processes are constantly revealing the interconnectedness of human populations and thereby undermining the credibility of the belief that each nation-state constitutes a distinct 'social body' (2000: 5, 23). This ties in with the theme in Urry's earlier work in which he and Lash traced the decline of corporatism, the system of extensive intervention and planning by the state in twentieth-century capitalist societies which was founded on the rationale that govern-ments could and should bring the various parts of the social body together.

Alongside the point about the increasingly internationalized nature of the contemporary world lies the other strand of criticism of the focus of com-parative social scientists on phenomena at the national level which emphasizes the processes of fragmentation to which individual societies are subject. Lash and Urry argue that 'Societies are being transformed from above, from below and from within', with one of the crucial results being that 'collectivity... melts into air' (1987: 313). Esping-Andersen has noted how the impetus behind the establishment of welfare states in many countries lay in the desire 'to foster national social integration' (1996: 2), but the perceived failure to achieve this in practice has led several commentators to detect the progres-sive fragmentation of societies as their constituent parts become competing communities. The polarization of citizens into winners and losers from social and economic change poses a threat to social cohesion to which one response may be a more extensive role for the state in managing market, family and policy interconnections (Esping-Andersen, 2001). Because states have achieved only limited success in moderating the process of social polarization, an alternative response has been the development of interest in the sphere of civil society or community with which people may more readily identify.

The criticism that focusing on national level phenomena leads to the neglect of the international dimension carries considerable weight. Sklair demonstrates this point by showing that of the 50 biggest economic entities in the world in 2000, only 15 are countries, the other 35 being transnational corporations. Sklair's more general argument is that 'The balance of power between state and non-state actors and agencies is changing'; as he notes, 'Research on small communities, global cities, border regions, groups of states, and virtual and mobile communities of various types provides strong evidence that existing territorial borders are becoming less important' (2002: 37, 8). Another way of putting this is to say that nation-states are less and less able to exercise sovereignty over their territories and populations, although Wallerstein's statement of this position attributes this change not to the power of transnational corporations but to 'the declining legitimacy accorded to the states by their populations' (1999: 75). Both positions are compatible with Urry's argument that what is being witnessed is a fundamental shift in the nature of the state, away from an institution concerned with imposing 'pattern, regularity and ordering' to one with the far more limited brief of general regulation without taking any interest in or responsibility for the detail of day-to-day life, a contrast that he captures in the distinction (borrowed from Bauman) between 'gardening' and 'gamekeeping' states (2000: 188–9). It follows that there is much that is missed, both above and below the level of the state, by taking an exclusively state-centred approach. Sklair (2002: 204) provides a telling illustration of this perspective by noting that it is not unusual for the advertising budgets of transnational corporations to exceed state expenditure on education in those societies in which they operate. His description of states as 'nominally sovereign' (2002: 5) conveys his sense that they function with very definite limits to their power.

If state-centred analyses are open to criticism for neglecting the global context within which governments act, they are also questionable for the assumptions that they embody about the capacity of states to control more local contexts. Scott's survey of large-scale schemes to bring about improvements in people's welfare that have failed includes analysis of Soviet collectivization, rural development in Tanzania, and the construction of new cities such as Brasília. On the basis of this survey he argues that the initiatives of modernist states were frequently flawed by the desire for standardization that paid no respect to local customs and traditions, but was instead driven by 'planning for abstract citizens' (1998: 345). What Scott calls 'seeing like a state' at best overlooked the various elements of civil society and at worst treated them as obstacles to be overcome and eradicated. The gulf between state officials and the people being administered has been greatest in authoritarian societies such as Stalinist state socialist ones in which citizens have little opportunity to organize autonomously (Crow, 1997:

ch. 5), but it is a potentially all-pervasive problem. Marshall was mindful of the danger that the state might be too distant from the lives of ordinary citizens to engage meaningfully with them when he noted that welfare states were not in a particularly strong position to encourage dutiful citizenship. This is because the national community that is appealed to 'is so large that the obligation appears remote and unreal' (1963: 123). The same concern lay behind Durkheim's promotion of intermediate bodies (such as occupational associations) that had the capacity to connect the individual to the wider collectivity, thereby reinforcing the sense of common purpose that he regarded as a crucial element of social solidarity (Crow, 2002).

In the context of this debate it is instructive to remember that Esping-Andersen's approach to comparing welfare state regimes was developed in order to avoid the error of being 'too narrowly preoccupied with just the welfare state'. Esping-Andersen is at pains to emphasize that 'Society's total welfare package combines inputs from the welfare state proper, markets (and especially labor markets), and families' (2001: 136). A surprising omission from this list is the sphere of voluntary organizations, civil society or community, the contribution of which long pre-dates the age of welfare states (de Swaan, 1988) and which the coming of welfare states by no means supplanted. Marshall's classic essay on citizenship and social class contains the observation that 'The original source of social rights was membership of local communities and functional associations' (1963: 81), and although the capacity of communities and associations to contribute to the welfare of their members became seriously circumscribed by the development of the market and of the state, it did not disappear completely. Esping-Andersen is thus overstating the case to suggest that the growth of markets brought with it a situation in which 'the welfare of individuals comes to depend entirely on the cash nexus' (1990: 21), and it is equally one-sided to go on to focus attention on the de-commodifying role of the state if doing so thereby neglects other responses to the spread of market relations. Much of the critique of Esping-Andersen's ideas that has been advanced by feminist writers has been concerned with the male bias implicit in his concept of the 'average worker' (1990: 50). The insistence that women are much more likely than men to be employed part-time or to be engaged in unpaid work in the home (Sainsbury, 1999) can be extended to include the point that voluntary work and community activism are also highly gendered (Deakin, 2001; Lister, 1997). The implication of doing so is to highlight still further the need to rethink Esping-Andersen's focus on state–market–family interconnections.

The reassertion of the continuing significance of the community dimension of welfare is an important corrective to the expectation, once widely-held, that it was in the process of being superseded by the expansion of state welfare. In many countries, particularly but not exclusively those of Western

Europe, the period 1960–1980 was one in which the 'growth of social entitlements was explosive' (Therborn, 1995: 92). This trajectory of rapid welfare state expansion proved unsustainable, and a good deal of discussion now revolves around whether the trajectory has not only slowed but gone into reverse. Taylor has argued that in the UK the state has been 'withdrawing from welfare and seeking ways of transferring responsibility for both delivery and financing of welfare to the market, family, community and individuals' (1995: 99). Whether these important shifts constitute the rolling back of the frontiers of the state that was an important component of the New Right's agenda depends on the definition of the state that is employed. Pierson's view is that 'The "traditional" welfare state in which mass services were delivered to the public by state employees in a largely non-contractual mode of public administration has been drastically reduced', but this reduction has been achieved only 'by creating a massive "quasi-state" or parallel state in its place' composed of 'quasi-non-governmental organizations' (1996: 103). A similar analytical problem faces researchers exploring the dramatic changes that are involved in the emergence of post-socialist societies, since what is under way there is a far more complex transition than a simple transfer of activity from state to civil society (Hann et al., 2002).

Re-conceptualizing state and society
There are several reasons why the concepts of state and society have been subjected to critical scrutiny in recent years. The concept of society is frustratingly vague in terms of both the relationship between its constituent elements and the boundaries marking its extent. Economic, political and cultural relationships do not in practice operate as a coherent whole with easily specified boundaries, and it has been claimed that the fictional nature of the idea of society has become ever-more apparent as the impact of globalization has increased. The concept of the state offers to go some way towards meeting the requirement for a more definite object of study, but state power is difficult to disentangle from other powerful influences on social and economic relationships, and a focus on the formal structures of state authority and their legislative and administrative activity is arguably too narrow to provide an explanation of how and why the welfare of populations varies. State-centred approaches have thus been challenged by attempts to capture the way in which states interact in a variety of patterns with the institutions of the market, family, community and civil society, in an attempt to counter the tendency to produce over-simplified generalizations.

The practice of comparative social science will continue to develop as a result of such debates. Already much has changed over the last half century. The crude contrast of capitalist, state socialist and underdeveloped societies that was used to make sense of the patterns of the 1950s was destined to break down as awareness grew of the increasing diversity present within each of these 'three worlds' (Crow, 1997). Esping-Andersen's identification of three distinct patterns of welfare capitalism illustrates this point nicely, as does the development of further and finer distinctions in response to his ideas, such as the notion that a distinct 'Southern' welfare state regime can be identified in countries like Italy, Spain, Portugal and Greece (Guillén and Álvarez, 2001). The breakdown of the 'three worlds' framework has also opened up the possibility of challenging the evolutionary assumption that the more developed societies showed the less developed ones an image of their future. Regarding developments in the field of community action, for example, it is not unusual for initiatives taking place in the poorer countries of the South to provide valuable lessons to observers in the richer Northern countries (Craig and Mayo, 1995; Porter, 2001). Educational policies as they relate to disability provide another example (Barton and Armstrong, 2001). The same rationale underlies the comparison of the institutions of civil society undertaken by Berger and his colleagues in which the countries studied include Chile, South Africa, Turkey, Indonesia, India and Taiwan as well as the USA, France, Germany and Japan from the advanced capitalist world and Hungary from the former state socialist bloc (Berger, 1998). The inclusion of Russia, South Africa and Hong Kong alongside Japan and Western European, North American and Australasian cases in Alcock and Craig's (2001) survey of international social policy is further evidence of the broadening of the research agenda in terms of both countries and topics being studied.

In responding to the opportunities and challenges that are emerging in their field, comparative social scientists need to be mindful of why comparison is undertaken in the first place. Baldwin's strictures against 'useless typologizing' are founded on his view that 'The growing sophistication of welfare state typologizing has left us in a position where the number of categories applied to, and the number of nations in, Europe are approximating to each other' (1996: 43, 40). In other words, the purpose of comparison is undermined if the main conclusion reached is that every case is unique. The identification of types of welfare state or of society is pursued in order to highlight broad patterns of similarity or difference, with a view to determining the crucial influences on their operation and trajectories. As Mills (1970: ch. 1) famously argued, it is important to avoid exchanging the shortcomings of ungrounded 'grand theory' for the equally unsatisfactory approach of descriptive 'abstracted empiricism'. Comparison always has a theoretical purpose, and requires the employment of appropriate methods of enquiry.

Theoretical innovations frequently run ahead of the methodological developments that are required to allow them to be tested against empirical evidence, as the current interest in the concept of 'civil society' may be taken to show. There is as yet no agreement on the most appropriate definition of civil society to use, as Hann and his colleagues note in their criticism of researchers who have 'tried to operationalize it by counting the number of "non-governmental organizations" and treating this as an index of the health of the society' (Hann et al., 2002: 9). Sklair makes essentially the same point about the global system, the operation of which is in his view obscured by 'dubious generalization about a host of discrete variables from societies' (2002: 3). The broadening out of comparative research to include concepts such as 'civil society' and 'the global system' promises to provide a more diverse set of tools with which to make sense of the world and to help overcome dependence on vague formulations about 'society' or unduly restrictive definitions of 'the state'. The response of comparativists to these developments is unlikely to be the abandonment of these two long-established terms, however, since there does not have to be an exclusive choice. A more probable response is that a good deal of comparative research will continue to be framed in terms of 'states' and 'societies', albeit in modified forms like Esping-Andersen's 'welfare state regimes' into which concept non-state elements were quite effectively incorporated. This outcome can be anticipated on several grounds. One is that the framework within which data are collected by governments and international agencies will continue to focus on nation-states as a prime unit of analysis, and the form in which data are available remains an important consideration. Secondly, a number of theorists consider the argument that globalization has undermined nation-states to have exaggerated the extent of the change, and consequently continue to focus at least part of their attention on them (Mann, 2000). And thirdly, the suggested alternatives to the concepts of 'state' and 'society' have problems of their own that prevent them from being ready substitutes, at least until further work is done on their operationalization. For all of these reasons, 'state' and 'society' are not about to disappear from the comparativists' lexicon.

References

Albrow, Martin (1996), *The Global Age: State and Society Beyond Modernity*, Cambridge: Polity.

Albrow, Martin (1999), *Sociology: The Basics*, London: Routledge.

Alcock, Pete and Gary Craig (eds) (2001), *International Social Policy: Welfare Regimes in the Developed World*, Basingstoke: Palgrave.

Anderson, Bridget (2000), *Doing the Dirty Work: The Global Politics of Domestic Labour*, London: Zed Books.

Baldwin, Peter (1996), 'Can we define a European Welfare State model?' in Bent Greve (ed.), *Comparative Welfare Systems: The Scandinavian Model in a Period of Change*, Basingstoke: Macmillan, pp. 29–44.

Barton, Len and Felicity Armstrong (2001), 'Disability, education and inclusion: cross-cultural issues and dilemmas', in Gary Albrecht, Katherine Seelman and Michael Bury (eds), *Handbook of Disability Studies*, London: Sage, pp. 693–710.

Berger, Peter (ed.) (1998), *The Limits of Social Cohesion: Conflict and Mediation in Pluralist Societies*, Boulder, Colorado: Westview Press.

Craig, Gary and Marjorie Mayo (eds) (1995), *Community Empowerment: A Reader in Partici-pation and Development*, London: Zed Books.

Crow, Graham (1997), *Comparative Sociology and Social Theory: Beyond the Three Worlds*, Basingstoke: Macmillan.

Crow, Graham (2002), *Social Solidarities: Theories, Identities and Social Change*, Bucking-ham: Open University Press.

Deakin, Nicholas (2001), *In Search of Civil Society*, Basingstoke: Palgrave.

De Swaan, Abram (1988), *In Care of the State: Health Care, Education and Welfare in Europe and the USA in the Modern Era*, Cambridge: Polity Press.

Durkheim, Emile (1982), *The Rules of Sociological Method*, London: Macmillan.

Esping-Andersen, Gøsta (1990), *The Three Worlds of Welfare Capitalism*, Cambridge: Polity Press.

Esping-Andersen, Gøsta (ed.) (1996), *Welfare States in Transition: National Adaptations in Global Economies*, London: Sage.

Esping-Andersen, Gøsta (2001), 'A welfare state for the 21st century', in Anthony Giddens (ed.), *The Global Third Way Debate*, Cambridge: Polity, pp. 134–56.

Gershuny, Jonathan (2000), *Changing Times: Work and Leisure in Postindustrial Society*, Ox-ford: Oxford University Press.

Giddens, Anthony (2001), 'Introduction', in Anthony Giddens (ed.), *The Global Third Way Debate*, Cambridge: Polity Press, pp. 1–21.

Guillén, Ana and Santiago Álvarez (2001), 'Globalization and the Southern welfare states', in Robert Sykes, Bruno Palier and Pauline Prior (eds), *Globalization and European Welfare States: Challenges and Change*, Basingstoke: Palgrave, pp. 103–26.

Hann, Chris, Caroline Humphrey and Katherine Verdery (2002), 'Introduction', in C.M. Hann (ed.), *Postsocialism: Ideals, Ideologies and Practices in Eurasia*, London: Routledge, pp. 1–28.

Hochschild, Arlie Russell (2001), 'Global care chains and emotional surplus value', in Will Hutton and Anthony Giddens (eds), *On The Edge: Living with Global Capitalism*, London: Vintage, pp. 130–46.

Inglehart, Ronald (1997), *Modernization and Postmodernization: Cultural, Economic and Po-litical Change in 43 Societies*, Princeton, NJ: Princeton University Press.

Keane, John (1998), *Civil Society: Old Images, New Visions*, Cambridge: Polity Press.

Kennett, Patricia (2001), *Comparative Social Policy*, Buckingham: Open University Press.

Kumar, Krishan (2001), *1989: Revolutionary Ideas and Ideals*, Minneapolis: University of Minnesota Press.

Lash, Scott and John Urry (1987), *The End of Organized Capitalism*, Cambridge: Polity Press.

Lister, Ruth (1997), *Citizenship: Feminist Perspectives*, Basingstoke: Macmillan.

Mabbett, Deborah and Helen Bolderson (1999), 'Theories and methods in comparative social policy', in Jochen Clasen (ed.), *Comparative Social Policy: Concepts, Theories and Methods*, Oxford: Blackwell, pp. 34–56.

Mann, Michael (1993), *The Sources of Social Power, volume II: The rise of Classes and Nation-states, 1760–1914*, Cambridge: Cambridge University Press.

Mann, Michael (2000), 'Has globalization ended the rise and rise of the nation-state?' in David Held and Anthony McGrew (eds), *The Global Transformations Reader: An Introduction to the Globalization Debate*, Cambridge: Polity, pp. 136–47.

Marshall, Gordon (1997), *Repositioning Class: Social Inequality in Industrial Societies*, Lon-don: Sage.

Marshall, T.H. (1963), *Sociology at the Crossroads and Other Essays*, London: Heinemann.

Mény, Yves (2001), 'Five (hypo)theses on democracy and its future', in Anthony Giddens (ed.), *The Global Third Way Debate*, Cambridge: Polity Press, pp. 259–68.

Mills, C. Wright (1970), *The Sociological Imagination*, Harmondsworth: Penguin.

Papastergiadis, Nikos (2000), *The Turbulence of Migration: Globalization, Deterritorialization and Hybridity*, Cambridge: Polity.

Pierson, Christopher (1996), *The Modern State*, Routledge: London.

Porter, Marilyn (2001), 'Something borrowed, something blue: learning from women's groups in Indonesia', *Sociological Research Online*, **6** (2), www.socresonline.org.uk/6/2/contents.html.

Ragin, Charles (1987), *The Comparative Method: Moving Beyond Qualitative and Quantitative Strategies*, Berkeley: University of California Press.

Roberts, Bryan (1995), *The Making of Citizens: Cities of Peasants Revisited*, London: Arnold.

Sainsbury, Diane (ed.) (1999), *Gender and Welfare State Regimes*, Oxford: Oxford University Press.

Scott, Alison (1994), *Divisions and Solidarities: Gender, Class and Employment in Latin America*, London: Routledge.

Scott, James (1998), *Seeing Like a State: How Certain Schemes to Improve the Human Condition Have Failed*, New Haven: Yale University Press.

Sklair, Leslie (2002), *Globalization: Capitalism and Its Alternatives*, Oxford: Oxford University Press.

Taylor, Marilyn (1995), 'Community work and the state: the changing context of UK practice', in Gary Craig and Marjorie Mayo (eds), *Community Empowerment: A Reader in Participation and Development*, London: Zed Books, pp. 99–111.

Therborn, Göran (1995), *European Modernity and Beyond: The Trajectory of European Societies, 1945–2000*, London: Sage.

Townsend, Peter (1993) *The International Analysis of Poverty*, Hemel Hempstead: Harvester Wheatsheaf.

Turner, Bryan (1999), *Classical Sociology*, London: Sage.

Urry, John (2000), *Sociology Beyond Societies: Mobilities for the Twenty-first Century*, London: Routledge.

Wallerstein, Immanuel (1999), *The End of the World as we Know It: Social Science for the Twenty-First Century*, Minneapolis: University of Minnesota Press.

Westergaard, John (1995), *Who Gets What? The Hardening of Class Inequality in the Late Twentieth Century*, Cambridge: Polity Press.

Williams, Raymond (1983), *Keywords: A Vocabulary of Culture and Society*, London: Flamingo.

7 The ethnocentric construction of the welfare state

Alan Walker and Chack-kie Wong

This chapter argues that welfare state regimes have been constructed specifically as capitalist-democratic projects and this has the effect of excluding societies which do not have either one or both of these particular economic and political systems. If a traditional social administration approach is adopted, a similar result occurs when a 'welfare state' is defined narrowly in terms of direct state provision.

Introduction

In recent years, there has been increased interest in the welfare systems of East Asian societies (Aspalter, 2001; Chan, 1996; Goodman and Peng, 1996; Goodman, White and Kwon, 1998; Jacobs, 1998; Jones, 1993; Lin, 1999; McLaughlin, 1993). However, whether the welfare systems of these societies should be classified as welfare states remains a controversial issue. Some writers (McLaughlin, 1993; Goodman, White and Kwon, 1998; Jacobs, 1998) avoid the issue altogether by not directly applying the label 'welfare state' to the East Asian welfare systems under study. For example, in the comparative social policy book *Comparing Welfare States: Britain in International Context*, McLaughlin (1993:105) uses the term 'welfare regime' to classify Hong Kong. In another book on East Asian welfare systems, the term 'Welfare Model' is preferred to that of 'welfare state' (Goodman, White and Kwon, 1998). Nevertheless, there are exceptions where the description 'welfare state' is applied to East Asian societies (Aspalter, 2001; Chan; 1996; Rose and Shiratori, 1986).

These recent exceptions apart, in the mainstream comparative social policy literature, definitions, theories and classifications of both welfare and the welfare state have been formulated with reference to only a small number of western industrialized or capitalist countries, which are particularly associated with advanced capitalism and membership of the Organization of Economic Cooperation and Development (OECD). Hence, this dominant approach to comparative social policy has been described as 'ethnocentric Western social research' (Jones, 1993:106) and the 'anglocentric frame of reference' (Powell and Hewitt, 1997:12). This ethnocentric construction of the welfare state paradigm reflects a Western bias and has the detrimental effect of excluding from comparative analyses not only the state welfare provisions of developing societies, but also those of some highly developed countries. This exclusion is particularly ironic in the case of the affluent East Asian economies because many of their welfare institutions resemble and, in many cases were modelled on, those found in Western welfare states.

Our argument is not that the governments of East Asian societies are eager to become members of the welfare state club, far from it (Lin, 1999:37). They do not regard their welfare systems as welfare states; this is particularly the case with respect to the governments and elites in Singapore and Hong Kong. These two city-states have attained the highest economic prosperity in recent years, second only to Japan in East Asia, in terms of per capita GDP. In these two societies, not only the elites but a majority of the general public as well, perceive state welfare as a burden on the economy, a social and economic 'infection' that has to be avoided for the sake of economic success. In this regard, it is not surprising to see the prevalence of a discourse about Asian values (Berger, 1987; Clammer, 1985) to support the argument for a particular welfare system that is different from that of the West – referred to variously in the comparative social policy literature as Confucian welfare states (Jones, 1993); the Confucian welfare cluster (Lin, 1999), or the Japan-focused East Asian welfare model (Goodman and Peng, 1996, p. 216). Of course science should not be divorced from its cultural and policy context, a stricture that applies as much to eastern social scientists as to their Western counterparts. However, and this is the crux of our argument, the exclusion of East Asian welfare systems from the mainstream comparative welfare state literature, including what is widely regarded as the core text on the subject (Esping-Andersen, 1990), artificially limits the scope of comparative social policy. Moreover, in the absence of a scientific rationale for this welfare state myopia the charge of ethnocentrism is hard to refute. This negation of East Asian welfare systems as welfare states begs the question precisely what is a welfare state? Although beyond the scope of this chapter it also reminds us that the term 'welfare state' has always been controversial not only in political but also scientific discourse (hence the fact that Titmuss always put it in quotation marks – see for example, Titmuss, 1958). This controversy is a global one.

Two seismic global events in the recent past which have, among other things, major implications for social policy and comparative research are the collapse of the former state socialist regimes of the Central and Eastern European bloc and the peaceful transition from an orthodox centrally planned economy to market socialism in China. The welfare systems of both the former state socialist countries and pre-reform China had long been excluded from comparative welfare state analysis because they were non-capitalist regimes and did not belong to the OECD club. However, the welfare systems of these countries had managed to provide for their citizens a wide range of universal entitlements; despite critical claims that their welfare provisions were out of all proportion to their resources and the fiscal capacity of the state (Kornai, 1997). (To some extent in accordance with this critique, following the collapse of state socialism some Central and Eastern European countries experienced a crisis of social protection.) In the case of transitional China, it has managed comparatively well in re-casting welfare responsibility especially in the urban areas, from a total reliance on the state to the incorporation of individual responsibility by social insurance and forced savings (Wong, 1999). Although it must be emphasized that this applies exclusively to urban areas – in social and economic terms the rural/urban division creates two nations in China. Despite the Tiananmen Square Incident of 1989, transitional China has been a relatively stable society; its welfare provisions, especially the newly installed safety-net system, are likely to have been a decisive factor in this stability.

The newly affluent East Asian capitalist economies, the former Central and Eastern European bloc and pre-reform China all have or had welfare institutions resembling those found in the Western welfare state club but they are not counted as welfare states. Thus, the exclusion of these countries from welfare state status is not due to the nature of their welfare institutions but, presumably, because they have neither a capitalist economy nor a fully fledged Western parliamentary democracy. If this is true, it tends to confirm our argument that the Western welfare state paradigm is an ethnocentric construction. Their exclusion is not based on the policy content or institutions of welfare in those countries, but on other institutional requirements that are not concerned with the welfare state *per se* but rather its cultural, economic and political *context*.

The main purpose of this chapter is to look closely at the ethnocentric assumptions behind the Western construction of the welfare state. It starts by examining the first assumption underpinning Western welfare states that they are a capitalist-democratic project. Then we look at the elasticity of the welfare state boundary in the Western construction.

Underlying institutional assumptions of the welfare state paradigm

The Western conception of the welfare state and descriptive studies of welfare state regimes usually neglect non-capitalist or non-democratic societies with state welfare components (Walker and Wong, 1996). Drawing on our original critique one recent analysis describes this ethnocentric bias:

> Whenever people from Northern and continental Europe talk about the welfare state, they have the very popular extensive/institutional welfare systems in mind that are predominant in that region of the world ... However the new usage of the

term 'welfare state', in its broader sense that includes residual welfare state systems, has not been accepted by a great number of people in Europe and Asia. (Aspalter, 2001:1–2)

However, the ethnocentric bias means that the liberal, residual welfare states of the USA, Canada, the UK (in some accounts the UK is a conservative welfare state regime) and the Antipodes are usually regarded as welfare states despite the fact that they deliver meagre benefits, on the basis of need, as a last resort to those who are unable to support themselves through market activities. Hence, it is not the content of the state welfare components or their impact that determines inclusion but the fact that welfare states are premised on two institutional arrangements: first it is a capitalist institution and second, it is embodied in a democratic (that is parliamentary) institutional structure. So, the state welfare components themselves are not sufficient, according to the Western paradigm, to qualify as a welfare state.

Democracy and capitalism are macro-institutions with their own underlying social principles. Equality of political rights among individuals, regardless of their status and means, is the basic social principle underlying democracy, while capitalism, the economic institution, depends upon the market as the principal method of distributing social and economic resources. Admittedly, these two macro-institutions have tensions between them. However, they have long been regarded as the two underlying and driving forces which affect the development of the welfare state. T.H. Marshall (1950) was the pioneer in this field with the idea of political citizenship that enables individuals to access a range of welfare benefits and provisions on an equal basis to their fellow citizens. Accordingly modern citizens are able to attain a decent living standard despite the unequal distribution of market-based incomes (Abrahamson, 1997:148). However, of course, Marshall's definition of citizenship has been criticized extensively, for example for failing to distinguish between the public and private spheres and, thereby, excluding many women in particular (Pascall, 1986; Williams, 1989; Lister, 1997). A more recent attempt to understand the assumptions underlying the welfare state and to distinguish its core components was made by Esping-Andersen (1990). He sees the welfare state and the different welfare state regimes in Western democracies as combining a system of stratification and strategies of decommodification to counteract the unequal and divisive market logic of capitalism.

Some writers (Gintis and Bowles, 1982; Jordan, 1996) also highlight the tension between capitalism and democracy, the two macro-institutions which dominate the development of the welfare state. According to Gintis and Bowles (1982:341) in their reference to Western capitalist economies, the welfare state is located at the interface of two distinct sets of rules, each contradicting the other. The first set of rules relates to the rights of citizens, which extend from the equal political status underlying democratic institutions. The second set of rules covers property rights which provide a framework for the capitalist market economy. Citizen rights are in persistent conflict with property rights. Despite this conflictual relationship between these two sets of rules, the welfare state is regarded by some writers, especially neo-Marxists (O'Connor, 1973; Offe, 1984; Gough, 1979), as fundamental to the very existence of capitalism, because it legitimizes the accumulation function of capital. In one author's words, 'The welfare state is [therefore] also the result of capital's requirements for the reproduction of labour power' (Ginsburg, 1992:3).

Despite the assumption with regard to democracy which underpins the welfare state paradigm, the most mature democratic capitalist countries were not the first to develop state welfare services (Esping-Andersen, 1990; Flora and Heidenheimer, 1982; Digby, 1989; de Swaan, 1988). For instance, Flora and Heidenheimer (1982:70) suggested that the first batch of countries which initiated the core welfare state programmes, the social insurance schemes, were non-parliamentary regimes in Western Europe such as Austria, Denmark, Germany and Sweden. In line with the neo-Marxist argument about the need to legitimize the accumulation function of capital, these governments used state welfare to consolidate the loyalty of the working class and compete with a growing and hostile labour movement. Thus the historical evidence does not support the idea that a democratic political institutional structure is the prerequisite for the development of state welfare programmes. This is exactly the case in today's East Asian countries and yesterday's Central and Eastern European Soviet bloc countries where, as argued earlier, similar state welfare institutions are and were established in the absence of Western-style parliamentary democracy.

In terms of inter-institutional relationships, welfare state programmes are usually regarded, in spite of being indispensable, as essentially in an adjunct position to the market economy (Titmuss, 1974:30–31; Martin, 1990:39). Despite its subordinate position, the welfare state is complementary to the market economy. The key is the fine-tuning of state intervention by the welfare state: it has to rectify market failures but stop well short of eradicating the market system (Walker, 1983). The essential feature of this sort of state welfare intervention is to enable any rules of the market system to remain intact; at the same time, it has also to limit the extent of accumulation on the part of capital by redistributing some to the less well-off. In other words, the welfare state and the market system have competing aims, but they also have complementary functions.

In this paradigm, the ideal type of a welfare state is one which can have the benefits of *both* macro-institutions: economic growth attained by the market system (the economic institution) with social interests being pursued by state welfare (the state institution). The contradictory nature of these two macro-institutions does not discourage theorists of the welfare state and comparative analysts to look for good examples of the ideal type. That is to say that the state can assume an extensive and strong role whilst it is complementary to the economy. In the literature of comparative welfare state analysis Sweden has long provided a model of a 'strong' welfare state without detriment to the economy (Therborn, 1986:18; Therborn and Roebroek, 1986:327). However, recent accounts by welfare state writers and theorists seem to be more cautious about the complementary relation between the two macro-institutions; they acknowledge the trade-off between economic growth and social interest (Esping-Andersen, 1999; Palme, 1999). For example, Esping-Andersen (2001, p. 358) asks the question 'why would the Nordic social democracies, so dedicated to decommodification, sponsor much weaker employment rights than do the Mediterranean polities, which are not exactly the prototypes of an advanced welfare state?' By asking this question, Esping-Andersen sees the contradictory nature of the welfare state regime as more prevalent than the complementary function between the welfare state and the capitalist economic system. Similarly in China, the state occupied an extensive role in the economy in its pre-reform era; now it believes that the state needs to be separated from the economy so that its accumulation function can be activated.

In contrast to the ideal type of the Swedish or Nordic model of the welfare state, the 'liberal' welfare states are usually the ideal type at the opposite end of the spectrum, in which the contradictory relationship between the state and the economy is more exaggerated. In this construction, the state and the economy should be operated as separately as possible from each other. In these liberal welfare states the residual public role of the state is assumed to be the public preference. Not only do we find the preference for a residual public role for the state among Western welfare states, such as the Anglo-Saxon English-speaking societies, the United States in particular, a similarly high regard for state residualism is also witnessed in the world's freest economy – Hong Kong. Nevertheless, it is necessary to differentiate the rhetoric of such a preference from the reality of welfare systems in which empirical evidence may prove the contrary. For instance, in Hong Kong the state has long occupied a major role with regard to housing, education and health care despite the fact that it is a non-welfare state East Asian economy (Wong, Chau and Wong, 2002).

The ideal postulate of welfare state regimes on the basis of the relation between the state and the economy seems to confirm the Western ethnocentric bias; it is the advent of Western parliamentary democracy that counts in deciding what is a welfare state. The dominant conceptualization of the welfare state as an adjunct to the market economy, despite the range of differences between the ideal types, looks more like the straightforward rationalization of an existing phenomenon than a scientific judgement based on empirical evidence of the political economy of state welfare. Because it is evident, as illustrated previously, that state welfare could be found in non-parliamentary and non-capitalist societies, so it follows that state welfare programmes are not exclusive to Western-style political democracies.

The 'elastic' welfare state boundary

The scientific construction of the welfare state as a democratic-capitalist project has suffered from the bias of excluding non-democratic and non-capitalist societies in comparative analyses. Moreover, the Western ethnocentric construction also has a narrow focus on one single institution, the state, and its role in social policy (Walker, 1984b). The ideal is seen as the institutional-redistributive welfare state, in Titmuss's (1974) terms, while at the other end is the residual role of alleviating poverty. The former indicates a strong role played by the state and represents the welfare state to aspire to; while the residual end consists of a weak or minimal role for the state and regards the welfare society as the primary provider of welfare. The supposed continuum between these two roles of the state and, indeed, also the dichotomy between welfare state and welfare society is not necessarily a realistic portrayal of empirical reality. In practice, the welfare state cohabits with the economy and many other social institutions such as the family and a range of private and quasi-private institutions, to form a welfare system. In fact, the co-existence of the welfare state and the welfare society has been referred to as the 'mixed economy of welfare' and this concept has been important in social policy analysis for many years (Johnson, 1987; Rose and Shiratori, 1986; Walker, 1984a).

The practical co-existence of the welfare state and the welfare society has not stopped the portrayal of the utilitarian or functional role-of-state continuum (or dichotomy) as forming the main theoretical paradigm for classifying Western welfare states. The social administration tradition is a case in point. The classic welfare state is portrayed as having the responsibility 'for securing some basic modicum of welfare for its citizens' (Esping-Andersen, 1990:18–19). This functional social administration tradition dates back to the work of Briggs (1961) and Marshall (1965). For example, Briggs (2000:18) suggested that,

> A welfare state is a state in which organized power is deliberately used in an effort to modify the play of market forces in at least three directions – first, by guaranteeing individuals and families a minimum income irrespective of the market value of their work or their property; second, by narrowing the extent of insecurity by enabling individuals and families to meet certain 'social contingencies' ... which lead otherwise to individual and family crises; and third, by ensuring that

all citizens without distinction of status or class are offered the best standards available in relation to a certain agreed range of social services.

This is a typical illustration of the social administration tradition and emphasizes the social democratic roots of this perspective by defining the responsibility of the welfare state in terms of the provision of a range of universal state welfare services. Nevertheless, the social administration tradition has several severe limitations. As noted by Walker (1981; 1983), the tradition's lack of a theoretical framework and especially its optimistic view of the functions of social policy and its narrow focus on state intervention have limited its comparative usefulness. There have been various attempts to define the welfare state from a more rigorous theoretical perspective. Titmuss (1974) was the forerunner and, in his welfare state framework, the residual, industrial achievement-performance, and institutional-redistributive approaches to welfare were formulated to illustrate the range of welfare state possibilities from selective to universal provision. The more recent account by Esping-Andersen (1990) is a sophisticated theorization based on de-commodification as the strategy to counteract the extent to which life chances are dependent on market principles and operations. On that basis, three clusters of welfare state regimes are identified: the Anglo-Saxon English-speaking 'liberal', the continental 'corporatist' and the Nordic 'social democratic' welfare states.

Despite the more rigorous than hitherto attempts of the utilitarian or functional approach to theorize welfare state regimes, it still encounters similar problems to those associated with the institutional approach. First of all, what exactly constitutes a welfare state or a welfare regime is still not precisely defined. It seems that if a society has institutionalized a range of social services and benefits to its citizens, it could qualify as a welfare state or welfare regime. However, the issue of precision in decisions about eligibility for inclusion as a welfare state is raised when some societies which have a substantial range of institutionalized social services and benefits are not classified as welfare states; the threshold question comes to the fore.

For instance, Japan is the only non-Western society that is often referred to as a welfare state (Lee, 1987; Rose and Shiratori, 1986; Esping-Andersen, 1990). It is certainly one of the most successful capitalist economies and also has a democratic polity. More importantly, perhaps, it is a member of the club of the rich countries, the OECD, and therefore has a kind of honorary Western status (it has had close links with the US since the Second World War). The case of South Korea is potentially interesting. It was excluded previously from scientific consideration as a welfare state along with the other three 'little dragons' – Hong Kong, Singapore and Taiwan. But now it has joined the OECD and has recently installed a Western-style democracy and, perhaps, it will be accorded welfare state status like Japan. Meanwhile the other 'little dragons' in East Asia, with a range of institutionalized social services and benefits (Jacobs, 1998), are usually not counted as welfare states. For example, Hong Kong has universal health services, universal and free basic education, extensive public housing programmes and an institutionalized social assistance scheme for its inhabitants; all these reflect the 'basic modicum' of welfare found in liberal welfare states. However, it is usually excluded from the 'club' of welfare states because it does not have one of the two essential institutional criteria – a Western-style political democracy – despite the fact that it is the freest economy on earth (Hong Kong SAR Government, 2002).

Critics might argue that Hong Kong is now part of China again but its exclusion from the welfare state category long pre-dates reunification. A similar case applies to transitional China itself, which lacks a western-style political democracy and is not a fully capitalist economy. In spite of these two institutional 'anomalies' from the perspective of the Western construction, it had managed and is still able to provide sufficient social protection to its urban population, albeit with enormous difficulties at the present moment. Back in the pre-reform era, comprehensive welfare was provided through the 'work-units' (that is, state-owned enterprises, government bureaux and so on) which could mirror the central idea of 'from cradle to grave' welfare of the classic perception of the idealized Western welfare state (Walker and Wong, 1996). Even in its reform era, the Chinese Government has made tremendous efforts to institutionalize social protection for its urban population. For example, a poverty line, with its accompanying benefit provisions, was first promulgated in 1993 in Shanghai and now covers all urban areas. Despite these advances China was and is not currently perceived as crossing the threshold of the welfare state group.

Second, if we take Briggs's first criterion – the guarantee of a basic minimum income – to examine the threshold question of the club of the welfare states, we may find that some well-established Western welfare states do not even cross this basic threshold. It is well acknowledged that the 'liberal' welfare states or welfare state regimes deliver meagre benefits, on the basis of need, as the last resort for those who are unable to support themselves through market activities. It is appropriate that this should be the lowest threshold that a welfare system has to cross to be classified as a welfare state. However, Greece, Spain, France and Italy, four European Union Member States, do not have formal universal rights to minimum income support (Ferrazzi, 1995). It is worth while to highlight that France and Italy are usually classified as the continental 'conservative' welfare states, a status with a higher level of de-commodification than the 'liberal' ones (Esping-Anderson, 1990). If the 'conservative' welfare states do not provide a universal social right to social protection to its citizens, it is not surprising to see that the largest 'liberal' welfare state, the USA, fares even worse. When the US reformed its social welfare system and capped the entitlement to social assistance benefits to two years within a lifelong five-year period in its 1996 Clinton welfare reform package, the basic guarantee criterion, as typically defined by Briggs (1961), was abandoned. Besides, the United States is the only major industrialized nation whose government does not guarantee the right of access to health care in time of need by providing universal and comprehensive health benefit coverage to its people. According to one source, 18 per cent of the population lack any form of health service coverage (Navarro, 1992). In contrast, Hong Kong is not a welfare state by the Western construction but it has guaranteed social assistance and universal health care. Again this begs the question of 'what constitutes a welfare state?'

Third, if we apply the most stringent criterion of Briggs (1961) – the provision of a range of universal state welfare services without regard to class or status – then perhaps the retreat of the state from welfare provision in many Western societies in the last two decades should deprive many of them of their status as welfare states (Pierson, 2001). The case is more obvious with regard to the application of workfare as the condition for state welfare. The introduction of 'workfare' is not confined to 'liberal' welfare states, even social democratic ones also apply it to promote active citizenship. Once state welfare is conditional, however, the basic guarantee criterion becomes obsolete. But neither the retreat of the state's role in welfare over the past decades nor the dire predictions of future austerity seem to have any implication for the status of the Western welfare states as welfare states (Pierson, 2001). Thus, in Western comparative analysis, the rule seems to be: once a welfare state, always a welfare state. In this regard, the elastic nature of the definition suggests that it cannot offer a precise threshold for comparative analysis because apparently it can be stretched to include all reformulations. The main problem of such a definition, therefore, is that it depends on the purposes of the authority using the concept.

Evidently, the welfare state definition is too elastic. A similar view is also voiced by British social policy analysts such as Glennerster (1995) and Powell and Hewitt (1997) on the British welfare state. They see the elasticity of the welfare state threshold as indicating the 'myth of the classic welfare state' and ask, for example by Powell and Hewitt (1997:22) 'at what point does the increase in means-testing or charging signal the end of classic welfare state?'

So, the myth, as it has been referred to, indicates the imperfection of the current welfare state definition at a very fundamental level. In our analysis it also indicates a flaw in terms of the unscientific and unfair exclusion of societies with state welfare programmes from being classified as 'welfare states'. The foregoing examples of Hong Kong and China in East Asia are cases in point. Also mentioned earlier were the former state socialist regimes of the Central and Eastern European bloc. They managed to provide comprehensive welfare to their citizens, in one authority's verdict, out of all proportion to their resources and the fiscal capacity of the state. Nevertheless, they had the essential state welfare programmes, and even in terms of the level of public expenditure, one of them, the former Yugoslavia, spent 19.75 per cent of its GNP on social spending in 1981 (Pusic, 1987). This was a proportion of national wealth devoted to social spending that was higher than many members of the welfare state club – the OECD countries. Thus, on theoretical as well as empirical grounds, the elasticity of welfare state definitions makes the Western ethnocentric construction of the welfare state open to challenge. On a more fundamental level, this implies that the terms 'welfare state' or 'welfare regime' lack the rigour that is usually required of a scientific tool for measuring empirical reality.

Fourth, the use of the effects of state welfare as the main criterion in defining the welfare state or welfare regime would encounter practical problems generated by the complexities of the actual programmes. Taking Esping-Andersen's de-commodification effects as a case in point, a state programme could have both positive and negative effects. For example, work-based pension schemes also have the effect of commodification as they require a job (that is, commodified labour) and the contributions of the worker (that is, market exchange operation and underlying principle) to the pension fund during their working life. Hence, there will inevitably be a subjective judgement about awarding a particular society the status of inclusion as a welfare state or welfare regime.

Likewise, in the comparative welfare state literature, there has been so much attention focused on the effect of income maintenance schemes in terms of de-commodification that the developmental aspect of state welfare has been overlooked. Perhaps this is the underlying reason for the exclusion of East Asian welfare systems from the group of welfare states: they are less generous than their western counterparts about social protection programmes against poverty and pay less attention to the elimination of social inequalities.

Fifth, the construction of the welfare state on the basis of the state's social policy effects is vulnerable to the criticism that it is based on too narrow a conception of welfare (Walker, 1981:225–50). The state sector is only one among the 'mixed economy of welfare' providers. Evidently, the state, the private market, the family and the voluntary sector have provided social services and benefits since the welfare state was created; and they will continue to do so. The state has to work closely with other non-statutory sectors in order to satisfy the needs of citizens. There can be a symbiotic relationship between the state sector and other non-statutory ones. The narrow focus on the functions and effects of the state sector tends to neglect the contributions of other non-statutory providers. The current discourses concerning 'welfare society', 'active social policy' or 'active society' (Burchell, 1995; Dean, 1995; Rodger, 2000) indicates a shift in the political and scientific consensus towards a 'mixed economy of welfare' (Wong, Chau and Wong, 2002); by doing so, it may help to rectify the longstanding statist bias. In the same vein, the use of the term 'welfare regime' instead of 'welfare state regime' in Esping-Andersen's recent book (1999) also signifies acknowledgement of the contribution of the 'welfare society' to welfare. Likewise, the feminist emphasis on the contribution of domestic labour to welfare, the relationship between unpaid work and paid work and welfare (Dominelli, 1991; Langan and Ostner, 1991; Lewis, 1992), and Titmuss's (1958) concept of the social division of welfare should also be welcomed.

Conclusion
This chapter has argued that the keystone of the foundations of comparative social policy, the concept of the welfare state, is a Western ethnocentric construction that has seriously hindered scientific inquiry in this field. The description 'welfare regimes' overcomes the narrow emphasis of social administration on the activities of the state but this too suffers from the same ethnocentric deficiency. We use the examples of East Asian societies, pre-reform China and the former state socialist countries of Central and Eastern Europe. A case could be made equally with regard to the welfare systems of many developing societies, although there will always be a threshold question with regard to some comparative analyses.

   In view of the evidence presented here it is tempting to conclude that the term 'welfare state' should be abolished from the comparative literature. That is unrealistic because Titmuss's (1958) early cautions were ignored and now the term is everywhere. In any case it is not clear how helpful that course would be to the comparative endeavour. A more potentially productive line would be to begin to define precisely what is meant by a welfare state, welfare system or welfare regime for the purposes of comparative analysis. Tentatively we suggest that the scientific construction of the welfare system or regime should fulfil the following criteria:

- a global perspective, to ensure that non-Western-style democracies and non-capitalist societies are included;
- inclusiveness with regard to modes of distribution and redistribution, to ensure that the full range of possibilities, from selective to universal, are counted;
- pluralism, to acknowledge the different range and combination of welfare providers in different countries and their distributional and other implications;

- a developmental perspective, to globalize the comparative analysis of welfare systems and recognize that, as well as de-commodifying effects, state welfare has a developmental role.

With regard to the 'welfare state', this term should be employed exclusively to refer to the various roles of the state in welfare (Titmuss's concept of the social division of welfare is particularly relevant to comparative analysis in this respect). Definitions of the welfare state should be clear about the threshold issue and, we suggest, the bottom line should be the guarantee of basic income protection to those resident in the society.

References

Abrahamson, Peter (1997), 'Combating poverty and social exclusion in Europe' in Wolfgang Beck, Laurent van der Maesen and Alan Walker (eds), *The Social Quality of Europe*, The Hague: Kluwer International, pp. 145–76.

Aspalter, Christian (2001), *Conservative Welfare State Systems in East Asia*, Westport, CT and London: Praeger.

Berger, Peter, L. (1987), *The Capitalist Revolution*, Hants: Wildwood House.

Briggs, Asa (1961), 'The welfare state in historical perspective', *European Journal of Sociology*, **2**(2), 221–58.

Briggs, Asa (2000), 'The welfare state in historical perspective', in Christopher Pierson and Francis G. Castles (eds), *The Welfare State: A Reader*, Cambridge: Polity Press, pp. 18–31.

Burchell, David (1995), 'The attributes of citizens: virtue, manners and the activity of citizenship', *Economy and Society*, **24**(4), 540–58.

Chan, Raymond K.H.(1996), *Welfare in Newly Industrialised Society: the Construction of the Welfare State in Hong Kong*, Aldershot: Avebury.

Clammer, John R. (1985), *Singapore: Ideology, Society, Culture*, Singapore: Chopmen Publishers.

de Swaan, Abram (1988), *In Care of the State*, Cambridge: Polity Press.

Dean, Mitchell (1995), 'Governing the unemployed self in an active society', *Economy and Society*, **24**(4), 559–83.

Digby, Anne (1989), *British Welfare Policy – Workhouse to Workfare*, London: Faber and Faber.

Dominelli, Lena (1991), *Women Across Continents*, Hemel Hempstead: Harvester Wheatsheaf.

Esping-Andersen, Gøsta (1990), *The Three Worlds of Welfare Capitalism*, Cambridge: Polity Press.

Esping-Andersen, Gøsta (1996), *Welfare States in Transition*, London: Sage.

Esping-Andersen, Gøsta (1999), *Social Foundations of Postindustrial Economies*, Oxford: Oxford University Press.

Esping-Andersen, Gøsta (2001), 'Multi-dimensional decommodification: a reply to Graham Room', *Policy and Politics*, **28**(3), 353–59.

Ferrazzi, Silva (1995), *The Condition of Women in European Social Assistance Policies: Italy and Great Britain Compared*, Centre for Research in European Social and Employment Policy, University of Bath.

Flora, Peter and Arnold J. Heidenheimer (1982), *The Development of Welfare States in Europe and America*, New Brunswick: Transaction Books.

Ginsburg, Norman (1992), *Divisions of Welfare*, London: Sage.

Gintis, Hubert and Samuel Bowles (1982), 'The welfare state and long-term economic growth: Marxism, neoclassical, and Keynesian approaches', *American Economic Review*, **72**(2), 341–5.

Glennerster, Howard (1995), *British Social Policy Since 1945*, Oxford: Blackwell.

Goodman, Roger and Ito Peng (1996), 'The East Asian welfare states: peripatetic learning, adaptive change, and nation building', in Gøsta Esping-Andersen (ed.), *Welfare States in*

Transition, London: Sage, in association with UN Research Institute for Social Development, pp. 192–224.

Goodman, Roger, Gordon White and Huck-ju Kwon (1998), *The East Asian Welfare Model: Welfare Orientalism and the State*, London: Routledge.

Gough, Ian ((1979), *The Political Economy of the Welfare State*, London: Macmillan.

Hong Kong SAR Government (2002), http://www.freeeconomy.org/freeeconomy/eng/main.htm.

Jacobs, Didier (1998), *Social Welfare Systems in East Asia: A Comparative Analysis including Private Welfare*, London: London School of Economics, Centre for Analysis of Social Exclusion.

Johnson, Norman (1987), *The Welfare State in Transition*, Brighton: Wheatsheaf.

Jones, Catherine (1993), *New Perspective on the Welfare State in Europe*, London: Routledge.

Jordan, Bill (1996), *A Theory of Poverty and Social Exclusion*, Cambridge: Polity.

Kornai, Janos (1997), 'Editorial: reforming the welfare state in post-socialist societies', *World Development*, **25**(8), 1183–6.

Langan, Mary and Ilona Ostner (1991), 'Gender and welfare', in Graham Room (ed.) *Towards a European Welfare State?*, Bristol, School for Advanced Urban Studies, pp. 127–50.

Lee, Hye Kyung (1987), 'The Japanese welfare state in transition', in Robert R. Friedman, Neil Gilbert and Moshe Sherer (eds), *Modern Welfare States*, Brighton: Wheatsheaf, pp. 243–63.

Lewis, Jane (1992), 'Gender and the development of welfare regimes', *European Journal of Social Policy*, **2** (3), 159–74.

Lin, Ka (1999), *Confucian Welfare Cluster: A Cultural Interpretation of Social Welfare*, Tampere: University of Tampere.

Lister, Ruth (1997), *Citizenship: Feminist Perspectives*, Basingstoke: Macmillan.

Marshall, Thomas H. (1950), *Citizenship and Social Class and Other Essays*, Cambridge: Cambridge University Press.

Marshall, Thomas H. (1965), *Social Policy*, London: Hutchinson.

Martin, George T. (1990), *Social Policy in the Welfare State*, Englewood Cliffs, NJ: Prentice-Hall.

McLaughlin, Eugene (1993), 'Hong Kong: a residual welfare regime', in Allan Cochrane and John Clarke (eds), *Comparing Welfare States: Britain in International Context*, London: Sage and Open University Press, pp. 105–40.

Navarro, Vicente (ed.) (1992), *Why the United States does not have a National Health Program*, New York: Baywood Publishing Co.

O'Connor, James (1973), *The Fiscal Crisis of the Welfare State*, New York: St. James Press.

OECD (1999), *A Caring World, The New Social Policy Agenda*, Paris: OECD.

Offe, Clau (1984), *Contradictions of the Welfare State*, London: Macmillan.

Palme, Joakim (1999), *The Nordic Model and the Modernisation of Social Protection in Europe*, Copenhagen: Nordic Council of Ministers.

Pascall, Gillian (1986), *Social Policy: a Feminist Analysis*, London: Tavistock.

Pierson, Paul (ed.) (2001), *The New Politics of the Welfare State*, Oxford: Oxford University Press.

Powell, Martin and Martin Hewitt (1997), 'Something happened. Conflicting descriptions of the new welfare state', paper presented at the 31st SPA Annual Conference, University of Lincolnshire and Humberside, Lincoln, 15–17 July.

Pusic, Eugen (1987), 'The development of the welfare state in Yugoslavia', in Robert R. Friedmann, Neil Gilbert and Moshe Sherer (eds), *Modern Welfare States*, Brighton: Wheatsheaf, pp. 151–73.

Rodger, John J. (2000), *From a Welfare State to a Welfare Society*, Hampshire: Macmillan.

Rose, Richard and Rei Shiratori (1986), *The Welfare State East and West*, New York: Oxford University Press.

Therborn, Goran (1986), *Why Some People Are More Unemployed Than Others*, London: Verso.

Therborn, Goran and Roebroek, Jacob (1986), 'The irreversible welfare state: its recent maturation, its encounters with the economic crisis, and its future prospects', *International Journal of Health Services*, **16** (3), 319–38.

Titmuss, Richard (1958), *Essays on 'the Welfare State'*, London: George Allen & Unwin.

Titmuss, Richard (1974), *Social Policy*, London: George Allen & Unwin.

Walker, Alan (1981), 'Social policy, social administration and the social construction of welfare', *Sociology*, **15** (2), 225–50.

Walker, Alan (1983), 'Labour's social plans: the limits of welfare statism', *Critical Social Policy*, **3** (3), 45–63.

Walker, Alan (1984a), 'The political economy of privatisation', Julian Le Grand and Ray Robinson (eds), *The Privatisation of the Welfare State*, London: Unwin & Hyman, pp. 19–44.

Walker, Alan (1984b), *Social Planning*, Oxford: Blackwell.

Walker, Alan and Wong, Chack-kie (1996), 'Rethinking the western construction of the welfare state', *International Journal of Health Services*, **26** (1), 67–92.

Walters, William (1997), 'The active society: new designs for social policy', *Policy and Politics*, **25** (3), 221–34.

Williams, Fiona (1989), *Social Policy*, Oxford: Polity Press.

Wong, Chack-kie (1999), 'Reforming China's state socialist workfare system: the cautionary and incremental approach and beyond', *Issues and Studies*, **35** (5), 169–94.

Wong, Chack-kie, Kin-lam Chau and Ka-yin Wong (2002), 'Neither welfare state nor welfare society: the case of Hong Kong', *Social Policy and Society*, **1** (4), 293–301.

8 The paradox of care: a Chinese Confucian perspective on long-term care

Julia Tao

Introduction

This chapter begins with a critical analysis of the paradox of care in the contemporary social policy approach to long-term care, arising from the institutionalization of care, the devaluation of care as an instrumental good, and the emphasis on autonomy as the central value of public care provision. It argues for an alternative moral framework, grounded in an ethic of human dignity, instead of in the supreme value of autonomy, to guide the provision of long-term care. It draws on the intellectual resources of the Chinese Confucian moral tradition to support the re-casting of dependency and caregiving as a moral good and re-conceptualizing the nature of human need and social obligation to allow for a more adequate response to long-term care in the final stage of life. Using Hong Kong as a case study, the chapter concludes by further examining how Confucian notions of care, human dignity and reciprocity have shaped a family-based approach to care-giving in a highly cosmopolitan Chinese society, thereby providing a sharp contrast to its Western counterparts where social policy is more generally guided by the values of rights and autonomy.

First paradox of care: care and dignity

Upholding the human dignity of the elderly person is widely accepted as an important goal of long-term care policies, across cultures and societies. Commitment to a measure of dignity in the final stage of human life is commonly found in government policy statements, public consultation documents, professional practice guidelines and relevant academic debates on long-term care policy.

For example, in Hong Kong in the 2002 Social Welfare Department Report on Services for the Elderly, it is stated that 'The mission of elderly services is to enable elderly people *to live in dignity* and to provide necessary support to them to promote their sense of belonging, sense of security and sense of worthiness' (Hong Kong Special Administrative Region Government, 2002a: 1, emphasis added). In the UK, the Report *With Respect to Old Age: Long Term Care – Rights and Responsibilities* published by the Royal Commission on reform of long-term care in March 1999 recommended that the aim of reform should be to promote 'maximum choice and *dignity* and independence' in long-term care through reforming the funding system and making the provision of personal care free, and non-means-tested (The Royal Commission, 1999, ch. 4, p. 12, para. 2, emphasis added).

However, it is also true that needing care can threaten to undermine human dignity, especially in the last stage of life. It can make the recipients of care appear to be needy, deprived, and lacking in self-sufficiency. In order to qualify for public care, very often the recipient has to meet the criterion of decrepitude or desolation, or both. For example, in Hong Kong, it is stated that in order to be eligible for admission to a care-and-attention home unit, the applicant must be without family members to provide the necessary assistance, or be causing great stress to the family (Hong Kong Government, 1994: 229). The first criterion implies accepting a self-admission of dependence, while the second criterion implies making a public declaration of desolation. Since care is a need of the needy, the decrepit and the desolate, not being in need of care is a sign of well-being and a measure of dignity. To have dignity is not to be in need of care. The cost of care is even greater to recipients of long-term care. This is the first paradox of care. It has often led to the denial, the refusal and the fear of care, especially public care, because of its perceived potential to undermine one's dignity and self-identity. And yet, dignity is one of the fundamental guiding values and objectives for long-term care policy in many modern societies. Does human dignity require care? *Or* does care deny human dignity?

Second paradox of care: care and autonomy

Autonomy is another important guiding moral ideal in the provision of care. In recent decades, it has come to acquire conceptual priority and practical relevance for social policy in general, and for long-term care in particular. On the one hand, it is viewed as a universal human need (see, for example, Doyal and Gough, 1991) which social policy has the obligation to fulfil because it is foundational to our moral agency. On the other hand, it is regarded as the moral standard and the ultimate goal for the provision of care which law and public policy have the obligation to guarantee.

A popular contemporary understanding of autonomy is self-determination. Immanuel Kant (1959) and John Stuart Mill (1972) are often cited as the philosophical source for a justification of this notion of autonomy. The core idea of Kant's autonomy, developed in his *Foundations of the Metaphysics of Morals*, is 'self-governance', meaning literally rational 'self-legislation', and is necessarily connected with morality. Although the central idea in Kant's concept is the autonomy of the will, contemporary interpretations tend to focus more narrowly on the Kantian notion of self-legislation to justify the claim of autonomy as self-determination. Mill, on the other hand, claims that individuals should be free to shape their lives in accordance with their own views in order to actualize their individuality within the limits of harming others or harming one's own ability to make free choices. This capacity to control and direct one's life is the central basis of the moral requirement of respect for persons. Self-determination in this sense is also equated with self-control and self-direction.

Such a concept of autonomy places a high premium on rationality. The assumption is that all human beings have the capacity to think rationally. It is this rational capacity that allows a human being to have superior power over all the rest of the creatures in the world. To recognize the humanity of a person is to recognize her rationality and to promote her autonomy. Social policy is often committed to the enhancement of autonomy as a necessary pre-condition for the realization of rationality or purposive agency. The argument is that human agency, or the ability to carry out our life plans, will be impaired if the need for autonomy is not satisfied through adequate opportunities for self-development and the removal of impairing conditions. In this way, human agency, rationality and autonomy are conceptually linked in a theory of human need which supports a vision of persons as robust, independent and free.

As a consequence of this emphasis on a universal value of autonomy as self-determination, choice and independence, paternalistic interventions to fulfil the requirement of care are increasingly viewed with suspicion because of their potential for undermining autonomy. This is further compounded by the important fact that in the case of long-term care, it entails paternalistic intervention from the outset. Moreover, it requires ever-increasing degrees of such intervention as physical and mental functions deteriorate. While this fact no doubt indicates a need for vigilance in regard to potential abuse, however, it also implies that the stronger the autonomy movement, the more the positive value of care-giving and long-term care will be viewed with suspicion and distrust. Ironically, the priority of autonomy seems to have led increasingly to the devaluation of care, especially in the context of long-term care. This constitutes the second paradox of care. Does care support autonomy? *Or* does autonomy devalue care?

Third paradox of care: care and justice
A defining feature of the modern welfare state is the institutionalization of care governed by a moral framework of justice. Turning to justice as the moral framework for guiding the distribution and the practice of public care is considered necessary for the protection of care recipients from the threats of paternalism. Because people are capable of moral autonomy, they are morally entitled and ought to be legally entitled to conduct their lives as they see fit. The justice framework shields the individual from the invasiveness of

the state. It helps to defend non-intervention – non-intervention which is essential to our personal autonomy. But it also shields us from the demands of others. Moreover, under the justice framework, claims about moral autonomy can also easily, though not necessarily, slip into claims about personal autonomy and self-sufficiency. All in all, these visions of autonomy and freedom produce a commitment to non-interference and so resist care as a public value (White, 2000: 51).

Furthermore, as a consequence of the institutionalization of care, 'a theory of justice is considered to be necessary for discerning among more or less urgent needs' (Tronto, 1993: 138). The further implication is that care comes to be increasingly perceived as a good, and justice is the means for distributing that good because the demand for care may exceed the 'supply'. Within the justice framework, there is increasing privatizing and devaluing of care by treating it as a good either for exchange in the market or for reallocation by the state. Treating care as a good rather than seeing care as a process is to miss the relational aspect of care, whereby empathy and benevolence, the essence of care, are easily left behind. In the context of long-term care, care becomes equated increasingly with the application of technology and medical assistance to maintain functional independence and to protect autonomy. What such an understanding of care overlooks is that very often the most dreaded threat to old age is the loss of significant relationships, affectionate ties, and personal engagements rather than the loss of choice, independent action or self-sufficiency.

As care becomes increasingly interpreted as an instrumental good distributed to those who are 'needy', 'care' is therefore not a 'good' that one looks forward to in old age. Receiving care is not a status which confers high self-esteem. Needing care, particularly in one's old age, brings fear of loss of dignity and diminished identity. Care-giving is considered to be first and foremost the obligation of the state through professional care-givers who are generally viewed with much suspicion and distrust, because of the potential for paternalism whereby the recipient of care is deligitimized because they are needy. This has also led to a static vision of the roles of care-givers and care-takers, resulting in a fixed division of labour between providers and recipients of care. Ironically, the institutionalization of care itself is becoming a source of deligitimation, and the demand of justice a source of devaluation of care. This constitutes the third paradox of care. Does justice deny care? *Or is care opposed to justice?*

Undignified human dignity in old age

The paradox of care is posing a serious challenge to the moral foundation of care as well as to the adequacy of the concept of autonomy as the defining moral value for social policy in general, and for long-term care in particular (see, for example, Pullman, 1999; Agich, 1993; Callahan, 1984). The reality of dependency in long–term care is one of the main reasons why an ethic of autonomy might fail the test of practical relevance, because of its inherent assumption that to maintain independence in the sense of autonomous choice and action is the highest good and goal of care. As Daniel Callahan wrote almost two decades ago '[a]utonomy should be a moral good, not a moral obsession. It is *a* value, not *the* value.' (1984: 42, original emphasis). Under an ethic of autonomy, care-giving is valuable only insofar as its goal is the restoration or maintenance of autonomous living. Instead of considering care-giving 'as good in-and-of-itself', we recognize care-giving as only instrumentally good. The merit of seeing care-giving as an instrumental good is that it can be distributed by the market in societies which emphasize freedom and individual responsibility, or reallocated by the state in societies which emphasize equity and collective responsibility. The drawback is that increasingly care has come to be seen less as a moral good, and is more and more regarded as degrading compensatory support for functional deficiencies associated with the 'undignified' human dignity in old age and dependency.

This is of course not to denigrate the value or to deny the importance of autonomy as a central guiding concept in the provision of care. But the problem remains that we need a more adequate moral framework which can enable us (1) to re-cast both dependency and care-giving as a moral good in old age; (2) to re-conceptualize the nature of human need and the role of social obligation; and (3) to re-capture the basic human dignity of a person on the simple fact that she is a human being, apart from her capacity to conduct herself as an autonomous human person. It is this simple fact that she is a human being which confers on her a fundamental value that demands our most careful moral consideration, even in the total loss of self-consciousness, in the complete absence of reflective awareness, and in the gradual surrender of basic autonomy. And yet, it is the nature of this basic human value which a doctrine of personal autonomy is unable to capture.

In the rest of this chapter, I want to examine how insights of the Chinese Confucian moral tradition may contribute to a different perspective on the paradox of long-term care, through re-casting the relationship between dependency and care-giving, re-conceiving the nature of human need and the role of social obligation, and recapturing the basic dignity of a person who has fundamental human value. The case of Hong Kong will be discussed to throw light on how the Confucian moral tradition has shaped care-giving to elderly persons in a Chinese society which, despite its highly cosmopolitan outlook and advanced development, seems determined to continue holding onto its traditional values in the care of the elderly. The case of Hong Kong is intriguing because it provides a sharp and interesting contrast with its Western counterparts on the one hand, and because it can throw light on the moral force of traditional cultures on social policy on the other.

Confucian account of human dignity and moral autonomy

The importance of the ideal of human dignity for the Chinese can be traced to the influence of Confucian moral philosophy which is focused on two central questions: (1) how are humans to be distinguished from animals? and (2) what is the ideal human way of life to achieve humanity? Confucius began with the initial premise that humans are distinguishable from animals because only humans have morality. Therefore to live a life distinguishable from that of a beast and befitting a human being is to follow morality. For Confucius, the ultimate point of life is not rationality or autonomy, but the realization of humanity, or human dignity by following morality. Confucius offered three arguments to support his claim that human beings have dignity which marks them off from animals or brutes. These arguments also explain the source of human dignity and its relationship to morality.

First, the Confucian account argues that the source of human dignity lies in the moral nature of human beings. It is this moral nature defined in terms of the capacity to follow morality in human relationships which distinguishes humans from animals. More importantly also, humans are self-conscious of their moral nature which Mencius, an important Confucian scholar, explained in this way: 'Slight is the difference between man and brutes. The common person loses this distinguishing feature, while the gentleman (moral person) retains it. Shun (ancient sage king) understood the ways of things and had a keen insight into human relationships. He followed the path of morality.' (Mencius, 1970, 4B: 19).

It is this self-awareness of, and a keen insight into, a human's potential capacity for making human relationships and for following the requirement of morality in the conduct of human relationships which distinguishes humans from beasts. The way to realize our humanity is to pursue morality in relating to our fellow human beings. Through cultivation of our moral nature, we learn to exhibit perfect human relations and thereby realize our humanity. Such cultivation is possible because, according to the Confucian thesis, we are all born with the same moral nature, the same potential for virtue, which is equally possessed by all. As the Master said: 'Heaven is the author of the virtue that is in me' (Confucius, 1979, 7: 23). (The word 'Heaven' or '*Tien*' in Chinese is just another name for the natural order, it has no anthropomorphic character.) This is the source of the intrinsic value of human beings which marks humans off from animals and brutes. Because of this common humanity, human beings deserve equal respect.

Second, according to Mencius, not only are ordinary human beings also capable of becoming sages, they are fundamentally like the sages. They are all born with the four 'seeds' (potentials) of humanity like the four limbs they possess at birth. In practice, of course, they all turn out differently in their achievements and development. The four seeds are the seeds of 'benevolence', 'righteousness', 'propriety' and 'wisdom' (Mencius, 1970, 2A: 6). Humans have the obligation to develop and realize their potentials through following virtues in their interactions and relationships with one another. Virtuous actions are actions guided by rules, rites, rituals or norms which enable us to recognize and express our mutual respect for the basic dignity that is inherent in each of us as members of the community of humanity.

Third, according to the Confucian moral thesis, not only are human relationships essential to our realization of our humanity, but family relationships, in particular, are especially important since it is within family relationships that we first learn about our humanity, recognize our dignity and develop our morality. Natural relationships within a family are the roots of morality. In particular, it is the parent–child relationship which can best enable us to gain insight into our own humanity as well as the concomitant moral requirement to treat human beings with due respect for their basic dignity. Mencius explained our self-consciousness of the moral requirement to treat with due respect the dignity in human beings in this way:

> Presumably there must have been cases in ancient times of people not burying their parents. When the parents died, they were thrown in the gullies. Then one day the sons passed the place and there lay the bodies, eaten by foxes and sucked by flies. A sweat broke out on their brows, and they could not bear to look. The sweating was not put on for others to see. *It was an outward expression of their innermost heart* (my italics). They went home for baskets and spades. If it was truly right for them to bury the remains of their parents, then it must also be right for all dutiful sons and men of humanity to do likewise. (Mencius, 1970, 3A: 5)

Mencius' story explains the genesis of the burying rites. It shows that these rites are grounded in our recognition that there is a morally right way, and a morally wrong way, of treating human beings, including even those who are dead and no longer living, which do matter to us as members of a common community. Human beings have dignity which requires us to treat them in a certain way in response to their dignity. Humans are also capable of having awareness as well as self-consciousness of the basic dignity which is inherent in humans qua humans. The moment of self-awareness is also a moment of self-consciousness of our common humanity and shared basic human dignity. It brings awareness of a moral obligation to respond with respect to basic human dignity. Such a moral obligation is self-imposed, uncoerced, unconditional and non-contractual in nature. The source of morality is internal rather than external. Morality is possible because of this self-awareness of human dignity. Human dignity on this understanding is grounded in the potential capacity of the human being for making self-imposed moral demands on himself or herself. Burying the dead where they are found unburied is today widely accepted as a common human obligation which applies even to strangers and unrelated others.

The Confucian account of human dignity emphasizes that we first learn how to treat others with respect in family relationships, especially in the parent–child relationship. Although there is a similar emphasis on human dignity in the moral philosophy of Immanuel Kant, the Confucian project stresses the role of the family and human relationships in supporting dignity and in cultivating humanity. Thus Confucius argued that a filial son or daughter has a moral duty not only just to satisfy the parents' physical needs by serving them with fine food, clothes, and shelter, but more importantly to care for the parents with a genuine respect: 'Nowadays for a man to be filial means no more than that he is able to provide his parents with food. Even dogs and horses are, in some way, provided with food. If a man shows no reverence, where is the difference?' (Confucius, 1979, 2: 7).

A genuine respect for one's parents is the key moral requirement of the parent–child relationship. But reverence or respect is due not only merely to one's parents or family members, but we are also urged to extend our reverence, our concern and respect to elderly parents other than our own. We must also learn to extend it to establish relations with others with whom we interact, until it becomes a way of life, a disposition. The ideal achievement, which Confucius expressed in this way, is that: 'while at home hold yourself in respectful attitude; when serving in an official capacity be reverent; when dealing with others give of your best' (Confucius, 1979, 13: 19).

It is therefore no surprise that Hong Kong social policy on long-term care emphasizes as the single overarching objective of care the promotion of human dignity. The mission, as stated earlier, is 'to enable elderly people to live in *dignity*' which is further defined in terms of a sense of *belonging*, a sense of *security* and a sense of *worthiness* (Hong Kong Special Administrative Region Government, 2002a: 1, emphasis added). With this understanding of dignity as the ideal of social policy for long-term care, rationality and autonomy have intrinsic value to the extent to which they contribute to constituting elements of human dignity. Such an emphasis provides a sharp contrast to the UK 1999 Report produced by the Royal Commission *With Respect to Old Age: Long Term Care – Rights and Responsibilities* which endorses 'independence as opposed to dependence' to be the overriding policy aim, and the promotion of 'maximum choice and dignity and independence' as the important goals of long-term care policy (The Royal Commission, 1999, ch. 4, p. 12, para. 2). Thus in the UK, 'dignity' is regarded as only one among three important values in long-term care, whereas in Hong Kong, dignity is the central, overriding value for the provision of care. The priority given to dignity implies a vision that needing care and holding onto a sense of dignity are now compatible with old age and dependency for human beings.

The enhancement of human dignity is an ideal of social policy in general, and of long-term care, in particular. In order to achieve one's humanity, or to live not as a mere animal among others, it is important to have self-awareness and to engage in interactions which respect our basic humanity.

Confucian account of dependency and care-giving as a moral good

In 1930, the renowned Chinese scholar Lin Yutang wrote that the contrast between the Chinese and Western family systems' treatment of the elderly was a major explanation for a general desire among the Chinese to grow old and to appear old because of 'the premium generally placed upon old age' (Lin Yutang, 1931 [1999]: 48–9). Young adults had a strong sense of obligation to care for their old parents. This was 'expressly defended on the sole ground of gratitude' for the many sacrifices their parents made for them when they were young. Such an attitude, he argued, was in sharp contrast to the emphasis on individualistic values in many other societies, which explained their emphasis on independence and their shame of being dependent on their children. According to Lin, the Chinese 'conception of life is based upon mutual help within the home; hence there is no shame attached to the circumstance of one's being served by his children in the sunset of one's life' (ibid.). Lin further pointed out that 'Rather it is considered good luck to have children who can take care of one' (ibid.). To what extent are Lin's observations still true today?

In the recently released *2001 Population Census Thematic Report – Older Persons* published by the Hong Kong Census and Statistics Department (Hong Kong Special Administrative Region Government, 2002c: 15), there were in 2001, 747 052 elderly persons (defined as those aged 65 and above) in Hong Kong which made up 11 per cent of the population. It was further reported that (ibid.: 45) among those living in domestic households, 487 319 (71.8 per cent) were living with non-elderly members, while 191 778 (28.2 per cent) were exclusively elderly person households. The total proportion of older persons living with their children was 56.8 per cent in 2001 while in 1991 it was 57.2 per cent. Statistics also show that the higher the age group of older persons, the higher the proportion of elderly persons living with child(ren) or living with other persons. Even for those who were 85 years old and above, 29.9 per cent of them were living with child(ren) alone, and 8.3 per cent were living with spouse and child(ren). Only 10.8 per cent of Hong Kong's elderly persons were living alone. Another 9.1 per cent were living in non-domestic households (which include old people's homes, hospitals, and penal institutions). These statistics regarding the living arrangements of the elderly population in Hong Kong indicate that family support of the elderly is still strong, and has remained quite stable over the past ten years, in spite of rapid societal changes.

In an even more recent report *Thematic Household Survey Report No. 11*, also published by the Hong Kong Census and Statistic Department (Hong Kong Special Administrative Region Government, 2003), one finds another interesting set of data on patterns of parent support in Hong Kong. According to the report (ibid.: 6–8), some 1 678 100 persons aged 15 and over had supported their parents' living in the past twelve months (that is in the year 2001), over half (57.6 per cent) were living with two dependent parents while 38.9 per cent were living with one dependent parent. Another 3.5 per cent were living with three and more dependent parents. The percentage of persons who had supported their parents' living was higher for males (34.8 per cent) than their female counterparts (25.6 per cent). For those persons who had supported the living of their parents whom they lived with, the median annual expenditure for supporting the dependent parents was HK$2500, whereas for those who had supported the living of their parents living apart, the median annual expenditure was HK$3000. Those in the age groups 20–29 and 30–39 had the highest proportion among those who had supported the living of dependent parents during the past 12 months, exceeding half of the population in these two age groups. There are some 1 117 000 dependent parents at the time of enumeration. But unlike Singapore, Taiwan, or even Mainland China, Hong Kong does not have laws which require adult children to be responsible for providing support and maintenance to their aged parents. In other words, the support provided by adult children to their parents in Hong Kong is done on an entirely voluntary basis.

It is indeed true that among the many relationships within the family, the Chinese philosophical discourse has focused most on the one between parents and children. Chinese Confucianism, in particular, is emphatic on the moral obligation of children towards parents, and particularly on grown children's obligation towards their aged parents. In contrast to many Western philosophers, filial obligation is not regarded as a moral obligation.

For example, to the question 'What do grown children owe their parents?' 'Nothing' is the reply given by the contemporary American philosopher Jane English (1979: 351). Her arguments are based upon the principles of 'consent' and 'voluntariness' (ibid.: 352–6). In her view, adult children do not have any moral obligations to support their elderly parents because what parents have done for their children are voluntary sacrifices, not favours, since children never requested what had been done for them by their parents. According to this view, a 'favour' done for one is based on one's request (consent), while a voluntary sacrifice made for one is not based on one's request. Such sacrifices create friendship between parents and children for voluntary assistance from each other, not a moral obligation on children to reciprocate care of their parents. They are not duties resulting from debts nor are they things owed in repayment. English's view was echoed by Norman Daniels (1988: 29), another contemporary American philosopher who argued that the parental obligation of caring for their young children is a self-imposed duty while children's obligation of caring for their parents is not self-imposed and thus cannot be morally required.

For the seventeenth-century British philosopher, John Locke, who recognized that grown children do have a moral obligation to their parents, the obligation was grounded in a notion of exchange or repayment of debt for past services. The parent–child relationship is understood as an exchange relationship. It exists for mutual gain and benefit for parents and children. They take turns in the relationship to be duty-bearers and service beneficiaries. In Locke's view, the son's honouring the father is a payment or reward for 'the care, cost and kindness in his education' provided by the father (1690 [1999]: 266). Therefore the degree of what is required of the obligation owed by the son to the father is determined by the past trouble and expense employed by the father upon his son. The parent–child relationship is a means of fulfilling individual needs during different life stages and to support individual development to attain full independence and freedom which are the highest liberal values.

It is therefore not surprising that caring for one's elderly parents in some societies is not culturally affirmed in the same way in which wanting and raising one's own children are. There is, in fact, in some of them no societal ethos concerning the obligations adult children have to their elderly parents. Because of this dearth of cultural discussion and public affirmation, or lack of societal endorsement, there also appears to be reluctance in society to embrace and value the role of 'caring' for one's parents as normative. 'Care' is therefore not a 'good' that one looks forward to in old age. Receiving care is not a status which confers high self-esteem. Needing care brings fear of loss of dignity and diminished identity.

In contrast, family support for the elderly has age-old cultural roots in China. This traditional culture provides the basis for the time-honoured 'feedback' mode of family support for the elderly in China. Under this cultural norm, the first generation of the family rears a second generation, which then supports the first generation in their old age and at the same time rears a third generation. Each successive generation thus 'feeds back' to the preceding generation and supports a new generation (Fei, 1996: 50–51). In contrast, it is argued that, under the influence of liberal values, Western cultural traditions generally support 'linear' family practices in which one generation rears another without receiving feedback in old age.

This cultural norm of the 'feedback' mode of family support is grounded in the Confucian notion of reciprocity whereby the moral obligation to care is understood as a two-way street rather than a one-way duty. The moral force of filial piety is not justified as an exchange or repayment to parents for past services, or the gift of life. Filial piety is valued as the reciprocation of 'good' for 'good': the son's or daughter's care and affection is a reciprocation of the parents' care and affection. It is within the parent–child relationship that a human agent learns to develop her benevolent nature and eventually comes to acquire a disposition for trust and reciprocity in social relationships.

In this sense, Confucian reciprocity is different from trading, or conscious exchange of goods and services. It involves, on the one hand, giving without consideration of return or obligation. On the other hand, it involves a straight moral obligation on the part of the recipient 'to return good for good'. It is what Becker refers to as a 'recipient good' (1986: 3). Such a notion of reciprocity is expressed in the often-cited Chinese proverbs: 'An earlier generation plants trees under whose shade later generations find shelter and rest'; and 'While you drink the water, you must not forget those who dug the well for you'. Under the Confucian system of ethics, the moral basis of reciprocity is not contract or utility, but our interconnectedness and interdependence. Importantly, such a notion of reciprocity can enable us to recognize our non-voluntary obligations – the obligations we acquire in the course of social life but acquire without regard to our invitation, consent or acceptance. Adult children always have a moral obligation for the welfare of their parents since their parents first showed benevolence towards them. The desire to care for and nurture his or her parent *as* parent is the adult child's own personal 'return' to the parent. Such a return is not specified in the way a car loan repayment is. Inability to return care to one's parents is one of life's greatest regrets. As pointed out by Lin Yutang, the greatest regret a Chinese person could have was the eternally lost opportunity of serving his/her old parents. This regret was expressed in two lines by a man who returned home too late only to find out his parents had already passed away: 'The tree desires repose, but the wind will not stop; the son desires to serve, but his parents are already gone' (Sommers and Sommers, 1993: 753).

The Confucian tradition of filial piety offers insight on a well-balanced reciprocity of dependency. It places a positive value on the dependency relationship and on the reciprocity of care between generations. The dependency of an aged parent upon his/her children is part of a reciprocal chain. It is a kind of long-cycled give-and-take which is supported by a collective memory in the form of the moral value of filial piety. Mutual interdependence is recognized as a phenomenological feature of human existence. Shifting the focus from autonomy to dignity enables us to focus upon the common dignity, which we share, rather than upon the relative autonomy and personal independence we have lost at a particular life stage.

Confucian account of human need and role of social provision

In the 1990s, Keith et al. conducted a number of studies in the three communities of Swarthmore (an affluent community in the mid-west, USA), Momence (a suburban community in Pennsylvania, USA), and Hong Kong to compare how successful ageing is perceived in these three communities. Their findings show that physical status – health and functionality – is an important reason that an older person is seen as doing well or poorly, whether in Hong Kong, or in Pennsylvania, or in the mid-west of the USA. But the relative significance given to physical status by the people in the two US communities is greater than in Hong Kong. This raises interesting questions about what is seen as more important in Hong Kong, and about why physical status is given such similar priority.

According to Keith et al., in Hong Kong, ill health is menacing in part because it threatens the ability to work. In the more affluent community of Swarthmore, ill health was dreaded because it threatened, not livelihood, but independence, hence, their fear of ill health and concomitant dependence. Furthermore, they pointed out that the many attributes people use to evaluate functionality in the United States included a cluster of abilities labelled as 'self-sufficiency', central to which was the ability to live alone. By contrast, in Hong Kong, people did not even see the sense of evaluating this ability: 'Why would anyone want to live alone?'. Moreover, in Hong Kong, people were far more likely to identify dependence, rather than independence, as a reason why an older person was doing well (Keith et al., 1990: 256). According to Keith et al., what they meant was that their dependency needs – financial, psychological and physical – were being met through the efforts of others, primarily members of their family.

Over half of the sample in Momence identified poor physical status as a reason that an older person is doing poorly. For the residents of Hong Kong, it was reported that 'personal characteristics' rather than physical status is the category of explanation used much more as the important reason for doing well or poorly in old age. A large proportion of the Chinese answers in this category refer to characteristics such as 'tolerant', 'easy-going', and 'not a nag' (ibid.). It was argued that this contrast in perspective implies a different emphasis on reasons for doing well in old age, as well as a different evaluation of dependency and independence in old age. The American perspective emphasizes the availability of the pre-conditions for self-sufficiency as an important indicator of well-being in old age, and these include self-sufficiency in meeting basic needs, independence in daily activities, and autonomy in decision making. The Hong Kong Chinese perspective emphasizes the cultivation of the personal characteristics of the elderly person, not being a burden, being considerate, and helpful.

According to Keith et al., in the United States family is less frequently described as a reason for problems in later life. The Chinese people talked more about family relations as reasons some old people were doing well in old age than older people themselves did. These differences have important effects on attitudes about needing care. In the two American communities, the old are concerned that they do *not* become dependent; the Chinese hope to raise proper children who *will* take care of them (ibid., p. 260).

A more recent study was conducted by the author and three other team members to investigate the Chinese cultural interpretation of human need and welfare choices in Hong Kong society. The study was based on focus group meetings and individual in-depth interviews through home visits paid to 100 randomly selected respondents living in a low-income, high-density area in Hong Kong in 1998 (Tao et al., 1996). The findings of the study show that there is no single unitary discourse on human need in Hong Kong society. There is a mix of vocabularies, expressions and languages in Hong Kong Chinese people's discussion on human need and welfare choices. And yet, notwithstanding these divergences, there is sufficient coherence of views which emerged from the divergent discourses to indicate some broadly shared conceptions of basic human needs and some common self-understanding among the local people in Hong Kong society. The basic needs which they name and which they define tend to converge around two main categories of needs: survival and identity. Survival needs include health and subsistence which are central to the biological life of a human agent. Identity needs include self-esteem and autonomy on the one hand, and care and relationship on the other. Identity needs are central to the biographical life of a human agent. There is no doubt that self-esteem and autonomy are considered basic human needs, but care and relationship are equally regarded by many respondents to be foundational which one of them explained in this way: 'Just institutions and mutual caring should be complementary, but mutual caring is more important, solidarity is strength, without commitment and participation, institutions are doomed to collapse' (Tao et al., 1996, Tape 143 TXT, Text Units 117–117, 1996).

In a separate but related Chinese values study conducted in three major Chinese cities, Hong Kong, Taipei and Beijing, between 2000 to 2001, 20 focus group meetings were organized in each of the three cities, to collect views and data from a total of 300 subjects (Chan et al., 2002; 2001). The findings also suggest that the Chinese in these three cities in general share a common core of values which are reflected in their conceptions of basic human needs, the provision of social care, the importance of meritocracy and the role of collective action. In terms of basic human needs, self-esteem is rated most highly, followed closely by mutual care, autonomy, personal freedom and family relations which were identified by the respondents as the most important human need in all three sites.

Findings in these studies also show that notwithstanding the emphasis on taking respectful care of the elderly people in Hong Kong society, the role of the state in the provision of care for the elderly, including long-term care, is supportive and supplementary only. In contrast to the UK where it was acknowledged, for example, in the 1999 Report of the Royal Commission on long-term care reform that 'Responsibility for provision now and in the future should be shared between the state and the individuals' (The Royal Commission, 1999: 1), the Hong Kong Government's policy is a 'family-based' elderly care policy. The Working Group on the Care of the Elderly, in announcing its proposal for reform, has further reaffirmed the decision to adopt the concept of 'the dignity of elderly persons' as the guiding principle but stresses at the same time that the government should continue to emphasize the present policy on elderly services which is to encourage caring for the elderly by family members within a family context and to strengthen support for care-givers (Hong Kong SAR Government, 2002a: 1). In terms of the division of responsibility, it calls for cooperation among three main policy actors, namely the state, the family and the individual. But it is very clear that the primary role of the state is to 'enable families to continue to assume the role of carers' (p. 10). The justification is that 'families should, as far as possible, reciprocate the love of their parents and care for them in their familiar environment when they grow old' (ibid.).

Earlier the Secretary for Health and Welfare also stated in the 2001 Report on Care for Elders Policy Objective and Key Result Areas that:

> Ensuring financial security for elders remains our fundamental policy. Hong Kong is fortunate in the sense that the family has always been the main source of financial and other support for the majority of our elders. We will continue to treasure and reinforce this traditional value. For those elders who lack means and family and other support, we will continue to provide the necessary financial and other assistance to meet their needs (Hong Kong SAR Government, 2001, http://www.info.gov.hk/hwb 'Message').

In reality, evidence of parental support by adult children in Hong Kong and the high proportion of elderly parents living with their adult children's family seem to confirm that the government's appeals for family support are not merely empty words.

It is, of course, important not to over-idealize the family traditional values. It has also been argued that elderly people's attitude towards family relationships and living arrangements are much more complex and dynamic than those usually conceived by traditional policy research (Chan and Lee Kin-ching, 1999). We should be open to the idea that many elderly people today may be more ready to accept independent living and no longer regard it as a kind of reluctant choice. It seems that more and more elderly people may be considering independent living for its intrinsic value to them. For this reason 'dependent living with the younger generation should not be taken for granted as the "best" choice for elderly lives, except when it is physically not feasible' (ibid:1). It is important to bear in mind that old people change with society, and hence the need to provide options for choice if we are serious about responding to basic human dignity. In fact, the elderly in Hong Kong are facing a dwindling network of community care, in which they have less accessibility to informal support provided by close relatives and friends. As a consequence, the elderly are more likely to be left on their own, or they can be left with little choice other than returning to their frustrated and stressful younger generation for family care. The 1994 Review on Care for the Elderly (Hong Kong Government, 1994) admitted that Hong Kong lacks sufficient home help services, community nursing care and residential care. It also admitted that 'the concept of care in the community or care in the family cannot be put into practical use without the provision of service support for the carers. Without such support, the victims of old age will be further victimized' (ibid.: x).

Another cautionary note about overemphasizing the ideal of the traditional family is that while the norm of long-cycled reciprocity seems to be still at work, yet it is also true that the sense of fulfilment at the final phase of the cycle does not always seem translatable into an anticipation of return from the younger generation. As has been pointed out in many studies, cultural, structural, economic and demographic changes have attenuated the binding force of long-cycled reciprocity which would ensure the aged parents the support and care of the filial generation. We are often reminded that 'more and more aged parents, while remaining "filiocentric" as far as their expressions of fulfillment are concerned, are muted as to their expectations for dependency upon their children' (Lebra, 1979: 351) It is also important to note that suicide rates among the elderly people of Hong Kong are among the highest in the world. In the 15 years from 1981 to 1995, the crude elderly suicide rate had remained quite stable and was reported to be 31.1 per 100 000, with the majority of the elderly suicide victims being also patients who suffered from chronic illness (Hong Kong Special Administrative Region Government, 2002b: 17).

Taking care of the aged generation has always been a social problem for civilized societies. The question is therefore not whether the elderly should be taken care of, but who should take care of them. If Daniels and English were right in saying that adult children do not have any more of a moral obligation to take care of their aged parents than any stranger on the street, or that such an obligation only has a voluntary basis, then most likely either the burden of care would be on the whole society, or the elderly who are disadvantaged would suffer. From a Confucian point of view, the family (interpreted in the broadest sense), as a natural institution, should play a mediating role between individuals and society.

In this regard, Confucian thinking may be an important source of conceptual resources that can be employed to 'see' interdependence and to prove useful for reassessing our approach to social policy. Its philosophical insights prompt us to search for answers in social policy oriented towards supporting reciprocity and creating mutual trust among actors, building individual and social identity, achieving personal security and sustaining interdependency. From this perspective, inclusion of the family in care provision need not mean the shifting of the burden from the state to the family; it could also be conceived as a shift from subsidizing the individuals as a separate entity to supporting the family as a whole.

Reframing care: Confucian ethics of human dignity and long-term care

The Confucian ethical account identifies the capacity to care and respect for others as the defining characteristics of our humanity. The giving and receiving of care are ongoing affirmations of our shared basic dignity and common humanity. Human dignity requires care and that is why care is a moral good. Human dignity should therefore be the moral framework for guiding and constraining care, in the contexts of both public and family care, especially during old age and extreme dependency.

For this reason, care should not be treated solely as an instrumental good, the responsibility for which is to be shared by the state and individuals. Confucian moral tradition emphasizes the positive value of family care which is defined as a process of reciprocation of 'good' between generations under the virtue of reciprocity. Emphasis on the virtue of reciprocity blurs the boundary between public care and family care, and diffuses the sharp division between the roles of care-giver and care-receiver in a reciprocal chain of care. Family care is essential for supporting identity and sustaining belonging while public care is often needed to enhance functional capacities and to improve material well-being in order to achieve 'holistic care' in old age and dependency. Caring is therefore the joint responsibility of the family, the individual and the state, although the family is always the primary carer in society. The Confucian ethical account supports a 'family-based' approach to long-term care which integrates family care with public care. It can be used to argue for a well-balanced reciprocity of dependency as the goal of social policy under the framework of holistic care.

The moral disposition of a community for care and reciprocity is just as important as the contestation of rights and autonomy in shaping the development of social policy. It can help us move out of the trap of increasing privatization of need, individualization of interest, and marketization of care. The family-based model, mediating between the state and the individual, has the promise of creating a more responsive social and economic long-term care infrastructure which can better integrate self-reliance, communal support and intergenerational reciprocity.

Human beings, in the Confucian account, possess basic dignity simply by virtue of their humanity. Importantly, such a perspective allows us to continue to care even in the face of total loss of self-consciousness and complete absence of reflective awareness. In a community that values mutual interdependence more highly, independence is not the only way in which the value of personal dignity might be expressed. An individual's sense of personal dignity could well be tied more closely to the mutual care and concern community members demonstrate to one another. Whereas an ethic of autonomy places a supreme value on choice and personal freedom, an ethic of dignity recognizes and values our mutual interdependence. Moreover, an ethic of dignity requires that each autonomous citizen assumes some paternalistic responsibilities to protect and enhance the dignity of others who may never have the capacity, are not yet capable, or who are no longer able, to care for themselves (Pullman, 1999: 41). For the Hong Kong community, providing security, promoting belonging and affirming worthiness are more important goals of long-term care than expanding choice, promoting autonomy and enhancing self-determination. Providing security, promoting belonging and affirming worthiness are essential for sustaining connectedness and membership in the human community – the source of our basic dignity. Human dignity is a basic respect required from each human being towards every other human being as a condition of basic common humanity. It is a communal value. In contrast, autonomy, choice, self-determination are individualist values. Under a Confucian ethic of human dignity, even as that autonomous, dignified self is fading further and further from our view, we continue to respond to the basic dignity we share with our elderly member in our long-term care policy through providing security, promoting belonging and affirming worthiness.

Acknowledgements

The research from which this chapter is derived was supported by City University RCPM Project 017 (2002), City University Strategic Research Grant Project 7000982 (2001), and Research Grant Council Competitive Earmarked Research Grant Project 9040246 (1996). Acknowledgement is also extended to the Governance in Asia Research Centre for funding our fieldwork in Taiwan. These projects have generated valuable findings on the Confucian moral concepts of reciprocity, obligations and needs. Valuable insights were also gained on how they have shaped the discourses of justice and welfare in providing the moral foundations of social policy among different contemporary Chinese communities. I am very grateful for these grants and the research which have led to the publication of several original papers on this subject matter.

References

Agich, George J. (1993), *Autonomy and Long-term Care*, New York: Oxford University Press.

Becker, Lawrence (1986), *Reciprocity*, London: Routledge & Kegan Paul.

Callahan, Daniel (1984), 'Autonomy: a moral good, not a moral obsession', *The Hastings Centre Report*, **14**(5), 40–42.

Chan, Kam-wah and James Lee Kin-ching (1999), 'Autonomy or dependence: housing the elderly in Hong Kong', Occasional Paper Series No. 9, May 1999, The Polytechnic University of Hong Kong.

Confucius: (1979), *The Analects*, D.C. Lau (trans.), London: Penguin.

Daniels, Norman (1988), *Am I My Parents' Keeper?* Oxford: Oxford University Press.

Doyal, Len and Ian Gough (1991), *A Theory of Human Need*, London: Macmillan.

English, Jane (1979), 'What do grown children owe their parents?', in Onora O'Neill and William Ruddick (eds), *Having Children: Philosophical and Legal Reflections on Parenthood*, New York: Oxford University Press, pp. 351–6.

Fei, Xiaotung (1996), 'Shehui diaocha zhibai' (Self-reflection on a social survey), in *Xueshu zhishu yu fansi* (*A Probe into Sociology*), Beijing: Sandian shudian, pp. 1–84.

Kant, Immanuel (trans. 1959), *Foundations of the Metaphysics of Morals*, L.W. Beck (trans.) Indianapolis: The Bobbs-Merrill Company, Inc.

Keith, Jennie, Christine L. Fry and Charlotte Ikels (1990), 'Community as context for successful aging', in Jay Sokolovsky (ed.), *The Cultural Context of Aging: Worldwide Perspectives*, New York: Bergin & Garvey Publishers, pp. 245–61.

Lebra, Takie Sugiyama (1979), 'Lemma and strategies of aging among contemporary Japanese women', *Ethnology*, vol. 18, 337–53.

Lin Yutang (1931), 'On growing old in China', in Laurence Houlgate (ed.) (1999), *Morals, Marriage and Parenthood: An Introduction to Family Ethics*, Belmont, CA: Wadsworth Publishing Company, pp. 47–50.

Locke, John (1690), 'The perpetual obligation to honour one's parents', in Laurence Houlgate (ed.) (1999), *Morals, Marriage and Parenthood: An Introduction to Family Ethics*, Belmont, CA: Wadsworth Publishing Company, pp. 266–7.

Mencius (1970), *Mencius*, D.C. Lau (trans.), New York: Penguin.

Mill, John Stuart (1972), 'On liberty', in *Three Essays*, Oxford: Oxford University Press.

Pullman, Daryl (1999), 'The ethics of autonomy and dignity in long-term care', *Canadian Journal on Aging*, **18** (1), 26–45.

Sommers, C. and F. Sommers (eds) (1993), *Vice and Virtue in Everyday Life*, Fort Worth, TX: Harcourt.

Tronto, Joan (1993), *Moral Boundaries*, London: Routledge.

White, Julie Anne (2000), *Democracy, Justice, and the Welfare State: Reconstructing Public Care*, Pennsylvania: The Pennsylvania State University Press.

Official Documents, Government Reports and Research Projects

Chan, Ho-mun, Julia Tao and Anthony Fung (2001), Project No.7000982, 'An Investigation on the Chinese Conception of Social Justice', Strategic Research Grant, City University of Hong Kong, 2001, with Chan Ho-mun as PI and Julia Tao, Anthony Fung as CI.

Chan, Ho-mun, Anthony Fung and Julia Tao (2002), Project Number RCPM 017, 'An Investigation into the Conception of Social Justice in Taiwan – A Comparative Study', with Chan Ho-mun as PI, and Anthony Fung, Julia Tao as CI.

Hong Kong Government (1994), Report of the Working Group on Care for the Elderly, August.

Hong Kong Special Administrative Region Government (1997–99), Report of the Elderly Commission, 1997–1999, http://www.hwfb.gov.hk/ch/committees/ec.htm.

Hong Kong Special Administrative Region Government (2001), Care for Elders – Policy Objective and Key Result Areas in *Policy Address 2001*, Health and Welfare Bureau.

Hong Kong Special Administrative Region Government (2002a), Social Welfare Department Report on Services for the Elderly.

Hong Kong Special Administrative Region Government (2002b), A Multi-disciplinary Study on the Causes of Elderly Suicide in Hong Kong, Elderly Commission.

Hong Kong Special Administrative Region Government (2002c), Thematic Report – Older Persons *Population Census 2001*, Census and Statistics Department, November.

Hong Kong Special Administrative Region Government (2003), Thematic Household Survey Report No.11, Census and Statistics Department, January.

The Royal Commission on Reform of Long-term Care, UK (1999), *With Respect to Old Age: Long Term Care – Rights and Responsibilities*, March, http://www.archive.official-documents.co.uk/document/cm41/4192/4192–gls.htm.

Tao, Julia, G. Drover, K. Chau and C.K. Wong (1996), RGC Competitive Earmarked Research Grant (CERG) Project 9040246, 'Needs and Welfare Choices in Hong Kong', with Julia Tao as PI and G. Drover, K. Chau and C.K. Wong as CI.

PART III

COMPARING AND CATEGORIZING SOCIAL POLICY, PROVISION AND REDISTRIBUTION

9 Robin Hood, St Matthew, or simple egalitarianism? Strategies of equality in welfare states

Walter Korpi and Joakim Palme

How should welfare states be organized in order to decrease inequality and poverty among citizens? In the long debates on this question in Western societies we find at least three types of answers. One recommendation is to follow the Robin Hood principle: take from the rich and give to the poor. A second alternative can be traced back at least to the gospel of St Matthew: to those that have shall be given, that is more to the rich than to the poor. A third proposal is a compromise between the noble robber and the apostle: give equally much to the poor as to the rich.

The above action alternatives in social policy embody what the British historian R.T. Tawney (1952) once called 'strategies of equality'. These strategies bring to the fore at least two different issues. One is whether social policies should be targeted or universal, that is, whether they should be organized for the poor only, or whether the welfare state should include all citizens. The second concerns the level of benefits to be accorded via social insurance, that is, whether benefits should be equal for all or related to previous earnings and income. Solutions of the latter issue determine to what extent the 'middle classes' are included in the welfare state in a way which protects their accustomed living standards. Scholars as well as policy makers have long been and continue to be divided on these two issues.

Assuming negative effects on labour supply and savings, economists have typically been cool towards earnings-related social insurance and have regarded programmes targeted at the poor as the most efficient way of reducing poverty and inequality.[1] According to Goodin and Le Grand (1987), the failure of social policies to reduce inequality lies precisely in the inclusion of the middle classes in the welfare state. If the goal of social policy is limited to the reduction of poverty, then universal programmes also benefiting the non-poor are a waste of resources. However, if we want to reduce inequality between the poor and the non-poor, their verdict is even more severe. 'In egalitarian terms ... the beneficial involvement of the non-poor in the welfare state is not merely wasteful – it is actually counterproductive. The more the non-poor benefit, the less redistributive (or, hence, egalitarian) the impact of the welfare state will be' (Goodin and Le Grand 1987: 215). This statement echoes T.H. Marshall's famous lectures on 'Citizenship and social class', where he compared the equalizing or class-abating effects of social insurance schemes involving the total population, insurance schemes limited to lower income groups, and means-tested programmes. Marshall's conclusion was that 'a total scheme is less specifically classabating in a purely economic sense than a limited one, and social insurance is less so than a means-tested service' (Marshall, 1950: 55).

The assumption that social policies directed at the needy constitute the most efficient strategy for reducing poverty and inequality has however been called into question. Thus R.H. Tawney argued that what he referred to as 'the strategy of equality' in a society should involve 'the pooling of its surplus resources by means of taxation, and the use of the funds thus obtained to make accessible to all, irrespective of their income, occupation, or social position, the conditions of civilization which, in the absence of such measures, can be enjoyed only by the rich' (Tawney, 1952: 130). According to Tawney, social policy should thus not be directed to the poor alone but should include all citizens.

In an early critique of the stress on targeting in American policy debate, Korpi contrasted a marginal social policy model with minimum benefits targeted at the poor with an institutional model based on universal programmes intended to maintain normal or accustomed standards of living. He argued that while a targeted programme 'may have greater redistributive effects *per unit of money spent* than institutional types of programs', other factors are likely to make institutional programmes more redistributive (Korpi, 1980a: 304, italics in the original, also 1980b). This rather unexpected outcome was predicted as a consequence of the type of political coalition formation that different models of welfare state institutions tend to generate. Since the marginal types of social policy programmes are directed primarily at those below the poverty line, a rational base is not found for coalition formation between those above and those below the poverty line. The poverty line, in effect, splits the working class and tends to generate coalitions between the better-off workers and the middle class against the lower sections of the working class, something which can result in tax revolts and welfare-state backlash. In an institutional model of social policy, however, most households will directly benefit in one way or another. Therefore this model 'tends to encourage coalition formation between the working class and the middle class in support for continued welfare state policies. The poor need not stand alone' (Korpi, 1980a: 305). In a study of pensions, Palme (1990) observed that universalistic and earnings-related pension systems tend to produce a lower degree of inequality in the distribution of final income among the elderly than flat-rate ones. He concluded that '*there is a paradox here* in the sense that comparatively unequal public pensions might produce the most equal income distributions by crowding out even more unequal income sources' (Palme, 1990: 154, italics added). Åberg (1989) shows how the distributive profiles of welfare states combine with their size to generate redistribution.

Since the 1980s, many social scientists in Europe as well as in America have come to view the targeting of social policies at the poor with increasing criticism. But while the support for targeting has decreased among social scientists, among policy makers in the Western countries it has instead been increasing. Thus, for example, in outlining its approach to social policy reform, the Conservative British government declared that resources should be directed more effectively to the areas of greatest need. On the international scene, institutions such as the International Monetary Fund and the World Bank have stressed the need for targeted transfers.

As the above review indicates, Western policy makers are renewing the old stress on the targeting of social policies, and social scientists disagree on the best strategy for reducing poverty and inequality. While universalism has gradually become accepted in many scholarly quarters outside economics, the earnings-relatedness of social insurance benefits is still strongly questioned. Within the countries of the European Union, this questioning has been strengthened by increasing pressures to reduce budget deficits in the public sector. In this context comparative analyses looking at the consequences for inequality and poverty of different types of welfare states are of central relevance.

In this chapter we analyse the capacities of what Titmuss (1974) referred to as different models of social policy to reduce inequality and poverty in the capitalist democracies. The analysis is centred on the role of the institutional structures of welfare states in the redistributive process. These institutional structures are here seen as reflecting differences in the roles for markets and politics in distributive processes within countries and as embodying, in Tawney's terms, different strategies of equality. The shape of societal institutions has been assumed to be affected by the actions of different interest groups, but we can also expect that institutional structures are of significance for the ways in which citizens come to define their interests and preferences.[2] Welfare state institutions can thus be viewed as 'intervening variables' (cf. Lazarsfeld, 1962). On the one hand reflecting causal factors such as actions by coalitions of interest groups, and, on the other hand, they potentially have feedback effects on distributive processes via their role in the formation of interests, preferences and coalitions among citizens. It would therefore appear to be a fruitful hypothesis that, while the institutions of the welfare state are to an important extent shaped by different types of interest groups, once in place they tend to influence the long-term development of definitions of interests and thereby coalition formation among citizens. This, consequently, makes it likely that institutional structures will have significant effects on redistributive processes and on the reduction of inequality and poverty.

The empirical parts of the chapter are based on two relatively new data sets. One is the *Social Citizenship Indicator Programme (SCIP)* containing information on the development of social insurance programmes in 18 OECD countries.[3] These countries are Australia, Austria, Belgium, Canada, Denmark, Finland, France, Germany, Ireland, Italy, Japan, the Netherlands, New Zealand, Norway, Sweden, Switzerland, the United Kingdom and the United States.[4] The second data set is the *Luxembourg Income Study (LIS)*, which contains micro-data on income distribution in a number of countries.[5] These two data sets represent major advances in the opportunity for the comparative study of social policies and their effects.

An institutional typology of welfare states

Welfare state institutions in the industrialized countries demonstrate differences as well as family resemblances which are likely to be of relevance for their redistributive consequences. The several attempts that have been made to capture these similarities by creating typologies of welfare states have run into familiar problems. By specifying ideal types, we can hope to crystallize similarities between countries and to gain a better understanding of the background to variations among them. However, ideal types will never have a perfect fit with existing realities, and typologies may thus obscure actual variations between countries. The fruitfulness of typologies therefore depends on our ability to base them on variables which are of heuristic value for the understanding of the background to and consequences of variations between ideal types and on the extent to which empirically observed variation between types are greater than variation within types.

Welfare state typologies can be used for different purposes and can focus on variables related to causes, institutions and/or outcomes. The clearly most influential attempt to create a welfare state typology has been that of Esping-Andersen (1990).[6] He uses the concept of welfare state regimes to characterize and to describe the complex of relationships between the state, the labour market and the family. By underlining the multi-dimensional nature of welfare state variation, Esping-Andersen's typology is innovative and very fruitful and it has stimulated much research. His trifold clusters of welfare states are labelled according to the main ideological currents assumed to underlie them, that is the Conservative, Liberal and Social Democratic welfare state regimes.

Since Esping-Andersen's primary interest was to describe the contours of the relationships between states, labour markets and families, his typology is based on a broad set of indicators referring to outcomes as well as to institutions.[7]

Our interest is primarily analytical, to study on the one hand, the causal factors affecting the institutional aspects of the welfare state and, on the other, the effects of institutions on the formation of interests, preferences and identities as well as on the degree of poverty and inequality in a society. For these purposes it is fruitful to base a typology of welfare states on their institutional characteristics. The major social insurance programmes catering for citizens' most important needs during the life course constitute a key part of the welfare state.[8] The institutional structures of two such programmes, old age pensions and sickness cash benefits, are here taken as bases for a welfare state typology. These two programmes respond to basic features of the human condition – the certainty of ageing and the risk of illness. Unlike, for example, unemployment and work accident insurance where the relevant risks differ greatly between socio-economic categories, old age pensions and sickness insurance are thus important for all citizens and households. The fact that they also have a major economic weight makes it likely that they are of great relevance for the formation of interest groups.

As a basis for our typology, the institutional structures of old age pension and sickness insurance programmes are here classified with primary reference to three aspects (Table 9.1). The first one is of relevance for the issue of targeting versus universalism. It refers to the definition of *eligibility for benefits* and involves four qualitatively different criteria reflecting whether eligibility is based on need determined via a means test, on contributions (by the insured or the employers) to the financing of the social insurance programme, on belonging to a specified occupational category, or on citizenship (residence) in the country.[9] These four criteria for eligibility to entitlements have been used in different combinations in different countries. The second aspect concerns the issue of to what extent social insurance benefits should replace lost income. It thus refers to the principles used for determining *benefit levels* and can be seen as a continuous variable, going from means-tested minimum benefits, to flat-rate benefits giving equally to everyone, and to benefits which in different degrees are related to previous earnings. The third aspect is a qualitative one, referring to the *forms for governing a social insurance programme* and receiving its significance via its combination with the previous two aspects. Here we create a dichotomy based on whether or not representatives of employers and employees participate in the governing of a programme.

On the bases of the above aspects of social insurance programmes we can delineate five different ideal types of institutional structures. In a rough chronological order according to their historical appearance in the Western countries, these ideal institutional types can be characterized as the *targeted, voluntary state subsidized, state corporatist, basic security,* and *encompassing models*. In Figure 9.1, we have attempted to characterize the ideal-typical

Table 9.1   Ideal-typical models of social insurance institutions

Model	Bases of entitlement	Benefit principle	Employer–Employee cooperation in programme governance
Targeted	Proved need	Minimum	No
Voluntary	Membership	Flat rate or earnings-related	No
State Subisdized	Contributions		
Corporatist	Occupational category *and* labour force participation	Earnings-related	Yes
Basic Security	Citizenship *or* contributions	Flat rate	No
Encompassing	Citizenship *and* labour force participation	Flat rate and earnings-related	No

features of these institutional structures. In this diagram the diamond-shaped figure symbolizes the socio-economic stratification system with high-income earners at the top and low-income earners as well as the poor at the bottom. Citizens with rights to flat-rate or minimum benefits are indicated by horizontal lines, and those with rights to clearly income-related benefits by vertical lines. Here it must however be noted that some social insurance programmes which formally give earnings-related benefits have relatively low benefit ceilings, in practice resulting in relatively equal benefits for a major part of the insured. In attempting to classify countries according to these models, we must remember that a typology based on ideal types can never be expected to fit the real world exactly. As a result of a century of efforts by different interest groups to place their stamp on the institutional structures of the welfare state, we must, in practice, expect to find cross-breeds, not purebreds; alloys, not elements.

In targeted programmes (1a) eligibility is based on a means test, resulting in minimum or relatively similar benefits (horizontal lines) to those who fall below a poverty line or who are defined as needy. Although targeted programmes have traditions going back to the old poor laws, the criteria for

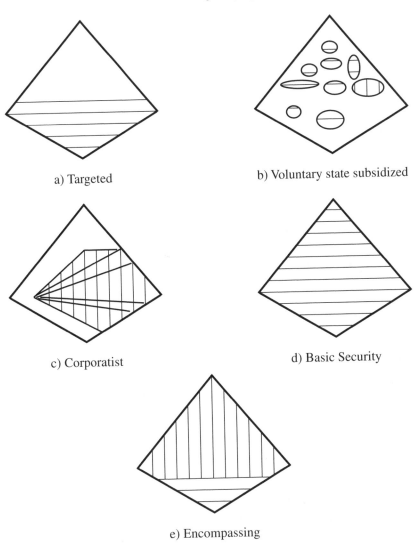

a) Targeted

b) Voluntary state subsidized

c) Corporatist

d) Basic Security

e) Encompassing

Note: The four-sided figures represent the social structure of society with high-income earners at the top and low-income earners at the bottom. White areas represent the non-covered population. Horizontal lines indicates flat-rate benefits. Vertical lines indicate earnings-related benefits. Ellipses in the voluntary state subsidized model indicate separate insurance programmes. Angled lines in the corporatist model indicate insurance programmes organized separately for different occupational categories.

Figure 9.1   Ideal-typical models of social insurance institutions

determining need can vary considerably in terms of punitiveness and generosity. During the course of this century, many countries came to relax the criteria used for means-testing. In recent years, in old age pensions and sickness benefits, the targeted model is found only in Australia, where targeting has gradually come to be focused on excluding top-income earners rather than on including only the poor. In the figure this possibility is indicated by thinner lines above the poverty line. Old traditions also characterize voluntary state-subsidized programmes (1b), where tax money is used to help mutual benefit societies and other voluntary organizations to provide insurance to protect their members against loss of earnings. Since eligibility for benefits is here based on voluntary contributions which give membership in the respective schemes, they have been more important for skilled workers and the middle classes than for the unskilled and the poor. Voluntary schemes can have flat-rate or earnings-related benefits; the latter however often approach the flat-rate ones because of relatively low ceilings for earnings replacements. This institutional model has been important in sickness as well as in unemployment insurance but has never worked in the area of pension; it is thus not dominant in any of our countries.

The pioneering social insurance programmes initiated in Germany by Bismarck in the 1880s broke with means-testing as well as with voluntarism by introducing programmes with compulsory membership giving specified occupational categories the right to claim benefits when their normal earnings were interrupted for reasons beyond their own control. In its institutional structure German social insurance came to follow the state corporatist model (1c) central to Catholic social teaching and nineteenth-century conservative thought.[10] Besides Germany, this model has been dominant in Austria, Belgium, France, Italy and Japan. The basic idea of the state corporatist model can be said to be to create 'socio-political communities' within different segments of the labour force and to induce cooperation between employers and employees within these segments. In the state corporatist model, programmes are directed at the economically active part of the population. Eligibility for benefits is based on a combination of contributions *and* belonging to a specified occupational category. Separate social insurance programmes with differing entitlements are organized for different occupations or branches of industry, creating a segmentation between occupational categories. Starting with the industrial working class, new occupational categories have gradually been added and accorded separate insurance programmes over the decades. Benefits are clearly earnings-related (vertical lines) but entitlements and rules can differ significantly between the programmes of different occupational categories. In contrast to the other four institutional types, and reflecting its basic idea of creating socio-political communities and cooperation between the potential antagonists on the labour market, in the state corporatist model programmes are governed by elected representatives of employees and employers, often with the state also present as a minor third party. They are also financed primarily via contributions from employers and employees. By being limited to the economically active population, this model came to exclude housewives and others outside the labour force. Typically, an income ceiling for coverage was also introduced, with high-income earners thus being expected to find private solutions.

In the basic security model (1d), eligibility is based either on contributions *or* on citizenship (residence). The basic security model comes close to central ideals expressed by William Beveridge (1942). One of these was to have flat-rate benefits or a low ceiling on earnings replacement in order to leave room for higher-income groups to protect their standard of living through private insurance programmes. According to Beveridge (1942: 121) 'the first fundamental principle of the social insurance scheme is provisions of a flat rate of insurance benefit, irrespective of the amount of earnings which have been interrupted ... This principle follows from the recognition of the place of voluntary insurance in social security ...'. Another basic idea was to achieve a large or universal coverage of the relevant population categories.[11] In 1985 the basic security model can be said to dominate in Canada, Denmark, Ireland, the Netherlands, New Zealand, Switzerland, the United Kingdom and the United States.

The encompassing model (1e) can be said to combine ideas from Bismarck and Beveridge into a new pattern. In this model eligibility is based on contributions *and* citizenship. Universal programmes covering all citizens and giving them basic security are thus combined with clearly earnings-related benefits for the economically active part of the population. This institutional organization is likely to reduce the demand for private insurance and has the potential to encompass all citizens within the same programme. In 1985 it is found in Finland, Norway and Sweden.

Institutions, strategies of equality and redistribution

The types of social insurance institutions outlined above can be expected to affect redistributive processes through differences in the role which they accord to markets and to politics but also through the direct and indirect ways in which they tend to encourage or discourage the formation of risk pools with varying degrees of homogeneity in terms of socio-economically structured distribution of risks and resources. The targeted model apparently involves the lowest degree of political interference with market distribution, followed by, in turn, the voluntary subsidized model and the basic security model, the latter establishing a basis upon which market-based stratification can be erected. The state corporatist model in turn involves a greater degree of encroachment upon market distribution than does the basic security model, but because of its occupational segmentation and the exclusion of the economically non-active and top-income earners it encroaches less than the encompassing model.

In traditional insurance terminology, social insurance involves the creation of risk pools within which risks and resources are shared. In the Western countries, economic risks and resources are unequally distributed along lines that tend to follow socio-economic cleavages. In social insurance the socio-economic structure therefore offers opportunities to delineate risk pools which are internally more or less homogeneous in terms of risks and resources. Our hypothesis is that the institutional structures of welfare states can emphasize differences in risks and resources by increasing homogeneity within risk pools in terms of their socio-economic composition, or they can play down these differences via the pooling of resources and the sharing of risks across socio-economically heterogeneous categories. Social insurance institutions can thereby come to frame and shape the processes of defining interests and identities among citizens, the rational choices they are likely to make, and the ways in which they are likely to combine for collective action.[12] Of special interest in this context is the extent to which institutional structures will discourage or encourage coalition formation between the poor and better-off citizens and between the working and the middle classes, thus making their definitions of interest diverge or converge. Such a divergence can be brought about directly through institutional structures which segment risk pools along socio-economic lines, or indirectly via redistributive strategies likely to create differences of interest between the poor and the non-poor, between workers and salaried employees.

Institutional structures can also be expected to affect coalition formation and the definition of interests among citizens in indirect ways through the various strategies of equality they can be seen as embodying. These strategies discussed in the introduction can be defined by their *degree of low-income targeting*, describing the extent to which budgets actually used for redistribution go to those defined as poor or as having low incomes. The degree of low-income targeting varies between institutional types. The targeted model can be said to follow the *Robin Hood Strategy* of taking from the rich and giving to the poor. The flat-rate benefits in the basic security model as well as in many voluntary subsidized programmes reflect a *Simple Egalitarian Strategy* with equal benefits for all, in relative terms, however, giving more to low-income earners than to the better off. The clearly earnings-related benefits found in the encompassing models follow instead the *Matthew Principle* of giving more, in absolute terms, to the rich than to the poor, and also, in relative terms, having only limited low-income targeting. The state corporatist and voluntary state subsidized models can be said to redistribute among relative equals.

By practising positive discrimination in favour of the poor, the targeted model creates what amounts to a zero-sum conflict of interests between the poor on the one hand and, on the other, the better-off workers and middle classes, who have to pay for the benefits of the poor without themselves receiving any benefits. The targeted model thus tends to drive a wedge between the short-term material interests of the poor and of the rest of the population, which has to rely on private insurance. It gives the better-off categories no rational basis for including the poor among themselves, leaving the poor to place their trust in the altruism of the more fortunate.

As made explicit by Beveridge (cf. above) in the basic security model flat-rate benefits are only intended to provide a safety net for the working class while the middle classes are expected to safeguard their standards of living via various forms of private insurance. Social insurance systems of the basic security type therefore tend to become a concern primarily for manual workers, while as in the targeted model, private insurance is likely to loom large for salaried employees and other better-off groups. The basic security model is therefore also likely to separate the interests of high-income strata from those of workers and the poor.

In contrast to voluntary or state corporatist programmes, the encompassing model includes all citizens within the framework of the same programmes. By giving basic security to everybody and by offering clearly earnings-related benefits to all economically active individuals, in contrast to the targeted and basic security models, the encompassing model brings low-income groups as well as the better-off citizens within the same institutional structures. Because of its earnings-related benefits, it is likely to reduce the demand for private insurance. The encompassing institutional model can thus be expected to have the most favourable outcomes in terms of the formation of cross-class coalitions which include manual workers as well as the middle classes. By providing sufficiently high benefits for high-income groups so as not to push them to exit, in the context of encompassing institutions the voice of the better-off citizens helps not only themselves but low-income groups also.[13]

The debate about the redistributive outcomes of welfare state programmes has been almost exclusively focused on how to distribute the money available for transfer and has not recognized the importance of variations in redistributive budget size, that is of the total sums made available for redistribution. In this context it is important to note that the degree of redistribution finally achieved depends on the size of the redistributive budget as well as on the degree of low-income targeting. Without specifying the functional form or all the other factors of relevance here, the redistributive formula indicating the degree of redistribution achieved can be seen as a multiplicative function of these two aspects, that is *Final Redistribution* is a function of *Degree of Low-income Targeting and Redistributive Budget Size.*

The neglect of budget size is all the more unfortunate, since, as the discussion above indicates we can expect a trade-off between the degree of low-income targeting and the size of the redistributive budget, so that *the greater the degree of low-income targeting, the smaller the budget tends to be.* This trade-off indicates that it is not possible to maximize the degree of low-income targeting and budget size at the same time. In so far as welfare state institutions contribute to the pooling of risks and resources and to coalition formation which includes the middle as well as the working classes and the poor, they are likely to affect the size of the budgets made available for redistribution.[14]

Encompassing institutions can therefore be expected to generate the broadest base of support for welfare state expansion and financing. However, while state corporatist institutions exclude the economically inactive and tend to segment different occupational categories, because of their earnings-related benefits, they can be expected to generate relatively large social expenditures. In spite of a high level of coverage, the basic security countries with relatively low benefits are expected to have lower expenditures than both the state corporatist and the encompassing types of welfare states. The lowest expenditure level is expected in the targeted welfare state.

It goes without saying that institutional structures are only one of many factors that affect the final distribution of income in a country.[15] Circumstances such as political traditions, demographic composition, labour force participation rates, levels of unemployment, wage-setting practices, and industrial structures are also of importance here.[16] At best we can therefore only hope for a partial agreement between our hypotheses and comparative empirical data. As is often the case in comparative research, we lack good quantitative indicators for some variables hypothesized to be of relevance and will have to use available proxies.

Redistribution

To test the above hypotheses empirically, we will start by looking at the overall relationship between institutional structures and outcomes in terms of the degree of inequality and poverty in the countries for which relevant data are available. For 11 of our 18 countries, we have been able to use microsurveys on household income included in the Luxembourg Income Study (LIS).[17] Data limitations have thus restricted this part of the analysis to the following countries (years for income data in parentheses): Australia (1985), Canada (1987), Finland (1987), France (1984), Germany (Federal Republic) (1984), the Netherlands (1987), Norway (1987), Sweden (1987), Switzerland (1982), the United Kingdom (1986) and the United States (1986). Analyses have been carried out for the total population, the working-age population (defined as those 25–59 years of age) and the elderly, defined as those above 65 years of age (cf. Appendix).

Table 9.2   *Inequality (Gini) and poverty rates in disposable income in 11 OECD countries c. 1985 in different population categories by type of social insurance institutions*

Type of social insurance institutions	Inequality (Gini) Population category			Poverty rate (%)[a] Population category		
	Total	25–59 years	65+ years	Total	25–59 years	65+ years
Encompassing						
Finland	.231	.205	.219	4.1	1.6	3.9
Norway	.232	.218	.241	3.5	2.9	2.6
Sweden	.215	.194	.182	4.9	2.6	1.4
Corporatist						
France	.292	.292	.287	8.5	8.0	1.9
Germany	.243	.235	.278	5.8	5.3	5.3
Basic security						
Canada	.279	.277	.257	10.9	10.9	4.9
Netherlands	.252	.254	.220	5.8	3.5	0.2
Switzerland	.320	.305	.355	7.4	5.8	11.9
United Kingdom	.293	.293	.242	13.2	11.0	9.2
United States	.333	.327	.355	17.9	17.8	17.5
Targeted						
Australia	.310	.301	.279	9.1	9.3	5.2

Note: [a] Percentage below 50% of median income.

The overall relevance of our institutional types of welfare states for income equality and poverty is indicated by the results from these analyses (Table 9.2). We find considerable differences in the degree of income inequality and the extent of poverty between countries with different institutional models. Whether we look at the total population or at the working-age population and the elderly, the lowest degree of inequality is found in the three encompassing countries, Finland, Norway and Sweden. Among the basic security countries, variation in Gini coefficients is relatively large, with the Netherlands having one of the lowest coefficients and the United States the highest one. The highest inequality figures appear in the basic security and targeted models, especially in the United States, Switzerland, Australia and the United Kingdom. The two state corporatist countries, France and Germany, occupy intermediate positions.

The same pattern emerges, by and large, for poverty rates. With only a few exceptions, the lowest poverty rates are found among the encompassing countries. As with the indicator of overall inequality, the variation among the basic security countries is very high. Thus the Netherlands, again, comes close to the encompassing countries, and the United States shows clearly the highest poverty rate of all countries, followed by the United Kingdom and Canada. With its targeted model, Australia also has comparatively high poverty rates. Again, the two state corporatist countries, France and Germany, fall into intermediary positions. The above results thus clearly follow the pattern predicted by our hypothesis about the overall role of welfare state institutions in the distributive processes of the Western countries.

Such an overall correlation between institutions and outcomes points to the need to open the blackbox of causal processes assumed to mediate the effects from institutions to redistributive outcomes. However, it is not possible for us, within the scope of this chapter and with the data now available, to take more than a partial look into this blackbox by following the subsequent stages in the causal processes and attempting to verify these different steps. Thus data not shown here tend to indicate that the largest redistributive budgets are found in the encompassing countries, followed in descending order by corporatist, basic security and targeted categories of countries (Korpi and Palme, 1998).

Do redistributive budget size and the degree of low-income targeting contribute to the reduction of income inequality in accordance with our hypotheses? To control for the effects of variations in factor income inequality between countries, we will here examine *income redistribution* in terms of the relative reduction of Gini coefficients when we move from market income to disposable income, that is after taxes and transfers (for definitions of terms cf. the Appendix). This has been done for the prime working-age population (25–59 years) as well as for the total population. Since the results for these two categories are quite similar, in the following only those for the total population are shown. *Redistributive budget size* in a country is measured as the percentage of the size of transfers to the size of gross income (defined as post-transfer but pre-tax income).

The bivariate plot between redistributive budget size and the degree of income redistribution achieved through the tax and transfer systems is shown in Figure 9.2. The correlation between these two variables is very strong (r = 0.92). The lowest level of redistribution is found in two basic security countries, that is Switzerland and the United States as well as in targeted Australia, countries which also have the smallest welfare states. Quite expectedly, the Netherlands and Sweden, which have the largest redistributive budgets, also have the highest redistributive effects. The two state corporatist countries, France and Germany, have fairly large transfer budgets and also achieve relatively large reductions in Gini coefficients.

In this context we do however run into problems of lack of comparability between different data sets, problems which are all too familiar to compara-

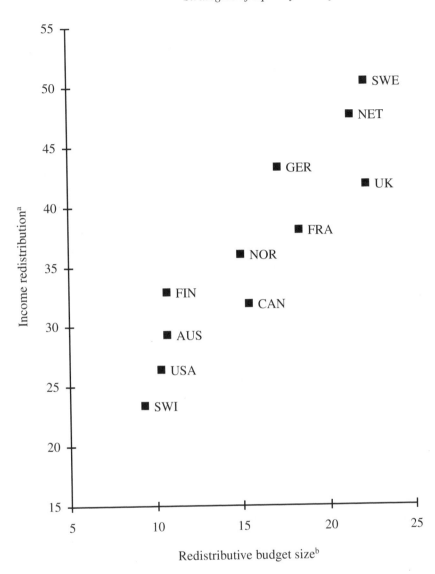

Notes:
[a]   Income redistribution = relative reduction of Gini from market to disposable income.
[b]   Redistributive budget size = transfer income as percentage of gross income.

Figure 9.2   Redistributive budget size and income redistribution in 11 OECD countries

tive social scientists. Thus, in terms of the LIS database, Finland with its encompassing institutions also appears among countries with small transfer budgets. This largely reflects the fact that in the LIS data set the Finnish earnings-related pension schemes are inappropriately treated as private ones. While the Finnish pension programmes are administered by private insurance companies, they have been created and are financed via legislation and should thus be regarded as public programmes. In the LIS data, Norway, despite its encompassing institutions, also appears as an average spender. This partly reflects Norway's high pension age (67 years), partly the use of legislated employer wage-continuation in sickness and work accident insurance, which in the LIS data set is defined as market income.[18] Canada has a medium-sized transfer rate but less redistribution than Norway. Contrary to what we could expect from other expenditure data, in the LIS data set the United Kingdom has a transfer size at the same level as that of Sweden and the Netherlands (Korpi and Palme, 1998).

Data not shown here indicate that (to some extent) increasing levels of targeting of redistributive budgets to low-income groups tend to be associated with decreasing levels of redistribution. The degree of redistribution is measured by the proportional decrease of inequality, when we look at the difference in the degree of inequality in market income and inequality in disposable income (Korpi and Palme, 1998: 667).

Income inequality among the elderly

In the analysis of the effects of the welfare state institutions on inequality and poverty, the elderly provide an interesting test case. The economic situation of the elderly is determined by their own previous economic activities as well as by public transfers. Their economic situation thus reflects the cumulative effects of forces operating in markets and in politics, yet with public transfers playing a greater role than in the working population. The goal of eradicating poverty and of achieving a relatively low income inequality probably commands more support with respect to the elderly than with regard to economically active citizens. Many have feared that 'earnings-related systems may ... perpetuate existing income inequalities over the life cycle' (Mitchell, Harding and Gruen, 1994: 324).

As discussed above, because of the clear relationship between benefits and previous income, public pensions are likely to have the highest degree of inequality in the encompassing and state corporatist countries, while pension inequality is expected to be lower in the basic security countries. In the targeted model, however, transfers will be directed primarily at low-income categories. Available data allow us to study the consequences of these differences in public pensions on inequality among the elderly in nine countries during the mid-1980s.[19] Thus in terms of our index of targeting of transfers, we find the highest positive values (that is the highest degree of inequality in favour of high-income groups) for public pensions in the three encompassing countries, Finland, Sweden and Norway, as well as in state corporatist Germany, all countries with relatively high maximum pensions (Figure 9.3). In the basic security countries, that is the United States, Netherlands, the United Kingdom and Canada, public pensions are relatively neutral in terms of distribution. In targeted Australia, however, as the negative value of the index of targeting indicates, public pensions clearly go primarily to low-income earners.[20]

Public pensions are however only one of the factors determining total income inequality among the elderly. When we look at the degree of inequality in total gross income (including private and occupational pensions as well as income from savings and earnings) among the elderly, the above picture is largely reversed. *The lowest inequality in total gross income* is in fact found in the four countries with *the most unequal public pensions*, that is Finland, Sweden, Germany and Norway. In contrast, Australia, with pensions targeted at low-income groups, turns out to have a much higher level of inequality in total gross income among the elderly, being second only to the United States. Countries with relatively flat-rate pensions, that is the Netherlands, the United Kingdom and Canada, also have higher inequality in total income among the elderly than have the clearly earnings-related countries.[21]

How are we to account for these rather surprising results? As indicated above, one of the factors generating differences in income inequality between various welfare state models is the relative role played by public and private transfer systems. Welfare state institutions can be expected to affect the type of public/private insurance mix in a country. In general, economically better-off citizens are more likely to acquire private pension insurance than are low-income earners. The demand for private pension insurance will therefore partly depend on the maximum benefit levels of the public systems, which determine whether public systems can give clearly earnings-related pensions to the middle classes and high-income earners or push them to exit into private pension programmes. The encompassing institutional type, which provides earnings-related benefits for all citizens, can thus be expected to generate the lowest level of private insurance. In contrast, the targeted or basic security countries are likely to have high levels of private insurance, since there high-income earners have to rely on private channels for income security. The demand for private insurance will be lower in the state corporatist model because of its earnings-related benefits for those insured. However, as a result of income ceilings for coverage and sizeable categories of non-covered citizens, we can expect private insurance to play a larger role in the state corporatist than in the encompassing model. These hypotheses are to a considerable extent verified

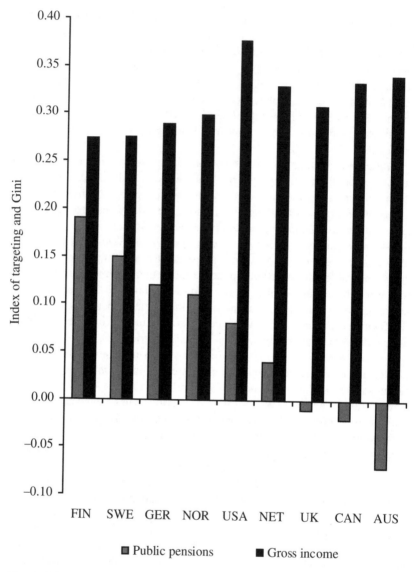

Figure 9.3   Index of targeting of public pensions and inequality in gross income (Gini) among the elderly in nine countries

in that the higher maximum pensions that can be paid out via the public pension systems, the lower does the relative size of private pension expenditure tend to be.[22]

The paradox of redistribution

The welfare state models outlined here have developed over a century of conflicts between different interest groups concerning the distribution of man's worldly goods (Korpi, 2001). They are associated with different types of strategies of equality and differing roles for markets and politics in distributive processes and can be shown to have differing consequences for income distribution and poverty among citizens. Our finding that, by providing high-income earners with clearly earnings-related benefits within encompassing social insurance institutions, we can reduce inequality and poverty more efficiently than by flat-rate or targeted benefits, may surprise many scholars and policy makers. The traditional arguments in favour of low-income targeting and flat-rate benefits have focused exclusively on the distribution of the money actually transferred, but have overlooked three basic circumstances. One is that the size of redistributive budgets is not necessarily fixed but tends to depend on the type of welfare state institutions in a country. A second factor is that there tends to be a trade-off between the extent of low-income targeting and the size of redistributive budgets. The third circumstance of importance here is that since large categories of citizens will not be able or willing to acquire private earnings-related insurance and because of the socio-economic selection processes in operation here, the outcomes of market-dominated distribution tend to be even more unequal than those found in earnings-related social insurance programmes (cf. Titmuss, 1955). Recognition of these factors helps us understand what we can call the *Paradox of Redistribution: The more we target benefits at the poor only and the more concerned we are with creating equality via equal public transfers to all, the less likely we are to reduce poverty and inequality.*

In a way which has only recently been possible thanks to the LIS and SCIP data sets, we have been able to test hypotheses on causal processes between welfare state institutions, redistributive processes and distributive outcomes. Yet, in view of the difficulties involved in carrying out comparative research in these areas, some of our results are primarily suggestive of fruitful future research. Our analyses indicate that in the generation of the paradox of redistribution, institutions of the welfare state are of key importance. These institutions affect the relative roles of markets and politics in distributive processes and the types of coalition formation among interest groups. As we expected, the effects on outcomes in terms of poverty and inequality appear to be largest in countries with encompassing institutions but low in the basic security countries. The Australian experience indicates that targeting by excluding the better-off citizens is not highly effective in reducing poverty, and that it is relatively inefficient in reducing inequality. In this respect the state corporatist countries tend to occupy an intermediary position. In all categories of countries, however, additional factors which cannot be considered here, such as the relative strength of political parties and economic factors affecting the distribution of factor incomes, are also likely to be of relevance for distributive outcomes. In some countries, such as the United States where cleavages along racial lines are correlated with income, institutional demarcations are likely to be reinforced by racial ones (Quadagno, 1994).

As discussed above, we view institutions as intervening variables, reflecting conflicts of interest between different interest groups on the one hand and, on the other, as being likely to have effects on the definitions of interests and coalition formation among citizens. In turn these coalitions and cleavages will have consequences for the size of budgets available for redistribution and the final degree of redistribution achieved. The empirical testing of macro–micro links between institutions and the formation of interests and coalitions provides a major challenge to social scientists. So far, we lack the comparative micro-data necessary for opening up this macro–micro blackbox. Here we can only draw attention to some relevant evidence indicating that this hypothesis, found in much institutional writing, is a fruitful one. Thus the historian Jürgen Kocka (1977: 49–53, 171–3, 1978: 66–7, 1981) has documented that the state corporatist model introduced in Imperial Germany with separate social insurance programmes for manual workers and salaried employees, thus privileging the latter, has significantly contributed to the cementation of the white/blue collar divide in Germany. Of indirect relevance in this context is also the fact that in the countries with encompassing institutions, surveys show that universal and encompassing programmes tend to receive considerably more support among citizens than do means- or income-tested ones (Svallfors, 1996; Kangas, 1995; Forma, 1996; Kangas and Palme, 1993).

Contrary to what many scholars have expected, earnings-related benefits would thus appear to be a condition of, rather than a hindrance to, the reduction of inequality. Because of their low ceilings for earnings replacement, not only targeted but also basic security programmes stimulate exit among the middle classes and increase their demand for private insurance. From the point of view of equality, the problem with the state corporatist model is not that benefits are earnings-related. The main difference between the state corporatist and the encompassing models is instead related to the fact that by organizing the economically active citizens into occupationally segmented social insurance programmes, the state corporatist model tends to give prominence to socio-economic distinctions between different categories of citizens and to create diverging interests between these categories. In contrast, encompassing institutions pool the risks as well as the resources of all citizens and thus tend to create converging definitions of interest among them. It is also evident that the encompassing countries tend to provide better basic benefits (Palme, 1998).

In the Western countries the stress on targeting has been increasing in recent years. If our goal is to reduce poverty and inequality this is an unfortunate development. Lawson and Wilson (1995: 706), reflecting on the experiences with the War on Poverty in the United States, argue that policies better suited to support the poor

> should begin with a new public rhetoric that does two things: focuses on the problems that afflict not only the poor, but the working and middle classes as well; and emphasizes integrative programs that promote the social and economic improvement of all groups in society, not just the truly disadvantaged segments of the population.

The analyses here support such a recommendation.

Our chapter suggests two empirically based conclusions. To paraphrase an old saying, if we attempt to fight the war on poverty through target-efficient benefits concentrated at the poor, we may well win some battles but are likely to lose the war. However, universalism is not enough. To have an effect, universalism has to be combined with a strategy of equality which comes closer to the preaching of Matthew than to the practices in Sherwood Forest.

Appendix

The distinction between basic security and encompassing programmes is here based on the degrees of earnings-relatedness and coverage. Because of the difference between short-term and long-term forms of income replacement in determining the degree of earnings-relatedness, different indicators have been used here for sickness and pension programmes. In sickness insurance, the indicator used is the relationship between gross maximum legislated benefit and the gross wage of an average production worker. In 1985, in the basic security programmes, this relationship ranges from 23 per cent in the United Kingdom to 70 per cent in Denmark, while in encompassing programmes it is 114 per cent or higher. In terms of coverage in the labour force, the 'insurance' subvariant of the basic security programmes has a coverage of 73 per cent in Ireland, 80 per cent in the United Kingdom, and 89 per cent in Canada. In the other basic security countries as well as in the three encompassing countries, coverage of sickness insurance is universal.

As a measure of *Maximum Pension*, we relate the net maximum pension to the net pension of an average production worker. In the eight basic security countries, the maximum pension falls below the pension for an average production worker except in Switzerland and the United Kingdom, where the ceiling is 105 and 125 per cent of an average production worker pension, respectively. In the encompassing countries the maximum pension in relation to the average worker pension is 143 per cent in Norway and 149 per cent in Sweden. In Finland, where no formal maximum pension (ceiling) is found, we have here used the pension level of a person with earnings three times the level of an average production worker. In basic security countries of the 'insurance' subvariant, pension coverage (as a proportion of the population 15–64 years) in Ireland, the United Kingdom and the United States was 52, 59, and 67 per cent, respectively. In the other basic security as well as the encompassing countries, pension coverage was universal.

In analyses based on the Luxembourg Income Study (LIS) on inequality and poverty in different population categories, our purpose has been to sample populations above or below normal pension age. Since the pension age differs between nations and is in practice associated with different degrees of flexibility, to improve comparability we have defined the elderly as those above 65 years of age (except for Norway, where the age limit was set at 67, that is equal to the normal pension age). In defining the working-age population we want to exclude students and young people living with their parents (for example, in Swedish income statistics, all persons above 18 years are defined as separate households). Hence, we defined the working-age group as those between 25 and 59 years of age.

The equivalence scale used here gives the weight of 1 to the first adult, 0.7 to the second and 0.5 to every additional person irrespective of age. This scale is used by the OECD and is in the 'middle of the road' compared to other alternatives. The choice of scale is of special importance when different kinds of household are compared, especially if families with children are compared with other families. It is less crucial when similar household categories are compared, for example the elderly. For a discussion of the effects of the choice of equivalence scales in a comparative perspective see Buhmann et al., (1988).

To control for the problem of variations in factor income inequality, we have examined *Income Redistribution* in terms of the relative reduction in inequality when we move from market income to disposable income, that is after taxes and transfers. Following Kakwani (1986) we thus define Income Redistribution = (Market Income Gini − Disposable Income Gini)/Market Income Gini. *Redistributive Budget Size* is here expressed as the relative size (per cent) of transfers to the mean size of gross income (post-transfer but pre-tax income). To get an indication of the way in which benefits are distributed among citizens with differing income, we have here used an *Index of Targeting of Transfer Income*. To compute this index we have ranked income units according to the size of gross income and then distributed transfers along this continuum. The Index of Targeting of Transfer Income is equivalent to what Fields (1979) has labelled the 'factor Gini coefficient' and what Kakwani (1986) has called the 'index of concentration'. It takes the value of −1 if the poorest person gets all the transfer income, 0 if everybody gets an equal amount, and 1 if the richest person gets all.

Notes

1. For example, Tullock (1983).
2. Hechter, Opp and Wippler (1990); Korpi (1980a, 1980b, 1985, 2001); March and Olsen (1989); Pierson (1995); Powell and DiMaggio (1991); Steinmo, Thelen and Longstreth (1992).
3. *The Social Citizenship Indicator Programme (SCIP)* is based at the Swedish Institute for Social Research, Stockholm University and is directed by the present authors. Cf. Korpi (1989) and Palme (1990) for presentations of the data files.
4. These countries are selected according to the principle of most comparable cases (Lijphart, 1975) and include only those with a history of non-interrupted political democracy during the post-war period and more than one million inhabitants.
5. For a presentation of the Luxembourg Income Study see Smeeding, O'Higgins and Rainwater (1990). Analyses are here restricted to the eleven countries for which *LIS*-data were available in 1994 and which included information detailed enough to enable us to follow the various steps in the income formation process.
6. Other attempts include Titmuss (1974), Korpi (1980b), and Mishra (1981).
7. Esping-Andersen (1990: 69–77) uses seven indicators for his typology, the number of occupationally distinct pension schemes, insurance coverage in the population, the difference between average and maximum benefit levels, and the size of expenditures in terms of the relative size of government employee pensions, means-tested benefits, private sector pensions, and private sector health care.
8. The social services constitute another significant part of the welfare state.
9. As a result of immigration, in most countries an increasing proportion of residents are not

citizens. For convenience, in this context we will however use the term 'citizens' to refer to residents as well.

10. For background to this model, see Leo XIII (1891 [1943]); Durkheim (1902 [1964]); Pius XI (1931 [1943]); Messner (1936, 1964). The term 'state corporatism' is here used in its original meaning of state-induced cooperation between employers and employees within specific sectors of industry. In the address of the German emperor to the *Reichstag* on 15 February, 1881, announcing the coming social insurance legislation, the term 'korporative Verbände' (corporatist associations) was used to describe this type of organization (Deutsche Reichstag, 1881).

11. Within the basic security model we do however find two subvariants with somewhat differing levels of coverage. In the 'citizenship' subvariant, eligibility is based on citizenship or residence, that is on the idea of 'People's Insurance' with universal coverage. In the 'insurance' subvariant, however, eligibility is acquired through contributions by the insured and/or employers, and here we find less than universal coverage. However, in contrast to the state corporatist model, where contributors in different occupational categories belong to different programmes, in the basic security model all insured are covered by the same programme. As will be discussed below, in the basic security model benefit levels have also come to vary to some extent. Relative to the variation found between the basic security, encompassing, and state corporatist models, the differences between these two subvariants would appear to be relatively small, but in some contexts they can certainly be of significance. For the present purposes, however, they are not likely to be of crucial importance.

12. The role of risk groups in the development of social policies stressed by Baldwin (1990) would thus not appear to be primarily as independent driving forces. Instead risk groups can be seen as in part created by social insurance institutions and, once formed, as acting to safeguard their specific interests.

13. The distinction between exit and voice here refers to the well-known distinction by Hirschman (1970).

14. Redistributive budgets are financed via taxation with different degrees of progressivity. This redistributive formula can thus be seen as applying also to the financing side of the redistributive process. We are here thus studying the combined redistribution achieved via the tax and transfer systems.

15. For recent reviews of the literature see, for example, Hicks and Misra (1993) and Huber, Ragin and Stephens (1993).

16. Some of these factors can partly be controlled for by an examination of the change in inequality when we move from factor income to gross and disposable income (cf. below).

17. The LIS data have unique qualities making possible primary analysis with great flexibility in terms of definitions and selection of income units and variables. The accuracy of the data is also much better than in previous studies. Yet, as discussed in the following, problems of comparability remain.

18. Also Germany has wage-continuation periods in sickness and work accident insurance.

19. Figures are from the LIS database except for Finland and Sweden, where we have had to re-analyse the original national data sets (Kangas and Palme, 1993).

20. In the 1970s, the degree of targeting in Australian social benefits tended to decrease, reaching a low in 1977/78. Since then targeting has gradually increased. In 1980 the income test for the age pension for those aged 70 had been reintroduced (Mitchell, Harding and Gruen, 1994).

21. An analysis of Finnish data sets over time indicates that the introduction of earnings-related pensions decreased income inequality among the elderly (Jäntti, Kangas and Ritakallio, 1996).

22. In 1980, the rank correlation between the size of private pension expenditure and total gross income inequality among the elderly is 0.83.

References

Åberg, Rune (1989), 'Distributive mechanisms of the welfare state. A formal analysis and an empirical application', *European Sociological Review*, vol. 5, 167–82.

Baldwin, Peter (1990), *The Politics of Social Solidarity. Class Bases of the European Welfare State 1875–1975*, Cambridge: Cambridge University Press.

Beveridge, William (1942), *Social Insurance and Allied Services*, London: HMSO.

Buhmann, Brigitte, Lee Rainwater, Günther Schmaus and Timothy Smeeding (1988), 'Equivalence scales, well-being, inequality and poverty: sensitivity estimates across ten countries using the Luxembourg Income Study (LIS) database', *Review of Income and Wealth*, vol. 34, 115–42.

Deutsche Reichstag (1881), *Stenographische Berichte über die Verhandlungen des Deutschen Reichstages*, IV. Legislaturperiode, Vierte Session (Microfiche).

Durkheim, Emilé (1902 [1964]), *The Division of Labor in Society*, Glencoe, Ill.: Free Press.

Esping-Andersen, Gøsta (1990), *The Three Worlds of Welfare Capitalism*, Cambridge: Polity Press.

Fields, Gary S. (1979), 'Decomposing LDC-inequality', *Oxford Economic Papers*, vol. 31, 437–61.

Forma, Pauli (1996), 'The politics of interest mediation. The case of universalistic social policy in Finland', Research Report, Department of Social Policy, University of Turku, Finland.

Fritzell, Johan (1991), 'The gap between market rewards and economic well-being in modern societies', *European Sociological Review*, vol. 7, 19–33.

Goodin, Robert E. and Julian Le Grand (1987), *Not Only the Poor*, London: Allen & Unwin.

Harrington Meyer, Madonna (1996), 'Making claims as workers or wives: the distribution of social security benefits', *American Sociological Review*, vol. 61, 449–65.

Hechter, Michael, Karl-Dieter Opp and Reinhard Wippler (1990), *Social Institutions. Their Emergence, Maintenance and Effects*, New York: Aldine de Gruyter.

Hicks, Alexander and Joya Misra (1993), 'Political resources and the growth of welfare in affluent capitalist democracies 1960–1982', *American Journal of Sociology*, vol. 99, 668–710.

Hicks, Alexander and Duane H. Swank (1984), 'Governmental redistribution in rich capitalist democracies', *Policy Studies Journal*, vol. 13, 265–8.

Hirschman, Albert O. (1970), *Exit, Voice, and Loyalty. Responses to Decline in Firms, Organizations, and States*, Cambridge, Mass.: Harvard University Press.

Huber, Evelyn, Charles Ragin and John D. Stephens (1993), 'Social democracy, Christian democracy, constitutional structure, and the welfare state', *American Journal of Sociology*, vol. 99, 711–49.

Jäntti, Markus, Olli Kangas and Veli-Matti Ritakallio (1996), 'From marginalism to institutionalism: distributional consequences of the transformation of the Finnish pension regime', *Review of Income and Wealth*, vol. 42, 473–91.

Kakwani, Nanak (1986), *Analyzing Redistribution Politics*, Oxford: Oxford University Press.

Kangas, Olli (1995), 'Attitudes to means-tested social benefits in Finland', *Acta Sociologica*, vol. 38, 299–310.

Kangas, Olli and Joakim Palme (1993), 'Eroding statism? Labour market benefits and the challenges to the Scandinavian welfare states', in Erik J. Hansen, Stein Ringen, Hannu Uusitalo, and Robert Erikson (eds), *Scandinavian Welfare Trends*, New Jersey: ME Sharpe, pp. 3–24.

Kocka, Jürgen (1977), *Angestellte zwischen Faschismus und Demokratie*, Göttingen: Vandehoeck & Ruprecht.

Kocka, Jürgen (1978), *Klassengesellschaft im Krieg. Deutsche Sozialgeschichte 1914–1918*, Göttingen: Vandehoeck & Ruprecht.

Kocka, Jürgen (1981), 'Class formation, interest articulation, and public policy. The origins of the German white-collar class in the late nineteenth and early twentieth century', in Susanne Berger (ed.), *Organizing Interest in Western Europe*, Cambridge: Cambridge University Press, pp. 63–82.

Korpi, Walter (1980a), 'Approaches to the study of poverty in the United States. Critical notes from a European perspective', in Vincent T. Covello (ed.), *Poverty and Public Policy*, Boston: Cambridge, Mass.: Schenkman, pp. 287–314.

Korpi, Walter (1980b), 'Social policy and distributional conflict in the capitalist democracies: a preliminary comparative framework', *European Politics*, vol. 3, 296–316.

Korpi, Walter (1983), *The Democratic Class Struggle*, London: Routledge.

Korpi, Walter (1985), 'Power resources vs. action and conflict: on causal and intentional explanation in the study of power', *Sociological Theory*, vol. 3, 31–45.

Korpi, Walter (1989), 'Power, politics and state autonomy in the development of social citizenship: social rights during sickness in 18 OECD countries since 1930', *American Sociological Review*, vol. 54, 309–28.

Korpi, Walter (1996), 'Eurosclerosis and the sclerosis of objectivity. On the role of values among economic policy experts', *The Economic Journal*, vol. 106, 1727–46.

Korpi, Walter (2001), 'Contentious institutions. An augmented rational-action analysis of the origins and path dependency of welfare state institutions in western countries', *Rationality and Society*, **13** (2), 235–83.

Korpi, Walter and Joakim Palme (1998), 'The paradox of redistribution and strategies of equality: welfare state institutions, inequality and poverty in the western countries', *American Sociological Review*, vol. 63, 661–87.

Lampman, Robert J. (1971), 'What does it do to the poor? A new test for national policy', *The Public Interest*, vol. 34, 66–82.

Lawson, Roger and William J. Wilson (1995), 'Poverty, social rights, and the quality of citizenship', in by Katherine McFate, Roger Lawson and William J. Wilson (eds), *Poverty, Inequality, and the Future of Social Policy*, New York: Russell Sage, pp. 693–714.

Lazarsfeld, Paul F. (1962), 'Interpretation of statistical relations as a research operation', in Paul F. Lazarsfeld and Morris Rosenberg (eds), *The Language of Social Research*, Glencoe: Free Press, pp. 115–25.

Le Grand, Julian (1982), *The Strategy of Equality. Redistribution and the Social Services*, London: George Allen & Unwin Ltd.

Leo XIII (1891 [1943]), *Rerum novarum*, Papal encyclical. Vatican City.

Lijphart, Arendt (1975), 'The comparable-cases strategy in comparative research', *Comparative Political Studies*, vol. 8, 158–77.

March, James and Johan P. Olsen (1989), *Rediscovering Institutions*, New York: Free Press.

Marshall, T.H. (1950), *Citizenship and Social Class*, Cambridge: Cambridge University Press.

Messner, Johannes (1964), *Die Soziale Frage in Blickfeld der Irrwege von Gestern, die Sozialkämpfe von Heute, die Weltentscheidungen von Morgen*, Innsbruck: Tyrolia Verlag.

Messner, Johannes (1936), *Die Berufständige Ordnung*, Innsbruck: Verlagsanstalt Tyrolia.

Mishra, Ramesh (1981), *Society and Social Policy. Theories and Practice of Welfare*, London: Macmillan.

Mitchell, Deborah, Ann Harding and Fred Gruen (1994), 'Targeting welfare', *Economic Record*, vol. 70, 315–40.

Palme, Joakim (1990), *Pension Rights in Welfare Capitalism*, Swedish Institute for Social Research Dissertation series No. 14, Stockholm University.

Palme, Joakim (1998), 'The welfare state and equality: pensions, poverty and income inequality among the elderly in western countries', paper prepared for the American Sociological Association Meeting, San Francisco, 21–25 August.

Pierson, Paul (1995), *Dismantling the Welfare State? Reagan, Thatcher and the Politics of Retrenchment*, Cambridge: Cambridge University Press.

Pius XI (1931 [1943]), *Quadragesimo Anno*, Papal encyclical, Vatican City.

Powell, Walter W. and Paul J. DiMaggio (1991), *The New Institutionalism in Organizational Analysis*, Chicago: Chicago University Press.

Quadagno, Jill S. (1994), *The Color of Welfare. How Racism Undermined the War on Poverty*, New York: Oxford University Press.

Smeeding, Timothy, Michael O'Higgins and Lee Rainwater (eds) (1990), *Poverty, Inequality and Income Distribution in Comparative Perspective: The Luxembourg Income Study*, New York: Harvester Wheatsheaf.

Steinmo, Sven, Kathleen Thelen and Frank Longstreth (1992), *Structuring Politics. Historical Institutionalism in Comparative Analysis*, Cambridge: Cambridge University Press.

Svallfors, Stefan (1996), *Välfärdsstatens moraliska ekonomi. Välfärdsopinionen in 90–talets Sverige* (The Moral Economy of the Welfare State. Social Policy Attitudes in Sweden of the 1990s), Umeå: Borea.

Tawney, R.H. (1952), *Equality*, London: George Allen & Unwin Ltd.

Titmuss, Richard (1955), 'Pension systems and population change', *Political Quarterly*, vol. 26, 152–66.

Titmuss, Richard (1974), *Social Policy*, London: George Allen & Unwin.

Tullock, Gordon (1983), *Economics of Income Redistribution*, Amsterdam: Kluwer-Nijhoff.

10 Gender, citizenship and welfare state regimes
Julia S. O'Connor

Introduction

All three elements of the title of this chapter – gender, citizenship and welfare state regimes – are contested concepts and this is particularly true when considered in relationship to one another either jointly or in total. The objective of this chapter is to provide an overview of the broad dimensions of the debates on these concepts as they relate to one another in the literature on comparing and categorizing social policy provision and redistribution cross-nationally. This entails a review of developments in the comparative analysis of welfare states, the elements of the citizenship debate as it relates to this and the gender-sensitive critique of, and contribution to, both. The structure of the chapter is as follows: section I is concerned with the welfare state concept and the cross-national variation of welfare states. This includes a brief discussion of the centrality of citizenship in welfare state development. Section II focuses on the welfare state regime concept. Section III presents a brief outline of the gendered analysis of the citizenship as rights and citizenship as obligation traditions, arguing that they are complementary and that both are essential to an effective analysis of welfare state regimes. Section IV is concerned with the overlapping gender critique of citizenship and welfare state regimes. Section V concludes with a brief overview of the current state of research on gender, citizenship and welfare state regimes.

I. The welfare state or welfare states?

The welfare state as we know it today in Western economically developed capitalist countries was developed primarily in the post-World War II period and is strongly associated with the 1942 British Government Beveridge report on *Social Insurance and Allied Services*, but the roots of many of the contemporary programmes were planted between the 1880s and 1920s in various Western Europe countries, most notably in Germany during the Bismark era, hence the contemporary reference to the 'Bismarkian welfare state' (Flora and Alber, 1981). State intervention in social policy type activity – that is, as a protection against total dependence on the market for survival – goes back several centuries (Polanyi, 1944).

The term 'welfare state' is usually used to refer to expenditure on health, education, personal social services and income maintenance programmes such as pensions, unemployment insurance, and social assistance or welfare as it is known in North America. These programmes are directed to lessening the impact of market forces on individuals and reflect social rights to certain minimum standards. While *the* welfare state so defined is a phenomenon of advanced capitalism and as such all developed capitalist economies can be identified as welfare states, it is important to recognize variation in the types of welfare states developed. This reflects the fact that different political choices have been made in different countries in response to the problems of reconciling production and distribution. These differences are reflected in differences in the scope and quality of social rights. One of the key arguments of this chapter is that the range and quality of social rights varies cross-nationally and that welfare state analysis must explain this variation. Our understanding of any particular welfare state is enhanced by analysing how and why it varies from other welfare states. Before outlining key theoretical approaches to the issue of welfare state development and variation it is necessary to consider the links between citizenship and welfare state development. The centrality of social rights in the definitions of the welfare state outlined above points to the inherent connection between the development of citizenship rights and welfare state development.

Citizenship rights, in particular social citizenship rights, are central to welfare states. The development of welfare states can be seen as a process of the transition from access to services and benefits entirely on the basis of class position and associated resources to access to certain categories of services and benefits on the basis of citizenship. Most contemporary discussions of citizenship take as their source the essay 'On Citizenship and Social Class' presented by T.H. Marshall in 1949 (Marshall, 1964: 65–122). On the basis of British history Marshall divided the development of citizenship into three stages: civil citizenship, relating to liberty of the person and property rights, is dated from the eighteenth century with the development of the judicial system and legal rights. Political citizenship, relating primarily to the right to vote and to organize, for example in trade unions, is dated from the nineteenth century. Social citizenship, which relates to rights to economic welfare and security, is dated from the twentieth century with the extension of the educational system and the development of the welfare state. Marshall identified social rights as essentially different from civil and political rights which had little direct effect on social inequality. Indeed, he identifies civil rights as necessary to the maintenance of class inequality (Marshall, 1964: 88). In contrast, he saw the extension of social citizenship rights as a process, directed towards the modification of 'the whole pattern of social inequality' within capitalist society (Marshall, 1964: 96). None of these rights evolved naturally; they were achieved through collective struggle. In the case of social rights this collective struggle was possible because of the existence of civil and political rights. This analysis and periodization relates to the British situation and it is problematic even when applied there because of its assumption of a universal category of citizens, all of whom equally benefit from achieved citizenship rights. For example, women achieved political and civil citizenship rights later than men and the struggle for political citizenship rights preceded the achievement of some civil rights (Walby, 1994). Furthermore, the exercise of all citizenship rights can be influenced by class position (Barbalet, 1988). Despite these limitations Marshall's analysis provides major insights into citizenship and provides the background for the conception of citizenship embodied in much of the welfare state literature, in particular, the comparative analysis literature. Citizenship is not just about rights, it is also about participation and obligations. Both dimension of the concept are considered in Section III.

II.   Welfare state regimes and citizenship

The welfare state regime concept is not new – in the 1970s Richard Titmuss identified three models of welfare state: residual; industrial achievement-performance; and institutional redistributive. In contrast to Wilensky and Lebaux (1958), who had pointed to a process of modernization from a 'residual', or least-developed welfare state, to an 'institutional', or well-developed welfare state, Titmus pointed to the simultaneous existence of the three regimes and pointed to an ideological basis of difference: policy choice, not level of economic development, determines the welfare state regime of a particular country. The work of Titmuss on social policy regimes is still influential but the recent growth in interest has been sparked by the work of Gøsta Esping-Andersen (1990, 1999), in particular his 1990 book: *The Three Worlds of Welfare Capitalism*. Citizenship rights are central to the welfare state regime concept outlined therein. Welfare regimes refer to clusters of more or less distinct welfare states in terms of the level and quality of social rights and bases of stratification on which the welfare state is built. 'The existence of policy regimes reflects the circumstances that short-term policies, reforms, debates, and decision-making take place within frameworks of historical institutionalisation that differ qualitatively between countries' (Esping-Andersen, 1990: 80).

Esping-Andersen has identified three welfare state regimes: social democratic as exemplified by Sweden, Norway, Denmark and Finland, since the 1960s, liberal as exemplified by Britain, Ireland, the United States, Canada, Australia and New Zealand and a conservative or status-based regime exemplified by Germany, France and Italy.

The *social democratic welfare state regime* is characterized by an emphasis on universalism, comprehensive risk coverage, generous benefit levels and egalitarianism.[1] This entails a strong role for the state as does its integration of social and economic policy and its emphasis on the primacy of full employment.[2] 'What is uniquely social democratic is firstly, the fusion of universalism with generosity and secondly, its comprehensive socialisation of risks' (Esping-Andersen, 1999: 79). This results in a strong emphasis on the provision of social services and the privileging of care for children and the aged. This in turn is associated with high levels of employment for women, particularly in the public sector (Huber and Stephens, 2001).

The *liberal welfare state regime* is characterized by state intervention that is clearly subordinate to the market. It has a relatively strong emphasis on income and/or means-tested programmes, and while there may be a commitment to universalism it is universalism with an equal opportunity focus. Using the distinction associated with Richard Titmuss (1974: 30–31) it is characterized by a marginalist as opposed to an institutional approach to social policy. Its residualist approach results in a narrow definition of eligibility as reflected in a relatively high level of needs-based social assistance, a narrow range of risks considered 'social' and a low level of family services and heavy reliance on the market for the provision of services.

The key characteristic of the *conservative welfare state regime* is the linkage of rights to class and status through a variety of social insurance schemes. There is a strong commitment to the maintenance of the traditional family, and social services tend to be provided only when the family's ability to cope is exhausted.[3]

The three regimes vary in terms of the degree of protection from total dependence on the labour market, that is de-commodification, the degree to which the organization of services contributes to social stratification and the primacy accorded to the state, the market and the family.

Esping-Andersen (1990, 1999) uses the term '*de-commodification*' to capture 'the degree to which welfare states weaken the cash nexus by granting entitlements independent of market participation. It is one way of specifying T.H. Marshall's notion of social citizenship rights' (Esping-Andersen, 1999: 43). De-commodification is central to the welfare state project and the associated historical struggles. Commodification of labour refers to the situation where the individual's ability to sell her/his labour solely determines her/his access to resources while de-commodification reflects a level of insulation from dependence on the labour market for survival and contributes to the ability of workers to resist this pressure. In other words, the citizenship entitlements reflected in social security payments and public services, which to varying degrees in different countries and at different time periods in individual countries are independent of class position, facilitate resistance to the pressures of the market.

The quality of social rights and the issue of *social stratification*, or the role of the welfare state as 'an active force in the ordering of social relations' (Esping-Andersen, 1990: 23), revolve around the criteria for access to, and duration of, benefits. These criteria are means and/or income testing, social insurance contributions and citizenship. Means and/or income testing is the criterion for access to social assistance benefits, that is access to benefits is based on need. This contrasts with social insurance-based benefits where contributions, generally related to labour force participation, are the criterion. Citizenship as a criterion 'offers a basic, equal benefit to all, irrespective of prior earnings, contributions, or performance' (Esping-Andersen, 1990: 23). The extent to which benefits based on any of the three criteria afford protection against dependence on the labour market for survival, that is are de-commodifying, depends on the level of benefits and the extent to which they insulate the individual from market pressures. The difference between means-tested social assistance and contribution-related social insurance has been identified in several studies. Both systems are associated with social divisions. Means and/or income testing is associated with the stigmatizing of recipients on the basis of demonstration of need. The social insurance model is associated with divisions related to income and/or occupational status. The citizenship criterion can also be associated with the creation and/or maintenance of social divisions. Specifically, low levels of citizenship-based benefits are likely to be associated with the purchase of additional private protection by those with ample resources.

All welfare states make use of the three criteria of eligibility but to a varying extent. In the social democratic welfare state the citizenship criterion is pervasive, the liberal welfare state is characterized by a strong emphasis on means-tested programmes and the conservative/status-based welfare state regime is characterized by a variety of class and status-based social insurance schemes. Each of these criteria for eligibility is reflected in a particular form of stratification.

Welfare state regimes also vary in the primacy they accord to *the state, the market and the family*: the social democratic regime relies heavily on state provision to meet social needs and the state espouses full employment as an integral part of the welfare state and is relatively active in its generation and maintenance; the liberal regime relies relatively heavily on the market and the conservative/status-based regime, with its commitment to the principle of subsidiarity, relies heavily on the family. A good example of these differences is child care, although there is variation within regimes. Taking Sweden and Denmark as exemplars of the social democratic regime, public child care provision is high, facilitating high female labour force participation. In the liberal regimes of the US and Canada, female labour force participation is also relatively high but the majority of working parents with child care responsibilities are dependent on market solutions. In Germany, an exemplar of the conservative regime, female labour force participation is low, reflecting the reliance on the family for child care.

The welfare regime concept as outlined by Esping-Andersen sparked an enormous and productive debate that is still continuing on welfare state regimes and the classification of welfare states within this framework (Abrahamson, 1999; Arts and Gelissen, 2002; Kauto, 2002). While it has inspired considerable innovative work on the comparative analysis of welfare states it has been the subject of some criticism, for example in relation to the inclusion of countries within the liberal regime and the exclusion from consideration of several southern European countries (Castles and Mitchell, 1992; Leibfried, 1993; Ferrera, 1996).[4] As a consequence of the fact that all welfare states are unique when examined in detail, disagreement in the classification of particular countries is not surprising. Despite differences in nomenclature there is broad agreement on the following clusters: social democratic/ Scandinavian/Nordic, liberal/residual/marginalist, conservative status-based/ continental/corporatist. It is now acknowledged that a fourth cluster – the Southern European welfare regime model – must be added. This refers to the welfare states of Spain, Portugal, Greece and Italy. This 'Southern model' is characterized by a fragmented income maintenance system with certain elements of marked generosity, for example in pensions, but significant gaps in social protection, a low degree of state penetration in the welfare sphere, a strong reliance on the extended family for care services, the persistence of clientelism and patronage systems but the development of significant, if partial, national health systems on universalistic grounds (Ferrera, 1996). Guillén and Matsaganis (2000) reinforce the argument for a unique 'Southern model' in their analysis of Greece and Spain in the context of membership of the European Union.

The most well-developed critique of the welfare state regime concept, especially the Esping-Andersen formulation, has been made by scholars interested in a gender-sensitive welfare state analysis. Before considering these issues I briefly outline key arguments relating to gender and citizenship.

III.   Gender and citizenship

Citizenship is about membership in society and the rights – civil, political and social – that characterize that membership. It is equally about obligations. These statements reflects the two historical traditions within which discussion of citizenship has taken place – these are the liberal individual rights tradition and the civic republican tradition with its emphasis on citizenship as obligation to participate in the political system in the interest of the common good. Most of the welfare regime-related debate has focused on the citizenship rights dimension as outlined by T.H. Marshall (see Sections I and V); the citizenship as obligations tradition tends not to consider the issues of social rights except in so far as obligations are considered as a corrective to individual rights. Increasingly it is recognized that both elements are essential for an effective analysis of welfare regimes (for example, Lister, 2001; Siim, 2000).

III.1   Citizenship: participation and obligations

The civic republican tradition emphasizes civic duty, the submission of individual interests to that of the common good and the primacy of the public sphere in which the citizen is a political actor. In its pure form civic republicanism is very demanding on the individual. Political activity is seen as an end in itself associated with the pursuit of the common good which is separate from the pursuit of individual interests or even particular group interests. The revival of the civic republican tradition since the 1980s reflects a reaction against the individualism of the liberal citizenship paradigm with its focus on rights and the pursuit of individual interests. Despite this, the rights and obligations traditions of citizenship analysis are complementary – they reflect two sides of the citizenship coin.

The problem with much of the analysis of citizenship as obligation is its failure to recognize the barriers to participation. This is particularly true of the New Right and some communitarian advocates of citizenship as obligation who have adapted the tradition to their own ends.[5] But there is also a critical but sympathetic debate on the civic republican tradition articulated by several feminist analysts. These analysts have sought to broaden the definition of political space and participation.

i.   The conception of political space: a major consequence of the traditional institutional focus of political analysis has been that women were largely excluded. The recognition of this exclusion, and the associated focus on women's political behaviour, implies a broadening of the concept of political action from 'formal interactions between the citizen and the state' to include the ways in which political space and political alliances are structured through interactions by individuals located in particular social situations 'who interact publicly and privately with each other and the state and other institutions' (Jones, 1990: 799). This has implications for the spatial dimension of citizenship which up to now has been largely institutional and has ignored those political processes associated with movements to transform public consciousness on issues such as sexual harassment, rape and pornography, which 'are examples of a definition of participation that is focused not on government action but on the reclamation of public space itself' (Jones, 1990: 803).

ii. The conception of political participation: defining participation purely in terms of active participation, and/or interest, in parliamentary politics is likely to under-represent the participation of women, particularly in some countries and in some communities in all countries. These indicators do not include participation in the informal political system of social movements and trade unions nor participation as client representatives 'in negotiating the content and forms of delivery of their entitlements' (Hernes, 1987: 189). Birte Siim has identified these informal political activities as 'power from below' in contrast to participation in formal politics or 'power from above' (Siim, 1988: 176). What is being called for in all these critiques of citizenship is movement towards a pluralistic concept of citizenship directed to 'analyze unequal power relations that impede an inclusive politics of diversity and to give voice to those who are underrepresented' (Sarvasy and Siim, 1994: 254).

The incorporation of gender into the analysis implies a broadening of what constitutes formally recognized political space and participation to take into account power or at least influence from various arenas of political action. This illustrates the importance of social citizenship rights as a facilitator of women's political mobilization (Hernes, 1987) and the mutual interaction of citizenship as rights, and citizenship as participation. Social reforms such as access to paid work on equal terms for women and men and the associated services such as child care and parental leave that facilitate labour force participation may be associated with increased political participation. Both Helga Hernes (1987) and Frances Fox Piven (1984) have identified the mobilization possibilities associated with welfare state development in the very different settings of a social democratic and liberal welfare state respectively. Birte Siim concludes that the Scandinavian research demonstrates a complex interaction between social reforms and women's political participation: 'social rights have been both the cause and the effect of women's political participation' (Siim, 1994: 292). In Denmark and Sweden social rights to child care and high female labour force participation preceded active political participation and mobilization, whereas in Norway political integration came first and social rights were an effect of this integration. While Siim argues that 'social reform without access to politics is an expression of paternalism' she acknowledges that such reforms in Scandinavia have created 'a power base that has stimulated women's access to politics and woman-friendly policies designed by women' (1994: 292). The concept of 'woman-friendly policies' aims to enable men and women to be 'autonomous individuals and parents'/caring individuals and also incorporates the idea of women's agency (1994: 301, note 5). Women's agency is the link between citizenship as participation and citizenship as rights (Siim, 2000).

III.2   Citizenship: participation and the exercise of rights
Variation in social citizenship rights is fundamental to welfare state regime differences. This is addressed in the next section. Here we outline briefly some general critiques of the liberal conception of citizenship as it relates to the sexual division of labour and the public–private divide. Carole Pateman (1989) is one of the strongest critics of the conventional gender-neutral conception of citizenship and builds her critique around the failure of the liberal conception of citizenship to take seriously the significance of the sexual division of labour. The narrowness of the dominant conception of the ideal citizen as full-time worker has implications for the conceptualization of paid work and its relationship to unpaid work. It also has implications for understanding caring work, the rights of those in need of care, and relations of dependence. Her critique of the public–private divide has been enormously influential although Biirte Siim is critical of its non-inclusion of women's agency, that is their active role in contributing to and forging change (Siim, 2000).

Ruth Lister's starting point is also the public–private divide, which she argues underpins the meaning of citizenship. Using a tripartite division of the public sphere she analyses women's position in relation to the paid economy, the state and the polity. She focuses on the implications for citizenship rights and obligations of the sexual division of paid and unpaid labour and concludes that women's citizenship is restricted in each of the public spheres by women's position in the private sphere. She concludes that the achievement of full citizenship for women is going to require 'radical' changes in both the public and private spheres and the relationship between the two. Specifically she argues that the sexual division of paid and unpaid work and time needs to be recast as does the social organization of paid work and politics (Lister, 1993). Like Pateman, she points to the limitations of both gender-neutrality and gender differentiation – the equality/difference formulation in relation to men and women – and argues instead for a gender-pluralism approach 'in which both women and men are seen as members of multiple groups'. Furthermore she argues for 'a critical synthesis of the rights and responsibilities of political participation' (Lister, 2001: 323).

III.3   Citizenship: participation, obligation and rights
Despite the limitations of the traditional citizenship as rights and as obligation approaches from a gender-sensitive point of view both are essential to a comprehensive understanding of citizenship and to the analysis of women's relationship to the state and public policy. Rights and obligations are not mutually exclusive. The fulfilment of obligations is dependent on rights and the enhancement of rights is dependent on political participation. We need to draw on both traditions but with a clear acknowledgement of the critiques of

both, which contribute to the re-framing of citizenship as rights and citizenship as participation and the fulfilment of obligations in a mutually reinforcing direction and as a positive contribution to the analysis of welfare state regimes.

IV.   Welfare state regimes, gender, class and citizenship

Gender refers to the socially constructed structural, relational and symbolic differences between men and women. The concern of gender-sensitive analysis is with 'how gender is involved in processes and structures that previously have been conceived as having nothing to do with gender' (Acker, 1989: 238). It is also based on the recognition that gender and class are produced within the same ongoing practices. 'Looking at them from one angle we see class, from another we see gender, neither is complete without the other' (ibid.: 239). Before considering the feminist critique of, and contribution to, citizenship and welfare regime analysis I outline briefly key insights of feminist analyses of the welfare state, which pre-date the welfare regimes debates but which influence those debates.

IV.1   Feminist analyses of the welfare state

There is no single feminist analysis of welfare states. Despite considerable theoretical variation amongst feminists, often paralleling traditional approaches, what is common to all feminist welfare state analysts is the recognition of gender as a fundamental structuring mechanism in contemporary societies and the recognition of gender as fundamental to understanding welfare states. The particular aspect of gender difference that is emphasized varies by theoretical orientation (Williams, 1989: Table 3.1).

Despite variation in the economic and social position of women in OECD countries (Norris, 1987) there are a number of common themes evident in feminist analyses of the welfare state irrespective of country of origin. The centrality of women for the welfare state, as paid workers and unpaid community care-givers, and also the centrality of the welfare state for women as clients and as employees has been demonstrated in numerous studies based on experience in several OECD countries with different kinds of welfare state regimes (see O'Connor, 1996, Chapter 1 for outline of this literature). Despite this double centrality most analyses of welfare states up to the 1990s not only ignored gender as an analytical category but also paid little attention to women as a distinct category and this is still true for much welfare state analysis. As a consequence much of the feminist analysis concentrates on making women visible in welfare states. This includes a growing body of research on women's role as social activists in women's organizations and bureaucracies in influencing the development of welfare states (Andrew, 1984; Skocpol, 1992; Thane, 1993; Gordon, 1994; Siim, 2000).

One of the major differences evident in feminist analyses relates to the conception of the welfare state vis-à-vis women. Some analysts conceive the welfare state as oppressive whereas others see it as a potential resource for women. The theme of the welfare state as oppressive and the stress on the limitations it imposes on women was strongly evident in the early work on women in welfare states. This work stressed the ideological bases of social policy and the issue of public partriarchy or the social control of women by welfare state bureaucracies. One of the earliest and most widely cited books analysing women in the welfare state is Elizabeth Wilson's (1977) *Women and the Welfare State*. It presents an historical analysis of the British welfare state stressing its ideological and social control aspects. Wilson argues that 'the Welfare State is not just a set of services, it is also a set of ideas about society, about the family, and – not least important – about women, who have a centrally important role within the family, as its linchpin' (ibid.: 9). Mary McIntosh, also on the basis of British experience, has identified the role of the welfare state in the maintenance of a particular family form – the male-breadwinner nuclear family – that is oppressive to women (McIntosh, 1978). In a similar vein many studies based on US and Canadian experience emphasize the oppressive and social control aspects of the welfare state for women (Fraser, 1989). In contrast, comparative studies and those based on Scandinavian experience, while recognizing marked gender inequalities even in well-developed welfare states, emphasize the possibility for empowerment of women through the welfare state (Ruggie, 1984; Borchorst and Siim, 1987; Dahlerup, 1987; Hernes, 1987; Norris, 1987). This difference may reflect differences in welfare state institutions across welfare state regimes. In liberal welfare states access to many benefits and services are income and/or means tested and the predominant encounter of many women with welfare state institutions is as social assistance clients whose benefits are relatively meagre. In contrast, the experience of women in the social democratic welfare state regime is more likely to be as employees and citizens with rights to services; this is reflected in a relatively optimistic view of state potential. For example, Helga Hernes, a Norwegian analyst, discusses the possibility of achieving a 'woman-friendly state', that is, 'a state where injustice on the basis of gender would be largely eliminated without an increase in other forms of inequality such as among groups of women' (Hernes, 1987: 15). Despite the overall relatively pessimistic view of the state that permeates work on women in liberal welfare states some analysts have identified the state as a resource for women and the possibility that social policy may provide opportunities for significant positive developments under particular historical circumstances even in liberal welfare states (Piven, 1984; Quadagno, 1990).

IV.2   Gender-sensitive analysis of citizenship and welfare state regimes
The gender-sensitive critique of welfare state regime analysis is inherently linked to the conception of citizenship underpinning the analysis, that is the focus on the citizen as worker. This is strongly linked to the critique of de-commodification, the welfare state as the conceptualization of a mechanism of stratification and state–market–family relations. These in turn relate to how relations between the public and private spheres are conceptualized and how the issues of caring and dependency are addressed. A related debate concerns the concept of the 'male-breadwinner regime' and its relationship to established welfare regime typologies.

De-commodification and access to the labour market   While de-commodification, as reflected in pensions and unemployment insurance for example, is a central protection for both men and women in the labour force it is important to recognize that before de-commodification becomes an issue it is necessary to be a labour market participant. The primary concern for many women is not de-commodification but commodification as reflected in labour market participation. If in the labour market, the gender-sensitive concern for social rights is likely to focus not just on pensions and unemployment insurance but also on provision for caring activities. This does not imply that caring is not relevant to all workers – it is a recognition of the reality of the widespread gender division of caring. Recognition of these facts implies a need to incorporate the relationship between unpaid and paid work into welfare state analysis. This means that analysis of de-commodification must be accompanied by analysis of services that facilitate labour market participation, such as child care and parental leave (O'Connor, 1993).

Limitation of access to the labour market may be the result of systemic discrimination or inequality of condition, such as that associated with the division of labour in caring responsibilities. Since both labour force participation and quality of employment are gender-linked and constrained by unpaid caring responsibilities, which are in turn gender-linked, those entitlements which facilitate labour force participation are of crucial importance to the economic and social rights of women and in the mitigation and/or prevention of dependence. Services related to 'the organization of daily life' may facilitate or hinder labour force participation (Hernes, 1987: 47). Policies relating to the length and flexibility of the working day, availability of child care and facilities for caring for other dependants, employment and pay equity, maternity and parental leave, training and re-training services facilitate, or make difficult, the articulation of production and reproduction or labour market and family. Public policies in these areas illustrate clearly the intersection of state, market and family and also the differences not only amongst but within welfare state regime clusters. There is considerable evidence that the state is of particular importance for women's employment; its action or inaction may facilitate, hinder or be neutral in regard to the level and quality of labour market participation (Ruggie, 1984). It has a crucial role as an agent of commodification of women: women's labour force participation is disproportionate in the public sector even in countries with relatively low levels of female labour force participation, and conditions and remuneration are generally superior in the public sector (O'Connor, Orloff and Shaver, 1999: Chapter 3).

Facilitating access to the labour market and enhancing the quality of employment addresses one element of the additional measure of state activity proposed by Ann Orloff to meet the needs of those with caring responsibilities. This is namely their capacity to form and maintain autonomous households: 'to survive and support their children without having to marry to gain access to breadwinners' income' (Orloff, 1993: 319) and to enhance women's power vis-à-vis men within marriages and families. In addition to labour market participation cash benefits from the state 'for staying at home to care for children or others, a citizen's wage, or a combination of employment and state benefits' could enhance the capacity to form and/or maintain an autonomous household (O'Connor, Orloff and Shaver, 1999: 33).

While de-commodification or protection from forced participation in the labour market irrespective of health, age, disability, care-giving requirements and the availability of suitable employment is a significant citizenship right for both men and women, it needs to be enhanced by the right to services facilitating access to the labour market and enhancing the quality of employment and the capacity to form and maintain an autonomous household.

Welfare states as systems of stratification   The criteria for access to benefits and services, namely means-tested social assistance, contribution-related social insurance and citizenship-based access, are mechanisms of social stratification and key distinguishing aspects of welfare state regimes. All welfare states make use of the three criteria of eligibility, however the dominance of one criterion or another differentiates welfare states. There is considerable evidence that, irrespective of welfare state regime, women constitute the vast majority of social assistance recipients and make claims on the basis of need, usually family need, rather than as individuals with citizenship and/or employment-related rights. In contrast, men are concentrated in the employment-related social insurance benefits category. While women are increasing their representation in this category these programmes have not always treated men's and women's work-based claims equally. Much equality legislation is directed to ensuring this. From a gender-sensitive perspective, stratification has two aspects: gender differentiation and gender inequality. 'Gender differentiation refers to the highlighting of gender difference and the underlining of gender identities through distinctions based on the gender division of labour. Creating gender inequality involves treating different gender roles differently or treating men and women differently' (O'Connor, Orloff and Shaver, 1999: 225).

States, market, family relations in provision of services In considering social services and benefits, the division in provision between state and market is readily recognizable because of the monetary values assigned to such benefits as pensions, and services such as health care. Yet, the family is a crucial site of social welfare in all welfare states but its role is not assigned a monetary value and its contribution tends to be taken for granted. This is particularly true in regard to care-giving, especially women's unpaid care-giving work (there is a huge body of gender-sensitive research on dependency and care-giving; see O'Connor, 1996: Chapters 2 and 3; Lewis (ed.) 1998; Daly (ed.), 2001). Yet, it is not sufficient to talk of the household in terms of the interaction between work in the household and in the labour market; it is necessary to recognize that participation in the public sphere is wider than labour market participation.

Participation and mobilization Each of the elements of the welfare state regime concept has been modified through the gender-sensitive analysis outlined above but this has focused for the most part on elements of the dependent variable, that is the variation in welfare state regimes. The independent variable has also been the focus of concern by gender-sensitive analysts (O'Connor, Orloff and Shaver, 1999: Chapter 6). This brings into focus the issue of agency and participation discussed in Section III.

The class politics perspective on social change that provides the explanation for variation and change in welfare regimes as outlined by Esping-Andersen (1990, 1999) focuses on collective action through trade unions and party control of government 'within frameworks of historical institutionalisation that differ qualitatively between countries' (Esping-Andersen, 1990: 80). The prospects for systemic change are seen as a function of the balance of class power at the political as well as at the economic level. This is not a denial of structural factors but recognition of the dual character of Western capitalist societies, that is the coexistence of a liberal democratic political system and a capitalist economic structure. The principal power resources of the working class are the right to vote and the right to organize for collective action (Korpi, 1989: 312). These power resources, expressed through trade union membership and labour or social democratic political party strength, may be used in coalition with other social forces, such as farmers or the middle class, to lead to political power that may partially offset the economic power of capital (Esping-Andersen, 1990). The welfare state is the essential element of the compromise with labour on the part of the capitalist class (Korpi, 1983; Stephens, 1979).[6] This leaves out of account other forms of mobilization that have influenced welfare state development, in particular the gender equality and anti-feminist movements. As was pointed out in Section III social citizenship rights that facilitate labour force participation may also facilitate political participation which in turn may enhance social and civil rights (Hernes, 1987; Koven and Michel, 1993; Siim, 2000).

IV.3   From male-breadwinner to 'adult-worker model family'

In an influential article in 1992, Jane Lewis (1992) argued that the idea of the male-breadwinner family model has historically cut across established typologies of welfare states and that the model has been modified in different ways and to different degrees in different countries. Services facilitating the labour force participation of women were absent or very limited in strong male-breadwinner states, such as Britain and Ireland, up to the 1990s whereas they were relatively well-developed in weak male-breadwinner models such as Sweden. This reflects the fact that weak male-breadwinner states are relatively successful in solving the issue of valuing caring work – women are compensated at market rates for caring work which is typically unpaid, or paid at very low rates, in strong male-breadwinner states. This difference is reflected in levels of public provision of child care and care for other dependent people and also in the payment rates for those, mostly women, who carry out this caring within welfare states.[7] The male-breadwinner model in its pure form never existed, that is women were not totally excluded from the labour market and totally dependent on male breadwinners for survival, yet all countries reflect elements of this ideology and it underpinned social policies assuming female dependency on a male wage and family law in the late nineteenth century and much of the twentieth century.[8]

Lewis (2001) argues that in the late twentieth century there was a shift in several economically developed countries to the 'one-and-a-half-earner family' and in some – she identifies Sweden and the United States – to an 'adult-worker model family' where it is assumed that all adult workers are in the labour market (ibid.: 163). While this is potentially more favourable to women than the male-breadwinner model the realization of this depends on appropriate policies to recognize care work, policies such as maternity and parental leave and child care. Sweden implemented such policies, the United States did not. Whereas the Swedish universalist welfare state grafted on *citizenship rights* to recognize 'difference' associated with child-bearing, child and other care activities, the residual US welfare state grafted the equal *citizenship obligation* of participation in the labour force irrespective of caring requirements on to its residual welfare state and associated residual entitlements. Lewis traces a shift towards an adult-worker family model in the Netherlands and the United Kingdom from the late twentieth century but points to considerable inconsistencies between labour market policies pushing towards participation on the one hand and the income maintenance and care policies, or the implementation of these, which would facilitate full participation on the other hand. Visser (2002) argues that the 'one-and-a-half-earner family' model that characterized the Netherlands in the late 1990s and early 2000s was not the result of deliberate policy but 'the outcome of "bottom-up" pressure and accommodating policy changes' linked to the late increase in married women in the labour force and the absence of child care provision (Visser, 2002).

While the male-breadwinner regime has never existed in pure form its various manifestations are now being modified and eroded through demographic and labour market change. The associated increasing commodification of women with caring demands is posing challenges for traditional patterns of de-commodification and welfare state stratification. Gender-sensitive analysis is essential to analyse effectively and understand these changes.

IV.4   Gender-sensitive analysis

Despite the variation in emphasis amongst feminist analysts, all are interested not only in making women visible in welfare state analysis but in incorporating gender, conceived in structural and relational terms, as a central analytical category in welfare state analysis. While much of the earlier research was in the 'women and the welfare state' mode, that is making women visible, much of the more recent research has been explicitly directed to the second project. This has been accompanied by an emphasis not only on the interaction of gender and class but also a recognition of the importance of race, in interaction with both gender and class, in structuring some welfare states, most notably the United States (Williams, 1989; Gordon, 1994; Quadagno, 1994). As with most of the feminist analyses of welfare states this work has tended to be country-specific historical analysis or comparative case studies. This is not surprising in view of the complexity of comparative work involving several key dimensions of difference. Recently, Fiona Williams (1995) has highlighted the absence of race in the analysis of welfare state regimes. She advocates an analysis of states' relationships through welfare states to the areas of family, work and nation as a means of understanding welfare settlements in different countries (Williams, 1995: 148). The nation dimension includes analysis of systems of migration, colonialism and imperialism and processes of inclusion and exclusion from the nation-state as reflected in citizenship rights. She argues that an analysis focused on all three areas is necessary to grasp the diversity of welfare settlements in different countries.

V.   Gender, citizenship and welfare regimes: moving towards an integrated multi-faceted analysis

In evaluating theories of the welfare state it is important to bear in mind that '[i]f a theory focuses upon a particular factor as historically important, then the empirical manifestations of that factor become important, and they are singled out for investigation' (Alford and Friedland, 1985: 398); in this process other factors are excluded or glossed over. This may be true of political or economic factors, of state-centred or society-centred factors. It was almost universally true of gender and race in welfare state analysis until recently. There is now some evidence of change, particularly in relation to gender but less so in relation to race. This change is in response, at least in part, to the very considerable amount of gender-sensitive analysis that has now become available. The change has also been conditioned by the realization that the family – both as a social institution and as decision maker – can no longer be assumed away. 'As the notion of a "second demographic revolution" indicates, and as all statistics demonstrate, the changing role of women and evolving new household forms are an intrinsic – possibly leading – part of the socioeconomic transformation around us' (Esping-Andersen, 1999: 12).

Irrespective of the basis of the change there is now a considerable body of work acknowledging and responding to the gender-sensitive critiques; those of Esping-Andersen (1999) and Korpi, (2000) are among the most noteworthy. The dialogue opened is likely to continue as the welfare regime concept is analysed (Abrahamson, 1999; Arts and Gelissen, 2002). Recent reviews conclude that the Esping-Andersen regime concept is still yielding useful insights and that further work is warranted on it and the associated modified typologies. Abrahamson (1999) suggests that the welfare regime concept may be particularly appropriate in the context of debates over globalization and European integration although he also points out that context matters in the sense that there may be some variation in regime typologies depending on the programme being analysed.

By their nature ideal types never are a perfect fit for the welfare state of any country nor are they intended to be such. Rather, they crystallize similarities and allow us to understand variation amongst the broadly similar, but they do not reflect exactly the characteristics of any particular welfare state.

> The fruitfulness of typologies ... depends on our ability to base them on variables which are of heuristic value for the understanding of the background to and consequences of variations between ideal types and on the extent to which empirically observed variation between types are greater than variation within types (Korpi and Palme, 1998: 667).

The preponderance of evidence indicates that despite variation within regime clusters, variation between clusters is greater. This means that the regime concept is a useful tool in understanding particular welfare states by sensitizing us as to how they vary from other welfare states in terms of de-commodification and services facilitating access to the labour market, stratification by class, gender and race and division of responsibility between state, market and family in the provision of services. In explaining this variation, the research on gender, citizenship and welfare state regimes indicates that it is necessary to have a broad interpretation of participation and mobilization that takes into account not only class mobilization but also other forms of mobilization.

In conclusion, while gender, citizenship and welfare state regime continue to be contested concepts they are now the subject of intense theoretical and empirical analysis that is yielding insights into the comparative analysis of welfare states, in particular, into the variation in the range and quality of social rights. Increasingly it is recognized that an undifferentiated concept of citizenship cannot be assumed, that gender, race and class and their interaction must be integral parts of the analysis.

Notes

1. It is noteworthy that Esping-Andersen (1999: 78) reserves the social democratic classification for the post-1960s welfare states in the Nordic countries. Their roots were with minor exceptions liberal, dating back like Britain to nineteenth-century poor relief, but there were elements of universalism relatively early.
2. Welfare and employment policy in the social democratic welfare state has consistently been couched in terms of 'productivism', that is 'maximizing the productive potential of the citizenry'. This is different from 'workfare' which implies conditionality of benefits. 'Productivism' implies that the welfare *state* must guarantee that all people have the necessary resources and motivation to work (and that work is available) (Esping-Andersen, 1999: 80).
3. The conservative/status-based welfare regime is sometimes identified as the continental [European] welfare states because of the countries it characterizes. It is also sometimes referred to, for example by Leibfried (1993), as Bismarkian. This reflects its historical origins and the influence of the insurance-based and corporatist elements characterizing the Bismarkian tradition.
4. I concentrate on the welfare regime typology formulated by Esping-Andersen (1990) but other typologies have also been formulated, for example Leibfried (1993) identifies four social policy regimes in the European Community: Scandinavian, Bismarkian, Anglo-Saxon and Latin Rim. The first three are similar but not identical to the social democratic, conservative-status based and liberal regimes respectively as identified by Esping-Andersen. The welfare state is identified as the employer of first resort (mainly for women) in the Scandinavian regime, as the compensator of first resort in the Bismarkian regime, as the compensator of last resort in the Anglo-Saxon countries. The Latin Rim regime covers the southern peripheral areas of Europe and is characterized as a 'rudimentary welfare state' – this characterization is disputed by Ferrera (1996). Korpi and Palme (1998) use the institutional structure of old age pension and sickness cash benefits as the basis for a welfare state typology. Based on these transfer payments arrangements they identify five institutional variants: targeted, voluntary state subsidized, conservative (corporatist), basic security and encompassing. These models reflect different views of the relative role of markets and politics in redistribution. While this typology provides differentiation of the Esping-Andersen typology it is consistent with it although based exclusively on transfer payment arrangements. Consequently, it has less general applica-

bility particularly in relation to services, which are of increasing importance in welfare regime analysis.

5. The New Right have argued for the primacy of work obligations over rights which should be contingent on the fulfilment of these obligations (for example Mead, 1986 and Novak, 1987) and the communitarians have argued for a re-balancing of duties and rights (for example Etzioni, 1993).

6. These 'historic compromises' are associated with change in the patterns and conceptions of 'normal politics' – for example in the right of workers to unionize, universal suffrage, the separation of political power from economic power that resulted from the accession to power of the Social Democrats in Sweden in 1932, and the post-Second World War settlement in Britain which included the National Health Service and the 1944 Education Act. All of these settlements or social contracts between capital, labour and the state reflect a shift in the basis of social rights from class to citizenship.

7. The second major issue related to unpaid work, namely, its division between women and men has not been addressed in any welfare state.

8. Diane Sainsbury (1994) extends the male-breadwinner model by identifying a number of neglected dimensions of variation amongst welfare states and constructing contrasting ideal types – the breadwinner and individual models. The latter is characterized by access to services on the basis of individual rights rather than through the male breadwinner. She identifies ten dimensions of variation in these models, for example, family ideology, basis of entitlement, unit of benefit and contributions, whether employment and wages policies give priority to men or are aimed at both sexes, whether care is primarily private or has strong state involvement and whether caring work is unpaid or has a paid component. Analysis based on these dimensions allows for recognition of greater variation amongst welfare states than does classification into strong, weak and modified male-breadwinner models.

References

Abrahamson, Peter (1999), 'The welfare modeling business', *Social Policy and Administration*, **33**(4), 394–415.

Acker, Joan (1989), 'The problem with patriarchy', *Sociology*, **23**(4), 235–40.

Alford, Robert and Roger Friedland (1985), *Powers of Theory*, Cambridge: Cambridge University Press.

Andrew, Caroline (1984), 'Women and the welfare state', *Canadian Journal of Political Science*, **XVII**(4), 667–83.

Arts, Wil and John Gelissen (2002), 'Three worlds of welfare capitalism or more? A state of the art report', *Journal of European Social Policy*, **12**(2), 137–58.

Barbalet, J.M. (1988), *Citizenship Rights, Struggles and Class Inequality*, Minneapolis: University of Minnesota Press.

Borchorst, Annette and Birte Siim (1987), 'Women and the advanced welfare state – a new kind of patriarchal power?', in Ann Showstack Sassoon (ed.), *Women and the State: The Shifting Boundaries of Public and Private*, London: Hutchinson, pp. 128–57.

Castles, Francis and Deborah Mitchell (1992), 'Identifying welfare state regimes: the links between politics, instruments and outcomes', *Governance*, **5**(1), 1–26.

Dahlerupe, Drude (1987), 'Confusing concepts – confusing reality: a theoretical discussion of the patriarchal state', in Anne Shocustack Sassoon (ed.), *Women and the State*, London: Hutchinson, pp. 93–127.

Daly, Mary (ed.) (2001), *Care to Work: The Quest for Security*, Geneva: International Labour Office.

Esping-Andersen, Gøsta (1990), *The Three Worlds of Welfare Capitalism*, Princeton: Princeton University Press.

Esping-Andersen, Gøsta (1999), *Social Foundations of Postindustrial Economies*, New York: Oxford University Press.

Etzioni, Amitai (1993), *The Spirit of Community: Rights, Responsibilities, and the Communitarian Agenda*, New York: Crown Books.

Ferrera, Maurizio (1996), 'The "southern model" of welfare in social Europe', *Journal of European Social Policy*, **6**(1), 17–37.

Flora, Peter and Jens Alber (1981), 'Modernization, democratization, and the development of welfare states in Western Europe', in P. Flora and A.J. Heidenheimer (eds), *The Development of Welfare States in Europe and America*, New Brunswick: Transaction Books, pp. 37–80.

Fraser, Nancy (1989), 'Women, welfare, and the politics of need interpretation', in Nancy Fraser (ed.), *Unruly Practices: Power, Discourse and Gender in Contemporary Social Theory*, Minnesota: University of Minnesota, pp. 144–60.

Gordon, Linda (1994), *Pitied But Not Entitled: Single Mothers and the History of Welfare*, New York: The Free Press.

Guillén, Ana M. and Manos Matsaganis (2000), 'Testing the "social dumping" hypothesis in Southern Europe: welfare policies in Greece and Spain during the last 20 years', *Journal of European Social Policy*, **10**(2), 120–45.

Hernes, Helga (1987), *Welfare State and Woman Power: Essays in State Feminism*, Oslo: Norwegian University Press.

Huber, Evelyne Huber and John D. Stephens (2001), *Development and Crisis of the Welfare State Parties and Policies in Global Markets*, Chicago: The University of Chicago Press.

Jones, Kathleen B. (1990), 'Citizenship in a woman-friendly polity', *Signs: Journal of Women in Culture and Society*, **15**(4), 781–812.

Kauto, Mikko (2002), 'Investing in services in Western Europe', *Journal of European Social Policy*, **12**(1), 53–65.

Korpi, Walter (1983), *The Democratic Class Struggle*, London: Routledge & Kegan Paul.

Korpi, Walter (1989), 'Power, politics, and state autonomy in the development of social citzenship: social rights during sickness in eighteen OECD countries since 1930', *American Sociological Review*, **54**(3), 309–28.

Korpi, Walter (2000), 'Faces of inequality: gender, class, and patterns of inequalities in different types of welfare states', *Social Politics*, **7**(2), 127–91.

Korpi, Walter and Joachim Palme (1998), 'The strategy of equality and the paradox of redistribution', *American Sociological Review*, vol. 63, 661–87.

Koven, Seth and Sonya Michel (eds) (1993), *Mothers of the World: Maternalist Politics and the Origins of the Welfare State*, London: Routledge.

Leibfried, Stephan (1993), 'Towards a European welfare state? On integrating poverty regimes in the European Community', in Catherine Jones (ed.), *New Perspectives on the Welfare State in Europe*, London and New York: Routledge, pp. 133–56.

Lewis, Jane (1992), 'Gender and the development of welfare regimes', *Journal of European Social Policy*, **2**(3), 159–73.

Lewis, Jane (ed.) (1998), *Gender, Social Care and Welfare State Restructuring in Europe*, Aldershot: Ashgate Publishing.

Lewis, Jane (2001), 'The decline of the male breadwinner model: implications for work and care', *Social Politics*, **8**(2), 152–69.

Lister, Ruth (1993), 'Tracing the contours of women's citizenship', *Policy and Politics*, **2**(1), 3–16.

Lister, Ruth (2001), 'Citizenship and gender', in Nash, K. and A. Scott (eds), *The Blackwell Companion to Political Sociology*, Oxford: Blackwell, pp. 323–32.

Marshall, T.H. (1964), 'Citizenship and social class', in T.H. Marshall, *Class, Citizenship and Social Development*, Westport, CT: Greenwood Press, pp. 64–122.

McIntosh, Mary (1978), 'The state and the oppression of women', in A. Kuhn and A. Wolpe (eds), *Feminism and Materialism: Women and Modes of Production*, London: Routledge & Kegan Paul, pp. 254–90.

Mead, Lawrence, M. (1986), *Beyond Entitlement: The Social Obligations of Citizenship*, New York: The Free Press.

Norris, Pippa (1987), *Politics and Sexual Equality: The Comparative Position of Women in Western Democracies*, Boulder, Colorado: Rienner and Wheatsheaf.

Novak, Michael (1987), *The New Consensus on Family and Welfare: A Community of Self-Reliance*, Washington, DC: AEI Press.

O'Connor, Julia S. (1993), 'Gender, class and citizenship in the comparative analysis of welfare state regimes: theoretical and methodological issues', *British Journal of Sociology*, **44**(3), 501–18.

O'Connor, Julia S. (1996), 'From women and the welfare state to gendering welfare state regimes', *Current Sociology*, **44**(2), 1–124.

O'Connor, Julia S., Ann Shola Orloff and Sheila Shaver (1999), *States, Markets, Families: Gender, Liberalism and Social Policy in Australia, Canada, Great Britain and the United States*, Cambridge: Cambridge University Press.

Orloff, Ann Shola (1993), 'Gender and the social rights of citizenship: the comparative analysis of gender relations and welfare states', *American Sociological Review*, vol. 58, 303–28.

Pateman, Carole (1989), 'The patriarchal welfare state', in C. Pateman, *The Disorder of Women: Democracy Feminism and Political Theory*, Cambridge: Polity Press.

Piven, Frances Fox (1984), 'Women and the state: ideology, power, and the welfare state', *Socialist-Feminism Today*, vol. IV, 11–9.

Polanyi, Karl (1957) [1944], *The Great Transformation*, Boston: Beacon Press.

Quadagno, Jill (1990), 'Race, class, and gender in the US welfare state: Nixon's failed family assistance plan', *American Sociological Review*, vol. 55, 11–28.

Quadagno, Jill (1994), *The Colour of Welfare: How Racism Undermined the War on Poverty*, New York: Oxford University Press.

Ruggie, Mary (1984), *The State and Working Women: A Comparative Study of Britain and Sweden*, Princeton: Princeton University Press.

Sainsbury, Diane (1994), 'Women's and men's social rights: gendering dimensions of welfare states', in Diane Sainsbury (ed.), *Gendering Welfare States*, London: Sage, pp. 150–69.

Sarvasy, Wendy and Birte Siim (1994), 'Gender transitions to democracy, and citizenship', *Social Politics*, **1**(3), 249–55.

Shalev, Michael (1983), 'The social democratic model and beyond: two "generations" of comparative research on the welfare state', *Comparative Social Research*, vol. 6, 315–51.

Siim, Birte (1988), 'Towards a feminist rethinking of the welfare state', in Kathleen B. Jones and Anna G. Jónasdóttir (eds), *The Political Interests of Gender: Developing Theory and Research with a Feminist Face*, London: Sage Publications, pp. 160–86.

Siim, Birte (1994), 'Engendering democracy: social citizenship and political participation for women in Scandinavia', *Social Politics*, **1**(3), 286–305.

Siim, Birte (2000), *Gender and Citizenship: Politics and Agency in France, Britain and Denmark*, Cambridge: Cambridge University Press.

Skocpol, Theda (1992), *Protecting Soldiers and Mothers: The Political Origins of Social Policy in the United States*, Cambridge, MA: The Bellnap Press of Harvard University Press.

Stephens, John D. (1979), *The Transition from Capitalism to Socialism*, London: Macmillan.

Thane, Pat (1993), 'Women in the British Labour Party and the construction of the welfare state', in S. Koven and S. Michel (eds), *Mothers of the World: Maternalist Politics and the Origins of the Welfare State*, London: Routledge, pp. 343–77.

Titmuss, Richard M. (1974), *Social Policy*, London: Allen and Unwin.

Visser, Jelle (2002), 'The first part-time economy in the world: a model to be followed?', *Journal of European Social Policy*, **12**(1), 23–42.

Walby, Sylvia (1994), 'Is citizenship gendered?', *Sociology*, **28**(2), 81–100.

Wilensky, Harold and Charles Lebaux (1958), *Industrial Society and Social Welfare*, New York: Russell Sage Foundation.

Williams, Fiona (1989), *Social Policy: A Critical Introduction: Issues of Race, Gender and Class*, Cambridge: Polity Press.

Williams, Fiona (1995), 'Race/ethnicity, gender, and class in welfare states: a framework for comparative analysis', *Social Politics International Studies in Gender, State and Society*, **2**(2), 127–59.

Wilson, Elizabeth (1977), *Women and the Welfare State*, London: Tavistock.

11 Structured diversity: a framework for critically comparing welfare states?

Norman Ginsburg

Introduction

In an earlier attempt to clarify my own thinking on cross-national analysis of social policy I used the term 'critical structured diversity' to try to get a grip on the task (Ginsburg, 1992: 28). I suggested that comparativists have to consider the uniqueness of the social policies of particular nation-states in their diverse, historical and political contexts, while at the same time acknowledging that social policy is shaped by supranational economic, political and social 'structures'. To many this may seem to be stating the completely obvious, but juggling a 'national diversity' and a 'structural' approach in practice is an almost impossible task, because, if interpreted purely they are incompatible, or at the very least, have quite different starting points. To this task I added the challenge of trying to develop a 'critical' approach, which perhaps interpreted rather narrowly meant a focus on the role of welfare states in shaping social divisions of race, class and gender. This chapter reviews and reflects upon the notion of structured diversity as a way of making sense of cross-national developments in social policy and the growing literature in this field. We proceed by discussing mainstream and critical interpretations of structure and diversity, taken individually, before moving on to the possibilities of combining them, and using them critically.

As a preliminary it is essential to reflect briefly on what is being held up for cross-national consideration, that is, the dependent variable(s) under the heading of 'social policy' or 'the welfare state'. Here the two terms are used almost synonymously and very broadly to include all activity and discourse in the public realm addressing the basic needs of individuals and households including needs for personal autonomy and safety, and freedom from oppression, as well as material welfare needs. Analysts sometimes make broad comparative statements about welfare states using very limited parameters, for example the proportion of GDP devoted to public social expenditure. Most cross-national studies are confined to very particular aspects of social policy, for example pensions, pre-school child care, immigration policy. Here it is assumed that all aspects of social policy can be addressed by cross-national analysis, but we have to proceed from there on by referring to a very limited selection of recent research. There are, of course, many areas of cross-national analysis of social policy, which are not even touched on below, such as health care and housing.

Structure

Structural thinking starts from assumptions about common, underlying socio-economic pressures and/or political responses across the welfare states. It puts much more emphasis on the similarities rather than the differences between welfare states. Inevitably there are many ways of thinking about cross-national analysis of social policy which can be described as structural. Here we delineate four contrasting ways of thinking about structure. First, there is a relatively pure structural approach, which would imply a developing convergence in the shape, extent and need coverage of different welfare states. Theories of industrialization/post-industrialization or of modernization/post-modernization often inform such approaches, sometimes implicitly, as discussed by Kennett (2001: 63–7). Structural analysis is often associated with macro-analysis of large data sets such as Wilensky (1975) but it can also inform qualitative approaches such as Rimlinger's (1971) great historical study. In recent times 'hard' globalization approaches have perhaps been most prominent in emphasizing structural thinking, best exemplified perhaps by Teeple (2000) and Mishra (1999).

A second widely deployed approach is to start from the common socio-economic pressures which welfare states appear to have experienced over the past quarter century. These changes or pressures can be considered 'structural' because they seem to be long established and universal, including:

- *Fiscal*: declining tax revenues due to falling employment; orthodoxy of corporate and national economic competitiveness demanding tax reduction and welfare 'cost containment'
- *Paid Employment*: much increased unemployment; decline of blue collar manual jobs; rise of service sector employment, including low-paid jobs; flexibilization and casualization; increased dispersion of wages and salaries; re-commodification of workers
- *Demographic*: stable or declining fertility; increasing proportion of pensioners; increasing numbers of care-dependent elderly people; increased economic and political pressures for and against inward migration
- *Household*: eclipse of the male-breadwinner norm, replaced by dual breadwinner/no breadwinner households with less capacity for informal care; increased lone mother households.

Contributors to, for example, Esping-Andersen (1996) and to Taylor-Gooby (2001) document the effects of some of these structural changes. Taylor-

Gooby (2001: 174) concludes from a survey of six West European welfare states that 'all are experiencing continuing and in most cases increasing tensions from the factors [above] and all have introduced changes which will weaken political and institutional obstacles to the redirection of welfare'. Such shifts in the policy consensus include 'the growth of private pensions, the expansion of means testing and similar targeting policies, and new measures designed to activate dependent populations of working age' (Taylor-Gooby, 2001: 181). 'Redirection' here implies a shift towards the neoliberal paradigm, involving lower public social expenditure, and a less universal, more disciplinary welfare state. Pierson talks of an 'essentially permanent austerity' descending on the welfare states in response to these structural pressures, which 'over the next few decades ... are likely to intensify' (Pierson, 2001: 411). Huber and Stephens (2001a) in their account of welfare 'retrenchment' during the 1980s and 1990s show that a wide range of states implemented significant cuts in welfare expenditures and entitlements, provoked principally by much increased levels of unemployment. But 'there were very few programs in any country where benefits in the mid 1990s were more than marginally lower than they had been in 1970' (Huber and Stephens, 2001a: 302). This is an important corrective to analyses which exaggerate the impact of the above structural pressures.

A third approach puts political 'structures' to the fore. Cross-national consideration of differing national responses to addressing basic needs and social injustices leads many comparativists to consideration of the political character and origins of welfare regimes. This, in turn, lends itself to notions of regime clusters or families of nations formed around distinctive political traditions and industrial models, the various worlds of welfare capitalism. Pierson (2001), Huber and Stephens (2001a) and Castles (2001) among others have all recently reiterated the significance of Esping-Andersen's (1990) classic delineation of three worlds of welfare capitalism, albeit with qualifications, extensions and modifications. Regime analysis or welfare modelling suggests that the various 'worlds' are structures in themselves, which shape quite fundamentally the ways in which states respond to needs and injustices.

Finally there is what has been dubbed 'critical' thinking about structures. Critical analysis focuses more on socio-economic outcomes and collective injustices. Here structures are forces shaping social policy, which underpin prominent social oppressions, injustices and inequalities. Hence as Young (2000: 95) suggests 'a person's social location in structures differentiated by class, gender, age, ability, race, or caste often implies predictable status in law, educational possibility, occupation, access to resources, political power and prestige ... one reason to call these structural is that they are relatively permanent'. Welfare states may be more or less successful in tackling structural injustices, which may be more or less prominent in particular national contexts, but they are social structures critically confronting them all. Critical analysts have focused most on class, gender and race as structural differences, reflecting respectively the powerful structures of capitalism, patriarchy and racism. The oppressions and injustices generated thereby are arguably the most universally experienced in the West, and are resisted by well-established social movements.

Diversity

This chapter is confined to considering cross-*national* analysis, setting aside the social policy diversities at the subnational level, and indeed the changing boundaries of the nation-state (for example German reunification, the 'break up' of the UK). It also focuses predominantly on the nation-states of 'advanced industrialism', also still known as 'the West'. Hence in this context the term 'diversity' is being used in relation to the diversity of only a few nation-states, and not the social diversities to be found within them.

Diversity thinking starts from the richness of national social policy discourses and welfare movements. In its purest form a diversity approach would be sceptical of the possibility of useful cross-national analysis of social policy by implying that each national regime is shaped within a particular culture, through which wider forces or structures are filtered and managed at some considerable distance. So, for example, studies of social policy history tend to focus on a national story, in which supranational elements play a relatively minor role – for example, economic recession in the international economy. This is hardly surprising given the centrality of the welfare state to the idea and legitimacy of the modern nation-state. In this context Kennett (2001: 7) talks of 'micro-studies which are more likely to use in-depth, qualitative techniques, and to emphasise cultural sensitivity, agency and reflexivity in the policy and research process'. Similarly Mabbett and Bolderson (1999: 49) refer to the 'case study approach', citing as an outstanding example Heclo (1974), a detailed historical account of the development of pensions and unemployment benefits in Sweden and Britain, showing how policy developed in parallel but contrasting directions. Here there is little explicit structural conceptualization, and there is a strong sense of governments responding to similar pressures for reform in very different political and social contexts. Heclo (1974) is an early example of what has been called the 'institutionalist' approach to cross-national analysis of social policy which is rooted in comparative politics. Social policy is considered as being shaped emphatically by and strongly reflective of its particular institutional context (Thelen and Steinmo, 1992: 2–9). Here 'institutions' can denote both formal organizations and 'informal rules and procedures', including the managerial capacity and the civil service culture of a particular state, and the culture of particular welfare professions. The concept of 'path dependence' has much in common with institutionalism. This suggests that nations rarely if ever develop policy in a ground zero situation. The path followed by policy change is shaped by historical and institutional context, and, once established, tends to stay in place, keeping reform within the boundaries of the path. Myles and Pierson's (2001) comparative account of contemporary pensions reform is a recent example of the 'path dependence' approach, showing that 'cross-national differences in the organisation and political capacities of the key constituencies affected by welfare states – workers, employers, women, private insurers and public officials – have an important impact on the character of reform' (Myles and Pierson, 2001: 306).

Structured diversity

The distinction between structural and diversity thinking is deliberately conveyed above for the sake of conceptual clarification. Most contemporary thinking on cross-national social policy takes some kind of structured diversity approach, attempting to combine notions of common structure(s) with acknowledgement of national diversities.

For example in relation to the structural socio-economic pressures, terms such as austerity and retrenchment tend to focus on the fiscal problem, but the other three factors listed above involve increased demands being made of the welfare state which in large measure contribute to fiscal pressure. So, while the structural pressures for austerity are common across the welfare states, the responses to the other factors are highly diverse. Hence, for example, Esping-Andersen (1996) showed that in the 1980s unemployment was soaked up in the US by the development of junk jobs, in Sweden by consolidation and expansion of public service employment, and in Germany by state-sponsored early retirement. Similarly Pierson's (2001) study of policy responses to permanent austerity recognizes 'the existence of quite different settings for the emerging politics of restructuring' (p. 428) so that 'there is not a single "new politics" of the welfare state but different politics in different configurations' (p. 455).

The regime analysis in Esping-Andersen (1990) is also, of course, a structured diversity approach with a strong 'critical' component with its focus on class outcomes, that is the social protection of workers from labour market risks or de-commodification. Hence he suggested that the extent to which welfare states protect workers from basic risks is linked directly to the strength (or weakness) of working class political and industrial mobilization sustaining them. This puts political structures to the fore, with the critical and normative message that social democratic regimes provide the best and most socially just protection against the risks of ageing, unemployment and sickness, while liberal regimes provide the least and most socially unjust protection. In his early work Esping-Andersen, alongside Korpi (1983), saw the welfare state as a product of 'democratic class struggle', a phrase with clear neo-Marxist connotations. More recently Esping-Andersen (1999: 29) talks of the 'declining correlates of class', seeing the diversity of welfare regimes as structured by the above plurality of socio-economic pressures within 'postindustrial economies' rather than the clash of class interests. The rest of this chapter reviews elements of what can be described rather cumbersomely as critical structured diversity approaches to cross-national analysis of social policy. Hence following Fiona Williams (1989: xiii), work, family and nation are taken as critical 'organizing principles in the development of the welfare state' which shape power structures, social movements and processes acting within and upon it. As she says 'it is through the state's relationship, through social policies (or the welfare state), to these three areas ... that we can begin to grasp the diverse configurations of multi-layered welfare settlements in different countries' (Williams, 2001: 151). There has, of course, been much academic and radical political discussion about the links between these three different power structures, movements and processes. As yet, however, critical cross-national social policy analysis has been largely confined to tackling just one of these dimensions at a time, which is how we will proceed here.

Class analysis
The neo-Marxist, class perspective on structural diversity sees social policy as the continually renegotiated outcome of the clash between the needs of capital and the basic needs of people for welfare and security. Hence as Gough (2000: 19) puts it 'the common "need" of capital is to make profits, but the institutional structures and policy patterns (the "specific satisfiers") which contribute to this can and do vary' so that 'different forms of capitalism' develop 'with different moral underpinnings and welfare outcomes'. Here there is more emphasis on the national diversity of capitalisms, reflecting the reality that 'property, markets and firms are "embedded" in wider social relationships' (Gough, 2000: 22). Focusing on the mobilization of capital as well as labour adds an important dimension to structural cross-national analysis of social policy, particularly as 'the structural power of capital has recuperated following a decline in the 1970s' (Gough, 2000: 18). The increasingly cross-national, structural power of capital has been fuelled by neoliberal and neo-conservative thinking which is hostile to social expenditure, indifferent to social inequality and injustice, and sceptical of 'the public realm' as a whole in social policy. Such thinking has thus far had much more influence in liberal states such as the US and the UK, than in the rest of Europe.

Huber and Stephens adopt a critical neo-Marxian perspective, which incorporates some gender dimensions. This suggests that social policy and welfare outcomes are principally shaped by the conflict between the interests and organizations of capital, and the interests and organizations of 'the subordinate classes and the subordinate gender' (Huber and Stephens, 2001a: 13). In these conflicts 'capitalist interests have a systematic advantage' which has been enhanced by the economic globalization of the last two or three decades. Alongside the critical, structural spine of their analysis, Huber and Stephens are at pains to emphasize the importance of national path dependence in policy formation and development, particularly the diversity of 'power-constellations' within each state. The power-constellation is shaped, principally, by the relative political and industrial strength of capital and labour, and by the socio-economic mobilization of women.

Huber and Stephens' work is supported by analysis of quantitative, cross-national data on social spending and welfare outcomes, as well as qualitative analysis of national political discourse and conflict. The quantitative data uses many more parameters (dependent variables) than Esping-Andersen (1990) to assess welfare state performance including public health care expenditure, income inequality and poverty. Their analyses confirm that distinct differences remain between the social democratic, Christian democratic and liberal regime clusters, reflecting diversities in the strength of labour vis-à-vis capital and in the presence of women in the workforce. However Huber and Stephens (2001b: 305) detect a 'narrowing of partisanship' over the 1980s and 1990s as all governments responded to similar socio-economic pressures by cost containment and some retrenchment. Yet they also note that, with the exception of the UK and New Zealand, 'the achievements of the welfare state in terms of income equalization and poverty reduction have largely been preserved' (Huber and Stephens, 2001b: 306). The salience of class power as a key structural factor in understanding the diversity of welfare states is illustrated powerfully by this data.

Gender analysis

Gender is obviously a major social, structural difference underpinning social policy. A critical perspective suggests that welfare states embrace fundamental and unjust gender differences in access to formal welfare, responsibility for informal welfare and in meeting women's basic needs, including reproductive rights and protection from violence. Much effort has been expended by feminist sociologists in trying to conceptualize what power structure or structures are involved in such processes. The application of such conceptualization to comparing welfare states is well summarized, for example, by Duncan (1995) and Daly (2000). The latter concludes accurately that 'the main thrust of current work appears to be more or less to abandon the search for a "grand theory"' (Daly, 2000: 34) in favour of empirical studies of particular states, which examine how 'differentiation and inequalities between men and women are generated, reproduced and institutionalised'. It could easily be concluded that the national diversity of welfare states has been the most prominent feature of the blossoming literature on gendered aspects of social policy over the past decade. Yet if we are left with the undoubted diversity of gender policy regimes amidst the diversity of welfare states, gender cannot really be claimed as a structural difference, which palpably it is across all the welfare states. Despite its widely recognized limitations, here we will use the word 'patriarchy' to describe this universal power structure.

The operation of patriarchy in cross-national analysis of social policy has been approached in several different ways. One approach starts from women as individuals whose personal autonomy is limited and constrained by patriarchal structures and processes throughout the public and private spheres. National social policy regimes have 'gendered logics' which are 'gendered patterns of stratification, social and civil rights and the social organisation of income and services' (O'Connor et al., 1999: 36) which underpin women's oppression and inequality. The diversity of welfare states is structured particularly by the extent to which a state denies women 'the capacity to form and maintain an autonomous household, ... an individual's ability to survive and support their children without being forced to marry or enter into other family relationships' (ibid.: 32). 'Women's autonomization' is a rather inelegant phrase by which to describe and measure the extent to which a welfare state challenges patriarchy.

O'Connor et al. (1999) deploy a gender autonomization perspective in a comparative study of four 'liberal' states. They suggest that both 'economic' and 'bodily' autonomy are essential to undermining patriarchy and developing the autonomous personhood of women. Hence for their concrete analysis as indices of economic autonomy they cite women's access to and status in paid employment, as well as state cash benefits which support and/or relieve women of some of the burden of informal care. As a parameter of bodily autonomy they use reproductive freedom, specifically abortion rights. The empirical analysis draws out the significant path dependencies of policy and its impact in the four states, while demonstrating that these liberal regimes have a distinct gender dimension which 'is most immediately evident in the privileging of the market over provision through the state'. This is evident in key areas of need such as child care and abortion services which are largely privately purchased, and maternity leave and parental care rights which are not underwritten adequately, if at all, as legal entitlements. The implication of this analysis is that gender autonomization, particularly in the liberal states, is severely constrained by the marketization of services and the absence of adequate care rights. The shift to 'gender sameness' in the labour market has reinforced class differences among women, so that only higher-income earners can achieve something close to gender autonomization.

A second approach starts not from women's individual personhood, but from the institution of the patriarchal household, obliging women to offer 'full-time' (that is, 24/7) informal, unpaid care to their husbands, children and other 'dependent' kin. A gender policy regime thus 'entails a logic based on the rules and norms about gender relations that influences the construction of policies' (Sainsbury, 1999a: 5). Gender policy regimes are structured according to 'ideologies that describe actual or preferred relations between men and women' (Sainsbury, 1999b: 77). The diversity of welfare states is structured by the extent to which they have moved away from the male-breadwinner model. According to Sainsbury (1999a: 5) the 'dimensions of variation' are structured around the 'familial ideology' and the extent to which welfare states depart from the norm of the male-breadwinner model with its strong gendered division of labour in the household, in which the husband provides financial support and women informal care with relatively little support from the state. 'Defamilization' or 'defamilialization' are again rather inelegant terms used to evaluate the extent to which welfare states advance women's interests in shifting from the male-breadwinner model. Defamilization is indicated by the extent to which policy supports an 'individual model', which 'has no preferred family form' with caring and financial support shared by both parents and the state.

The 'defamilization' perspective in cross-national analysis of social policy is particularly associated with the work of Lewis (1992, 1997) and Sainsbury (1996). As with the autonomy perspective a key parameter structuring differences between welfare states is the extent and status of women's presence in the labour market. Beyond this there are two other major parameters. First, the extent to which entitlement to benefits, fiscal welfare and services is prescribed on an individual or a familial basis, the latter almost inevitably strengthening women's economic dependency. The second parameter is the extent to which informal care is socialized in the form of support payments for informal care and/or by provision of social care services. Reviewing a range of data on these parameters for states across a diversity of welfare regimes, Sainsbury (1999c: 252) suggests that the UK, the Netherlands and Germany are 'exemplars of strong male-breadwinner countries'. France and Belgium had strong indicators of defamilization on some parameters, and adhered to familialism on other counts. Denmark, Finland and Sweden had gone furthest towards defamilization. Hence the gendered diversity of welfare states does not coincide very well with the regime clusters identified by Esping-Andersen. Most obviously the 'Christian democratic' or 'conservative' states are differentiated according to those which have followed a pro-natalist path generating some defamilization, and those which have remained more firmly rooted in the male-breadwinner tradition. While three of the Nordic social democratic states have moved furthest towards defamilization, Norway has in some respects retained more of the male-breadwinner model.

A third approach to pinning down gender structures for cross-national analysis of social policy focuses solely on women's economic status in different welfare states, which ostensibly allows more precise, quantitative comparison of welfare state performance. The economic status and well-being of lone mothers is a particularly salient indicator of the extent to which welfare states support both women's autonomy and departure from the male-breadwinner model. Using Luxembourg Income Study data for the mid-1990s Huber et al. (2001) compared the performance of 14 OECD states in reducing poverty among single mothers and in equalizing married women's wages relative to their spouses. The results suggest a very familiar and distinct clustering of regimes in which 'the social democratic regimes are highest on women's earnings and lowest on single mothers in poverty; the Christian democratic welfare states are lowest on women's earnings and intermediate on [lone mother] poverty; and the liberal welfare states are intermediate on women's earnings but highest on [lone mother] poverty' (Huber et al., 2001: 17). Hence the diversity of gender regimes using economic parameters seems to be structured by the conventional divergences in national political mobilization identified in Esping-Andersen's regime analysis. Yet this does not mean that gender outcomes can be read off from the conventional regime analysis. It simply suggests that feminist pressure and women's movement mobilization have more impact in a social democratic context than elsewhere. Thus, for example, the 'sex role equality' debate initiated by women within the Swedish labour and social democratic movement in the 1960s had a long-term impact on the welfare state provision of benefits, services and employment opportunities facilitating women's autonomization and defamilization (Ginsburg, 2001: 214).

Here we have briefly reviewed three contrasting approaches to feminist cross-national policy analysis, all of which demonstrate that patriarchy is a social structure which shapes social policy across the welfare states, but to different extents and in different forms in particular regimes. Gender policy regimes continue also to be structured according to mainstream political mobilization patterns, with social democratic regimes making more inroads into patriarchy than other welfare 'models'.

'Race' analysis

The role of social policy in furthering and mitigating racial and ethnic divisions is obviously a hugely significant, structural dimension of critical analysis, though it has had much less prominence in the cross-national analysis of social policy literature than class and gender. There are obvious reasons for this. First, minority ethnic groups are, by definition, minorities whose political mobilization is more limited inasmuch as it is constructed around an ethnic identity rather than anti-racism. Second, welfare states tend to have policies which either exclude racialized groups or seek to assimilate them. Both processes involve denial of the significance of race and ethnicity in welfare, and certainly results in lack of useful data. Third and most important there is a great diversity of 'ethnic-making situations' (Fenton, 1999: 32) and, hence, a great diversity of racialization processes and of racisms.

Following Fenton (1999: 44), in shaping modern welfare states three historical 'structures' have been prominent: slavery/post-slavery, colonialism/ post-colonialism, and nation-state capitalism, all of them inspired more or less by notions of white supremacy and/or ethnically based nationhood. The racialization inherent in modern welfare states has been shaped by a particular national blend of these historical processes and discourses. They continue to undermine the emergence of multi-ethnic or deracialized welfare states. Obviously the US in the segregationist era and Nazi Germany are particularly prominent examples of explicitly racist social policy regimes in advanced industrial societies. In the contemporary era, for African Americans the post-slavery dimension continues to structure policy processes, while in Britain post-colonialism continues to loom large in the institutionalization of racism within the welfare state. In Sweden and Germany social policy discourse has been shaped more by ethnically based notions of nationhood. In Sweden this can be seen in the construction of the People's Home in the 1930s (Ginsburg, 2001: 209) and in the strong emphasis on assimilationist measures for the minority ethnic groups of the post-war era. In Germany it was reinforced by the division of the country in the Cold War, which fostered the notion of the ethnic German identity and legitimated comparatively exclusionary socio-economic measures (Ginsburg, 1994). One might simply conclude from this that the development and character of racialized welfare states is 'path dependent', that is largely shaped by nationally specific histories and politics. Nevertheless some attempts have been made to analyse how this diversity may be structured in ways which embrace historical processes but go beyond the particularity of path dependence.

Looking for dependent variables for cross-national analysis of social policy in this field is hampered by lack of data and by the limitations of each particular parameter. There are a large number of social processes which are conceivably relevant to such analysis, as discussed by Williams (2001: 150). In concrete terms the following indices seem particularly salient: immigration/citizenship policy and processes; socio-economic outcomes for racialized groups; anti-discrimination/equal opportunities policies; racial violence and responses to it; racialized reproductive rights. In Ginsburg (1992) I offered a very brief review of data and policies in these areas for four welfare states, without being able to suggest whether cross-national differences were structured in any way beyond path dependence because of the methodological obstacles. Focusing on immigration/citizenship policy excludes 'indigenous' groups, such as African Americans. Racialized data on socio-economic outcomes is not collected by most governments, so a focus on this aspect is severely limited. Many states have very limited anti-discrimination/equal opportunity measures, and, even where they are well established, critical evaluation is often limited by inadequate data and the particularities of political and legal mobilization of minorities. Nevertheless some aspects of race regimes have been amenable to some cross-national analysis of social policy, most notably post-war immigration and settlement policies. By the 1970s many of the Western welfare states had experienced considerable inward labour migration, involving the more or less permanent settlement of ethnicized or racialized minorities. The policy responses of governments to this were structured by particular 'conceptions of nationhood' (Williams, 2001: 146), involving the historical, cultural and political traditions of states and, hence, were strongly 'path dependent'. Nevertheless some reasonably distinct models could be identified. Studies by Castles and Miller (2003) and by Joppke (1999) suggest that there were three different approaches, which can be described as settler, exclusionary and post-colonial. The settler regimes accepted without much difficulty the notion of immigration leading to permanent settlement and assumed long-term assimilation and naturalization, sometimes facilitated by the state through policies of 'prescribed multiculturalism'. Commonly cited examples of settler regimes include the US, Canada, Australia and Sweden, though, of course the conceptions of nationhood in each case are enormously divergent. At the other extreme, the exclusionary regimes did not conceive of themselves as countries of immigration, seeing migrants as guestworkers and/or temporary residents, and hostile to long-term settlement. Here the conception of nationhood is built upon a relatively unyielding notion of an ethnic community. Commonly cited examples of exclusionary regimes include former guestworker states such as Germany, Austria and Switzerland, as well as Japan. Post-colonial regimes recruited labour from colonies and former colonies, conceived in many respects as a continuation of colonial relations in a domestic context. This suggests full citizenship in formal terms but maintains powerfully racialized, institutional discrimination within social policy processes, not least in immigration control itself. Frequently cited examples of post-colonial regimes include France, the UK and the Netherlands.

Though they continue to have a profound influence in shaping policy processes and discourses, in the 1980s and 1990s the distinctiveness of the exclusionary and post-colonial regimes began to fade for several reasons. First, post-colonial and guestworker labour migration were brought to an end by more restrictive and racialized immigration policies in North Western

Europe passed in response to rising unemployment and violent racism in the 1970s. Second, in the 1970s and 1980s the post-colonial regimes acknowledged more fully the reality of permanent settlement and embraced assimilationism and the formal enfranchisement of established minority ethnic communities into the welfare state. Such processes also began to become more prominent in the exclusionary regimes in the 1990s. These changes were a response to the increasingly effective political mobilization of minority ethnic communities. Third, from the late 1980s onwards 'new' and more diverse forms of migration emerged, at least in Western Europe, made up of both asylum seekers/refugees and migrant workers. These developments were prompted by the renewed demand for labour, particularly in the wake of the long economic boom of the 1990s, alongside the increasing numbers of people able to flee brutal regimes and war zones for the promise of human rights in the West.

It would appear that, over the past two decades, there have been two distinct and perhaps contradictory processes at work across the Western welfare states in terms of policies and processes shaping racism and racial injustices. First in all the welfare states there is a shift towards a deeper multi-culturalism and away from stronger forms of assimilationism. This may have been more pronounced in the settler states and least pronounced in the exclusionary states, but it appears to be a universal and, hence, perhaps 'structural' shift. At the same time, and equally important, there has been a strengthening of racialized, exclusionary immigration/asylum policies, accompanied by worsening, or at best unchanging, socio-economic inequalities between minority ethnic communities and the majority, and the menacing activity of overtly racist political movements and the racist violence which they promote. In the states of the EU, for example, the 'successful' economic integration of states such as Ireland and Spain has been accompanied by an upsurge of racism directed against migrant workers. Racism appears to be structurally endemic within the capitalist welfare state, whether the economy is booming or in recession, whether the government is to the left or the right of centre. As the peoples of the Western welfare states become more multi-ethnic, so the importance of both multi-cultural and racist structural processes will increase.

Conclusion

Critical structured diversity suggests that social policy often acts to reinforce and legitimate structural social injustices and inequalities, alongside efforts to mitigate them. As we have seen, a handful of critical writers have addressed particular social divisions, but there have been few, if any, attempts to look at the situation across a number of structural divisions, Williams (2001) being an outstanding, if brief, exception. Feminist analysis has thrived relatively in the past decade, but even here the approach is mostly particularist. Marxian class analysis has been in retreat in the face of various related onslaughts, not least the end of the cold war and the rise of neoliberalism. This is so despite its increased relevance in the context of increasing class inequalities and increasing commodification of welfare. Anti-racist approaches have remained relatively marginalized and separated from mainstream policy analysis. Despite the undoubted challenges, critical structured diversity analysis is worth pursuing because it suggests that some regimes are more successful than others in undermining structural injustices, while recognizing that each regime is driven by its own welfare movements, as well as by structural pressures. At the risk of overgeneralization, the evidence suggests, un-surprisingly, that European social democracy is far more effective in mitigating structural injustices and in responding justly to welfare movements than those regimes closer to the liberal model, currently so much under the spell of neoliberalism. This is certainly the case in respect of class divisions, and more uncertainly in the case of gender and, particularly, 'race'.

Structured diversity is really just a benchmark device which suggests that comparative analysts of social policy should juggle the universalities of cross-national structural forces with the particularities of national (and subnational) administrations and movements. This may seem obvious to many readers, until one considers the current tendency to cite globalization or even Europeanization as pre-eminent structural factors shaping social policy. At the other extreme, there is the rubbishing of regime analysis or other structural ideas derived from 'grand theories' in favour of the particular national case study approach. The literature on international social policy has a preponderance of case studies by national experts on particular needs, policy areas or services. The student is so often left to draw out cross-national comparison intuitively. Structured diversity is easily caught between these two poles. Yet it is worth pursuing because it tries to capture the clash between structural forces and active welfare subjects (social movements) which shapes the making, implementation and impact of social policy, allowing meaningful cross-national comparison.

Bibliography

Castles, F. (2001), 'On the political economy of recent public sector development', *Journal of European Social Policy*, **11**(3), 195–211.
Castles, Stephen and Alistair Davidson (2000), *Citizenship and Migration*, London: Sage.
Castles, Stephen and Mark J. Miller (2003), *The Age of Migration*, Basingstoke: Macmillan.
Daly, Mary (2000), *The Gender Division of Welfare*, Cambridge: Cambridge University Press.
Duncan, S. (1995), 'Theorizing European gender systems', *Journal of European Social Policy*, **5**(4), 263–84.
Esping-Andersen, Gøsta (1990), *Three Worlds of Welfare Capitalism*, Cambridge: Polity.
Esping-Andersen, Gøsta (1996), 'After the Golden Age? Welfare state dilemmas in a global economy', in Gøsta Esping-Andersen (ed.), *Welfare States in Transition*, London: Sage, pp. 1–31.

Esping-Andersen, Gøsta (1999), *The Social Foundations of Postindustrial Economies*, Oxford: Oxford University Press.

Fenton, Steve (1999), *Ethnicity: Racism, Class and Culture*, Basingstoke: Macmillan.

Ginsburg, Norman (1992), *Divisions of Welfare*, London: Sage.

Ginsburg, Norman (1994), 'Ethnic minorities and social policy in Germany', in Jochen Clasen and Richard Freeman (eds), *Social Policy in Germany*, Hemel Hempstead: Harvester, pp. 191–206.

Ginsburg, Norman (2001), 'Sweden: the Social Democratic case', in Allan Cochrane, John Clarke and Sharon Gewirtz (eds), *Comparing Welfare States*, London: Sage, pp. 195–222.

Gough, Ian (2000), *Global Capital, Human Needs and Social Policies*, Basingstoke: Palgrave.

Heclo, Hugh (1974), *Modern Social Politics in Britain and Sweden*, New Haven: Yale University Press.

Huber, Evelyne and J. John Stephens (2001a), *Development and Crisis of the Welfare State*, Chicago: Chicago University Press.

Huber, Evelyne and J. John Stephens (2001b), 'The social democratic welfare state', in Andrew Glyn (ed.), *Social Democracy in Neoliberal Times*, Oxford: Oxford University Press, pp. 276–311.

Huber, Evelyne, John Stephens, David Bradley, Stephanie Moller and François Nielsen (2001), *The Welfare State and Gender Equality*, Luxembourg Income Study Working Paper No. 279, www.lisproject.org.

Joppke, Christian (1999), *Immigration and the Nation State*, Oxford: Oxford University Press.

Kennett, Patricia (2001), *Comparative Social Policy*, Buckingham: Open University Press.

Korpi, Walter (1983), *The Democratic Class Struggle*, London: Routledge.

Lewis, J. (1992), 'Gender and the development of welfare regimes', *Journal of European Social Policy*, **2**(3), 159–73.

Lewis, J. (1997), 'Gender and welfare regimes: further thoughts', *Social Politics*, **4**(2), 160–77.

Mabbett, Deborah and Helen Bolderson (1999), 'Theories and methods in comparative social policy', in Jochen Clasen (ed.), *Comparative Social Policy*, Oxford: Blackwell, pp. 34–56.

Mishra, Ramesh (1999), *Globalization and the Welfare State*, Cheltenham, UK and Brookfield, US: Edward Elgar.

Myles, John and Paul Pierson (2001), 'The comparative political economy of pension reform' in Paul Pierson (ed.), *The New Politics of the Welfare State*, Oxford: Oxford University Press, pp. 305–33.

O'Connor, Julia, Ann Orloff and Sheila Shaver (1999), *States, Markets and Families*, Cambridge: Cambridge University Press.

Orloff, A. (1993), 'Gender and the social rights of citizenship: the comparative analysis of gender relations and welfare states', *American Sociological Review*, **58**(3), 303–28.

Pierson, Paul (2001), 'Coping with permanent austerity: welfare state restructuring in affluent democracies', in Paul Pierson (ed.), *The New Politics of the Welfare State*, Oxford: Oxford University Press, pp. 410–56.

Rimlinger, Gaston V. (1971), *Welfare Policy and Industrialization in Europe, America and Russia*, New York: John Wiley.

Sainsbury, Diana (1996), *Gender, Equality and Welfare States*, Cambridge: Cambridge University Press.

Sainsbury, Diana (1999a), 'Introduction', in Diana Sainsbury (ed.), *Gender and Welfare State Regimes*, Oxford: Oxford University Press, pp. 1–11.

Sainsbury, Diana (1999b), 'Gender and social-democratic welfare states', in Diana Sainsbury (ed.), *Gender and Welfare State Regimes*, Oxford: Oxford University Press, pp. 75–114.

Sainsbury, Diana (1999c), 'Gender, policy regimes and politics', in Diana Sainsbury (ed.), *Gender and Welfare State Regimes*, Oxford: Oxford University Press, pp. 245–75.

Taylor-Gooby, Peter (2001), 'Polity, policy-making and welfare futures', in Peter Taylor-Gooby (ed.), *Welfare States Under Pressure*, London: Sage, pp. 171–88.

Teeple, Gary (2000), *Globalization and the Decline of Social Reform*, Toronto: Humanity Books.

Thelen, Kathleen and Sven Steinmo (1992), 'Historical institutionalism in comparative politics', in Sven Steinmo, Kathleen Thelen and Frank Longstreth (eds), *Structuring Politics:*

Historical Institutionalism in Comparative Analysis, Cambridge: Cambridge University Press, pp. 1–32.

Wilensky, Harold (1975), *The Welfare State and Equality*, Berkeley: University of California Press.

Williams, Fiona (1989), *Social Policy: A Critical Introduction*, Cambridge: Polity.

Williams, Fiona (2001), 'Race/ethnicity, gender and class in welfare states: a framework for comparative analysis', in Janet Fink, Gail Lewis and John Clarke (eds), *Rethinking European Welfare*, London: Sage, pp. 131–62.

Young, Iris Marion (2000), *Inclusion and Democracy*, Oxford: Oxford University Press.

12 Social development and social welfare: implications for social policy

James Midgley

While international social policy was previously regarded as an exotic and highly specialized activity to be pursued by experts who were uniquely equipped to travel to distant regions and understand unfamiliar cultures, comparative inquiry has today become commonplace. Mirroring the ready accessibility of global information, and the ease with which people travel and communicate internationally, publications on international social welfare now appear with what seems to be monotonous regularity, international content is increasingly incorporated into local journals and textbooks, students are routinely exposed to developments in other countries, and international issues are even debated at local conferences and meetings.

These developments reflect a rapidly expanding interest in international social welfare in Europe and North America. Social policy scholarship in the Global North now routinely transcends the preoccupation with domestic activities that previously characterized Western social policy inquiry. Social welfare systems in other nations have been extensively documented and analysed, typologies that classify different state welfare systems have been constructed and causal factors responsible for welfare effort have been identified. As a result of these activities, social policy scholarship has evolved and expanded its interests in ways that are compatible with the emergent realities of a global, one-world system.

However, comparative social policy inquiry is still challenged by problems that have not been adequately recognized, let alone addressed. One problem concerns the way comparative social policy has been defined and shaped by scholars in the Global North. This has resulted in what may be called a 'mainstream' approach that focuses almost exclusively on state welfare and uses a Western 'institutional' or welfarist perspective to conceptualize and define the field. Although this discourse has engaged neoliberalism, the other powerful discourse in Western social policy thinking, it has paid little attention to other discourses that address indigenous welfare phenomena in other regions of the world. By failing to engage these discourses, mainstream scholarship has impeded the emergence of a multifaceted perspective that recognizes hybridity, incorporates diverse insights and promotes a truly global understanding of social welfare.

Another problem is that mainstream comparative social policy inquiry has neglected normative and practical issues, preferring instead to pursue classificatory and explanatory activities. Normative references embedded in these activities are implicit rather than explicit and do not, accordingly, provide an adequate basis for social policy formulation. Similarly, because the implicit normative preferences in mainstream scholarship reflect the dominance of Western ideologies, they are of limited use in assessing social welfare in societies where different cultural and social traditions are valued. Nevertheless, they pervade the subject and exert a subtle but decisive influence in determining what, in social policy terms, is desirable. This is unfortunate in view of the urgent need for appropriate normative frameworks that can address the persistence of global poverty, mass deprivation, oppression and other pressing social problems.

These issues have been raised before, but they need to be more extensively debated. Mainstream inquiry also needs to recognize and seek to accommodate the alternative discourses about social welfare which emanate from other societies, groups and communities. This requires a greater knowledge of indigenous social welfare perspectives, a receptivity to the contribution of cognate fields such as cultural and development studies, and an awareness of the activities of the international development agencies which have exerted considerable influence on social policy thinking in non-Western societies. Innovations in policy formulation and implementation in other parts of the world can also inform these debates.

One innovation of this kind is social development which emerged in the developing countries of the Global South in the post-war years, and has since been actively promoted by the United Nations and other international agencies. However, it has been almost totally disregarded by mainstream social policy scholars. By focusing on the social development approach and considering how it addresses firstly, the issues of indigenization and secondly, the need for a normative framework that can address global social needs, this chapter discusses some of the issues arising out of a broadened vision for comparative social policy. It also considers social development's potential to contribute to the emergence of a one-world perspective that does not depend on the adoption or emulation of Western approaches.

Contributions and deficiencies of comparative social policy

Writing in the mid-1980s, Jones (1985) identified a handful of books that were explicitly devoted to the subject of comparative social policy. It seems that the first of these books were published in the 1960s. Today, this handful has multiplied many times over and, as was suggested earlier, books dealing with social policy in a comparative and international context have now become commonplace. In addition to these books, the number of articles and chapters on international social welfare in social policy journals and edited collections have proliferated.

The growth of interest in the field is not only reflected in an increase in the quantity of comparative publications, but in the diversity of topics covered. Today, material on a wide range of international and comparative social welfare issues is available. For example, comparative social policy scholars have extensively documented the nature, extent and costs of state welfare provision in different countries. The number of country case studies of national welfare systems has increased exponentially and detailed, descriptive information about many more nations have become available. The inclusion of non-Western countries as varied as Hong Kong (Jones, 1990a; Tang, 1998), Malaysia (Doling and Omar, 2000), Mexico (Ward, 1986), Nigeria (Onokerhoraye, 1984), South Africa (Patel, 1992) and Taiwan (Aspalter, 2002; Ku, 1995) to name but a few, is indicative of the extended coverage of this approach. Previously, country case studies and transnational comparisons were largely limited to Europe and the United States.

Analyses of how social welfare institutions have evolved in different countries, of how they function, and how they affect people's lives have, in turn, produced a substantive body of descriptive and theoretical literature about social welfare at the transnational level. This type of inquiry goes well beyond the documentation of welfare systems in different countries and the production of descriptive comparisons. Building on descriptive county case studies and cross-national comparisons, comparative social policy has generated conceptual approaches that have sought to classify and comprehend different welfare systems and explain the causal determinants of state welfare engagement.

The classification of welfare systems in terms of the construction of taxonomies has been a major preoccupation in comparative social policy scholarship. Abstracted from Wilensky's and Lebeaux's (1965) characterization of social welfare in the United States as evolving from a residual to institutional form, many comparative social policy scholars, beginning with Titmuss (1974), have augmented or redefined the residual–institutional dichotomy. Despite numerous criticisms of their inadequacies, taxonomic exercises continue to feature prominently in mainstream comparative social policy scholarship; indeed, since the publication of Esping-Anderson's celebrated typology in 1990, these activities have dominated the field.

The typological preoccupation in Western comparative social policy has propelled the subject beyond its previous engagement with explanatory theory. For many years, mainstream comparative social policy scholarship was primarily concerned with analysing the complex factors that appeared to be causally associated with the rise in public social expenditures and the expansion of government social programmes during the twentieth century. In addition to complex factor analyses based on the manipulation of statistical data (Aaron, 1967; Cutright, 1965), a number of plausible theoretical accounts of the reasons for increased public welfare effort have been published. These include functionalist, Marxist, pluralist and other interpretations. Although none provide a definitive explanation of the determinants of welfare effort, this scholarship reveals the impressive degree of analytical sophistication the subject has achieved (Higgins, 1981; Fitzpatrick, 2001; Kennett, 2001; Midgley, 1997; Mishra, 1977; O'Brein and Penna, 1998).

Since the 1980s, comparative social policy inquiry has also been concerned with the tendency of governments in various parts of the world to reduce social expenditures and retrench social programmes. The nature of the trend has been subjected to critical scrutiny and while some scholars are persuaded that there is a 'crisis' in government welfare, others are not convinced that the state welfare programmes are, in fact, being dismantled (Esping-Anderson, 1996; Mishra, 1984; Munday, 1989; Pierson, 1991; Goldberg and Rosenthal, 2002). Nevertheless, a good deal of comparative social policy scholarship has sought to document this trend, and many have pointed to the increasing influence of neoliberal ideology which has prompted many governments to reduce public expenditures, retrench social spending, impose more demanding eligibility requirements, and require recipients of income benefits to engage in paid employment (Goldberg and Rosenthal, 2002; Pfaller, Gough and Therborn, 1991; Pierson, 2001). More recently, the ambiguous concept of globalization has been employed by comparative social policy writers to examine this issue (Mishra, 1999).

Challenges for mainstream comparative inquiry
As these examples reveal, comparative social policy inquiry in Europe and North America has produced a substantial and significant corpus of knowledge. However, the field still faces numerous challenges. As has been argued already, one challenge concerns the way the dominant discourse of mainstream comparative social policy inquiry is infused with a particularistic, Western perspective that reflects a long-standing preoccupation with state welfare and an implicit commitment to institutional welfarist thinking. Since the waning of Marxist influences in mainstream comparative social policy scholarship, this orientation has been consolidated.

Mainstream comparative scholars have paid little attention to the alternative discourses emanating from the Global South and other regions of the world, and in other fields of academic inquiry, which utilize different cultural perspectives, values and assumptions to address social welfare. If recognized, these discourses could inform and elucidate the field. Cognate academic subjects such as development studies and cultural studies have provided useful insights into welfare phenomena in other societies but this work has been largely ignored. The efforts of feminist and post-modernist social policy scholars to promote an alternative international discourse has also made little impression. The work of researchers and policy makers in the international development agencies, which has significantly influenced social policy in the Global South, has been given little attention. The writings of comparativists within social policy who have previously used alternative perspectives such as international structuralism to analyse social welfare issues have received little attention.

Neglectful of these alternative perspectives, mainstream comparative social policy scholarship continues to use Western theories and conceptual frameworks to categorize, analyse and explain social welfare institutions in different parts of the world. However, it is unlikely that analytical inquiry into social welfare phenomena in culturally different societies can be effectively pursued by the exclusive application of Western constructs and theories. The use of Western preconceptions to determine the subject matter of inquiry fails to ask appropriate questions or to address the most pertinent realities of non-Western countries. Because of its failure to understand indigenous welfare realities from the perspective of the 'other', mainstream comparative social policy is unlikely to properly comprehend welfare phenomena in the world's many different cultures.

The problem is revealed in the widespread use of Western taxonomies, and even the 'welfare state' construct, to classify government welfare programmes in non-Western societies. Although the notion of a 'welfare state' is of dubious validity when characterizing Western nations, it pervades mainstream social policy discourse with unhelpful results. For example, comparative accounts of what are sometimes referred to as the East Asian 'welfare states' reveal the extent to which Western constructs and taxonomies fail to elucidate complex realities. Of course, it is questionable whether East Asian societies such as Hong Kong, Singapore, Taiwan and Malaysia can or should be classed as 'welfare states'. Several of the region's political leaders, most notably Lee Kuan Yew of Singapore, have publicly denigrated Western welfarism (Lee Kuan Yew, 2000) and some social policy scholars have reported difficulties when seeking to understand social welfare provision in East Asian countries by using established Western approaches (Goodman and Peng, 1996; Wilding and Mok, 2001). The frequent use of the residual construct in Western social policy to characterize social policy in Hong Kong has, for example, been questioned by scholars such as Chow (1998) who points out that while state welfare in Hong Kong does have residual features, it also has institutional features. Midgley (1984) reached the same conclusion almost fifteen years earlier. Similar difficulties have been encountered by attempts to build on the Esping-Anderson typology and to identify a unique East Asian welfare model. While some scholars have happily classified the

East Asian societies into one or more of Esping Andersen's categories (Aspalter, 2001), others have concluded that there is, in fact, no distinctly East Asian welfare model and that efforts to expand Esping-Andersen's typology by creating a fourth, East Asian welfare category, are futile (Goodman, White and Kwon, 1998). The result is a muddle that hardly enhances comparative knowledge of social welfare in this region of the world.

Another example of the problematic way mainstream ideas have been used in comparative social policy inquiry is the adoption of Western explanatory theories to account for the evolution of state welfare institutions in different parts of the world. As was noted earlier, explanatory theories have been extensively employed to account for the expansion of government welfare effort. However, while these theories may illuminate social policy development in Europe and other industrial nations, it is doubtful that they can provide plausible interpretations of the determinants of welfare effort in the Global South. Indeed, attempts to test the veracity of these theories have not been particularly successful. For example, studies of the evolution of social security in Latin America, which have used these theories, have reached quite different conclusions (Mesa-Lago, 1978; Malloy, 1979), and in Midgley's (1986) account of the factors responsible for the growth of government welfare in the East Asian 'tiger' economies, established Western theories were found to offer few explanatory insights. Similarly, Tang's (1998) account of the expansion of state welfare in Hong Kong found that no established theory provided a satisfactory explanation of social policy development in the territory. However, these limitations have not prevented social policy scholars in the Global South from using these theories to explain indigenous realities. One example is Ku's (1995) reliance on Marxism to provide a paradigmatic basis for analysing government social welfare in Taiwan. Although the author's use of theory is impressive, the role of culture and other indigenous factors are given little attention.

Some social policy writers have sought to examine welfare realities in other countries, and notably the nations of the Global South, by using discourses originating in development studies. One of the most significant was MacPherson's (1982) application of international structuralist theory to analyse social policy in the developing countries. This account, as well as Midgley's (1981) analysis of Western influences in the development of social work in the Third World, anticipated a subsequent plethora of social science inquiry into the impact of colonialism on contemporary realities. Although both development studies and post-colonial studies could provide useful insights for comparative social policy analysis, this work has been largely ignored. Similarly, studies such as MacPherson's, and several subsequent accounts focusing specifically on the Global South (Hardiman and Midgley, 1982; Jones, 1990; MacPherson and Midgley, 1987) have attracted little attention in mainstream comparative social policy circles.

As was argued earlier, a related problem is the failure of mainstream comparative social policy to engage actively with normative concerns. Indeed, mainstream comparative social policy scholarship has been remarkably indifferent to normative and practical issues, preferring to pursue typological and explanatory interests. This is not to deny that mainstream comparative scholarship implicitly addresses normative issues. For example, many accounts in the comparative literature have examined, and regretted, the shift from collectivist institutionalism to neoliberal individualism in many countries (Glennerster and Midgley, 1991; Mishra, 1984; Munday, 1989). While these accounts do evoke normative issues, they remain implicit, offering few if any proposals that can effectively challenge the hegemony of neoliberal ideas. Mainstream inquiry is also detached from the type of advisory endeavour that practical social policy formulation requires if it is to generate humane responses to pressing social needs. Indeed, despite an awareness of the impact of neoliberalism, mainstream social policy has not counteracted its diffusionary impact. Today, neoliberal social policy advisors from Western countries and agencies such as the International Monetary Fund and the World Bank actively promote the adoption of approaches that denigrate state intervention, ignore cultural traditions based on familial and solidaristic community institutions, and promote the radical individualism which seems now to be increasingly celebrated in the West.

It has been argued already that the implicit normative assumptions in mainstream comparative social policy are rooted in the experience of European welfare statism. This preference has established an implicit, international normative standard against which other welfare systems are evaluated. Consequently, accounts of non-Western welfare systems by both local and international scholars are often critical, or even apologetic, if local approaches do not comply with this standard. It is not uncommon for social policy scholars in other societies to complain that the public welfare systems of their countries do not conform to the European 'welfare state' ideal. Even studies that do not seek explicitly to compare local welfare provision against the idealized Western 'welfare state' standard often make implicit normative comparisons revealing the inadequacies of local welfare institutions (Ramesh, 2000).

The way mainstream comparative social policy scholarship has focused almost exclusively on state welfare institutions when seeking normatively to assess welfare phenomena in other societies has resulted in the neglect of the many other institutional mechanisms that contribute to the well-being of individuals, families, communities and societies as a whole. As feminist scholarship has shown, the preoccupation with state welfare provision and its historic emphasis on the role of the male breadwinner has failed to explicate the contribution of women and familial forms of caring in social welfare

(Bryson, 1992; Dominelli, 1991; Sainsbury, 1994). Consequently, normative assessments of state welfare have been seriously biased. Non-formal, 'traditional' institutions that play a far more important role in meeting social needs than government social programmes in non-Western societies have also been ignored. It is unfortunate that a rich body of normative as well as analytical research into these welfare institutions, generated largely by anthropologists, remains beyond the scope of mainstream comparative social policy scholarship (von Benda Beckmann et al., 1988; von Benda-Beckmann and von Benda-Beckmann, 1994; Midgley, 1994; van Ginneken, 1999).

Of course, this is not to suggest that comparative social policy inquiry should ignore the role of governments in social welfare. The state is a major contributor to social welfare provision and its contribution obviously requires attention and analysis. But to focus exclusively on state welfare, as most mainstream comparative social policy scholars have done, is to offer a partial and inaccurate account of the many complex realities that contribute to human well-being in different societies. Since these institutions play a particularly significant role in the Global South, comparative scholarship must be cognizant of their role.

The failure to interpret non-Western welfare systems in terms of criteria that reflect the realities of culturally different societies, rather than external normative standards originating in mainstream Western thinking, has impeded the development of normative theories which can facilitate the formulation and implementation of appropriate social policies and programmes. There is an urgent need for comparative social policy to contribute, in practical ways, to the formulation of policies and programmes that incorporate indigenous welfare approaches and accommodate social, cultural, economic, demographic and other differences. Because social policy is ultimately an applied field, it is not unreasonable to suggest that mainstream comparative inquiry should be more directly involved in practical matters. While analytical preoccupations need not be abandoned, the persistent problems of global poverty, hunger, exploitation, conflict and oppression demand normative frameworks that can provide a basis for appropriate social policy making in different societies and ultimately at a global level as well. But, because comparative social policy scholarship is so preoccupied with typological and explanatory endeavours, and so infused with the normative preferences of Western welfare statism, this goal is far from being realized.

Social welfare and social development in the Global South

Half a century ago, at the end of the Second World War, governments in many parts of the world broke with conventional beliefs about the virtues of non-intervention and began more confidently to direct economic affairs and expand a range of social provisions designed to promote the well-being of their populations. In the industrial nations, enhanced state intervention was closely associated with post-war reconstruction. In the developing nations, government engagement was closely linked to the struggle for independence from European imperialism. Nationalist movements, which had gathered strength before the war, now aggressively asserted the right to national self-determination. While this trend was resisted with bitter consequences in some places by some of the imperial powers, it did not halt the inexorable struggle for freedom from foreign domination. In some regions of the world such as Latin America, which had secured independence from European rule many decades earlier, and in other nations which had never been colonized, the struggle for self-determination found expression in greater efforts to assert national autonomy and achieve economic and social modernization.

It was in this context that the idea of development gained a new vibrancy. Drawing on nineteenth-century social evolutionary ideas as well as older beliefs about the possibility of progress and the ability of human agency to shape the future, the independence movements embraced economic planning and sought to address the pressing problems of mass poverty and deprivation which characterized their societies after what the imperial powers claimed was a period of progressive and 'civilizing' rule. For various motives, some of the metropolitan powers supported these efforts. Focusing chiefly on territories without sizeable settler colonies, they provided aid and technical assistance to create economic planning agencies and introduced limited social services. Many of the nationalist independence movements were inspired by European socialism believing that state direction of the economy, centralized five-year planning, nationalization, public welfare provision and other forms of intervention would promote economic and social modernization.

At the time, social conditions in most of the colonial territories were appalling. While European settlers and colonial officials enjoyed a high standard of living, poverty and deprivation among the indigenous population was widespread. Many local people suffered from debilitating communicable diseases, infant mortality was high, life expectancy was low, and few were literate. Access to health, education and social services was limited. Although some colonial administrations had established education and welfare provisions in the years preceding the war, missionaries were historically responsible for running hospitals and clinics, for managing schools and for providing residential social welfare services to those with physical disabilities, the destitute elderly, orphans and others. However, the hospitals, clinics, schools and welfare facilities operated by the missionaries catered only for a small proportion of those in need (MacPherson, 1982).

With independence, many of the nationalist movements hoped to address the pressing social needs of their people through expanding social service provisions. Many leaders had been inspired by the rapid growth of the public social services in the industrial nations and aspired to create their own 'welfare states'. However, it was clear that rapid economic development would be required to generate the funds needed to increase social provision on a significant scale. Accordingly, it was widely believed that economic development should be given the highest priority and that consumption should be deferred. Although this goal was not, in fact, realized, partly because of growing political pressures for access to modern health and educational services, economic development was viewed by political as well as administrative elites as a primary objective of government.

It was in this context that limited welfare services were introduced by the governments of the newly independent states (Hardiman and Midgley, 1982; MacPherson, 1982). In some cases, existing colonial welfare provisions were augmented by national governments. Generally, this involved the creation of social insurance and provident funds for civil servants and workers in regular wage employment, and social assistance and residential care for the urban poor. The introduction of social welfare services for the urban poor was closely associated with professional social work. Social work had achieved recognition in the industrial nations as a modern approach to dealing with social problems and although it had previously been introduced into India, South Africa and several Latin American countries, several metropolitan governments assisted in the creation of professional training opportunities, and in the development of agencies that would employ these professionals.

The role of social work in the creation of the social development approach to social welfare in the newly independent, developing nations was critical. The realization that individualized casework treatment could not begin to address the problem of mass poverty and its associated ills of hunger, ill-health, illiteracy and landlessness in the developing countries, facilitated the introduction of community-based interventions which focused on mobilizing local people to address social needs and to engage simultaneously in productive economic activities that would raise their incomes. Known as community development, this approach fused with other social interventions to comprise an approach that the British Colonial Office in 1954 dubbed social development (United Kingdom, 1954). The term was used to connote the linking of social welfare with the overriding commitment to economic development which then characterized nation-building efforts in the Global South.

Social development was actively promoted in the colonial territories by the British government but, with the waning of European imperialism, the United Nations assumed international leadership (Midgley, 1995). The organization actively promoted economic planning in the newly independent developing countries and provided technical assistance for this purpose. It also encouraged social policy development. In the early 1950s, the United Nations subscribed to the widely held view that professional social work should be introduced to the developing countries to meet the need for modern social service provision. However, it also recognized that community development should form an integral part of the social services, particularly in the rural areas where the majority of the population resided. Accordingly, remedial social work services were emphasized for urban areas while community development was given greater priority in the rural areas.

By the 1960s, the United Nations had begun to reassess this approach and it gradually began to place more emphasis on macro-development planning that integrated national economic policies with social welfare provisions (Midgley, 1995). Governments were now encouraged and provided with aid and technical assistance to adopt policies that would transcend social work and community-based interventions and instead focus the activities of their powerful central planning agencies on social objectives. In terms of this approach, which was known as unified socio-economic development, economic development would be targeted at meeting social objectives. Economic growth achievements would no longer be measured in terms of industrial investments or increases in exports or per capital income growth but in terms of social outputs such as employment creation, improvements in nutrition, gains in health status, increases in literacy and educational achievements and other social improvements.

Together, the community-based and centralized planning approaches formed the core of social development's agenda. Although they co-existed uneasily, these twin perspectives provided a normative basis for social policy in many countries of the Global South. Through its influence over member states in the Economic and Social Council, and the adoption of numerous resolutions by the General Assembly, the United Nations played a key leadership role in promoting the adoption of social development. Many of the metropolitan nations supported these efforts through their own aid programmes and, in addition, other multilateral organizations such as the World Health Organization, the International Labour Organization and the World Bank also facilitated the adoption of the social development perspective (Midgley, 1995).

By the 1960s, community-based projects concerned with social and economic improvements were commonplace throughout the developing nations of the Global South. The community development approach was also infused into health care and became a primary mechanism for promoting health and nutritional improvements in many countries. At the same time, national planning agencies created social sectoral programmes concerned with health, education, housing and social welfare services. In addition, social planners skilled in promoting social development planning goals were recruited and trained. Social indicators were refined and widely adopted to measure the attainment of social development goals (Baster, 1972; Estes, 1985; Morris, 1979).

While social development exerted a pervasive influence in the Global South, it was not universally adopted or always effectively implemented. In many developing countries, social policy development was incremental and haphazard and in others, serious economic difficulties, widespread ethnic and political conflict as well as corruption impeded the implementation of this approach. In many others, social development coexisted uneasily with other approaches. Indeed, the dominant institutional welfarist approach which advocated the adoption of European style welfare statism, remains influential.

In addition, international economic difficulties in the 1970s increased developing country indebtedness and weakened the ability of governments to expand social provision. These problems were exacerbated by the diffusion of neoliberal ideology emanating from academics and political leaders in Britain, the United States and other countries. As the International Monetary Fund and World Bank became increasingly committed to neoliberal ideologies, structural adjustment programmes were imposed, national planning agencies were dismantled or debilitated, social expenditures were curtailed and social programmes retrenched. These various factors undermined the social development project.

As a result of these developments, a new approach to social development has emerged. Instead of government planners and community development workers directing social development, the field is now dominated by aid officials, international development experts and consultants. Funded by international donor agencies and national governments in the Global North, social development is now largely focused on local non-profit organizations and community groups which manage a variety of development projects. Many social development projects supported by international donors are concerned with health, children and gender issues and many are directed at poor women. Many seek to implement local income-generating projects. Social development personnel are also involved in large-scale development projects to ensure that the 'human factor', as it is called, is taken into account when large-scale transportation, hydroelectric and industrial projects are constructed. They are employed to assess the social impact of these projects, and are also involved in project appraisal and evaluation, and stakeholder and gender analyses. Gender issues now feature prominently in social development practice.

Believing that social development efforts had become increasingly fragmented, and that it had lost its original purpose, the United Nations sought in the 1990s to reinvigorate the social development approach. In 1990, it published the first of a series of reports on what was now called 'human' rather than social development (United Nations Development Programme, 1990). Nevertheless, the commitment to social progress through harmonizing economic and social development efforts, and through directive state intervention combined with community participation, were affirmed. The publication of these reports was accompanied by political efforts directed at member states that would again promote social development ideals on an international scale. These steps were a prelude to the convening of the World Social Summit on Social Development.

The Summit was held in Copenhagen in March 1995 and was attended by 186 government delegations including 117 heads of state, with the noticeable exception of President Clinton of the United States and British Prime Minster John Major. It resulted in the adoption of the Copenhagen Declaration which commits the world's governments to achieve eight major goals. These are first, the creation of an enabling economic, political and legal environment which will promote social development; second, the eradication of poverty; third, the promotion of full employment and sustainable livelihoods; fourth, the enhancement of social integration; fifth, the achievement of gender equity and the full participation of women in political, economic, civil and cultural life; sixth, the achievement of universal and equitable access to education and health; seventh, the acceleration of economic and social development in Africa; and eighth, the mitigation of structural adjustment programmes through social measures (United Nations, 1996).

Although the Copenhagen Declaration was accompanied by a Plan of Action designed to ensure that policies and programmes to achieve these goals were implemented, few would claim that a great deal has been achieved. In June 2000, when the United Nations General Assembly met in Geneva to review progress in implementing the Declaration, the results were, to say the least, uneven. Many countries had failed to adopt poverty eradication strategies let alone targets, and ethnic conflicts had continued in many parts of the world impeding efforts towards social integration. Economic adversity in many countries had slowed employment generation and with budgets cuts, access to the social services had been curtailed. In many countries, gender discrimination had not been reduced and economic and social conditions, particularly in Africa, had deteriorated. In addition, several countries, noticeably in East Asia and Latin America, were seriously affected by economic crises associated with international speculative finance capitalism. Indeed, meetings of the World Trade Organization have attracted far more media attention than the Geneva meeting.

On the other hand, the Copenhagen Declaration has created an agenda for social policy at the global level. While the formulation of specific policy programmes and goals may be the responsibility of individual governments, they are situated within an international framework of collaborative policy formulation and implementation that ultimately transcends national activities. In addition, social improvements have been recorded in many countries where steady economic growth has been combined with effective social policies and programmes. Despite economic upheavals in many parts of the world, improvements in life expectancy, nutrition, health, literacy and educational achievements are still being recorded in many parts of the world. This perpetuates the long-term trend towards improved social conditions which has been recorded globally since the middle years of the last century. The major difference today is that the overall trend towards social progress is now characterized by more significant deviations from the norm. In some regions, such as Africa, economic stagnation has been pervasive while in others, such as Latin America, economic growth has been accompanied by an exacerbation of the region's historic inequalities in income and wealth.

Despite setbacks, social development is hardly defunct. Indeed, efforts to ensure its vitality have continued at the political level and academic levels. Its essentially pragmatic prescriptions have been augmented by attempts at theory building and various conceptual formulations of the social development ideal have appeared (Midgley, 1995). The populist, community-based approach which provided the foundations on which social development thinking emerged in the 1950s, was subsequently enhanced by the incorporation of radical community action. More recently, social capital theory has been incorporated into social development theory. These ideas have since been formalized, giving social development an intellectual identity and coherence. The statist version of social development which emerged in the late 1960s has also been formalized in the guise of conceptualizations known variously as Unified Socio-Economic Planning, Basic Needs and Redistribution with Growth (Midgley, 1995; Miah and Tracy, 2001). A more recent development is the interest in local entrepreneurship and the promotion of micro-credit and micro-enterprises by which poor people can engage more vigorously in economic activities (Rainford, 2001). Although this approach reflects the influence of neoliberal thinking, it has fused with the populist, community development tradition to promote cooperative, community-based enterprises which involve larger numbers of people. Post-modernist themes may also be discerned in these activities.

Attempts have also been made to synthesize these different perspectives into a unified 'institutional' approach which recognizes the role of governments, communities and markets in the promotion of well-being in the context of economic development efforts (Midgley, 1995). Rather than treating these different normative positions as antagonistic, some admittedly optimistic proponents of social development believe it is possible to integrate their respective approaches so that all contribute to a comprehensive and sustainable process of development in which social and economic interventions are purposefully linked and harmonized. However, the need for economic development remains paramount. For the proponents of social development, economic growth is a vital dynamic in the production of social welfare. But a distinctive type of economic growth that maximizes employment, spreads benefits widely and invests in human capabilities is needed. This requires state intervention, participation and redistribution. Of course, this approach is antithetical to the neoliberal perspective which requires a limited role for government, maximum opportunities for entrepreneurs to pursue profits without hinderance, and a faith in a trickle-down effect which, it is claimed, will of its own accord, bring prosperity to all.

An important element in the conceptualization of social development is the growing emphasis on welfare productivism. Since social development ideas were first implemented in community-based interventions in the Global South more than 50 years ago, social welfare has been viewed as an inextricable component of economic development. It was believed that local social needs could best be met through an engagement in local economic activities. However, it was also believed that social interventions should not only be compatible with economic activities, but should be productivist in their own right. In more recent articulations of these ideas, the notion of social investments which enhance individual, family and community capabilities has been stressed (Midgley, 1999a).

As will be recognized, the ideas attending social development have been controversial and have been contested both within the development community and by proponents of alternative normative perspectives, particularly neoliberalism and post-modernism. Neoliberals view social development's statism as antithetical to economic progress while post-modernists regard social development's commitment to social change and progress as just another failed meta-narrative arising from Enlightenment thought (Midgley, 1999b). For the anti- or post-development school, which has drawn extensively on post-modernist thinking, every idea of progress is anathema (Rahnema and Bawtree, 1997; Munck and O'Hearn, 1999). However, it is precisely because social development comprises one of many alternative discourses in comparative social policy, that its approach needs to be recognized, examined and comprehended.

Social development: indigenization and normative relevance

The preceding discussion of social development and its relation to comparative social policy inquiry is intended to serve an illustrative rather than informative purpose. It shows that social development comprises an alterative discourse about social welfare at the international level that, together with other discourses, deserves to be recognized and understood in mainstream comparative social policy inquiry. The fact that the 1995 Copenhagen World Summit was attended by representatives of the vast majority of the member states of the United Nations, and by more than two-thirds of the world's heads of state, suggests that social development is not a peripheral activity. It represents many voices that should be heard. By accommodating social development, the comparative study of social welfare can be enriched.

However, social development is only one of many discourses about social welfare that are relevant to comparative social policy scholarship. It has been noted already that feminist scholarship has generated a discourse which, in the form of a critique of mainstream thinking, has revealed the need for a broadened vision of social welfare based on social care, familial institutions and the uniqueness of gender roles. Similarly, post-colonial studies provide insights which can inform a long-standing concern with issues of immigration, cultural identity and racism in social policy scholarship in the industrial nations. Although this scholarship has not been adequately linked to comparative inquiry, it is of obvious relevance to the field (Midgley, 1998).

By paying attention to these and other discourses, the limitations of comparative social policy inquiry can be addressed. As has been argued already, the lack of both indigenization and appropriate normative frameworks that can inform efforts to respond to pressing social needs are major limitations of mainstream comparative inquiry. Social development is concerned with both issues. Its roots are indigenous to the Global South and it gives vigorous expression to a body of normative theory that seeks to address the serious social problems facing millions of people in the world's poorest countries.

Social development has been cognizant of indigenous influences and, despite its Modernist roots, may be regarded as a distinctly 'Third Worldist' approach to social welfare. Although the initial impetus for social development came from expatriate colonial officials involved in promoting the introduction of social work, they recognized that urban-based remedial interventions which relied on bureaucratic social service provision and professional expertise were of limited relevance to the problems facing the majority of the population located in the rural areas. The formulation of a community-based approach revealed an understanding of the importance of agrarian life in the Global South as well as the importance of community networks and cultural commitments, both of which are often based on indigenous family forms. The participatory emphasis in community development drew on culturally institutionalized patterns of mutual aid based on reciprocal obligations and created an intervention that made limited use of professional and bureaucratic provisions. The emphasis on self-determination and cooperation, which formed an integral element of community development, was also highly compatible with indigenous culture. Indeed, in some countries such as India, community development was directly influenced by Gandhi and Tagore's nativism. The statist interventionism which subsequently became prominent in social development thinking also had an indigenous aspect, harmonizing social policy with the nationalist populism that characterized the ideology of the anti-colonial, independence movements.

By being cognizant of the way indigenization can inform the comprehension of welfare institutions in other societies, mainstream comparative social policy scholarship may become more sensitive to cultural realities and transcend its current preoccupation with typological categorization and the use of Western theories to explain the origins and functions of state welfare. Fortunately, there are indications that some mainstream comparative scholarship is moving in this direction. For example, recent accounts of the evolution of social welfare in Ireland and Sweden have utilized categories of this type, placing far more emphasis on the role of culture than before (Gould, 2001; Peillon, 2001). Similarly, although criticized, Jones's (1990b; 1993) exploration of the role of indigenous culture in East Asian welfare transcended conventional approaches and may foster future and more incisive accounts of cultural dynamics.

Social development is also overtly normative. It places more emphasis on articulating value assumptions and formulating responses to social problems than on categorization and explanation. While the normative engagement of social development writing may be viewed by some social policy scholars as a second-order activity that should follow analytical endeavour, social development proponents believe that the pressing social problems of our time demand solutions based on appropriate and workable normative theories. Unlike much mainstream comparative social policy scholarship, social development has energetically sought to explicate normative assumptions and policy prescriptions.

The willingness of social development proponents to declare normative preferences in social development should encourage those engaged in mainstream comparative social policy scholarship to explicate their own implicit preference for institutionalist welfarism. The tendency in mainstream comparative social policy to assume the moral superiority of the institutional, welfarist position has resulted in a failure to affirm normative commitments and to articulate, in a coherent way, a defensible normative position. The failure to do so has resulted in an inability to confront the continuing diffusion of neoliberalism. It has also impeded the formulation of a reconstructed neo-institutional position that can meet neoliberalism's challenge. By ignoring the normative implications of other approaches in comparative analysis, mainstream social policy has not exploited its potential to contribute to the formulation of a reconstructed normative conceptualization of state welfare engagement that may challenge neoliberalism.

For example, the productivist commitment in social development offers a viable response to neoliberal claims that social expenditures impede economic development. There is a wealth of evidence to show that social expenditures that invest in human capabilities promote economic growth and, as Midgley (1999a) suggested, have positive redistributive implications. For example, antimalarial campaigns in India and Sri Lanka in the 1950s not only reduced mortality and morbidity but increased agricultural production (Schultz, 1981). Similarly, investments in human capital are today regarded as an essential component of economic development, and social capital generated by community interventions have the same effect (Midgley, 1995). By utilizing this evidence to demonstrate that social expenditures can promote economic growth, competitiveness and prosperity, social policy scholarship could provide a normative alternative which progressive policy makers could use to repackage conventional welfarist ideals. Unfortunately, the extensive experience of social development practitioners with social investments of this kind has not attracted much attention in mainstream social policy scholarship. But a normative engagement with neoliberalism is only one aspect of the wider challenges arising from civil conflict, oppression, ethnic hatreds and gender and other forms of discrimination. Mainstream comparative social policy has not even begun to address these endemic problems preferring instead to focus on formal government welfare programmes. But these programmes have little meaning for those whose daily lives are characterized by violence, brutal oppression and perpetual suffering. Issues of public welfare provision have little meaning for African villagers who do not know whether they will be slaughtered by marauding gangs of militia funded by political leaders from different ethnic groups, or for slum dwellers on the outskirts of Latin American cities who scavenge in landfills for their subsistence, or for Palestinian families who cower in terror as Israeli tanks demolish their neighbourhoods, or for impoverished Asian families who live in oppressive feudal conditions and are compelled to sell their children into debt bondage. While it is obviously desirable that comparative social policy scholars be concerned with typological and explanatory activities, these pressing problems demand attention.

Finally, a familiarity with the social development perspective can also help promote the goal of developing a one-world approach to social policy. Although the literature on this issue is still underdeveloped, the subject has been discussed particularly with reference to the pressures being exerted by economic globalization on national welfare systems. However, debates on this topic are still framed in terms of mainstream 'welfare state' criteria except that the role of international organizations rather than national governments is now being emphasized (Deacon, Hulse and Stubbs 1997; Mishra, 1999). While these debates touch on issues relevant to social development to a greater extent than before, they nevertheless perpetuate conventional statist preoccupations and fail to recognize the heterogeneity of welfare institutions and the diverse ways in which these institutions have been conceptualized and analysed by scholars working outside the mainstream.

A truly global perspective on social policy must accommodate diverse discourses. It has been argued already that social development is only one of many discourses that provide insights into the complex and heterogeneous realities of social welfare around the world. The construction of a truly one world perspective cannot legitimately proceed by seeking to impose one approach on efforts to conceptualize global social policy. Nor can it use only one interpretive mode to understand the complex reality of social welfare in the world's many, diverse societies. Similarly, attempts to subsume this reality within a unitary normative perspective such as institutionalism or neoliberalism are meaningless. Instead, efforts to promote the emergence of a one world perspective on social welfare should begin by recognizing the claims of many discourses, assessing them in a discursive dialogue and ultimately by promoting hybridity based on relative rather than absolute criteria. This does not deny the need for absolute standards relating to the alleviation of suffering, oppression, the eradication of poverty and the assertion of freedoms. But it should recognize that these goals may be achieved through different institutional mechanisms in different social, economic and cultural contexts. The acceptance of hybridity may result in the creation of a flexible conceptual framework that can accommodate diverse perspectives. Eventually, it may also promote a fusion of these diverse positions and result in the emergence of a truly one-world approach. By understanding the social development approach as an example of an alternative discourse, and recognizing its contribution to comparative social policy, efforts to achieve this goal may be furthered.

References

Aaron, Henry (1967), 'Social security: international comparisons', in O. Eckstein (ed.), *Studies in the Economics Income Maintenance*, Washington, DC: Brookings Institution, pp. 13–48.

Aspalter, Christian (2001), *Conservative Welfare State Systems in East Asia*, Westport, CT: Praeger.

Aspalter, Christian (2002), *Democratization and Welfare State Development in Taiwan*, Aldershot: Ashgate.

Baster, Nancy (1972), *Measuring Development*, London: Frank Cass.

Benda-Beckmann, Franz, Keebet Benda-Beckmann, Otto B. Brun and Frank Hirtz (1988), *Between Kinship and the State: Social Security and Law in Developing Countries*, Dordrecht: Foris Publications.

Benda-Beckmann, Franz and Keebet Benda-Beckmann, (1994), 'Coping with insecurity', *Focaal*, **22/23** (1), 7–34.

Bryson, Lois (1992), *Welfare and the State*, London: Macmillan.

Chow, Nelson (1998), '*The making of social policy in Hong Kong before and after 1997*', Paper presented at the Conference on *New Prospects for Social Welfare Systems in East Asia*, Taiwan. Cited in P. Wilding and K. Mok (2001), 'Hong Kong: Between State and Market', in P. Alcock and G. Craig (eds), *International Social Policy*, New York: Palgrave, pp. 241–56.

Cutright, P. (1965), 'Political structure, economic development and social security programs', *American Journal of Sociology*, **70** (4), 537–50.

Deacon, Bob, Michelle Hulse and Paul Stubbs (1997), *Global Social Policy: International Organizations and the Future of Welfare*, London: Sage Publications.

Doling, John and Roziah Omar (2000), *Social Welfare East and West: Britain and Malaysia*, Aldershot: Ashgate.

Dominelli, Lena (1991), *Women Across Continents: Feminist Comparative Social Policy*, Hemel Hempstead: Harvester Wheatsheaf.

Esping-Andersen, Gøsta (1990), *Three Worlds of Welfare Capitalism*, Cambridge: Polity Press.

Esping-Andersen, Gøsta (1996), *Welfare States in Transition: National Adaptations in Global Economies*, London: Sage Publications.

Estes, Richard (1985), *The Social Progress of Nations*, New York: Praeger.

Fitzpatrick, Tony (2001), *Welfare Theory: An Introduction*, New York: Palgrave.

Glennerster, Howard and James Midgley (1991), *The Radical Right and the Welfare State*, Hemel Hempstead: Harvester Wheatsheaf.

Goldberg, Getrude S. and Marguerite G. Rosenthal (eds) (2002), *Diminishing Welfare: A Cross-National Study of Social Provision*, Westport, CT: Auburn House.

Goodman, Roger and Ito Peng (1996), 'The East Asian welfare states: peripatetic learning, adaptive change and nation-building', in G. Esping Andersen (ed.), *Welfare States in Transition: National Adaptations in Global Economies*, London: Sage Publications, pp. 193–224.

Goodman, Roger, Gordon White and Huk-ju Kwon (1998), *The East Asian Welfare Model: Welfare Orientalism and the State*, New York: Routledge.

Gould, Arthur (2001), *Developments in Swedish Social Policy: Resisting Dionysus*, New York: Palgrave.

Hardiman, Margaret and James Midgley (1982), *The Social Dimensions of Development: Social Policy and Planning in the Third World*, New York: John Wiley & Sons.

Higgins, Joan (1981), *States of Welfare: Comparative Analysis in Social Policy*, London: Basil Blackwell.

Jones, Catherine (1985), *Patterns of Social Policy*, London: Tavistock.

Jones, Catherine (1990a), *Promoting Prosperity: The Hong Kong Way of Social Policy*, Hong Kong: Chinese University Press.

Jones, Catherine (1990b), 'Hong Kong, Singapore, South Korea and Taiwan: oikonomic welfare states', *Government and Opposition*, **25** (4), 447–62.

Jones, Catherine (1993), 'The Pacific challenge: Confucian welfare states', in C. Jones (ed.), *New Perspectives on the Welfare State in Europe*, New York: Routledge, pp. 198–217.

Jones, Howard (1990), *Social Welfare in Third World Development*, London: Macmillan.

Kennett, Patricia (2001), *Comparative Social Policy*, Buckingham: Open University Press.

Ku, Yuen-wen (1995), *Welfare Capitalism in Taiwan: State, Economy and Social Policy*, New York: St. Martin's Press.

Lee Kuan Yew (2000), *From Third World to First: The Singapore Story 1965–2000*, New York: HarperCollins.

MacPherson, Stewart (1982), *Social Policy in the Third World: The Dilemmas of Underdevelopment*, Brighton: Harvester.

MacPherson, Stewart and James Midgley (1987), *Comparative Social Policy and the Third World*, Brighton: Wheatsheaf.

Malloy, James (1979), *The Politics of Social Security in Brazil*, Pittsburgh: University of Pittsburgh Press.

Mesa-Lago, Carmelo (1978), *Social Security in Latin America*, Pittsburgh, PA: University of Pittsburgh Press.

Miah, Mizan R. and Martin B. Tracy (2001), 'The institutional approach to social development', *Social Development Issues*, **23** (1), 58–64.

Midgley, James (1981), *Professional Imperialism: Social Work in the Third World*, London: Heinemann.

Midgley, James (1984), *Social Security, Inequality and the Third World*, Chichester: John Wiley & Sons.

Midgley, James (1986), 'Industrialization and welfare: the case of the four little tigers', *Social Policy and Administration*, **20** (4), 225–38.

Midgley, James (1994), 'Social security policy in developing countries: integrating state and traditional systems', *Focaal*, **22/23** (1), 219–30.

Midgley, James (1995), *Social Development: The Developmental Perspective in Social Welfare*, Thousand Oaks, CA: Sage Publications.

Midgley, James (1997), *Social Welfare in Global Context*, Thousand Oaks, CA: Sage Publications.

Midgley, James (1998), 'Colonialism and welfare: a post-colonial commentary', *Journal of Progressive Human Services*, **9** (2), 31–50.

Midgley, James (1999a), 'Growth, redistribution and welfare: towards social investment', *Social Service Review*, **77** (1), 3–2.

Midgley, James (1999b), 'Postmodernism and social development: implications for progress, intervention and ideology, *Social Development Issues*, **21** (3), 5–13.

Mishra, Ramesh (1977), *Society and Social Policy: Theories and Practice of Welfare*, London: Macmillan.

Mishra, Ramesh (1984), *The Welfare State in Crisis*, Brighton: Wheatsheaf.

Mishra, Ramesh (1990), *The Welfare State in Capitalist Society*, Hemel Hempstead: Harvester Wheatsheaf.

Mishra, Ramesh (1999), *Globalization and the Welfare State*, Cheltenham, UK and Northampton, MA, USA: Edward Elgar.

Morris, D. M. (1979), *Measuring the Conditions of the World's Poor*, Oxford: Pergamon Press.

Munck, Ronaldo and O'Hearn, Denis (eds) (1999), *Critical Development Theory: Contributions to a New Paradigm*, New York: Zed Books.

Munday, Brian (1989), *The Crisis in Welfare: An International Perspective on Social Services and Social Work*, New York: St. Martin's Press.

O'Brein, Martin and Sue Penna (1998), *Theorising Welfare: Enlightenment and Modern Society*, Thousand Oaks, CA: Sage Publications.

Onokerhoraye, Andrew G. (1984), *Social Services in Nigeria*, London: Routledge and Kegan Paul.

Patel, Leila (1992), *Restructuring Social Welfare: Options for South Africa*, Johannesburg: Ravan Press.

Peillon, Michel (2001), *Welfare in Ireland: Actors, Resources and Strategies*, Westport, CT: Praeger.

Pfaller, Alfred, Ian Gough and Goran Therborn (1991), *Can the Welfare State Compete? A Comparative Study of Five Advanced Capitalist Countries*, London: Macmillan.

Pierson, Chris (1991), *Beyond the Welfare State: The New Political Economy of Welfare*, Cambridge: Polity Press.

Pierson, Paul (ed.) (2001), *The New Politics of the Welfare State*, New York: Oxford University Press.

Rahnema, Majid and Victoria Bawtree (eds) (1997), *The Post-development Reader*, New York: Zed Books.

Rainford, W. (2001), 'Promoting welfare by enhancing opportunity: the individual enterprise approach to social development', *Social Development Issues*, **23** (1), 51–7.

Ramesh, M. with M. G. Asher (2000), *Welfare Capitalism in Southeast Asia*, New York: St. Martin's Press.

Sainsbury, Diane (1994), 'Women and men's social rights: gendering dimensions of welfare states', in Diane Sainsbury (ed.), *Gendering Welfare States*, Thousand Oaks, CA: Sage Publications.

Schultz, Theodore W. (1981), *Investing in People*, Berkeley, CA: University of California Press.

Tang, Kwong Leung (1998), *Colonial State and Social Policy: Social Welfare Development in Hong Kong 1842–1997*, Lanham, MD: University Press of America.

Titmuss Richard M. (1974), *Social Policy: An Introduction*, London: Allen & Unwin.

United Kingdom, Colonial Office (1954), *Social Development in the British Colonial Territories*, London: HMSO.

United Nations (1996), *Report of the World Summit for Social Development: Copenhagen, 6–12 March 1995*, New York.

United Nations Development Programme (1990), *Human Development Report 1990*, New York.

Van Ginneken, Wouter (1999), *Social Security for the Excluded Majority: Case Studies from Developing Countries*, Geneva: International Labour Office.

Ward, Peter (1986), *Welfare Politics in Mexico: Papering Over the Cracks*, London: Allen & Unwin.

Wilding, Paul and Ka-ho Mok (2001), 'Hong Kong: between state and market', in Pete Alcock and Gary Craig (eds), *International Social Policy*, New York: Palgrave, pp. 241–56.

Wilensky, Harold and Charles Lebeaux (1965), *Industrial Society and Social Welfare*, New York: Free Press.

13 Social policy regimes in the developing world

Ian Gough

Introduction

This chapter starts from the absence bemoaned by James Midgley in the previous chapter, but addresses it using a methodological approach which he dismisses. The continuing absence of scholarly debate on social policy in development contexts is as remarkable as it is regrettable. Social policy studies have continued to develop an institutionalist framework reflecting a particularistic Western perspective. Of course, development studies have filled the gap and made notable contributions, but no sustained dialogue has occurred between Northern social policy studies and development studies. It is this bridge that this chapter attempts to construct.[1]

Midgley accuses 'mainstream comparative social policy' of neglecting normative, explanatory and practical issues in favour of 'classificatory activities'. Elsewhere with Len Doyal I have tried to construct a universal normative framework via a theory of human needs (Doyal and Gough, 1991). In subsequent articles I have applied this theory to the evaluation of different economic systems as frameworks for satisfying human needs, and to a statistical analysis of cross-national variations in need-satisfaction (Gough, 2000, chapters 2 and 5). These issues are not directly addressed here, though they inform some of what follows.

My concern in this chapter is positive and explanatory, yet it begins from a classificatory approach. The aim is to reconceptualize the welfare regime paradigm developed within Northern social policy studies to provide a rich, open and rewarding framework for understanding the nature and diversity of social policies in the South. Midgley has rightly criticized the relevance of the welfare regime paradigm to social policy dilemmas in much of the world, so this approach may seem perverse and will need defending. The intention is certainly not simply to 'apply' it to the South, but to radically recast it. My basic reason is that it offers the way out of a classic dilemma in understanding social policy and social development across the world. By developing a variegated middle-range model it avoids both over-generalization and over-specificity. A regime approach can recognize, on the one hand, the commonalities across the countries and regions of the South, while on the other hand identifying systematic qualitatively distinct patterns within the

South. It can also provide a bridge between thinking about social policy in the North and the South, without imposing Northern frameworks and solutions on the rest of the world.

In adopting a regime approach we are placing ourselves within the historical–institutional school of social research. This attempts to steer a middle way between teleological or functionalist approaches (both modernization and Marxist) on the one hand, and post-modern approaches emphasizing uniqueness and diversity on the other hand. It integrates structures and actors within a framework which promises a comparative analysis of socio-economic systems at different stages of development and different positions in the world system. Similarly it seeks to reconcile the rival 'structural' and 'actor' approaches within development sociology (Long and van der Ploeg, 1994). We recognize that structures are socially constructed, reproduced and changed through the actions of people in real time, but that, at given points in time, actors occupy different interest and power positions within structures, generating different goals, levels of autonomy and clout.

The chapter is in three parts followed by a conclusion. First, it introduces the 'welfare regime' paradigm initially developed to understand the post-war welfare states of the West. Its underlying assumptions are revealed and shown to be manifestly inapplicable to much of the less developed, the developing and the transitional worlds of the South and the East. Second, two alternative ideal-type models are constructed: an *informal security regime* and, very briefly, an *insecurity regime*. This provides a richer framework for the comparative analysis of social policy in the modern world system.[2] Third, I briefly apply our model to four regions of the world – Latin America, East Asia, South Asia and Africa. In each case their regime characteristics are summarized and (very briefly) interpreted using a framework of historical political economy which gives due weight to external and internal factors in their evolution.

To maintain a clear distinction between the three ideal-type regimes, and between these and real-world regimes, I shall use the generic term 'social policy regime' to refer to all of them.[3] However, 'social policy' is necessarily defined much more broadly than in conventional Northern analysis. For the sake of clarity I adopt the following definition. Social policy:

1. is a *policy*, that is, an intentional action within the public sphere to achieve certain goals, not just whatever people do to secure their livelihoods;
2. is oriented to *social welfare* goals, that is, some positive conception of human well-being, whether defined in terms of human needs, capabilities, flourishing, active participation, equity, justice, and so on;

3. operates through a wide variety of policy *instruments* across a number of sectors, that is, it may include land reform, agricultural support, work programmes, food subsidies, tax expenditures, as well as health, education and social protection programmes;
4. is formulated and implemented by a wide spread of *actor*s acting within a public sphere. This means that the field of social policy is not confined to the nation-state, but may extend downwards through regions to localities and associations wherever there is a recognizable 'public sphere', and upwards to transnational and global actors.

The welfare regime model

A welfare regime is an institutional matrix of market, state and family forms, which generates welfare outcomes. According to Esping-Andersen (1990, chapters 1, 3) these are shaped by different class coalitions working within a context of inherited institutions. Welfare regimes are characterized by a) different patterns of state, market and household forms of social provision, b) different welfare outcomes, assessed according to the degree to which labour is 'de-commodified' or shielded from market forces, and c) different stratification outcomes. The last component provides positive feedback: the stratification outcomes shape class coalitions, which tend to reproduce or intensify the original institutional matrix and welfare outcomes. 'Existing institutional arrangements heavily determine, maybe even over-determine, national trajectories' (Esping-Andersen, 1999: 4).

Esping-Andersen identifies three welfare regimes in advanced capitalist countries with continual democratic histories since WW2: the liberal, conservative-corporatist and social-democratic. He summarizes their characteristics as shown in Table 13.1 (Esping-Andersen, 1999, Table 5.4).

This welfare regime paradigm has spawned an immense amount of empirical work and has attracted volumes of critical commentary and theoretical reworking, which can be divided into the following critiques (Gough, 1999):

*   The identification of just three regimes and the allocation of countries between them is disputed. For example, it has been argued that Australia and New Zealand are not liberal, that the Mediterranean countries are different from North European countries, and that Japan cannot be encompassed in such a 'Western' framework.
*   In concentrating on income maintenance and labour market practices it overlooks critical social programmes like health, education and housing which do not conform to these welfare regime patterns and which, further, may reveal that national patterns of social policies are programme-specific. For example, 'liberal' Britain still retains a universal National Health Service.

Table 13.1   The three worlds of welfare capitalism

	Liberal	Conservative-corporatist	Social democratic
Role of:			
Family	Marginal	Central	Marginal
Market	Central	Marginal	Marginal
State	Marginal	Subsidiary	Central
Welfare state:			
Dominant locus of solidarity	Market	Family	State
Dominant mode of solidarity	Individual	Kinship Corporatism Etatism	Universal
Degree of de-commodification	Minimal	High (for breadwinner)	Maximum
Modal examples	US	Germany, Italy	Sweden

- In defining welfare outcomes in terms of de-commodification – insulation from market forces – it ignores other components of well-being, in terms of autonomy and need satisfaction, and other sources of ill-being.
- In concentrating on class analysis, it ignores other sources of stratification such as religion, ethnicity and gender.
- In particular, the effects of the gendered division of labour and household forms are ignored at all three levels (social programmes, welfare outcome and stratification effect).
- In emphasizing the reproduction and stability of class coalitions, social programmes and welfare outcomes it cannot handle dynamic changes and shifts in welfare regime (such as took place in Britain in the 1980s).
- In focusing on domestic institutions and coalitions it ignores the growing constraints of the global political economy and the growing role of supranational institutions.

This debate has encouraged modification of the regime approach even in its OECD heartlands. It is not our intention to review these criticisms systematically here, but three issues should be considered and incorporated before we proceed.

First, the dominant emphasis on labour markets and social protection programmes is related to the reliance on de-commodification as the measure of welfare outcomes. But modern welfare states also deliver health and other social services designed to ameliorate harm or suffering caused by illness, accident and frailty – what Bevan (2004a) calls 'life processes'. A major result in the West is a sprawling 'health state' (Moran, 1999), with interests, institutions and dynamics of its own. Second, the modern state undertakes human investment and self-development through education, training, work experience and allied programmes. Heidenheimer (1981) contends that the early development of the mass education state in the US provided an alternative path of social development to the welfare states of Europe. More recently, interest has grown in the OECD in 'active' alternatives to traditional 'passive' welfare programmes. Room (2000) interprets these activities as 'de-commodification for self-development', thus linking them conceptually to Esping-Andersen's original framework. Third, another important failure of Esping-Andersen's original idea of welfare regime, in the eyes of many, was its blindness to gender. The fact that women undertake the vast bulk of unpaid labour across the developed world, that this establishes a gendered division of labour embracing paid work, that caring duties reproduce inequalities between men and women within households and that this in turn entails a sharp split between the public and private spheres of social life – these social facts are now impinging on the analysis of welfare regimes. Disputes continue however on whether welfare regimes as defined above map closely onto such gender differences (see O'Connor, Orloff and Shaver, 1999).

In what follows I shall extend the idea of (what I now call) social policy regime to incorporate provisions that ameliorate harmful life processes and invest in human capacities. In developing countries these may well extend beyond traditional health and education services. Furthermore, we shall assume that gendered life processes shape the welfare mix, welfare outcomes and stratification effects in all welfare regimes.

In my view this framework (incorporating these prior modifications) offers a useful starting point for studying social policy in development contexts for four reasons. First, the welfare regime approach is precisely concerned with the broader 'welfare mix': the interactions of public sector, private sector and households in producing livelihoods and distributing welfare: a dominant theme in the development literature. Second, it focuses not only on institutions but outcomes – the real states of well-being or ill-being of groups of people. Third, it is a 'political economy' approach which embeds welfare institutions in the 'deep structures' of social reproduction: it forces researchers to analyse social policy not merely in technical but in power terms, and this has much to offer. Fourth, it enables one to identify clusters of countries with welfare features in common; it holds out the promise of distinguishing between groups of developing countries according to their trajectory or paths of development.

To tap this potential, we must first stand back and distil its essentials. We contend that the following nine elements are integral to the welfare regime paradigm.

1. The dominant mode of production is capitalist. There is a division of labour based on the ownership or non-ownership of capital; the dominant form of coordination is *ex post* via market signals; the technological base is dynamic, driven by a never-ending search for profit.
2. A set of class relations is based on this division of labour. The dominant form of inequality derives from exploitation by asset owners of non-asset owners.
3. The dominant means of securing livelihoods is via employment in formal labour markets; conversely, the major threats to security stem from interrupted access to labour markets (and from 'life processes').
4. Political mobilization by the working classes and other classes and 'democratic class struggle' shapes an inter-class 'political settlement'.
5. There is a 'relatively autonomous state' bounded by the structural power of capital but open to class mobilization and voice and able to take initiatives on its own behalf.
6. These factors, together with inherited institutional structures, shape a set of state institutions and practices which undertake social interventions. This state intervention combines with market and family structures and processes to construct a 'welfare mix'.
7. This welfare mix de-commodifies labour to varying degrees (and provides social services and invests in human capital).
8. Together the welfare mix and welfare outcomes influence the definition of interests and the distribution of class power resources, which tend to reproduce the welfare regime through time.
9. Within each regime, 'social policy' entails intentional action within the public sphere to achieve normative, welfare-oriented goals.

Every one of these elements must be examined when our attention turns from the North to the South.

The informal security regime

This section develops the idea of an informal security regime, drawing heavily on the work of my colleagues Geof Wood (2004) and Pip Bevan (2004a, 2004b). I summarize this work here by starkly contrasting each of the nine elements of the welfare regime framework above to an ideal-type informal security regime model.

First, the division of labour is not uniquely determined by a capitalist mode of production. On the one hand, other forms of production persist, develop and interact with capitalism: direct production of food and other goods and services, employment in informal labour markets, the cultural resources of communities, kin connections, smuggling and other illegal activities and so on. The social formation is more variegated and over-determined. On the other hand, external capitalism (international market forces and transnational actors) heavily influences the environment of these political economies. The capitalist world system and its actors is of course not without importance in understanding advanced capitalist countries, but in the South there is a lack of congruity – the world system does not necessarily transform them into developed capitalist social formations.

Second, and related to this, two other forms of domination bulk large alongside exploitation: exclusion and coercion. *Exclusion* refers to processes of 'shutting out' certain categories of people from major social forms of participation (such as cultural activities and political roles) on the basis of their ascribed identity. A wide range of exclusionary practices – closure, monopolization and opportunity hoarding – are alternative sources of disadvantage. *Coercion* refers to 'all concerted application, threatened or actual, of actions that commonly cause loss or damage' (Tilly, 1999: 36). It can vary from discrete threats to the full-scale destruction of people and communities. In much of the developing world, economy-based exploitation relations are interwoven with other systems of inequality and domination.

Third, the idea of livelihoods replaces that of labour markets. Individuals and families use diverse strategies to make a living, involving various types of labour. Standing (2000) distinguishes alongside wage labour: sharecropping, peasant agriculture, tribal cultivation, nomadic pastoralism, artisans, outworking, family working and bonded labour. In addition, migration for labour, petty trade, begging and petty crime also coexist. The modern peasant moves between different forms of employment and ways of life; in Kearney's (1996) term they are 'polybians' akin to amphibeans moving between aquatic and terrestrial environments. Another important difference from the ideal modern capitalist model concerns the lack of a clear division between production and reproduction and the significance of 'non-productive' activities, including investment in social networks.

Fourth, political mobilization takes different forms. Class power resources and mobilization can no longer be privileged. Ethnicity, region, religion, caste, age groups, clan or kinship groups and other interpersonal networks can all form the basis of identity and mobilization. In Parson's terms ascribed status remains as important as achieved identity. The complexity of sources of identification, and the existence of excluded groups outside the political system altogether, confounds or precludes the emergence of political class settlements. Political stability reflects political equilibrium rather than a negotiated compromise.

Fifth, 'states' are at best weakly differentiated from surrounding social and power systems. Political relationships are particularistic and diffuse, are based on interpersonal obligations, mix together economic, instrumental and political elements of exchange, yet are premised on deep inequalities in power between patrons and clients (Eisentstadt and Roniger, 1984: 48–9). This patron-clientelism engenders a widespread form of political incorporation of subordinate classes. The result is a dependence of the powerless on relationships which may offer a measure of security in the short run but prevent their longer-term liberation and ability to enhance their security and welfare. In Wood's phrase (2001), they are 'adversely incorporated'.

Sixth, the institutional landscape of the welfare mix becomes problematic. At one level, a wider range of institutions and actors are involved in modifying livelihood structures and their outcomes. At the domestic level, 'communities', informal groups and more formal NGOs, figure as informal actors and add a fourth institutional actor to the state–market–family trinity. More important, all four elements have important counterparts at the *supranational* level: outside economic actors such as transnational corporations or semi-illegal traders, international governance organizations such as the IMF, the World Bank, the WTO, the arms of powerful nation-states such as the US and international aid bodies, international NGOs. Even the household sector has an international dimension, through migration and remittances. Thus a broader 'institutional responsibility matrix' emerges as in Table 13.2.

But the complexity does not stop there. The informal security model does not presume the degree of institutional differentiation of the classic welfare regime model. On the contrary, the different institutions do not operate inde-

Table 13.2   Components of the institutional responsibility matrix

	Domestic	Supranational
State	Domestic governance	International organizations, national donors
Market	Domestic markets	Global markets, MNCs
Community	Civil society, NGOs	International NGOs
Household	Households	International household strategies

pendently of each other in terms of rules and pervading moralities. Self-interest is not confined to the market realm, loyalty to the family realm and group interests to the political realm. Instead there is *permeability*. Behaviour is frequently not different when acting within the state, the market, the community or the family. As Wood (2004) puts it: 'Markets are imperfect, communities clientelist, households patriarchal and states marketised, patrimonial and clientelist'.

Seventh, 'de-commodification' becomes even less suitable as a measure of welfare outcomes than in the OECD world. The very notion of de-commodification does not make sense when economic behaviour is not commodified and where states and markets are not distinct realms. As already argued, the goal and measure of welfare needs to expand to take on board protection against 'life processes', amelioration of exclusion and active investment for self-development. More than that, the fuzzy distinction between *development* and welfare and the wider range of threats to security (such as from violence and physical insecurity) entail nothing less than an audit of basic and intermediate need satisfaction (Doyal and Gough, 1991, chapter 8).

Eighth, the notion of path-dependent development has a broader applicability. Countries dependent on overseas aid or NGO-based provision or remittances from migrant labour or clientelist networks will develop group interests and alliances which may act to continue and extend the private benefits these generate. Even societies with persistent civil and cross-border wars may organize livelihoods and develop forms of collective provision which adapt to war and reproduce through time. However, the vulnerability of poorer countries in the face of an uncontrollable external environment undermines path dependency and frequently replaces it with uncertainty and unpredictable change. The likelihood of stable political settlements is also undermined – instead unstable political equilibria are more common.

Lastly, the very idea of social policy as a conscious countervailing force in Polanyi's sense, whereby the public realm subjects and controls the private realm in the interests of collective welfare goals, is thrown into question. Social policy in the West is based at some level on the idea that behaviour in one sphere can be successfully deployed to modify behaviour in another sphere. More specifically mobilization in civil society can, via the state, impose collectivist values on the pursuit of individual interests in the market (and the family). Like Ulysses tempted by the Sirens, citizens and voters voluntarily chain and restrict their ability to pursue their short-term desires in the pursuit of longer-term collective needs (Elster, 1979). However, if permeability rules and the principles of different domains 'contaminate' each other, then social policy cannot act as an independent countervailing force, or will reinforce privilege, private short-term gain, exclusion or domination. In this situation 'all are prisoners' (Wood, 2000).

The net result of these nine features of the peasant analogue is an 'informal security regime', as far removed conceptually from the original idea of a welfare regime as in reality. Table 13.3 summarizes these contrasts.

Table 13.3   Ideal-type welfare and informal security regimes compared

	Welfare regime	Informal security regime
Dominant mode of production	Capitalism: technological progress plus exploitation	Informal economies within peripheral capitalism: uneven development
Dominant social relationship	Exploitation and market inequalities	Variegated: exploitation, exclusion and domination
Dominant source of livelihood	Access to formal labour market	A portfolio of livelihoods, including subsistence, cash crops, self-employment and informal employment
Dominant form of political mobilization	Class coalitions, issue-based political parties and political settlements	Diffuse and particularistic based on ascribed identities: patron-clientelism
State form	Relatively autonomous state	'State' weakly differentiated from other power systems
Institutional landscape	Welfare mix of market, state and family	Broader institutional responsibility matrix with powerful external influences and extensive permeability
Welfare outcomes	De-commodification plus health and human investment plus poverty/exclusion	Adverse incorporation, insecurity and exclusion
Path dependent development	Liberal, conservative and social democratic regimes	Less autonomous path dependency: patron-clientelism and external influence
Nature of social policy	Countervailing power based on institutional differentiation	Less distinct policy mode due to permeability and contamination

We should stress that the above account of the informal security regime is an ideal-type counterposition to what is after all an ideal-type welfare regime model. Nevertheless, this now establishes two poles between which we may range real-world countries and regions in the present epoch. This is our goal in the next section.

However, we are not finished yet. For there is a third ideal-type regime where neither formal nor informal security obtain: an *insecurity* regime. According to Bevan (2004a, 2004b), this is characterized by chronic conflict and exterminatory wars, 'vampire' states, shadow states and absent states, mobilization via militarization, wide gaps in institutional responsibility, absent social policies and extreme suffering. In this (non-)ideal-type, chronic insecurity is the norm and such social policy as there is is the province of humanitarian aid regimes. As we shall see, real-life approximations to this ideal-type are distressingly prevalent in today's world.

Regional social policy regimes: a preliminary map

In the remaining section, I offer a sketch of the social policy regimes in three regions of the world – Latin America, East Asia and Africa – and in Bangladesh, part of South Asia. It thus ignores several world regions outside the OECD: the ex-Soviet Union and Eastern Europe, China, much of the Arab world, and the remainder of South Asia. In each case I sketch their histories, economies and polities. The implicit approach used is that of historical political economy which gives due weight to external and internal factors in their evolution. Much of this draws on material from Gough and Wood et al. (2004).

Latin America: from conservative-informal to liberal-informal welfare regimes

According to Barrientos (2004), there is enough commonality across Latin America to identify a modal welfare regime, and one with some similarities to those in developed capitalist societies. (This does not apply to most of the Caribbean countries, which gained independence only after World War II and which are more influenced by their colonial inheritance.) Early de-colonization and political independence in the region and the development of export economies plus partial industrialization developed a capitalist class and an urban proletariat alongside the land-owning class. The devastating inter-war crisis brought about a switch from export economies to import substitution strategies. At the same time it fostered the emergence of social insurance and employment protection schemes for formal sector workers, which gained an institutional autonomy. On this basis an alliance of industry, public sector workers and urban industrial workers emerged which acted to protect and extend these incipient welfare institutions.

As a result, a welfare regime emerged in post-war Latin America, most clearly in the more developed Southern Cone, not unlike that of Southern Europe. There were aspirations towards universal access in health and education. Social insurance and employment protection institutions provided a substantial degree of protection against risk for formal sector workers and their dependants. However, the dualized economy left the mass of informal sector workers unprotected, reliant on unregulated labour markets, residual public assistance programmes and above all their own resources. Throughout the region, household provision and livelihood mixing was important, and the private sector was not clearly distinguished from the public.

This can be characterized as a *conservative-informal welfare regime*. It was a *welfare* regime along European lines in that there was a conscious attempt to mitigate market forces for privileged classes of worker. It was a *conservative* welfare regime because of the segmented nature of the social protection (education and health provision aspired to be universal but in practice was not). It was conservative-*informal* due to the absence of protection and the high insecurity of the millions of peasants, landless labourers, urban unemployed and marginal workers.

This welfare regime was transformed in the 1990s, Barrientos argues. The import substitution strategy was fatally undermined by the neoliberal redirection of global economic governance in the 1970s and the crisis this induced. High interest rates and debt crises led to the imposition of structural adjustment programmes in the early 1980s. The import substitution model, increasingly ill-adapted to the liberalization of trade, investment and finance, was replaced by export-oriented growth models. At the same time, from the mid-1970s to the mid-1980s, military-authoritarian-bureaucratic rule spread across the continent. In the face of this combined onslaught the political constituency of industry, public sector and formal sector workers crumbled.

As a result the welfare regime began to shift to a 'liberal-informal' one in the 1990s. Employment protection withered in the face of labour market deregulation, social insurance began to be replaced by individual saving and market provision, and private financing and provision of health and education was encouraged. 'The change in development model undermined support for social insurance from the state and employers, while at the same time reducing the political influence of urban industrial workers and public sector workers' (Barrientos, 2004). At the same time, the resurgence of political democracy across the region offers opportunities for new, perhaps more inclusive, social programmes and forms of social development to emerge.

East Asia: economic miracle and productivist social policy
East Asia here refers to the 'long strip of coastal capitalist states stretching down from South Korea to the eastern edge of the Indian Ocean' (Anderson,

1998: 300). All except Siam were colonized but by a variety of different powers: Portugal, Spain, the Netherlands, France, Britain, the US and Japan. The atomic end of the Japanese attempt to build an East Asian imperium ushered in a period of political instability paradoxically coupled with unprecedented economic development. According to Anderson (1998, chapter 14), there were four external 'conditions-of-possibility' for the post-war East Asian miracle: first, the Cold War, contested US hegemony and aid; second, propinquity to the extraordinarily dynamic Japanese economy which fostered trade then investment; third, the isolation of China for four decades; and fourth, the role of the overseas Chinese in developing entrepreneurial networks which were yet barred from political power.

These external circumstances impacted upon relatively large states with different colonial and pre-colonial institutional and cultural legacies. Due to Japanese occupation, revolutionary movements and authoritarian responses to these movements, landowners and capitalists have been relatively weak as a class. On the other hand, states have periodically been able to raise themselves as an independent force above society. East Asian states are relatively autonomous and have been despotically powerful, if not always infrastructurally strong. In the countries of Northeast Asia closest to Japan (Korea and Taiwan), strong group-coordinated economies emerged guided by developmental states wherein elite policy makers set economic growth as the fundamental goal and pursued coherent strategies to achieve it. In the city-states of Hong Kong and Singapore different forms of state-guided development took place. The second wave of emerging market economies in Southeast Asia (Malaysia, Thailand, the Philippines and Indonesia) also exhibit relatively strong states but with fewer policy levers. Compared with Northeast Asia, business is more internationalized and more in the control of a separate Chinese business class. State policies are more reactive, to secure state legitimacy or elite loyalty.

Modifying Holliday (2000) I characterize the dominant regional regime as a *productivist social development* regime (Gough, 2004). Social policy is subordinated to economic policy and the pursuit of economic growth. Rapid employment growth and rising wages means that commodification, not decommodification, is the primary welfare strategy. What social policy there is is focused almost entirely on social investments in primary education and basic health. Social protection is largely absent and household savings, family provision and private welfare play a large role. In Northeast Asia, post-war land redistribution provided the basis for a relatively equitable distribution of primary incomes and good welfare outcomes. Here in recent years, democratization and higher value-added production is laying the basis for an emerging productivist *welfare* regime.

Southeast Asia differs in several respects. Economies are more open and less developed, with large informal sectors. However, agriculture is also more extensive and dynamic. Rural industrialization permits family strategies which can successfully mix different livelihoods. State social policies are extremely underdeveloped and, apart from the rich, even private provision is limited. Informal security mechanisms are extensive. Yet the dynamic capitalization of the economy has enabled many families to pursue strategies that combined elements of the capitalist and the peasant models in what was, for many until recently, a virtuous circle – a productivist social development regime. (The Philippines stands out from this pattern and has in several respects more in common with Latin American welfare regimes.)

In 1997, the East Asian financial crisis posed the question whether such a regime was sustainable. The open economies of the region were exposed to short-term inflows of hot money from the US and Japan which financed unsustainable bank lending and investment projects. The ultimate collapse of the Thai *baht* triggered a currency and banking crisis with major impacts upon incomes, poverty and living standards. As a result, the absence of social protection measures and the lack of social investment in higher education was exposed. It remains to be seen whether and how this transforms the productivist social development regimes in the region.

Bangladesh and South Asia: aid and informal security

Davis (2001, 2004) presents a detailed study which applies our regime model to Bangladesh. Though distinct in significant ways this offers some pointers to the rest of the sub-continent. The extreme poverty of the region and the relative absence of sustained economic development until recent years has parallels with Africa. Development discourses dominate and 'welfare' strategies are nested within wider 'development' programmes. Yet, by contrast with many parts of Africa, the British colonial legacy bequeathed several states with recognizable territories and competences. A formal system of law and, within India, liberal-democratic practices are also well established. This combination of 'stateness' alongside absent or uneven capitalist development and rural poverty enables us to identify a distinct informal security regime in South Asia.

The dominant political economy of Bangladesh is of rural class relations based on land-holding coupled with elite control over resources and opportunities at both national and local levels. A history of state monopolies has fostered widespread rent-seeking and corruption. As a result, reliance on networks, linkages, informal rules, personal favours and discretion is pervasive (Wood, 2000). Political parties are segmental, factional and non-ideological. Despite recent growth and some flourishing export sectors the dominant policy environment is one of poverty and over-population.

> In a context where the emerging capitalist system does not enjoy political stability and general acceptance, where the state is not strong enough to enforce order by

force and where civil society is failing to create the ideological support for the emergence of capitalism, patron–client networks which organise payoffs to the most vociferous opponents of the system are an effective if costly way of maintaining political stability (Kahn, 1998: 115).

The Bangladeshi regime is characterized by a bewildering range of actors: over 1200 officially registered NGOs; a large number of international donor organizations (who also provide much of the finance for the domestic NGOs); informal, community-based welfare and development organizations; and burgeoning labour migration to the Middle East and elsewhere generating growing household remittances. An integral feature of this regime is the interrelation between the international donors and actors and internal elites and patrons. All operate within, adapt to, and in turn influence the vertical patron–client relationships that structure interest representation in Bangladesh. Foreign aid can both improve welfare outcomes but at the same time harm the potential for poor people to participate and organize for longer-term social development. 'A psychology of plunder prevails where unholy alliances of *de facto* illicit beneficiaries get away with as much as donors will let them'. The lack of a citizenship link between the funding of programmes and their disbursement prevents the emergence of a positive feedback link characteristic of Western welfare regimes (Davis, 2001, 2004).

The informal security regime also rests on a plethora of informal entitlements provided by kinship and community groups, including *zakat*, *fitra*, gifts, loans, employment, meals, help with dowry and medical costs, hospitality, land, help in resolving disputes and physical protection. However, Davis (2004) and Wood (2004) conclude that socio-economic change and modernization is breaking down the informal support provided by kin and community. In the absence of more institutionalized official programmes, the result is new forms of social exclusion and extreme poverty.

Sub-Saharan Africa: a regional insecurity regime
The dominant historical legacy in Africa south of the Sahara is of European colonialism – late, brief and rivalrous – superimposed on a prior system of kingdoms and stateless societies. The prime motive for the establishment of colonies was economic, and the colonies became dependent on foreign capital and trading companies. The colonial legacies of the British, French, Belgians, Portuguese and others differed, but a common factor was a lack of both sustained economic development and investment in education and human services. Significant European settlement in Southern and Eastern Africa modified this legacy and introduced later bifurcated and racialist forms of development, notably in South Africa.

Decolonization occurred late – mainly in the 1960s – and nowhere was political independence prepared for in a sustained and meaningful way. Many small states were created, superimposed on a mosaic of livelihood systems. The new states emerged in a continent dominated by the Cold War and external players. Discourses of modernization and industrialization dominated in the early years and there was a significant effort to improve and widen education provision. However, the openness to international forces, the predominantly pre-industrial social formations and the lack of state capacities engendered unbalanced development alongside rapid urbanization. Patron–clientelist political relations flourished in place of class movements. Above all, a harsher economic climate in the 1970s (for all but oil-producing countries) engendered disillusionment and crisis. The IMF and other powerful players imposed structural adjustment programmes in the 1980s which stalled economic development and began to reverse aspects of social development.

The outcome in the 1990s, according to Bevan (2004a, 2004b), is a regional *insecurity regime* across much of the continent. The dominant forms of livelihood are agriculture and informal urban activities. The two main ways of mitigating risks are first the efforts of individuals within families, households and clans and second patrimonial relations. The importance of the latter leads to a continuing investment in social networks and role of local leaders in offering some security, if at the price of 'adverse incorporation' into hierarchical and disempowering relationships. Above all, a wide range of external agencies increasingly intervene in the welfare mix: supranational governmental organizations (the World Bank, the IMF, the United Nations and its related agencies), regional associations, powerful Western governments, international donors of many kinds, international NGOs, and so on. These may alleviate suffering but can also reinforce dependency relations, inequality and domination. The outcomes have been deteriorating health and rising poverty in many areas. Superimposed on this, in many parts of the continent, the HIV-AIDS pandemic or/and war and civil conflict have generated extreme levels of suffering.

More than this, the regime label can only in certain respects be applied at the national level, according to Bevan (2004b). Major areas of Africa resemble more an open field of play for powerful external interests: governments, multinational corporations, development agencies, criminal gangs and private armies, among others. Many states are 'incoherent' in two senses: they are not institutionally differentiated from the societies within which they are embedded, and they lack meaningful territorial borders. As a result, the external players intrude into and enmesh with domestic elites in a novel and menacing way. This can enhance the power of the military, criminals and informal elites in ways which establish a perverted form of path dependency. The World Bank and the IMF, recently converted to pro-poor growth, now earnestly wish to reverse this downward spiral, but this entails confronting the results of past international involvements.

The picture is of course variegated across Africa. Some countries of North Africa and elsewhere resemble more stable informal security regimes with small welfare and productivist elements. But the whole continent from Algeria to Angola is perhaps best viewed as an unstable, dynamic mix of informal security and insecurity regimes.

Conclusions

This chapter has sought to adapt and apply the welfare regime approach, developed to provide a comparative analysis of social policy and welfare outcomes in the OECD region, to the developing world. I hope to have demonstrated that there are critical differences between social policy regimes across the developing world (and this still excludes China, the transitional countries of Eastern Europe and Central Asia, and significant other parts of the South). Those countries with more developed capitalist sectors and relatively autonomous states exhibit partial welfare regimes (Latin America) and distinct productivist social development regimes (East Asia). Those countries less integrated into global capitalism and with less legitimate states exhibit a wide variety of informal security regimes, such as in South Asia and privileged parts of Africa. Those regions, notably though not exclusively in Africa, with the least institutionalized and least stable links to the global economy and the least autonomous or absent states, labour under chronic insecurity regimes.

This is not to deny that there remain critical commonalities which distinguish the countries and states of the developing and transitional world from the OECD world. One recurring theme is their vulnerability to external forces. This power inequality is of two sorts, based on exit and voice. First, the structural power of capital has grown over the last two decades as a result of liberalization of trade, foreign exchange and capital markets. Capital can now more easily 'exit' from any jurisdiction if it considers an alternative one more favourable to its profitability, security and growth (Gough and Farnsworth, 2000). This enhances its power relative to nation-states and national actors such as trade unions, NGOs and social movements. Second, and related to this, the 'voice' and political leverage of external actors has strengthened, notably of the US government and other powerful states and of the IMF, World Bank and other international financial institutions. Both forms of transnational power tightly constrain Southern states.

The very idea of welfare states and welfare regimes entails the conscious imposition by public actors of collective values and choices on unplanned market outcomes. Thus, it might be concluded, 'globalization' fatally undermines the prospects for further welfare regime development across the world. And indeed this is a recurring theme in much contemporary literature. Yet, as regards the North, evidence to back up this assertion is remarkably thin. On the contrary, the conclusion of comparative studies of OECD countries is that global pressures are effectively mediated by the different welfare regimes: common pressures generate distinct policy reactions according to the domestic pattern of institutions, interests and ideas. Nation welfare regimes appear to be quite resilient in the face of transnational forces (Gough, 2001).

It would be quite Panglossian to assume that the same conclusion can be drawn for the South. Indeed many are pessimistic. Deacon (2000), for example, concludes that the preconditions to build cross-class political coalitions are fatally weakened by the opportunities available to Southern elites and middle classes to 'exit' from national social policies and programmes. It would take another article or more to address this question. Yet, our approach offers some support against this dystopian scenario. It is likely that, across much of the world, nation-states will remain crucial sites of contestation, including contestation over social policies. But actors will not contest them under circumstances of their own choosing. It makes no sense to apply a 'one-size-fits-all' model to analyse the nature of social policy and social development across these countries and regions, let alone to conceive and promote alternative social policies.

Notes

1. This chapter is an earlier and shorter version of 'Welfare regimes in development contexts: a global and regional analysis', which appears in *Insecurity and Welfare Regimes in Asia, Africa and Latin America: Social Policy in Development Contexts*, by Ian Gough and Geoff Wood, with Armando Barrientos, Philippa Bevan, Peter Davis and Graham Room (Cambridge University Press, 2004). My analysis has been revised in certain significant respects since this was submitted to the *Handbook* for publication. The other contributors to our book are of course not responsible for my arguments and presentation here.
2. Though this is not presented here – see Gough (2004a) for a simple cluster analysis of developing and transitional countries.
3. In Gough (2004a) this term is replaced by the term 'welfare regime' used in a generic sense to distinguish it from 'welfare state regime'.

References

Anderson, Benedict (1998), *The Spectre of Comparisons: Nationalism, Southeast Asia and the World*, London: Verso.

Barrientos, Armando (2004), 'Latin America: towards a liberal informal welfare regime', in Gough and Wood et al.

Bevan, Philippa (2004a), 'Conceptualising in/security regimes', in Gough and Wood et al.

Bevan, Philippa (2004b), 'The dynamics of Africa's in/security regimes', in Gough and Wood et al.

Cammack, Paul, David Pool and William Tordoff (1993), *Third World Politics: A Comparative Introduction*, second edition, London: Macmillan.

Davis, Peter (2001), 'Rethinking the welfare regime approach: the case of Bangladesh', *Global Social Policy*, **1**(1), 79–107.

Davis, Peter (2004), 'Rethinking the welfare regime approach in the context of Bangladesh', in Gough and Wood et al.

Deacon, Bob (2000), *Globalization and Social Policy: The Threat to Equitable Welfare*, GASSP Occasional Paper 5, Helsinki, March.

Doyal, Len and Ian Gough (1991), *A Theory of Human Need*, London: Macmillan.

Eisentstadt, S.N. and L. Roniger (1984), *Patrons, Clients and Friends: Interpersonal Relations and the Structure of Trust in Society*, Cambridge: Cambridge University Press.

Elster, Jon (1979), *Ulysses and the Sirens: Studies in Rationality and Irrationality*, Cambridge: Cambridge University Press.

Esping-Andersen, Gøsta (1990), *The Three Worlds of Welfare Capitalism*, Cambridge: Polity Press.

Esping-Andersen, Gøsta (1999), *Social Foundations of Postindustrial Economies*, Oxford: Oxford University Press.

Gough, Ian (1999), 'Welfare regimes: on adapting the framework to developing countries', *Discourse: A Journal of Policy Studies*, **3**(1), 1–18.

Gough, Ian (2001), 'Globalization and regional welfare regimes: the East Asian case', *Global Social Policy*, **1**(2), 163–89.

Gough, Ian (2004a), 'Welfare regimes in development contexts: a global and regional analysis', in Gough and Wood et al.

Gough, Ian (2004b), 'East Asia: the limits of productivist regimes', in Gough and Wood et al.

Gough, Ian and Kevin Farnsworth (2000), 'The enhanced structural power of capital: a review and assessment', in Ian Gough, *Global Capital, Human Needs and Social Policies: Selected Essays 1994–99*, Basingstoke: Palgrave.

Gough, Ian and Geoff Wood, with Armando Barrientos, Philippa Bevan, Peter Davis and Graham Room (2004), *Insecurity and Welfare Regimes in Asia, Africa and Latin America: Social Policy in Development Contexts*, Cambridge: Cambridge University Press.

Heidenheimer, Arnold J. (1981), 'Education and social security entitlements in Europe and America', in Peter Flora and Arnold J. Heidenheimer (eds), *The Development of Welfare States in Europe and America*, Transaction Publishers, pp. 269–306.

Holliday, Ian (2000), 'Productivist welfare capitalism: social policy in East Asia', *Political Studies*, **48**(4), 706–23.

Kahn, M. (1998), 'The role of civil society and patron–client networks in the analysis of corruption', in S.H. Kpundeh and I. Hors (eds), *Corruption and Integrity Improvement Initiatives in Developing Countries*, New York: UNDP/PECD Development Center.

Kearney, M. (1996), *Reconceptualising the Peasantry*, Westview: Boulder.

Long, N. and J.D. van der Ploeg (1994), 'Heterogeneity, actor and structure: towards a reconstitution of the concept of structure', in D. Booth (ed.), *Rethinking Social Development: Theory, Research and Practice*, London: Longman, Chapter 3, pp. 62–89.

Moran, Michael (1999), *Governing the Health Care State: A Comparative Study of the United Kingdom, the United States and Germany*, Manchester: Manchester University Press.

O'Connor, Julia, Ann Shola Orloff and Sheila Shaver (1999), *States, Markets, Families: Gender, Liberalism and Social Policy in Australia, Canada, Great Britain and the United States*, Cambridge: Cambridge University Press.

Polanyi, K. (1944), *The Great Transformation*, New York: Rinehart: republished (1957), Boston: Beacon Press.

Room, Graham (2000), 'Commodification and decommodification: a developmental critique', *Policy and Politics*, **28**(3), 331–51.

Standing, Guy (2000), Background paper prepared for ILO In Focus Programme on Socio-Economic Security, http://www.ilo.org/public/english/protection/ses/index.htm.

Tilly, C. (1999), *Durable Inequality*, Los Angeles: University of California Press.

Wood G.D. (2000), 'Prisoners and escapees: improving the institutional responsibility square in Bangladesh', *Public Administration and Development*, vol. 20, 221–37.

Wood, G.D. (2001), 'Desperately seeking security', *Journal of International Development*, vol. 13, 523–34.

Wood, G.D. (2004), 'Informal security regimes: social policy and the search for a secure institutional landscape', in Gough and Wood et al.

PART IV

THE RESEARCH PROCESS

14 Crossing cultural boundaries

Linda Hantrais

Cooperation in the social sciences between researchers from different cultural backgrounds is never straightforward or unproblematic. The difficulties of crossing cultural boundaries are accentuated when language barriers also have to be overcome. The European Research Area, launched in 2000, affords a particularly fertile terrain in which to analyse the comparative research process, due to the great diversity of economic, political and socio-cultural contexts contained within its borders. These differences are reflected in research traditions, which, in turn, impact on working methods. Whereas the natural sciences are dealing with concepts and language that are common, if not universal, the object of study for social scientists is socially constructed. Concepts therefore need to be located and understood within the national, regional, local and disciplinary contexts that produce them, and within which policy is formulated and implemented.

This chapter focuses on the ways in which the cultural and linguistic knowledge and experience of researchers impact on their approaches to comparative studies that cross national boundaries. It examines disciplinary traditions, theoretical and methodological issues, the choice of countries for comparison, as well as the practicalities of working in international teams. Attention is also devoted to the ways in which the research process and its outcomes are monitored and evaluated, involving an appraisal of the linkages made between research and policy.

Understanding research cultures

Within the Western world, differences have been identified at the epistemological level between three dominant 'intellectual styles' of research: Saxonic, Teutonic and Gallic. Although his depiction is not based on hard data and the aim is to represent 'ideal types' in the Weberian sense, Johan Galtung (1982) has drawn a useful distinction between the three styles by focusing on how different research tasks are performed. He identifies four sets of tasks: those involving the exploration of paradigms (what kinds of phenomena exist); empirical tasks associated with the description of phenomena; theoretical tasks carried out by researchers in the quest for explanation; and the commentary they produce on the performance of tasks by other intellectuals. The emphasis attributed to each task serves to characterize members of the three major research communities. For Galtung, the Saxonic style is strong on data collection and facts but weaker on the philosophical basis and theory formation, whereas the Teutonic and Gallic intellectual styles are more cerebral. The Anglo-American social science tradition, as it is also termed, which extends to the Nordic fringe of Europe, is generally considered to be empirical, while the continental European tradition, especially in Germany and France, and also in Southern European countries, is more philosophical.

Within his classification, Galtung makes a further distinction between the American variant of the Saxonic style, founded on large-scale statistical analysis, but where individual units are not investigated in any detail, and the British variant with its emphasis on case studies, ideographic history and social anthropology. Both approaches share the conviction that knowledge rests on documentation. Within the cerebral styles, Galtung distinguishes between a Teutonic variant, with its 'search for the axiomatic pyramid that facilitates the much honoured pursuits of *Zurückführung* and *Ableitung*', and the more complex Gallic variant, involving 'pyramidal exercises couched in highly embroidered, artistic forms of expression where *elegance* plays a key role as a carrier of conviction power' (Galtung, 1982: 26, original italics). Here, data are for illustration rather than confirmation.

Examples abound to show that Galtung's broad-brush classification is undoubtedly overstated. However, it serves a useful purpose in drawing attention to an issue that is often disregarded when embarking on multinational projects: the need to take account of the research cultures within which team members are trained and operate. Galtung argues that the emphasis placed by the Teutonic style on different theoretical options is associated with dissent and disharmony between researchers and, therefore, leads to divisiveness, whereas the Saxonic approach lends itself to dialogue between researchers based on consensus.

At the time when Galtung was writing in the 1980s, he was associated with the European Coordination Centre for Research and Documentation in Social Sciences in Vienna, which funded large-scale multinational social science projects, involving East and West European countries with very different political and economic regimes. As Michel Lesage (1987: 1) argued from experience of the same organization, East–West comparison was a difficult and delicate task due to ideological differences and the lack of reliable source materials, which created problems in cooperating across the ideological divide. Again from the Western standpoint and while working at the Vienna Centre, Ralph Kinnear (1987: 9) commented on 'differences in the assumptions and preconceptions which the researchers adopt because they are the product of a particular ideological context'. During the Soviet era, social science researchers were severely constrained by the Marxist view of social and economic phenomena. Kinnear (1987) has shown how the problems of interference from the researcher's background were easier to overcome in

East–West research in disciplines such as geography and anthropology where the major aim of researchers was to understand societies other than their own. By contrast, economists were reluctant to compare countries across East–West boundaries and, if they did so, tended to view the East from the standpoint of the West and without paying attention to diversity as an object of study in its own right. The major differences in research cultures between East and West generally militated against anything other than a pragmatic approach to cross-national comparisons. The studies undertaken were, consequently, generally confined to the collection of vast amounts of disparate descriptive data, which did not allow for meaningful comparative analysis or interpretation with reference to the socio-cultural environments from which they were derived. The end of the Cold War and the development of plans for enlargement of the European Union to the East in the 1990s provided a new impetus for researchers from Central and Eastern Europe to participate in European projects. They are now being exposed to formidable challenges as they seek to build international class research infrastructures, adapt to multiple Western mindsets and construct cross-cultural alliances within European networks.

While considerable effort is being expended to prepare researchers in former Soviet states for the epistemological leap from East to West, less attention has been paid to the barriers to effective cooperation between neighbouring countries within the European Union. Jean Tennom's (1995) analysis of differences in cultural backgrounds between French (Gallic style) and British (Saxonic style) researchers, to take one example, shows that Franco-British cooperation is far from being unproblematic. He argues that the very different research traditions and contexts of British and French researchers inform their approaches to international cooperation. In a similar vein, Pierre Joliot (2001), the grandson of Pierre and Marie Curie, contrasts the state-protected, introvert and closed French research environment with the competitive liberal environment of the United States of America, which stimulates outward and inward geographical mobility. The status of civil servants conferred on the 11 000 researchers employed by the Centre National de la Recherche Scientifique (CNRS) in France affords protection from external interference, giving them the opportunity to concentrate on fundamental research, theoretical and conceptual work, and the production of new knowledge. Although, increasingly, they too are being exposed to competitive pressures, CNRS researchers have not, hitherto, been required to take account of the major economic, political and social concerns of the day. Nor have they been obliged to attract external funding to be able to engage in research on topics of their own choosing. In a situation where evaluation does not directly determine funding, they have lacked the incentive to disseminate their findings widely through international publications.

British researchers, by contrast, have long been driven by the market demands of productivity, 'maximum output for minimum input', as Tennom (1995: 275) expresses it, forcing them to become entrepreneurs. They are more likely than their French counterparts to concentrate on applied, policy-relevant research and the user interface and to avoid theoretical excursions and intellectual adventurousness. They operate within a context where researchers are expected to be publicly accountable and where taxpayers must be seen to receive value for money from their investment. In Britain, researchers know that their performance is being constantly monitored, assessed and called into question, which tends to encourage them to adopt an instrumental approach to their work, maximizing opportunities to cooperate with industry and other potential funders and engaging with end-users in the policy arena.

Although the barriers created by the cultural background of researchers are rarely insuperable and may be an interesting object of study in their own right, they can lead to delays and misunderstandings. Many of these problems might be avoided if members of international teams were more explicit about one another's culturally and linguistically determined assumptions and mindsets. Researchers who have experience of working on cross-national projects and who are aware of the barriers to effective cooperation due to differences in intellectual styles are careful to develop networks within which consensus can be achieved on the basis of shared objectives and compatibility of approach. If coordinators do decide to constitute a team of researchers representing different intellectual styles, it is usually in the knowledge that the confrontation of different research cultures can be a source of fruitful dialogue rather than dissent, particularly if participants are encouraged to discuss methods and materials at all stages of project design, data collection and analysis, and if they are able to respect diversity and bring new perspectives to the topic.

Disciplinary traditions in comparative research

Galtung's different intellectual styles are to some extent reflected in disciplinary preferences for particular research designs. Much of the comparative research undertaken in the early post-war period, especially the large-scale studies carried out by political scientists in the United States, in line with Galtung's broad-brush Saxonic style, aimed to track and map the development of socio-political and economic phenomena across the world. The intention was to produce generalizations, often from the North American experience, that were assumed to be universally applicable. The theory was grounded in the assumption that universal characteristics could be identified in social phenomena, independent of a specific, cultural context (Rose, 1991). Following in this tradition, Harold Wilensky and Charles Lebeaux (1965) used regression analysis of welfare effort and economic development to test grand theory about the logic of industrialism, arguing that Western societies would undergo the same evolutionary process and ultimately converge.

By contrast, the culturalist approach, which also developed in the United States, focused on national uniqueness and particularism, and cross-cultural contrasts and differences. In line with Galtung's second Saxonic variant, culturalism, as practised in Britain, has drawn heavily on ethnographic accounts to illustrate diversity and divergence rather than similarity and convergence (Chamberlayne and Rustin, 1999).

Following on from the neo-evolutionists (for example Parsons, 1966), again in the United States, a body of theory developed that took account of the efficiency of different societies in adapting to evolutionary advances. It was argued that general theories could be formulated if the diversity and mutual interdependence of social structures is recognized and if phenomena are situated in relation to their spatial and temporal locations. The assumption was that systems are not unique and social reality may be partly explained by phenomena extrinsic to the system, enabling more general or universal factors to be identified (Przeworski and Teune, 1970). Pursuing this line of argument, researchers from the British Saxonic tradition applied the approach in disciplines such as organizational behaviour (Lammers and Hickson, 1979) and industrial relations (Hyman, 1998) to demonstrate the effect of the national context on the object of study. Their purpose was to determine the extent to which generalizations can be made from the theoretical models and hypotheses they are seeking to test empirically.

Adaptations and developments of these three approaches to cross-national comparisons can be found among researchers who are the product of the Gallic and Teutonic intellectual styles. In his analysis of Western European welfare states since the Second World War, Peter Flora (1986) from Germany, for example, combined a configurational analysis of institutional variations, where countries were considered as cases, with analysis of empirical data to test specific hypotheses. He argued that basic structures themselves change and lead to new processes. He concluded that the development of welfare states was long-term and irreversible, but that institutional variation was persistent and would continue to be fundamental in determining solutions to the challenges posed by low- or no-growth economies.

The so-called 'societal' approach was perhaps most fully articulated in the cerebral Gallic style by Marc Maurice (1989) and his co-workers in industrial sociology in France. They stressed the importance of analysing the relationship between the macro and the micro, implying an interaction between a plurality of causal factors, on the basis that actors cannot be separated from structures and vice versa, since they are all socially constructed.

Societal analysis has proved to be particularly valuable for cross-national comparisons in social policy. This is an area where, as Jochen Clasen (1999:

3) has pointed out, in the latter part of the twentieth century, the large-scale correlational approach (American Saxonic) was progressively declining in favour of cross-national case studies (British Saxonic), which place greater emphasis on understanding the policy process. Deborah Mabbett and Helen Bolderson (1999) support the view that regime analysis can be most fruitfully pursued through case studies, arguing from their own work that the multi-dimensional modelling tradition of social welfare systems does 'not survive confrontation with the complex detail of actual arrangements', while case studies can 'yield generalizable theoretical insights' (Mabbett and Bolderson, 1999: 47, 50). Case studies in social policy (for example Heclo, 1974) have long demonstrated the value of the concept of path dependency in analysing the constraining or enabling effect of decisions made in the early state of a policy or institution on the future choices available to policy makers. More recently, interest in the case study approach and in the concept of path dependency has been stimulated among social policy analysts by the acceleration of the European integration process and by the need for the applicant states to meet the economic, social and political criteria laid down for membership. Governments in East and West have found a new incentive to look for opportunities for cross-border learning, requiring a discriminating and contextualized analysis of the relationship between macro- and micro-level structures.

Language barriers to cross-cultural comparisons

Whatever their disciplinary orientation, British researchers do, as Tennom (1995) acknowledges, have the immense advantage over other national research communities of possessing a *lingua franca*, which facilitates their participation in the international arena and explains their frequent leadership role in European research networks and projects. Another characteristic of the Anglo-Saxon research culture, which is increasingly being adopted by the Nordic states and the Netherlands, as well as by countries like Portugal, is the need to publish in internationally refereed journals. Here too, British researchers have what might be considered an advantage over other countries because of their language and training. In conjunction with financial and academic pressures, these factors may help to explain the relatively high ranking of British social science research, as measured by international performance indicators derived from publications indices (Adams et al., 1998). Publication ratings are calculated from databases originally established by the Institute for Scientific Information in the United States for bibliographic searching, and are generally acknowledged to have a strong bias towards Anglo-American English-language literature. The impact factor of individual articles thus reflects the extent to which different research communities have sought to internationalize their output by publishing in English-language journals, thereby increasing the chances that their findings will be widely read and cited. In the social sciences, the work of Dutch, Finnish and Swedish researchers, who routinely publish in English, is, for example, much more widely read beyond national borders than work in French, German or Spanish (Husso et al., 2000).

In social science disciplines, monolingual speakers of English are, however, at a disadvantage. Researchers whose native language is English, tend, as in the natural sciences, to believe that the concepts transmitted through their language are universally understood. The difficulty that many social scientists encounter in studies that cross linguistic boundaries, as argued by Edmond Lisle in the 1980s, is that:

> language is not simply a medium to carry concepts. It is itself the very matter of scientific observation and discourse. When we study a particular country, we are examining it with the only instruments available, namely a conceptual system and set of ideas produced within and by the society we are investigating, reflecting its history, its institutions, its values, its ideology, all of which are expressed in that country's language. By definition, that overall system and those concepts have no exact equivalents in other societies. When we engage in cross-national comparative studies, therefore, we have to find the nearest approximation ... (Lisle, 1985: 24).

Lisle goes on to argue that research on different societies that is confined to using English results in loss of information and inaccuracy, since English cannot accurately express all the concepts and ideas generated in other cultures and conveyed in other languages. Approximation may, he suggests, result in misinterpretation. The thought processes and mindsets underlying different modes of expression (French is more abstract and Cartesian than English) imply that different approaches and interpretations are being called into play.

The development of a European Research Area[1] within the European Union and the extension of its boundaries to Central and Eastern Europe have undoubtedly created a new openness to the rich variety of cultures and languages that it contains. At the same time, it has reinforced the dominance of British researchers as project coordinators, and of English as the working language of trans-European networks and teams, but without dispelling the impression that British researchers are insular and not fully committed to the European concept. Even if project members are fluent in two or three languages, it is unlikely that researchers involved in multinational projects will have an equal command of all the languages concerned, particularly when few European projects or networks in the social sciences are limited to only three or four language communities. It is axiomatic that researchers who can operate in only one language will have to rely on intermediaries to provide them with filtered and selective access to other cultures.

The cultural baggage of researchers shapes not only their formulation of the research question and the theoretical assumptions underlying it, but also the choice of data with which they will be working and their interpretations of findings. The researcher's cultural environment is usually considered to be less problematic in projects dealing with description and large-scale quantitative data, where language is primarily seen as an instrument for obtaining facts. In multilingual projects, it cannot, however, be assumed that the facts collected represent the same reality. Not only linguistic but also conceptual equivalence is needed to ensure that questionnaires and interview schedules accurately reflect the intentions of their designers (Harkness, 1999). Translation of survey instruments has to be aimed at expressing questions in such a way that the stimulus has an equivalent meaning and purpose and provokes an equivalent reaction in different societies. Good translation practice must, therefore, direct effort towards achieving conceptual equivalence rather than lexical comparability by close scrutiny of the context within which language is used and develops.

The unit of expression is not necessarily the same across languages, as exemplified in the field of welfare where, for example, the denotations and connotations of vocabulary for different benefits vary considerably from one national context to another within the European Union. These variations have been illustrated by the comparison of family allowances and child benefits in EU member states (Hantrais, 2000: 107–9), the concept of flexibility in Western and Eastern Europe (Wallace and Cousins, 2001), and residualism and universalism in welfare systems (Mabbett and Bolderson, 1999: 47). Many key concepts in social policy at EU level are contested: poverty line, social exclusion and inclusion, training, unemployment, part-time work, parental leave, lone parenthood, caring and take-up of benefits (Brown, 1986; MacGregor, 1993; Hantrais, 2004). In the EU applicant states, the experience of transition has shown how important it is to take account of within-country changes and to revisit earlier data, since their reliability and interpretation have often been called into question, especially in areas where concepts are politically and ideologically charged, as for example with unemployment (Kutsar and Tiit, 2000).

If the aim of a study is to describe and map benefits systems in different countries and provide a detailed account of entitlements, as in the annual publications on social protection produced by the Mutual Information Systems on Social Protection in the European Union (MISSOC) for the European Commission, it is not too difficult to characterize national benefits systems. For the purposes of comparison, however, the advice given by Richard Titmuss (1967: 57) in the 1960s still holds, namely that national social policies should be treated 'not by discussing the details for this or that country, but with the aid of concepts and models, principles and goals, and in terms of categories of benefits, contributions and users'. The most meaningful units of analysis, he suggests, should be 'classes of benefits, kinds of entitlement, patterns of utilisation, and differences in goals and objectives'. In qualitative studies involving fine-grain analysis, the ability to understand the way these units are socially constructed and expressed through language is critical in gaining a proper understanding of other cultures, their defining characteristics and their identities.

Selecting countries for cross-cultural analysis
Proposals submitted for European funding are required to involve at least two different member states or one member state and one associated state. The European Commission is also generally looking to ensure that 'less favoured' member states are well represented, and it is interested in encouraging candidate countries to become part of the European Research Area. The reasons given by project coordinators for selecting particular mixes of countries for projects in the social sciences are generally pragmatic rather than having a scientific basis (Hantrais, 2001). In view of the cultural, disciplinary and linguistic issues raised above, coordinators often prefer to draw on existing networks and partners with whom they know they can cooperate. A more scientific justification may be the interest of a particular geographical mix in the context of the development of welfare regimes. The choice of countries may be intended to illustrate the possible effects of diversity in provision, or to uncover examples of good practice, for instance by comparing the situation in EU member and applicant states.

The number and mix of countries and the variables selected have several consequences for the research process and for the findings. The number affects the depth of analysis: the broader the country coverage, the greater the likelihood is that generalizations can be drawn from the findings but that only a small number of within-country variations and contexts can be examined. The smaller the number of countries included, the greater the contextual detail, and the easier it is to be consistent in specifying and applying concepts and in using qualitative evidence. Findings will differ depending on the mix of countries and the variables selected. As already suggested, projects that include EU candidate countries from Central and Eastern Europe are likely to come up with different results from those that confine their coverage to EU member states or particular regions in the Union. A country that appears to be an aberrant case in one grouping may be closer to the mean in another cluster.

According to the principle of 'variable distance', developed by Georg Simmel (1980), the distance from the object under observation affects the way it is observed. The long-distance perspective can be exemplified by the large-scale quantitative studies in political science coordinated from the United States, the socio-economic projects of the Vienna Centre or European Foundation for the Improvement of Living and Working Conditions in Dublin, the European Commission's reports on demographic trends, employment and social protection across Europe, based on Eurostat data, and also the information provided by national correspondents for the European Commission's observatories. Of necessity, these accounts are often confined to description; their purpose is to provide snapshots of situations in a large number of different countries at a given point in time or for selected variables over time.

By contrast, a 'close-up' comparison of a social phenomenon within a country may reveal differences attributable to region, class, age, sex or ethnicity, for example in population ageing, levels of poverty or access to social entitlements, that may not be apparent when aggregated national-level data are being compared from a distance. The close-up view allows identification of subnational variations that may result in greater similarities being found across countries than within them. Although most social policies are framed at national level, they are often implemented at local level, providing scope for regional disparities, as exemplified by minimum income, welfare to work policies or the provision of child and elder care. What emerge as significant differences within and between countries may pale into insignificance when the EU member states are compared to countries in the less developed world.

The contours of the long-distance view may also change over time. Just as earlier waves of EU membership from the North and South altered the European 'mean' and changed territorial boundaries, further expansion to Central and Eastern Europe has once again changed the shape of the Union, creating new cultural boundaries that have to be crossed and leading to new intellectual alliances. In the past, Central and Eastern European countries tended to be considered as a bloc because they shared in common their experience of the Soviet regime. The close scrutiny to which they have been subjected since transition reveals, however, that their social development during the Soviet era, and subsequently, has been very different. Estonia, for example, which forcefully opposed Soviet rule, has moved rapidly towards the Nordic social model, as typified by Finland, despite the strong German influence on its higher education system and research culture. By contrast, Poland's strong religious base and intellectual traditions align it more closely with the Mediterranean countries and Ireland, as illustrated by its social policy stance.

Linkages between research and policy
Analysis of research cultures suggests that differences in intellectual styles and disciplinary backgrounds impact on the ways in which the relationship between research and policy is conceptualized and expressed. Again the United Kingdom and France can be taken to exemplify two diametrically

opposite approaches to this relationship. British social scientists almost routinely build a policy dimension into their research proposals. They are generally required to be familiar with the policy agenda of their 'customers' or 'end-users', and to identify a policy forum where they will disseminate their findings. In France, by contrast, the social science research community demands that its intellectual freedom and independence should be respected and that its work should not be constrained or tainted by political interference, even though researchers rely on government departments for funding support, and they launch research initiatives with a policy focus. French researchers expect to be able to adopt a critical stance and to choose the extent to which they engage with the policy process. Hitherto, the European tradition was believed to be closer to the French model but, progressively, the drive for public accountability has resulted in the requirement that the policy dimension of European-funded research should be made explicit and that research should inform policy debates.

This shift was formalized when the European Commission announced the creation of a European Research Area in 2000. A major objective was to increase the international impact of the European research effort by strengthening the relationship between research activities and policies. Already between 1995 and 1999, some 250 000 transnational cooperational links had been established, but the Commission was looking for something more. It wanted to encourage closer intergovernmental consultation over science policy as a means of removing obstacles to the free movement of researchers, knowledge and technologies in Europe. The intention was to coordinate the implementation of national research programmes at EU level. The link between research and policy is clearly articulated: it is legitimate to use public funds to support research activities if the findings are of public benefit, the more so if research makes a contribution to the implementation of public policies or helps to resolve the problems confronting society. Another important principle legitimating public funding of research is the added value of European cooperation: it should produce economies of scale by creating critical mass, by bringing together complementary expertise and by underpinning EU priorities and interests.

Although researchers undertaking European-funded research projects are increasingly aware of the need for the policy relevance of their work to be made more explicit, the ways in which the policy dimension is incorporated into projects is variable. Cross-national social science research projects may help to improve understanding of socio-economic change among policy actors. They may provide a tool, for example in the form of a database, that can be used to support policy analysis and policy development. Large-scale quantitative projects may be looking for causal linkages between variables to support particular policy options. Research may serve to heighten awareness of the possible implications of socio-economic change for policy, or identify policy as an explanatory factor in change. The aim of the research may be to evaluate policy measures, to look for examples of good practice or improve the efficacy of policy responses (Hantrais, 2001).

The growing importance attributed to policy relevance creates a further complication in what is already an immensely complex process by highlighting the ideological dimension in comparative social policy. The main obstacle to East–West comparisons in sociology in the 1980s was the politicization of the discipline, which was considered as part of the establishment process. Researchers therefore had to engage in self-censorship and regulation if they wanted to avoid losing their political patronage (Kinnear, 1987). Alain Desrosières (1996) has shown how differences in political and institutional styles influence national statistical systems and, consequently, data collection and the interpretation of findings. He characterizes Britain by its empiricism and relatively uncodified system, described as 'political arithmetic'. German legalism, by contrast, has rooted statistics in the formal description of states, while French centralism has resulted in a high level of legitimacy being attributed to statistical institutions, which was also the case in Spain during the Franco era.

The relationship between researchers and policy actors is not always easy to manage. Bruce Stafford (2001) suggests that it should not be taken for granted that policy makers always welcome research-based evidence. As he points out, policy-relevant research may contain both 'good' and 'bad' news. The findings from commissioned research may be politically embarrassing or call into question power relations in the policy process, as demonstrated by the reactions of governments to findings that appear to undermine policies on sensitive issues such as unemployment or poverty. Policy actors may resist changes that researchers recommend on the basis of their evidence. Researchers and policy actors may be working to very different time horizons and agendas. For political actors the painstaking analysis of past trends is only of academic interest, whereas researchers may be reluctant to draw hasty conclusions from their observation of current trends or speculate about future developments on the basis of headline statistics. Policy actors are likely to be more concerned about whether they have got a policy right, with an eye on the next elections and the reactions of the media. Researchers may prefer to devote their efforts to unravelling a methodological or theoretical point with a view to securing the next refereed journal publication.

The extent to which meaningful dialogue has developed between researchers and policy actors at different levels (local, national and international) and in different disciplines is not easy to determine. The onus would seem to be on researchers to initiate an exchange of views and to bring their findings to the attention of policy makers. Researchers who have mastered the skills needed to operate effectively in international networks that cross research cultures may find that they are also well equipped to cross the boundaries that separate researchers from policy actors.

The challenges of cross-cultural comparisons

This chapter has illustrated the ways in which the cultural and linguistic knowledge and experience of researchers affect their approach to comparative studies across cultural boundaries. It has shown how research and disciplinary traditions, theoretical and methodological issues, the choice of countries for comparison, as well as the practicalities of working in international teams can shape the research process, and influence findings and dissemination strategies. Questions have been raised about the motivation of researchers in undertaking cross-cultural comparisons and, more especially, in joining multinational teams, when the effort involved does not always seem to be commensurate with the rewards. It is most probably easier to work with partners who share the same assumptions, objectives and perceptions, and adopt similar working practices, than it is to communicate across ideological and intellectual divides, whether they are national or disciplinary.

To a much greater extent than in the past, social science researchers in Europe are being forced by the advent of the European Research Area and the incorporation of the countries of Central and Eastern Europe to follow the model of the natural sciences by forming large-scale multinational consortia (critical mass). They are actively encouraged to seek external funding and build an international dimension into their research. In return, they are exposed to the pressures of accountability and productivity, and required to demonstrate policy relevance and added value through research cooperation. The evidence provided in the present chapter suggests that the ensuing challenges for social scientists within Europe are considerable, not least because language and culture are at one and the same time the object and medium of study. The inability to understand other languages and cultures can serve as a selective and exclusionary mechanism, determining membership of teams and working arrangements, and ultimately the interpretation of findings.

The rewards for those who rise to meet the challenge of crossing cultural boundaries are also considerable. Far from resulting in cultural levelling, the opportunity exists for researchers to develop new insights, knowledge, understanding and awareness of cultural diversity, to learn from the exchange of information and experience and, thereby, to contribute to the development of an international research area.

Note

1. In recognition of the centrality of research in a knowledge-based society, the aim of the European Research Area is to increase the impact of European research efforts and, thereby,

prevent Europe from falling behind the United States. The objective is to strengthen the coherence of research activities and policies conducted in Europe by coordinating activities at national and EU level (Commission of the European Communities, 2000).

References

Adams, Jonathan, Tim Bailey, Louise Jackson, Peter Scott, David Pendlebury and Henry Small (1998), *Benchmarking of the International Standing of Research in England: report of a consultancy study on bibliometric analysis*, Leeds and Philadelphia: Centre for Policy Studies in Education, University of Leeds/Institute for Scientific Information.

Brown, Joan (1986), 'Cross-national and inter-country research into poverty: the case of the First European Poverty Programme', *Cross-National Research Papers*, **1**(2), *Research Methods in Comparative Public Policy*, pp. 40–51.

Chamberlayne, Prue and Michael Rustin (1999), *From Biography to Social Policy: final report of the SOSTRIS project*, London: University of East London, Centre for Biography in Social Policy.

Clasen, Jochen (1999), 'Introduction', in Jochen Clasen (ed.), *Comparative Social Policy: concepts, theories and methods*, Oxford: Blackwell, pp. 1–12.

Commission of the European Communities (2000), 'Making a reality of the European Research Area: Guidelines for EU research activities (2002–2006)', Communication from the Commission, COM (2000) 612 final.

Desrosières, Alain (1996), 'Statistical traditions: an obstacle to comparisons?', in Linda Hantrais and Steen Mangen (eds), *Cross-National Research Methods in the Social Sciences*, London and New York: Pinter, pp. 17–27.

Flora, Peter (ed.) (1986), *Growth to Limits: the Western European welfare states since World War II*, vols 1 and 2, Berlin and New York: W. de Gruyter.

Galtung, Johan (1982), 'On the meaning of "nation" as a "variable"', in Manfred Niessen and Jules Peschar (eds), *International Comparative Research: problems of theory, methodology and organization in Eastern and Western Europe*, Oxford: Pergamon, pp. 17–34.

Hantrais, Linda (2000), *Social Policy in the European Union*, 2nd edn, Basingstoke and New York: Macmillan and St Martin's Press.

Hantrais, Linda (ed.) (2001), *Researching Family and Welfare from an International Comparative Perspective*, Luxembourg: Office for Official Publications of the European Community.

Hantrais, Linda (2004), *Family Policy Matters: Responding to Family Change in Europe*, Bristol: The Policy Press.

Harkness, Janet (1999), 'In pursuit of quality: issues for cross-national survey research', *International Journal of Social Research Methodology: theory & practice*, **2**(2), 125–40.

Heclo, Hugo (1974), *Modern Social Politics in Britain and Sweden: from relief to income maintenance*, New Haven and London: Yale University Press.

Husso, Kai, Sakari Karjalainen and Tuomas Parkkari (2000), *The State and Quality in Scientific Research: a review of scientific research and its environment in the late 1990s*, Helsinki: Monila Oy/Eriloispaino Oy.

Hyman, Richard (1998), 'Recherche sur les syndicats et comparaison internationale', *Revue de l'IRES*, no. 28, Special issue, 43–61.

Joliot, Pierre (2001), *La recherche passionément*, Paris: Odile Jacob.

Kinnear, Ralph (1987), 'Interference from the researcher's background in comparisons across the ideological divide', *Cross-National Research Papers*, **1**(4), *Comparative Social Research: the East–West dimension*, pp. 9–14.

Kutsar, Dagmar and Ene-Margit Tiit (2000), 'Comparing socio-demographic indicators in Estonia and the European Union', *Cross-National Research Papers*, **6**(2), *Spatio-Temporal Dimensions of Economic and Social Change in Europe*, pp. 27–34.

Lammers, Cornelius J. and David J. Hickson (1979), *Organizations Alike and Unlike: international and inter-institutional studies in the sociology of organizations*, London, Boston and Henley: Routledge & Kegan Paul.

Lesage, Michel (1987), 'Comparison. Communication. Confidence', *Cross-National Research Papers*, **1**(4), *Comparative Social Research: the East–West dimension*, pp. 1–7.

Lisle, Edmond (1985), 'Validation in the social sciences by international comparison', *Cross-National Research Papers*, **1**(1), *Doing Cross-National Research*, pp. 11–28.

Mabbett, Deborah and Helen Bolderson (1999), 'Theories and methods in comparative social policy', in Jochen Clasen (ed.), *Comparative Social Policy: concepts, theories and methods*, Oxford: Blackwell, pp. 34–56.

MacGregor, Susanne (1993), 'The semantics and politics of urban poverty', *Cross-National Research Papers*, **3**(2), *Polarisation and Urban Space*, pp. 65–78.

Maurice, Marc (1989), 'Méthode comparative et analyse sociétale: les implications théoriques des comparaisons internationales', *Sociologie du travail*, no. 2, 175–91.

Parsons, Talcott (1966), *Societies: evolutionary and comparative perspectives*, Englewood Cliffs, New Jersey: Prentice Hall.

Przeworski, Adam and Henry Teune (1970), *The Logic of Comparative Social Inquiry*, New York: John Wiley.

Rose, Richard (1991), 'Comparing forms of comparative analysis', *Political Studies*, **39**(3), 446–62.

Simmel, Georg (1980), *Essays as Interpretation in Social Sciences*, Manchester: Manchester University Press.

Stafford, Bruce (2001), 'Analysing and assessing the family–welfare relationship', in Linda Hantrais (ed.), *Researching Family and Welfare from an International Comparative Perspective*, Luxembourg: Office for Official Publications of the European Community, pp. 85–6.

Tennom, Jean (1995), 'European research communities: France vs. the United Kingdom', *The Puzzle of Integration. European Yearbook on Youth Policy and Research* (CYRCE), vol. 1, 269–81.

Titmuss, Richard M. (1967), 'The relationship between income maintenance and social service benefits – an overview', *International Social Security Review*, **20**(1), 57–66.

Wallace, Claire and Christine Cousins (2001), 'Households, work and flexibility', in Linda Hantrais (ed.), *Researching Family and Welfare from an International Comparative Perspective*, Luxembourg: Office for Official Publications of the European Community, pp. 46–53.

Wilensky, Harold L. and Charles N. Lebeaux (1965), *Industrial Society and Welfare*, New York: Free Press.

15 Living with imperfect comparisons[1]

Else Øyen

Together with the scope and extent of research, the number of comparative studies has increased greatly in recent years. As more and more countries are brought into such studies a growing array of social phenomena, variables and processes are being compared. Globalization, educational exchange programmes, access to megasize databanks, speedy electronic communication and increasing intellectual curiosity about ethnic and cultural differences can all be seen as part of this picture. The unfortunate thing is that comparative methodology has not developed at the same speed as new information and information technology.[2] While there are now masses of empirical material available and more power to incorporate large amounts of variables in a comparative analysis, basic methodological questions remain unsolved. For example, how do we know that one variable in one country carries the same cultural understanding in another country and therefore can be compared directly? How are we to understand the differential impact of the social context on a variable that is seemingly similar in different countries? How is it possible to control for the cultural impact of researchers on the formulation of research questions and interpretations of results? How can countries be compared where the lacunae in data give priority to better understanding of those countries that are rich in data? This is of particular importance since many countries in the South suffer from lack of data and are likely to do so for a long time to come. Is it at all possible to draw comparisons between highly industrialized countries and countries with a low level of industrialization? Does it make sense to compare countries with different dominant religious or political orientations? When can a nation be considered a more appropriate unit of analysis than a region or a community or a certain social group? The questions are many, and at present there are no standard answers that can be formulated into a fully satisfying comparative methodology. For example, using a demographic indicator such as birthrate in a certain population seems straightforward enough, provided one has the relevant and correct data. However, explaining why birthrates vary is a different matter that brings forward the kind of questions raised above. Using a more complex variable such as a definition of poverty brings out all the problems connected with non-equivalence. Even the simplest definition of poverty raises the issue of non-equivalence. If poverty is defined as a lack of access to potable water, the number of wells and other sources of water provision can be mapped, the quality of the water can be judged, actual consumption of water per person can be investigated, as can the price. The processes whereby poor people have less access to water than the non-poor, need more time to fetch it, may have to pay more for it and have less command over how water is distributed, are at the core of poverty production. Some of these processes are culture-specific. Others are of such a general nature that they can be recognized worldwide. The former needs extensive investigations if several countries are part of the study and numerous variables need to be identified if direct comparisons are to take place. The latter needs thorough empirical material from the former, helped by theoretical shortcuts.

Comparative researchers have approached these various problems in different ways. Some will acknowledge the fact that within a national setting there may be an endless number of variables interfering with the phenomenon they have selected to study. As a consequence they focus on getting as many of these variables under control as possible. Sophisticated computer technology is brought in to analyse and compare available statistical data as well as new data collected for the study in case. However, the methodological gremlin is not deceived. For every single variable collected, the same unpleasant question can be raised: how do we know that one variable in one country expresses the same qualities and is perceived the same way as a variable with the same kind of characteristics found in another country? Ironically, the problem is magnified as more variables are brought in, variables that were supposed to solve another one of those questions in comparative studies.

Other researchers turn to in-depth studies of the phenomenon to be compared in order to understand better whether the phenomenon can be said to be the same in different countries, or how the variations are to be understood. The social context in which the phenomenon operates will likewise be scrutinized, variable by variable, interacting process by interacting process. The danger is that the myriad of information brought forward clutters up the picture, is difficult to organize and blurs the intended comparisons.

Most comparative researchers find their position somewhere in between these two extremes of simplification and complexity. Some are acutely aware of the many hurdles built into comparative studies. They try to overcome such obstacles wherever possible and in the final analysis discuss their assumed impact on the results of the study. Other researchers just go ahead with their comparative projects, follow the rules of a traditional scientific approach and treat comparative studies as any other social science project.

In the following I shall use comparative research on poverty as a frame of reference for the discussion. The context of research on poverty highlights the difficulties, but also the advantages of adopting a comparative focus.[3]

Obstacles to comparative research

Traditional methodological problems

Social science is based on comparisons, whether it is comparisons between different groups, different social phenomena, or different processes. Fundamentally, there ought to be little difference in the methodology used for doing comparative studies within a country and that of doing comparisons between countries. All the methodological baggage of problems found in comparisons in one context carries the same weight in another context. However, there are some additional problems that need to be taken into consideration.

The choice of unit of analysis, for example, needs to be questioned. Can a country be considered a more appropriate unit of analysis than a region or a community or a certain social group? One definition of a country is an administrative unit with well-defined geographical borders. Some such countries are bound together through a joint history, a set of national norms, a common infrastructure, a loyalty towards the ruling power, an integrated economy, a shared religious belief, and so forth. But even so, a country is likely to be a very heterogeneous structure, even under the 'best' of circumstances. How can such a complex conglomerate of different social structures, norms and behaviour be compared with another country that has a completely different composition? Even when certain elements in two or more countries are selected for comparisons, the eternal question remains: how to account for the impact of such heterogeneity on the results of a comparative study?

Another matter that needs to be taken into account is the cultural impact on the formulation of research questions and interpretation of results. For example, can poverty manifestations in one country be compared to poverty manifestations in another country, and if they look alike, also be considered to be alike and have the same meaning for the poor? If, as is often the case, the manifestations do not look alike, how can the differences be accounted for in such a way that comparisons are still possible? The many attempts to develop universal measures of poverty across time and space are faced with such obstacles. Elaborate scales of equivalence have been constructed to smooth out the effects of cultural differences in consumption patterns and other kinds of behaviour. To minimize cultural differences hard-core definitions of poverty have been introduced which include only the very basic necessities a person needs to survive. The World Bank definition of 'a dollar a day' as a universal definition of extreme poverty is an example of a hard-core definition – which in spite of its simplicity (and adjusted purchasing power parity) still falls under the spell of differential economic and social behaviour in a country. Databanks developed in the West rely on a set of social and economic indicators that can be standardized to make them useful for international comparisons of poverty (and other social phenomena). The paradox of the increasingly omnipotent databanks is the trade-off between simple indicators which can easily be collected and standardized, and the arduous and costly collection of complex indicators which better reflect differential realities but are difficult to weigh and assemble in a comprehensive and reliable picture. Both kinds of indicators are culture-sensitive in ways we have not yet learned to overcome. Also, it should be added, they are culture-laden in the sense that the concept and methodology are developed within a Western mode of thinking that at times are alien to non-western cultures.[4]

Epistemological problems

The many lacunae in the systematic understanding of reason and rationality in the social and phenomenological space that poverty occupies is problematic to overcome in comparative studies where differences in culture and perceptions play an important role in the analysis.

The history of how an understanding of poverty has developed over time has not yet been written. Historians have been challenged by the broader issues of humanism and compared them under different regimes and ideological impacts. But to the extent that poverty has been drawn into the analysis, it has been perceived more as a nuisance than as a phenomenon to be analysed along the same lines as other social phenomena. Poverty reduction as a social phenomenon has received even less historical attention. While it can be assumed that the British Poor Law must have had a sizeable impact on the understanding and definition of poverty in the British colonies, little systematic knowledge is available on this process of influence.[5] In modern times the introduction of poverty lines in for example Australia and the United States must likewise have had an impact on the understanding and acceptance/rejection of the poor by the population at large. Again, this is an area that is under-researched, while the actual methodology of creating poverty lines can well be characterized as over-researched. The latter has developed into an international and comparative field of research with a worldwide impact on how to measure and define poverty. Lately the professional understanding of poverty and the poor has come to the forefront, through as diverse approaches as ethical discussions on the convergence of values between social workers and clients, participatory research as an expression of grassroot democracy, and the limitations of bureaucrats when they try to reach out to the poor (Chambers, 1996).[6]

Theoretical knowledge about poverty processes is limited altogether. Although 'everybody' has his or her own theory about the cause(s) of poverty, the scientific foundation for poverty understanding is still weak. The fact that popular perceptions of who the poor are, how they behave and why they are poor, may be one of the major obstacles as to why a scientific approach to poverty has been slow to develop. It has not been considered necessary to invest in research and systematic production of knowledge on a topic where the answers seemed to be already in place.

As a result, the definitional tools needed for poverty research have not been well developed. A recent survey has brought out more than 200 poverty-related definitions or understandings of poverty.[7] A review of poverty studies shows that the definitions used in the various studies vary. This could be expected where the aims of the studies vary. However, many standard definitions are adopted uncritically and do not fit the declared aim of the study in question. Not uncommonly, variations in the use of a definition are found also within a particular study. It is as if the notion of poverty is considered an accepted norm that needs not to be spelled out in detail. For those engaging in comparative poverty research, many of those studies make comparisons fruitless.

The difficulties of methodological problems mentioned in the previous section hamper the use of definitions as analytical instruments as well. Together with an inconsistent application of definitions in empirical studies and theory formation, the comparative value in building up a theoretical coherent body has been undermined. Such lack of a theoretical framework leads to a situation where neither the 'right' questions, nor the 'wrong' questions become relevant to pose. Social scientists brought up in a tradition of dominant paradigms wander into a fuzzy field of theoretical fragmentation and everyday beliefs that blur their visions.

Another barrier to a more basic understanding of the poverty phenomena is the preoccupation with an administrative understanding of poverty that dominates current research. Poverty-reducing strategies become the property of those administrators and policy makers who are responsible for doing poverty reduction. Like the rest of us they need tools for their trade, and the development and implementation of poverty-reducing tools become their particular focus of attention. A large body of research has sprung up around the technicalities of poverty lines, the effects of one strategy as compared to another, the notion of best practices,[8] the use of discretion versus entitlements, measurements of need and the number of poor people, the impact of different strategies on unemployment and employment, and of course, the economy and budgetary drains of using different strategies. Very little of this research touches for example on the cognitive maps or the rationality of the actors involved in poverty reduction.

Apart from political philosophy's early studies there has been little research interest in state construction and its impact on poverty. It is only recently that political scientists have taken an interest in the welfare state construction.[9] The writings of Marshall (1964) and Titmuss (1968) on citizenship set a framework for a discussion on individual rights that was important for the understanding of the nature of poverty.[10] It will be interesting to compare those discussions to current discussions on documents such as the *International Covenant on Economic, Social and Cultural Rights* which is an attempt to establish citizenship rights for poor people world-wide, as part of the Declaration of Human Rights. The early writings of social scientists like Lewis (1966), Moynihan (1968), Piven and Cloward (1971), Rawls (1971) and Gans (1973) set the poverty phenomenon in a larger social context which brought forward questions about the nature of poverty and the invisible functions it fulfils, also in societies which argue otherwise.[11]

Contextual poverty, that is the relationship between the poor and the non-poor and their institutions, is another ignored feature of poverty. Within this mode of thought the non-poor play an important role in setting the context for the lives of the poor, through the way decisions are made concerning infrastructure and use of public resources, and through the pervasiveness of their norms. The images the non-poor have of poverty and the poor will influence their relationship with the poor and their willingness to engage in poverty reduction. Their social and moral bonds to the poor will be another factor influencing the politicization of poverty and bringing poverty reduction on the political agenda (de Swaan, 1988).[12]

It is interesting to note that the major part of the objective, subjective, empathic and analytic knowledge about the poor and their lives is found in the literature, classic as well as modern, on the stage and on the screen, and to a certain extent also in the media. It is evident that the abstract world of the poor belongs also to the non-poor. Why this is so is also a matter about which we know very little. How is it that the non-poor take so much interest in abstract poverty that a literary market portraying and analysing misery can be sustained for generations? Is it only the non-poor's built-in fear of becoming poor, their past history, their victory over poverty or the pleasant background it provides for their present lives, which keep this market alive? There are plenty of hypotheses here that can be of use in comparative studies.

Implementational problems[13]

Those who engage in comparative studies are in for a long time- and energy-consuming process. Linking up with the right kind of partners, sorting out the academic content of the project, and carrying out the many practical details necessary for a successful project, much of it done at a physical and electronic distance with limited face-to-face contact, calls for more patience than most researchers are willing to undertake. Along the way, guidelines have to be established on how duties, responsibilities, resources and results are to be allocated and shared. It is a prime example of decision making under a high degree of uncertainty.

Comparative studies involve per se researchers from different cultures. They are brought up within different frameworks of norms and expectations and have been subjected to different political and social realities. Within an academic setting it may mean, for example, that the researchers are subjected to different structures of reward and academic loyalties. Some will gain more from adhering to the expectations of their academic institutions, while others may gain more by adhering to the expectations of non-academic or semi-academic institutions. When the different sets of expectations are contradictory, the stage is set for conflicts between the collaborators.

There is a long-standing reluctance to the Western hegemony in the social sciences amongst some third world scholars. Many Latin American social scientists, for example, have for a long time been sceptical of their Western colleagues. In the 1950s and 1960s Western theories of development and modernization, in sociology as well as in political science and economics, zoomed in on the 'undeveloped' countries and paved the way for an analysis coined in Western terms. Latin American scholars in good faith were instrumental in adapting for political implementation the ideas embedded in these theories. The analysis and conceptual tools proved inadequate, theoretically as well as politically, and the results were disastrous (Calderon and Piscitelli, 1990).[14]

African social scientists launched the concept of 'Afro-pessimism'. On the one hand, it expresses the extreme frustration of living in a battered continent, begging the North for mercy, and knowing that the future holds very little in store for the majority of those living in poverty. On the other hand, it expresses a weariness with verbally well-meaning colleagues in the wealthier countries who never become de-coded enough to enter a real dialogue about the specific nature of African culture. Tired of begging for understanding there are now African scholars who have withdrawn from the international scene, to try to develop an 'African social science' (Mutiso, 1991[15]). Only trust and face-to-face contact developed over a long time is likely to help alleviate some of these problems in collaborative research projects. To achieve this aim trade-offs have to be developed, some of which are likely to have an impact on the direction of the research questions, methodologies and choice of data. While these trade-offs are necessary for continued collaboration and implementation of the project, they may not be optimal from a research point of view.

The field of comparative studies on poverty is permeated by other sets of ethical issues that are seldom made visible. These issues run as an undercurrent in the relationship between researchers from affluent countries and poor countries. At times this undercurrent is so strong that it hampers the carrying out of joint studies and influences the results of the studies. It can be argued that studying ethical issues and their impact is part of the methodology of doing comparative studies.

Researchers from the North are on average more affluent and control a more powerful infrastructure than researchers from the South. They are also brought up within a social science tradition that for a long time has taken its superiority for granted. These circumstances are likely to create an asymmetrical relationship between researchers from developed countries and researchers from developing countries.

In a collaborative research effort such as comparative study, the two or more parties have a common interest in the outcome of the project. They are striving towards a joint framework, whilst at the same time accommodating for personal, local and external interests. This calls for long-term interaction. It also calls for a comprehensive exchange of information. If one party controls more economic resources, more technology, more manpower, more access to library facilities and more expertise than the other party, an asymmetrical relationship is introduced. This asymmetrical relationship can be modified, either by sharing these resources in a more equal manner, or by developing coping strategies that ease the interaction between the parties. In either case it calls for ethical guidelines to be made visible for the parties involved.

A comparative project is an ad hoc formation developed to reach a certain goal. The ordinary stratification patterns and lines of command may not be the best instrument to reach such a goal. There is no evidence supporting the fact that the party controlling the most resources in a comparative research project is also the party best equipped to command the project, but empirically this is a likely outcome. More subtle issues can be just as important for the relationship. For example, who commands the right to give advice to whom? From the outside, donors may interfere in a finely balanced relationship when they assign authority to the party accountable for the use of resources.

A conflict of interest often observed in collaborative research projects with participants from the North and the South is whether the project should be research-driven or action-driven. Researchers from countries where poverty is dominant can rightfully ask if it is fair to emphasize theoretical and methodological issues when so much needs to be done to reduce poverty. It may be difficult to gain acceptance in the surrounding community for time-consuming basic research in an environment where resources are scarce and the social problems overwhelming. Applied research focusing on immediate problems seems to be a more appropriate option than comparative poverty research aimed at a wider understanding of poverty problems.[16]

Vested interests in poverty research
Still another obstacle to comparative poverty research is located in the many outside interests in the outcome of the research and the consequences the results may have for the outside actors' own interests. The examples are numerous. It is not uncommon for governments to stamp research reports on

poverty confidential, deny researchers and the public access to poverty-related data or to doctor official statistics. It is not uncommon that political parties denounce results showing the depth and intensity of poverty and instead redirect public attention by throwing doubt on the methodology used in the analysis. The Swedish public refused to believe the results of the first level-of-living study because it disclosed serious poverty traps in the best welfare state in the world, and so challenged the methodology used.[17] Conservative groups in Australia did not like the new transfer system implied in the Henderson poverty line and so mounted a ferocious attack on both the methodology and the researchers involved.

Several types of vested interests in how poverty should be defined can be identified. One is tied to policy interests. Those actors who can command a definition of poverty can also influence who are to be the beneficiaries of poverty-reducing measures and how much aid is needed before the beneficiaries are no longer defined as poor. History is full of examples of who are defined as 'deserving poor' and who are to be defined as 'undeserving poor'. In Norway definitions of sorting the deserving needy from the non-deserving can be traced all the way back to the thirteenth century.[18] Wherever an official poverty line is established, it serves the same purpose of sorting the needy from the not-so-needy. The World Bank poverty definition during the last 20 years of 'one-dollar-a-day' has influenced a worldwide understanding of poverty based on a crude and minimalist definition.

Another set of vested interests in poverty definitions are tied to professional interests. The disciplines emphasize and define poverty differently and in accordance with the paradigms within which they work. While there is a general agreement that none of the singular disciplinary definitions describes poverty and the poor adequately, the academic traditions give little room for integrating definitions brought forward in disciplines outside one's own discipline. Rather, it becomes a mark of excellence for some researchers to keep their definitions 'clean'.

For practical purposes a single cause model is often used. When poverty is presented as a lack of access to clean water, then the best poverty-reducing strategy is to invest in wells. When poverty is presented as illiteracy, then basic education is the best remedy. When poverty is presented as moral decay, then birth control and increased policing seems the best strategy.

Statistical units likewise have their vested interests because time series and trend analyses have to be based on past definitions. Since earlier definitions of poverty were characterized by simplicity, in accordance with a more simplified perception of poverty than is the case in academia today, outdated definitions of poverty keep on influencing decisions made on statistical data. For other decision makers, scarcity of data and resources forces the use of simple definitions. Large Western databanks demonstrate their newly won electronic power to develop still more elaborate and complex indicators that can disseminate a more realistic picture of poverty than hitherto, but this leaves the decision makers unable to cope with the overflow of information and the concrete implementation of the many facts.

International agencies and donors often have their own agenda for poverty intervention. Consultants of many kinds feed on these agencies and develop their own agenda of vested interests.

All these interests, whether crude and direct or low-keyed and indirect, influence our thinking about poverty and the way we relate to poor people. They also affect the design and practicalities of a poverty study. Their impact becomes magnified in a comparative poverty study because the number of actors with vested interests increases, as does the magnitude of vested interests at stake.

Gains of comparative studies

With all these obstacles and problems accounted for above, is it still possible to carry through comparative studies of poverty and other topics across national boundaries? How can the gains of such studies possibly make up for all the methodological, practical, ethical and political barriers that have to be overcome? One answer to these questions is that since comparisons are in the nature of the social sciences then all units ought to be subjects of analysis, including nation-states. Another answer is that there is no other way to go. Neither our methodological tools, nor our theoretical tools, are good enough at present. If we want to develop better tools and more explanatory power we shall need to go on trying them out in different contexts and compare the outcomes. Still another answer is that comparative studies yield additional gains to those performed on smaller and more homogeneous arenas.

Increased general knowledge

So far the major part of poverty research has been carried out within a national context, leaving the impression that causes and manifestations of poverty have their roots in specific cultures. This is partly true, in so far as certain cultures create specific poverty problems, as well as emphasize certain individual and collective responses to poverty and set the limits for poverty-reducing strategies. But poverty can also be seen as a more universal phenomenon that is found in all cultures and whose causes and manifestations get modified through cultural impact. If this is the case, new poverty understanding of a more basic nature can be teased out through comparative studies. There are questions that can only be answered through comparative studies. One set of questions concerns the universal versus the culture-specific aspects of causes of poverty and manifestations of poverty. Which parts of the poverty phenomenon are of such a nature that they can be said to be inherent in all societies? For example, when causes of poverty are seen to change, do the manifestations stay the same? How culture-specific are certain manifestations and how robust are they to change, as judged from manifestations in other cultures?[19]

One of the immediate gains of comparative poverty studies lies in the simple fact that they help create a better overview of the many different local and national approaches to poverty understanding and make visible the variation in the conditions under which pro-poor and anti-poor strategies may develop. That is in itself valuable, because so far this is scarce and unsystematic knowledge.

All the empirical information from national studies contains data and theoretical elements that are needed for a broader and more general understanding of poverty. While there is no reason to expect any kind of all-embracing social theory for the explanation of poverty (poverty is as diverse a phenomenon as non-poverty), there is still a need to develop a more comprehensive theoretical foundation for the understanding of poverty. National studies alone provide only limited theoretical insights because they tend to get caught in their own cultural paradigms.

Much of foreign aid has not been successful in reducing poverty in the South. The lack of a more fundamental understanding of the complex relationship between causes of poverty, coping strategies of the poor, reactions of the non-poor and the interplay with other social phenomena, makes it difficult to create sustainable social institutions for efficient poverty reduction. It has been argued that donors and others responsible for poverty reduction are not knowledgeable enough to conduct such interventions. That may be true. Like other actors they are likely to be caught in their own cultural and professional paradigms, and sometimes also in their vested interests. But it can also be argued with a great deal of authority that the necessary knowledge for powerful interventions is still not available.

Comparative studies have the advantage that they provide the opportunity to evaluate and rethink all the many elements in the process of poverty production under different cultural impacts (Øyen, 2002). When variations arise in one element in one context and not in the same element in another context, it triggers new hypotheses and explanations. Ideally, the entire sequence of reasoning and project design have to be checked and questions asked whether a variation is due to deficiencies in the research tool, or can be explained through cultural characteristics.

Still another gain of comparative studies is the set of new questions that emerge. This may be particularly true in an under-researched field such as poverty. On the one hand, applied poverty research has a long tradition in the Western world. On the other hand, poverty research in the South is limited and has only developed recently. The voids in poverty research in those countries have been filled with an understanding of poverty developed in the West. In countries in the South imported hypotheses and methodologies have often led to dead ends, and at times have even been disastrous. In Western countries researchers are now becoming increasingly aware of the shortcomings of earlier approaches. This illustrates not only the fact that all academic import needs to be scrutinized carefully before it is put to use in a different culture. It also illustrates the fact that outsiders pose questions in a different way than insiders, for good and for bad. In principle this is a healthy practice that is encouraged through comparative studies. However, it does call for research partners in developing countries who are strong enough to counterbalance unwarranted Western influences on their endogenous knowledge and regional theorizing.

New questions can be raised concerning globalization. Like so many other social phenomena, poverty formation has increasingly become influenced by global forces. The relationship between those forces and the formation of poverty is at present an open issue, compare for example the comprehensive, controversial and inconclusive discussion on the effects of economic growth on poverty reduction. However, it is not too controversial to argue that changing technology and a more differentiated labour market are but two of the forces that will diminish the opportunities for the poorest and unskilled segment of the population. Global developments can only be studied through an international effort of research projects covering several countries, and preferably as many as possible. Most comparative studies cannot be labelled international since usually they include only a few countries. However, they are the pathways to an internationalization of research. When still more studies are added the contours of a global picture are drawn which can further the understanding of those causes of poverty which are tied to increasing globalization in the economic, political and social sphere.

Country-specific knowledge
Country-specific knowledge increases through comparative studies. Through a background of studies from other countries national studies can be analysed in a larger perspective and the lacunae of knowledge can temporarily and cautiously be supplemented with knowledge from such external studies. From a policy view comparative studies and the increased contact between experts in the field can provide new inputs on pro-poor policies, and best practices in poverty reduction can be provided. Increased awareness of a shared problem is another benefit that throws light on a more general phenomenon and its solutions.

From another angle comparative studies may help penetrate the moralistic and stereotyped atmosphere that has always surrounded poverty issues. For example, in spite of the many verbal commitments to anti-poverty strategies, a certain amount of poverty is directly of value for some non-poor groups.[20] When this kind of vested interests documented in one country study match vested interests in studies from other countries, it can become legitimate to shift a causal analysis based on moral deficiency of the poor to an analysis of the non-poor and their role in sustaining poverty. When results of such controversial analyses are repeated in comparative studies they gain a momentum that cannot be brushed off as a national anomaly. Research on poverty among the urban poor in several countries has documented that the poor experience an added vulnerability beyond their actual poverty, because they are exposed to a set of risks stemming from the majority society. Health risks arise from the spatial juxtaposition of industrial pollution, high traffic density, lack of sanitary installations, and a generally poor infrastructure where the poor live and work. Poor people often experience the state in negative ways: as an oppressive bureaucracy that attempts to regulate their activities without understanding their needs, as corrupt police officers, or as planners who make plans without an understanding of how the poor live and survive. As a result poor people tend to avoid contact with official representatives of the majority society, thereby marginalizing themselves further.[21] This picture has emerged through the comparison of results from different studies, and has become part of the generalized knowledge about present day poverty life in the cities. It seems to be a basic pattern with local variations. This is valuable knowledge for people and organizations working towards efficient poverty-reducing measures. Since the knowledge has also been obtained independently in other countries it is likely to have greater validity than isolated knowledge obtained locally. For those who are engaged in poverty reduction it means they can concentrate on sorting out the local variations and seek confirmation of what has been observed elsewhere. Also, it gives the information more credibility, a fact that should not be overlooked in the politics of poverty reduction. Since a phenomenon has been observed in several countries it cannot be as easily ignored and dismissed as a local anomaly. For those working with theory building such parallel phenomena observed through comparative studies provides fertile soil for more general hypotheses about poverty formation.

Concluding remarks

Comparative methodology has not made major leaps forward. This is in spite of refinements in other methodologies, new information technology and masses of empirical data available through huge databases and a myriad of comparative studies. The shortcomings are such that the yield of comparative studies can rightly be questioned. At the same time it can be argued that there are other sizeable gains in carrying out comparative studies. They increase general knowledge, offer a critical background for limited national studies, and provide the opportunity to raise new issues. Altogether the 'migration of ideas' expands the horizon of researchers and users of the studies.

Other indirect effects of comparative studies are the dissemination of expertise and country-specific insights that are created throughout a project where partners from different countries work together over a lengthy period. Successful cooperation tends to create sustainable networks and continued exchange of knowledge. This is a form of globalization that most academics are likely to welcome.

It is interesting to note that researchers who engage in comparative studies of poverty after a while seem to go beyond their disciplinary borders, break with traditional ways of thinking and develop a broader spectre of academic expertise than that found in their original discipline. This seems to be particularly true where comparative studies involve partners in the South whose education is less mono-disciplinary. This gives reason to develop a hypothesis that increased internationalization in research experience is one avenue towards increasing interdisciplinarity.

Notes

1. Comparisons are here defined as comparisons between countries/nations.
2. More than a decade ago I edited a book where a group of experts in the field wrote essays that updated our knowledge about the then current methodology of comparative studies. Those essays are still very relevant: Øyen (ed.) (1990). Some of the writings on comparative methodology still in use as textbook material date back to the 1970s and 1980s and include Przeworski and Teune (1970); Macintyre (1973); Ragin and Zaret (1983); Ragin (1987); Collier (1991); Collier and Mahon (1993) and Dogan (1994).
3. This is an area that demonstrates all the problems of comparative research. It is also the one with which I am the most familiar; see www.crop.org for more information on CROP, The Comparative Research Programme on Poverty.
4. These and several other methodological problems of the same kind are well documented in the social science literature and need not be further discussed here.
5. Michael Ward, 'Perceptions of Poverty: The Historical Legacy', Paper presented at International Conference on What Can Be Done About Poverty?, IDS, Sussex, June 1998.
6. Robert Chambers (1996).
7. David Gordon and Paul Spicker (eds) (1998). The volume is now under revision in order to incorporate newer definitions, in particular in Latin America.
8. Else Øyen et al. (2002).
9. See for example Erik Oddvar Eriksen and Jørn Loftager (1996).
10. T.H. Marshall (1964); Richard M. Titmuss (1968).
11. Oscar Lewis (1966); Daniel P. Moynihan (ed.) (1968); Frances Fox Piven and Richard A. Cloward (1971); John Rawls (1971); Herbert J. Gans (1972).
12. Abram de Swaan (1988).
13. The discussion in this part of the chapter is based on Else Øyen (1996).
14. F. Calderon and A. Piscitelli (1990).
15. Roberta M. Mutiso, Nairobi, Kenya, private conversation 1991.
16. In order to get around this difficult issue, the concept of 'action research' has developed as some kind of compromise. On the one hand, action research lends it legitimacy from the fairly prestigious arena of academic knowledge production. On the other hand, action research gets legitimacy through its moral emphasis on intervention. However, the loss of mixing two incompatible strategies outweighs the gain of two compatible and valuable goals, and a sound methodology for action research has not yet been developed.

290 A handbook of comparative social policy

17. Sten Johansson (1970).
18. Magnus Lagabøtes landslov 1274–76. (Law given by King Magnus the Lawmaker.)
19. Else Øyen (1992).
20. Gans (1973).
21. Ellen Wratten (1995); World Bank (2000).

References

Calderon, F. and A. Piscitelli (1990), 'Paradigm crisis and social movement: A Latin American perspective', in Else Øyen (ed.), *Comparative Methodology: Theory and Practice in International Social Research*, London: Sage, pp. 81–95.

Chambers, Robert (1996), 'Poor people's realities: the professional challenge', in Yogesh Atal and Else Øyen (eds), *Poverty and Participation in Civil Society*, Paris: UNESCO and ISSC/CROP.

Collier, David (1991), 'The comparative method: two decades of change', in Dankwart A. Rostow and Kenneth Paul Erichson (eds), *Comparative Political Dynamics: Global Research Perspectives*, New York: Harper Collins.

Collier, David and James Mahon (1993), 'Conceptual "Stretching" revisited: adapting categories in comparative analysis', *American Political Science Review*, 4(87), 845–55.

Dogan, Mattei (1994), 'The use and misuse of statistics in comparative research. Limits to quantification in comparative politics: the gap between substance and method', in Mattei Dogan and Ali Kazancilgil (eds), *Comparing Nations*, Oxford: Blackwell, pp. 35–71.

Eriksen, Erik Oddvar and Jørn Loftager (1996), *The Rationality of the Welfare State*, Oslo: Scandinavian University Press.

Gans, Herbert J. (1972), 'The positive functions of poverty', *American Journal of Sociology*, 78(2), 275–89.

Gordon, David and Paul Spicker (eds) (1998), *The International Glossary on Poverty*, CROP International Studies in Poverty Research, London: Zed Books.

Johansson, Sten (1970), *Om levnadsnivåundersökningen*, Stockholm: Almänna Förlaget.

Lewis, Oscar (1966), *La Vida*, New York: Random House.

Macintyre, Alasdair (1973), 'Is a science of comparative politics possible?', in Alan Ryan (ed.), *The Philosophy of Social Explanations*, Oxford: Oxford University Press.

Marshall, T. H. (1964), *Class, Citizenship and Development: Essays*, New York: Doubleday.

Moynihan, Daniel P. (ed.) (1968), *On Understanding Poverty*, New York: Basic Books.

Øyen, Else (ed.) (1990), *Comparative Methodology: Theory and Practice in International Social Research*, London: Sage Publications.

Øyen, Else (1992), 'Some basic issues in comparative poverty research', *International Social Science Journal*, vol. 134, 615–26.

Øyen, Else (1996), 'Ethics of asymmetrical relationships evolving from doing comparative studies in poverty research', in *Science, Éthique & Societé*, Fédération Mondiale des Travailleurs Scientifiques, Paris: UNESCO, pp. 67–71.

Øyen, Else (2002), 'Poverty production: a different approach to poverty understanding', in Nicolai Genov (ed.), *Advances in Sociological Knowledge over Half a Century*, Paris: International Social Science Council, pp. 351–71; also in Nicolai Genov (ed.) (2003), *Advances in Sociological Knowledge*, Berlin: Lesket Budrich, and on www.crop.org. Published also in Spanish, Portuguese and German. Contact author for more details.

Øyen, Else et al. (2002), *Best Practices in Poverty Reduction: An Analytical Framework*, CROP International Studies in Poverty Research, London and New York: Zed Books.

Piven, Frances Fox and Richard A. Cloward (1971), *Regulating the Poor: The Functions of Public Welfare*, New York: Pantheon.

Przeworski, Adam and Henry Teune (1970), *The Logic of Comparative Social Inquiry*, New York: Wiley.

Ragin, Charles and David Zaret (1983), 'Theory and method in comparative research: two strategies', *Social Forces*, 61(3), 731–54.

Ragin, Charles (1987), *The Comparative Method: Moving Beyond Qualitative and Quantitative Strategies*, Berkeley: University of California Press.

Rawls, John (1971), *A Theory of Justice*, Cambridge, Mass: The Belknap Press of Harvard University Press.
Swaan, Abram de (1988), *In Care of the State: Health Care, Education and Welfare in Europe and the USA in the Modern Era*, Oxford: Polity Press.
Titmuss, Richard M. (1968), *Commitment to Welfare*, London: Allen & Unwin.
World Bank (2000), *World Development Report 2000–2001: Attacking Poverty*, Oxford: Oxford University Press.
Wratten, Ellen (1995), 'Conceptualising urban poverty', *Environment and Urbanization*, **1**(7), 11–36.

16 Constructing categories and data collection
Patricia Kennett

The construction of concepts, categories and definitions of contemporary social issues is a central issue in comparative social research. Not only is it vital to ensure that the concepts and categories being compared mean the same or something similar across the societies being investigated, it is also vital to analyse the processes through which a phenomenon becomes defined as a problem. As Jessop argues, selective narratives of past events generate distinctive accounts of current economic, social and political problems, from which emerge 'a limited but widely accepted set of diagnoses and prescriptions for the economic, social and political difficulties now confronting nations, regions, and cities and their populations' (Jessop, 1996: 3). Representations of social issues are subject to political manipulation, and numbers play a central role in constructing and reinforcing discourses around specific social 'problems', determining what aspects of a problem are responded to and in what way. May (1997) points to three important elements in the construction of a 'social problem' – culture, history and social power. He argues that power is not evenly distributed between groups. The recognition that a 'problem' exists and the way that it is defined is often a product of 'the relative power that the people who define the social problem have over those who are defined.' (p. 47). Thus it becomes vital to 'examine the process through which a phenomenon became defined as a problem' (p. 47), rather than just accept given definitions. This chapter begins by considering the issues of equivalence in the construction of concepts, categories and definitions. It then goes on to focus on debates around and measurements of homelessness in both a national and a cross-national context.

Concepts, categories and equivalence of meaning
The issue of cross-societal equivalence of concepts is prominent in the literature and is clearly a crucial factor in cross-national research given that phenomena or relationships may have different meanings in other societies. In order to compare something across systems it is necessary to have confidence that the components and their properties being compared are the 'same' or indicate something equivalent. As Beals (1954) argues

> Unless initially we use precisely comparative conceptualisations and methodologies, comparative studies are a waste of time, for they will never add up to proof,

disproof, or reformulation or anything. Rather we will emerge, not with one set of culture-bound theories and concepts, but with a multitude of culture-bound theories (Beals, 1954: 308 in Marsh, 1967: 268).

According to Rose (1991) 'Concepts are necessary as common points of reference for grouping phenomena that are differentiated geographically and often linguistically' (Rose, 1991: 447). He points out that without concepts information collected about different countries provides no basis for relating one country to another. 'In order to connect empirical materials horizontally across national boundaries, they must also be connected vertically; that is, capable of being related to concepts that are sufficiently abstract to travel across national boundaries' (Rose, 1991: 447).

Appropriateness, then, refers to the methods employed and the conceptualization of issues when undertaking comparative research. As Armer (1973) explains 'appropriateness requires feasibility, significance and acceptability in each foreign culture as a necessary (but not sufficient) condition for insuring validity and successful completion of comparative studies' (pp. 50–51). Thus, issues of appropriateness and equivalence in the conceptualization of issues are key factors within the research process (May, 1997).

Marsh (1967) differentiates between *formal* equivalence and *functional* equivalence of concepts, pointing out that using identical formal procedures when comparing different societies may produce functionally non-equivalent meanings. In order to compare something across countries it is, of course, vital to have confidence that the components and their properties being compared are the 'same' or indicate something equivalent. Pickvance (1986) points to the lack of familiarity one might have with other national contexts which may lead to the omission or misinterpretation of an important feature and have a strong causal influence on the subject of analysis. Iyengar (1993) reinforces this point and is particularly concerned with conceptual rigour in multi-language studies. He argues that linguistic diversity can be a barrier when carrying out both cross-national and single-country studies because of the lack of robust concepts and the difficulties of analysing data in more than one language. He considers linguistic equivalence and measurement equivalence to be vital elements of the cross-national research process. He describes linguistic equivalence as 'validity *within* languages' but argues that measurement equivalence requires that the linguistic equivalence of concepts 'is operationalised as reliability *across* the languages concerned' (p. 174, original emphasis). What he is emphasizing here is that care must be taken not only to ensure that concepts developed for use in each particular language are up to measuring what they set out to investigate, but also that the range of conceptual frameworks can be integrated and analysed systematically. As discussed earlier, it may well be that concepts when translated and operationalized in a range of national contexts may vary in order to capture the 'language of expressions'. However, 'unless it can be demonstrated that the indices in one particular context are applicable to other contexts, comparison is of little value' (Iyengar, 1993: 173).

Carey-Wood (1991) has indicated that equivalence in meaning and concepts is not necessarily obtainable by correct translations because of the semantic, cultural and societal differences inherent in words and concepts. Conceptual equivalence, according to Hantrais and Ager (1985), requires intimate knowledge of context and culture, whilst for Warwick and Osherson 'linguistic equivalence is inseparable from the theory and concepts guiding the study, the problems chosen, and the research design' (Warwick and Osherson, 1973: 31). As Hantrais and Mangen (1996) argue, drawing on the work of Lisle (1985) 'language is not simply a medium for conveying concepts, it is part of the conceptual system, reflecting institutions, thought processes, values and ideology, and implying that the approach to a topic and the interpretation of it will differ, according to the language of expression'(p. 7).

Not only might issues which are held to be important in one national context not be of significance in another, but values and interpretations of phenomena differ from society to society. It is important that the researcher does not assume a 'value consensus' across societies, nor 'impose' meaning and interpretations on a particular social phenomenon, influencing interpretations about what is legitimate and normal, and therefore what is deviant (May, 1997). Lewis (1999) highlights the profound differences in the nature of the debates about lone mothers in Britain, and other European countries. In Britain (and the USA) lone mothers have been characterized as welfare dependent, morally feckless and ineffective mothers. Their status, according to Lewis (1999), has evolved from one of 'social problem' to 'social threat'. In other European countries lone mothers have not been singled out as a problem category, or demonized by the media and are also better off in material terms. The reasons for this are complex and varied. Demographic factors, including the larger populations of lone mothers in Britain and the USA, as well as the kinds of lone mothers which predominate in different countries in terms of previous marital status and the age of unmarried mothers, have contributed to the tone of the debate. Lewis (1999) indicates that extra-marital birth rates are highest in Scandinavian countries (46.4 per cent in 1990), whilst England and Wales have a much higher percentage of teenage mothers (33 per cent in 1990) than other European countries, though not as high as in the USA (59.4 per cent). She also highlights the dynamics of class and race in the discourse around lone mothers, pointing out that 'in the United States, unmarried mothers are disproportionately black and on benefit', and in Britain, unlike other European countries, 'they are disproportionatley poorly educated and unskilled and also on benefit' (Lewis, 1999: 185). The welfare dependency of lone mothers in Britain is a product of 'the poverty of their social wage [child care provision, parental leave for example] compared to so many of their counterparts in other European countries' (p. 197). Whilst demographics and the characteristics of lone mothers may offer some explanation for the differences in the nature of debates between countries, the key to understanding national differences in policies and the diverse dynamics of integration of lone mothers is the political ideologies within which welfare regimes and family policies have been established and are maintained.

Appreciating the specificity of national contexts and the recognition of alternative and dynamic discourses around perceived 'social problems' is the key to developing robust and appropriate concepts. The remainder of this chapter focuses on the development of debates associated with homelessness and the fragility and flexibility of definitions and concepts used to construct and measure homelessness across the globe.

Conceptualizing and quantifying homelessness

For a more diverse section of the population post-industrial capitalism offers exposure to new types of processes of marginalization and exclusion. Restructuring, rationalization and globalization have tended to reinforce social divisions and have contributed to a 'new dynamic of inequality' (UNCHS (Habitat), 2001: 71). During the last 30 years the growth in the numbers of people experiencing homelessness – one of the most acute forms, if not the most acute form of social and housing exclusion – in many cities worldwide has been emblematic of these new dynamics of inequality and what Castells refers to as 'the Fourth World' (Castells, 1998) of informational capitalism.

Just as poverty and social exclusion have proved controversial concepts, so has homelessness proved to be a fundamentally unstable category. There is no universally accepted definition of homelessness. Extensive debates have been generated over the precise definition and the appropriate means of measuring the extent of homelessness (see Bramley, 1988, Jacobs et al., 1999; Burrows, Pleace and Quilgars 1997). The processes and context of homelessness are complex, multifarious and vary with different national settings. And as Doherty, Edgar and Meert (2002) point out the difficulties of measuring homelessness are further exacerbated because of the hidden and dynamic nature of the phenomenon. 'People may be homeless for short periods in their lives, some people may have recurrent episodes of homelessness and others may be homeless for long periods of time' (p. 4). Thus, the exact number of homeless people is difficult to quantify given the multitude of ways in which the phenomenon is conceptualized and experienced. As Marsh and Kennett (1999) have argued

All statistical measures are socially negotiated, but in the case of homelessness – along with other key political issues like crime and unemployment – the fragility of official definitions and measures is particularly stark. Societies with different socio-political traditions are likely to come to very different understandings of the term (Marsh and Kennett, 1999: 3).

And indeed, there is by now abundant evidence drawing on a range of definitions and methodologies to suggest that throughout the 1980s and 1990s homelessness escalated dramatically (for example: Ferrand-Bechmann, 1988 (France); Schuler-Walner, 1986 (Germany); Bramley, 1988; Kennett and Marsh, 1999 (UK); Dear and Wolch, 1987, Bingham, Green and White, 1987 (USA); Daly, 1996, NCFH, 1986, Glasser, 1994 (general) to name but a few). In the USA, according to Hoch (2000), there are between 5 000 000 to 1 million homeless people on any night, depending on the type of measurement used. These figures for the USA represent a decline in the rate of growth since the early 1990s, but indicate a continued increase in the number of homeless people. In Japan, the homelessness phenomenon did not become an issue until the 1990s when the numbers of homeless people in the five Japanese cities of Yokohama, Kawasaki, Nagoya, Tokyo and Osaka rose consistently throughout the 1990s reaching approximately 17 000 by 1999 (Kennett and Iwata, 2003). As in many other studies in other parts of the world attempting to enumerate the extent of the problem the homeless were narrowly classified as 'rough sleepers'. In the case of Japan homelessness was constructed as a circumstance predominantly experienced by unemployed day labourers, by excluded and marginalized residents of the *yoseba* districts, and by men. Whilst the vast majority of rough sleepers are male, it is also the case that in Tokyo the number of women sleeping rough has increased year on year since 1997. In 1999 the number stood at 123 women. However, the focus on identifying only those living on the streets as homeless and on characterizing the phenomenon as 'male' has ensured that the number of females recorded as homeless is low or completely absent. It is well documented that women are less likely to take to the streets than men for fear of violence and abuse. As Watson (1999) argues

> ...how homelessness is understood in each society reflects the ways in which the society is organised and in patriarchal society, these are necessarily gendered ...If homelessness is defined in terms of men's experiences and practices or men's subjectivities then women's homelessness becomes invisible (Watson, 1999: 84, 87).

And such is the case in Japan. Giamo (1995) argues that there is very little 'tolerance and compassion for those who, for one reason or another, slip off the ladder of social obligation' (p. 35). For homeless women this experience is particularly stark. Traditional attitudes in Japan firmly link the female and the family, and define her identity and sense of self in relation to other household members. To be outside this relationship of obligation, to be without a home, is particularly damaging and stigmatizing for women. As Guzewicz (2000) explains in his account of street homelessness in Tokyo:

> There is no simple way to look into the face of a filthy young woman on the street. We are saddened or repelled, guilty if not resentful, and then avert our eyes from her. In a society that disdains women even in the best of curcumstances, we are at times overwhelmed by those women who belong to no one and no place; those who in the very state of their existence violate all conventional notions of femininity. If they are 'crazy' all the more reason to hurry past, cross the street or avoid them all together (p. 76).

And commenting more generally on the tendency to reduce homelessness to sleeping rough Cloke, Milbourne and Widdowfield argue that

> Quantifying rough sleeping as a measure of the homelessness problem helps to sustain negative images and perceptions in which homelessness is reduced to a set of key issues centred around begging, street drunkenness and other perceived 'anti-social' behaviour. With such criminalisation and distortion of homelessness, it is hardly surprising that homelessness and homeless people are discussed in pejorative terms (2001: 270).

A study carried out by the United Nations Centre for Human Settlement, which attempted to estimate the number of homeless people worldwide in the mid-1990s, featured a range of interpretations of homelessness and estimates of the numbers of people experiencing homelessness. They concluded that it was somewhere between 100 million to 1 billion, depending on how the categories were defined. It is worth citing the following quote in full as an indication of the flexibility and instability of the term:

> The estimate of 100 million would apply to those who have no shelter at all, including those who sleep outside (on pavements, in shop doorways, in parks or under bridges) or in public buildings (in railway, bus or metro stations) or in night shelters set up to provide homeless people with a bed. The estimate of 1 billion homeless people would also include those in accommodation that is very insecure or temporary, and often poor quality – for instance squatters who have found accommodation by illegally occupying someone else's home or land and are under constant threat of eviction, those living in refugee camps whose home has been destroyed and those living in temporary shelters (like the 250 000 pavement dwellers in Bombay). The estimate for the number of homeless people worldwide would exceed 1 billion people if it were to include all people who lack an adequate home with secure tenure ... and the most basic facilities such as water of adequate quality piped into the home, provision for sanitation and drainage' (UNCHS (Habitat), 1996: 229)

Within the countries of the European Union some 18 million people were considered to be homeless or badly housed. This figure was based on the broad, fourfold classification of homelessness developed by the European Observatory on homelessness, run by the European Federation of National Organisations Working with the Homeless (FEANTSA). The classification includes a) rooflessness or sleeping rough; b) houselessness (living in institutions or short-term accommodation; c) insecure accommodation; and d) inferior or substandard housing. However, according to Doherty, Edgar and Meert (2002) in no country of the European Union is it possible to obtain figures on homelessness based on each of the dimensions of the FEANTSA definition. They also point out that there is no single and consistent method of collecting data on homelessness employed by the national statistical offices or other official sources of statistics in the member states. Indeed '... in some countries there are simply no official statistics on homelessness (for example Austria, Greece, Spain)' (p. 4). So, despite this broad definition the most commonly used data to emerge from the Observatory is based on research drawn from each member country which is then collated to provide an overall picture. The figure of 1.8 million people shown in Table 16.1 covers only those people who have used public or voluntary services for temporary shelter or who squat or sleep rough. As Avramov (1996) points out, however, it

Table 16.1   Estimates of number of persons homeless in Europe

Country	Homeless on an average day	In the course of a year
Austria	6,100	8,400
Belgium	4,000	5,500
Germany	490,700	876,450
Denmark	2,947	4,000
Spain	8,000	11,000
Finland	4,000	5,500
France	250,000	346,000
Greece	5,500	7,700
Ireland	2,667	3,700
Italy	56,000	78,000
Luxembourg	194	200
The Netherlands	7,000	12,000
Portugal	3,000	4,000
Sweden	9,903	14,000
UK	283,000	460,000
	1,133,011	1,836,450

Source: Based on Avramov (1996).

tends to be those countries with relatively good provision for the homeless that come out with the highest number of homeless people. Harvey suggests that these estimates may be more an indication of 'efficient information-gathering, as much as the size of the problem itself' (Harvey, 1999: 278). Nevertheless they provide sufficient evidence to indicate that homelessness is a significant problem in many countries of the European Union and highlight the relevance of recent work being undertaken by FEANTSA to develop conceptual and measurement issues in order to facilitate more effective and comparative analysis across European countries.

When considering any estimate of homelessness then it is important to question how the figures were obtained. The remainder of the discussion focuses on the British experience to highlight the necessity of incorporating into the cross-national analysis a consideration of how a specific social problem has been constructed, understood, quantified and responded to in a specific national context.

The construction of homelessness in the UK

Homelessness in Britain is not a new or transient phenomenon. The vagrants, indigents and 'wards of the community' of the nineteenth century, the transient workers and mobile poor of the early twentieth century and the 'victims' of the depression during the 1930s are all indications of the various ways in which the phenomenon has been constructed at different times. Following the second world war poverty and homelessness were seen as a thing of the past, and the prevailing ideology was that income and housing need had been met. In 1960, only a few thousand households were accepted by local authorities as homeless, the great majority in London. The situation has been transformed since then and homelessness has emerged as a problem affecting different kinds of areas from the inner city to rural villages and has involved a widening spectrum of the population. The extent of homelessness, according to Marcuse (1993), can no longer be linked to changes in economic conditions, especially in the USA. For Marcuse (1993) homelessness today is

> large scale, permanent and independent of the short-term business cycle, a combination never before existing in an advanced industrial society. It represents the inability of the state to care for the most basic needs of significant segments of the population…, and their subsequent complete exclusion from or suppression in the spatial fabric of a technologically and economically advanced city. It may fairly be called 'advanced homelessness' (p. 353).

The end of full employment, the erosion of the welfare safety net, and the marketization and residualization of the welfare state have all contributed to an environment in which a growing section of the population have found it difficult to access and maintain adequate, secure, affordable accommodation.

Britain is unusual in having a statutory definition of homelessness. The operational definition applied by the government and local authorities in dealing with homelessness derives from the 1977 Housing (Homeless Persons) Act, incorporated into the 1986 Housing Act in England and Wales and 1987 in Scotland. The Act represented a fundamental shift in policy and practice away from the 1948 National Assistance Act which, according to Greve (1997), had 'inherited and perpetuated much of the philosophy of some of the practices of the hated Poor Law' (p. 1). The new legislation acknowledged homelessness as a housing problem rather than a welfare problem and gave housing departments responsibility for re-housing those considered to have met the statutory criteria. However, even in countries with 'official' definitions of homelessness like Britain, where local authorities have a duty to respond to those defined as homeless, the legislation excludes many single households, and others considered not to be in 'priority need'.

The statutory definition is relatively narrow and whilst it defines a concept of homelessness, it then delimits it to exclude certain categories. The Act imposes a duty on local authorities to secure accommodation for persons who are assessed as actually or imminently homeless, who are not *intentionally* homeless, who are in *priority* need and who have a local connection. *Priority need* is defined as: families with dependent children, pregnant women, people who are vulnerable because of old age, disability, young people at risk, people made homeless by emergence (for example fire). Recent changes to the homeless legislation (2002 Homelessness Act) has extended the priority category to include those leaving institutionalized settings, and those experiencing domestic violence.

During the last 20 years homelessness reached its peak in 1992 when 179 410 households were accepted by local authorities as homeless (see Figure 16.1). As Figure 16.1 shows the numbers then proceeded to fall until 1997, but began to increase thereafter. In 1999 the number of local authority homeless acceptances was approximately 134 000[1] households. And there is significant evidence to suggest that homelessness is highly significant for ethnic minority groups (Harrison, 1999). In 1998, 59 per cent of households accepted by local authorities in inner London were from ethnic minorities.

The official definition then consists of those households, most often families with children, who have been accepted as homeless by a local authority. Approximately 70 per cent of acceptances of those in priority need are households with dependent children or with a pregnant member. The most common immediate causes are recorded in Figure 16.2. A consistent cause of homelessness has been that parents, relatives or friends have no longer been willing or able to provide accommodation. Whilst still the major reason precipitating homelessness since the mid-1990s, other factors such as breakdown of a relationship with a partner and loss of private dwelling have

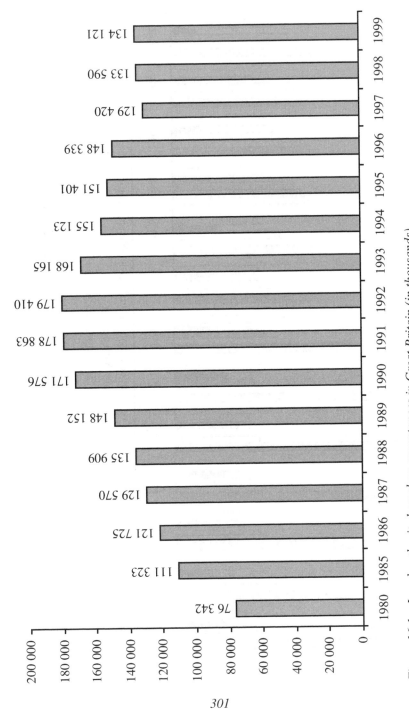

Figure 16.1   Local authority homeless acceptances in Great Britain (in thousands)

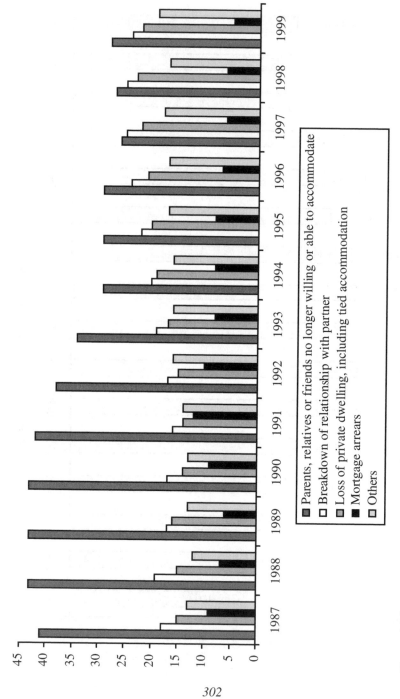

Figure 16.2   Reasons for homelessness in England (in percentages)

become almost as influential in affecting an individual's or household's ability to maintain a home. The numbers experiencing homelessness because of mortgage arrears reached a peak in 1991. This coincided with a period of economic instability, recession and high interest rates in England, a situation that has been in reverse since the late 1990s. The number of statutory homeless people citing mortgage arrears as the immediate cause of their homelessness it is now much less than in the early 1990s but it is still the case that in the year 2000 there were 22 610 repossessions, 91 630 households were 3–6 months in arrears, 45 680 households were 6–12 months in arrears and 18 830 households were 12 months or more in arrears (Wilcox, 2001).

Whilst these figures provide a useful snapshot of the immediate causes of statutory homelessness, it could also be argued that in many ways the data simply represent administrative categories and rather than revealing, they often disguise the complex processes which have precipitated these events. For most people events such as losing a job, increasing debt or the breakdown of a relationship will not result in such extreme consequences as homelessness. However, in the risk society (Giddens, 1991; Beck, 1992; Culpitt, 1999) of contemporary capitalism, it is increasingly the case that for those with limited personal and financial resources and little by way of social networks or social capital on which to draw the descent down the 'spiral of precariousness' (Paugam, 1995; Forrest, 1999) is given added momentum. Official figures do not reveal the complexity and diversity of these processes and individual pathways into homelessness.

It is also the case that there is considerable local discretion in the way the legislation is interpreted. Indeed, as Marsh and Kennett (1999) point out

> beyond a core of households whose circumstances would mean that they would be treated as homeless by the vast majority of local administrations, there is a range of households whose status as officially 'homeless' depends entirely upon which locality they find themselves in. Whether a household is considered by a local authority to be statutorily homeless and eligible for assistance is likely to depend on a number of contingent factors such as the political complexion of an authority or the demand for social housing locally (p. 3).

A negative effect of the legislation is that people assessed as not in the priority need categories generally do not get material help in finding accommodation. This mostly affects single homeless people and couples without dependent children. The total numbers falling into these categories are substantial. Shelter (a UK homelessness charity), for example, estimates that there are some 41 000 people who are living in hostels and squats who are not included in the figures (Shelter, 2000). Homeless legislation clearly treats single homeless households with less priority than homeless families. When they do emerge in policy discourse, the tone is often one of individual blame and deviancy on behalf of the homeless person as demonstrated in more recent government policies directed at 'rough sleepers' (Social Exclusion Unit).

In Britain the official definition of homelessness constructs the issue in a particular way which in turn influences the nature of the homeless population and the causes of the phenomenon. It is generally single and non-family households that make up the vast majority of those considered to be the non-statutory homeless. And it is from amongst this group that the majority of those sleeping on the streets or in hostels is to be found. There can be little doubt that official statistics on homelessness are a useful starting point for the researcher. However, whether official statistics or census or survey data are being utilized they should be subject to critical analysis and supported by data from other contexts and international sources.

Conclusion

Drawing on the phenomenon of homelessness this chapter has sought to show the elasticity and fragility of concepts both nationally and internationally. It has emphasized the importance of recognizing and understanding the processes through which an issue becomes defined in a particular way and the implications of this for data collection and cross-national analysis.

In a social world that is increasingly fluid and fragmented, individualized and polarized the recognition of appropriate points of reference and orientation through which individuals understand, experience and make sense of the world around them is vital. The development and implementation of appropriate, robust concepts and frameworks is more relevant than ever if comparative social policy analysis is to capture the reality of the lived experience in the contemporary world and explain and understand the nature of social divisions in different societies.

Note

1. This figure represents 111 750 households accepted as homeless in England and 4171 in Wales in 1999. The 1990 figure of 18 200 households is used for Scotland, as 1999 figures were not available.

References

Armer, M. (1973), 'Methodological problems and possibilities in comparative research', in M. Armer and A. Grimshaw (eds), *Comparative Social Research: Methodological Problems and Strategies*, New York: Wiley.

Avramov, Dragana (1996), *The Invisible Hand of the Housing Market*, Brussels: FEANTSA.

Beals, R.L. (1954), 'A review of Miner', *American Anthropologist*, vol. 56, pp. 307–8.

Beck, Ulrich (1992), *Risk Society: Towards a New Modernity*, London: Sage Publications.

Bingham, Richard D., Roy E. Green and Sammis B. White (eds) (1987), *The Homeless in Contemporary Society*, Newbury Park, CA: Sage.

Bramley, Glen (1988), *Homelessness and the London Housing Market*, Occasional paper 32, SAUS Publications, Bristol.

Burrows, Roger, Nicolas Pleace and Deborah Quilgars (1997), *Homelessness and Social Policy*, London: Routledge.

Carey-Wood, Jennifer (1991), *Leaving Home: Housing for Young People in England and France*, Unpublished Ph.D. Thesis, University of Bristol, UK.

Castells, Manuel (1998), *End of Millenium*, Oxford: Blackwell.

Cloke, P., P. Milbourne and R. Widdowfield (2001), 'Making the homeless count? Enumerating rough sleepers and the distortion of homelessness', *Policy and Politics*, **29**(3) 259–79.

Culpitt, Ian (1999), *Social Policy and Risk*, London: Sage.

Daly, Gerald (1996), *Homelessness: Policies, Strategies, and Lives on the Street*, London: Routledge.

Dear, Michael, J. and Jennifer R. Wolch (1987), *Landscapes of Despair; from Deinstitutionalization to Homelessness*, Princeton, NJ: Princeton University Press.

Doherty, Joe, Bill Edgar and Henk Meert (2000), *Review of Statistics on Homelessness in Europe*, Brussels: FEANTSA.

Doherty, Joe, Bill Edgar and Henk Meert (2002), *Homelessness Research in the EU: A Summary*, Brussels: FEANTSA.

Ferrand-Bechmann, Dan (1988), 'Homelessness in France: public and private policies', in Jurgen Friedrichs (ed.), *Affordable Housing and the Homeless*, Berlin: Walter de Gruyter, pp. 147–55.

Forrest, Ray (1999), 'The new landscape of precariousness', in Patricia Kennett and Alex Marsh (eds), *Exploring the New Terrain*, Bristol: The Policy Press, pp. 17–37.

Giamo, B. (1995), 'Order, disorder and the homeless in the United States and Japan', *American Studies International*, **XXXIII**(1), 19–41.

Giddens, Anthony (1991), *Modernity and Self-identity: Self and Society in the Late Modern Age*, Cambridge: Polity Press.

Glasser, I. (1994), *Homelessness in Global Perspective*, New York: G.H. Hall.

Greve, John (1997), 'Preface: homelessness then and now', in Roger Burrow, Nicolas Pleace and Deborah Quilgars (eds), *Homelessness and Social Policy*, London: Routledge, pp. xi–xvii.

Guzewicz, Tony D. (2000), *Tokyo's Homeless: A City in Denial*, Huntingdon, New York: Kroshka Books.

Hantrais, Linda and Dennis Ager (1985), 'The language barrier to effective cross-national research', in Linda Hantrais, Steen Mangen and Margaret O'Brien (eds), 'Doing cross-national research', *Cross-National Research Papers*, **1**(1), 29–40, Aston University, Birmingham, UK.

Hantrais, Linda and Steen Mangen (1996), *Cross-National Research Methods in the Social Sciences*, London: Pinter.

Harrison, Malcolm (1999), 'Theorising homelessness and race', in Patricia Kennett and Alex Marsh (eds), *Homelessness: Exploring the New Terrain*, Bristol: The Policy Press, pp. 101–21.

Harvey, Brian (1999), 'Models of resettlement for the homeless in the European Union', in Patricia Kennett and Alex Marsh (eds), *Homelessness: Exploring the New Terrain*, Bristol: The Policy Press, pp. 267–92.

Hoch, Charles (2000), 'Sheltering the homeless in the US: social improvement and the continuum of care', *Housing Studies*, **15**(6), 865–76.

Iyengar, Shanto (1993), 'Social research in developing countries', in Martin Bulmer and Donald P. Warwick (eds), *Social Research in Developing Countries*, London: UCL, pp. 173–82.

Jacobs, Keith, Jim Kemeny and Tony Manzi (1999), 'The struggle to define homelessness: a constructivist approach', in Susan Hutson and David Clapham (eds), *Homelessness: Public Policies and Private Troubles*, London: Cassell, pp. 11–28.

Jessop, Bob (1996), 'The entrepreneurial city: re-imaging localities, re-designing economic governance, or re-structuring capital?', Paper presented at *Urban Change and Conflict Conference*, Glasgow, January.

Kennett, Patricia and Alex Marsh (eds) (1999), *Homelessness: Exploring the New Terrain*, Bristol: The Policy Press.

Kennett, Patricia and Masami Iwata (2003), 'Precariousness in everyday life: homelessness in Japan', *International Journal of Urban and Regional Research*, **27**(1), 62–74.

Lewis, Jane (1999), 'The "problem" of lone motherhood in comparative perspective', in Jochen Clasen (ed.), *Comparative Social Policy: Concepts, Theories and Methods*, London: Blackwell, pp. 181–99.

Lisle, Edmond (1985), 'Validation in the social sciences by international comparison', *Cross-national Research Papers*, **1**(1), 11–28.

Marcuse, P. (1993), 'What's so new about divided cities?', *International Journal of Urban and Regional Research*, **17**(3), 355–65.

Marsh, Alex and Patricia Kennett (1999), 'Exploring the new terrain', in Patricia Kennett and Alex Marsh (eds), *Homelessness: Exploring the New Terrain*, Bristol: The Polity Press, pp. 1–15.

Marsh, R. (1967), *Comparative Sociology: A Codification of Cross-societal Analysis*, New York: Harcourt, Brace.

May, Tim (1997), *Social Research: Issues, Methods and Processes*, 2nd edition, Buckingham: Open University Press.

NCFH (National Campaign for the Homeless) (1986), Homelessness in the European Community, EEC Commission Seminar on Poverty and Homelessness, Cork.

Paugam, Serge (1995), 'The spiral of precariousness: a multidimensional approach to the process of social disqualification in France', in Graham Room (ed.), *Beyond the Threshold: The Measurement and Analysis of Social Exclusion*, Bristol: The Policy Press.

Pickvance, C.G. (1986), 'Comparative urban analysis and assumptions about causality', *International Journal of Urban and Regional Research*, **10**(2), 162–84.

Rose, R.(1991), 'Comparing forms of comparative analysis', *Political Studies*, vol. 39, 446–62.

Schuler-Walner, Gisela (1986), *Homelessness in the Federal Republic of Germany – a Contribution to the International Year of Shelter for the Homeless*, Institute of Housing and Environmental Research, Darmstadt.

Shelter (2000) *Housing and Homelessness in England: The Facts*, available at www.shelter.org.uk.

UNCHS (Habitat) (1996), *An Urbanising World. Global Report on Human Settlements*, Oxford: Oxford University Press.

UNCHS (Habitat) (2001), *Cities in a Globalizing World: Global Report on Human Settlements 2001*, London: Earthscan Publications

Warwick, Donald, P. and Samuel, Osherson (eds) (1973), *Comparative Research Methods*, Englewood Cliffs, NJ: Prentice Hall.

Watson, Sophie (1999), 'A home is where the heart is: engendering notions of homelessness', in Patricia Kennett and Alex Marsh (eds), *Homelessness: Exploring the New Terrain*, Bristol: The Policy Press.

Wilcox, Steven (2001), *Housing Finance Review 2000/2001 CIH/CML/JRF*, Coventry, London.

17 'Fit for purpose?' Qualitative methods in comparative social policy

Steen Mangen

Each person can only claim one aspect of our character as part of his knowledge. To everyone we turn a different face of the prism. (Lawrence Durrell, *Justine*, London, Faber & Faber, 1968, page 105)

As the chapter demonstrates, in the last decade qualitative methods have increasingly contributed to clarification of both theoretical concerns and social policy and planning agenda in cross-national settings. This review will examine research that crosses cultures and languages,[1] or in the case of single countries, investigations undertaken by a non-native. Among the issues to be addressed are the link between methods and theory, management of multinational teams, problems of language, sampling, selection of methods and the processing of data. The focus will largely be research within the European Union: apart from limitations of space, this choice is defended on the grounds that, in the period under consideration, there has been a substantial growth in the comparative enterprise in this region in all aspects: such as model building, hypothesis generation, more refined integration of qualitative and quantitative methods – an acceleration of the effort noted by Øyen (1990) in the 1970s and 1980s. This activity has been prosecuted under the direct or indirect stimulus of the construction of the European Union in line with the promotion of the convergence objective, prompting the search for 'lesson learning' based on more holistic evaluations that respect differences of culture, context and power (Mabbett and Bolderson, 1999). Beyond the EU imperative, comparative qualitative research in this region has also been both a response to and reflection of wider globalization.

What is distinctive about the cross-national approach is not the method per se but the focus on space and, often, time. By eschewing top-down, highly aggregated analyses that prioritize parsimony at the cost of meaning – a bias in too many global quantitative strategies – qualitative methods offer the possibilities of bottom-up, open-ended, flexible and exploratory formulae for understanding phenomena in different environments. Many of these methods seek to privilege the experiential comparative worlds of actors through the spoken or written word and entail a profound change in the traditional relations between researcher and researched. Indeed, a concern about these sensitivities is a notable feature of much recent comparative literature, and not simply that reporting interpretative methods, with the critical advantage being the real sense of dynamism that can be infused, both in method and analysis relating to welfare systems. This is, perhaps, particularly the case with biographic methods, although the case study focus, in general, offers the potential for a sensitive treatment of the cumulative impact of time as witnessed, for instance, in the imposing study by Baldwin (1990) of risk-sharing interest coalitions in determining the evolution of European social insurance. Equally beneficial is the scope for differentiating institutional stability of welfare systems from the effects of episodic political volatility, with implications for more effective assessment of the impact of socio-economic transformations on individuals and groups, embracing gender, age, class and ethnicity dimensions (Chamberlayne, 1997; Veit-Wilson, 2000).

A noticeable feature of recent qualitative projects has been the attempt to accommodate the linguistic, cultural and politico-institutional problematic by resort to multi-disciplinary input which has encouraged the integration of multiple methods, thereby, where feasible and appropriate, assisting the aim of triangulation.[2] Of course, such developments are not without costs, not least in terms of parsimony, with the inevitable expansion of the range of variables incorporated to match the widening of the research problem. Nonetheless, an audit of recent cross-national research activity would suggest considerable advances in the range of innovative, middle-range theory-driven methods and in processing capacities through software packages.[3] Admittedly, less reassuring in too much of the relevant literature is the impression that the scientific 'black box' remains at the level of 'coal-face' interpretation of the data, which unavoidably impacts on the validity and, indeed, objectivity of analytical presentation.

Linking methods, context and theory
The heart of the qualitative approach to comparative social policy is the explicit recognition of the dynamic plural, cultural attributes of welfare systems – at all tiers of governance – in determining the linkages between inputs, process and outcomes. It follows that deconstruction of 'whole systems' and investigation of interconnectedness across policy sectors should be to the fore, with an explicit respect for specificity, reflexivity and agency. Accordingly, for Ashenden (1999), qualitative methods, at their best, can serve as an antidote to a one-dimensional misapplication of overly generic concepts in what are diverse situations. This assists a more valid dissemination of differential popular, professional and bureaucratic values and interests *within* and *between* countries (Knowles, 1999; Rustin, 1999).

Several pragmatic solutions to contested interpretations of welfare processes across nations have been proposed. Tizot (2001), for example, postulates a 'case-centred' approach to comparative analysis by concentrating on the *operational* level of a specific policy sector. For him, this 'functional analysis' is especially indicated in sectors which manifest high international transfer – in his case urban problems and regeneration interventions: I could add de-institutionalization programmes in mental health (Mangen, 1985). This sectoral approach is also proposed by Esping-Anderson (1993), in response to critiques of his welfare regime analysis and, in particular, the narrow and relatively static approach to 'de-commodification'. Through it he argues the purchase of examining welfare sectors in terms of the wider interactive impact of families, civil society, the market and the state. Complementing this approach in terms of 'fit for specific purpose' is the suggestion by Svallfors (1997), among others, in favour of a cross-sectoral research design to investigate dimensions such as race and gender whose overall effect may significantly compromise conventional institutionally based 'welfare regime' distinctions. Such recommendations would go some way to remedying sampling errors due to the fluidity of 'boundary specification' in standard classifications. Furthermore, they may alleviate what Abrahamson (1999) complains is a negative 'propinquity factor', his example being other Scandinavians who find the Swedo-centric conceptual equivalence of the Nordic democratic model problematic. They would also counter a 'league table' interpretation of welfare states by more specifically addressing the quality (rather than quantity) of welfare through examining actual experiences of social citizenship.

These kinds of difficulties, of course, arise directly from the practical limits of sample size: in typical qualitative comparative research arenas a variety of factors conspire to expand the range of variables included, whilst restricting the number of countries or localities sampled which tend to be heavily reliant on preconceived systemic classifications. The consequences are data management dilemmas due to high intra-class variation: in other words, how to cope with very different 'sames' (Nissen, 1998; Johnson and Rake, 1998). The most cited example of these problems is the 'conservative corporatist' welfare regime of Esping-Andersen (1990) which includes countries with as diverse a welfare history as Spain, France and Germany.

Cross-national qualitative sampling, then, has to take account of the interaction between the *unit* and the *level* of analysis which is all the more important in the move from large to small numbers of cases and the consequent problems of specifying the relationship between dependent and independent variables (Ragin, 1987). The case study, of course, permits the retention of a wide range of factors and, by privileging causal linkages, has remained pivotal for hypothesizing in international contexts. Its advantages are well aired in the literature: for instance, its eminent flexibility and the ease of incorporating a range of methods, including quantitative data. Nissen (1998) has surveyed the strengths and limitations of a variety of approaches: atheoretical case studies where description is paramount; an interstitial theory 'confirming' or 'infirming' framework; with the ultimate being interpretive and hypothesis-generating case studies. In comparative research the latter have proven particularly insightful in highlighting deviant cases. Nonetheless, there have been extensive critiques of case studies in terms of limited possibilities for the production of generalizable data: Heidenheimer and his colleagues (1990) are among the many who assert that the consequence is a failure to generate valid comparators for cross-national treatment. On the other hand, detailed critical case studies put context right at the heart of the enterprise, facilitating an examination of how endogenous and exogenous factors may interact. For Wilson (2001) they aid a real incorporation of power relations: whose history or culture counts? To be sure, context may be more important at different stages of the research act than at others: Chamberlayne and Spanò (2000), for example, adopted a flexible approach in their biographic study of risk strategies (see below): in the early stages of their interpretation micro-dynamic processes were the prime concern, whilst later the wider context was central. However, both Revauger (2001a) and Tizot (2001) caution against an excessive concentration on context which could lead to mere essentialism and the neglect of extraneous 'converging' impacts on social policies. Sartori (1978) puts forward a reconciliation of these considerations through the construction of a tailor-made 'ladder of abstraction', prompting the researcher to make explicit trade-offs between empirical 'extension' (denotation) and analytic 'intension' (connotation). The benefits for Sartori are the reductions of the dangers of 'conceptual stretching' in which culture-bound interpretations are imposed on cross-national data. His preference is for one of the middle rungs: that is, a medium-level of abstraction in order to develop what he terms, more robust intermediate categories permitting the integration of relevant material from higher and lower down the analytic scale, thereby retaining contextual relevance – the strength of critical case studies – while searching for generalizations – the strength of middle-range theories.

Managing collaboration, aegis and language

That most immediately pragmatic cross-national research design, the 'safari' method, has been a favoured, often initial-phase, strategy particularly employed for research themes with a relatively well-defined problematic and where the impact of intervening cultural factors may already be well understood. Safaris have normally taken the form of national or international teams undertaking brief stays in the country of investigation, with the typical aim of engaging in elite interviews and collection of documentation. Whilst undoubtedly cheap in terms of time, the possible overcoming of language problems, the securing of responder compliance and the enhanced access to information, there are several limitations. There are dangers that the technique descends into the 'touristic', reliant on steretypes, engaging only with respondents who reflect official discourse, and naïve to the different values of professional cultures that affect policy implementation styles. These problems are compounded in the common situation where investigators wish respondents to be both interviewees, gatekeepers, the source of advice and a launch-pad for 'snowballing'.

Often building on the safari, the hitherto conventional approach of EU-sponsored research has entailed 'parallel' reports prepared by national experts accompanied by a collaborative comparative synthesis. Rapid generation of data is an obvious advantage. Furthermore, many studies report the invaluable contextual explanations provided by national teams. The research environment promoted by EU institutions, with tight funding, strict and often hastily imposed deadlines, contractual obligations to include all member states, and so on, will ensure the approach a certain longevity, but these constraints should be factored into research designs. This being said, there has recently been a welcome move away from parallel description to more integrated analysis and formal evaluation since there can be no argument that 'parallel' methods fall short of the ideal. The demands for rapid execution of international projects exacerbates fundamental differences in research approaches: Galtung (1982) has parodied divergent intellectual styles in Europe and beyond (see Linda Hantrais, Chapter 14, this volume) which can severely frustrate effective collaboration. In this regard, Ettore (2000) recounts her experience of being the lead manager in an undisclosed EU project which is redolent of the politics of networking, problems of power relations, the different prestige and motivations of professionals and researchers in the selected countries, the effects of opting for a dominant language and the differential status internationally of 'applied' research. She presents a strong case for mentoring and explicit training for which she proposes a framework of objectives.

Parallel strategies, by exploiting aegis, may, of course, afford privileged access to research material. The issue of aegis has been the object of considerable discussion in the international literature. On the one hand, the independent researcher may be isolated and encounter serious problems with access and may, perforce, have to rely on lengthy 'snowballing' tactics which may compromise original research aims (Zulauf, 2001). On the other hand, aegis can be a mixed blessing by imposing preconditions and steering access. This proved the case in a UK–USSR investigation of child care where the collaboration of Soviet officialdom frustratingly restricted the freedom to consult (Harwin, 1987). Similarly, Jones Finer (2000) records the cost of privileged access to a personal archive where serious differences of opinion between the researcher and the object of the research (an internationally well-respected worker with Neapolitan street children) was compounded by her admitted relative ignorance of the machinations of the local political environment.

Apart from coping with aegis, a central problem of comparative research is the treatment of language and, in particular, issues about translation and the use of interpreters. Some investigators try to avoid these limitations by selecting only native tongue documentation or respondents with a knowledge of their language. However, the latter option puts the onus on interviewees and may not necessarily eradicate a knowledge of their language if the researcher is not to be misled: in my own experience, respondents who are eager to 'practise their English' – assisting access, of course – may rely on many 'false friends' in translations; in my cross-national study of inner city regeneration, I recall several Spanish respondents referring to the 'deception' of the socialist government in urban policy, simply because 'deception' is a false friend of the English 'disappointment'. There is also the additional problem of differential change in meanings among languages: the elements of what are contemporarily understood by 'urban regeneration' spring to mind. As a general guideline, investigators should not foist responsibility for language problems on the respondent, even if this means exploiting a relatively limited command of language or even the interpolation of translated key terms in interviews conducted in their native language.

The use of interpreters is inevitably more intrusive than translation. Jentsch (1998) provides an extensive discussion of their various effects: including the imposition of distance between the researcher and researched, choice of a fellow national or native, interpreter-led translation, and the value of recording interviews for subsequent third-party verification.

Beyond the data collection stage, several researchers have urged retaining multilingual texts for processing and analysis: Lisle (1985) proposes 'polygonal syntheses' – bilateral analyses of several languages; Ungerson (1996), if not multilingual publication, then at least its retention until the write-up stage; Revauger (2001a) suggests leaving problematic terms untranslated.

Whatever the pragmatic device adopted, reliance on translation and interpreters is always a second-best option impoverishing the quality of analysis, albeit one of necessity, given expanding international research remits. The investigator remains naïve to the subtle cognitive, connotational and functional specificities of language such as metaphor, litotes, aphorisms, euphemisms, hyperbole, innuendo and irony are neglected. Crucially, s/he cannot independently verify the processed material by means of supplementary contextual sources. Nor is the growing English language domination of the international agenda necessarily a salvation: Chamberlayne and colleagues (2000) worry about the perversities of an English-based 'Eurospeak' giving the semblance of common terminology whilst undermining subtle, cultural differences in meanings. This Anglo-Saxon hegemony is evident, for instance, in the international imposition of the concept of 'gender' which has been loosely translated into languages where it does not possess strict linguistic equivalence (Letablier, 1989). The wider issue of power relations in translation and the social construction of meaning is taken up by Wilson (2001), for whom they are central to the post-modernist problematic of cross-national social policy.

Sampling 'fit for purpose'

The matter of sample selection of countries in comparative qualitative research is rendered even more paramount by the exigencies of the typically limited range incorporated. Most commentators argue the case for a 'most similar' selection to test for specificity, with perhaps the inclusion of 'within-system' deviant cases to extend interpretive capacities. 'Most similar' methods aim to test for specificity. There are seductive arguments favouring this approach: for example, in research sensitive to expressed emotion the responses of near neighbours may seem easier to interpret. Furthermore, 'most similar' strategies tend to cope better with problems of functional, conceptual and contextual equivalence, although even here significant differences have been noted: for example in meanings of welfare terms in France and Britain (Revauger, 2001b) and the functional equivalence of 'nursing' in Britain and Germany (Zulauf, 2001). In comparison, 'least similar' strategies for welfare research, testing for universalities, are typically more costly and usually more speculative. However, Manning (1993) is among those who castigate resorting to the 'most similar' sampling base for its implicit reliance on welfare typologies that have been too narrowly drawn, thereby eliminating key variables where significant variance may be located. A similar line is taken by Kennett (2001) who sees in the over-dependence on the technique the danger that objects of sampling which do not fit preconceived suppositions will tend to be neglected, with evident consequences for 'lesson learning'. And Nissen (1998) warns of difficulties in interpreting variance in the targeted phenomenon in cases of close sequential causation: that is, where the object of study is present in a country because it has already occurred in a near-neighbour.

Choosing amongst methods

This discussion is necessarily limited to assessing methods that are most commonly employed in comparative social policy research[4] and refers to the degree of intrusiveness of design, cultural acceptability, ease of access and management.

Largely for practical reasons, and particularly where research is concerned with meso and macro-level policy-making, documentary material may be the only feasible means of investigation. Documentary research is one of the least intrusive, relatively cheap and eminently flexible methods: one can set one's own research pace; re-consult; re-analyse and disaggregate for sensitized content analysis. Computer scanning and software packages can be a vital aid for the rapid incorporation of large volumes of material and for 'whole text' analyses. These practicalities aside, the prime consideration has to be the social contexts in which documents are produced. Documentary and archival material is, by definition, selective in total coverage, highly edited and structured to serve specific purposes, which entails extra work on the part of the researcher in terms of wider contextualization in order to avoid naïve interpretation. Aegis is important here: whether documents are produced by officialdom or by pressure groups, for example. Depending on its nature there may be problems of corroborating evidence. Jones Finer (2000), in working through the personal archive referred to earlier, complains of a lack of independent commentary covering the whole period, as well as the need for a prolonged grounding in the local political scenario. There has been a growing resort within documentary research to 'grey literature': unofficial or semi-official, often ephemeral material with limited circulation. Contextualization is even more important in this framework and it has generally been employed in combination with interviews with experts and users. This was the case in a study of elder care in Britain and Germany (Schunk, 1996) and in my project on inner city regeneration in the EU (Mangen, 2004). Survey methods in international settings, whilst frequently the only means of obtaining data, often encounter the problems of differential response rates. Snowballing, albeit imposing costs as discussed earlier, is, nevertheless, a pragmatic means of reaching more respondents, especially where research relates to sensitive subjects. Commonly, surveys rely on questionnaires. Their advantages lie in the ability to test variants of the schedule, and to engage in forward and backward translation with obvious advantages in terms of contributing to the establishment of acceptable levels of inter-rater reliability. Yet, there are several considerations to bear in mind in their use in comparative research. Consent to respond to informal questionnaires can vary significantly among cultures and sub-cultures. This reluctance to comply has been noted in former totalitarian regimes such as Russia (Chubarova, 2002), although it undoubtedly applies more generally. Problems may be exacerbated by the request for supplementary tape recording, an issue also relevant to other methods. Questionnaires may be the victim of subtle differences in cultural specificity: questions may not convey the same meaning, with implications for the range of responses elicited. This is especially problematic when using fixed formats, although problems may be alleviated if they are supplemented by clarificatory interviews. For these reasons the World Health Organization employs multinational 'quality of life' questionnaires to avoid a particular cultural domination in content (Serra-Sutton and Herdman, 2001). Another solution, proposed by Hantrais (1989), is for a battery of questions around one theme, particularly when the aim is to combine subjective and objective measures.

Serra-Sutton and Herdman (2001) make the case for the translation of well-established questionnaires, both on cost grounds and the fact that, if reliability and validity are established, they can facilitate a more rapid international comparison. Forward and backward translation is essential for determining the reliability of linguistic, semantic and cultural equivalence. They suggest that two translations are best undertaken either by professionals or bilingual translators whose mother tongue is the target language, to assess equivalence, supported by 'expert' verification, either through focus groups or panels, with the aim of reconciling differences in order to arrive at an agreed third version. Hayashi and colleagues (1992) provide detailed examples of forward and backward translation techniques of questionnaires, as between Japanese and English, including problems of questions that could not be understood, even when 'properly' translated.

Apart from documents and questionnaires, the favoured qualitative method design is the semi- or relatively unstructured in-depth interview. In cross-national terms there are two overarching considerations: the degree of intrusiveness and, as already discussed in relation to questionnaires, response equivalence. In this approach linguistic competence is paramount. For many research themes prior consultation of extensive contextual material is also indispensable. Few international projects rely on an entirely unstructured method, although biographical techniques, discussed below, may come close. Whatever their format, in-depth interviews are time consuming – other things being equal, with implications for sample size – and raise ethical questions about expectations of time devoted by the respondent. In general, the non-native interviewer working in a second language is likely to be in a more passive position than a native and must confront the stress involved in exposing lack of linguistic or cultural competence. The potential for these 'distortions' in data collection should be factored into the analysis.

The biographical approach to intensive interviewing offers significant purchase in comparative frameworks through its focus on unravelling linkages between individuals and welfare processes internationally. This stems directly from the appreciation of the plurality of experiences, agency and, critically, reflexivity and, at its best, contributes to post-modernist, non-reductionist interpretations of welfare (Kennett, 2001). The approach seems eminently suitable, for example, for investigations of the complexities of social exclusion, given that this represents a process of external discrediting of personal biographies and disengagement from access to valued resources.

A commendable series of investigations derives from the 'Sostris' project which examined individuals' confrontation of a range of risks arising from socio-economic transformations in seven EU countries. The Sostris studies ambitiously attempt to link structure and agency in a concrete fashion, through what the authors term interpretive 'socio-biographic' techniques. The Sostris team claim that this offers a more effective exploitation of grounded theory which, hitherto, has been too rooted in 'micro' singularity; in contrast they examine the link with 'macro' structural dimensions connecting families, localities, regions, nations and the more global level. Interviews with subjects of risk management are supplemented by a similar method engaging leading members of new innovative 'flagship' agencies serving the targeted clientele. The approach offered the potential for an effective management of time perspectives, with biographies documenting experiences of social change, privileging reflexivity and the locating of the individual in their past, present and likely future. Although largely non-directive, interviewing methods were sufficiently standardized to avoid undesired international variation in application (Chamberlayne and Rustin, 1999; Chamberlayne et al., 2000).

The Sostris collaborators emphasize that their method combined the potentials of relatively unstructured data collection with a well-defined process for analysis, recorded and transcribed interviews being intensively and sequentially interpreted, typically by a team of national researchers. In this way, hypotheses and contextual issues could be introduced and assessed in a systematic, stage-by-stage manner.

Admittedly, Sostris' prime sample for intense data processing amounted to only 50 respondents spread over six risk categories (such as redundancy and lone parenthood), although material from the remaining 250 interviews was used for further background. As the authors concede, there was a danger that even the limited briefing that respondents were given about the interview could have introduced biases. In particular, the potential to over-dramatize events could not be entirely discounted. Intensive interviewing of this kind is, of necessity, intrusive and may only be productive through manifestly high levels of empathetic relations between researcher and researched. This carries the danger of positive 'halo effects': respondents may edit their narratives to portray the most socially acceptable or 'helpful' image to the interviewer, a conscious or unconscious tendency in which Durrell's observation heading this chapter undoubtedly plays a part. There is, as the authors acknowledge, the limitation that certain types of respondents could not be reached by this approach. Finally, the need for empathy and the background of the interviewer could preclude certain types of research topics being undertaken: sexual crime springs to mind.

Vignettes, brief case scenarios composed from fictional or true life predicaments, have gained increasing currency as a comparative quasi-experimental method. Projects adopting them have made substantial inroads into challenging their reputation as a makeshift method and, given their economic use of scarce research resources, in a globalizing social policy research environment, they are likely to prove increasingly attractive. There appear to be convincing benefits accruing to their adoption, not least their contribution to hypothesis generation. Among the many other advantages cited are flexibility in the pre-determined degree of refinement and specification of details, and a less intrusive method for respondents who, through the maintenance of depersonalization, are reassured that their confidentiality is being maintained, thus stimulating a higher response rate. In this regard, Schoenberg and Ravdal (2000) discuss studies about health promotion in sensitive areas where vignettes overcame problems of cross-cultural communication.

This being said, Johnson and Rake (1998) complain of the markedly reduced capacity to make valid generalizations, given that responses may be sensitive to the artificially narrow, perhaps stereotypical, specification of predicaments. Moreover, cross-national problematics may demand adaptation in the depiction of representative cases to suit national circumstances, with the potential loss of comparability. Barter and Renold (2000) note the conflict between the benefit of the non-directiveness of case depiction, prompting respondents to provide contextual information on how they arrived at assessments, and the scope for encouraging socially desirable responses. A further problem may arise from respondents' reluctance to make assessments due to a lack of specificity about what can be perceived by them as artificial description (Schoenberg and Ravdal, 2000). Pre-testing and semi-structured interviews for elucidation could help to counter these problems, as might the test–retest and back translation methods involving user–professional dimensions, as described in international studies of child protection (Cooper, 2000) and divorce (Bastard et al., 1989).

As a general assessment, in cross-national settings, it appears that the vignette works best with professional samples where there is a high level of shared practice (for example Soydan, 1996). However, Warman and Millar (1996) repeat a relatively frequent observation that it can be the least successful component of research design, due to a lack of clarity on the part of respondents about what kind of responses are being elicited.

Comparative evaluation

Evaluative research is the most difficult comparative qualitative enterprise; in particular, prospective experimental methods are largely unrealistic in a majority of international settings. This being said, there have been growing funding incentives to undertake evaluation. Attention has been paid to reducing real scientific problems through, for example, greater consideration of the role of evaluators: their distance from the research setting, and the cost–benefits of neutral passivity or a more active involvement. A noticeable feature of the contemporary research agenda – mirroring the emphasis on bottom-up participatory social planning, as opposed to top-down interventions – is the attempt effectively to incorporate stakeholders at all stages of research activity. Greene (2001) strongly affirms that this new-found 'insider–outsider' dialogue is essential for inclusive engagement, principally to understand power relations in data generation: in short, it is part of the democratization of the research act. Moreover, it can strengthen the commitment of all stakeholders, in part by aiding mutual understanding of the variety of motives at play in any environment; it also promotes post-modernist assessment, incorporating uncertainty and diversity into the evaluative act.

In some measure, insider–outsider (IO) evaluation may go some way to reassuring Cooper (2000) who asserts that until 'the relationship between outcomes and reflexive understandings within particular complex cultural systems is better understood ... comparative "outcome" study is likely to produce more harm than good' (p. 105). Bartunek and Louis (1996) have extensively reviewed the benefits of IO approaches, including easing access to the research site and sustained cooperation. They describe management tactics ranging from the treatment of equality between the parties and a partial or differential IO format for particular stages of the research act when confidentiality, for example, could be a concern. The model espoused by Baslé (2000) is claimed to permit iteration in the evaluatory act and, thereby, a sensitive understanding of causal mediation. Similar assertions are made by Kuipers and Richardson (1999) who maintain that IO methods combine an open qualitative strategy with constant active dialogue with participants, permitting mutual learning by both parties through the retention of the critical link with ground-level experience: in this way differences of experience become an essential part of the problematic. And, by incorporating implicit or 'local' theories, which are brought to the heart of the research, alongside the more generalizable theories of the evaluator, IO techniques have the potential for generating more diverse evaluative scenarios or, as Bartunek and Louis (1996) put it, 'interpretive lenses'. These latter authors sum up the strength of the IO strategy as offering the insight of the 'marginal person' – no participant in the interaction being either fully inside or outside – the outcome being a reduced risk of 'context-free generalizations'. There is space here to cite only two relevant studies in this tradition. The evaluation by Saraceno (1999) of the EU 'LEADER' rural development initiative concluded that participation is especially important in identifying locally defined objectives and actions required by stakeholders from different perspectives within horizontal and vertical partnerships. This was vital in order to formulate, monitor and provide effective feedback in area-based interventions. She argues the primacy of qualitative methods in this context because what was important was process: how innovation came about, how networks were strengthened and how empowerment was achieved. Her methods, she claims, preserve the integrity of disaggregated data to match the scientific challenge of territorial diversity. Hetherington (1999), in a qualitative investigation of French and English child protection, recounts that an IO approach was employed to stimulate practitioners and service users to interpret their own experiences in the light of processes of the counterpart welfare regime: everyone was simultaneously a research subject and a researcher.

It must be said that leadership in some cross-national IO projects has proved an issue, particularly in sustaining close working relations in conflictual environments. Here, where there may be almost irreconcilable differences of perspectives and values, the approach is tested to the limit. Hundt (2000), for example, reports a study of maternal and child health services in Gaza and the Negev, where the consideration of local, national and international sensitivities was paramount. She notes that this extended even to the level of the political descriptors for geographical units. Contested discourse and meanings dogged all stages of the research, including the versions of the final publications sanctioned.

Processing and interpreting the data
In all but a few studies, at the data processing phase qualitative data in whatever form are converted into text which, of course, is also the principal medium for its dissemination. This stage requires careful management, in order to avoid too 'heavy' an attempt to impose highly structured harmonized coding on comparative data which, rather than contributing to highlighting meaning, may actually fragment it (Coffey and Atkinson, 1996). The work of Ragin (1987) has stimulated considerable discussion about processing strategies, especially with regard to separating 'variable' and 'case' coding. In this regard, for the Sostris team, the 'case-oriented' strategy, rather than a 'variable-oriented' approach, proved one of the most rewarding experiences in undertaking their comparative study of risk and social policy (Chamberlayne and Spanò, 2000).

Sivesind (1999) promotes what he terms his 'structured qualitative comparison' which introduces formalized distinctions between 'variable' and 'theme' coding on the one hand and 'code' and 'content-oriented' analysis on the other. He argues that variable coding of text content should be avoided, since this reduces multi-dimensional data to a single dimension. However, variable coding of background information is recommended, together with theme coding of the text content, without this corruption. In this way the many potential levels of meaning can be preserved throughout the research process. Sivesind maintains that by overcoming the problem of 'singularity' – non-hypothesis generating description that applies only to the cases studied – and by achieving a content analysis not oriented towards an imposed pattern of codes, grounded theory is not reduced to a function of the narrow 'data' but is liberated to interact more effectively with wider context.

Final comments

In assessing 'fit for purpose' some things are clear: apart from rare ideal situations, cross-national qualitative research involves compromises about the problematic, unit and level of investigation, methods employed, processing of material and subsequent analysis, to say nothing about dissemination.

Scepticism about a lack of transparency – and, hence, ease of reproduction of the methods employed – leads to the accusation that qualitative approaches are 'soft' in terms of various dimensions of reliability and validity or are, at best, preliminary to 'harder' quantitative strategies, a viewpoint rejected here. However, methods such as documentary research which eliminate interaction between investigator and data producer, whilst being less intrusive, are, as I have argued, a mixed blessing. On the other hand the more intrusive methods, such as in-depth interviewing or observation, may require an empathy between researcher and the researched that renders them unsuitable for certain types of problematic, either because of the problem of accessing subjects or effectively interacting with them. These kinds of considerations strengthen the argument for multiple methods and, allied to this, the rejection of any rigid and unproductive ideological preference for qualitative over quantitative approaches.

As for trajectories for qualitative methods, Wilson (2001) has speculated about the scope for future extensive exploitation of the Internet; certainly the growing and easy availability of mass qualitative data sets offers virtually countless opportunities to engage in comparative investigations. She foresees the prospect of multilingual tools aiding instant access to archives throughout the world. In this increasingly realistic scenario what constitutes 'fit for purpose' becomes ever more critical.

Notes

1. There can be some compensation between opting for geographical propinquity while coping with the consequences of language difference. In fact, whilst language differences are certainly exacerbated by distance, there is equally the potential that cultural differences may be underestimated among far-flung countries ostensibly speaking the same language.
2. Kelle (2001) reviews literature and provides examples cautioning against naïve attempts to achieve triangulation.
3. Lee and Esterhuizen (2000) provide a brief review of computer software packages, as well as assessing their general potential – the ability to handle large volumes of data, mass entry of written material, in part through the use of scanners – and pitfalls – set-up costs and the mass generation of non-theoretically grounded categorizations. Extensive information on packages is available at http://caqdas.soc.surrey.ac.uk/.

    Personal experience of processing documentary and interview material prompts me to cite NUD*IST, now in its fifth version as N5. This proved capable of coping with enormous amounts of multilingual texts in various formats and offered rapid and easy coding procedures. From the same company comes the newer NVivo, advertised as offering fine-detailed analysis. NVivo can import directly from word processor files and, among other things, can link to multi-media files (for example tapes). It offers a range of visual displays of theoretical linkages. I am informed that the software is particularly adaptable in coping with non-European scripts. However, it is limited to 1000 documents.

There is no doubt that software packages are a major innovation in qualitative research particularly in grounded theorizing, although Richards and Richards (1995), authors of NUD*IST, provide cautionary examples of the unreflective misuse of the data disaggregation potential of their programme.

4. Omitted are ethnographic and/or participant observation, diaries and biographies, panel studies, group or focus group material, as well as a range of audio-visual sources, including the Internet and CD roms. One readily available source – newspapers – argues MacGregor (1993) can provide valuable insights into widely circulating semantics about social policy, her example being social exclusion.

References

Abrahamson, P. (1999), 'The welfare modelling business', *Social Policy & Administration*, **33**(4), 394–415.

Ashenden, Samantha (1999), 'Habermas on discursive consensus: rethinking the welfare state in the face of cultural pluralism', in Prue Chamberlayne, Andrew Cooper, Richard Freeman and Michael Rustin (eds), *Welfare and Culture in Europe: Towards a New Paradigm in Social Policy*, London: Jessica Kingsley, pp. 216–39.

Baldwin, Peter (1990), *The Politics of Social Solidarity – Class Bases of European Welfare States: 1875–1975*, Cambridge: Cambridge University Press.

Barter, C. and E. Renold (2000), '"I wanna tell you a story": Exploring the application of vignettes in qualitative research with children and young people', *International Journal of Social Research Methodology*, **3**(4), 307–23.

Bartunek, Jean M. and Meryl Reis Louis (1996), *Insider/Outsider Team Research*, Qualitative Research Methods Series, No 40. London: Sage.

Baslé, M. (2000), 'Comparative analysis of quantitative and qualitative methods in French non-experimental evaluation of regional and local policies', *Evaluation*, **6**(3), 323–34.

Bastard, B., C. Vonèche and M. Maclean (1989), 'Women's resources after divorce: Britain and France', *Cross-National Research Papers*, **1**(5), 29–38.

Chamberlayne, P. (1997), 'Social exclusion: sociological traditions and national contexts', *Sostris Working Paper No 1: Social Strategies in Risk Societies*, pp. 1–11.

Chamberlayne Prue and Michael Rustin (1999), *From Biography to Social Policy: Final Report of the SOSTRIS Project*, London: University of East London.

Chamberlayne, P. and A. Spanò (2000), 'Modernisation as lived experience: contrasting case studies from the SOSTRIS project', in Prue Chamberlayne, Joanna Bornat and Tom Wengraf (eds), *The Turn to Biographical Methods in Social Science: Comparative Issues and Examples*, London: Routledge, pp. 321–36.

Chamberlayne, P., J. Bornat and T. Wengraf (2000), 'Introduction: the biographical turn', in Prue Chamberlayne, Joanna Bornat and Tom Wengraf (eds), *The Turn to Biographical Methods in Social Science: Comparative Issues and Examples*, London: Routledge, pp. 1–30.

Chubarova, Tatiana (2002), *Occupational Welfare in Russia with Special Reference to Health Care*, University of London Ph.D.

Coffey, A. and Atkinson, P. (1996), *Making Sense of Qualitative Data: Complementary Research Strategies*, London: Sage.

Cooper, Andrew (2000), 'The vanishing point of resemblance: comparative welfare as philosophical anthropology', in Prue Chamberlayne, Joanna Bornat and Tom Wengraf (eds), *The Turn to Biographical Methods in Social Science: Comparative Issues and Examples*, London: Routledge, pp. 90–108.

Esping-Andersen, Gøsta (1990), *The Three Worlds of Welfare Capitalism*, Cambridge: Polity.

Esping-Andersen, Gøsta (1993), 'The comparative macro-sociology of welfare states', in Luis Moreno (ed.), *Social Exchange and Welfare Development*, Madrid: Consejo Superior de Investigaciones Científicas, pp. 123–36.

Ettore, E. (2000), 'Recognizing diversity and group processes in international, collaborative research work: a case study', *Social Policy & Administration*, **34**(4), 392–407.

Galtung, J. (1982, 'On the meaning of "nation" as a variable', in Manfred Niessen and Jules

Peschar (eds), *International Comparative Research: Problems of Theory, Methodology and Organisation in Eastern and Western Europe*, Oxford: Pergamon, pp. 17–34.

Greene, J.C. (2001), 'Dialogue in evaluation: a relational perspective', *Evaluation*, **7**(2), 181–7.

Hantrais, L. (1989), 'Approaches to cross-national comparison', *Cross-National Research Papers*, Special Issue, pp. 9–19.

Harwin, J. (1987), 'Child care in the USSR and England and Wales: some theoretical and practical issues', *Cross-National Research Papers*, **1**(4), 43–56.

Hayashi, Chikio, Tatsuzo Suzuki and Masamichi Sasaki (1992), *Data Analysis for Comparative Social Research: International Perspectives*, Amsterdam: Elsevier.

Heidenheimer, Arnold, Hugh Heclo and Carolyn Teich (1990), *Comparative Public Policy: The Politics of Social Change*, London: Macmillan.

Hetherington, Rachael (1999), 'Patients' experiences of child welfare in England and France: getting help and having rights', in Prue Chamberlayne, Andrew Cooper, Richard Freeman and Michael Rustin (eds), *Welfare and Culture in Europe: Towards a New Paradigm in Social Policy*, London: Jessica Kingsley, pp. 118–31.

Hundt, G.L. (2000), 'Multiple scripts and contested discourse', *Social Policy & Administration*, **34**(4), 419–33.

Jentsch, B. (1998), 'The "interpreter effect": rendering interpreters visible in cross-cultural research and methodology', *Journal of European Social Policy*, **8**(4), 275–89.

Johnson, P. and K. Rake (1998), 'Comparative social policy research in Europe', *Social Policy Review*, **10**, 257–78.

Jones Finer, C. (2000), 'Researching a contemporary archive', *Social Policy & Administration*, **34**(4), 434–47.

Kelle, U. (2001), 'Sociological explanations between micro and macro and the integration of qualitative and quantitative methods', *Forum: Qualitative Social Research*, **2**(1), (on-line journal available at: http://qualitative-research.net/fqs/fqs-eng.htm).

Kennett, Patricia (2001), *Comparative Social Policy*, Buckingham: Open University Press.

Knowles, Caroline (1999), 'Cultural perspectives and welfare regimes: the contributions of Foucault and Lefebvre', in Prue Chamberlayne, Andrew Cooper, Richard Freeman and Michael Rustin (eds), *Welfare and Culture in Europe: Towards a New Paradigm in Social Policy*, London: Jessica Kingsley, pp. 240–54.

Kuipers, H. and R. Richardson (1999), 'Active qualitative evaluation: core elements and procedures', *Evaluation*, **5**(1), 61–79.

Lee, R.M. and L. Esterhuizen (2000), 'Computer software and qualitative analysis: trends, issues and resources', *International Journal of Social Research Methodology*, **3**(3), 231–43.

Letablier, M-T. (1989), 'Women's work and employment in France and Britain: problems of comparability from a French perspective', *Cross-National Research Papers*, Special Issue, pp. 24–33.

Lisle, E. (1985), 'Validation in the social sciences by international comparison', *Cross-National Research Papers*, **1**(1), 29–40.

Mabbett, D. and H. Bolderson, (1999) 'Theories and methods in comparative social policy', in Jochen Clasen (ed.), *Comparative Social Policy: Concepts, Theories and Methods*, Oxford: Blackwell, pp. 34–56.

MacGregor, S. (1993), 'The semantics of urban poverty', *Cross-National Research Papers*, **3**(2), 65–78.

Mangen, Steen (1985), *Mental health care in the European community*, London: Croom Helm.

Mangen, S.P. (2004), *Social Exclusion and Inner City Europe: Regulating Urban Regeneration*, Basingstoke: Palgrave.

Manning, N. (1993), 'The impact of the EC on social policy at national level: the case of Denmark, France and the UK', *Cross-National Research Papers*, **3**(1), 15–32.

Nissen, S. (1998), 'The case of case studies: on methodological discussion in comparative political science', *Quality and Quantity*, vol. 32, 399–418.

Øyen, Else (1990) (ed.), *Comparative Methodology: Theory and Practice in International Social Research*, London: Sage.

Ragin, Charles C. (1987), *The Comparative Method: Moving beyond Qualitative and Quantitative Strategies*, Berkeley: University of California Press.

Revauger, J.P. (2001a), 'Editorial', *International Journal of Social Research Methodology*, **4**(4), 261–4.

Revauger, J.P. (2001b), 'Translating English and French social policy concepts: a personal view from France', *International Journal of Social Research Methodology*, **4**(4), 327–38.

Richards, T. and L. Richards (1995), 'Using hierarchical categories in qualitative data analysis', in Udo Kelle, Gerald Prein and Katherine Bird (eds), *Computer Aided Qualitative Data Analysis: Theory, Methods and Practices*, London: Sage, pp. 80–95.

Rustin, Michael (1999), 'Missing dimensions in the culture of welfare', in Prue Chamberlayne, Andrew Cooper, Richard Freeman and Michael Rustin (eds), *Welfare and Culture in Europe: Towards a New Paradigm in Social Policy*, London: Jessica Kingsley, pp. 255–74.

Saraceno, E. (1999), 'The evaluation of local policy-making in Europe: learning from the LEADER community initiative', *Evaluation*, **10**(5), 439–57.

Sartori, G. (1978), 'Faulty concepts', in Paul Lewis, David Potter and Francis Castles (eds), *The Practice of Comparative Politics: A Reader*, London: Longman, pp. 228–65.

Schoenberg, N.E. and H. Ravdal (2000), 'Using vignettes in awareness and attitudinal research', *International Journal of Social Research Methodology*, **3**(1), 63–74.

Schunk, Michaela (1996), 'Constructing models of the welfare mix: care options of frail elders', in Linda Hantrais and Steen Mangen (eds), *Cross-National Research Methods in the Social Sciences*, London: Pinter, pp. 84–94.

Serra-Sutton, V. and M. Herdman (2001), 'Methodology of cross-cultural adaptation of instruments for measuring health related quality of life', *Informatiu AATM* (Catalan Agency for Health Technology Assessment and Research), vol. 24, 18–20.

Sivesind, K.H. (1999), 'Structured, qualitative comparison: between singularity and single-dimensionality', *Quality & Quantity*, vol. 33, 361–80.

Soydan, H. (1996), 'Using the vignette method in cross-cultural comparisons', in Linda Hantrais and Steen Mangen (eds), *Cross-National Research Methods in the Social Sciences*, London: Pinter, pp. 120–28.

Svallfors, S. (1997), 'Worlds of welfare and attitudes to redistribution: a comparison of eight Western nations', *European Sociological Review*, vol. 13, 283–304.

Tizot, J.Y. (2001), 'The issues of translation, transferability and transfer of social policies: French and British "Urban Social Policy": finding common ground for comparison?', *International Journal of Social Research Methodology*, **4**(4), 301–17.

Ungerson, Clare (1996), 'Qualitative methods', in Linda Hantrais and Steen Mangen (eds), *Cross-National Research Methods in the Social Sciences*, London: Pinter, pp. 63–5.

Veit-Wilson, J. (2000), 'States of welfare: a conceptual challenge', *Social Policy & Administration*, **34**(1), 1–25.

Warman, A. and J. Millar (1996), 'Researching family obligations: some reflections on methodology', *Cross-National Research Papers*, **4**(4), 23–31.

Wilson, G. (2001), 'Power and translation in social policy research', *International Journal of Social Research Methodology*, **4**(4), 319–26.

Zulauf, Monika (2001), *Migrant Women Professionals in the European Union*, Basingstoke: Palgrave.

18 The quantitative method in comparative research

Mattei Dogan

Comparative observation can replace direct experiments by altering the circumstances of a series of observations. Through quantifications the comparative method can become a substitute for the experimental method. The method of concomitant variations described by J.S. Mill contained the logic of statistical correlations and multiple regressions that social scientists use today. Among the many issues that could be raised I have selected eight to discuss briefly. I shall not look at the entire field of comparative politics, only at efforts of quantification and at the limits of the statistical method. I shall abstain from commenting on the other end of the comparative spectrum – the castles of grand theories. I shall also leave aside the literature on mathematical modelling, and any discussion on the gap between method and theory, an issue which raises enormous problems. Instead I will concentrate on the links between data and method.

The eight issues to be discussed are as follows: the significance of the national average, the potentials and limits of survey research, the worldwide statistical analysis, the gross national product as a fallacious indicator, the scoring and scaling as a substitute for formal statistics, the need to replace isolated indicators by composite indices, the temporal lag between cause and effect, and the problem of the shadow economy in comparative research. These eight issues, among others, are chosen because of their relevance in the specific domain of quantitative comparisons.

1. National averages and intra-national diversities

With very few exceptions, cross-national comparisons use national averages. But, as is well known, when on the Gauss curve the distance between average, mean and mode is great, an average is not a significant statistical value. In a distribution the average does not reflect skewness. The assumption is that the internal diversity of countries is less significant than the differences between them. But in reality most countries are characterized by important internal diversity, either regional or vertical in terms of social strata. Some of the most significant characteristics are distributed unevenly. Internal diversities can be ethnic, linguistic, religious, social or economic. Almost all countries could be ranked according to their position on the continuum of homogeneity to heterogeneity. In some matters, like pluralism, internal diversity is an essential dimension. The internal diversity of countries is not necessarily related to their size. Some small countries are very heterogeneous and some large countries relatively homogeneous. Regional diversities are visible in all European countries. There are three Belgiums, four Italys (Dogan, 1967: 147), eight Spains, (Linz and de Miguel, 1966: 267–320). In Finland there are old regional contrasts. Yugoslavia has exploded into six pieces, and instead of a single national average for the entire Soviet colossus, there are today 15 independent nation-states, and as many national averages.

Geographical diversity may be expressed in survey research by the notion of social context. When these contexts are taken into consideration the risk of the 'individualistic fallacy' (Scheuch, 1966) is seriously reduced, particularly in ethnically diverse countries (Verba, 1971: 309). The individualistic fallacy emerges when the researcher takes into consideration only the characteristics of the individuals, ignoring the impact of the social milieu. For the analysis of intra-national diversities statisticians and geographers long ago elaborated adequate indices, like the Gini index of inequality, translated into Lorenz curves and coefficients of dispersion. We have the appropriate tools but the standardized statistical data on internal diversity were, until recently, scarce. An important indicator of internal diversity is the degree of linguistic homogeneity, which has been quantified for a large number of countries.

Many political phenomena cannot be explained by national averages. Take, for instance, the level of poverty. People do not revolt against poverty as such, they revolt against injustice; they do not revolt against the national average of poverty. In statistical terms social inequalities may be expressed in standard deviations. In some developing countries, governments have been reluctant to collect and publish data on inequalities in terms of regions, ethnic groups or social strata. Nevertheless, the World Bank has published data on income inequality for about 80 countries (Jain, 1975), and so has the OECD for 15 Western countries. Regional disparities have been studied in many fields, including voting behaviour. Today we can do better. We have more data on many more countries and we know much more about the diversity within countries. It is very likely that in the future, more attention will be given to intra-national disparities because, for many significant variables, intra-national differences are larger than differences between countries. In this way it is possible to explain a larger part of the variance.

2.   Potentials and limits in survey research

'Like telescopes in astronomy, and microscopes in biology, surveys have features that make them a fundamental data collection method for the social sciences. No other method for understanding politics is used more often, and no other method has so consistently illuminated political science theories with political facts' (Brady, 2000: 47) In the literature on comparative survey research many theoretical and methodological issues are carefully discussed (Scheuch, 2000). Here I shall raise only one: given the errors which are theoretically admitted in random sampling, how much statistical treatment might be applied to survey data? It is necessary to remember an elementary rule in the theory of probabilities, a rule that students are supposed to know, but that eminent scholars forget all too often. In a sample of 1000 individuals the chances are 95 in 100 that the sampling error is not larger than 5 percentage points in the case of a dichotomous category (men versus women for instance). Theoretically the error increases rapidly if the sample is divided into four or five categories (age groups for example). It increases even more in the case of a triple cross-tabulation (for example age groups by gender across political parties). We should not neglect the errors generated by sampling procedures, weighing of data, unclear questions, insufficient training of interviewers, and so on. Given such a theoretical margin of error within the data, is it reasonable to treat survey results by sophisticated statistical methods? The gap between the softness of the data and the sophistication of the technique used to treat it denotes an uncritical reasoning and the forgetting of the theory of probability.

In *The Silent Revolution* Ronald Inglehart gives a good example of the limits to sophistication in the statistical treatment of survey data (1977: 26): A fruitful method for analysing survey data was proposed long ago by Paul Lazarsfeld, particularly the refinement of the analysis by a chain of cross-tabulations. His methodology, based on critical reasoning, avoids the risks of overquantification. Lazarsfeld has not practised factor analysis and rarely regression analysis. Lazarsfeld's method consists in transforming the samples into a series of typologies. The richness of studies based on survey research depends on the validity of the theoretical framework and the pertinence of the questions asked, and very little on the power of statistical techniques used for the treatment of the data (Harding et al., 1986; Stoetzel, 1983; Turner, 1992; Inglehart, 1977; Barnes and Kaase, 1979; Dogan, 1988). None of these uses sophisticated techniques of analysis. *Political Action* by Barnes and Kaase (1979) has avoided unnecessary methodological complications. None of the nine contributors to the edited collection has gone beyond mean scores, mean coefficients of dissimilarity, attitudes scales, and a variety of typologies. Nonetheless, the book includes interesting tables and graphs. The same is true for Inglehart's *Culture Shift* (1990) and Stoetzel's *Les valeurs du temps présent* (1983). The tree-analysis, which consists in a chain of dichotomies, is the only methodological pedantry that can be found in *Electoral Behavior*, edited by Richard Rose (1974), which is very rich, full of empirical evidence with tables and graphs on most of its 745 pages. The book edited by Charles Glock, *Survey Research in the Social Sciences* (1967), concentrates on reasoning and logic and not on statistical techniques for analysing the data. Survey research has pushed forward the frontiers of comparative research. Important aspects like regime legitimacy, trust in rulers, religious feelings, national identities, perception of national symbols and many others are analysed cross-nationally today by survey research. Enormous progress has been achieved since the old *Civic Culture*, by Almond and Verba (1963). By 1969, in an inventory of comparative surveys, Rokkan et al. (1969) had counted 982 cross-national surveys. In a bibliographical follow-up, published three years later, several hundred titles were added (Delatte and Almasy, 1972). The first European Values survey (1981) covered some twenty countries; the World Values survey (under the leadership of Ronald Inglehart 1990–1998), about forty countries. The book edited by Loek Halman on European Values (2001) covers 32 countries.

Survey data and aggregate data should be combined wherever possible. Such a combination requires standardized indicators, not as yet pressed far enough and largely limited to the efforts of individual scholars. A good strategy for combining aggregate data and survey research has been proposed by Erwin Scheuch (1966), Juan Linz (1969), and Dogan and Rokkan (1969) who distinguish between primary data and derived data, and between individuals and territorial units (Dogan and Rokkan, 1969: 5).

3.   World-wide statistical comparisons

'The principal problems facing the comparative method can be succinctly stated: many variables, small number of cases', wrote A. Lijphart in 1971. More than three decades later, looking back on progress in comparative politics, such a statement remains convincing only for certain types of comparisons. With 202 independent nations in 2000, the number of cases does not look so small. In the last decades many insignificant variables have been abandoned, and other indicators, because of their interchangeability, have been combined in indices.

The literature on comparative politics can be divided into several categories: case studies in a comparative perspective; binary analyses; comparisons of similar countries; comparisons of contrasting countries; the conceptual homogenization of a heterogeneous field and worldwide correlational analyses (Dogan and Pelassy, 1990; Dogan, 2001). Not all of these six strategies are eminently statistical. Worldwide analysis, called by Raoul Naroll (1972) holonational, (adapted from the anthropological term hologeistic) consists of the study of whole societies, counts each country as one case, computes formal mathematical measures of relationships among variables and uses these measures to test general theories (Naroll, 1972). The larger the number of countries included in the comparison, the greater the need for quantitative data. Worldwide correlational analysis has experienced a period of stagnation and today is out of breath, a saturate form of research. The main reason for this decline is the discrepancy between the quality of statistical data for the advanced countries and for the developing ones. Scholars became aware that in comparing the two sets of countries they were dealing with material of unequal accuracy. It became clear that the lower the level of development, the lower the validity of quantitative data. The difficulties encountered in world-wide correlational analyses mark one of the limits to statistical approaches in comparative politics. The limits of worldwide statistical comparison can be explained also by the fact that it is based on national averages, which hide internal diversities.

4.   From gross national product (GNP) per capita to purchasing power parities (PPP)

The GNP is one of the most frequently used indicators in comparative analysis. It has been defined by economists as the market value of all final goods and services produced by the economy during a given year. It does not measure the standard of living, but rather the commercial value of goods and services produced. It is a valid indicator in economic comparisons. Applied to comparative politics it loses a large part of its validity, for several reasons. The proportion of goods that are commercialized varies according to the level of industrialization. Agricultural production is underevaluated. The work of women is another source of distortion in international GNP per capita statistics, for instance between Muslim countries and Western countries. If a housewife goes to work and hires a maid, she increases the GNP by two incomes where there were none before. Baking bread at home does not raise the GNP, but buying it in a shop does. The GNP per capita can theoretically be weighted according to the importance of the agricultural sector and the proportion of women in the workforce, but such a correction has rarely been attempted. As M.D. Morris puts it, 'the less developed a society, the smaller the proportion of goods and services that are produced for, and exchanged in the market. The GNP is an appropriate measure of output, but not a very satisfactory measure of welfare. As a measure of welfare, the GNP is fundamentally flawed' (Morris, 1979:13).

Moreover, by convention the GNP is calculated in US dollars, into which monetary statistics are converted. The fluctuation of the dollar can modify the difference between the USA and most other countries. This distortion was recognized long ago. The distortion has been noted, but conversion into dollars continues. It has been demonstrated that the resulting underestimation could range from 10 per cent to 300 per cent. The lower the GNP per capita, the higher the underestimation. The distortion is of such magnitude that it defies common sense. When the GNP per capita for a given year, for instance, is valued at $300 for India and at $9000 for Canada, it has to be taken in its narrow commercial sense. In reality the gap cannot be so enormous. It is sufficient to calculate in local currency by various sociological methods the minimal subsistence level for survival, to conclude that in comparative politics the GNP per capita has much less meaning than in monetary economics, and consequently should not be taken as an accurate indicator.

Furthermore, the statistical comparisons based on the GNP per capita between advanced and developing countries are misleading because of a well-known statistical artefact, too often forgotten. In growth percentage terms, an increase from $10 000 to $11 000 per capita is equivalent to a change from $200 to $220 per capita, that is 10 per cent. Statistical evidence is indispensable in comparative research, but we should always remember that equal increases in percentages can mean a greater gap in absolute terms.

The GNP tends to become an instrument of measurement in international relations. For instance, in 1992 at the Rio UN conference it was proposed that every country allocate 0.7 per cent of its GNP to the United Nations Fund for the Environment. Because of the size of its economy, but also because the American GNP is comparatively inflated by the value of the dollar, the United States would have had to contribute to such a Fund as much as 80 times that of the smaller or poorer countries. For several decades, the GNP per capita has been a privileged indicator in dozens of studies on development. But in recent years it has been severely criticized, even by economists. To replace it, several composite indices have been proposed.

The OECD's Purchasing Power Parities (PPP), intended to replace the classical GNP, is an improvement. For instance, calculated in GNP per capita, the standard of living appears 40 times higher in France than in India ($300 against $12 790 in 1987). Calculated in purchasing power parity, the distortion is diminished to 13 times ($1050 against $13 960) (United Nations Development Programme, 1990: 0–131). But for political comparisons the PPP remains a deception. First because it is limited to OECD countries, whereas the underestimation of the standard of living is heavier for the poor countries. Second, it covers only the currency conversion. It ignores the real differences in price levels between countries and does not evaluate the real differences in national production and consumption. As its title indicates, the objective is the monetary purchasing capacity. The field of quantitative comparative politics is still deprived of an appropriate tool for measuring the wealth of nations.

5.   Scoring and scaling as a substitute for formal statistics

Many of the most significant aspects of political life cannot be treated in statistical terms. The alternative is scaling by experts. The recourse to judgemental rankings, and to scoring finds a justification in a statement by the mathematician Tukey: 'Far better an approximate answer to the right question, which is often vague, than an exact answer to the wrong question, which can always be made precise' (cited by Banks and Textor, 1963: 7).

The translation of qualitative aspects into measurable variables requires scaling by judges. The involvement of judges raises the question of coder reliability: how likely are two or several judges to rate the same situation in the same manner? If an expert says that country A is more democratic than country B, and this last more than country C, (s)he must admit also that A is more democratic than C. The reliability of an expert can be tested by the consistency of her/his rankings. To show the potential of scoring and judgemental rankings, three examples are selected here from the literature.

The first one is from Phillips Cutright's 'National Political Development: Measurement and Analysis' (1963: 253–64). This article is one of the most cited in the literature on comparative politics and one of the few still relevant today among those published three decades ago. With the help of experts Cutright constructed an index of political development. He allocated for each country two points for each year in which a parliament existed and where the minority party had at least 30 per cent of the seats. He allocated only one point when the minority party was weaker, and no points for each year when no parliament existed. He did the same scoring for the executive branch. Over a period of 22 years a country could accumulate 66 points. Cutright used a simple but pertinent index. The validity of his scoring can be tested retrospectively. For 1963 he found an imbalance for Chile, the Philippines, Indonesia, Nicaragua and Guatemala: political development was higher than socio-economic development. In the following years the façade of democracy in these countries collapsed. The opposite was true for Spain, Portugal, Czechoslovakia and Poland. These countries were supposedly ripe for democracy. Cutright's analysis based on scores and simple statistical models should be compared with many other articles published roughly at the same time which disappeared from the literature despite the mountains of statistics on which they were built. Cutright's method of scores could be applied today to Eastern Europe: the implosion in 1989–90 can be explained by the gap between the relatively high socio-economic level (education, health, urbanization, industrialization) and the low level of political development. A second example of scoring as a substitute to formal statistics is the voluminous book by Banks and Textor, *A Cross-Polity Survey* (1963). They proposed a series of 57 dichotomized variables, most of which were directly political: interest articulation and aggregation, leadership charisma, freedom of group opposition, freedom of the press, role of the police, character of the bureaucracy, *personalismo*, westernization and others. The authors preferred significant aspects of political life to quantified but unimportant variables, even if their dichotomization was uncertain. They gave approximate answers to good questions.

Another codification of variables which are not directly quantifiable was adopted by Irma Adelman and Cynthia Taft Morris in their *Society, Politics and Economic Development: A Quantitative Approach* (1971). This book has been severely criticized by some scholars (Kingsley Davis among others) and appreciated by others. These contrasting evaluations can be explained by the fact that it consists of two parts. The first (pp. 1–129) contains an interesting discussion of 41 variables, most of which were and remain not directly quantifiable. The second part consists of a confusing factor analysis.

I shall give as a final example a series of volumes *Freedom in the World*, by Raymond D. Gastil 1979–1990), who has ranked countries with the help of experts according to two basic dimensions: political rights and civil liberties. The rating is on a seven-point scale by univocal ranking. Published annually since 1979, this series has become an important source of documentation for comparative politics in general and for empirical quantitative research in particular.

After decades of progress in comparative research we still face this dilemma: to take recourse to judgemental variables or to neglect some of the most important aspects of social and political life.

6.   From isolated indicators to composite indices

Single isolated indicators are often misleading. When a researcher relies on only one or two indicators to measure a complex phenomenon, these are likely to be ineffective measures. An example: some still use the number of radios per 1000 population as an indicator of the development of the entire communications network of a nation. While such extrapolation may have been valid several decades ago for many nations, there are today cases where this indicator is obsolete. A relatively poor country could rank in radios per 1000 inhabitants as high as a relatively rich country. At the same moment the rich country could rank very high in television sets, computers and daily newspaper circulation per 1000. Except for comparisons between the 50 or 60 poorest countries the indicator might well be abandoned today.

The same problem is evident in many other areas where there are complementary items, such as in the transportation network. Cars, trains, buses, boats and aeroplanes all fulfil similar functions. The relative frequency in the use of one or more of these modes of transportation is influenced by geography, average distance, cost and cultural preference. In Europe the rail system is more developed than in the US, there being shorter distances to cover and higher population densities. Trains are not seen as a lowly form of transportation in Europe, as they are in the US. It would be misleading, then, to use air traffic as an indicator of the development of the transportation system. While many social scientists have assumed that the number of cars per thousand inhabitants is a valid indicator of development, they may not have recognized the importance of the fact that there are alternatives available.

Energy consumption per capita is another variable which needs an index to help integrate various energy data. The consumption of energy can reflect many social indicators: industrialization, mechanization and even mass communication. Forms of energy include oil, electricity, coal, gasoline and nuclear energy. For purposes of international standardization, the index of energy expresses data in coal equivalents to oil, natural gas and electric energy.

Another aspect of relevance of indices is whether certain variables can meaningfully be quantified. It is not enough to assign numbers to events. The second edition of the *World Handbook of Political Indicators* (Taylor and Hudson, 1972) contains quantified data on indicators of political protest. Aside from problems of accuracy, these data are of questionable validity: do they really measure unrest in a society? Even if we grant that demonstrations, riots, armed attacks, deaths from domestic violence, and governmental sanctions can be accurately quantified, it is still questionable whether we can assume that these categories represent the true level of unrest in a society. Discontent may not appear without a spark to bring it out into the open. Even more fundamentally, the indicators of unrest fail to acknowledge the role of suppression in affecting the statistics. Dictatorial governments around the world suppress the expression of unrest. The existence of this underlying level of unrest was demonstrated by the crises in East Germany, Czechoslovakia, Poland and Hungary, Romania and Baltic countries in 1989–90.

By compounding various indicators in an index, the sociological significance of statistical data could be enhanced. Too often isolated indicators are still treated by complex methods, even when a simple statistical treatment of indices would be sufficient. By combining isolated indicators into indices, quantitative comparative analysis would be facilitated, since the number of variables would be reduced and their explanatory power enhanced. We possess today quantified indicators difficult or impossible to obtain in the 1970s for a large number of countries, for instance for life expectancy, access to safe water, number of people per hospital bed, or school enrolment at age 10–12 for developing countries. It is also the case, however, that certain indicators do not need to be combined into indices, because their explanatory power is sufficient, as attested to by numerous empirical analyses. Among these privileged indicators is infant mortality. One does not need sophisticated factor analysis to understand why, sociologically, infant mortality is one of the best indicators in comparative research. Worldwide statistics published by the UN, the World Bank, and other specialized institutions demonstrate the soundness of the above assertion.

7.   The temporal dimension: causal relationships are staggered over time

Time dimension is important for the understanding of political processes and effects. Rates of change are essential for the analysis of political development. Rapid changes may have different effects than slow ones. The impact of some indicators may be immediate. Other indicators suggest staggered consequences. The GNP per capita and school enrolment, for instance, have different time dimensions. Comparisons of rates of change may reveal important differences. Nevertheless, most comparative research over the last quarter century has used synchronic data, often because they seemed to be the only ones available. For a long time most survey data were synchronic; only recently have comparative time-series become available. Synchronic political analysis was an important step, but often it could only explain a fraction of the variance. This is the reason why many analyses reached insignificant results. Time lags are crucial in understanding causality or probabilistic influence. Everything in politics takes time, and so do all changes in society. No social change is instantaneous. Even if communications take place with electronic speed, the social impact of political decisions takes time. Even revolutions need time to engender social consequences (Dogan and Higley, 1998).

A technical means for dealing with the time-consuming aspects of human communication and response is the use of lagged variables. If we assume for theoretical reasons, or from experience, that a change in variable A will have an impact on variable B, we must still ask how much later this impact will take place and have observable results. We must compare variable A and B not at the same time but variable A at a certain moment with B at some later time. This delay may be quite long. Historians have pointed out that the introduction of compulsory primary education in several Western countries around the 1860s was followed by the rise of the popular press in the 1890s. The historian Daniel Vernet has demonstrated that in France, during the 18th century, revolutionary ideas and behaviour spread in the countryside two decades after the rise of radical ideas in the main cities. Legislative changes in education, health, and welfare need many years to become social realities.

Other time lags may be shorter, depending on the scale of the processes involved, but some lag is always to be expected. For instance, the attainment of power by social democratic or similarly welfare-oriented parties – often in the form of coalitions – has been linked by several authors to the enactment of additional social welfare legislation and to an actual rise in welfare benefits. Many of these studies, however, have not given enough weight to time lags, and hence underestimated the actual impact that occurred. The time lags involved include the time between the formation of the government, enactment of a specific legislation, its promulgation, its effective implementation at the administrative level and the time it takes the public to learn to make full use of the opportunities under the new laws. The rise in the number of social security beneficiaries partly illustrates this process. In all Western democracies social expenditures have changed slowly, by an incremental trend (see Flora and Heidenheimer, 1981; Flora, 1983; Taylor and Jodice, 1983). A phalange of comparativists have tried to ascertain the importance of the Social Democratic parties in the growth of government, but having neglected the time dimension and the delayed, incremental social consequences of the participation of Social Democrats in power, they have succeeded to explain only a small part of the variance.

The vexed question of economic development and the prerequisites for the establishment of stable democratic regimes also involve considerable time lags, too often neglected. Causal relationships in contemporary demographic trends in the Third World would emerge more clearly if urbanization and literacy were considered at a certain time and birth rates and infant mortality one generation later. Such staggering does not require sophisticated statistical techniques. The neglect of the temporal dimension has long limited the explanation of variance. Its inclusion in research designs could enhance the potential for comparative quantitative analysis.

8.   The shadow economy

Inaccurate statistics used in comparative politics often originate from the shadow economy, also called the underground economy, black market, submerged economy, clandestine work, parallel economy, concealed, informal, hidden, illicit, unobserved, dual economy. The official GNP includes all economic activities which are paid for with money, which pass through some sort of market and are reported to the government, supervised and taxed by it and form the basis of all trade statistics. Yet these indicators understate the volume of many economically significant activities. They omit the self-consumption of households in agriculture, goods and services exchanged informally through barter, exchanged in transactions not reported to authorities. In some advanced countries, the consumption of peasant households of their own produce is partially included in official estimates of the social product. This is done by estimating the portions of agricultural output.

An important part of the shadow economy is the monetary transactions concealed from the government and therefore missing in its statistics. With regard to goods, these are usually referred to as being on the 'black market'. In regard to labour and services, one often speaks of the shadow economy. The total of the two varies greatly from country to country and from time to time. It has been estimated higher for Britain than for France, and as high as 30 per cent for Italy (because of high taxation) and nearly half for a country like India (because of small land holdings). Without estimates of the extent of the shadow economy the GNP is a deceptive measure.

Higher taxes and extensive governmental controls are likely to drive more economic transactions underground. Increased levels of unemployment tend to have similar effects; so does the lag in the income of workers and low-level civil servants behind the cost of living, which impels them to seek second jobs. Compulsory health and welfare contributions motivate employers to offer jobs at lower rates or lower side costs. The problem is illustrated by a remark by President Mitterrand in 1984, to the effect that 'the higher the level of taxation, the less income the state can extract from it' (perceived as a criticism of the policy adopted by his own Government in 1981/83).

The implications for comparative analysis are obvious. In OECD statistics, the British are on average still richer than the Italians. In reality it may well be that the standard of living in Italy, except in the deep South and Sardinia, is higher than it is in Britain. How much does the vigorous Italian shadow economy contribute to the outcome? Tuscany and Emilia, where the shadow economy may produce one third of the local GNP, are in reality much richer than the figures in the official statistics would suggest. In general, the shadow economy reflects the activities of artisans and small businessmen/women, and the production of agriculture and food. Much of the latter stays within the country. According to the wise beliefs of certain Italian politicians 'as long as the government tolerates the shadow economy, people may be more willing to tolerate the government'.

Clearly, better estimates and new indicators are needed here for studies both of developing and highly industrialized countries. Family and household surveys, such as India's annual 25 000 family survey, may offer useful starting points. Without estimates of the size of the shadow economy, real economic growth or decline is hard to assess. The shadow economy limits the potential of quantification: how might one quantify accurately what is by definition clandestine? Obviously the shadow economy has a direct impact on the calculation of the gross national product per capita, but this impact is too often neglected in quantitative comparative analysis. Sociologists should not worship this golden calf fabricated by economists for their own needs.

Final comment: what cannot be compared in statistical terms
The appropriate dose of quantified data depends on the kind of question that you ask and the goals pursued by comparing. For instance, a reply to the question 'Is the gap between poor and rich countries increasing?' has to be based on solid statistical data, carefully analysed. On the other hand, when Samuel Huntington asks, 'Will more countries become democratic?', the analytical reasoning becomes more important than the statistical evidence.

In some cases, statistical data are pertinent revealers, or even true discoverers of historical trends. A good example is the indicator 'infant mortality' in the Soviet Union between 1958 and 1990. The rate of infant mortality was halved between 1958 and 1971, from 41 per thousand to 23 per thousand. But later, within a decade, it had risen to 32 per thousand. Retrospectively, the rate of infant mortality appears as premonitory of real social conditions in the ex-Soviet Union at that time.

But excessive recourse to quantified data can be of little help in finding answers to some major questions. Why did China not collapse into rival feudalities, as did the Roman Empire? The explanation by the existence of mandarins should not go so far as some non-quantitative comparativists have proposed, who proclaim that: 'Almost all important questions are important precisely because they are not susceptible to quantitative answers'. This is a gross exaggeration.

Some observable phenomena are not quantifiable. Take, for instance, political corruption. There cannot be statistics on a phenomenon which by its very nature is concealed. For certain phenomena, quantification is unnecessary; or not the most pertinent approach. For instance, to compare the condition of women in Islamic countries and in Western countries, dozens of observations could be made without need of statistical data. When the contrast is obvious the differences in percentage points becomes superfluous.

According to certain theories based on social and economic indicators, India should not be a democratic country. The social infrastructure of this country does not respond to the traditional models in comparative sociology. Some interesting theories in comparative research cannot be tested statistically. The attempts to test with regression equations the 'dependency theory' have not resulted, despite the great statistical expertise of the authors, in a great advance of the theories, as it was formulated previously without powerful statistical techniques. Nor should we forget the Weberian comparison by ideal-types, which played a seminal role in the past, and which is in practice the opposite of the inductive statistical method. Because of the kind of questions that they have asked, none of the great classic comparativists have used the statistical techniques available in their time, not even Durkheim.

Briefly stated, the degree of quantification is conditioned by the balance between data and method. If the data is inaccurate, the degree of statistical technique should not be too ambitious. If the data is reliable, the sophisticated methodological design is justified and recommended.

Bibliography

Adelman, Irma and Cynthia Taft Morris (1971), *Society, Politics and Economic Development: A Quantitative Approach*, Baltimore: The Johns Hopkins Press.

Almond, Gabriel and Sidney Verba (1963), *The Civic Culture*, Princeton: Princeton University Press.

Banks, Arthur S. and Robert B. Textor (1963), *A Cross-Polity Survey*, Cambridge: The MIT Press.

Barnes, Samuel H. and Max Kaase (eds) (1979), *Political Action: Mass Participation in Five Western Democracies*, London: Sage.

Brady, Henry (2000), 'Contribution of survey research to political science', *Political Science and Politics*, **XXXIII**, 1 March, 47–57.

Cutright, Philips (1963), 'National political development: measurement and analysis', *American Sociological Review*, vol. 28, 253–64.

Delatte, J. and E. Almasy, (1972), *Comparative Survey Analysis: A Bibliographical Follow-Up*, Paris: International Social Science Council.

Dogan, Mattei (1967), 'Political cleavage and social stratification in France and Italy', in S.M. Lipset and S. Rokkan (eds), *Party Systems and Voter Alignments*, New York: Free Press.

Dogan, Mattei (ed.) (1988), *Comparing Pluralist Democracies, Strains on Legitimacy*, Boulder, Co, Westview Press.

Dogan, Mattei (2001), 'Strategies in comparative sociology', *Comparative Sociology*, **6**(1), 63–92.

Dogan, Mattei and John Higley (1998), *Elites, Crises and the Origins of Regimes*, Boulder, CO: Rowman and Littlefield.

Dogan, Mattei and John D. Kasarda (eds) (1988), *A World of Giant Cities* and *Mega-Cities* London: Sage (two volumes).

Dogan, Mattei and Dominique Pelassy (1990), *How to Compare Nations*, 2nd edn, Chatham: Chatham House.

Dogan, Mattei and Stein Rokkan (eds) (1969), *Quantitative Ecological Analysis in the Social Sciences*, Cambridge, MA: The MIT Press.

Flora, Peter (ed.) (1983), *State, Economy and Society in Western Europe – A Data Handbook*, Frankfurt: Campus Verlag.

Flora, Peter and Arnold J. Heidenheimer (eds) (1981), *The Development of Welfare States in Europe and America*, New Brunswick: Transaction Books.

Gastil, Raymond D. (1979–1990), *Freedom in the World, Political Rights and Civil Liberties*, Westport, CT: Greenwood Press, various volumes.

Glock, Charles Y. (ed.) (1967), *Survey Research in the Social Sciences*, New York: Russell Sage Foundation.

Halman, Loek (2001), *The European Values Study: A Third Wave*, Tilburg: Tilburg University Press.

Harding, S., D. Phillips and M. Fogarty (1986), *Contrasting Values in Western Europe*, London: Macmillan.

Heidenheimer, A.J., M. Johnston and V.T. Le Vine (eds) (1990), *Political Corruption*, New Brunswick: Transaction Publishers.

Huntington, Samuel P. (1968), *Political Order in Changing Societies*, New Haven: Yale University Press.

Inglehart, Ronald (1977), *The Silent Revolution*, Princeton: Princeton University Press.

Inglehart, Ronald (1990), *Culture Shift in Advanced Industrial Society*, Princeton: Princeton University Press.

Jain, Shail (1975), *The Size Distribution of Income: A Compilation of Data*, Washington: The World Bank.

Lijphart, Arend (1971), 'Comparative politics and the comparative method', *American Political Science Review*, vol. 65, 682–93.

Linz, Juan J. and Amando de Miguel (1966), 'Within-nation differences and comparisons: the eight Spains', in R. Merritt and S. Rokkan (eds), *Comparing Nations*, New Haven: Yale University Press, pp. 267–320.

Linz, Juan J. (1969), 'Ecological analysis and survey research' in M. Dogan and S. Rokkan (eds), *Quantitative Ecological Analysis in the Social Sciences*, Cambridge, MA: The MIT Press, pp. 91–131.

Morris, M. David (1979), *Measuring the Condition of the World's Poor*, New York: Pergamon Press.

Naroll, Raoul (1972), 'A holonational bibliography', *Comparative Political Studies*, **5**(2), July, 211–30.

OECD (1992), *Purchasing Power Parities and Real Expenditures*, Paris: OECD.

Phillips, Derek L. (1971), *Knowledge From What? Theories and Methods in Social Research*, Chicago: Rand McNally.

Rokkan, S., J. Viet, S. Verba and E. Almasy (1969), *Comparative Survey Analysis*, Paris: Mouton.

Rose, Richard (ed.) (1974), *Electoral Behavior: A Comparative Handbook*, London: Macmillan.

Russett Bruce et al. (1964), *World Handbook of Political and Social Indicators*, I, New Haven: Yale University Press.

Scheuch, Erwin K. (1966), 'Cross-national comparison using aggregate data: some substantive and methodological problems', in R. Merritt and S. Rokkan (eds), *Comparing Nations*, New Haven: Yale University Press.

Scheuch, Erwin K. (1969), 'Social context and individual behaviour', in M. Dogan and S. Rokkan (eds), *Quantitative Ecological Analysis in the Social Sciences*, Cambridge, MA: The MIT Press, pp. 133–55.

Scheuch, Erwin K. (2000), 'The rise of ISSP for comparative research', Fifth International Conference on Social Science Methodology, Cologne.

Stoetzel, Jean (1983), *Les valeurs du temps présent: une enquête européenne*, Paris: Presses Universitaires de France.

Taylor, Charles L. (ed.) (1980), *Indicator Systems for Political, Economic and Social Analysis*, Cambridge: Oelgeschlager Publishers.

Taylor, Charles L. and Michael C. Hudson (1972), *World Handbook of Political and Social Indicators*, II, New Haven: Yale University Press.

Taylor, Charles L. and David A. Jodice (1983), *World Handbook of Political and Social Indicators*, III, New Haven: Yale University Press.

Turner, Frederick C. (ed.) (1992), *Social Mobility and Political Attitudes: Comparative Perspectives*, New Brunswick: Transaction Publishers.

United Nations Development Programme (1990), *Human Development Report 1990*, Oxford: Oxford University Press.

Verba, Sidney (ed.) (1971), 'Cross-national survey research, the problem of credibility', in Ivan Vallier (ed.), *Comparative Methods in Sociology*, Berkeley: University of California Press, pp. 309–56.

PART V

THEMES AND ISSUES

19 The international and comparative analysis of social exclusion: European perspectives

Graham Room

Introduction

The analysis of social exclusion raises three methodological questions. First, how is social exclusion to be conceptualized? As a lack of financial resources, perhaps; or as poor housing, health and diet; or as detachment from the major institutions of society? Second, how is social exclusion to be measured? By reference to some financial poverty line; or in terms of the length of time for which an individual or household endures poor social conditions; or in terms of the range of social networks on which such a household can call in times of adversity? What are then the implications for organizations – especially public bodies – charged with the regular collection of data on such matters? Third, by reference to what theoretical and policy purposes is the investigation and analysis of social exclusion to be conducted? As a tool for allocating public resources between more or less deserving households or localities? As a means of illuminating competing theories of social deprivation?

These three types of question are not of course peculiar to the study of social exclusion: they arise across many other areas of applied social science. Nor are they peculiar to international and comparative research. Nevertheless, this international and comparative dimension does give them a particular twist. In conceptualizing social exclusion, how far is it necessary to relate the analysis to the specific social and cultural features of the different countries being compared? If social exclusion is measured by reference to particular financial poverty lines, should these be nationally specific or make reference to some international standards? Finally, what policy purpose can such comparative analyses serve? Are they intended primarily to illuminate for individual national governments the comparative performance of their neighbours, so as to assist in cross-national lesson drawing? Or with the growth of international and supranational organizations, having a policy remit of their own, are such comparative and international studies intended primarily to furnish such organizations with the information base for their own initiatives?

These are of course large questions. In order to provide a more delimited focus for this chapter, it will concentrate primarily upon the initiatives taken forward during recent decades under the auspices of the EU institutions. Only in the closing section do we consider the possible implications for wider efforts to conduct comparative and international investigations in this field.

The analysis of social exclusion: EU initiatives in retrospect

The first European anti-poverty programme (1975–80) included as its principal element a number of locally-based pilot projects, intended to demonstrate innovatory methods of combating poverty (Dennett et al., 1982). Many had various forms of research and evaluation to accompany and illuminate the action. These in turn drew upon the rich variety of methodologies of action-research that had developed during the 1960s and 1970s: some from the American War on Poverty and the British Community Development Project (CDP), others from German critical theory, others again from Italian traditions of de-institutionalization (Room, 1986: Chapter 4). As significant in some countries – Italy, for example – in stimulating national debate were the nine national reports on poverty and anti-poverty policy, accompanied by a first attempt at estimating levels of income poverty in the various member states according to a common methodology (European Commission, 1981). Alongside the action projects and these national studies, researchers such as Peter Willmott were responsible for cross-national studies on particular aspects of poverty – in his case, unemployment, social security and poverty in France, Germany and the UK (Mitton et al., 1983). It was, moreover, this first Poverty Programme that sponsored the first of a series of reports on the perceptions of poverty held by citizens in different European Community countries in the mid-1970s, with attitudes in the UK proving to be particularly harsh (European Commission, 1977).

With the European Parliament calling for action not words, the Commission planned the second programme (1986–89) with cross-national action-research projects as the centrepiece. These provided some valuable models of cross-national policy learning (Room et al., 1993). Although the programme had no research element as such, studies of national policies were commissioned as part of the evaluation of the action programme and these echoed the national reports of the first programme. As part of the same evaluation, O'Higgins and Jenkins (1987) ventured a new estimate of the total number of persons and households across the Community falling below a poverty line defined, as in the Commission's 1981 report, as 50 per cent of equivalent disposable income in each of the countries concerned. This in turn prompted the statistical office of the Commission, Eurostat, to begin a programme of work on the long-term improvement of poverty indicators, initially by working with national statistical offices to use household budget surveys for producing comparable data on low-income groups.

The third programme (1990–94), as well as continuing the cross-national action-research, saw the reinstatement of a series of cross-national studies.

Also of significance was the so-called 'Observatory' on policies to combat social exclusion (Room et al., 1991, 1992; Robbins et al., 1994). This Observatory, involving a network of research institutes, was a response to the 1989 Council of Ministers Resolution, which had committed member states to combatting social exclusion (Council of Ministers, 1989). Like the other activities of this programme, it was brought to an untimely end, when in 1994 the German government insisted that as poverty and social exclusion had never an explicit part of the EU Treaties, such actions were inappropriate.

Within this series of initiatives, how were poverty and social exclusion conceptualized? During the 1970s and 1980s, the EU had been operating with a notion of poverty broadly indebted to such writers as Townsend (1970): poverty was to be defined in terms relative to the living standards customary in the society concerned, and the resources required to participate within it. However, this was then operationalized in terms of financial poverty lines, defined relative to the income distribution of each country, as the principal point of reference for purposes of cross-national comparison. Financial poverty lines, defined in relative terms, also drove the efforts of Eurostat to improve the cross-national comparability of official statistics. The action projects that had figured prominently in this series of European initiatives had, it is true, provided a picture of poverty which was multi-dimensional, rather than just financial, and which was concerned as much with the processes by which poverty was generated as with the outcomes. Nevertheless, to add to research was only a secondary aim as far as these projects were concerned, and neither statisticians nor academic researchers gave their efforts in this regard much attention.

By the 1990s, however, in part under the influence of Commission President Delors, the EU authorities were increasingly couching their concerns in the language of 'social exclusion'. In part this was a semantic shift: on the one hand, the enthusiasm of Delors and the French government for the language of inclusion; on the other, the long-standing sensitivity by many national governments, including notably the UK and Germany, to the suggestion that poverty could be found in their countries. Nevertheless, this was also a shift of substance, involving perhaps five principal elements (Room, 1999):

- it was concerned with a *multi-dimensional* notion of inadequate living conditions;
- it was concerned with *dynamic* processes: on the one hand, changes in the poor population between one time period and the next; on the other, investments in future consumption and security, not just current consumption;
- it recognized that people's living conditions depended not just on their personal and household resources but also on the material and cultural *collective* resources to which they had access;

- it focused attention on the *relational* as much as the distributional dimensions of stratification: on the one hand, making explicit that consumption and investment take place within particular social relationships; on the other, recognizing that relationships are themselves a component of human well-being, and their breakdown or absence can therefore be a deprivation;
- it directed attention to those individuals, households and communities who were suffering multi-dimensional disadvantage and the degradation of the collective resources and relational links on which they could draw: long-term and to a considerable degree irreversible, except perhaps in face of special and disproportionate interventions.

If the conceptualization of poverty and social exclusion was changing, so also were the preferred methods of measurement. During the 1980s Eurostat had promoted the use and comparability of national household budget surveys for purposes of producing Community-wide poverty estimates: during the 1990s it moved on to multi-dimensional and intertemporal data instruments, in particular through the new generation of panel studies that were now emerging. At a national level, there is a growing number of such panel surveys, along with research studies which analyse their data. Various attempts have been made to set alongside each other the findings emerging from different national panels and to draw comparative conclusions (Leisering and Walker, 1998; Goodin et al., 1999). These various studies show that most poverty is short term: there is plenty of income mobility, although many of those who escape from poverty remain on its margins and may subsequently descend into it once more. These panel studies can also identify those most at risk of falling into poverty and staying there: people who are poorly educated, unemployed or disabled, and lone mothers. Factors related to employability are crucial in determining who escapes. From 1994 onwards, these national panel studies were complemented by a new European Community Household Panel (ECHP), data from which have become a key instrument for social monitoring at European level.

Nevertheless, some of the other conceptual shifts set in motion by the debates on social exclusion were much slower to re-shape the data instruments and methods of measurement that were being promoted by the European authorities. Action projects working in local communities had been a prominent feature of these European programmes, and researchers concerned with social exclusion were giving increasing recognition to the collective resources within those communities, which helped to shape the living conditions of individual households (see, for example, some of the contributions to the seminar on the measurement of social exclusion sponsored by the European Commission and the UK Department of Social Security in 1994: Room,

1995, Chapters 8–11). However, notwithstanding the interest of the EU authorities in area-based policies, there has as yet been little or no attempt on their part to develop data instruments which bring together measures of household and neighbourhood resources. So also, while the European Community Household Panel allows some analysis of the social relationships and networks on which people can call for support, this is very limited, compared with some of the pioneering work done by such researchers as Paugam (1995, 1996).

Finally, the research into poverty and social exclusion conducted under this series of European initiatives was oriented to a shifting agenda of theoretical and policy purposes. The earlier programmes were concerned with information gathering and exchange of good practice in action-research, but without any very clear over-arching theoretical or policy purpose. Poverty and social exclusion were absent from the research and policy agenda of the EU, save for these special programmes, and national agendas showed enormous variation. However, as the pressures towards a strengthened European social dimension developed in the late 1980s, this situation also began to change, with the Commission drawing in part on its experience with these pilot programmes when preparing proposals for the social dimension.

The 1989 Council of Ministers Resolution on social exclusion brought these issues one step closer to the main EU policy agenda. Under the resolution, the Commission as already mentioned established an Observatory: to monitor how far member states were honouring their Resolution commitments, to assess the effectiveness of national policies to combat social exclusion and to highlight examples of good practice for purposes of cross-national policy learning. However, whatever the progress in monitoring final outcomes (poverty rates and so on), the EU authorities had made next to no progress in establishing a common approach to monitoring policy outputs and effectiveness. The Observatory was therefore heavily constrained in what it could do and in general limited itself to describing policy intentions and recording social conditions.

During the latter part of the 1990s, the EU policy agenda shifted still further, as did the direction of the international and comparative analysis of social exclusion which EU policy makers would henceforth sponsor. Social exclusion became a formal concern of EU policy under the Amsterdam Treaty of 1997. At least as important, however, was the Lisbon process, the so-called open method of coordination (OMC), which developed during 2000, and which took policies for social inclusion as a major point of reference.

The European Council of Lisbon, in March 2000, established the OMC as a novel but key mode of policy coordination, intended to benchmark best practice and promote policy convergence (De la Porte, Pochet and Room, 2001). It involves:

- fixing guidelines for the Union, combined with specific timetables for achieving the goals which they set in the short, medium and long term;
- establishing, where appropriate, quantitative and qualitative indicators and benchmarks against the best in the world and tailored to the needs of different member states and sectors, as a means of comparing best practice;
- translating these European guidelines into national and regional policies by setting specific targets and adopting measures, taking into account national and regional differences;
- periodic monitoring, evaluation and peer review, organized as mutual learning processes (European Council, 2000).

In this process, the Commission is meant to play a coordinating role, by presenting proposals on the European guidelines, organizing the exchange of best practices, presenting proposals on potential indicators, and providing support to the processes of implementation and peer review.

Poverty and social exclusion have been singled out as a quasi-separate area of action under the OMC. Within a set of common objectives defined and endorsed by the Nice European Council, each member state was required by June 2001 to present a national action plan to combat poverty and social exclusion. This was to include national level indicators, selected to take account of the multi-dimensionality of the phenomenon, and to measure progress in relation to national and regional targets and the overall European objectives. Peer review and supranational monitoring and evaluation are an integral part of the exercise, creating pressure to converge towards European level objectives. The exercise is to be repeated on a biannual basis (European Commission, 2002). It is to be accompanied by a new Community Action Programme, intended to enhance the exchange of information and best practices among member states (European Commission, 2000).

The most sensitive issue has been the establishment of commonly agreed indicators. During the latter part of 2001, under the Belgian Presidency, various working groups and expert reports contributed to an agreed portfolio of indicators (Social Protection Committee, 2001; Atkinson et al., 2002). These indicators focus upon social conditions such as the risk of financial poverty, the proportion of people unemployed, those in poor housing. There is some reference to intertemporal and dynamic aspects, although the impending demise of the ECHP, and its replacement by EU-SILC (Statistics on Income and Living Conditions: see Eurostat, 2001) limits what can be proposed. There are brief references to the territorial and relational dimensions of social exclusion but no more: no doubt in part because of the absence of appropriate comparable data on these matters. Moreover, while these indicators focus on social conditions – and therefore, it can be argued, on the ultimate outcomes of policy – they do not touch directly on policy inputs and outputs: by themselves, therefore, they will not enable comparisons of the effectiveness of different national policy mixes.

Before considering how these limitations might be overcome – the task of the next section of this chapter – it is worth concluding this discussion, by considering what trends and benchmarks of comparative performance these recent developments have served to highlight. How far, moreover, do they differ from those produced within the research paradigms favoured by earlier phases in this European odyssey? The answer is that as far as headline indicators are concerned, both the comparative indicators and the cross-national patterns that they reveal have remained remarkably constant.

Financial poverty lines, defined as a percentage of the mean or median equivalent disposable income in each of the countries concerned, have enjoyed pride of place: from the first estimates in 1981 (European Commission, 1981) to those in the most recent Joint Report on Social Inclusion (European Commission, 2002). The former, taking 50 per cent of mean disposable income, estimated just over 30 million people in poverty in the then nine member states; the latter, using 60 per cent of the median, estimated 60 million or 18 per cent in the 15 member states. Income poverty was highest in the southern member states and Ireland, lowest in the Benelux countries and Scandinavia. Between these two dates a series of similar estimates were produced, under the sponsorship of DG Employment and Eurostat in particular, varying according to the statistical definitions used, but apparently immune to the larger shifts in the language of the debate from poverty to social exclusion.

One more fundamental dilemma that did emerge in these estimates, however, concerned the reference point for relative poverty lines: the respective member state was conventionally used, but at least one attempt was also made to treat the whole Community as a single entity for the purpose of defining the relative poverty line (Eurostat, 1990). This, of course, produced an apparent increase in the amount of poverty in the poorer member states and a reduction in the richer. Whether this was a more or less appropriate point of reference was never resolved: and indeed, taking the whole Community as a reference point thereafter disappeared from view. What seems clear is that here, as always, it must be by reference to the theoretical and policy purpose of the investigation that the indicators and points of reference must be chosen: but with these policy purposes even now not entirely clear, it was unsurprising that this particular nettle was never properly grasped.

What the debate on social exclusion has done is to prompt a range of additional indicators concerned on the one hand with the persistence of financial poverty among particular households, on the other with non-financial aspects of deprivation. However, as yet at least, these have not delivered a statistical portrait of social exclusion to match the apparent solidity of the financial poverty estimates. It remains to be seen whether the new set of common indicators agreed under the Belgian Presidency ushers in a new era.

Prospects

The indicators of social exclusion which are being promoted by the EU are concerned primarily with the risks of multi-dimensional disadvantage at the level of persons and households, some account being taken of dynamic changes over time. This is the focus of the OMC process, guided by DG Employment: it is also the focus of Eurostat's recent statistical publications on social exclusion (Mejer, 2000). However, in important respects this generates an impoverished research agenda, focused on the social arithmetic of misery and insufficiently informed by broader debates on social inclusion. The value of research on household conditions is not in doubt: however, it is worth questioning whether it is sufficient.

First, as well as identifying the numbers of persons or households falling below such thresholds of multi-dimensional disadvantage, it would seem important *to provide data on relative life chances and livelihood strategies across the whole social spectrum*. There are dangers (Levitas, 1996) that the language of social exclusion will otherwise lead researchers and policy makers to focus on the divide between mainstream and excluded, overlooking the patterns of stratification and inequality *within* the supposed 'mainstream'. It is also important to make sense of the different life trajectories along which individuals and households located at different places in this system of stratification typically move, depending on the insecurities to which they are exposed, the opportunities available, and the resources and supports which they typically command, including those mediated by social and public policies (Room, 2000). Not least, it can be argued that the livelihood strategies and life projects pursued by more advantaged groups can have negative consequences for the life trajectories of the less advantaged, thereby producing the very processes of social exclusion in which we are supposedly interested. 'Exclusion' is, in part at least, the result of such a zero-sum struggle, rather than being a label to attach to the casualties of some impersonal process of urban-industrial change.

Second, the indicators of social exclusion which are being promoted by the EU are in general concerned with low levels of consumption: *they say little if anything about assets and investments*. However, the ability of a person or household to survive adversity and to take up opportunities depends heavily on their portfolio of assets. The ECHP, the prime instrument currently available at European level for general comparable statistics on social exclusion, includes next to no information on savings and capital ownership; and while it does include data on education and health, investments in a person's human capital, this is in nothing like the sort of detail as the data on income and consumption. As Barnes et al. (2002) have highlighted, in their recent studies of social exclusion dynamics in the EU, these data need to be strengthened with several key considerations in mind: the strategies that families adopt for supporting their young people in their education, re-affirming thereby the inter-generational bargain within each family; and the pursuit of education and human capital not just as a means of securing consumption streams in the future, but also as positional goods, enabling the holder to monopolize access to privileged positions (Room, 2002).

Third, as well as individual assets, *collective assets and investments shape well-being at the individual level*: these also therefore need to be monitored, along with patterns of differential access to such resources. This suggests that household surveys and panel studies need to include questions on the availability or non-availability of these local community resources, if we are to understand the differential vulnerability of different individuals and households to social exclusion and disadvantage. No less important are local traditions of mutual aid, self-help organizations and other elements of development potential; or, more negatively, local sub-cultures which may limit and undermine the capacity of local people to take up opportunities and to take control of their lives (Moulaert, 1995). This is of obvious relevance for policy makers, who must consider what actions they will take to invest in these local community resources – this social capital – alongside policies which are targeted on particular individuals and households. Yet it is not just local communities and neighbourhoods which can be sources of such support. Workplaces and occupational communities can offer occupational welfare in its broadest sense also. And of course, extended family networks offer patterns of support which vary markedly between different European countries (Paugam, 1996; Paugam and Russell, 2000).

Fourth, while the development of improved statistics of the conditions of individuals and households is welcome, this may say little about *the institutional processes by which these conditions arise*. Unemployment, a prime risk factor in social exclusion, is not a randomly distributed event: it is the result of a decision by an employer who is pursuing certain strategic goals for his enterprise, within a particular set of labour market conditions and legal regulations. Retirement, another important risk factor, involves the end of normal employment earnings: but whether or not it leads to deprivation depends on pensions provisions, social services and the patterns of informal support in the local community. The cohort and panel studies on which mainstream social exclusion studies rely may include some data which can be used to draw inferences about these institutional processes, but they are no more than that: intuitively plausible inferences. The basis they provide for inferences for policy is similarly tenuous.

Public policy reform involves re-shaping the strategic environment of key institutional actors. Government legislates on employment protection: employers find it more difficult to dismiss workers on regular contracts and they may make increasing use of irregular labour. Government legislates on child protection: social service directors give this greater priority, even if services to other needy groups are in consequence reduced. We need to understand how, on the one hand, the strategies of these institutional chiefs are shaped by public policy, and how, on the other, these strategies then affect individuals and households. Only then can we draw policy inferences from data about these household conditions.

What sorts of data about institutional strategies would be required? We would need to find out about the strategic goals of the institutions in question, the resources and techniques at their disposal, the investments they are making in new skills and resources, and relevant aspects of the broader political, social and economic environment. How would such data be obtained? One approach might involve a 'panel' study, but one addressed not to households but to organizations and their heads: enterprises, educational institutions, local authorities and health services, local community organizations. Thus, for example, during the 1990s the UK Workplace Industrial Relations Panel Survey (WIRS) collected data through a national survey of British workplaces, including a substantial panel element tracking changes between the years 1990, 1994, 1998 (Cully et al., 1999). Even within this panel survey, some of the workplace issues that are investigated – payments systems, equal opportunities, flexibility – are relevant to an analysis of risks of social exclusion. To extend this approach to other key institutions which shape the risks of social exclusion, and to conduct it on a cross-national basis, would certainly pose practical and methodological challenges, but there would seem to be no reason why these should be insurmountable.

A second approach to the analysis of institutional strategies is exemplified by Davies's study (2000) of secondary schools in Sheffield. He traces how the strategy and the resources of each school were re-shaped by the Conservative reforms of the 1990s, with each school being obliged to become an entrepreneur in search of pupils, even while the latter shopped around for the 'best' school. He then traces the consequences for the various competing schools: the vicious and virtuous spirals of decline or expansion, in terms of pupil numbers and funding. He also points to specific tactics employed by the schools in pursuit of their strategies: excluding difficult pupils; marketing themselves with a specific eye on affluent homes. From his analysis follows, on the one hand, an explanation of the association between social origins and educational success; on the other, specific policy recommendations for those who might wish to make 'equal opportunity' for those from different backgrounds more of a reality.

A further approach would be to investigate the interplay of organizational strategies and household trajectories within particular communities. Numerous examples could be taken from the action-research projects that took part in the series of European programmes discussed earlier in this chapter (see, for example, Dennett et al., 1982, Part 2). Initial efforts by these projects commonly involved local household surveys, aimed at mapping those households who were suffering deprivation and experiencing family dysfunction. However, the results of these surveys commonly suggested that the roots of deprivation lay in various institutional process and organizational strategies. In many cases, for example, local municipalities were pursuing strategies of re-development, which gave little attention to the needs or voice of local residents. It was also common to find that household deprivation and income insecurity were directly related to labour market fluctuations: local employers accommodated to fluctuations in demand by laying off or taking on local unskilled labour. Each of these organizational strategies was framed in a specific political and economic context and might therefore have been different, had public policy set different requirements in terms of redevelopment planning on the one hand, and employment protection on the other.

In short, these approaches focus not so much on those who are, or are at risk of becoming, excluded, but on the strategies of those who do the excluding and including in the first place: on organizations, that is, whose strategies shape the trajectories of inclusion and exclusion which people experience, either enabling them to take up opportunities, or multiplying the adversities that they encounter. Without research into these organizational strategies, we will end up with supposed policy recommendations which are, however, ignorant of the structural and institutional context of the society in question. Such policy recommendations tend to focus on handing out social benefits to the casualties of urban-industrial society, rather than considering how the processes going on in that society should be modified, to prevent such high rates of casualty.

Conclusion

Social research is influenced in a variety of ways by the agendas of governmental bodies. Public policy makers powerfully shape the agenda of public debate, which social researchers may seek both to inform and criticize. Public policy makers direct some of the major data-gathering agencies in the fields of social and economic policy, so that the content, scope, timeliness, quality and accessibility of such data have important implications for what social researchers can do. Public policy makers also, of course, fund much social research, whether directly through government departments or indirectly, through research councils and similar bodies.

As this chapter has demonstrated, the EU institutions have played a significant role in shaping the context of comparative research into social exclusion, as European policy goals have changed. The chapter has also pointed to the European data systems which have slowly developed, and the way these have been shaped by these same policy concerns. And we have seen how these EU institutional strategies have served to include some research approaches and exclude others, thereby providing both opportunities and constraints for the development of research relevant to both policy and theory.

It is not only the broad policy goals – in this case of the EU institutions – that drive their institutional strategies in relation to the research environment. Bureaucratic politics also plays a role. DG Employment (formerly DGV) may be the lead Directorate-General for policy initiatives on poverty and social inclusion, but with social inclusion now a core part of the OMC, the economic DGs seem to be exercising a powerful role (De La Porte et al., 2001). Since the mid-1980s Eurostat has sought, on the one hand, to develop data systems to serve EU policy goals in this field; on the other, to manage the politics of its relations with the national statistical offices. The decision not to continue with the ECHP seems in part to have been taken because of difficulties in securing a strong commitment to its timely implementation by some of these national offices. Meanwhile DG Research has included studies of social exclusion in its Framework IV and V programmes. The overall coherence of these separate initiatives is not always apparent and would be an interesting and worthwhile topic of investigation in its own right.

We can summarize this stocktaking of the European social exclusion agenda – and in particular the context and direction it sets for research – as follows:

- A strong EU policy focus is now in place, centred on the OMC, and therefore involving common indicators of inclusion and exclusion, a cycle of national reporting and comparison, and efforts to promote cross-national policy learning;
- The indicators which have been chosen for the OMC focus on final outcomes and may not by themselves suffice for policy comparison and policy learning;
- At a European level, statistical indicators are needed of the relational aspects of social exclusion, and the significance of collective resources for household well-being; the prospects for dynamic tracking of changes in household circumstances are unclear, with the end of the ECHP and the launch of a new cross-sectional survey, the EU-SILC;
- Investment is also needed in the development of common approaches to the evaluation of policy effectiveness and to the analysis of the relationship between policy outputs and final social conditions;

- The traditions of cross-national action-research which are the legacy of earlier EU initiatives could now offer a valuable instrument for promoting cross-national policy learning, the ultimate goal of the OMC.

At the beginning of the story which this chapter has told – the first anti-poverty initiatives of the 1970s – what was striking was that poverty should figure at all on the European Community's policy horizon, venturing as it did beyond the narrow confines of a social policy supportive of the labour market. With the Amsterdam Treaty and the Lisbon process, poverty and social exclusion have moved centre stage. This is thus a key moment to have taken stock of the political context and dominant paradigms shaping international and comparative research into social exclusion. We have, in particular, suggested that the politically dominant approaches to data and to policy learning, in terms of national reporting by reference to common indicators of exclusion and inclusion, may be quite inadequate as a basis for policy monitoring and cross-national policy learning. Nevertheless, some of the other traditions of policy analysis and cross-national action-research which our history has re-called could, suitably employed, be used to provide some powerful processes of comparative policy evaluation. This is turn could serve the larger purposes of policy scrutiny and public accountability which should, in part at least, be the ultimate concern of social research (De la Porte et al., 2001).

References

Atkinson, A.B., B. Cantillon, E. Marlier and B. Nolan (2002), *Social Indicators: the EU and Social Inclusion*, Oxford: Oxford University Press.

Barnes, Matt, Christopher Heady, Sue Middleton, Jane Millar, F. Papadopoulos, Graham Room, and Panos Tsakloglou (2002), *Poverty and Social Exclusion in Europe*, Cheltenham, UK and Northampton, MA, USA: Edward Elgar.

Council of Ministers (1989), 'Resolution on combating social exclusion (89/C277/01)', *Official Journal*, 31 October, Brussels.

Cully, Mark, S. Woodland, A. O'Reilly and G. Dix (1999), *Britain at Work. As Depicted by the 1998 Workplace Industrial Relations Panel Survey*, London: Routledge.

Davies, N. (2000), *The School Report*, London: Vintage.

De la Porte, C., P. Pochet and G. Room (2001), 'Social benchmarking, policy-making and new governance in the EU', *Journal of European Social Policy*, **11**(4), pp. 291–307.

Dennett, J., E. James, G. Room and P. Watson (1982), *Europe Against Poverty: the European Poverty Programme 1975–80*, London: Bedford Square Press.

European Commission (1977), *The Perception of Poverty in Europe* (V/171/77–E), Brussels.

European Commission (1981), *Final Report from the Commission to the Council on the First Programme of Pilot Schemes and Studies to Combat Poverty*, (COM(81)769): Brussels.

European Commission (2000), *Proposal for a Decision of the European Parliament and of the Council establishing a Programme of Community action to encourage cooperation between Member States to combat Social Exclusion* (presented by the Commission), COM (2000) 368 final, 16 June.

European Commission (2002), *Joint Report on Social Inclusion*, Luxembourg: European Communities.

European Council (2000), Lisbon European Council, *Presidency Conclusions*, 23–24 March.

Eurostat (1990), *Poverty in Figures: Europe in the 1980s*, Luxembourg: European Commission.

Eurostat (1993), *European Community Household Panel: Strategy and Policy*, Luxembourg.

Eurostat (2001), *EC Household Panel Newsletter* (1/01), Luxembourg: Eurostat.

Goodin, Robert E., B. Headey, R. Muffels and H-D. Dirven (1999), *The Real Worlds of Welfare Capitalism*, Cambridge: Cambridge University Press.

Leisering, Lutz and Robert Walker (eds) (1998), *The Dynamics of Modern Society*, Bristol: The Policy Press.

Levitas, R. (1996), 'The concept of social exclusion and the new Durkheimian hegemony', *Critical Social Policy*, Vol 16, pp. 1–20.

Mejer, L. (2000), *Social Exclusion in the EU Member States*, Luxembourg: Eurostat.

Mitton, Roger, Peter Willmott and Phyllis Willmott (1983), *Unemployment, Poverty and Social Policy in Europe*, London: Bedford Square Press.

Moulaert, Frank (1995), 'Measuring socioeconomic disintegration at the local level in Europe: an analytical framework', in Graham Room (ed.) (1995), *Beyond the Threshold: The Measurement and Analysis of Social Exclusion*, Bristol: The Policy Press.

O'Higgins, Michael and S. Jenkins (1987), 'Poverty in Europe: estimates for the numbers in poverty in 1975, 1980, 1985', Bath: University of Bath.

Paugam, Serge (1995), 'The spiral of precariousness', in Graham Room (ed.), *Beyond the Threshold: The Measurement and Analysis of Social Exclusion*, Bristol: The Policy Press.

Paugam, S (1996), 'Poverty and social disqualification: a comparative analysis of cumulative disadvantage in Europe', *Journal of European Social Policy*, **6**(4), 287–304.

Paugam, Serge and H. Russell (2000), 'The effects of employment precarity and unemployment on social isolation', in Duncan Gallie and Serge Paugam (eds), *Welfare Regimes and the Experience of Unemployment in Europe*, Oxford: Oxford University Press.

Robbins, D. et al. (1994), *National Policies to Combat Social Exclusion* (Third Annual Report of the European Observatory on Policies to Combat Social Exclusion), Brussels: European Commission.

Room, Graham (1986), *Cross-National Innovation in Social Policy*, London: Macmillan.

Room, G. (1999), 'Social exclusion, solidarity and the challenge of globalisation', *International Journal of Social Welfare*, **8**(3), 166–74.

Room, Graham (2000), 'Trajectories of social exclusion: the wider context for the third and first worlds', in Dave Gordon and Peter Townsend (eds), *Breadline Europe: The Measurement of Poverty*, Bristol: The Policy Press.

Room, G. (2002), 'Education and welfare: recalibrating the European debate', *Policy Studies*, **23**(1), 37–50.

Room, Graham (ed.) (1995), *Beyond the Threshold: The Measurement and Analysis of Social Exclusion*, Bristol: The Policy Press.

Room, Graham et al. (1991), *National Policies to Combat Social Exclusion* (First Annual Report of the EC Observatory on Policies to Combat Social Exclusion), Brussels: European Commission.

Room, Graham et al. (1992), *National Policies to Combat Social Exclusion* (Second Annual Report of the EC Observatory on Policies to Combat Social Exclusion), Brussels: European Commission.

Room, Graham et al. (1993), *Anti-Poverty Action-Research in Europe*, Bristol: SAUS.

Social Protection Committee (2001), *National Action Plans against Poverty and Social Exclusion (NAPsincl) 2001/03*, (Ref:SPC/01/01/02_EN Council Ref:5366/00), Directorate E2 DGH EMPL (J27 1/201), Brussels.

Townsend, Peter (1970), *The Concept of Poverty*, London: Heinemann.

20 Shelter, housing and inequality

Ray Forrest

Introduction

How do we construct the housing question from a comparative perspective? How do we begin to map out variations over space and time in the processes which shape patterns of housing provision and housing inequalities? This chapter offers an introductory exploration of these issues. Initially, it outlines a general framework for understanding some of the special features of housing as a focus of social policy and government intervention. It then proceeds to define the nature of the contemporary housing policy debate, primarily but not exclusively, in (post-) industrialized societies and outlines how this debate can be approached for purposes of international comparative research. The remainder of the chapter then concentrates on three processes which are central to the contemporary housing question: *social change and economic uncertainty*; *demographic ageing*; *housing commodification and social disadvantage*.

The nature of housing and the contemporary housing policy debate

Unlike policy areas such as education, health or social security, housing provision is most typically dominated by market processes in both construction, use and exchange. Moreover, housing as a physical entity is immobile, generally durable and encompasses wide variations in style and function. As a social creation and in its everyday use it is intimately local and the key site of daily routine and family life. At the other extreme, investment in housing and the flows of funds into and out of the residential sphere have significant ramifications for household finances, national economies and global financial flows. Housing is both globalized big business and the private sphere of the home. It is pivotal to social status, processes of social and spatial segregation, daily social interaction as well as a key sector in capitalist economies. Indeed, the state of the residential property sector is increasingly seen as a bell-wether of the general health of national economies. A depressed housing market is likely to be associated with a general downturn in consumer and business confidence and symptomatic of wider economic problems. An analysis of house price busts by the IMF concludes that falling residential property markets have more severe impacts on the wider economy than falling stock and shares.

Private consumption fell sharply and immediately in the case of housing price busts while the decline was smaller and more gradual after equity price busts. These findings are consistent with recent research which found larger short term (impact) and long run effects of changes in housing wealth compared with equity wealth (IMF, 2003: 14–15).

At the time of writing, policy and political debate in Britain is preoccupied with the apparently unstoppable surge in house prices paralleled by a decline in manufacturing output, a crisis in pension funds and a thoroughly depressed stock market. There are daily and contradictory commentaries on the inevitable property crash which is looming in the context of growing consumer debt fuelled by an ever rising stock of housing-related equity. At the same time, much of the Asian world is struggling to escape the aftermath of a financial crisis occasioned in great part by unregulated overinvestment in residential property development. The contrasting fortunes of different property markets are increasingly interconnected as funds flow from across the globe with investors seeking better alternatives to stocks and shares.

This pervasive discourse of investment, capital gains, booms and busts, positive or negative equity is, however, symptomatic of a wider change in the way in which housing is provided and whose interests are dominant in policy debates. It is a debate in which the interests of home owners and mortgage financiers take precedence over traditional housing policy priorities. Concerns with the homeless, the poor in need of some form of subsidized housing and with addressing the basic provision of adequate, affordable shelter for those unable to compete in the housing market have tended to be progressively sidelined. Why is this?

We can point to the following underlying factors which explain the tone of contemporary housing policy debate. First, national governments in varying economic circumstances and of varying political persuasion have embraced individual, mortgage-financed home ownership as the most appropriate form of provision for the majority of households. Second, home ownership apparently meshes most comfortably with neoliberal economic doctrines and with fiscal pressures associated with the global competitiveness. Third, the rise of home ownership has meant that it has become in many national contexts the housing tenure of the majority, or at least the housing tenure of those with the greatest political and economic bargaining power. Fourth, and related to the previous point, those in need of non-profit, social or public housing are most typically households on the economic margins with limited bargaining power in the knowledge-intensive labour markets of the twenty-first century. Here, we are referring to minorities, often ethnic minorities, in core capitalist economies or to the disposable labour of large swathes of Asia and Latin America. Fifth, and as intimated above, the health of the residential economy is of increasing importance in what Boyer has referred to as nascent 'property owning regimes' – capitalist economies fuelled by spending power rooted in stocks, shares, bonds and housing equity. Retail sales and small business start-ups are intimately connected with the undulations of property prices. As the IMF report emphasizes, the effects of soaring or falling residential property values ripple positively or negatively through macro-economies. And unsurprisingly, the price paid by governments for the promotion of home ownership and the retreat from state intervention in housing provision is a loss of direct control and leverage. This becomes apparent when housing markets fall into severe recession and home-owning households plead in vain for their governments to act decisively to counteract these recessionary trends – or when economists provide contradictory predictions of imminent price trends.

The financial aspects of housing, housing as exchange value and investment, are therefore increasingly dominating influences in housing policy debate. This trend is part and parcel of a less benign world in which market influences are more prevalent and in which inequalities in wealth and income are resurgent. The 1980s and 1990s saw a divergence of incomes, particularly in countries such as the USA and the UK, as tax regimes became less progressive and the demand for skilled labour rose relative to unskilled (Castells, 1998; Cochrane, 1993). These divergent trends in income and wealth were particularly marked in the major cities of the capitalist core (see for example, Hamnett, 2003).

Temporally, we can detect a strong shift from the shape of housing policy of the post-World War II period in which the public sector was an important force in addressing absolute housing shortages and unacceptable housing conditions and opportunities. And spatially, the most evident patterns are ones of segregation and division of concentrations of impoverished and disconnected communities paralleled by a trend towards defensive and defended communities of the rich (Blakely and Snyder, 1997). Between those two extremes lie the middle masses in varying conditions of economic security. This is, of course, inevitably a broadbrush description of the shape of housing and housing policy across the world but it is our starting point and one echoed by the most recent assessment by the United Nations Centre for Human Settlement (Habitat). In its 2001 report on the state of the urbanized world it observes that in contrast to the post-war period, few countries provide government-supported housing to a wide cross-section of their populations. It may be that public provision on a broad scale is no longer necessary but the social consequences appear to have been generally negative. 'The unwillingnesss to subsidize "unproductive" investment in housing is a consequence, at least in part, of the pressures felt by governmental leaders from perceived global competition; it has led to heightened segregation and inequality in housing provision around the world' (UNCHS, 2001: 39).

Constructing the housing question comparatively

It has often been said that housing is an essentially local issue. An official European Union Communique in 1989 (European Union, 1989) stressed that the pursuit of a common European housing policy was not only complex but also inappropriate. On the principle of subsidiarity, housing matters were best left to lower tiers of government which would have the knowledge of local housing needs and requirements and of the shape of local markets to deal most effectively with housing matters. Certainly, in physical terms, dwellings are uniquely located. However uniform the design or layout, no one dwelling is exactly the same as another. Even in the apparently homogeneous environment of somewhere like Hong Kong with its blocks of pencil-thin skyscrapers, floor level and view distinguishes one flat from another. People will often have subtle preferences which favour one property rather than another. As has been stressed above, housing is a major element of a contemporary political economy in which the vicissitudes of property investment both reflect but increasingly act upon production and consumption. But it is also an intensely intimate ingredient of our social life. Where we live, what we live in, who we live with, who lives beside us and how secure we feel in our residential surroundings are of utmost importance to an individual's sense of well-being, belonging and identity. The house as home connects in a myriad of ways to all the other elements of everyday life. To be homeless is to be extensively disconnected and, in most cases, profoundly excluded from the social norms of the majority. In comparative terms these norms will inevitably vary as will definitions and experiences of homelessness. But we should have at the forefront of our analysis this pivotal role of housing as the receptacle for most of our material goods and many of our activities and memories. Major inequalities in housing provision thus resonate throughout social structures and social relations and it is for this reason that housing has so often been at the forefront of popular struggles for social justice (Castells, 1983).

In more general terms, when we are exploring housing issues comparatively both within and between nation-states, we need to take account of what will be a unique mix of 'local' ingredients. These will include the nature of the dwelling stock, dwelling quality, policy histories, institutional structures, demographic patterns, cultural norms and levels of affluence. For example, a society with a rapidly ageing population living mainly in city apartments with a substantial public rented sector and a relatively underdeveloped mortgage finance system will have a very different set of policy issues and possibilities compared with a demographically younger society with a predominance of home owners living in family houses in suburbs with high levels of residential mobility and where employers are important providers of direct and indirect subsidies. This is not to say that there are such stark contrasts between actually existing housing systems but there are strong path dependencies in the options available to policy makers. The dwellings produced and the policies pursued in one epoque will heavily circumscribe the shape of policies in the next.

The most obvious contemporary example relates to privatization policies. The strong dose of neoliberalism which began to impact on social and housing policy in the early 1980s in many countries promoted disinvestment in direct state provision and the sale of publicly owned dwellings to sitting tenants, other private individuals or to private companies. Both Ronald Reagan and Margaret Thatcher were strong advocates of such policies. However, the UK had a long history of direct housing provision by local authorities and a substantial stock of high-quality dwellings occupied by a large swathe of the British working class. There were attractive dwellings to sell and tenants who could afford to buy them. By contrast, US policy enthusiasm could not overcome the reality that their state housing represented minority provision for overwhelmingly poor, ethnic minority households. There simply were insufficient dwellings to sell, they were not attractive assets and tenants could not afford them. There can therefore be a convergence of policy discourse in very different contexts and with quite divergent outcomes.

Similarly, whilst there is a strong relationship between space standards and per capita income there is no necessary connection between GDP per capita and levels of individual home ownership. In a European context, Switzerland and pre-unification West Germany have relatively low levels of individual ownership. The explanation lies in a particular policy and institutional mix which has not favoured mortgaged purchase to the same degree as in many other affluent, (post-) industrial societies (Kemeny, 1995).

The housing question is constructed therefore in distinctive ways over space and time. There are both sharp contrasts and striking similarities between the issues at the forefront of housing debates today and the policy preoccupations of the immediate post-war period. Perceptions of change depend, of course, on who is constructing the question and for which part of the world – Birmingham, UK in 1950 or Manila in 2000? What unifies these two locations is that they are quintessentially urban, and housing problems are primarily urban problems. This is not to diminish the significance of poor conditions and poor housing opportunities in more rural areas. But by the end of the twentieth century the majority of the world's population were living in cities. Those cities are growing larger and more dominant. And as we move into this century, housing policies in terms of design, location and quality are inevitably and increasingly connected to issues of environmental sustainability and quality of life. Governments in a variety of contexts and with different levels of resources face rising problems of overcrowding, traffic congestion, environmental pollution and energy conservation. Over half a century or so it is appropriate to detect a significant degree of continuity in the nature of the housing question. Essentially, it has been associated with progressive but geographically uneven urbanization.

There are, however, inevitably rather different problems of mature urbanization in, say, Northern Europe as opposed to the exploding cities of Asia and South America. In the former there are particular problems associated with the ageing residential infrastructure of a previous industrial era and with processes of redevelopment which can have significant impacts on the social morphology of contemporary cities. However, in many of the rapidly growing cities of the developing world rural–urban migration remains the dominant force for urban growth with associated street homelessness, an absolute shortage of dwellings and serious problems of environmental health. The accelerated pace of urbanization and the commercialization of land markets in these parts of the world involve new pressures of eviction and displacement of vulnerable populations (see, for example, Pacione, 2001 for an extended discussion of these issues).

Housing standards in the core capitalist countries have improved markedly for most people over the last half century or so but the continuing reality for millions across the globe is subsistence living, marginality and severe housing deprivation. As has been emphasized elsewhere (Forrest, 2003), on the large global canvas the picture of the contemporary housing question is not so different from one which would have been painted a century ago. The geography of urbanization has changed but the movement of populations from rural areas into expanding cities with attendant changes in lifestyles, social practices, work environments and living conditions remains at the core of housing problems and debates.

The remainder of this chapter will concentrate mainly on issues of shelter and inequality associated with what has been referred to as mature urbanization. In general terms the housing problems associated with older cities do not derive from rapid population expansion but from internal pressures of the expanding numbers of households and from more brutal competition for the prime residential space between the increasingly affluent and the increasingly disadvantaged (see, for example, Marcuse and van Kempen, 2000).

The housing infrastructure of these older cities is therefore facing new pressures of demography, competition for space between social groups and changes in working patterns and practices. The social and technological infrastructure required for the new informational age collides with a built environment constructed for a different set of social and economic conditions (Graham and Marvin, 2001). This tension between the fixity of the built form and the fluidity and volatility of social and economic change is not novel (Harvey, 1978). The residential sphere is in a continual state of recomposition. For much of the last century the key issues of shelter inequality revolved around the provision of basic amenities, general living conditions and absolute numbers of dwellings. Today, however, in the mature cities of the industrialized or post-industrialized world the pressures on the housing stock derive from processes of economic restructuring, changes in social behaviour associated with the second demographic transition (Bongaarts and Bulatao, 1999) and a new set of economic conditions which threatens to compromise existing housing institutions and practices. For the purposes of this chapter three particular issues stand out for further examination: *social change and economic uncertainty*; *demographic ageing*; *housing commodification and social disadvantage*.

Social change and economic uncertainty
The economic conditions facing residential property markets appear to be more volatile. The conventional fissions between those who rent and those who own have become more blurred over time as many societies have seen a growth in individual home ownership. The development of more accessible forms of mortgage finance, state assistance to gain access to home ownership via low-cost loans or other indirect forms of financial aid and various privatization policies has involved a recruitment of households in a wide variety of economic circumstances. Mortgaged home ownership (to be distinguished from more historically rooted traditional forms of often rural home ownership) has come to encompass a wider cross-section of the population. In Great Britain, for example, home ownership grew by some 18 percentage points between 1970 and 1999 – from an essentially middle-class tenure to a form of provision which catered for the mass of the population. At the same time, the conditions which had fuelled the growth of home ownership in the post-war period gradually gave way to a rather contrasting set of circumstances. Put simply, a minority tenure associated primarily with younger households in relatively secure forms of white collar and professional employment in conditions of real income and GDP growth became a mass tenure of households moving across the life course in the context of price and employment volatility. Two points should be emphasized at this juncture. First, we should be cautious about exaggerating the extent of this transformation in the UK or elsewhere. There has not been a widespread malaise but rather a patchworked impact of income or job loss on those who own residential properties. Nevertheless, housing problems which have in the past been primarily associated with the rental tenures have increasingly spilled over into home ownership. This has been evident in a number of countries where at different times there have been rising possessions and mortgage debt and in the most extreme cases, homelessness. Whereas in the past social policy in housing has typically been preoccupied with assisting access into residential property ownership, the emphasis in this new era is turning to issues of security and sustainability in relation to residential property ownership.

In macro terms, across a wide range of societies, there is a complicated mix in the housing sphere of asset accumulation, asset devalorization, social and spatial exclusion and state withdrawal. A previous narrative of modernization and class mobility in which rising affluence and a widening of employment opportunities, often associated with public sector employment, fuelled a middle-class expansion of home owners has been transformed into a more confused and uncertain scenario. Hirayama (2001), for example, describes changing circumstances in Japan where a longstanding recession, employment loss and restructuring and an associated fall in property values has coalesced with, and provoked, new social divisions and cultural transformation. What he refers to as the previous 'social mainstream' of male-breadwinner households, corporate employment and family home ownership was a significant layer of the social glue of post-war Japanese society. The high price of Japanese housing had necessitated high household debt but in a situation where for the 'social mainstream' the salary levels of secure jobs rose with seniority, those debts were assumed to be manageable over a lifetime's employment. In an economic environment where secure work and rising incomes cannot be assumed, rather different social configurations emerge. For example, rising female participation rates are partly fuelled by the necessity to maintain mortgage payments because of reduced or absent male earnings in the household. But that process is only one element in the increased role of women in the labour market. Similarly, more affordable housing enables groups previously excluded to access home ownership – most notably professional single women. The crisis in home ownership in these ways acts to transform previous gender relations.

Intergenerational relations also come under pressure. One cohort of ageing home owners have accumulated significant household wealth. At the other end of the life course, new entrants to the housing and labour market confront fewer job opportunities, less assured income progression and may adopt quite contrary housing strategies through choice or constraint. This is most evident in the falling levels of residential property ownership among younger Japanese. Thus, on the one hand, youth are becoming more independent in their attitudes and social norms. On the other, and Japan is not exceptional, there is increasing dependence of a younger generation on the accumulated assets of their parents or grandparents.

The severity and longevity of the recession in Japan and its distinctive social structure make these transformations particularly noteable in that society. The reshaping of gender and generational inequalities in housing is, however, a more widespread phenomenon. In many European societies the process of departure from the family home is being delayed and compromised. A long period in which each successive generation gained housing independence at an earlier age is, at least to a degree, in reverse (Datamonitor,

2003). Reduced state benefits for young people, longer and more financially onerous periods in full-time education, more precarious and lower earnings for those lacking the necessary skills and qualifications and housing opportunities more determined by market processes all combine to make the transition from youth to adulthood more problematic.

The particular impacts of social, economic and policy changes on the housing opportunities of young people point to a more general set of issues and relationships which are important in considering contemporary patterns of inequality and disadvantage in housing. Different cohorts in any population encounter different social, policy and economic environments in terms of housing opportunities. These cohort effects vary over both space and time. We can contrast, for example, a cohort entering the housing market under conditions of real income growth, strong state intervention, growing employment opportunities and high house price inflation. This cohort will then progress across the life course encountering a distinct set of economic conditions and policy change. Under those conditions of entry one might expect a generally strong upward trajectory in their housing careers. Opportunities for house purchase might have been complemented by a relative abundance of public or non-profit housing accommodating many of the housing needs of both low- and middle-income households. With direct and indirect financial support for both renters and purchasers, the risks of job loss or unexpected and damaging changes in financial or personal circumstances for this cohort are mitigated by a relatively high degree of security in housing.

We can contrast the experiences of this cohort with a group further back in the convoy. They may encounter a less benign environment with greater competition for jobs, a more uneven pattern of income growth within and between employment sectors, less state assistance for both renting and purchase within a general ethos of financial stringency and state cutbacks and a property market which rapidly goes from boom to bust. Under those conditions, the prospect is of a more fragmented and unpredictable pattern of housing histories and trajectories, greater social and spatial divisions and less secure housing circumstances to mitigate adversity in other aspects of life. These contrasting sets of circumstances describe the kind of differences which are associated with cohorts which moved through housing systems during the period of general economic expansion and a later cohort which has experienced the more deregulated, privatized and deflationary late 1980s and 1990s. There are, of course, major variations between societies with similar cohorts passing through very different policy regimes and economic transformations. Nevertheless, it is as important to consider aspects of division *across* cohorts rather than simply *within* cohorts of the same generation when analysing contemporary patterns of housing inequality.

More specifically we can contrast an era where the conditions for the promotion of individual home ownership involved relatively affluent households experiencing rising real incomes, high inflation and growing job security with a new age in which a more competitive global capitalism exerts a strong downward pressure on inflation, state social expenditure, public sector employment and requires more flexible labour market policies. The ideal conditions for home ownership are stability and growth in employment and high general inflation. In such circumstances, borrowing is cheap and debts are quickly eroded through general inflation. Dymski and Isenberg (1998) contrast the 'golden age' with the 'global age' as being centrally about the breakdown of the varying social contracts which were brokered by governments in the post-war period. These social contracts encompassed 'methods of providing adequate housing stock' and 'a set of housing finance mechanisms, including government transfers, subsidies and financial instruments and institutions for accumulating savings or taking on debts' (p. 220). As they emphasize, each nation solved the problem of maintaining housing supply and providing affordable and available finance in unique ways. The most prominent examples of these 'Fordist' institutions are the major state providers of indirect and direct housing assistance such as British council housing, the Japanese Housing Loans Corporation, the Hong Kong Housing Authority or the Northern Ireland Housing Executive. Such institutional forms are, however, rapidly disappearing in the global age through policies of privatization and deregulation. The social contracts of the past are giving way to more diffuse and fragmented social arrangements in which risks are being increasingly individualized. In housing terms, Dymski and Isenberg usefully differentiate between entry risks, tenure risks and re-entry risks (p. 223). These risks tend to be associated with different life-cycle stages and to involve different forms of financial risk. The general point is that individual household exposure to all three areas of risk has been accentuated with the withdrawal or erosion of state housing assistance in the context of more marketized housing systems.

Demographic ageing
Societies are ageing. Demographic compositions vary and the pace of ageing varies but the trend is common and unambiguous. While historical and contemporary responses of market and state institutions to housing needs and problems have been enormously varied, demographic change presents a relatively common backcloth for policy development. The statistics are striking. The combination of declining fertility and greater longevity is producing major shifts in demographic structures. Fukayama (1999), for example, observes that 'Some countries, like Spain, Italy, and Japan, have fallen so far below replacement fertility that their total population in each successive

generation will be more than 30 per cent smaller than in the previous one' (p. 39). In a period of just 20 years, from 1997, the percentage of the population aged 65 and over will increase by some 5 percentage points in Singapore and Hong Kong (Tan, 2000). And Thorns (2002) notes that it will be Europe which is most affected by these changes – 'where the percentage of children will fall from 18 per cent (1998) to 14 per cent (2050) and southern Europe, especially Italy, Greece and Spain, will have the oldest populations' (p. 47). These trends have major implications for, *inter alia*, labour supply, pension and social security arrangements and for traditional bonds of reciprocity between the generations.

Housing policy makers in the post-war period were faced with a rather different demographic scenario in which a severe absolute shortage of housing meshed with a baby boom and a rapid increase in the need for family housing. In the contemporary world, falling birth rates, greater longevity and diversity of household structures and the ageing of the large cohorts of the post-war period place new pressures on housing systems. These pressures include issues of design and adaptation for the very elderly (the post-1918 boom generation), different locational priorities for households when children leave home and as they enter or near retirement, the costs of maintenance and repair of dwellings and the differential resources available to an ageing generation. It is this latter issue which is of most relevance to us. And it is relevant in a number of ways. For most households their dwelling is likely to be their principal cost and, for home owners, their principal asset. The housing circumstances of the older generations also impact on their younger counterparts. Parents who are relatively well housed may provide an important resource for their children, either directly as somewhere to live if independent accommodation is unattainable or indirectly through cash gifts and loans to enable that independence to be achieved (Forrest and Murie, 1995). Conversely, children may find their parents in need of their direct or indirect assistance in housing terms. It is also the case that the erosion of traditional kinship links may mean that such assistance is not forthcoming in either direction.

What is evident is that where government resources are less freely available to provide assistance for disadvantaged households, the family becomes a more important safety net. An ageing population enters retirement with a highly differentiated portfolio of resources to draw upon. Some will have generous occupational pensions, significant savings and valuable, appreciating dwellings. Others will be lifelong renters, dependent on small private or state pensions or social security and have virtually no savings. Moreover, as the ageing population itself ages, it is inevitable that an increasingly higher proportion will be female. The prospect is therefore of rising gendered poverty in old age given the generally weaker financial position of women in the labour market (and thus beyond) and the prospect of depleted incomes with the death of a male spouse.

The consequences in terms of housing inequality will depend on the particular mix of institutional arrangements in place. As in any area of social policy, there is no inevitable determinacy of demographic change. Secure, low-cost and high-quality rental options may be available. The overall proportion of relatively affluent home owners in a population may be substantial. Mortgages may have been paid off and housing costs will be minimal. Social security and pension provision in old age will also vary.

While the most prominent fault lines of housing inequality in old age are most likely to be between those who own and those who rent, poverty and disadvantage will not map neatly onto such a divide. In the UK for example, the growth of home ownership, which was particularly marked from the 1950s to the 1990s, has meant that the level of residential ownership has steadily risen in the older age groups. Forrest and Leather (1998) estimated that between 1996 and 2011, the number of older home owners in England would increase by 37 per cent, with the highest rate of increase among those aged 80 or over. The number of older, single-person home-owning households aged 80 or over will rise significantly, the majority of which will be women.

Burrows (2003) has recently examined the relationships between poverty and housing tenure in Britain and found that whilst the incidence of poverty is higher in the rental tenures, the absolute numbers are greater in the home ownership sector. This is a function of the sheer size of the home-owning population. His work does not highlight old age as a particular dimension but outright owners (who are most likely to be older households) account for some 15 per cent of households in poverty. The incidence of poverty among home owners is particularly associated with those with a manual socio-economic background, black and ethnic minority groups, lone parents, and the divorced and separated. As a more diverse home ownership sector ages, the incidence of poverty among ageing home owners will inevitably increase with the need for new, tailored policy responses.

Moving targets: housing commodification and social disadvantage
Much of this chapter has concentrated on difficulties associated with access to and survival in the home ownership sector. Typically, however, housing problems in most industrialized societies have been associated with the rental sectors. This emphasis on mass home ownership reflects the shifting terrain of the housing problem. In the pre- and immediate post-war period the 'problem', certainly in the European context, was most closely associated with private landlords and private landlordism. This is understandable since it was the majority tenure. The last half of the twentieth century, however, saw a decline of private rental sectors in many countries paralleled by the rise of

other forms of provision in the forms of social renting and mortgaged home ownership. The extent of the decline and the growth of alternative tenures varies substantially between nations. But lack of investment and deteriorating housing conditions, deficiencies in institutional capacity to respond to rising expectations and rapid urbanization, difficult landlord–tenant relations, policy and subsidy support for other forms of provision and more attractive forms of investment have all contributed to the sector's decline. The UK provides one of the extreme examples. Private renting accommodated more than half of all households in 1951 but only just over 7 per cent in 1991. In other countries, the downward trajectory may have been less steep but the direction of change has been similar. The changed political and economic climate of the post-Second World War world combined with the necessities for extensive reconstruction and upgrading of the housing stock saw greater support for direct state intervention in the housing market. The particular housing policy pathways pursued by different governments in the capitalist core countries of western Europe, North America and Australasia require, however, detailed exploration beyond the scope of this chapter. For example, Harloe's (1995) examination of the rise and fall of social renting shows how the shaping of housing policy is embedded in specific political, economic and institutional circumstances. These varied conditions explain the uneven growth and varied forms of social rental sectors and the relative importance and survival of private landlordism. In this context we can contrast, for example, the former West Germany and the Netherlands. In the mid-1990s both were notable for having a majority of households in the rental tenures. However, 74 per cent of German tenants were in the private sector whereas 78 per cent of Dutch tenants were in the social rental sector (Freeman et al., 1996). Of course, such crude labels conceal complicated definitional problems which are discussed elsewhere in this book. It is, for example, debatable how *private* a rental sector is when a significant level of government subsidy and regulation is involved – as was the case in West Germany's post-war private rental sector arrangements. Nevertheless, the general direction of historical change has been from one in which households paid rent to a private individual or company to one in which an increasing proportion of households pay off a mortgage borrowed from a bank, insurance company or specialist housing finance institution. In addition, and in parallel, social or public rental sectors have in some contexts provided significant rental opportunities on a non-profit basis.

These developments can be understood theoretically as a progressive shift from one form of market-based provision (private *rentier* capital) to another (mass home ownership). At this level of abstraction, it can be argued that the role of direct state intervention in housing on a significant scale can be seen as performing an enabling and facilitating role during this process of transition. Empirically, this process of commodification (Forrest and Williams, 1984) or re-commodification (Harloe, 1981)) can be seen in the post-war expansion of public rental sectors in the European context at a time when the social and economic institutions were not capable of delivering home owner-ship to the majority of the population. Subsequently, as conditions changed, processes of privatization and deregulation signalled the maturation of this new form of mass provision and the progressive demise of mass public housing. Harloe (1995) in his discussion of developments in Europe and the USA refers to this 'golden age' of direct state intervention in housing in the following terms.

> The third, relatively decommodified form of large-scale provision, social rented housing, was seen as the product of a relatively brief period, notably the years after the Second World War, when the private rental market's inability to provide mass housing was already well advanced (and made worse by the effects of war), but when the necessary economic and other conditions for the growth of mass home ownership were still absent from the societies in question (p. 6).

Over time therefore we have seen disadvantage rooted in income, gender, ethnic and class inequalities overlain on a shifting terrain of housing provi-sion. Housing poverty has at different times been most strongly associated with residual private rental sectors, residual public or social rental sectors and, more recently, has spilled over into mass home-ownership sectors. For the future this raises issues of the role of government in what are likely to be increasingly individualized and private housing problems and the extent to which housing provision exacerbates or ameliorates inequalities generated elsewhere in social systems. Problems of homelessness, possession, default and unforeseen changes in personal circumstances require a new mix of regulation and intervention if politically unacceptable consequences for the home-ownership sector are to be avoided. The reference to political accept-ability is intended to suggest that the repercussions of widespread payment default among home owners or a rise in homelessness among former owners would have more damaging political repercussions than similar plights asso-ciated with poorer renters. Equally, as was suggested earlier, governments which have promoted more market-oriented housing forms of provision can find themselves relatively powerless when a price bust sends values tumbling. When negative equity hit the economic heartland of the UK in the late 1980s and early 1990s, the government soon found itself up against the boundary of legitimate and feasible intervention. Home owners demanded solutions and policies but little could be done other than wait for more benign market circumstances. Similarly, when home owners in a similar predicament took to the streets in Hong Kong in the late 1990s with placards proclaiming 'Save Us From Negative Equity' the only response was to progressively cut public housing and subsidized home ownership schemes. The developers may have benefited (Fung and Forrest, 2002) but home owners there are still waiting for prices to recover.

Against this background it is evident that housing and social welfare policies in countries with dominant home-ownership sectors will increasingly have to address issues of social and economic stability for those who already own rather than being focused in the main on first-time purchasers or those seeking to buy. The physical deterioration of older established owner-occupied areas is also expanding. Policies to dispose of public housing in countries such as Great Britain, Northern Ireland and in some former state socialist societies have resulted in both a sharp rise in the home-ownership level and in the number of low-income home owners. The coincidence of these developments is likely to occasion the need for new policy interventions in the future. But this has to be set against the background of greater institutional vulnerability in the private sector. Savings, investments and property values appear less secure as major financial institutions reel from the effects of falling stock markets, changes in climatic patterns, natural disasters, health epidemics, war and international terrorism.

And outside differentiated home-ownership sectors are the deeply entrenched pockets of poverty most closely associated with, but not confined to, the public rental sectors (see, for example, Madanipour et al., 1988). This can be perceived as the traditional housing problem of poor people unable to access mainstream housing. Privatization programmes, build for sale policies and low-cost access schemes have enabled many working-class households to gain home ownership status. But the promise of progressive recruitment to home-ownership has not always been fulfilled and the familiar problems of visible and less overt housing disadvantage have simply moved around the housing system with varying spatial manifestations. Those households unable to take advantage of the opportunities for home ownership have tended to be channelled into a downgraded form of public housing provision, often in badly serviced, high-rise, peripheral locations. Sometimes, most notably in the USA, they have taken the form of black, inner-city ghettos. Elsewhere, for example in the UK, visible housing poverty is more ethnically diverse and may be as strongly associated with the poorest and least skilled sections of the ethnic majority as with minority ethnic groups. The processes which have generated these contemporary forms of housing disadvantage also seem more deeply entrenched, more multi-dimensional and more resistant to policy intervention. For Castells (1998) the rise of these socially excluded places and groups within the industrialized capitalist core countries is a product of a combination of trends and developments. These include the differential impact of deindustrialization, privatization trends and their selective impact on social and spatial mobility, the rise of the knowledge-intensive economy and the declining market worth of unskilled labour. In a knowledge-based economy sections of societies are being bypassed in an economic system in which they seem to be increasingly economically irrelevant. As always, poor housing in poor locations is merely a symptom of wider processes of disadvantage and discrimination. However, in deindustrialized, service sector-intensive economies it is difficult to see where new opportunities will arise for those with the least marketable skills. Sections of the population thus face increasing housing disadvantage because they confront housing sectors which are more market based in conditions of falling real incomes.

These developments have created major challenges for policy makers in many countries. The policy trend in places such as Britain and France has been to seek 'joined up' interventions with housing provision being part of a wider set of policy initiatives in which employment creation, educational investment and improvements in health and the general environment are all part of the regeneration strategy. Unfortunately, the creation of employment opportunities is so often swimming against the tide of global economic trends. Jobs fail to appear, the housing stock continues to deteriorate and such areas can become policy-intensive, special cases full of state, quasi-state and voluntary organizations and progressively devoid of shops, banks and other retail infrastructure of mainstream economic life. Again, Castells (1998) provides a characteristic and dramatic description of the global nature of this 'fourth world' – 'the multiple black holes of social exclusion throughout the planet'. While whole areas of Sub-Saharan Africa and Latin America fall within the scope of his description he emphasizes that 'it is also present in literally every country, and every city, in this new geography of social exclusion. It is formed of American inner city ghettos, Spanish enclaves of mass youth unemployment, French banlieues warehousing North Africans, Japanese Yoseba quarters, and Asian mega-cities' shanty towns.' (p. 164). The housing issues are, of course, very different for workers being drawn into the factories of Asia or Latin America, often women moving from rural areas, than for their disadvantaged counterparts in the generally affluent, industrialized world. But proletarianization and deindustrialization are two sides of the same coin with different geographies – low-quality dormitories in one location and deterioriating housing estates in the other. That is an extreme comparison, perhaps, but it serves to underline the historical and contemporary embeddedness of housing policy issues in wider economic questions.

Concluding comments

This chapter has attempted to provide an overview of the changing contours of housing inequalities and disadvantage. It has stressed the need to appreciate the specific policy, institutional, cultural and economic contexts for housing provision and housing opportunities in particular societies when cross-national research is being undertaken. It has also highlighted some key 'drivers' of housing policy change, particularly the ageing of societies and the more fragile relationship between the promotion of home ownership as a common policy goal and the shifting economic fortunes of national economies. New fault lines are emerging, with different societal contours shaped by particular policy regimes, cultural traditions and institutional histories. While the privatizing and deregulating orthodoxies of global players such as the IMF and the World Bank have produced some commonality in policy responses to contemporary housing needs and inequalities, it remains the case that housing policy remains overwhelmingly national or even local in character. It is also the case, however, that globalization conceived of in terms of financial flows and more rapid shifts in employment opportunities is producing new challenges for national governments. These challenges include the problems which can be generated by both rapid depreciation and appreciation of property values, the stubborn enclaves of housing poverty found in major Western cities and the environmental and social impacts of rapid urbanization in Asia and Latin America. For comparative analysis of housing inequalities and policy the imperative is to fuse an understanding of the 'global' with a subtle and nuanced account of the 'particular'. That demands an analytical approach which identifies the key drivers of social change with a sensitivity to factors such as family and cultural tradition, institutional linkages and the historical evolution of housing policy debate.

References

Blakely, Edward and Mary Gail Snyder (1997), *Fortress America: Gated Communities in the United States*, Washington: Brookings Institute Press.

Bongaarts, J. and R. Bulatao (1999), 'Completing the demographic transition', *Population and Development Review*, **25** (3), 515–29.

Boyer, R. (2000), 'The political in the era of globalization and finance: focus on some regulation school research', *International Journal of Urban and Regional Research*, vol. 24, 274–322.

Calverley, J. (2002), 'The power of asset prices', *The International Economy*, **16** (1), 55–7.

Castells, Manuel (1983), *The City and the Grassroots: A Cross Cultural Theory of Urban Social Movements*, London: Edward Arnold.

Castells, Manuel (1998), *End of Millenium*, Oxford: Blackwell.

Cochrane, Alan (1993), 'Looking for a European welfare state', in Alan Cochrane and John Clarke (eds), *Comparing Welfare States: Britain in International Context*, London: Sage, pp. 239–68.

Datamonitor (2003), *Young Adults Living Arrangements*, London: Datamonitor Ltd.

Dymski, Gary and Dorene Isenberg (1998), 'Housing finance in the age of globalization: from social housing to life cycle risk', in Dean Baker, Gerald Epstein and Robert Pollin (eds), *Globalization and Progressive Economic Policy*, Cambridge: Cambridge University Press, pp. 219–39.

European Union (1989), 'Final communiqué of the First Informal Meeting of Housing Ministers', Lille, 18–19 December.

Forrest, Ray (2003), 'Some reflections on the housing question', in Ray Forrest and James Lee (eds), *Housing and Social Change: East/West Perspectives*, London: Routledge, pp. 1–19.

Forrest, R. and P. Leather (1998), 'The ageing of the property owning democracy', *Ageing and Society*, vol. 18, 35–63.

Forrest, Ray and Murie, Alan (1990), *Selling the Welfare State: The Privatisation of Public Housing*, London: Routledge

Forrest, Ray and Alan Murie (eds) (1995), *Housing and Family Wealth: Comparative International Perspectives*, London: Routledge.

Forrest, R. and P. Williams (1984), 'The commodification of housing', *Environment and Planning*, A, 16, 1163–80.

Forrest, R., P. Kennett and M. Izuhara (2002), 'Home ownership and economic change in Japan, *Housing Studies*, **18** (3), 277–93.

Fukayama, Frances (1999), *The Great Disruption: Human Nature and the Reconstitution of Social Order*, New York: The Free Press.

Fung, K.K. and R. Forrest (2002), 'Institutional mediation, the Asian financial crisis and the Hong Kong housing market', *Housing Studies*, **17** (2), 189–208.

Graham, Stephen and Simon Marvin (2001), *Splintering Urbanism: Networked Infrastructures, Technological Mobilities and the Urban Condition*, London: Routledge.

Hamnett, Chris (2003), *Unequal City: London in the Global Arena*, London: Routledge.

Harloe, Michael (1981), 'The recommodification of housing', in Michael Harloe and Elizabeth Lebas (eds), *City, Class and Capital*, London: Edward Arnold, pp. 17–50.

Harloe, Michael (1995), *The People's Home? Social Rented Housing in Europe and America*, Oxford: Blackwell.

Harvey, D. (1978), 'The urban process under capitalism', *International Journal of Urban and Regional Research*, **2** (1), 101–31.

Hirayama, Yosuke (2001), 'Housing policy and social inequality in Japan', paper presented at Anglo-Japanese Workshops, *Social Policy in the 21st Century*, March, University of Bristol, UK.

International Monetary Fund (2003), *World Economic Outlook*, Washington: IMF.

Kemeny, Jim (1995), *From Public Housing to the Social Market*, London: Routledge.

Madanipour, Ali, Goran Cars and Judith Allen (1988), *Social Exclusion in European Cities*, London: Jessica Kingsley.

Marcuse, Peter and Ronald van Kempen (2000), *Globalizing Cities: A New Spatial Order?*, Oxford: Blackwell.

Pacione, Michael (2001), *Urban Geography – A Global Perspective*, London: Routledge.

Tan, Gerald (2000), *Asian Development*, Singapore: Times Academic Press.

Thorns, David C. (2002), *The Transformation of Cities: Urban Theory and Social Life*, London: Palgrave.

UNCHS (1996), *An Urbanising World – Global Report on Human Settlements*, Oxford: Oxford University Press.

UNCHS (2001), *Cities in a Globalising World*, London: Earthscan Publishing.

21 Globalization and crime[1]

David Nelken

Ihr, die ihr euren Wanst und unsre bravheit liebt
Das eine wisset ein für allemal.
Wie ihr es immer dreht und wie ihr's immer schiebt
Erst kammt das Fressen, dann kommt die Moral
(Brecht/Weil, *The Threepenny Opera*, 1928)[2]

Introduction

One of the most striking features of globalization is the way talking about crime helps construct the 'global village'. Today's papers in the sleepy (and remarkably crime-free) Italian University town where I teach are full of a potent mixture of crime stories from near and far (but mainly from far). These project a variety of anxieties about security arising from challenges to the social, political and moral order. Everyday stories of burglary and mugging assume a new-found salience when they are associated not with other Italians but attributed rather to so-called 'extra-community' immigrants (in practice those who are non-EU and poor). But the main news stories are more impressive. We are told about eight North Africans allegedly linked to Bin Laden's Al Qaeda terrorist organization who have been arrested in Rome accused of planning to add cyanide to the water system. We are invited to follow the proceedings at the International War Crimes Tribunal at the Hague where former Serbia president Milosevic (who, we learn, enjoys listening to Sinatra's 'I did it my way') is defending himself (rather astutely) against charges of war crimes by arguing that the alleged crimes took place in the course of a civil war. Discussions of the ways we should be responding to crime also no longer respect frontiers. American methods of crime control such as the idea of 'zero tolerance' are invoked as the best means of responding to street crime. The Minister of Justice announces that he is attracted by the tough American provision of life sentences based on the principle of 'three strikes and you are out'; though he also does concede that it may not be too workable in the formalistic Italian criminal process.

Criminal law and criminal procedure still remain crucial symbolic elements of political sovereignty. But, as this glimpse of Italian preoccupations reveals, the changing nature of crime threats means that it is less and less possible to formulate the response to crime in purely national terms. Within the European Union for example Justice and Home Affairs has now become a key component of the European Union's 'Third Pillar' activities. In particular organized 'transnational', crime, terrorism and illegal immigration have become central political issues for the EU as well as for the other G-8 most powerful industrialized countries. The terrorist attacks on the United States on 11 September, 2001 (what European Commission President Prodi labelled 'the dark side of globalization') – as well as the continuing response to that attack – mean that there is now nothing metaphorical about talk of waging a 'war on crime'.

This problem of how to defend societies against transnational organized crime and terrorism has tended to dominate most discussions of the globalization of crime. Without denying the significance of these dangers, however, my purpose in this chapter will be to show the need for an agenda of research which also ranges more widely. Students of social policy need to look carefully at how arguments referring to the globalization of crime influence a variety of local, national and international interventions. This will obviously involve consideration of the role of politicians, administrators, police forces and the secret services. But we also need to examine the part played by the media and by commercial organizations such as banks and businesses (in Britain lorry drivers have been fined heavily for carrying illegal migrants across the Channel, though the courts have now stepped in to stop this).

In addition, special attention must be given to the discourses of practitioners and criminological experts because of the way responses themselves shape the problem of crime. Crime, crime control and criminology are interrelated in complex ways. Globalization produces or exacerbates a series of difficult challenges for national and international policy makers. But policy decisions or (as often) non-decisions in dealing with social problems also help shape globalization. Thus political, official and public talk about crimes which transcend frontiers – as well as the increasingly global spread of fears of more ordinary crime – are themselves elements of the phenomenon which needs to be investigated. This means that the globalization of crime needs to be examined not only;

a)   as a feature of objective changes in the nature of criminal behaviour and threats; but also
b)   as an aspect of changes in the approaches which are used to combat or to study crime.

In what follows I shall first say something about what I mean by globalization and offer an outline of possible links between globalization, crime and crime control. In the second part of the chapter I shall go on to say something about the rise and implications of what I call 'globalizing criminology' in relation both to transnational organized crime and to more locally based crime threats.

1 Globalization, crime and crime control

The various developments referred to as globalization are the subject of an enormous literature. While it is impossible to review this here it may be helpful to give a few preliminary conceptual notes of how I shall be using the term (readers are also referred to earlier chapters of this handbook). I shall be treating globalization as a name given to complex and contradictory processes regarding the overcoming and reconfiguring of economic, political and cultural boundaries. Law both registers and sometimes seeks to limit the impact of these developments (Heyderbrand, 2001; Santos, 1995). While globalization can make it more difficult to draw political and moral boundaries it may also create all the more need for them. Crime and crime control are of interest not least because of the important and occasionally fundamental role they play in challenging and redrawing such boundaries (see further Nelken, 1997, 2003).

In many respects, globalization can be seen as no more than the latest stage in the expansion of capitalism and the spread of 'modernity'. Little of what is ascribed to globalization in relation to crime or anything else is totally without precedent. There have been other periods, such as the early years of the twentieth century, which witnessed widespread levels of concern about international drug traffic, accompanied by xenophobia about foreign threats (though Britain and Holland were amongst the countries then accused of profiting from the trade). As far as crime control is concerned it is enough to think of the spread of Beccaria's ideas about punishment in the eighteenth century, or the flurry of international exchange visits in the nineteenth century to compare styles of prison building.

Nor is globalization the homogenizing juggernaut it is often portrayed as being. References to globalization sometimes confuse trends towards internationalization, Americanization and Europeanization. Moves to greater unity within the ever enlarging European Union or the signing of the NAFTA trade agreement can be seen both as a sign of globalization and as a reaction to it. If globalization sometimes produces similarities and convergence of behaviour and ideas, it also often presupposes and even heightens differences (Nelken, 1997). Globalizing processes which encourage convergence have objective and subjective aspects (but these do not always coincide). And global trends can have different – perhaps even opposite – meanings and outcomes in different local – or glocal – contexts. In practice the alleged universalism associated with globalization usually comes down to the imposition or imitation of some dominant group or groups' *local* practices (Santos, 1995).

Thus globalization in the sense of growing convergence is not inevitable. Talking about it as if it is may often be part of a political strategy, for example when police seek greater resources. There are already some early signs of a return to economic protectionism; and many national, regional and cultural identities are growing stronger. Resistance movements objecting to decision-making by dominant states, corporations and NGOs have already acquired large followings. On the other hand, even those 'no global' groups most committed to fighting the evils of globalization are forced, or choose, to adopt many of the techniques and logos developed by globalizing companies.

If we wish to plan interventions which can limit the negative effects of globalization we shall need to construct theories of the middle range aimed at showing how crime-related phenomena are affected by and affect larger trends. In this chapter I shall seek to unsettle the widespread assumption that globalization inevitably leads to more crime and that this leads ineluctably to the need for more in the way of international police action. I shall argue that globalization leads to changes in opportunities for crime control as well as crime, and thus, depending on methods and circumstances, may or may not increase or reduce crime. The nation-state may indeed be weakened by globalization but it is also strengthened by reacting to global crime threats. At the same time, 'resistance' to globalization (and not only globalization itself) may itself involve criminal behaviour or otherwise serve to increase crime.

Linking crime and globalization

Greater contacts through trade, travel and communication can give rise to *new types* of crime such as those connected to transnational organized crime or to sexual tourism. More commonly, however, globalization affects the way more ordinary crimes can be committed, and has implications for the levels and distribution of such crimes. It is self-evident that globalized markets have consequences for the size of crimes. Foreign dealings helped produce the multi-million pound losses which brought down the Daiwa bank in Japan or the English Barings bank. (On the other hand the USA home grown 'Savings and Loans' debacle dwarfs these crimes). Increased legal trade also helps camouflage the growth in illegal trade. And illegitimate business as much as legitimate business can gain from customs frontiers being eliminated (as in the EU or NAFTA). Globalization in manufacturing and service industries involves the specialization and integration of differentiated units which can involve legal and illegal businesses alike. Where markets expand but other legal barriers persist, this allows businesses more opportunities to shop around for more favourable regimes of regulation so as to have impunity for what would be white collar crimes at home (Michalowski and Kramer, 1987). On the other hand, too often it is only the criminogenic aspects of opening up markets which get discussed. It is rarely noted that the same developments can also reduce some opportunities for organized and professional criminals. For example, the abandonment of internal custom barriers means that there is less chance for lucrative schemes of smuggling, contraband, and subsidies frauds within the EU. And market opportunities can weaken the hold of local organized crime monopolies (Nelken, 1997).

One important way globalizing trends contribute to crime is by exacerbating the differences between more or less economically successful or favoured countries (those in the centre of capitalism as opposed to those in the periphery) as well as between different regions, different cities and, even, or especially, parts of cities (Davis, 1990). In its impact on developed societies globalization can be seen as an aspect of the decline in Fordist methods of industrial production and trade, linked to the relative exhaustion of the home market for Fordist goods (Taylor, 1999). The loss of the manufacturing base and the possibility of finding substitute work is an important variable in the chain of crime causation. It explains the reduced opportunities, ghettoization, marginalization and social exclusion which provide both the conditions and alibi for much crime.

According to Taylor, as industrial areas decline there is less factory work for young men and much of the part-time work that becomes available is deemed more suited to women. This leads to a crisis in masculinity, the gender order and parenting. With so many women working there are also fewer people around to exercise surveillance and provide unpaid voluntary work in and for the community. As locally based social control declines, property crime and black economy activity increases and escapist routes of alcohol and drugs become tempting (Taylor, 1999). On the other hand, there are also those fortunate enough to benefit from the better economic opportunities presented by globalization. These typically seek to safeguard their families in bubbles of security in defined areas of housing and shopping which are fortified against the risks posed by those members of the population who have been displaced from the economy by processes of global change (Bottoms and Wiles, 1996).

A key feature of crime and crime control in the current phase of globalization is the often contradictory and frequently cruel attempt to increase the circulation of goods and money whilst blocking the transfer of people from less favoured to more favoured countries. From the 1970s onwards international police collaboration and databases have been overwhelmingly focused on blocking illegal immigration. Newspaper reports tell us that immigrants who enter without permission have been drugged and sent back like parcels from France; would-be immigrants have died in their hundreds in the straits of water off southern Italy and Spain, and others have suffocated hiding in container lorries trying to reach the UK.

In Continental Europe the growth of irregular immigration has led to an increase in registered crime but, even more important, to considerable changes in the make up of the officially classified criminal population outside and inside prison (Ruggiero et al., 1995). The offences for which immigrants are convicted are often connected with the irregularities of immigration itself. Otherwise their crimes usually involve small-time drug dealing which is often the only way immigrants can pay their passage (Geopolitical Drugs Watch, 1996). They are also convicted for other (relatively) low-level offences for which most locals would normally be able to avoid prison with the help of competent lawyers and the benefits which the penal process offers to those with a stable address and other guarantees. But there are, it must be said, also many examples of more serious crimes in which immigrants are well represented, both as perpetrators and as victims (Freilich et al., 2002). Attempts to expel or extradite offenders often fail because of difficulties of identification and lack of collaboration from home countries. Meanwhile, the barely acknowledged presence of a large number of irregular immigrants willing to accept work at any price puts enormous pressure on regular immigrants to continue to accept poor wages and conditions.

There are also less obvious, and perhaps more auspicious, ways in which globalization affects crime. Crime is not always simply the product of globalization – it can itself be a factor in producing globalization. Sometimes globalization helps bring offences into existence. The laws against what is aptly named 'insider trading' were introduced at the time of the so-called 'big bang' liberalization of the London stock exchange. They were required so as to maintain the impression of predictability and trustworthiness of the globalized City of London once it was opened up to outsiders. Globalization here led to the criminalization of behaviour which not long before had been considered as acceptable, or at least containable within acceptable limits, as long as it was confined to 'insiders'.

'Globalizing moral panics' about crime problems range from paedophilia to political corruption. These anxieties may not necessarily have any common denominator but their very existence is significant of the way crime reconstructs moral boundaries beyond the nation-state. This is also demonstrated by the creation of International Criminal Courts, such as the War crimes Tribunal at the Hague, and now the permanent Court based at Rome (though for the present these courts have only narrow jurisdiction and the Rome court does not yet enjoy the support of important states such as the US). Traces of global moral concerns are also increasingly to be found in domestic law. Some states have thought fit to pass laws reducing the burden of proof in criminal cases dealing with sex tourism. On one view this increased protection for victims abroad could be taken as a sign of a broadened definition of who counts as a 'neighbour' – one result of the way television has made our conscience global. On another we might dismiss this as more of an emotional reaction to the health and other dangers represented by returning sex tourists (it should be noted that there is widespread toleration of under-age prostitutes working in European countries).

Controlling crime in a globalizing world

Many of the trends associated with globalization have direct consequences for crime policy. This is true most obviously of the 'hollowing out' of the state, the privatization of public services, and the emergence of the so-called 2/3 or 3/4 society with its quota of surplus labour force. As economic actors become more independent of the nation-state this reduces the tax base, and the locus of political decisions, including those to do with crime control, moves up to the super-national level or down to regional and local levels. There is a reconfiguration of the responsibilities for crime control between government and civil society, between state and non-state actors, and between the public and private spheres (Crawford, 1997). The extent to which states adopt neoliberal strategies to stay competitive also correlates highly with the way they handle crime. The retreat from Keynesian economics goes together with the abandonment of 'penal welfarism' and the growth of popular punitiveness towards street crime (Garland, 1996, 2000). 'Inclusionary' social policies go into retreat. The focus of political attention shifts from the offender to the victim. While sexual and other so-called kinds of lifestyle deviance grow in acceptability, the remedying of inequality is no longer seen as the prime task of the state (Young, 1999). On the other hand, though this is less discussed, there can be continuing tolerance of business crimes – as in many countries' reluctance to crack down on money laundering so that their financial systems do not suffer competitive disadvantage.

The globalization of crime control is often thought to mark the decline of the nation-state or at least the need for it to pool sovereignty. But the opportunity to respond to organized crime and terrorism can also offer a way of (re)legitimating the nation-state and even of reversing neoliberal policies. This can be seen in the American reply to the Al Qaeda attack on the centre of international finance in New York and military headquarters in Washington on 11 September 2001. The re-nationalization of airline security and the creation of the office for homeland security are only two of the most obvious manifestations of the re-found centrality of the Federal state. Even with more local threats the promise to provide greater security against crime and incivilities – which is connected, rightly or wrongly, with immigration – has been a crucial determinant of voting in recent national elections in Italy, France, Germany, Holland and Belgium. Holding prisons are being constructed for unwanted immigrants, and second generation immigrants become targets for public order policing. On the Continent crime has gained new salience as a social issue as compared to its more established role in elections in most English-speaking countries. In Britain, domestic social policy finds its direction and funding increasingly re-defined in terms of its implications for crime policy – with results which include the risks of increasing levels of criminalization. One important example of this is New Labour's approach to young people in trouble in England and Wales where youth offending teams are constantly reminded that their priority is crime reduction and not children's welfare as such.

Much the same can be said for the way globalization is pushing the development of communications technologies. Technology plays an increasingly important part in facilitating crime, but it also has at least as much of a role in stopping it. New forms of information technology which construct flows and exchanges in cyberspace serve both as a support for crime and an environment for crime beyond boundaries. The Internet spreads knowledge of crime techniques and facilitates the possibilities for organizing or committing crimes (news reports concentrate on paedophilia, money laundering, terrorism, bomb making, violent racism and hate crimes or even hacking, but the major risk still arises from the age-old crimes of theft and fraud). As important though, the same technological progress which facilitates crime beyond boundaries can also be used for purposes of crime control. Governments increase their surveillance of international traffic through ECHELON and other unaccountable forms of listening devices. Cryptography is used by Governments even more than by criminals. More and more criminals are traced through their incautious use of mobile phones. And the relatively few sites of child pornography offer an excuse for censorship of the many more sex sites (Wall, 2002). Otherwise it is unclear how social control will develop in this area. The initial euphoria over the unregulated communal togetherness which could be created in virtual space has largely dissipated. But the possibilities for individuals to forge virtual relationships have certainly expanded and, in general, though these relationships may sometimes be abused or abusive, so-called 'netizens' bring with them their existing normative values rather than treat the net as a moral wilderness. We may also witness increasing examples of informal control and regulation by, in, and for the 'virtual community'.

2 The spread of globalizing criminology

Images of American types of crime, and crime control, circulate ever more widely. 'Miami vice' pistols are sold in Warsaw, the most violent slum in Abidjan is called Chicago, and so on. But the same applies to the influence of ways of talking about crime amongst the elites. Globalization appears to be helping to produce an increasingly administrative and technocratic approach to crime from which few experts seem willing to dissent. On the one hand, the 1990s saw a major campaign concerned with the menace of ex-communist transnational organized criminals, shared not only by sympathizers with the American secret services (who were in search of a new role) but also by otherwise anti-establishment sociologists such as Manuel Castells in his description of what he calls 'The Perverse Connection; the Global Criminal Economy' (Castells, 1998). On the other hand, as will be seen, even ordinary and everyday crime threats are presented as a new international scourge to which the only answer is the Anglo-American type of criminal justice state.

Two opposing fears

For many writers the key fact about globalization is the enormous opportunities it is creating for business and organized crime. Locally based criminal justice systems, it is said, struggle to keep up with this challenge and perhaps are always destined to be behind. There is a long list of so-called transnational crimes. These include terrorism, espionage including industrial espionage, theft of intellectual property, fraud, criminal bankruptcy, infiltration of legal business, drugs and arms trafficking, aircraft hijacking, the international wholesaling of pornography and prostitution, smuggling and trade in children, women, immigrants, bodily organs, cultural artefacts, flora and fauna, nuclear materials and cars; counterfeiting, crimes related to computer technology, international fraud and other financial crimes, tax evasion, theft of art, antiques and other precious items, piracy, insurance fraud, crimes against the environment, trade in endangered species, and internationally coordinated racial violence. Radical conclusions are drawn from this challenge. The legal institutions of the world, it is claimed, are still bound to the nation-state but the forces of coercion are transnational; existing state-based legal systems therefore cannot protect citizens from the new authoritarian threat provided by transnational organized crime. According to this view the globalization of crime thrives on the inability of the criminal law to globalize.

Although they are given much less publicity, it is also possible to find some consideration of opposing concerns. The claim here is that police forces are in fact using these worries about transnational crime to forge non-democratically accountable alliances. America has long given a lead by exporting its war against drugs and terrorism, but the attempts by the European Union to organize police cooperation in the absence of European-wide parliamentary accountability is another good example. Even before the events of September 2001, European Community members, individually and collectively, had already developed a 'fortress' mentality. One author claims that it is by looking at the enforcement practices of the transnational law enforcement enterprise that we can best come to understand the political form of the emergent transnational world system (Sheptycki, 1995; see also Anderson and De Boer, 1994; Nadelmann, 1993). Research shows that police forces reach their own consensus on the main categories of criminality which need to be pursued even though the criminal law has not been harmonized. The powers and techniques demanded or taken in order to deal with the threat of major forms of organized crime often end up being used against more low-level or local forms of criminality (Sheptycki, 2002). Often they are adapted to keeping out those immigrants who in the present economic climate are once again assumed to be surplus to requirements. It is noticeable that illegal immigration is always now included alongside drugs and terrorism as a major threat against which 'Fortress Europe' needs to be defended.

The global penal gaze

But the effects of globalization on criminology (and vice versa) are not limited to the problem of international and transnational crime. Economic and political developments are also promoting a trend towards a European or even worldwide homogeneous understanding and control of more ordinary and conventional crimes such as mugging or burglary. This ambition is not in itself unprecedented. Many criminologists have long believed that they were pursuing what was in principle a universalizable science. What is significant is the continuation of this endeavour even after the alleged discrediting of Enlightenment or Marxist meta-narratives of progress, when many practitioners of the social sciences have come instead to embrace 'the interpretative turn' towards cultural studies. Perhaps crime, like the discourse of rights or victimization, with which it is of course connected, has assumed such prominence precisely because of the relative decline of more utopian ideologies?

An important example of such globalizing criminology (and not only because of its auspices) is provided by the recently published United Nations' sponsored global survey of crime and crime control (Newman, 1999). The survey displays impressive scope and ambition, offering not only to distil the 'best practice' implications of criminological research but also to summarize the results of an international victim survey of the views and experiences of no less than 155 thousand victims in 54 countries. It starts out by seeking to prove that the crime problem is experienced more or less similarly everywhere. Worldwide, it says, opinion polls show the crime problem to be a worry second in importance only to unemployment. And – crucially – it argues that people are worrying about the same thing. The evidence for this is found in an alleged worldwide 'almost perfect correspondence in ranking of crimes' as reflected in similar ideas about the seriousness of car theft, robbery with a weapon as compared to robbery without a weapon and so on (Newman, 1999: 28). Its vision for a (re)ordered world depends on this premise – what it calls 'crime as a universal concept'.

This sort of globalizing criminology draws on all the world for its data. We are told for example that 'over a five-year period two out of three inhabitants in big cities will be victims of crime at least once'. Much the same explanations of crime, it is proposed, can be applied to both poor and rich countries – and this forms part of a determined effort to re-appraise the link between crime and modernity. It used to be thought that a growth in levels of property crime was the inevitable price to be paid for modernization. But the UN Report claims that the level of theft in less economically developed countries, especially in large towns, has been underestimated (because where people do not trust the police they report less). The Report argues therefore that increasing the level of affluence in poorer countries would indeed lead to *less* crime. The exceptions are where rich and poor live alongside one another, or where affluence leads to more going out at night and hence, just as in more developed societies, increases the risk of exposure to crime. The message is mainly optimistic. In richer countries there is more violence than was thought and this is rising. But property crime is beginning to decline because the market for small consumer goods is saturated, and it is more difficult to move electrical items such as televisions which have now become larger. Crime is also being discouraged by privately arranged security (whereas developing countries have less money to pay for this).

Without denying the value of the Report as a 'synthesis' of knowledge about crime it is important to see how this sort of work seeks not only to document but also to *produce* 'global facts'. Adopting the partial representation of 'crime' current in the debates over 'crime prevention' in developed economies, nothing is said about preventing the harms caused by the boardrooms of company directors or the practices of corrupt politicians. Even the apparently objective task of gathering comparative statistics without ulterior purpose can have itself an independent effect on systems of criminal justice. Thus, after comparative figures on relative rates of incarceration emerged in the 1970s Finland sought to reduce its prison population, whilst other nations such as Italy felt able to do the opposite. But those responsible for organizing large-scale cross-national victim surveys also *deliberately* deploy their findings as much as a tool for achieving social change than as a search for understanding variability. The political goal, which is now seen to be applicable on a worldwide scale, is the need to increase the status of the victim and especially that of 'repeat victims'. The views of victims are assumed to be not only *the* appropriate basis for determining how well police and other aspects of the criminal justice system are operating but also the measure of how they should be made to operate (see further Van Dyke, 2000).

Prescribing the future
What are the implications of all this for the state monopoly of crime control? There is a key ambiguity in the recommendations put forward by globalizing criminologists. On the one hand, their arguments could be seen to strengthen the nation-state. After all, what is mandated is the universal introduction of the Western model of the criminal justice state. The appropriate way of dealing with crime is taken to be 'policing plus prevention', a well-organized mix of public policing public, private crime prevention and community initiatives. As opposed to those such as Garland who announce the inevitable end of penal welfarism the global penal gaze offers a 'top-down' and easy (too

facile?) mixing of the older rehabilitative approach with more 'state of the art' advice about crime prevention. As the UN report puts it, 'promoting social control and responsibility, investing in youth and family, breaking the cycle of violence, city action and innovative policing have become synonymous with best practice in crime reduction' (Newman, 1999: 220). But although the report describes a range of projects which it is claimed will work effectively in reducing crime, there is strangely no discussion of the many reasonably sounding interventions which do not in fact work. Nor does it hint at the difficulties even the most economically developed societies have in organizing unbiased and effective methods of evaluation so as to be able to distinguish the one from the other.

As with other types of international aid efforts the impression given is that organizing an appropriate response to crime is much like setting up a successful health or road system. Perhaps because of the diplomatic requirements of United Nations sponsorship there is no discussion of the problem of state crime, or the participation or collusion of governments in the crimes of their citizens (Cohen, 2001; Friedrichs, 1998). There is also no acknowledgement of the ambiguous role of states in politically, ethnically, religiously or otherwise deeply divided societies. No allowance is made for the intensely political stakes in the construction of consensus for criminal justice interventions, whether, as in the past, against the 'dangerous classes', or, as now, against immigrants and ethnic minorities. Reading the UN report it is easy to forget that what is good for some may not be in everyone's interest. Private sector involvement in crime prevention is seen as only a good thing. No problems are raised about potentially conflicting public and private interests, the danger that private security tends to go only to those who can pay for it, or that those who supply it may have a vested interest in increasing rather than reducing fear of crime.

The emphasis on the need to centralize social control in the hands of the state also seems to give too little attention to the important role played by types and forms of social control within social groups, workplaces and neighbourhoods. Indeed it goes in the opposite direction to the conclusion which has been reached in those societies such as the USA which have most experience of governmentally organized criminal justice remedies. Here we are told that those who respond to crime 'can no longer rely on "state knowledge", on unresponsive bureaucratic agencies, and upon universal solutions imposed from above' (Garland, 2000: 285).

On the other hand, and at the same time, there are many ways in which this sort of globalizing criminology potentially undermines the sovereignty of the state. The UN report speaks in the name of victims and their priorities for crime control rather than in terms of the state's claim to monopoly authority as regulator of disputes. The state is not being encouraged to 'govern through crime control' but rather to improve its services to victims. More generally, the Report presupposes that states need to accept the requirements of the United Nations as a supranational body and the universal criterion and standards it claims should be applied. The use of criminology in the Report – much like the use of science in the Green movement (Yearley, 1996) – is intended to make a given transnational political programme seem natural and universal. As in the attempted imposition of worldwide standards against under-age labour or sexual exploitation – many would consider the projects in themselves of value, even if often unrealistic. But, whatever its good intentions, we need to recognize that the globalizing penal gaze, like the related discourse of human rights, is also part of a scheme of world governance.

Like so many purported examples of universally applicable ideas, globalizing criminology presupposes Western (and even what are largely Anglo-American) models of criminal justice and discourses of criminology. But the USA and even Europe are hardly models of success when it comes to crime control. Even if there is no sign of this in the UN report these societies have themselves sometimes looked to less economically developed ones for approaches to crime more rooted in the community. There is much more to be done in learning from the different forms taken by crime and crime control in other places (Nelken, 1994, 2000, 2002). To make progress in this direction we will need to avoid the opposing errors of assuming either that other societies are – or should be – necessarily like ours, or presupposing that they are – and always will be – inherently different (Cain, 2000). Notwithstanding the obstacles, this will also require the promotion of social policy as a dialogue by which it is possible to listen to, and not only instruct, 'the South' (Santos, 1995).

We have seen in this chapter that both the phenomenon of crime and the way it is studied are undergoing important changes in the context of globalization. But I have also argued that much talk of the globalization of crime serves ideological ends. In a world in which resources are distributed so unequally, the wealth and freedoms of the better off are – and, even more, are often seen to be – connected by action and inaction to exploitation and suffering elsewhere. The current focus on the world threat from terrorism is only the latest example of how talk of the globalization of crime tries to conceal this. Some time ago one astute commentator prophesied that international terrorism would take the place of human rights as a central concern because terrorism can be presented as the ultimate abuse of human rights (Gearty, 1996: xviii). In trying to make the world safe for all (but, we should ask, against whom?) globalizing criminology is first of all also trying to make the world safe for us (and so we need to ask, safe to do what?). In practice, whether or not this is acknowledged, the struggle against crime at the international, national, subnational or local level regularly overlaps with the attempt to maintain privilege, and tame diversity.

Note

1. This chapter was submitted on 17 June 2002 and therefore does not take account of the many developments – most of them negative – since then.
2. 'You who love your paunches and our virtue
   just learn this truth once for all
   no matter how you twist or turn it
   first comes the grub, then comes the morals'.

References

Anderson, Malcolm and Monica de Boer (1994), *Policing across National Boundaries*, London, Frances Pinter.

Bottoms, Anthony and Paul Wiles (1996), 'Crime and insecurity in the city', in Cyril Finjaut et al. (eds), *Changes in Society, Crime and Criminal Justice in Europe Volume I*, Amsterdam: Kluwer.

Cain, Maureen (2000), 'Orientalism, occidentalism and the sociology of crime', *British Journal of Criminology*, vol. 40, 239–60.

Castells, Manuel (1998), *The Information Age: Economy, Society and Culture Vol. III: End of Millennium*, Oxford: Blackwells.

Cohen, Stan (2001), *States of Denial*, Oxford: Polity Press.

Crawford, Adam (1997), *The Local Governance of Crime*, Oxford: Oxford University Press.

Davis, Mike (1990), *City of Quartz*, New York: Vintage.

Freilich, Joshua, D., Graeme Newman, S. Giora Shoham and Moshe Addad (eds) (2002), *Migration, Culture Conflict and Crime*, Aldershot: Dartmouth.

Friedrichs, David (1998), *State Crime* (Two Vols.), Aldershot: Dartmouth.

Garland, David (1996), 'The limits of the sovereign state: strategies of crime control in contemporary society', *British Journal of Criminology*, vol. 36, 445–71.

Garland, David (2000), *The Culture of Control*, Oxford: Oxford University Press.

Gearty, Conor (1996), *Terrorism*, Aldershot: Ashgate.

Geopolitical Drugs Watch (1996), *The Geopolitics of Drugs*, Boston: Northeastern University Press.

Heyderbrand,Wolf (2001), 'From globalisation of law to law under globalisation', in David Nelken and Johannes Feest (eds), *Adapating Legal Cultures*, Oxford: Hart, pp. 117–40.

Michalowski, Raymond J. and Ronald C. Kramer (1987), 'The space between laws: the problem of corporate crime in a transnational context', in Piers Bierne and David Nelken (eds), *Issues in Comparative Criminology*, Aldershot: Dartmouth.

Nadelmann, Ethan (1993), *Cops across Borders*, University Park, PA: Penn State University Press.

Nelken, David (1994), 'Whom can you trust?', in D. Nelken (ed.), *The Futures of Criminology*, London: Sage, 220–44.

Nelken, David (1997), 'The globalization of crime and criminal justice: prospects and problems', in Michael Freeman (ed.), *Law at the Turn of the Century*, Oxford: Oxford University Press, pp. 251–79.

Nelken, David (ed.) (2000), *Contrasting Criminal Justice*, Aldershot: Dartmouth.

Nelken, David (2002), 'Comparing criminal justice', in Mike Maguire, Rod Morgan and Robert Reiner (eds), *The Oxford Handbook of Criminology* (3rd edn), pp. 175–202.

Nelken, David (2003), 'Crime's changing boundaries', in Peter Cane and Mark Tushent (eds), *The Oxford Handbook of Legal Studies*, Oxford: Oxford University Press, pp. 250–70.

Newman, Graeme (ed.) (1999), *Global Report on Crime and Justice*, Oxford: Oxford University Press.

Ruggiero, Vincenzo, Mick Ryan and Jo Sim (eds) (1995), *Western European Penal Systems*, London: Sage.

Santos, de Sousa, Boaventura (1995), *Against Common Sense*, London: Routledge.

Sheptycki, Jim (1995), 'Transnational policing and the makings of a postmodern state', *British Journal of Criminology*, vol. 35, 613.

Sheptycki, Jim (2002), *In Search of the Transnational Police*, Aldershot: Dartmouth.

Taylor, Ian (1999), *Crime in Context*, Oxford: Polity Press.
Van Dyke Jan (2000), 'Implications of the international crime victims survey for a victim perspective', in Adam Crawford and Jo Goodey (eds), *Integrating a Victim Perspective within Criminal Justice: International Debates*, Aldershot: Dartmouth, pp. 97–124.
Wall, David (ed.) (2002), *Cyberspace Crime*, Aldershot, Dartmouth.
Yearley, Stephen (1996), *Sociology, Environmentalism, Globalization*, London: Sage.
Young, Jock (1999), *The Exclusive Society*, London: Sage.

22 Informational society, e-governance and the policy process

Ian Holliday

The rapid development of information technology (IT) is currently affecting many spheres of economic, social and political life. In social policy sectors, the impacts are already considerable, and seem likely to intensify as existing IT applications are implemented and further advances are made. This chapter analyses the current and prospective implications of informational society and e-governance for the policy process in general, and social policy in particular. It begins by examining the nature of informational society and e-governance before turning to key policy issues.

Informational society

For some analysts, the IT advances of the past half-century or so, and particularly of the past two decades with the emergence first of the personal computer and secondly of the Internet, constitute nothing less than a revolution that will transform every aspect of human life. Castells, the leading information age guru, argues that the IT revolution is 'at least as major an historical event as was the eighteenth-century industrial revolution' (Castells, 2000a: 29). Its sheer speed and reach mean that its effects may be even greater than the industrialization changes that have swept the globe since about 1750. As Castells notes, 'dominant functions, social groups and territories across the globe are connected at the dawn of the twenty-first century in a new techno-logical system that, as such, started to take shape only in the 1970s' (Castells, 2000a: 33). Although information age impacts are not yet universal even in societies at the forefront of IT progress, and in many under-developed societies are hardly felt at all, the prospects for change are considerable. For Castells, the product of the IT revolution is 'informational society', permeated and structured by knowledge-based information in much the same way as industrial society is dominated by manufacturing industry. The new society, he argues, is 'informational, global, and networked': informational because of the pervasive role of knowledge-based information; global because core activities are organized on an international scale; and networked because key interactions now take place in networks with global extent and reach (Castells, 2000a: 77). Indeed, his 'over-arching conclusion' is that 'as an historical trend, dominant functions and processes in the Information Age are increasingly organized around networks' (Castells, 2000a: 500). Today, Castells contends, '*the unit is the network*, made up of a variety of subjects and organizations, relentlessly modified as networks adapt to supportive environments and market structures' (Castells, 2000a: 214; author's emphasis). Informational society is network society.

Castells defines a network as 'a set of interconnected nodes', and a node as 'the point at which a curve intersects itself' (Castells, 2000a: 501). A network has open structures, and is capable of expanding without limit. It has two fundamental attributes: connectedness and consistency. Connectedness identifies a network's 'structural ability to facilitate noise-free communication between its components'. Consistency specifies 'the extent to which there is a sharing of interests between the network's goals and the goals of its components' (Castells, 2000a: 187). In informational society, presence or absence in a network is critical, with exclusion constituting powerlessness. Furthermore, within a network power can certainly be unequal, but it can never be wholly concentrated in one place. All nodes, without exception, are interdependent. Finally, between networks interconnecting switches are privileged instruments of power (Castells, 2000a: 500–501, 2000b: 363).

The major organizational and policy process impacts of the IT revolution are to be found in the prevalence of networks. For Castells, the paramount organizational form in informational society is the 'network enterprise' (Castells, 2000a: ch. 3). 'Every period of organizational transformation has its archetypical expression', he maintains. 'It may well be that the business model of the Internet-based economy will be epitomized by Cisco Systems' (Castells, 2000a: 180). What makes Cisco Systems special is its 'global networked business model' within which the Internet and related innovations are exploited to ensure that relationships are key, information is shared, and a 'networked' fabric is created. Inspired by corporate developments pioneered in Silicon Valley in the 1990s, many firms are now engaging in structural reconfigurations that place essential elements of the IT revolution, notably a web site, at the heart of their activities. 'The core of Cisco Systems operation', claims Castells, 'is its web site' (Castells, 2000a: 181). It is not necessary to take on board all that Castells writes. The notion that organizational categories with which we have been familiar for years – class, state, nation – are ceding place wholly to networks is extreme. Indeed, empirical research suggests that emergent information age networks are embedded in pre-existing social structures (Van Dijk, 1999; Halavais, 2000; Slack and Williams, 2000; Rantanen, 2001). Similarly, the contention that the entire world is becoming integrated and interdependent strikes something of a post-9/11 chord. But it also looks rather facile in the face of the unilateralist options that remain open to the US in many spheres (Brooks and Wohlforth, 2002), as well as the continuing exclusion of numerous societies from global dialogue or concern. However, although Castells may take things too far in arguing that the unit is now the network, he is clearly right to focus on the growing importance of networked forms of organization in informational society. This is a key context for any exploration of the impact of the IT revolution on the policy process and social policy sectors.

E-governance

Turning to states, information age impacts are often captured in the notion of e-government, an umbrella term covering many distinct applications of IT to public-sector operations. In a major empirical survey, the UN and the American Society for Public Administration (ASPA) define e-government as 'utilizing the internet and the world-wide-web for delivering government information and services to citizens' (UN/ASPA, 2002: 1). In now familiar fashion, they also argue that analysis should not be confined to e-government, but should expand to embrace e-governance. 'Governance is not necessarily government as a physical entity, nor is it the act of governing through individuals. It is more realistically understood to be a process: the process by which institutions, organizations, and citizens "guide" themselves'. Accordingly, they define e-governance as public sector use of IT, including the Internet, 'to deliver to all citizens improved services, reliable information and greater knowledge in order to facilitate access to the governing process and encourage deeper citizen participation' (UN/ASPA, 2002: 53–4).

Surveying e-government progress in 2001, the UN and ASPA found that out of 190 UN member state governments, 169 (89 per cent) used the Internet to some extent. From this, they drew perhaps their most important conclusions. 'Like the personal computer,' they noted, 'the internet has become an indispensable tool in the day-to-day administration of government'. '[F]or a large majority of countries,' they further argued, 'national e-government program development is occurring in a swift and dynamic manner and for now change is the only constant' (UN/ASPA, 2002: 1, 4). Within these broad statements they also sought to determine degrees of progress, splitting the 169 member states into four broad categories. At the bottom end of the scale, 32 (17 per cent) had *emerging* e-government, meaning that they had simply established an official online presence. Next up the scale, they found that 65 (34 per cent) had *enhanced* e-government, with a number of government sites providing more dynamic information. Moving up still further, they found that 55 (30 per cent) had *interactive* e-government, enabling users to download forms, e-mail officials and interact with government through the web. Finally, they found that 17 (9 per cent) had *transactional* e-government, enabling users to pay for services and conduct other transactions online. No UN member state had *seamless* e-government, with full integration of e-services across administrative boundaries.

In 2001 the clear e-government leader was the United States, followed at some distance by Australia, New Zealand, Singapore, Norway, Canada, the UK, the Netherlands, Denmark and Germany (UN/ASPA, 2002: 2–3, 12). The survey estimated that in 2001 there were 50 000 official government sites on the World Wide Web. It further estimated that 22 000 were US federal government sites, and that close to another 10 000 were US state and local government sites (UN/ASPA, 2002: 5, 16). A separate analysis of the US, published in 2001, noted that 'Today, every state and major city is on-line' (Barrett and Greene, 2001: 15). Ten years on from Al Gore's path-breaking 1993 National Performance Review analysis of government reinvention through application of IT, US leadership is as substantial in this domain as in many others (Gore, 1993).

Although the general tone of the UN/ASPA report was upbeat, it also contained many elements of criticism. Despite creative initiatives, national e-government progress was 'overwhelmingly at the information provision stage'. Development was often 'desultory and unsynchronized', with a 'compelling lack of coordination' across administrative and policy boundaries. Within national public administrations there was a 'significant digital divide'. Across many states there was a 'considerable lack' of public awareness campaigns to inform citizens about online service delivery (UN/ASPA, 2002: 2–4). A 2000 study of US municipal government, published in 2002, was also cautionary, noting that 'e-government has been adopted by many municipal govern-ments, but it is still at an early stage and has not obtained many of the expected outcomes ... that the rhetoric of e-government has promised' (Moon, 2002: 424). A 2002 analysis of e-government in East and Southeast Asia reported variable progress (Holliday, 2002). Nevertheless, the 17 e-government leaders identified in the UN/ASPA report were at least demonstrating the contemporary possibilities of e-government. Their transactional presence com-prised a single entry portal linked to citizen-centric sites that were updated regularly and allowed services like obtaining a passport, paying utility bills and filing and paying taxes to be conducted online (UN/ASPA, 2002: 19–20). They also pointed to the future possibilities of e-governance in which partici-pation in politics and policy is enhanced by the informational and transactional capacities of the Internet. 'E-government potentially increases citizen in-volvement in the process of governance at all levels by introducing new voices in the dialogue through online discussion groups, thus expanding outreach and influence while enhancing the rapid development and effective-ness of interest groups' (UN/ASPA, 2002: 9).

In the most advanced e-governments, policy and policy process impacts are already being registered. Elsewhere, they are likely to be increasingly felt as information age dynamics work their way through political systems. Fur-thermore, the e-governance to which the UN/ASPA survey points is emerging through the growth of e-citizenship (Hill and Hughes, 1998), e-legislatures (Coleman, et al., 1999) and e-democracy (Coleman, 1999; Hague and Loader, 1999; Dahlberg, 2001). Civic networking and citizen empowerment are clear themes of emergent information age analyses (Tambini, 1999; Bucy and Gregson, 2001). It is in these contexts of changing political and institutional environments, driven by rapid technological advance, that the rest of this chapter seeks to assess how policy processes and social policy sectors are being reshaped in the information age.

The policy process in the information age
Capturing the nature of the policy process before the dawn of the information age was already difficult. Trying to work out how the IT revolution might change things is harder still. Against this, it helps that one dominant strand in the policy studies literature emphasizes precisely the kinds of links that Castells argues are critical in informational society. For many years now, the concepts of policy network and policy community have been at the heart of policy studies (Dowding, 1995). They loom larger in analyses stressing the closed and elitist nature of the policy process than in analyses premised on openness and pluralism. Nevertheless, even in porous and fluid policy worlds they play a part. Here, the relevant question is how IT advances are likely to reshape policy networks. This question is best addressed from three separate angles. First, to what extent are inputs to policy networks and the policy process more generally being affected? This is essentially an agenda-setting analysis. Secondly, in what ways are links between key players within policy networks changing? This is really a 'policy-making' analysis. Thirdly, to what degree are policy networks expanding their remit to embrace delivery issues? This is mainly an implementation analysis.

There is no consensus concerning agenda setting. What for, say, Sabatier and Jenkins-Smith is a rather closed policy world dominated by advocacy coalitions is for Kingdon much more open and characterized by fluid policy streams. However, both approaches rely on the linked notions of policy community or network. For Sabatier and Jenkins-Smith (1993), policy space is largely controlled by policy communities. For Kingdon (1995), it is individuals from policy communities who contribute ideas to the policy primeval soup, and who, if lucky, emerge to become successful policy entrepreneurs. The impact of the Internet on agenda setting is clearly to expand the possibilities for participation in policy making (Tambini, 1999: Bucy and Gregson, 2001). This is not to say that such an expansion will take place, because existing occupants and owners of policy space still have strong incentives to exclude outsiders. Nevertheless, the chances are that in the information age they will find it harder to do this. The wealth of information now available on the web, and the direct access to both policy materials and policy actors that it affords, mean that exclusive strategies are likely to be harder to manage. Agenda setting is becoming, then, more open in informational society. Both dramatic and largely hidden instances of this have been witnessed in recent years. Among the most dramatic were violent anti-globalization protests at summits of the WTO in Seattle in November–December 1999, the World Bank and IMF in Washington DC in April 2000, the IMF in Prague in September 2000, the EU in Gothenburg in June 2001, and the G8 in Genoa in July 2001. In each case virtual links were said to have facilitated mobilization. When G8 leaders met in Okinawa in July 2000, the vast majority of e-mails sent to the summit web site formed part of a campaign coordinated by Jubilee 2000 to 'drop the debt'. Alongside these very visible forms of virtual and virtually-inspired protest are much more hidden forms of input into the policy process. A US survey conducted by Pew in January 2002 estimated that 42 million Americans had used government web sites to research public policy issues, 23 million had used the Internet to send comments to public officials about policy choices, 14 million had used government web sites to gather information related to voting, and 13 million had participated in online lobbying campaigns (Pew Internet & American Life Project, 2002: 1). The policy impact of these new forms of citizen activism is of course extremely difficult to measure. Furthermore, existing power elites have already taken steps to isolate themselves from the most destructive forms of virtually-organized protest, with the G8 for example holding its June 2002 summit in Kananaskis, in the remote Canadian Rockies.

Nevertheless, the potential for ordinary people to at least register concerns with policy makers through virtual, non-violent channels is now considerable. Moreover, the ease of sending e-mail to governments and international organizations means that popular input to agenda setting is likely to increase considerably.

Policy making is hard to distinguish from agenda setting, which is why the 'stages heuristic' is rarely used today (John, 1998: 22–37). Nevertheless, if we take policy making to involve reasonably established actors within a policy network – 'insiders' rather than 'outsiders' – then some degree of analytical separation can be made. Here connection possibilities clearly extend with the development of virtual links, and networks can expand. However, in this sphere Internet impacts may turn out to be rather limited. On the one hand, prior advances like the invention of the telegraph, telephone, photocopier, fax machine and video cassette recorder made linkage within policy networks reasonably smooth even before the advent of the Internet. On the other, the wealth of information now available on the web may actually be to the advantage of insiders, and to the disadvantage of outsiders. Whereas insiders often used to rely on information provided by intermediaries, they can now gather material directly and in pure form. Furthermore, consultation, a key element of policy-making, is much easier in the information age, and enables insider actors to engage with outsiders on their own terms. In some ways, then, it is possible that the policy grasp of core network actors will be enhanced, or at least not diminished, by the development of the Internet. At a time when policy making is increasingly evidence-based, technological advances are an important means by which core network actors can expand their capacity and extend their ability to direct policy.

Evidence for non-change is never easy to come by, but any survey of policy networks even in societies at the forefront of the information revolution is likely to reveal that stability, or at least predictable change, is the norm. In all societies, policy networks are of course affected by long-term trend changes such as the challenge to technocracy, the decline of the professions and the emergence of citizen activism. In democratic societies, political shifts such as the election of a new party to government may also impact on policy networks. The Reagan effect in the US, the Thatcher effect in the UK and the Mitterrand effect in France are all instances. Setting aside these sorts of reshaping changes, the impact of the information age on established policy networks appears, so far, to be limited. Policy networks in the US are not qualitatively different today from what they were, say, five or ten years ago. In the wired societies of East Asia, where Internet usage consistently ranks among the highest in the world (Nielsen/Net Ratings, 2002), the coming of the information age has had little or no visible impact on core power holders and policy makers. In Japan, Liberal Democratic Party networks are as pervasive and important as ever, and a Koizumi effect, launched in part on information age themes, is conspicuous by its absence. In South Korea and Taiwan, change to policy networks has been driven less by technology and more by politics, notably the transitions to democracy of the late 1980s and the peaceful power shifts of 1997 (with the election of Kim Dae-jung in South Korea) and 2000 (with the election of Chen Shui-bian in Taiwan). In Singapore, the controlling power of the People's Action Party is as secure now as it was before the information age. Finally, in China, not at the forefront of IT advance but nevertheless a key case, the Internet is being successfully exploited in commercial spheres while being carefully supervised in social and political domains (Dai, 2002; Zhang, 2002). Within policy networks, then, the potential for information age change looks quite limited.

As with agenda setting and policy making, implementation is not an entirely secure category, and has no clear boundaries (Hill and Hupe, 2002). Street-level bureaucrats can also shape agendas and make policy. Nevertheless, for analytical purposes a separation can again be made. Here Internet impacts could be considerable, as policy makers at central levels of government gain the ability to become part of local service delivery networks, and as individual service users are able to interact in quite direct ways with officials. Furthermore, in this sphere the informational resources available online start to operate against established actors and in favour of citizens. In many areas of service delivery, users are now able easily to equip themselves with information that hitherto was either unavailable or difficult to amass. They are also able to undertake some transactions wholly online. An activist citizenry, engaged in policy issues of direct relevance to individuals' everyday lives, is a strong possibility in informational society.

From the evidence to date, bottom-up changes appear to be more substantial than top-down changes. Central actors are getting involved in local implementation issues. One instance from the UK was a 1998 initiative called Better Government for Older People, which brought together a network of actors from all tiers of government and from the non-profit sector (Holliday, 2001: 323). However, time and other resource constraints mean that the real extent of central involvement in such networks will always be limited. Probably more significant is citizen engagement with the public sector. When Pew asked American Internet users about this kind of activity in September 2001, they revealed a strong preference for seeking information online, rather than completing transactions. Thus, 77 per cent of users had sought tourism and recreational information, 70 per cent had done research for work or school, 62 per cent had sought information about a public policy or an issue of interest, 49 per cent had got advice about a health or safety issue, and so on. Only 16 per cent had filed taxes, only 12 per cent had renewed a driver's licence or auto registration, and only 7 per cent had renewed a professional license (Pew Internet & American Life Project, 2002: 7). In summer 2000, Ho found similar government–citizen interactions in US cities (Ho, 2002). It is probable that this profile of citizen activism is currently being repeated in other emergent informational societies. In time, however, a growth in transactional engagement is likely.

Pulling all this together, the pattern of information age impacts on the policy process appears to be variable, with new networks and links being constructed in agenda setting and implementation, but with established policymaking networks being less affected. Such an assessment is in conflict with the persistent belief among information age analysts that IT advances are rapidly fragmenting all elements of the policy process. Writing at the start of the 1990s, Taylor and Williams speculated that the 'centralist drift' of British politics witnessed in the 1980s might be reversed by the emergence of the information polity (Taylor and Williams, 1991: 188). By the end of the 1990s, Frissen was arguing that all forms of command and control were now effectively redundant. 'The traits of [the] techno culture are postmodern: it is fragmented, varied, decentred and non-hierarchical.' His verdict was that 'the only thing governments can do is contingent steering… Surfing on the Internet … seems more suitable than drawing up serious policy programmes and documents' (Frissen, 1998: 41, 46). Little of this post-modernist psycho babble is borne out by developments in nascent informational societies. Rather, what is being witnessed is, for sure, enhanced citizen engagement but also continuing control of much policy space by established actors. The chances of this changing in the foreseeable future seem slim.

Social policy in the information age

Social policy sectors have already been touched upon in the more general analysis of information age policy impacts. Looking more deeply into those sectors, the evidence of change is mixed. IT-led healthcare reforms in the US, the UK and Ecuador, for instance, have all generated both good and bad outcomes (Iglehart, 2000; Ballantine and Cunningham, 1999; Salazar, 1999). Moreover, as much research is undertaken from public management perspectives, it tends to focus on service delivery, and to say little about citizen engagement at the front end of the policy process. Nevertheless, even within these restrictions reforms are clearly taking place. Prominent among them is the emergence of 'one-stop' service centres seeking to make administrative boundaries invisible to service users and government seamless. Single service delivery platforms are increasingly the norm in leading e-governments, and in municipalities throughout the developed world (UN/ASPA, 2002; Ho, 2002; Vardon, 2002: Dionysius, 2002). Many 'back office' changes are also taking place, with IT advances affecting procurement, outsourcing, training and so on.

To get a clearer sense of information age impacts, the rest of this section focuses on a social policy sector that appears to have great potential for reform, and already to be experiencing considerable change: healthcare. Getting advice about a health or safety issue was the only social policy issue actually identified in the Pew US survey of September 2001. Furthermore, in taking a close look at citizens' online activities, Pew placed at the top of its list a 'new urgency for health information'. It speculated that this reflected trust of government on health issues, but also noted that 'those who trust government the least look for health information as much as those who trust it the most' (Pew Internet & American Life Project, 2002: 11). It should be added that these findings were registered before the anthrax alerts that swept the US soon after 11 September 2001, and before the onset of the winter flu season. Healthcare also has the advantages of being information-rich and policy-complex.

Although much of the existing literature on information age healthcare policy change has been developed in the US context, reflecting both US leadership in the information age and the continuing search for solutions to US healthcare problems, analysis does not need to be restricted to that single case. However, it does make sense to draw on themes that are prominent in the US literature, for they define the territory better than any other. Four of those themes address distinct dimensions of the broad policy and management framework for healthcare, examining Internet impacts on policymaking, regulation, provision and funding. The fifth theme looks inside the healthcare sector, and inside the surgery, at the implications of the Internet for physician–patient relations. Eventually, this may have policy significance, but for now it is best treated separately.

In the US, the major argument about healthcare policy making contends that the government has been slow to engage with the numerous issues generated by the IT revolution, and that most policy actors in both Congress and the executive branch continue to focus on pre-information age agendas (Iglehart, 2000). The result is a dearth of Internet-related policy activity, and an absence of perspectives on the Internet's potential to transform the US healthcare system. Clearly structural features of the US system, including fragmentation both of government and of the healthcare sector, play key roles here. Elsewhere, more attention has been paid to Internet potentials. In the UK, for instance, where the National Health Service (NHS) has one million employees and presides over a much more unified healthcare system, the wealth of information placed online by public-sector agencies is close to overwhelming. Some is reasonably straightforward, with the Department of Health, the NHS itself, and devolved health authorities and delivery agencies using web sites to communicate mainly routine information to citizens and patients. This is undeniably useful, but it does not count as path-breaking. However, some information is considerably more advanced. The NHS Information Authority site links to the National Electronic Library for Health (nhsia.nhs.uk). The NHS Modernisation Agency site contains extensive information about clinical governance (modernnhs.nhs.uk). The Commission for Health Improvement site reports on clinical governance reviews undertaken throughout the NHS (chi.nhs.uk). The National Institute for Clinical Excellence site contains state-of-the-art clinical guidelines monitored by healthcare institutions and actors not only in the UK but also elsewhere (nice.org.uk). And so on. Even within healthcare systems dominated by the private sector, public-sector web-based initiatives are now being seen. In Taiwan, where private-sector provision is extensive, the Department of Health in 2002 launched an ambitious e-health project, with a timeline stretching to 2006. The Health Information Network that is central to this initiative has a backbone funded by central government, and permits local users in both the public and private sectors to participate on a self-paying basis. Drawing on US experience, it seeks to promote electronic medical records, based on a smart card system, so that information can flow to all parts of the healthcare sector. A Healthcare Certification Authority, created in 2002, oversees the initiative. In the narrower sphere of regulation, concerns are expressed in the US literature about the failure of regulatory agencies to keep pace with Internet-related developments. Goldsmith (2000) notes that the Internet generates many potential regulatory problems, ranging from licensing e-health practitioners to monitoring information quality in a virtual world with no boundaries. Fried et al. (2000) detail some of the obstacles placed in the way of e-health by existing regulations, holding that individuals and organizations must navigate a maze of rules and codes, old and new, if they wish to implement fresh ideas and approaches. Kassirer's (2000) prediction is that the courts will play a role when substandard medical advice provided through web sites or e-mail yields poor medical outcomes. He believes that courts will be especially important when professional advice is given without a direct patient encounter, or when state lines are crossed. Some of these issues are clearly US-specific, but many have much wider relevance. In many parts of the world limitations are placed on e-consultations, with face-to-face physician–patient contact being required before any specific healthcare information or advice can be given. In Japan, for instance, physicians are prohibited from answering any questions about healthcare or disease by e-mail or telephone. By contrast, in Taiwan the Department of Health operates a Taiwan e-Hospital site to provide free online medical advice to patients (taiwanedoctor.doh.gov.tw). Currently, 237 medical practitioners and 11 nutritionists from 31 public hospitals form a consulting team to answer questions about 29 specialities. Patients seeking general medical advice can send questions to a particular practitioner, and receive feedback online or by e-mail. However, for the foreseeable future in many jurisdictions, online consultation, though technically feasible, is likely to be restricted by professional concerns. Limitations are also frequently placed on information sharing and exchange, with privacy considerations looming large. In Singapore, patients requiring repeat prescriptions can place an order online and have the medications delivered to their homes. Only after six months do they have to return to the healthcare system to consult a physician. In many other countries, this practice is illegal.

Linked to the regulatory theme, analysts also debate the limitations currently imposed on healthcare provision through the Internet. Kleinke (2000) argues that the Internet will not contribute to a solution to the administrative redundancies, economic inefficiencies, and quality problems that have long plagued the US healthcare system. Instead, it will exacerbate the cost and utilization problems of a system in which patients demand more, physicians are legally and economically motivated to supply more, and public and private purchasers are expected to pay the bills. Goldsmith (2000) holds that the challenges of standardizing coding and formats for clinical information, and protecting patient privacy, will hinder the realization of network computing potentials in healthcare. The problems to which these and other authors point are structural. Economic, organizational, legal, regulatory, and cultural conflicts rooted in the US healthcare system are all barriers to e-healthcare provision. Nevertheless, there is a burgeoning amount of healthcare information online, and provision has to count as one of the spheres of greatest progress. The amount of material placed online by the UK's state-dominated healthcare system has already been mentioned. Equally, in Taiwan many private hospitals have online question-and-answer services for patients. In addition, the KingNet Second Opinion WebHospital (webhospital.org.tw) and the Taiwan Physicians' Net (doctor.com.tw) provide free online medical advice to patients. Established in 1998, the WebHospital has some 200 voluntary physicians answering questions from the public. The Taiwan Physicians' Net brings together about 1500 physicians, whose information and advice are posted on the web. In the sphere of healthcare funding, Shortliffe (2000) criticizes Congress for focusing on short-term benefits, arguing that research investment for e-health must be balanced between basic and applied analyses. Robinson (2000) examines the effect of distinct forms of capital on the development of the healthcare Internet. In the late 1990s, venture capital flooded into the e-health sector, rising dramatically from $3 million in early 1998 to $335 million in late 2000. In the same period, 26 e-health firms went public, raising $1.35 billion at their initial public offerings. However, the technology-sector crash in late 2000 hit the e-health sector especially hard, prompting an extended period of consolidation between e-health and more conventional firms. US funding problems thus relate to both public and private sector sources. In other societies the funding dynamics are very different. The UK, with its state-funded healthcare system, has to look to public resources, which have grown considerably in recent years. Advanced East Asian societies tend to be characterized by developmental states that play key roles in guiding private-sector involvement in hi-tech projects (Mathews and Cho, 2000).

Finally, analysts have looked inside the surgery at physician–patient relations. Kassirer (2000) argues that the Internet will change this relationship in unpredictable ways, with some aspects of electronic communication enhancing the bond and others threatening it. Goldsmith (2000) believes patients have most to gain from the emergence of the Internet, arguing that it will rebalance the steeply asymmetrical medical knowledge held by patients and physicians. Using information gained through Internet searches, patients can now open their dialogues with physicians at a much higher level than before, and thereby gain leverage in the care process. Ball and Lillis (2001) also discuss the potential challenges the Internet presents to physicians. As Internet searches often generate as many questions as answers, physicians are likely to find themselves under increased workload pressures. Existing survey data show that among patients performing online searches, 54 per cent of those with a chronic disease ask their physician about specific treatments that they have read about on the web. As more patients go online, increasing numbers will turn up in surgeries with Internet-fuelled questions and concerns. Meeting the growing expectations of these individuals will be a significant challenge for physicians. In a similar vein, Zupko and Toth (2000) hold that physicians sometimes encounter a form of cultural shock when confronted by well-informed patients. It is therefore perhaps not surprising that an April 2002 US survey found that physicians are much more reluctant than patients to use the Internet for healthcare interactions. While 90 per cent of patients wanted to exchange e-mail with their doctors, only about 15 per cent of doctors actually did so. Physician–patient confidentiality, time concerns and increased exposure to malpractice liability were cited as primary reasons for doctors' wariness (Hafner, 2002). In the face of this mounting speculation and evidence, Lumpkin (2000) is sanguine, however, contending that the physician–patient encounter is little changed, despite widespread Internet usage in healthcare.

Social policy in informational society

Castells argues that alongside the crisis of the state prompted by the information revolution and the shift to networked forms of organization, there is also a crisis of democracy. For him, democracy has always been predicated on a sovereign body. With sovereignty flowing out of states and into networks, democracy has become an 'empty shell' (Castells, 1997: 349). Yet, at the same time as the political participation afforded by standard liberal democracy comes under challenge, so new possibilities are generated by the informational capacities of the Internet (Tambini, 1999; Bucy and Gregson, 2001). The extent to which those possibilities are currently being tapped must of course not be exaggerated. Digital divides exist both within and among all contemporary societies. IT-driven government reinvention faces many barriers (Heeks and Davies, 1999). Nevertheless, the potential is considerable. The most important social policy impacts will be registered when that potential is realized.

To generate interactive forms of social policy-making in which citizens make a real input to policy and play a genuine partnership role in delivery – to shift, in short, to e-governance in social policy – it is necessary to tackle the structural inequalities that currently dominate emergent informational societies. Although the UK government has one of the most advanced programmes to tackle social exclusion, it still presides over a significant digital divide. Indeed, Selwyn contends that the entire programme has been given an underlying economic rationale that means it will never generate a fully inclusive society (Selwyn, 2002). Against this, however, there are also positive UK developments.

The government's July 2002 e-democracy consultation paper, *In the Service of Democracy*, floated proposals for extensions of e-voting and e-participation based on five main principles: inclusion, openness, security and privacy, responsiveness, and deliberation. It invited UK citizens to join the government in shaping broader forms of political participation and improved modes of access to the policy process. It pledged to develop the Citizen Space initiative, created at ukonline.gov.uk in 2001, which enhances direct citizen participation in the policy process (HM Government/UKonline, 2002). More widely, experience at the cutting edge of the information age suggests that within advanced societies digital divides may prove to be essentially temporary phenomena. At the start of 2002, a US survey reported 'rapidly growing use of new information technologies across all demographic groups and geographic regions' (US Department of Commerce, 2002: 1).

In these circumstances, attention turns to the very deep international digital divides that currently exist, and strategies for promoting social inclusion on a global scale. Here there is no escaping the fact that poverty is the major determinant of exclusion from informational society, though politics can also play a role as governments use firewall and filtering technologies to restrict or channel the Internet access of entire nations. Nevertheless, even in the absence of concerted international action to tackle global income and wealth inequalities, steps can be taken to put disadvantaged or remote communities online and promote sustainable human development (Harris et al., 2001). If Castells is right to argue that presence in or absence from international networks is crucial to the exercise of power in the information age, then initiatives to reduce global digital divides become imperative.

In this dimension of contemporary social change we can also find an important research agenda for social policy analysts. The emergence of genuinely global networks suggests that analysis of social policy should build on recent trends to develop fully comparative studies. This is not to deny that there are clear national borders on the World Wide Web (Halavais, 2000), or that it is being given distinctively national characteristics (Sy, 2001; Dai, 2002). It is simply to argue that the Internet as a public sphere has immense social policy possibilities not only within societies but also across and among them (Papacharissi, 2002). The challenge and opportunity for comparative research is to capture the ways in which social policy networks and processes are being reshaped both nationally and internationally.

As traditional forms of political participation are superseded, new forms may, then, take their place. This will of course only happen if both governments and citizens seek to make it happen, within societies and among them. However, once the full potential of the information age is exploited, new forms of policy making and of social policy become possible. Within established policy settings, it seems likely that the greatest opportunities for citizen involvement lie in agenda setting and policy implementation networks. By contrast, the core policy actors who tend to oversee actual policy making may be less affected. Yet this would still be a significant change, for agenda setting is known to be a critical part of the policy process, and gaining a voice in service delivery is precisely the sort of social policy role that many individuals seek. Outside established policy settings, in international networks of social policy actors, even greater change is possible.

In informational societies of the twenty-first century, and in transnational virtual networks, policy processes are likely to be very different from those we came to know in the twentieth century. The impacts on social policy will also be extensive. The key challenge for both governments and active citizens is to ensure that the potentials of the IT revolution are realized for the benefit of all the members of the 'informational, global, and networked' world currently being created by IT advance.

References

Ball, M.J. and J. Lillis (2001), 'E-health: transforming the physician/patient relationship', *International Journal of Medical Informatics*, vol. 61, 1–10.

Ballantine, Joan A. and Nigel Cunningham (1999), 'Strategic information systems planning: applying private sector frameworks in UK public healthcare', in Richard Heeks (ed.), *Reinventing Government in the Information Age: International Practice in IT-enabled Public Sector Reform*, London: Routledge, pp. 293–311.

Barrett, Katherine and Richard Greene (2001), *Powering Up: How Public Managers Can Take Control of Information Technology*, Washington, DC: CQ Press.

Brooks, S.G. and W.C. Wohlforth (2002), 'American primacy in perspective', *Foreign Affairs*, **81**(4), 20–33.

Bucy, E.P. and K.S. Gregson (2001), 'Media participation: a legitimizing mechanism of mass democracy', *New Media and Society*, vol. 3, 357–80.

Castells, Manuel (1997), *The Information Age: Economy, Society and Culture*, Volume II, *The Power of Identity*, Oxford: Blackwell.

Castells, Manuel (2000a), *The Information Age: Economy, Society and Culture*, Volume I, *The Rise of the Network Society*, 2nd edn, Oxford: Blackwell.

Castells, Manuel (2000b), *The Information Age: Economy, Society and Culture*, Volume III, *End of Millennium*, 2nd edn, Oxford: Blackwell.

Coleman, S. (1999), 'The new media and democratic politics', *New Media and Society*, vol. 1, 67–74.

Coleman, Stephen, John Taylor and Wim Van de Donk (1999), *Parliament in the Age of the Internet*, Oxford: Oxford University Press.

Dahlberg, L. (2001), 'Democracy via cyberspace: mapping the rhetorics and practices of three prominent camps', *New Media and Society*, vol. 3, 157–77.

Dai, X. (2002), 'Towards a digital economy with Chinese characteristics?', *New Media and Society*, vol. 4, 141–62.

Dionysius, Judith (2002), 'Brisbane: a reflection on a journey', in Eileen M. Milner (ed.), *Delivering the Vision: Public Services for the Information Society and the Knowledge Economy*, London: Routledge, pp. 63–85.

Dowding, K. (1995), 'Model or metaphor? A critical review of the policy network approach', *Political Studies*, vol. 45, 136–58.

Fried, B.M., G. Weinreich, G.M. Cavalier and K.J. Lester (2000), 'E-health: technologic revolution meets regulatory constraint', *Health Affairs*, vol. 19, 124–31.

Frissen, Paul H.A. (1998), 'Public administration in cyberspace', in I.T.M. Snellen and W.B.H.J.

Van de Donk (eds), *Public Administration in an Information Age: A Handbook*, Amsterdam: IOS Press, pp. 33–46.

Goldsmith, J. (2000), 'How will the internet change our health system?', *Health Affairs*, vol. 19, 148–56.

Gore, Al (1993), *Creating a Government that Works Better and Costs Less: Reengineering Through Information Technology*, Report of the National Performance Review, Washington, DC: Government Printing Office.

Hafner, K. (2002), 'Doctor–patient e-mail slow to develop', *International Herald Tribune*, 7 June, p. 16.

Hague, Barry N. and Brian D. Loader (eds) (1999), *Digital Democracy: Discourse and Decision Making in the Information Age*, London: Routledge.

Halavais, A. (2000), 'National borders on the World Wide Web', *New Media and Society*, vol. 2, 7–28.

Harris, R., P. Bala, P. Songan, E.G.L. Khoo and T. Trang (2001), 'Challenges and opportunities in introducing information and communication technologies to the Kelabit community of North Central Borneo', *New Media and Society*, vol. 3, 270–95.

Heeks, Richard and Anne Davies (1999), 'Different approaches to information age reform', in Richard Heeks (ed.), *Reinventing Government in the Information Age: International Practice in IT-enabled Public Sector Reform*, London: Routledge, pp. 22–48.

Hill, Kevin A. and John E. Hughes (1998), *Cyberpolitics: Citizen Activism in the Age of the Internet*, Lanham, MD: Rowman and Littlefield.

Hill, Michael and Peter L. Hupe (2002), *Implementing Public Policy: Governance in Theory and in Practice*, London: Sage.

HM Government/UKonline (2002), *In the Service of Democracy: A Consultation Paper on a Policy for Electronic Democracy*, 02/8085, London: HM Government.

Ho, A.T-K. (2002), 'Reinventing local governments and the e-government initiative', *Public Administration Review*, vol. 62, 434–44.

Holliday, I. (2001), 'Steering the British state in the information age', *Government and Opposition*, vol. 36, 314–29.

Holliday, I. (2002), 'Building e-government in East and Southeast Asia: regional rhetoric and nation (in)action', *Public Administration and Development*, vol. 22.

Iglehart, J.K. (2000), 'The internet promise, the policy reality', *Health Affairs*, **19**(6), 6–7.

John, Peter (1998), *Analysing Public Policy*, London: Pinter.

Kassirer, J.P. (2000), 'Patients, physicians, and the internet', *Health Affairs*, vol. 19, 115–23.

Kingdon, John W. (1995), *Agendas, Alternatives, and Public Policies*, 2nd edn, New York: HarperCollins.

Kleinke, J.D. (2000), 'Vaporware.com: the failed promise of the healthcare internet', *Health Affairs*, vol. 19, 57–71.

Lumpkin, J.R. (2000), 'E-health, HIPAA, and beyond', *Health Affairs*, vol. 19, 149–51.

Mathews, John A. and Dong-Sung Cho (2000), *Tiger Technology: The Creation of a Semiconductor Industry in East Asia*, Cambridge: Cambridge University Press.

Moon, M.J. (2002), 'The evolution of e-government among municipalities: rhetoric or reality?', *Public Administration Review*, vol. 62, 424–33.

Nielsen/Net Ratings (2002), Nielsen/Net Ratings Global Internet Index, accessed at nielsen-netratings.com, 20 July 2002.

Papacharissi, Z. (2002), 'The virtual sphere: the Internet as a public sphere', *New Media and Society*, vol. 4, 9–27.

Pew Internet & American Life Project (2002), *The Rise of the E-citizen: How People Use Government Agencies' Web Sites*, Washington, DC: Pew Internet & American Life Project.

Rantanen, T. (2001), 'The old and the new: communications technology and globalization in Russia', *New Media and Society*, vol. 3, 85–105.

Robinson, J.C. (2000), 'Financing the healthcare Internet', *Health Affairs*, vol. 19, 72–88.

Sabatier, Paul A. and Hank C. Jenkins-Smith (eds) (1993), *Policy Change and Learning: An Advocacy Coalition Approach*, Boulder, CO: Westview Press.

Salazar, Angel (1999), 'Evaluating information systems for decentralisation: health management reform in Ecuador', in Richard Heeks (ed.), *Reinventing Government in the Information*

Age: International Practice in IT-enabled Public Sector Reform, London: Routledge, pp. 156–74.

Selwyn, N. (2002), '"E-stablishing" an inclusive society? Technology, social exclusion and UK government policy making', *Journal of Social Policy*, vol. 31, 1–20.

Shortliffe, E. (2000), 'Networking health: learning from others, taking the lead', *Health Affairs*, vol. 19, 9–22.

Slack, R.S. and R.A. Williams (2000), 'The dialectics of place and space: on community in the "information age"', *New Media and Society*, vol. 2, 313–34.

Sy, P. (2001), 'Barangays of IT: Filipinizing mediated communication and digital power', *New Media and Society*, vol. 3, 296–312.

Tambini, D. (1999), 'New media and democracy', *New Media and Society*, vol. 1, 305–29.

Taylor, J.A. and H. Williams (1991), 'Public administration and the information polity', *Public Administration*, vol. 69, 171–90.

United Nations/American Society for Public Administration (UN/ASPA) (2002), *Benchmarking E-government: A Global Perspective*, New York: UN/ASPA.

US Department of Commerce (2002), *A Nation Online: How Americans are Expanding Their Use of the Internet*, Washington, DC: US Department of Commerce.

Van Dijk, J.A.G.M. (1999), 'The one-dimensional network society of Manuel Castells', *New Media and Society*, vol. 1, 127–38.

Vardon, Sue (2002), 'Centrelink, changing culture and expectations', in Eileen M. Milner (ed.), *Delivering the Vision: Public Services for the Information Society and the Knowledge Economy*, London: Routledge, pp. 39–62.

Zhang, J. (2002), 'Will the government "serve the people"? The development of Chinese e-government', *New Media and Society*, vol. 4, 163–84.

Zupko, Karen A. and Cheryl L. Toth (2000), 'Physicians get on line', in Douglas E. Goldstein (ed.), *E-Healthcare: Harness the Power of Internet E-Commerce and E-Care*, Gaithersburg, MD: Aspen, pp. 296–322.

Index

absolutism, monarchical 51
academic discipline, social policy as an 92
action projects, EU anti-poverty programmes 343, 344
administrative capacity, of state 52
administrative understanding, poverty research, preoccupation with 280
adult-worker family model 194–5
aegis, issue of 311–12, 314
affluence, and crime 283
Africa
    dysfunctional aspects of social life 53
    pessimism of social scientists 282
    pressures of globalization 57
    regulatory weakness of state 54
    residual social policies 56
    see also Sub-Saharan Africa
ageing
    demographic, and housing 364–6
    perceptions of successful 143–4
agency, social change 31
agenda-setting, impact of Internet 392–3
aid, Bangladesh and South Asia 252–3
Amsterdam Treaty 353
Anglo-American social science tradition 262
anti-discrimination/equal policy measures, cross-national policy analysis 212
anti-globalization protests 393
anti-poverty programmes (EU) 342–8
appropriateness, research methods 293
Asia
    dysfunctional aspects of social life 53
    see also East Asia; South Asia
assets, social exclusion indicators 348–9
assimilationism 211, 212, 213
atheoretical case studies 309–10
Australia, SPM 68, 70–73, 82, 83–4, 85
autonomy
    and care
        failure of practical relevance 135

    as guiding moral ideal 132–3
    see also bodily autonomy; economic autonomy; moral autonomy

Bangladesh, aid and informal security 252–3
basic security model, welfare 158, 159, 161
    income inequality
        among elderly 169
        and poverty 165, 166
    strategies of equality 161, 162, 163
biannual bonuses, Japanese wage system 76
biographical approach, intensive interviewing 315
bodily autonomy 208
boundaries, comparative social policy 3, 91–4
Bretton Woods System 33
bubble economy, Japan 75
budget size, income redistribution 164
burying rights, self-consciousness of moral requirement 137

Canada, redistribution 168
capitalism
    cross-national policy analysis 206–7
    as driving force of welfare states 119–20
    see also liberal capitalism; organized capitalism; welfare capitalism
care, *see* long-term care
care-giving
    as an instrumental good 134, 135
    as a moral good 139–43
case study approach 204, 266, 308–10
causal relationships, time dimension 334–5
Central America, neo-patrimonial regimes 55–6
Central and Eastern Europe
    exclusion from club of welfare states 126